Accountability for International Humanitarian Law Violations:
The Case of Rwanda and East Timor

Mohamed C. Othman

Accountability for International Humanitarian Law Violations: The Case of Rwanda and East Timor

Springer

Mohamed C. Othman
Judge, High Court of Tanzania
P.O. Box 14789
DAR ES SALAAM
Tanzania
mwamady@yahoo.com

Reprint of cover pictures by courtesy of
Dr. Alessandro Caldarone and ICTR

ISBN-10 3-540-26081-1 Springer Berlin Heidelberg New York
ISBN-13 978-3-540-26081-3 Springer Berlin Heidelberg New York

Cataloging-in-Publication Data
Library of Congress Control Number: 2005929337

Springer is a part of Springer Science+Business Media

springeronline.com

Printed in Germany

Hardcover-Design: Erich Kirchner, Heidelberg
Layout: Schreib- und Korrekturservice Manuela Ebert, Mannheim

SPIN 11431343 64/3153-5 4 3 2 1 0 – Printed on acid-free paper

Preface

The main objective of this book is to make available to an informed audience a legal and policy oriented study on accountability for serious human rights and international humanitarian law violations. It is an attempt to share the lessons learnt in accountability for atrocity crimes as conducted by the International Criminal Tribunal for Rwanda (ICTR), and the United Nations Transitional Administration in East Timor (UNTAET). The former established subsequent to egregious atrocities that took place in 1994, and the latter following the massive outburst of violence in 1999. The book is based on two cases: Rwanda and East Timor. It is expected that it will serve as reference literature to both the legal community and policy makers on accountability for heinous international crimes.

As the international community and States, following serious human rights and international humanitarian law violations have painfully come to terms with their obligations to bring to justice persons in high offices or leadership positions, de jure or de facto, alleged to have committed such crimes, it has also become imperative that beginners mistakes be avoided. When the International Criminal Tribunal for the Former Yugoslavia (ICTY) was established in 1993, and the ICTR in 1994 and commenced their pioneering mandates there was no template on which the prosecution of individuals most responsible or with the greatest responsibility could be cast. Accountability had to be experimental. Ten years later, this book subjects the accountability process by the ICTR and UNTAET to testing cross examination. It exposes, from a legal and policy perspective, the accumulated experiences of accountability for the atrocities committed in Rwanda and East Timor. The need to ensure effective, impartial, transparent and fair prosecutions is warranted for at least one basic reason. International tribunals and courts are able to guarantee accountability only for a very few. Less than a fraction of the hundreds and thousands of perpetrators who constitute front-line criminals. As concerns the ICTR for example the plans are for it to prosecute around 70 accused persons by 2010. This will have been after a 16 years life-tenure. The Extraordinary Chambers in the Courts of Cambodia for the Prosecution of Crimes Committed during the Period of Democratic Kampuchea (i.e. Khmer Rouge Tribunal) once functional envisions holding accountable up to 10 accused during its planned three year tenure.

A work of this nature can only be the result of tangible support. First and foremost I wish to fully acknowledge the assistance of the United States Institute of Peace without which this book would have been incomplete. A word of appreciation also goes to the Chr. Michelsen Institute of Development and Human Rights and the Max Planck Institute for Foreign and International Criminal Law for unheeded access to their vast library resources, and to the Tanzania Red Cross.

I am personally indebted to a number of persons who offered advice, comments, encouragement, guidance, and most important critique. Others to be thanked include all those who agreed to be interviewed, and to share information or materials. Particular appreciation goes Judge Navanethem Pillay former President of ICTR, Judge Eric Mose it current President, Adama Dieng its Registrar, Professor Albin Eser, Alessandro Caldarone, Astri Suhrke, Catherine Cisse, William Egbe, Professor Kai Ambos, Adam Kimbisa, Oyvind Olsen, Dr. Michael Polannen, Ambassador Juma Mwapachu, Mathias Marcussen, Maxwell Nkole, Nathalie Ndongo-Seh, Roland Amoussouga, Rashid S. Rashid, Taylor Seybolt, Gunar Sorbo, Karim Ahmad Khan, Shyamala Alagendra, Marko Kalbush, Stanley Zankel and Mwamy Sykes. Finally I must also express my most sincere appreciation to my wife Saada, and children, Said, Aysha and Amin whose petitions to spend time together I simply had to dismiss or at best, adjourn.

Mohamed Chande Othman

Table of Contents

Selected Abbreviations

ABRI	Angakatan Bersenjata Republik Indonesia (Armed Forces of the Republic of Indonesia)
BABINSA	Village Guidance non commissioned officers
BRIMOB	Brigada Mobil (Mobile Brigade), i.e. Indonesia Riot Police).
CDR	Coalition pour la defence de la republique et de la democratie
COMINTERFET	Commander of the International Force in East Timor
CIVPOL	United Nations civilian police
CNRT	Concelho Nacional de Resistencia Timorense (Naional Council of Timorese Resistance).
Dandim	Commander of the District Military Command.
Danramil	Commander of Sub district Military Command
Danrem	Commander of the Sub regional Military Command.
DRC	Democratic Republic of the Congo, formely Zaire.
ESM	Ecole Superieure Militaire, Senior Staff College.
FALANTIL	Forcas Armadas de Liberacao Nacional de Timor Leste (Armed Forces for the National Liberation of East Timor)
FAR	Forces Armee Rwandaise (Rwandan Armed Forces)
FRETILIN	Frente Revolucionaria de Timor Leste Inde pendente(Revolutionary Front for an Independent East Timor)
FPDK	Forum Persatuan Demokrasi Dan Keadilan (Forum for Unity, Democracy and Justice)
ICC	International Criminal Court
ICTR	International Criminal Tribunal for Rwanda/Rwanda Tribunal

ICTY	International Criminal Tribunal for the Former Yugoslavia
ICRC	International Committee of the Red Cross
INTERFET	International Force in East Timor
Kapolda	Chief of Police Area
Kapolres	Chief of Police District
Kapolsek	Chief of Police Sector
Kapolwil	Chief of Police Region
KODAM	Regional or Area Military Command
KODIM	District Military Command
KOPASSUS	Komando Pasukan Khusus (Special Forces Command of the Indonesian Armed Forces).
KORAMIL	Sub-District Military Command
KOREM	Sub- Region Military Command
KOSTRAD	Komando Strategis Angkatan Darat (Strategic Reserve Command of the Indonesian Armed Forces)
KPP HAM	Komisi Penyelidik Pelanggaran HAM di Timur -Timur (IndonesianCommission of Investigation into Human Right in East Timor)
MDR	Movement democratique republicain
MRN	Former a single party, Mouvement revolutionnaire nationa pour le developpement (National Revolutionary Movement for Development), it was rebaptised in July 1991 as Movement republicaine national pour la democracie et le developpement; National Republican Movement for Democracy and Development.
Pangdam	Commander of Regional/Area (Udayana) Military Command, i.e. covered East Timor
Panglima	Panglima Angkatan Bersenjata Republik Indonesia/Panglima Tentara Nasional Indonesia;; Commander of the National Army of Indonesian Commander of the Indonesian Amed Forces
PDC	Parti democrate Chretien
PKF	United Nations Peacekeeping Force

POLDA	Police Area
POLRI	Polisi Republik Indonesia; Indonesian, Indonesian National Police
POLRES	Police District
POLSEK	Police Sector
POLWIL	Police Region
PPI	Pasukan Perjuangan Integrasi; Integration Fighting Forces
PSD	Parti social democrate
RPF/RFA	Rwandan Patriotic Front, the political movement opposed to the Rwandan Government under President Habyarimana. The name of its armed wing is the Rwanda Patriotic Army (RPA).
RTLM	Radio Television Libre des Milles Collines
SCIU	Serious Crimes Investigation Unit
SGI	Satuan Tugas Intelijen (Indonesian Combat Intelligence Unit)
TNI	Tentara Nasional Indonesia (National Army of Indonesia or Indonesian Armed Forces)
UNAMET	United Nations Assistance Mission in East Timor
UNGA	United Nations General Assembly
UNTAET	United Nations Transitional Administration in East Timor
UNMISET	United Nations Mission of Support in East Timor.
UNSC	United Nations Security Council

East Timor Militia Groups

ABLAI	Aku Berjuang Lestikaran Amanat Intergrasi; I will Fight to Preserve the Mandate for Integration.
AITARAK	Thorn militia group, based in Dili.
BESI MERAH PUTIH	Red and White Iron rod, based in Liquica.
DADARUS MERAH PUTHI	Red and White Typhoon, based in Maliana.
DARAH MERAH	Red Blood, based in Ermera.

FIRMI MERAH PUTIH	Stand Firm with the Red and White
HALILINTIR	Thunderbolt, based in Maliana.
KAER MERAH PUTIH	Capture the Red and White
LAK SAUR	Flying Eagle, based in Suai
MAHIDI	Mati Hidup Demi Integrasi ; Dead or Alive for Indonesia, based in Ainaro.
SAKUNAR	Scorpion, based in Oecussi.
TIM ALFA	Team Alpha, also known as Jeti Merah Putih; Authentic Red and White
TIM SERA	Team Sera
TIM SAKA	Super Team

Chapter 1
Introduction

This book is in essence a legal and policy study on accountability for serious human rights and international humanitarian law violations committed in Rwanda in 1994, and East Timor in 1999. It is a contribution to attempts aimed at narrowing the impunity gap through the prosecution of persons individually responsibility for such egregious atrocities. It is partly driven by the challenge put forward by the former UN High Commissioner for Human Rights Ayala Lasso that "we must rid this planet the obscenity that a person stands better chance of being tried and judged for killing one human being than for killing 100,000.[1] The book is a focused examination of accountability conducted under the authority of the United Nations Security Council by the International Criminal Tribunal for Rwanda (hereinafter referred to as ICTR or Rwanda Tribunal),[2] and that provided for by the United Nations Transitional Administration in East Timor (UNTAET)[3] following the mayhem in East Timor. It provides a critical review of accountability, of the institutional arrangements and the legal frameworks set up. It analyses and examines the strategies and policies adopted; all aimed at bringing to justice those allegedly responsible for orchestrating widespread and systematic violence. The issues addressed are pertinent to the exercise of jurisdiction, both national and international, for genocide, crimes against humanity, and war crimes. They are also of interest to accountability by the International Criminal Court (ICC).[4] It is no longer tenable to claim as Slobodan Milosevic, the former President of Yugoslavia did, at

---

1 Annual Report of the ICTR to the SC and UNGA, UN Doc. A/51/292S/1996/665, 16 Aug. 1996, para 5.

2 International Criminal Tribunal for the Prosecution of Persons Responsible for Genocide and Other Serious Violations of International Humanitarian Law Committed in the Territory of Rwanda and Rwandan Citizens responsible foe genocide and other such violations committed in the territory of neighbouring States between 1 January 1994 and 31 December 1994, SC res. 955, 8 November 1994, UN SC Doc. S/RES/955 (1994), (ICTR), Statute Annexed; reprinted in 33 ILM 1602 (1994). Its counterpart, The International Tribunal for the Prosecution of Persons Responsible for Serious Violations of International Humanitarian Law Committed in the Territory of the Former Yugoslavia since 1991, was established by UNSC resolution, UN Doc. S/25704, Annex (1993), reprinted in 32 ILM 1192 (1993.

3 Established by UN SC resolution 1272, 15 September 1999.

4 Rome Statute of the International Criminal Court, UN Doc.A/CONF.183/9, at www.un.org/law/icc/romefra.htm.

his initial appearance before the ICTY that such institutions are “false”.[5] They have become a permanent undertaking. As held by the Appeal Chamber of the Special Court for Sierra Leone in *P. v. Charles Ghankay Taylor*, the principle is now established that sovereign equality of State does not prevent a Head of State from being prosecuted before an international tribunal or court, and his international prosecution as an incumbent Head of State at the time when the criminal proceedings are instituted against him is not a bar to his prosecution.[6]

A word needs to be said of the uniqueness of the subject matter of the book. The establishment by the United Nations Security Council of the two ad hoc International Criminal Tribunals in the first half of the 1990s was then a new undertaking. There was also a total lack of basic facilities: no courtroom, no prison, no budget, no computers, no law clerks, no rules of procedure and no judges’ robes.[7] The legal and policy issues with which they have been confronted must be measured against that of any newly born offspring. At the beginning the two UN ad hoc Tribunals had no precedents to rely upon, and trial and error was inevitable.[8] Although, when they were established, there was a resounding echo of the International Military Tribunal at Nuremberg (Nuremberg Tribunal), established fifty years earlier, the UN had no direct hands-on experience in the investigation and prosecution of serious human rights and international humanitarian law violations. Its specialized Agencies were also not conversant with arteries of international criminal justice. Furthermore, the United Nations administrative and financial rules provided little guidance. The book is thus driven by lessons learnt in accountability. It captures developments up to 31 December 2004.

A number of essentials mark each of the two specific situations studied, namely, Rwanda and East Timor. First, the book generally deals with accountability for atrocity crimes by three classes of perpetrators namely, the “*big, medium and small fish*”. Its focus however, is on the legal and policy issues related to the prosecution of those with the “*greatest responsibility*”. It is this class of perpetrators that is the primary concern and priority of international accountability. That said accountability for atrocity crimes also concerns intermediate level perpetrators. They provide the connecting tissue between those with leadership responsi-

---

5 Cf. “I consider this Tribunal a false Tribunal and the indictment a false Indictment”, Ini tial Appearance, *P. v. S. Milosevic,* Case no: IT- 02-54, 3 July 2000; Following suggestions of her possible accusation in Serbia his wife, Mirjana Markovic had this to say: “I’m just waiting to be accused of provoking the conflict in Chechnya, floods in India the abduction of Aldo Moro or freezing temperatures in Serbia”. The Guardian (UK), 20 July 2001.

6 *P. v. C. G. Taylor*, Motion made under protest and without waiving Immunity to a Head of State requiring the Trial Chamber to quash the Indictment and declare null and void the warrant of arrest and order for the transfer of detention of 23 July 2003 [Immunity Motion], A.C, Case no: SCSL-03-01-1-059, 31 May 2004; For Indictment See, Case no: SCSL-2003-01-I, 7 March 2003.

7 Cassese A, (2004) The ICTY: A Living and Vital Reality, International Journal of Criminal Law vol. 2 p. 585.

8 Goldstone R in Dixon R, Khan K (2003) Archbold International Criminal Courts, Practice, Procedure and Evidence, Sweet and Maxwell, London, p. vii.

bility (i.e. the planners and organizers) and those who directly executed the crimes. The case of low-level perpetrators will also be examined. Evidence from recent conflicts has plainly demonstrated that large numbers of such perpetrators (i.e. the "small fish") are often involved as executioners. They consist of individuals most visible at crimes scenes, and present at massacre sites. In Rwanda many thousands, mostly former interahamwe and impuzamugambi militia have been detained since 1994 and are awaiting trial or gacaca proceedings. In East Timor the initial group of suspected arrestees consisted of "small fish" pro-autonomy militiamen who had been identified as suspects by the civilian population from their own communities. The book will also high-light experiences of accountability related to these very classes of perpetrators. It is expected that the issues raised will contribute to the serious on-going debate on fast forward means of enhancing accountability for atrocity crimes.

This book is not about and does concern itself with any alleged criminal responsibility or guilt of any suspect or accused. That is the sole mandate of lawfully constituted courts; national, mixed or international. Nor does it suggest any incriminating or exculpatory evidence. It is settled law that the presumption of innocence is a cardinal principle of criminal law. The book only examines legal, policy and procedural issues, as well as accountability strategies for atrocity crimes. These have been defined as crimes whose pattern is one of significant magnitude (i.e. widespread or systematic, and involves a relatively large number of victims) that occur in times of armed conflict (international or non international), violent social upheaval or even during peace-time and that must be identifiable as the crime of genocide, a violation of the laws and customs of war, or crimes against humanity.[9] They must also have been led in their execution by powerful elite, in society, who planned their commission; and for which the law applied to such crimes is regarded under customary international law as holding individuals criminally liable for the commission of such crimes.[10] The book is a contribution to national and international criminal justice in that mid-life into the tenure of the two UN ad hoc tribunals, it re-examines the arrangements, law, policies and practices that have steered the investigative and prosecutorial course of the ICTR, and accountability for serious crimes in East Timor. The sharing of experiences exposed in the book should also be seen in the light of the requirement by United Nations Security Council for both the ICTY and the ICTR in principle to wind up all judicial activities by 2010, under each institution's Completion Strategy.[11] Following independence on 20 May 2002 the new East Timor Constitution has transitionally extended the mandate and timeframe of the judicial mechanisms for the accountability of those responsible for atrocity crimes.

---

9 Scheffer D J (2003) The Future of Atrocity Law, Suffolk Transnational Law Review, vol. XXV/3, pp. 399-400.

10 Pp. 399-400 Id.

11 Completion Strategy for the ICTR, 8th Annual Report of the ICTR to the UNSC and GA, UN Doc. A/58/140, S/2003/707, 11 July 2003; 4th version of Strategy issued by ICTR on 19 November 2004, at www.icrr.org.

Chapter 2 serves as a curtain raiser. It provides, in giant leaps, the background and context in which atrocity crimes were committed in Rwanda in 1994 and East Timor in 1999. Deciphering the pattern of violence is the entry point for an effective accountability process. The chapter discusses accountability for some of the unique events that precipitated the atrocity crimes, such as the shooting down of the Presidential plane over Kigali on 6 April 1994 that led to the death of Rwandan President, Juvenal Habyarimana, the Burundian President Cyprian Ntaryamira, and others. An incident acknowledged as the most immediate triggering event that ignited the genocide in Rwanda.

Chapter 3 deals specifically with Rwanda. It explains the urge for justice, and details the framework of accountability for atrocity crimes committed there. It reviews the institutional arrangements opted for, discusses the merits and demerits of a common Prosecutor for both the UN ad hoc Tribunals, and cooperation between the ICTR and Rwanda. An unresolved thorny issue, accountability relating to Rwandan Patriotic Army (RPA)[12] soldiers, is addressed in this chapter. This is a modern day equivalent of the "victor's justice" controversy that still haunts the Nuremberg Tribunal.

Chapter 4 deals with East Timor. It reviews the institutional arrangements for the accountability of atrocity crimes that took place before and after the popular consultation in 1999. It analyses the prosecution strategy, and highlights pertinent issues related to the dual track model of accountability in which East Timor and Indonesia were each tasked by the United Nations Security Council to undertake prosecutions. The question of prosecution by Indonesia, of its nationals comprising senior military and police commanders, as well as pro autonomy militia commanders who remain at large in West Timor, Indonesia is also examined. The chapter also considers the prospects, if any, of accountability for those within the ranks of the Indonesian Armed Forces (TNI) and the Indonesian Police Force (POLRI) and of militia commanders for the planned campaign of systematic violence in East Timor.

In addressing accountability under UNTAET and successor mission, UNMISET, two issues are specifically dealt with. First that of the detention of suspected militia. Dealing with the post conflict incarceration of suspects represents a particular challenge to accountability, more so when atrocities involve mass criminality and justice is locally dispensed. Neither Rwanda nor East Timor has been spared this problem. Recently, in Iraq, too, where United States Armed Forces had swept up into the dragnet a number of Iraqi leaders and hundreds of civilians, effective accountability is yet to be satisfactorily realized.[13] There, arrests were followed by incomplete interrogations, or none at all, lack of an efficient trial-or-release system, makeshift and deplorable detention conditions, con-

---

12 It was originally named Rwanda Patriotic Front (RPF).

13 Bush and Blair promised justice in Iraq. Another lie, The Guardian (UK), 30 June 2003.

stant buck-passing, and sloppy paperwork by authorities.[14] Not to mention the abhorrent and illegal treatment of civilian detainees and prisoners at Abu Ghraib.[15]

The second issue concerns accountability for suspected militia refugees based in West Timor, Indonesia. Accountability for militia in such a situation is linked to the wider question of justice and post conflict national reconciliation. This is a hot subject that still divides many East Timorese. As a direct result of the 1999 violence in East Timor, some 250,000 East Timorese were forcibly dragged into West Timor. This was conducted primarily by pro autonomy militia, acting in concert with the Indonesian Armed Forces. There the refugees remained and still remain captive to militia groups. As with the interahamwe who held, under siege, the Rwandan refugee population in the Democratic Republic of Congo, immediately after the atrocity crimes in Rwanda in July 1994, accountability for this group of perpetrators is essential to any restoration of the rule of law. The task is one of 'separating the predators from the prey, the wolves from the sheep, which is a precondition to even beginning to deal with the wolves'.[16] The accountability lessons from East Timor are of guidance in dealing with this troublesome issue.

Chapter 5 focuses on the profiling of perpetrators. It examines the various approaches considered by Prosecutors and States in the classification of perpetrators. These have ranged from official and non-official lists of alleged ring-leaders, to a deck of 55 playing cards. Among the issues dealt with is the question whether there is any marked difference between the standpoint of the United Nations Secretary-General Kofi Annan and the United Nations Secretariat in recommending the prosecution of persons "*most responsible*", and the preference, on the other hand, of Security Council Member States (including the United States) for accountability only for those with the "*greatest responsibility*". The chapter traces ICTR's prosecution strategy in the light of its officially designated mandate: the prosecution of persons with the highest level of responsibility atrocity crimes in Rwanda. The same category the East Timor serious crimes process aimed to hold accountable.

Chapter 6 exhaustively deals with conspiracy to commit genocide. It offers an in-depth inquiry into conspiracy to commit genocide in Rwanda. One which the Prosecutor at ICTR alleges involved senior officers of the former Government of Rwanda, cabinet members, top military and gendarmerie commanders, leaders of political parties, senior civil administrators, media stakeholders and journalists, and the militia. The chapter contains a full-blown account of the law of conspiracy, and the conspiracy strategy of the office of the Prosecutor. A strategy that led

14 It was punishment without trial, The Guardian (UK), 15 August 2003.

15 US Prisoner Abuse: How Lessons of WWII Were Thrown Out of the Window; Highly Paid Private Soldiers Doing US Military's Dirty Work, The East African, January 24-30, 2005; In December 2003, of 7,000 prisoners detained by Coalition Forces, there were 2,200 "criminal detainees", and 4,800 "security internees" and those deemed to pose a threat to those Forces or Iraqi's in general. None had been charged or had access to a lawyer. See Bringing the Old Regime to Trial, The Economist 11 December 2003, www.economict.com/agenda on 15 September 2005.

16 Statement of the Representative of Czech, UN Doc. SC/ PV.3453, 8 November 1994, p. 7.

to the abortive attempt to charge 29 persons, most alleged to have had greatest responsibility for the 1994 atrocity crimes, in a joint indictment that resembled the Nuremberg accusation. Conspiracy to commit genocide is discussed as a crime as well as a tool for accountability. The chapter finally touches on the doctrine of joint criminal enterprise and the other forms of co-perpetration embodied in the Statute of the International Court and assesses whether they provide an effective alternative to conspiracy.

Chapter 7 deals with superior responsibility, an effective accountability tool for persons in authority and command. These are the individuals that are of interest and priority in terms of international accountability. Used to indict Jean Kambanda, Theoneste Bagosora, Slobodan Milosevic, Radovan Karadzik, General Ratko Mladic, General Radislav Krstic, Colonel General Ante Gotovina, General Wiranto and Charles Taylor, among others, it is now a well-established norm of criminal liability. The Chapter draws on the experiences of the accountability process at the ICTR and in East Timor on superior responsibility. It discusses a number of defences, some of which were used by generals within the Indonesian Armed Forces to exculpate their involvement or that of their troops.

Chapter 8 examines guilty pleas in the practice of the two UN ad hoc Tribunals. It details the case law and the trial of four accused that have pleaded guilty before the ICTR in the first ten years of its existence. One that of Jean Kambanda the Prime Minister of the Interim Government of Rwanda was the first by a former Head of Government to have pleaded guilty for genocide and conspiracy to commit it, before an International Criminal Tribunal. His admission of guilt and the responsibility of his Government in the genocide of the Tutsi in Rwanda momentarily dislodged revisionists. The chapter examines whether it can be ranked as a crowing achievement of that Tribunal. It also inquires whether the non-lenient life sentence imposed upon Kambanda, a Prime Minister who "joined a moving genocide train" was excessive or not. It is argued that the decision, which reflected an unpredictable departure from conventional judicial wisdom, has acted as a disincentive to other accused who might have volunteered to plead guilty before the ICTR. Of recent, only one accused has stepped forward and confessed. The chapter also compares guilty pleas before the ICTY, where the Prosecutor's charging and sentencing concessions to accused pleading guilty, and generally a more lenient sentencing attitude by Trial Chambers has led to 17 guilty pleas to date.

Chapter 9 is the conclusion. It provides an executive summary of the main findings of the study, and offers a set of matrix of accountability for atrocity crimes.

Chapter 2
Rwanda and East Timor: Pattern of Violence

A legal and policy analysis of accountability for serious human rights and international humanitarian law violations that took place in Rwanda in 1994 and East Timor in 1999 requires a chronicle of key historical and socio-political developments that had a bearing on the commission of atrocity crimes in those two states. This provides a better understanding of the pattern of violence, and the policy or policies, be they of a state, an entity or an organization behind the systematic or widespread commission of such egregious crimes. *All atrocity crimes have a political character. Invariably they are the result of state action, in-action, omission, or policy.* Appreciating this is important in conducting any inquiry into the elements of the crimes committed. It is also the starting point for the design of the prosecution strategy for the accountability of alleged perpetrators, no matter the category; "big, medium, or small". The resume of events summed up in this chapter is intended to highlight only the essentials. It is not meant to be an essay on the root causes of the Rwanda and East Timor conflicts. Well-documented and narrative accounts of the atrocities committed in Rwanda in 1994, and in East Timor in 1999 exist.[1] The author brings to surface in gigantic leaps, the sequence of events and highlights developments that will ultimately be linked to the examination of prosecution strategies, policies, and core legal issues surrounding accountability. While accountability measures include justice, truth and reconciliation, this book only focuses on the first. The inquiry will inevitably touch on state organs and institutions that may have been implicated, as well other non state actors, such as para-military organizations, militia, and even private individuals. The book examines major events which culminated into unprecedented human catastrophes, and what may best explain the planned, organized, systematic and large-scale character of the crimes carried out in Rwanda and East Timor.

---

1 On Rwanda, see, African Rights (1994) Death, Despair and Defiance, London; Human Rights Watch/Federation International des Ligues des Droit de L'Homme (1999) Leave None to Tell the Story, N.Y; Gourevitch P (1998) We Wish to Inform You That Tomorrow We Will Be Killed With Our Families: Stories From Rwanda, Farar, Strauss and Giraux, N.Y.; Prunier G (1997) Rwanda Crisis 1959-1994: History of a Genocide, Hurst, N.Y.; Anyidoho H K (1999) Guns over Kigali, Woeli Publishing Services, Accra; On East Timor, see, Dunn J (1996) Timor. A People Betrayed, ABC Books, Sydney; Martinkus J A (2001) Dirty Little War, Random House, Australia; Greenlees D and Garran R (2002) Deliverance: The Inside Story of East Timor's Fight for Freedom, Allen and Unwin (Australia) Pty Ltd.

Rwanda

The most recent history of Rwanda, since the dawn of colonization, is one marked by political and social antagonism, as well as intermittent ethnic clashes between Tutsi and Hutu. The marking point was the 'social' revolution of 1959, which led to the death in Rwanda of an estimated 20,000 Tutsi, and the fleeing of thousands to Burundi, Democratic Republic of Congo (DRC), Tanzania and Uganda. A direct result of the revolution was the abolition of the Tutsi monarchy, and the end of the domination of the state by an exclusive Tutsi elite.[2] The revolution was a strong rural movement whose political objective was to end the caste system, which accorded the monopoly of power to an ethnic minority, and to replace a predatory or exploitary monarchy with a democratic republic.[3] Rwanda achieved political independence on 1 July 1962. A pro-Hutu party, MDR-PARMEHUTU[4] gained dominance, and its leader Gregoire Kayibanda became the first President of the Republic of Rwanda on 26 October 1961. This period saw the exclusion of all Tutsi from political life, and a growing authoritarianism practiced by a Hutu power base that became increasingly centralized.[5] Independence was characterized by a discriminatory regime, a government that remained ethno-centric, with democracy available for only a fraction of the population.[6] The revolution drew on the frustrations of a politics of exclusion under the monarchy, but then failed to install in its place, a politics of inclusion.[7] A quota system was imposed on the Tutsi who were allocated only 10% of the places in schools, the civil service, and in private enterprise.[8] During the early post independence period, political power rested with Hutus of central and southern Rwanda.

Rwanda, landlocked within the Great Lakes region, had before 1994 an estimated population of 7.5 million, inhabitants Hutu comprising 91%, Tutsi 8%, Twa 0.4, all speaking the same language, Kinyarwanda, a Bantu language of the interlacustrine zone, and sharing a common history, culture and traditional beliefs.[9] Rwanda has a bi-polar ethnic situation having within its midst two ethnic groups

---

2 Newbury C, Newbury D (1999) A Catholic Mass in Kigali: Contested Views of the Genocide and Ethnicity in Rwanda, Canadian Journal of African Studies, vol.33/2-3, p. 297.

3 Gasana J K La guerre, la paix et la démocratie au Rwanda. In Guichaoua A (1995) Les crises politique au Burundi et au Rwanda (1993-1994), Université des Sciences et Technologies de Lille, p. 212.

4 Mouvement démocratique republicaine-Parti de Mouvement de l'emacipation hutu; Repiblican Democratic party-Hutu Emacipation Movement Party.

5 Destexhe A (1995) Rwanda and Genocide in the Twentieth Century, Pluto Press, London, East Haven, CT, pp. 44.

6 Gasana E, Butera J B, Byanafashe D, Karfikzi A Rwanda. In Adedeji A (1999) Comprehending and Mastering African Conflicts. The Search for Sustainable Peace and Good Governance, Zed Books, London and N.Y, pp. 155.

7 Newbury C, Newbury D (1999) p. 297.

8 Destexhe A (1995) p. 44.

9 Rwanda Government 1991 Census, in ICTR Yearbook 1994-1996, ICTR, Arusha.

having different and heavy demographic weights.[10] The origin of the violence is connected to how Hutu and Tutsi were considered as political identities by the colonial state, Belgium; with Hutu as indigenous and Tutsi as alien.[11] Historical accounts indicate that all lived together in present day Rwanda from about 900 AD. [12] Explanations of the difference between Hutu, Tutsis, and Twa through measured characteristics, biotopes or migratory factors, as those offered during German and Belgium colonization remain scientifically unimpressive.[13] Asymmetric relationship in size between the Hutu and Tutsis may only explain why so many people were killed in 1994.[14]

In early 1973 ethnic violence between Tutsi and Hutu erupted, resulting in the exodus of Tutsi. Ethnic tension and violence, internal regional divide, and the "rotting" of the political situation[15] led to a military coup on 5 July 1973 by General Juvenal Habyarimana, then Minister of Defence and Chief of Staff of the Armed Forces. This shifted the rule from civilian to the military and from Hutu of central Rwanda to those of the northern prefectures of Gisenyi and Ruhengeri. President Habyarimana founded the MRND (Mouvement revolutionnaire national pour le developpement) a single political party on 5 July 1975. This state party was an all-inclusive political organization with all Rwandans considered members, including babies.[16] The clergy also became party members. For almost a decade the Archbishop of Kigali, Vincent Nsengiyumva, served in its central committee.[17] He was assassinated in Kigali between 3 and 5 June 1994.

The Government used a system of ethnic and regional quotas in the education and public administration sectors to increasingly discriminate against Tutsi, and Hutu from regions outside the northwest. Throughout almost the entire Habyarimana years there was not to be a single Tutsi *Bourgmestre* or *Prefet.* There was only 1 Tutsi officer in the entire army, there were 2 Tutsi in Parliament out of 70 members, and there was only 1 Tutsi minister out of a cabinet containing between 20 to 30 members.[18] It was the Belgians, world quota specialists of political meas-

---

10 Reyntjens F Akazu <<escadrons de la mort>> et autres <<Réseau Zéro>>: un historiques des résistances au changement politiques depuis 1990. In Guichaoua A (1995), p. 265.

11 Mamdani M (2001) When Victims become Killers. Colonialism, Nativism and the Genocide in Rwanda, Princeton University Press, Princeton, N.Y, pp. 16, 34.

12 Twagiralimana A (1998) Hutu and Tutsi, The Rosen Publishing Group, Inc. N.Y., p. 11.

13 Cf. Belgium Congo and Ruanda-Urundi Information and Public Relations Office (1960), Ruanda-Urundi, Geography and History, Brussels.

14 Lema A Causes of Civil War in Rwanda: the Weight of History and Socio-Cultural Structures. In Braathen E, Boas M, Saether G (2000) Ethnicity Kills? The Politics of War, Peace and Ethnicity in Sub Saharan Africa, Macmillan Press, London, p. 72.

15 Gasana J K La guerre, la paix et la democratie au Rwanda (1989-1993). In Guichaoua A (1995), p. 213.

16 Prunier G (1997) The Rwandan Crisis, p. 76.

17 He resigned from the party in 1990 on the eve of the Pope's visit to Rwanda, See, Braeckmann C (1994), Rwanda. Histoire d'un genocide, Librairie A.Fayard, France, p. 92.

18 Prunier G (1997) p. 75.

urements and balanced involvement who suggested giving each group proportional representation according to its numerical importance.[19] The Habyarimana Government thus allocated the Tutsi 10 % of administrative and teaching posts, the Twa 1 %, while the rest was earmarked for Hutu. In the 1980s people from Gisenyi and Ruhengeri occupied the most important positions in the military, political, economic and administrative sectors of Rwandan society. This developed into a particular system of political governance and control, clientelism.[20] By the 1990s an inner circle of relatives and close associates of the President, and mostly connected with his wife, Agathe Kanziga, usurped power and monopolized both legal and illegal commerce and trade.[21] This select group, known as *Akazu* ("little house") composed mostly of Hutu and persons from the same area and region (Bushiru, Gisenyi) as the President and his wife, became a network of parallel power.[22]

On 1 October 1990 the Rwanda Patriotic Front (RPF), composed mostly of Tutsi refugees, launched an attack from Uganda into Rwanda. This marked the beginning of armed hostilities between the Rwandan Armed Forces (FAR) and RFP, which led during a period of a little less than four years to numerous cease-fires, a peace agreement, recommencement of armed hostilities, and genocide.

Identifying the Enemy

Extremists within the Government, including elements in the army, seized the occasion of the October 1990 invasion to promote two goals; namely, a significant expansion of the armed forces, whose strength rose from 7,000 to 30,000 troops in 1994, and to brand all Tutsi in Rwanda as internal supporters of the RPF.[23] As a counter measure to the RPF invasion, a strategy of polarising ethnic division between Hutu and Tutsi was also conceived and implemented. The conflict was presented as a confrontation between two clearly defined ethnic groups, each homogenous within, and utterly distinct from the other. [24] The Tutsi population at

19 "C'est sont les Belges, spécialistes mondiaux des quotas, des dosages politique et des équilibres alambiques, qui ont suggérer de donner a chaque group une représentation proportionnelle a son importance numérique", Braeckman C (1994), Rwanda, Histoire d'un genocide, p. 83.

20 Guichaoua A (1998) L'administration Territoriale Rwandaise, Rapport "expertise, ICTR, Arusha, pp. 33-35. Such a social system is dependent on relations of patronage and loyalty.

21 Gasana E, Butera J B, Byanafashe D, Karfikzi A, Rwanda. In Adedeji A (1999) Comprehending and mastering African Conflicts, p. 159; see also, Braeckmann C (1994) Rwanda Histoire d'un Genocide, pp. 104-111, id; Storey A (2001) Structural Adjustment, State Power and Genocide: the World Bank and Rwanda, Review of African Political Economy, no: 89, pp. 367-369.

22 Reyntjens F Akazu<<escadrons de la mort>>. In Guichaoua A (1995), pp. 265-273. For a list of alleged members, see p. 765.

23 Newbury C, Newbury D (1999) p. 304.

24 P. 304, Id.

large, as well as moderate Hutu political opponents was increasingly targeted. A memorandum issued to military commanders on 21 September 1992 by Colonel Deogratius Nsabimana, FAR's Chief of Staff, defined and identified the 'principal enemy', as:

"The Tutsi inside and outside the country, extremist and nostalgic for power, who have never recognized and will never recognize the realities of the 1959 social revolution and who wish to reconquer power by all means necessary, including arms". [25]

Partisans of the enemy were defined as those who supported the principal enemy. The memorandum further specified that the enemy and its supporters were recruited principally among the Tutsi refugees, the National Resistance Army (i.e. Uganda Government army), Tutsi inside the country, Hutu dissatisfied with the presidential movement in power, and foreigners married to Tutsi wives.[26]

The identification of the enemy, and those who supported them became a virulent drumbeat of extremist leaders of political parties, as the political impasse accentuated. As the conflict became pronounced, the RPF was labelled "inyenzi" literally meaning cockroach. This term, which had a negative or pejorative connotation, acquired through usage, an extended meaning as referring to Tutsi as a group. According to socio-linguists the meaning of a word depends on the context (i.e. the set of factors and circumstances surrounding the production of speech), in which the word is used.[27] Ascribing a particular meaning to a word is not a political decision as such, but a function of usage, which in turns brings about its acquired meaning.[28] Similarly although the RPF initially referred themselves as "inkotanyi"; literary meaning an ardent warrior or warrior, the word eventually came to mean not only the RPF army but also to Tutsi in general or Tutsi as a whole group.[29] The term also referred to Tutsi their sympathizers whether they were Tutsi or Hutu, Rwandan or non Rwandan.[30] Progressively, and by 1993 "Inyenzi-Inkotanyi" meant inkotanyi who were Tutsi, as well as Tutsi in general. Two other words were trumpeted before and during the genocide. The first "ibyitso" (accomplices), came to be understood by the Rwandan population as from 1993, as referring to Tutsi or Hutu favourable to, or as a sympathizer of the RPF or somebody in agreement with its opinion or policies.[31] The other, a verb "gukora", which literary meant "to work", acquired a more fateful meaning. Used during the 1959 'social revolution' to mean "to destroy" someone's dwelling, it meant in 1994, simply, to kill.[32]

---

25 Human Rights Watch/FILDH (1999) Leave None to Tell the Story, p. 62.

26 P. 63, Id.

27 Expert Testimony, ICTR, Transcript, Dr M. Ruzindana, *P. v. J. B. Barayagwiza, F. Nahimana & H. Ngeze*, ICTR case no: 99-52-T (Joinder), 96-11-T, 97-27-T, 97-19-T, 20 March 2002, pp. 21, 29.

28 Dr M. Ruzindana, Expert Testimony, ICTR, Transcript, p. 68.

29 Pp. 51, 57, 65, 67, Id.

30 Pp. 51, 57, 65, 67, Id.

31 Pp. 80-83, Id.

32 Pp. 100-104, Id.

In the face of external pressure, President Mitterrand's encouragement of multi-parties through his speech during the summit of Francophone States, at La Baule, and internal political developments led to the legalization of political parties on 18 June 1991. A new constitution was adopted by the Counsel national pour le developpment (National Council for Development) [i.e. the National Assembly] on 10 June 1991. The single party was renamed Movement republicaine national pour la democratie et le development (National Republican Movement for Democracy and Development) (MRND) in July 1991. The other parties that were formed, and which subsequently became a part of the Rwandan political scene were the Movement Democratique Republicain (Republican Democratic Movement) (MDR), Parti Social Democratique (Social Democratic Party) (PSD), Parti Liberal (Liberal Party) (PL), and Parti Democrate Chretien (Christian Democratic Party) (PDC). Another party Coalition pour la Defence de la Republique et de democratie (Coalition for the Defence of the Republic and Democracy) (CDR), a by-product of the hard line wing of the MRND was founded on 22 March 1992, but was not accorded any place within the Arusha Accords transitional institutions. A first transitional government was formed consisting exclusively of MRND members, following the refusal of other parties to join. A second transitional government was formed in 1992, with MRND holding nine of nineteen ministerial portfolios.

The media occupied a privileged place in the exacerbation of politico-ethnic tension, and in the name of free expression was manipulated by the Hutu extremists both in the official and private media.[33] The strategy of incitement to ethnic hatred, fear and denigration of Tutsi through the media, which was conceived in the 1990s, was put into motion by these extremists. In the campaign to deepen hatred of Tutsi, extremists played upon memories of past domination by the Tutsi minority and on the legacy of the revolution that overthrew their rule in 1959.[34] By hatred is meant an aversion carried out to a point at which there is a desire to injure or destroy the object of the emotion.[35] The propaganda also targeted Tutsi women as gender stereotypes. It portrayed them as calculated seductress-spies bent on dominating and undermining the Hutu.[36] Incitement became a deliberate political technique to rally supporters and distract attention from domestic problems.[37] The setting up of a 'privately owned' and 'commercial' radio station, 'Radio Television Libre', was conceived on or about 13 July 1992. The company, Radio Television Libre des Milles Collines (RTLM S.A.), was incorporated on 8 April 1993. It was owned largely by members of MRND party, with President Juvenal Habyarimana as the largest shareholder.[38] Its principal ideologist was Fer-

---

33 Guichaoua A (1995) p. 36, Id.

34 Human Rights Watch/FILDH (1999) Leave None to tell the Story, p. 3.

35 Sardar M I K M (1978) Law Terms and Phrases Judicially Interpreted, Law Publishing Co., Lahore, p. 243.

36 Human Rights Watch (1996) Shattered Lives. Sexual Violence during the Rwandan Genocide and its Aftermath, New York, p. 18.

37 Berry C P, Berry J A (eds.) (1999) Genocide in Rwanda. A Collective Memory, Howard University Press, W.D.C., p. 3.

38 *P. v. F. Nahimana et all.*, Judgement, T.C, Case no: ICTR-99-52-T, 3 Dec. 2003, para. 30.

dinand Nahimana.[39] The real purpose for the establishment of RTLM was to defend Hutu "pawa" (power).[40] Direct and public incitement by senior politicians and leaders, and the media, played an instrumental role in propelling atrocity crimes in Rwanda.[41] By direct, we mean specifically urging another individual to take immediate criminal action rather than merely making a vague or indirect suggestion.[42] By public, we mean that the call for criminal action is communicated to a number of individuals in a public place or to members of the general public at large.[43] Known as "Radio Machete", after 6 April 1994, RTLM broadcasts not only engaged in ethnic stereotyping in a manner that promoted contempt and hatred for the Tutsi, but also called explicitly for the extermination of the Tutsi ethnic group. [44]

Among its original founders and shareholders were Felician Kabuga, Ferdinand Nahimana, Joseph Nzirorera, Andre Ntagerura (Minister of Telecommunication), George Rutaganda (Vice President, Youth Wing MRND) Simon Bikindi (Ministry of Youth staff and music composer), and Jean Bosco Barayagwiza. All have been indicted by the ICTR. Of the fifty original founders, forty were from the three Prefectures of northern Rwanda, and all but seven of those from Gisenyi and Ruhengeri, the regions identified with Habyarimana.[45] An agreement between the Rwandan Government and R.T.L.M. SA to establish and operate the radio station was signed on 30 September 1993. The radio began broadcasting on 8 July 1993.

A newspaper, Kangura ("to awaken"), with a circulation of up to 9,500 copies, was set up in order to unite and defend all Hutu, and promote extremist Hutu ideology.[46] Its founding members also included Ferdinand Nahimana, Jean Bosco Barayagwiza and Felician Kabuga. Its owner, founder and editor-in-chief was Hassan Ngeze. Its first issue was published in May 1990, its last in 1995. From March 1992 it expressly made propaganda for the CDR, an extremist party belonging to the presidential movement.[47] CDR promoted killing of Tusti, and it did not open its membership to Rwandans of Tutsi ethnicity.[48] Kangura and CDR functioned as partners in a Hutu coalition.[49] The newspaper was printed at the National Printing Press owned by the Government. It had an anti Tutsi editorial pol-

---

39 Para. 83, Id.

40 The term is said to have been introduced in Rwanda's political vocabulary by Froduard Karemera, Vice President of MDR, during a rally in Kigali in October 1993.

41 See, Schabas W A (2000-2001) Hate Speech in Rwanda: The Road to Genocide, McGill L.J, vol. 46, pp. 141-170.

42 Barboza J (1999) International Criminal Law, Recueil des Cours, T.278, Academie de Droit International, La Haye, p. 45.

43 Barboza J (1999) p. 45.

44 *P. v. F. Nahimana et all.*, Judgement, T.C, paras. 26, 63, 99.

45 Human Rights Watch/FILDH (1999) Leave None to tell the story, p. 68.

46 Chrétien J P (ed.) (1995) Rwanda. Les Medias du Génocide, Karthala and Reporteurs sans Frontières, Paris, p. 17.

47 Reyntjens F Akazu. << escadrons de la mort.>> In Guichaoua A (1995) p. 271.

48 *P. v. F. Nahimana et all.*, Judgement, T.C, para. 22.

49 Para. 62, Id.

icy, used anti Tutsi language, and was one of the most virulent voices of hate.[50] It published the 'Ten Commandments of the Bahutu' in Issue No. 6 in December 1990. The Commandments conveyed contempt and hatred for the Tutsi ethnic group and for Tutsi women in particular as enemy agents.[51] They spelled out that every Hutu who took a Tutsi women as a concubine, secretary or protégée was a traitor; that every Hutu must know that every Tutsi businessmen was dishonest, and that he only aimed at supremacy of this ethnic group; that any Hutu who makes an alliance with a Tutsi businessman, or who borrowed from a Tutsi, or who gave him any business favour was equally a traitor; that strategic posts, as well as political, administrative, economic, military and security posts must be put in Hutu hands; that the education sector must be Hutu in majority; that the Rwandan Armed Forces must be exclusively Hutu, and a Hutu soldier cannot take a Tutsi women as a wife; that Hutu must be firm and vigilant against their common enemy, Tutsi; and that the 1959 social revolution, the 1961 Referendum and the Hutu ideology must be to every Hutu and at all levels. Kangura further extensively used caricature to reinforce a culture of violence through words and lies.[52]

In early 1991 more than 1,200 Bagogwe, a clan stemming from the Tutsi were massacred in North West Rwanda. In March 1992 Hutus attacked Tutsi in the southern part of the country. A phenomenal incident of incitement to ethnic hatred and violence was the speech by Leon Mugesera, MRND Vice President for Gisenyi Prefecture, delivered in Kabaya, Gisenyi, on 22 November 1992, and broadcasted over Radio Rwanda. His threat to the Tutsi: "I am telling you that your home is in Ethiopia, that we are going to send you there quickly, by the Nyabarongo [River]" [53] became one of the violent methods of the commission of atrocity crimes in Rwanda in 1994.[54] In her testimony in *P. v. J. P. Akayesu* Alison Des Forges, Expert Witness for the Prosecution opined that the systematic throwing of Tutsi into the Nyabarongo river, a tributary of the Nile river had as underlying intention to "send the Tutsi back to their place of origin", to "make them return to Abyssinia", in keeping with the allegation that the Tutsi are foreigners in Rwanda, where they are supposed to have settled following their arrival from the Nilotic regions.[55] On 19 April 1994, during a public rally, on the occasion of the installation of the new Prefet of Butare, President Sindikubwabo declared:

---

50 Human Rights Watch/FILDH (1999) Leave None to Tell the Story, p. 66; Expert Testimony, ICTR, Transcript, Dr M. Ruzindana, pp. 107- 110.

51 *P. v. F. Nahimana et all.*, Judgement, T.C, para. 16.

52 Chrétien J P (ed.) (1995) Les Medias du Génocide, p. 361.

53 "*Je te fait saviour que chez vous c'est en Ethipie et que vous y'en verra par la Nyabarongo*", See also, Human Rights Watch (1999) Propaganda and Practice, www.hrwor/reports/1999/rwanda/Geno1-3-10.htm.

54 See, *Decision dans la Cause Contre Leon Mugesera et Le Ministre de la Citoyenneté et de l'immigration*, Décision et Motifs de M. Pierre Turmel, Arbitre, Dossier No. QML-95-00171, Montreal, 11 Juillet 1996; This decision was overturned on appeal to the Canadian Federal Court of Appeal. The Govt. of Canada has appealed to the Supreme Court.

55 *P. v. J. P. Akayesu*, Case No. ICTR-96-4-T, Judgement, 2 September 1998, para. 120.

"I do not want you to take our messages, speeches and lessons as if they were mere words spoken in the air; these are important messages since we are in a period of war. What does this mean? What this mean is that those who are waiting for the others to work, they should watch us work without being part of our team. If someone feels like saying, 'I am not concerned, that does not concern me, I am afraid, that person should move away from us".[56]

In that context the word "work" clearly meant "to kill".[57]

Arusha Peace Agreement

Negotiations between the Government of Rwanda and the RPF, coordinated by the Organization of African Unity (OAU) and 'facilitated' by Tanzania, led to the signing of the Peace Agreement between the two Rwandan parties in Arusha on 4 August 1993. [58] The parties agreed that war between them had been brought to an end; that the Rwandan Constitution of 10 June 1991, and the Peace Agreement constituted indissolubly the fundamental law which was to govern Rwanda during the transitional period, and that the transitional institutions (i.e. Presidency, National Transitional Assembly and a Broad-Based Transitional Government (BBTG), were to be set up within 37 days of the signing of the agreement.[59] The main objectives of the Arusha Peace talks were to end the civil war and to construct a post war peace agreement in a situation short of total victory and absolute defeat.[60] It was meant to provide room for the RPF and other political forces so that they could occupy political, military and economic space. Under the Accords the incumbent President was to remain in office until the outcome of elections to be conducted towards the end of the transitional period. To this effect Habyarimana took the constitutional oath of office as interim Head of State on 5 January 1994. The Accords reserved the position of President to MRND, and that of Prime

---

56 Dr. M. Ruzindana, Expert Testimony, ICTR, Transcript, pp. 15-16.

57 P. 104, Id.; see also HRW/FILDH (1999) Leave None to Tell the Story, pp. 454-461.

58 Peace Agreement between the Government of the Republic of Rwanda and the Rwandans Patriotic Front. The agreement includes six protocols concluded and signed as part of the Arusha talks, namely The N'sele Ceasefire agreement of 29 March 1991, as amended in Gladolite on 16 Sept. and Arusha on 12 July 1992, Protocol of agreement on the rule of law, signed at Arusha on 18 Sept. 1992, Protocol of agreement on power-sharing signed at Arusha on 30 October 1992, and 9 January 1993, Protocol of agreement on the repatriation of refugees and resettlement of displaced persons, signed at Arusha on 9 June 1993, Protocol of agreement on the integration of the armed forces of the two parties, signed at Arusha on 3 August 1993, and the Protocol of agreement on miscellaneous issues and final provisions signed at Arusha on 3 August 1993 by which the parties reached agreement on the appointment of Prime Minister, and the transitional period which was set at 22 months. UN Doc. A/48/824-S/26915, 23 Dec.1993.

59 Arts. 1, 2 & 7. This was to be followed by a second phase that would cover national elections, to take place 22 months after the installation of the transitional government.

60 Suhrke A (1997) UN Peace-Keeping in Rwanda in Sorbo G, Vale P (1997) Out of Conflict. From War to Peace in Africa, Nordiska Afrikainstitutet, Uppsala, p. 103.

Minister was allocated to MDR. The distribution of ministerial portfolios and membership to the Transitional Assembly was also proportionately distributed among five political parties and the RPF.[61] Also of significance the post of Minister of Defence was earmarked for MRND, that of Interior to RPF, and Foreign Affairs to MDR.

The Accords provided for the formation of a single national army and a new gendarmerie consisting of 13,000 men from both the Rwandan Armed Forces (FAR) and the Rwandan Patriotic Front (RPF).[62] The RPF was to constitute 40% of the new integrated military forces, and FAR the remaining 60%. The sharing of the army officer corps positions was to be 50% for each group. It also provided that during the transitional phase an RPF security battalion of 600 troops was to be cantoned in Kigali.[63] The creation of the newly integrated army meant immediate demobilization of thousands of soldiers and gendarmerie. It was like serving an unemployment notice.[64]

In order to assist in the implementation of the peace agreement, the parties agreed on the presence of a neutral international force, and a neutral military observer group under the responsibility and command of the United Nations. The responsibilities allocated to the proposed force included assistance in ensuring overall security in Kigali and in the recovery of all weapons distributed to or illegally acquired by civilians, and monitoring the observance of formalities for a definite cessation of hostilities.[65] To facilitate implementation of the accord, the United Nations Security Council, on 5 October 1993 established a United Nations Mission in Rwanda (UNAMIR).[66] The Mission was mandated to contribute to the security of Kigali; to monitor the cease-fire agreement which called for the establishment of cantonment and assembly zones; to monitor the security situation during the final period of the transitional Government's mandate leading up to the elections, and to investigate non-compliance with the Peace Agreement.[67]

UNAMIR was a watchdog aimed at ensuring implementation of the Arusha Agreement.[68] It was established as a peacekeeping operation under Chapter 6 of the UN Charter. It was based on the consent of the parties (i.e. the Rwandan Government and the RPF), and did not have an enforcement mandate. It was authorized to use force only as a last resort and in self-defence. The Arusha Peace

61 The distribution of Ministerial portfolios was MRND (5), RPF (5), MDR, including Prime Minister (4), PSD (3) Pl (3) and PDC (1). For that of the Transitional Assembly MRND (11), RPF (11), PSD (11), PL (11), PDC (4) and other regional parties (1 seat each). Arts. 6, 55, 57, 63, Protocol of Agreement on Power Sharing.

62 Arts. 2 & 147 (Demobilization process), Protocol on the Integration of the Armed Forces of the Two Parties, Arusha Peace Agreement.

63 Art. 72, Id.; The battalion arrived in Kigali on 28 Dec.1993.

64 Mamdani M (2001) p. 210.

65 Arts. 53 & 54, Arusha Peace Agreement.

66 UN SC resolution 872 (1993), 5 October 1993; extended by UN Sc resolution 909 (1994), 5 April 1994.It was further extended to 29 July 1994.

67 Id.

68 Khan S M Learning the Lessons from Genocide in Rwanda, The East African, 9-15 February 1999.

Agreement considered the return of Rwandan refugees to their country as an inalienable right and that it constituted a factor of peace, national unity and reconciliation.[69] Returning refugees were entitled to repossess their property on return, but the parties recommended that refugees who left the country for more than ten years should not reclaim their properties.[70] In a joint declaration issued on 10 December 1993 the Government of Rwanda and RPF reaffirmed their commitment to the Arusha Peace Agreement, and agreed to set up a Broad Based Transitional Government and a Transitional National Assembly before 31 December 1993. By that date however, it had not been constituted, nor installed due to inability of the parties to settle their political differences.

Hutu extremists including several of President Habyarimana's close associates vehemently opposed the power sharing arrangements of the Accords. The President himself, in a speech in Ruhengeri on 15 November 1992 rejected Protocol I on the power sharing arrangements. He publicly characterized it as nothing but "a scrap of paper".[71] The Peace Agreement challenged Hutu power interests. It provided for a greater political role for Tutsi, which Hutu extremists portrayed as an unfair democratic over-representation.[72] There was also discontent within the Rwandan Armed Forces. Officers from the north feared not only loosing key positions to RPF, but also of the return of officers from the south who had been removed from the army, but who now had the support of the opposition parties.[73] That the Habyarimana's Government was still pursuing the logic of armed conflict rather than the spirit of the Arusha Peace Agreement is reflected in the Government's procurement of conventional arms and ammunitions immediately before, as well as after, the signing of the Accords. On 9 July 1993 less than 5 weeks before the signing of the Agreement it signed a 13.5 million USD contract for the purchase of arms. The order included 10,000 hand grenades, 20,000 rifle grenades, and 5,000 anti personal mines from Denel International Marketing of South Africa a division of Denel (PTY) Ltd. This contract was not executed due to the withdrawal of the mandatory arms permit by the Government of South Africa on 28 March 1994. Similarly the Government signed another contract to the tune of 10.8 million USD with Egypt on 7 February 1994 six months after the Arusha Peace Accords. A contract that was also not honoured by Egypt following the events of April 1994. In discussions with the United Nations Secretary-General's political mission to Rwanda in May 1994, the 'head' of the interim Government of Rwanda argued that the Accords rested on the fallacious premise that tensions in Rwanda would be resolved by a political formula when the fundamental problem was ethnic; the historic animosity between the majority Hutu who in the past had been

---

69 Art. 1, Protocol on the Repatriation of Refugees.

70 Art. 4, Arusha Peace Agreement. The Government was to provide compensation by putting land at the disposal of such persons.

71 "ni masezerano ki? Si ibi papuro", Nsengiyareme D 'La Transition Démocratique au Rwanda (1989-93)', p. 258 in Guichaoua A(1995) Les crises politique; Braeckman C (1994) p. 138.

72 Klinghoffer A J (1998) The International Dimension of Genocide in Rwanda, New York University Press, N.Y, p. 116.

73 Braeckmann C (1994) p. 170.

ruled by the minority Tutsi, and that the accords granted the RPF far more political power than their demographic proportion of 15 % justified.[74]

It has been submitted that three aspects of the Arusha Peace Agreement contributed to the polarization of political tension in Rwanda.[75] First hardliners in the government insisted that President Habyarimana had given up too much to the RPF who had been allocated 5 out of 20 ministerial portfolios and 11 out of 70 seats in the transitional national assembly. Secondly they drew upon uncertainties and insecurities in the army that would result from the demobilization of two-thirds of FAR troops and the lack of an effective policy and clear plans for the re-integration of soldiers into civil society. Thirdly the stipulation that refugees had a right to return and to reclaim their property resurfaced a class issue that raised the concern of land security for all Rwandan peasants.[76] To Andre Guichaoua, the Accords represented military peace,[77] and constituted a negotiated victory for the RFP. [78]

Events in Burundi also had an impact in Rwanda. On 21 October 1993, Burundi's first democratically elected Hutu President, Melchior Ndadaye, was assassinated by members of the Tutsi controlled army upon his return from a Francophone Summit in Mauritius. Thousands of Hutu were killed in subsequent violence in which the army was extensively involved. The killing reinforced the claim by Hutu extremists in Rwanda that power sharing with Tutsi was not possible. It deepened the level of mistrust, and had a negative effect on the prospect of peaceful co-existence with RPF, which had direct and secret links with the Burundi Army.[79] The assassination of Ndadaye led to violent retaliation by Hutu extremist and the systematic massacres of the Tutsi in that country; two elements of regional memory that played an important role after the death of Habyarimana

Extremist Hutu opposition to the Arusha Agreement and intra-party factionalism, especially within the Liberal Party (PL), resulted in prolonged delays in establishing the transitional institutions. Among those ferociously against the accords was CDR. It was not a party to the Arusha peace talks, and demanded a post of Deputy to the Transitional Assembly; the demand of which was supported by President Habyarimana but opposed by RPF which considered that party, "a crypto-fascist gang that would not even allow anyone with a Tutsi grandparent to

---

74 Report of the Secretary-General on the situation in Rwanda, reporting on the political mission he sent to Rwanda to move the warring parties towards a ceasefire, par. 30, UN Doc. S/1994/640, 31 May 1994.

75 Newbury C, Newbury D (1999) p. 308.

76 Newbury C, Newbury D (1999) p. 308.

77 See, Guichaoua A (1995) pp. 19-51; Cf. " Les solutions avancees…notammnent dans l'accord de paix d'Arusha, visaient a metre fin a la guerre, sans garantir la fin du conflict qui en est la cause", Gasana G La guerre, la paix, et la democratie au Rwanda. In Guichaoua A (1995) p. 236.

78 Andre Guichaoua: L'asassinat du president Habyarimana a ete programme des 1993, Le Monde, 06.05.2004.

79 Nsengiyaremye D Le Transition Démocratique au Rwanda. In Guichaoua A (1995) p. 261.

join".[80] Mamdani submits that the Arusha Peace Agreement was signed "still-born", mainly because it failed to take account of the extremist CDR, either by including it or containing it.[81] Furthermore political differences and repeated delays contributed to the deterioration of the security situation. Frequent violations of the weapons free zone established in and around Kigali took place. Party militias were secretly trained by the Rwandan Armed Forces, and in concert with their parties stockpiled weapons. Between October 1990 and January 1993 at least 2,000 civilians became victims of extra judicial, summary, or arbitrary executions.[82] It been submitted by Andre Guichaoua that violence was also attributable to the RPF, and that between July 1991 and September 1992 forty five assassinations were carried out by them, including renewed attacks which were carried out between March and May 1993.[83] The Minister of Public Works and Executive Secretary of PSD was assassinated on 21 February 1994. On the following day a crowd in Butare lynched the President of CDR.[84]

The worsening political climate and mounting insecurity became a more imminent threat to the peace process itself. UN Secretary-General Boutros Boutros Ghali regarded the delay in the transitional process a "persistent impasse" and a "serious impediment" to the peace process.[85] On 14 March 1994 Willy Claes, Belgium Foreign Minister, qualified it as a political deadlock.[86] By then the other transitional institutions, such as the various Commissions foreseen in the Arusha Peace Accords were still not in place. In fact there was no indication when they would be instituted.

80 Melvern L (2000) A People Betrayed. The Role of the West in Rwanda's Genocide, Zed Books, London, p. 54.

81 Mamdani M (2001) p. 211; " The key lesson of the Arusha Agreement is that one cannot put an end to the civil war by excluding one party to it, especially the party most entrenched in its partisan ideology", at p. 278.

82 Report by the Special Rapporteur on extrajudicial, summary and arbitrary executions on his mission to Rwanda, 8-17 April 1993, UN Doc. E/CN.4/1994/7 Add.1, 1993, para. 27.

83 Andre Guichaoua: L' assasinat du president Hanyarimana a ete programme des 1993, Le Monde, 06.05.2004.

84 General R. Dellaire, Testimony, ICTR, Transcript, *P. v. J. P. Akayesu*, Case no: ICTR-95-4-T, 25 February 1998, p. 55.

85 United Nations (1996) The United Nations and Rwanda. 1993-1996, Department of Public Information, pp. 242-243; UN Doc. S/1994/360, para. 9, 30 March 1994; See also Statement of the President of the Security Council expressing concern over delays in establishing transitional government and the deteriorating security situation in Rwanda, UN Doc. S/PRST/1994/8, 17 Feb.1994.

86 Letter dated 14 March 1994 from the Minister of Foreign Affairs of Belgium to the UN Secretary-General, Doc. 34, in United Nations (1996) The UN and Rwanda, p. 224.

Genocide: Its Beginnings

On 6 April 1994 the plane carrying President Habyarimana back to Kigali from Dar es Salaam, Tanzania, where he had attended a regional Summit, was shot down at 2020 hrs on its approach to Kigali Airport. It exploded and crashed into the garden of the presidential residence at Kanombe, Kigali. All passengers, including the President of Burundi Cyprien Ntaryamira were killed. Under the Arusha Peace Agreement the Transitional Government was to have been installed on 8 April 1994. On the ever of his travel to Dar es salaam, Habrayimana had met the United Nations Secretary General's Special Representative to Rwanda, Jacques-Roger Booh Booh (Cameroon), and discussions had taken place on the imperative to put in place soonest the remaining institutions of the transitional government. A UN Security Council meeting in New York on UNAMIR's fate was scheduled to take place on 5 April 1994.

Although initially referred to as an "air crash"[87], a "tragic accident",[88] a "tragic incident"[89] or a "disastrous incident"[90], the shooting down of the Presidential aircraft was a criminal act of dire consequences for Rwanda. It was the 'spark to the power keg'[91] that set off the formal beginning of the genocide. Accountability for this criminal conduct is a prime requirement for the clarification of facts on the conflict. It is also essential to revelation of the truth about the atrocity crimes committed in Rwanda in 1994. We note this since the question of an effective investigation of the downing of the Presidential plane, and the wilful killing of two Heads of States, of Burundi and Rwanda, and others still hangs in the air. We shall discuss the place for such an investigation within the strategy and priorities of any international Prosecutor and of accountability for atrocity crimes.

The relevance of this tragic incident, and for that matter any singular act or acts responsible for the immediate ignition of atrocity crimes for the purposes of accountability, is whether it be considered an mandatory entry point for investigations, or that it is only a factor be taken into consideration in the overall investigations of persons responsible for the crimes committed. The experience of the ICTR has it that a triggering event such as the April 6, 1994, shooting down of the Presidential plane, erroneously lead criminal investigations to an inquiry and the gathering of evidence on what happened as of that date onwards, rather than what previously transpired that could have led to that fateful event, or the identification of persons, groups or agencies responsible for prior planning and organization of

---

87 Statement by the Secretary-General expressing grief over the deaths of the Presidents of Burundi and Rwanda, UN Press Release SG/SM/5259, 7 April 1994.

88 Statement by the President of the Security Council regretting the deaths of the Presidents of Rwanda and Burundi and condemning all acts of violence in Rwanda, particularly the deaths of 10 Belgium peace-keepers, UN Doc.S/PRST/1994/16, 7 April 1994.

89 UN SC resolution 912(1994), UN Doc. S/RES/912 (1994), 21 April 1994.

90 Letter of the Secretary General to the President of the Security Council, UN Doc. S/1994/518, 29 April 1994.

91 Report on the situation of human rights in Rwanda submitted by Mr Rene Degni-Segui, Special rapporteur of the Commission on Human Rights, UN Doc. E/CN.4/1995/7, 28 June 1994, para. 58.

atrocity crimes. In East Timor a singular event, the announcement of the outcome of the popular consultation on 4 September 1999, which resulted in immediate large-scale violence, was also taken as the starting point of the initial criminal probe by United Nations Civilian Police (CIVPOL) investigations. Amiss in the case of East Timor was the evidential built-up, as early as January 1999, of the widespread and systematic intimidation, threat and violence against pro-independence supporters that took place from the beginning of that year, and which later engulfed that island state. *A prosecution strategy for atrocity crimes requires a gestational gathering of facts.* It requires a gathering of evidence of events prior to the triggering act or acts. As we shall illustrate in Rwanda, the planning of the genocide can only be ascertained by the conduct of an inquiry into events, at least from the outbreak of the armed conflict in October 1990.

In East Timor atrocity crimes could only be judicially explained by investigating as early as 27 January 1999, when President B. J. Habibie of Indonesia announced that East Timorese would be permitted to decide, whether they accepted or not special autonomy within the Unitary State of the Republic of Indonesia. Although these events explain certain conduct, they only have significant value when fully investigated in the context of their proper occurrence; not as isolated incidents. Atrocity crimes invariably involve the use of governmental, party, military, para-statal, and civil apparatus, assets and resources. They also encompass a policy element of a political or military kind. As a matter of investigation and prosecution of those with the greatest responsibility this requires as a must, an examination of past conduct or acts.

It took until the later part of May 1994 for UNAMIR to be able to go to the site of the plane crash, since the Presidential Guard had categorically refused access.[92] It also took time to establish that it was in fact missiles that brought down the President's plane.[93] UNAMIR never initiated an investigation, although RPF had agreed as early as the 7 April 1994 for a neutral country to send a team of investigators.[94] As noted, criminal investigations into the singular triggering incident of the 1994 events in Rwanda remains an unfinished affair. Although not a sole prerogative of the ICTR Prosecutor, it is perhaps the sole independent organ that could have delivered an impartial answer. Justice is also a question of transparency and truth which legitimizes the prosecution of individuals no matter what side they may belong to. To the former ICTR President Judge Pillay, the non-investigation of the plane crash is a serious omission which should not affect the current trials.[95] For her the assassination of a President, which in the case of Rwanda took place within the Tribunal's temporal jurisdiction, is a serious crime that should have been investigated.[96]

It is proper that one discusses the attitude of the International Criminal Tribunal for Rwanda on the investigation of the shooting down of the Presidential plane,

---

92 General R. Dellaire, Testimony, ICTR, Transcript, p. 122.

93 P. 122, Id.

94 P. 123, Id.

95 Interview by author, The Hague, 19 June 2003.

96 Id.

and the repeated demand by accused persons to the Prosecutor and the Tribunal to disclose to them information on investigations of that tragic incident. All parties, both the Prosecution and the Defence, unanimously agree that the assassination of President Habyarimana was what triggered, if not precipitated the events that occurred in Rwanda between April and July 1999. The articulation of nearly all indictments by the Prosecutor, and confirmed and accepted by the Tribunal as well as the Defence, contain a statement to the "pivotal" effect of that incident to the atrocity crimes committed in Rwanda. That statement has generally been considered a broad statement of fact with no causal link to any incriminating allegation against an accused in all the indictments so far issued by the Prosecutor.

That said, a number of accused have expressly demanded the Tribunal to order the Prosecutor to investigate the plane crash, in that it is fundamental to a clear understanding of the planning and execution of the massacres of which some of the accused have been charged with, and for a fair and proper administration of justice.[97] Generally, Trial Chambers have held that in these requests, the Defence had failed to establish any causal link between the requested investigation into the responsibility for the plane crash and the acts and omissions which form the basis of the charges against the accused in the indictment; that the Chambers have no authority, under the Statute or the Rules, to order the Prosecutor to open any such investigation, and that the issue is one solely for the discretion of the Prosecutor.[98]

Following the transmission by the United Nations Headquarters in New York, to the Tribunal, of a three page report by a former investigator of the Office of the Prosecutor whom Deputy Prosecutor Bernard Muna categorized as a "fire raiser",[99] on a summary of an investigation report on that incident, accused persons before the Tribunal also sought from the Prosecutor the disclosure of its contents on the ground that it was material to their cases. The Prosecution on its part argued that the report was not in its possession and thus not subject to disclosure, and moreover that any such information in her possession would be a report, memorandum or internal document prepared by the Office of the Prosecutor in connection with its investigation and preparation of the case as envisaged by Rule 70 and thus not subject to disclosure. The Trial Chamber, while making no finding as to the relevance of the report, in the interest of justice, decided to invoke the inherent powers of the Tribunal, and ordered the release and disclosure of the report

---

97 Defence Motion Seeking Supplementary Investigations, *P. v. G. Kabiligi*, Case no: ICTY-97-34-I, 5 January 1999; Defence Motion for an order to the Prosecutor to investigate the circumstances of the crash of President Habyarimana's place, *P. v. J. Nzirorera*, Case no: ICTR-97-20-I, 8 December 1999.

98 Decision on the Defence Motion Seeking Supplementary Investigations, para 19-20, *P. v. G. Kabiligi*, Case no: ICTR –97-34-1, 1 June 2000; Decision on the Defence Motion seeking An Order to the Prosecutor to Investigate the circumstances of the Plane crash of president Habyarimana's plane, *P. v. J. Nzirorera,* Case no: ICTR-97-20-I, 2 June 2000, p. 3.

99 Arusha Tribunal Will Not Investigate Habyarimana's Death, Panafrican News Agency, 4 April 2000; Statement by the President. Plane Crash in Rwanda in April 1994, Press Release, ICTR/INFO-9-2-228STA.EN, 17 April 2000.

to both the Prosecution and the Defence.[100] They considered the circumstances exceptional and not precedent setting.

An interesting dimension of the legal problematic involved in the above is reflected in the Trial Chamber *Decision on the request of the Defence for an Order for service of a UN Memorandum.*[101] There, on Bagilishema's request for a copy of the memorandum the Prosecutor had argued that the plane crash was a mere historical fact of common knowledge and thus no disclosure obligation arose. On his part, Bagilishema submitted that the Prosecutor had presented its case on the basis that the plane crash triggered the subsequent massacres that took place, including those in which he is charged (i.e. Kibuye). The Trial Chamber held:[102]

> "irrespective of whether the Memorandum will in the event have a bearing on the outcome of the case, the Chamber is of the opinion that, to deprive the Defence, at this stage of the trial, of access to specific document, which is now in the possession of the Tribunal, may affect the right of the accused in the presentation of his case fully and fairly. Reference is made to Article 20 of the Statute which guarantees the right of the accused to a fair trial".

It directed the Registrar to serve forthwith a copy of that memorandum to the defence and to make available a copy to the prosecution, if it so desired.[103] In a separate and dissenting opinion Judge Mehmet Guney considered that a document which is in its nature so uncertain cannot, in principle, be useful for the manifestation of the truth in general and in particular for the defence of an accused.[104] Furthermore, that it did not establish a cause-specific effect relation between the plane crash and his acts or omissions which formed the basis of the accusations against him in his quality as Bourgmestre of Mabanza Commune, and that in the absence of a causal link between the authors of the plane crash and the authors of crimes alleged in the indictment that request had no merit.[105]

A recent turn of events on the shooting of the Falcon F 50 Presidential plane registration (registration number 9XR-NN) is the storm unleashed by the publication in Le Monde, a leading French newspaper on 10 March 2004 of parts of the report and findings of the French Investigating Judge Jean-Louis Bruguiere's 6 years investigations on the incident.[106] The newspaper which had access to the 220

---

[100] Decision on Ntabakuze's Motion for Disclosure of Material, *P. v. G. Kabilgi & A. Ntabakuze*, Case no: ICTR-97-34-I, 8 June 2000, paras. 23 & 25; Decision on Kabiligi's Supplementary Motion for Investigation and Disclosure of Evidence, *P. v. G. Kabiligi & A. Ntabakuze*, Case no: ICTR-97-34-1, 8 June 2000, paras. 16 & 18.

[101] *P. v.I .Bagilishema*, ICTR-95-1A-I (Judges E. Mose and Asoka de Z. Gunawardane, Judge M. Guney *Dissenting*), 8 June 2000.

[102] Id.

[103] Id.

[104] Id.

[105] Id.

[106] Le recit de láttenat du 6 avril 1994 par un ancient member du "network commado"; Lénquete sur láttentat qui fit basculer le Rwanda dans le genocide, Le Monde, Le Monde 09.03.2004; Rwanda: revelations d' un expert de la justice international, Le Monde, 06.05.2004; See also Guichaoua A Migrants, refugies et deplaces en Afrique cenrale et orientale, Editions Karthala, Paris, p. 165.

pages report dated 30 January 2004, titled "Result of the investigation of the National Anti-Terrorist Division of the General Directorate of the Judicial Police" revealed that it imputed responsibility for that incident to the Rwandan Patriotic Front, and particularly Rwanda's President Paul Kagame as the principle decision-maker of the that plane crash, as well as 10 senior RPF commanders and the 2 launchers of the surface-to-air missile that fired and the shot it.

These judicially untested allegations in Bruguiere's report are based on the investigation he conducted and from admissions by made Captain Venuste Josue Abdul Ruzibiza a member of the "Commando Network" who claimed responsibility for that incident. The captain has further alleged that this network, a secret structure within RPF and commanded at its highest level, consisted of a reconnaissance, logistic and an execution group. According to his narration between September 1993 and February 1994 three preparatory meetings took place in Mulindi, the RPF base to prepare the same. The article revealed that one of the material links to the shooting was provided to Bruguiere from Russian Military Prosecutors, is trace of the SA 16 low altitude surface-to-air missiles which were part of the consignment of 40 such missiles manufactured in April 1987 and sold by the Soviet Union to Uganda through a "state to state" trade deal and which were passed on to the RPF in January 2004. The two missile tube launchers recovered from the plane crash were also used to trace to source of the arms used.

The article published on the eve of President Kagame's state visit to Belgium drew strong indignation from Rwanda's Head of State who in a press conference with Belgium Prime Minster Guy Verhofstadt held on 11 March 2004 virulently denied any personal involvement, including that of RPF.[107] He blamed France for diverting attention on the eve of the 10th anniversary of the commemoration of the genocide so that it is eclipsed by the shooting of the Presidential plane, an event that triggered the pre-planned atrocity crimes. He further accused France for furnishing arms, active participation in the preparation and killing of Tutsi, and of fleeing its responsibility in their extermination. These developments underscores the very point made earlier that without an impartial investigation by a technically competent and authoritative body it is almost certain that any result or finding by a national authority of any State will be contested or challenged by one party or the other. Additionally, without such an investigation accountability for the criminal act and its truth will remain ever elusive.[108]

Immediately following the shooting down of the Presidential plane over Gregoire Kayibanda International Airport in Kanombe, Kigali, a number of senior officers of the Rwandan Armed Forces, including Theoneste Bagosora, then *Directeur de cabinet* of the Minister of Defense, pushed for a military take over, but that option was rejected by some of the others. The Special Representative of the Sec-

---

[107] Le president rwandais Paul Kagame recuse avec virulence lénquete Bruguiere, Le Monde 12.03.2004; Genocide: le president rwandais accuse la France, Le Monde, 16.03.2004; Paul Kagame relance la polemique sur la passé de la France au Rwanda, Le Monde, 17.03.2004.

[108] War Crimes Court asked to summon Kagame over 1994 assassination, AFP, 27 November 2003.

retary General (SRSG) in Rwanda Jacques-Roger Booh-Booh, UNAMIR Commander General Delaire, and some members of the diplomatic community, in particular the United States, in meetings with Bagosora and other senior military and gendarmerie officers discouraged that option. Instead an interim Government, under the 10 June 1991 Constitution, and through the umbrella of Rwanda's five main political parties was set up. Pursuant to Article 42 of the Constitution of Rwanda (1991), the Chairman of the National Development Council, Theodore Sindikubwabo, assumed office as the President of Rwanda. An interim Government headed by Jean Kambanda, as Prime Minister, was sworn-in on 9 April 1994, with MRND holding 9 ministerial portfolios, including the President of the Republic, and the remaining 11 portfolios, including that of Prime Minister, allocated to the "pawa" (power) factions of the other parties. The cabinet contained no Tutsi as members.

The SRSG and the UNAMIR Force Commander met Bagosora on the night of the 6th April 1994, and asked him to abide by the strict application of the Arusha Accords to allow the government to manage the crisis as well the need for Prime Minister Agathe Uwilingiyimana to be involved in the handling of the crisis and for her to address the people on the radio. She had planned to address the nation at 09:00 hrs on 7 April 1994, and appeal for calm while steps were being taken by authorities to control the situation[109] She had planned to do that via the Government Radio, the other radio station, RTLM, having bluntly refused. Bagosora who "took charge"[110] immediately after the death of President Habyarimana, categorically refused to meet the Prime Minister, alleging that she no longer had the necessary credibility with the nation.[111] A number of Ghanaian peacekeeping soldiers, and a Togo military observer, as well as 10 Belgium peacekeeping soldiers who were dispatched to provide additional security, and escort her to the radio station were overpowered by Rwandan Armed Forces soldiers. They were disarmed, arrested, and taken to Kigali military Camp a short distance from her residence. The Prime Minister and her immediate family fled her residence. She sought refuge in the house of a Senegalese United Nations Volunteer. She and her husband were discovered, dislodged, and taken back to her residence where they were killed.[112] As events unfolded, the 10 Belgium peacekeeping soldiers were killed by FAR soldiers at Camp Kigali, where Major Bernard Ntuyahaga had taken them. [113] The Headquarters of the Rwandan Armed Forces and the Reconnaissance Battalion were located at the Camp.

The shooting down of the presidential plane, and the death of President Habyarimana triggered on 7 April 1999 the selective killing of Tutsi and moderate

---

109 Rwanda: enquete sur un genocide oblie, Le Monde, 31 mars- 4 avril, 1998.

110 Human Rights Watch/FILDL (1999) Leave None to Tell The Story, p. 197.

111 Castonguay J (1998) Les Casques Blues au Rwanda, Editions L'Harmattan, Paris, p. 108.

112 It has been alleged that she was shot by a Lieutenant of he national Police on the orders of a Presidential Guard Captain, See, Human Rights Watch/ FILDH (1999) Leave None to Tell the Story, pp. 187 – 191; L'Assasinat D'Agathe Uwilingiyimana Premier Ministre. In Guichaoua A (1995) pp. 694-696.

113 See, Castonguay J (1998) pp. 105 –126.

Hutu in Remera quarters in Kigali by Presidential Guard soldiers. Some Ministers like Andre Ntagerura Minster of Transport and Cizimir Bizimungu Minister for Health were evacuated to safety by President Guard and other soldiers.[114] Others like Faustin Rucogoza Minister for Information who had warned RTLM officials in November 1993 and on 10 February 2004 about the broadcast of hate material that could incite ethnic hatred, and Landoald Ndasingwa Minister of Social Affairs were arrested and executed on that day.[115]

The incident became the most immediate excuse offered for the violence.[116] In the first 24 hours the entire moderate opposition could no longer be found; they had either been killed, had fled, or went into hiding.[117] Roadblocks by Presidential Guards, the interahamwe, and sometimes by the Rwandan Armed Forces and Gendermerie were set up within hours of the plane crash, the first by Presidential Guards in Kigali, as early as 21:18 hrs on 6 April 1994.[118] At these roadblocks identity cards were checked, and those identified or perceived to be Tutsi were takėn away and killed.[119] In Remera and Kimihurura quarters in Kigali, elements of the Presidential Guards searched for and selectively eliminated Tutsi and moderate Hutu leaders. On the other hand they evacuated to safety MRND politicians and their families.

On 7 April1974 at around 16:00 hrs, the 600 RPF soldiers who had been stationed since 28 December 1993 at the Conseil national de developpement (CND) (i.e. National Assembly) compound left their cantonment area and engaged FAR, including elements of the Presidential Guard. On or about the 7th of April, RPF troops then based in Mulindi, Rwanda, near the Ugandan border, advanced towards Kigali. At that time, it was estimated that RPF had about 12,000-13,000 troops deployed in three groups, two groups in the western flank of the demilitarized zone, and one in the eastern flank with 6 independent battalions (i.e. a reconnaissance battalion, an air defence battalion with heavy weaponry, a missiles battalion, ground-to-ground missiles and a mortar battalion).[120] The Rwandan Armed Forces had an estimated strength of 35,000 troops, 23,000 of which were in an area about 5 to 10 kilometres in the southern area of the demilitarized zone, with a heavy concentration in Byumba and Ruhengeri[121] In Kigali they had about 7,000 troops, among which there was an artillery battalion, the reconnaissance bat-

---

114 Rwanda; Wife of Former Constitutional Court President Tells of Husband's Capture, Hirondelle News Agency (HNA), 27 Nov. 2003; There were previous attempts to Murder my Husband, says Witness, HNA, 28 Nov. 2003.

115 Id.

116 *P. v. Omar Serishago*, Reasons for Judgement, Appeal Chamber, ICTR case no: 98-39-A, 6 April 2000, para. 5.

117 General R. Dellaire, Testimony, ICTR, Transcript, p. 205.

118 Report of the Secretary General on the investigation of serious international humanitarian law violations committed in Rwanda during the conflict, UN Doc. S/1994/867, para. 5, 25 July 1994.

119 Para. 5, Id.

120 General R. Dellaire, Testimony, ICTR, Transcript, p. 43.

121 P. 44, Id.

talion, and the military police.[122] There was also a 6,000 strong Gendarmerie for the whole of Rwanda.[123]

For security reasons the interim Government moved from Kigali to Gitarama on 12 April 1994. In the first week of the events an estimated 20,000 people, the majority of whom were Tutsi were killed in Kigali alone.[124] By 28 June 1994 between 200,000 and 500,000 people had been killed throughout Rwanda.[125] It has been estimated that in the southern prefecture of Butare, 65,000 people were murdered during between 10:00 and 15:30 hrs a figure that translates to about 13,000 deaths an hour, or over 200 victims a minute.[126] And by 31 July 1994 an estimated 800, 000 people had been slaughtered as a result of the atrocities.

In the atrocity crimes that ensued, that persons in leadership positions also took direct part is typified by the acts of Niyitegeka, then Minister for Information, and a member Cabinet in the Interim Government. On 20 May 1994, he shot and killed a girl of 13-15 years of age in Bisesero by the Gisovu-Kibuye road. [127] That the atrocity crimes were the result of planning and were directed is borne out by his involvement.[128] In his case based on the totality of the evidence presented, the Trial Chamber found that on or about 10 June 1994, between 9.00 a.m. and 10.00 a.m., he attended a meeting at Kibuye Prefectural Hall as one of the leaders, together with Kayishema the Prefet of Kibuye, and others. The meeting's objective was to find ways to kill all Tutsi in Bisesero. At that meeting he promised to provide weapons for the killing of the Tutsi in Bisesero. The following week, he attended another meeting at Kibuye Prefectural Hall, with, amongst others, the Prefet. That meeting was held to permit him to answer questions posed at the previous meeting, including in relation to his promise to supply weapons. At this meeting, he distributed the weapons to group representatives for use in the planned killings. He told those attending that the attack would take place the next day in Bisesero. He then presented the attack plan on a blackboard: a circle with "Bisesero" written in the circle. Around this circle were written the names of the designated leaders of each group of attackers and the points of departure for the five groups of attackers, which were Karongi, Rushishi, Kiziba, Gisiza and Murambi. He encouraged people to participate in the attack, and was himself a leader for the Kiziba group. The next day the plan was carried out in the attack at Kiziba, and against Tutsi in Bisesero, which attacks resulted in many victims amongst the Tutsi refugees. From his actions and omission the Chamber held him criminally responsible.

---

[122] P. 44, Id.

[123] P. 45, Id.

[124] Preliminary Report of the Independent Commission of Experts established in accordance with SC res.935 (1994), UN Doc. S/1994/1125, para. 57, 4 Oct.1994.

[125] Para 24, Report on the Situation of Human rights, UN Doc. E/CN.4/1995/7, 28 June 1994.

[126] Martin A, Rwanda's Biggest Lesson from the 1994 Genocide: Look After Yourself or Peril, The East African, 21-27 April 2003.

[127] *P. v. E. Niyitegeka*, Judgement, T.C, Case no: ICTR-96-14-T, 16 May 2003, para. 302.

[128] For findings see, paras. 225, 416- 419, 427, Id.

As mentioned earlier the remit of this book is only on legal and policy issues of relevance to accountability for atrocity crimes. An in-depth narration of the horrors committed is beyond its scope. Nonetheless to provide a brief appreciation of the mode in which crimes were committed, and a profile of the kind of authorities and persons involved we cannot escape high-lighting a few judicially tested examples. This includes acts attributable to Eliezer Niyitegeka former Minster of Information in the Interim Government, Jean Paul Akayesu Bourgmester of Taba Commune, and Father Elizaphan Ntakiritumane an elder priest.

In the ICTR's first trial *P. v. J. P. Akayesu* the Trial Chamber had occasion to consider whether the acts of violence that took place in 1994 constituted genocide. It was of the view that the main intention of the atrocities was to wipe out the Tutsi group in its entirety.[129] This it inferred from a number of material facts, including the fact that newborn babies were not spared; even pregnant women, including those of Hutu origin, were killed on the grounds that the foetuses in their wombs were fathered by Tutsi men, for in a patrilineal society like Rwanda, the child belongs to the father's group of origin. It opined that this took place was also grounded by Akayesu's public statement to the effect that if a Hutu woman were impregnated by a Tutsi man, the Hutu woman had to be found in order "for the pregnancy to be aborted". On other occasions he expressed the same opinion in the form of a Rwandese proverb according to which if a snake wraps itself round a calabash, there is nothing that can be done, except to break the calabash' (" Iyo inzoka yiziritse ku gisabo, nta kundi bigenda barakimena).

In the context of the Rwandan events of 1994, this proverb in Kinyarwanda meant that if a Hutu woman married to a Tutsi man was impregnated by him, the foetus had to be destroyed so that the Tutsi child which it would become should not survive. In Rwandese culture, it should be noted, breaking the "gisabo", which is a big calabash used as a churn was considered taboo. Yet, if a snake wraps itself round a gisabo, obviously, one has no choice but to ignore this taboo in order to kill the snake. That apart, widespread atrocities committed included the cutting of Achilles tendons of many wounded victims in order to prevent them from fleeing, acts that demonstrated the resolve of the perpetrators of the massacres not to spare the life of any Tutsi.[130] In the opinion of the Chamber, it was indeed a particular group, the Tutsi ethnic group, which was targeted; the victims chosen not as individuals but, indeed, because they belonged to said group, selected as such.[131] In Court, Alison Des Forges of Human Rights Watch testified that the Tutsi were killed solely on account of having been born Tutsi.[132]

Women were subjected to widespread and systematic sexual violence, including individual and gang rape, sexual slavery, and torture by civilians, FAR sol-

[129] *P. v. J. P. Akayesu*, Case No. ICTR-96-4-T, Judgement, 2 September 1998; For findings see, paras. 121-124.

[130] Para. 111, Id.

[131] Para. 124, Id.

[132] Paras. 120 & 124, Id.

diers, including Presidential Guard, and the party militia.[133] It is estimated that at least 35% of Rwandan soldiers were HIV positive before April 1994.[134] Victims were often killed, tortured or mutilated after being sexually assaulted and raped. These acts were mostly directed against Tutsi women because of both their gender and ethnicity.[135] Sexual violence against women has in a number of conflicts been a deliberate weapon of war. In the conflict in former Yugoslavia as many as 20,000 women may have been raped.[136] In the Sierra Leone conflict, girls were forced to become partners of combatants or were otherwise held as sexual slaves and forced to bear unwanted pregnancies and children at a young age.[137] There were, for every person with limbs amputated, 10 to 100 girls abducted or abused.[138] In Rwanda during the events rape was the rule; its absence the exception.[139]

That sexual violence was directly encouraged by civil administrators is evidenced in what happened at the Taba Commune, Kigali Prefecture, and before Akayesu.[140] Then the Commune's Bourgmestre, he watched two Interahamwe drag a woman to be raped between his office, the bureau communal and the bureau's cultural centre. Two commune policemen in front of his office who had also witnessed the rape did nothing to prevent it. On two occasions a victim was brought to the communal bureau's cultural centre to be raped, she and the group of girls and women with her were taken past the Akayesu, on the way. On the first occasion he looked at them, and on the second occasion he stood at the entrance to the cultural centre. On this second occasion, he said, "Never ask me again what a Tutsi woman tastes like." When he made those remarks he talked "as if someone were encouraging a player." More generally he was the one "supervising" the acts

133 Human Rights Watch (1996) Shattered Lives. Sexual Violence during the Rwandan Genocide and its Aftermath, p. 1; See also, Askin K D (1999) Sexual Violence in Decisions of the Yugoslavia and Rwanda Tribunals: Current Status, vol. 93/ 1 A.J.I.L, pp. 97-123; See also, Meron T (1993) Rape as a crimes under International Humanitarian Law, A.J.I.L., pp. 424-428.

134 Richeter-Lyonette (ed.) (1997) Women after the genocide in Rwanda, In the Aftermath of Rape: Women's Rights, War Crimes and Genocide, 2nd ed., The Rwanda Coordination of Women Advocacy, p. 107 cited in Jones A (2002) Gender and Genocide in Rwanda, Journal of Genocide Research, vol. 4/1, p. 82 and fn. 89.

135 Human Rights Watch (1996) Shattered Lives. Sexual Violence during the Rwandan Genocide and its Aftermath, pp. 2, 18; In relation to the Former Yugoslavia, See, Sellers P, Okuizumi K (1997) International Prosecution of Sexual Assaults, Transitional Law and Contemporary Problems, vol. 7/1, pp. 45- 70.

136 Bassiouni C, McCormick M (1996) Sexual Violence: An Invisible weapon of War in the Former Yugoslavia, Occasional Paper No. 1, International Human Rights Law Institute, De Paul University College of Law, p. 6.

137 Ad hoc Working Group on Conflict Prevention and Resolution in Africa, The Situation in Africa, UN Doc, S/PV.4577, 18 July 2002, p. 15.

138 P. 15, Id.

139 Report on the Situation of Human rights in Rwanda by the Special Rapporteur of the Commission on human rights, UN Doc. E7CN.4/1996/68, 29 January 1996, para 16.

140 *P. v. J. P. Akayesu*, Judgement, T.C Case No. ICTR-96-4-T, 2 September 1998; For findings see para. 696 & Count 13.

of rape. When another victim and two other girls were apprehended by Interahamwe in flight from the bureau communal, the Interahamwe went to him and informed him that they were taking the girls away to sleep with them. He responded: "take them." He also told the Interahamwe to undress a woman and march her around. He laughed and happily watched. Afterwards he told the Interahamwe to take her away and said "you should first of all make sure that you sleep with this girl." In all about 28 girls and women had been raped in the cultural centre of bureau communal or near the bureau communal.

From all of the above the Chamber held him criminally responsible under the provisions of the Statute. In his case the Chamber held that it was proved beyond a reasonable doubt that he had reason to know and in fact knew that sexual violence was taking place on or near the premises of the bureau communal; that women were being taken away from the bureau communal and sexually violated, and that he did not take any measures to prevent acts of sexual violence or to punish the perpetrators of sexual violence. It opined that in fact on the contrary there was evidence that he ordered, instigated and otherwise aided and abetted sexual violence.

Response by the International Community

The killing of the 10 Belgium peacekeeping troops, and the specific threats to its soldiers, led to the unilateral withdrawal by Belgium of its contingent with UNAMIR.[141] It brought UNAMIR to the brink of disintegration.[142] In a real sense the "American syndrome" afflicted Belgium: pull out at the first encounter with trouble.[143] On 13 April 1994 Belgium announced that its continued deployment would expose its troops to unacceptable risks.[144] It also considered that the continuation of UNAMIR's operations in Rwanda had become pointless, and that it was imperative that UNAMIR's activities be forthwith suspended.[145] Belgium further stated that its recommendation for the withdrawal of UNAMIR was based on an intimate knowledge of the political and military situation in the field. One in which a lasting ceasefire was unlikely, and in which UNAMIR would be exposed to serious risks and powerlessness in the face of a worsening situation.[146] Other

[141] The decision to withdraw was communicated to the UN Secretary-General by the Belgium Foreign Minister in Bonn, Germany on 12 April 1994.

[142] See, Report of the Independent Inquiry into the actions of the United Nations during the 1994 Genocide in Rwanda, 15 December 1999, http://www.un.org/News/ossg/Rwanda_report.htm.

[143] Boutros-Ghali B (1999) Unvanquished: A US-UN Saga, Random House Press, New York, serialized in The East African, Part II, 25-31 October 1999.

[144] Letter from the Permanent Representative of Belgium to the United Nations addressed to the President of the Security Council, UN Doc. S/1994/430, 13 April 1994.

[145] Id.

[146] Letter from Belgium Deputy Prime Minister and Minister of Foreign Affairs addressed to the President of the Security Council, and Letter dated addressed to the Secretary-General, UN. Doc. S/1994/446, 15 April 1994.

Permanent Members of the Security Council, in particular the United States haunted by the 'phantom' of Somalia where during its 1993 intervention, it had lost eighteen soldiers from its elite unit, and accordingly was equally reluctant to be engaged.[147] On 15 April 1994 the US State Department instructed its Mission in New York that "highest priority" must be given to full orderly withdrawal of all UNAMIR personnel as soon as possible. The United States also prevented the effective deployment of a robust UN force in Rwanda by prevailing upon other governments to withhold funding for the Rwandan peacekeeping operation.[148]

The lack of political will to act in response to the events in Rwanda become all the more deplorable in the light of the reluctance by key members of the international community to acknowledge that the mass murder in Rwanda constituted genocide.[149] The non-recognition of the massacre of the Tutsi as genocide was scandalous.[150] Any recognition of the genocide would have meant an obligation to act.[151] Rules of customary international law impose 'community' obligations (i.e. obligations that are owed to all member states of the international community), and at the same time confer upon any state the right to require that acts of genocide be discontinued. [152] It was only on 4 May 1994 that the UN Secretary General in a televised interview finally mentioned the word 'genocide'.[153] On 31 May 1994, in his report to the Security Council on the political mission he had sent to Rwanda to urge the warring parties towards a cease-fire, the UN Secretary General observed that there was little doubt that the magnitude of human calamity that had engulfed Rwanda constituted genocide, since there had been large scale killings of communities and families belonging to a particular ethnic group.[154]

---

147 Des Forges A, Face au génocide: une reponse désastreuse des Etats –Unis et des Nations Unies. In Guichaoua A (1995) p. 458.

148 Boutros-Ghali B (1999) Unvanquished: A US-UN Saga, reprinted in The East Africa, Part II & III; Cf. "At the UN, the Security Council, led unremittingly by the United States, simply did not care enough about Rwanda to intervene appropriately", OAU (2000) Report of the International Panel of Eminent Personalities created by the Organization of African Unity to investigate the Genocide in Rwanda, Executive Summary (E.S), para 33, see, www.oau.oua.org.

149 See, Report of the Independent Inquiry into the Actions of the United Nations during the 1994 Genocide in Rwanda.

150 Martin I (2002) Justice and Reconciliation: Responsibilities and Dilemmas of Peacemakers and Peace-builders. In Hankin A H (2002) The Legacy of Abuse. Confronting the Past, Facing the Future, The Aspen Institute/N.Y. University School of Law, N.Y, p. 84.

151 Cf." No State should have ratified the Genocide convention if there was an obligation to use military force.....There were catastrophic political failures with respect to Rwanda and Srebrenica, but not legal failures", Scheffer D (2003) The Future of Atrocity Crimes, p. 420.

152 Cassese A Genocide. In Cassese A, Gaeta P, Jones J R W D (2002), The Rome Statute of the International Criminal Court: A Commentary, vol. 1, Oxford University Press, Oxford, pp. 337-338.

153 Report of the Independent Inquiry into the Actions of the UN.

154 Report of the Secretary General on the situation in Rwanda, para. 36, UN Doc. S/1994/640, 31 May 1994.

Earlier during April 1994 the Security Council could not agree on the use of the term genocide. It circumvented the issue by including a paraphrase of the Genocide Convention's definition of genocide in the Statement of the President of the Security Council of 30 April 1994.[155] On 17 May in resolution 918 (1994) the Security Council also avoided direct reference to that term.[156] Partial recognition of the term was made on 8 June 1994, in SC resolution 925 (1994) where it belatedly noted with grave concern the reports indicating that "acts of genocide" had occurred in Rwanda, and recalled that genocide constituted a crime punishable under international law.[157]

A discussion on the knowledge of the United Nations of an impending genocide would be unfaithful without reference to the 11 January 1994 code cable from UNAMIR Commander, General Romeo Delaire, to the UN Secretary General's Military Adviser in New York and shared among others with Kofi Annan, then Under Secretary General for Peacekeeping Operations.[158] The cable stated that UNAMIR was in contact with a top interahamwe trainer (set up by then Prime Minister designate, Faustin Twagiramungu), who had been ordered to register all Tutsi in Kigali, which he suspected was for extermination and that his group of 1,700 trained men, divided into groups of 40 dispersed throughout Kigali, was able to kill up to 1,000 Tutsi in 20 minutes. He further informed UNAMIR that interahamwe, in a previous demonstration, had intended to provoke the withdrawal of the Belgium contingent by killing one of its members, and that he was prepared to show UNAMIR a major weapons cache with at least 135 weapons (G3 and AK 47 rifles) if his family was given protection. General Delaire informed the UN Secretariat in New York that it was UNAMIR's intention to take action within the next 36 hours, and requested guidance on how to proceed with regard to the protection of the informant. In a subsequent cable from UNAMIR, dated the same day, Delaire further stated that he was prepared to pursue the operation in accordance with military doctrine with reconnaissance, rehearsal and implementation using overwhelming force.

Replies from UN Headquarters on 10 and 11 January 1994, from Kofi Annan, but signed by Assistant Secretary-General, Iqbal Riza, stated that no reconnaissance or other action, including response to protection should be taken by UNAMIR until clear guidance was received from Headquarters, and that they could not agree to the operation as in their view it was beyond the mandate en-

---

155 "In this context, the Security Council recalls that the killing of members of an ethnic group with the intention of destroying such a group, in whole or in part, constitutes a crime punishable under international law", UN Doc. S/PRST/1994/21, 30 April 1994.

156 "*Recalling* in this context that the killing of members of an ethnic group with the intention of destroying such a group, in whole or in part, constitutes a crime punishable under international law", UN Doc. S/RES/918(1994), 17 May 1994.

157 UN Doc. S/RES/925 (1994), 8 June 1994. "According to notes from the consultations, the original draft's use of the word genocide was changed to "acts of genocide" as a compromise after China objected to use of the term genocide on its own", Report of the Independent Inquiry into the actions of the UN, Id.

158 For Details, see, Report of the Independent Inquiry into the Actions of the United Nations During the 1994 Genocide in Rwanda.

trusted to UNAMIR under UNSC resolution 872 (1993). Instead the SRSG Jacques-Roger Booh Booh and General Delaire were instructed to request an urgent meeting with President Habyarimana, and to inform him that they had received apparently reliable information of interahamwe activities, which represented a clear threat to the Arusha peace process. On 12 January the President was duly informed of the illegal activities of the interahamwe carried out in violations of the Peace Agreement and the Kigali weapons free area, as were the Belgian, French and United States Embassies in Kigali. In New York, however, neither was the UN Secretary General briefed nor was the Security Council informed of the UNAMIR cables.

An accurate picture of impending genocide was not assessed at UNHQ mainly because political developments were not accurately evaluated from the field.[159] It did not detect the actors or the substance of the conspiracy to commit genocide, which had been planned before 6th April 1944. The Security Council remained reluctant to intervene before the overt acts were fully transacted upon. The concept of genocide is so alien to human experience, and so outrageous to contemplate, that its signs were simply not absorbed.[160] The world that mattered to Rwanda, its Great Lakes Region neighbours, the UN, and all major western powers knew exactly what was happening, and that genocide was being masterminded at the highest levels of the Rwandan Government.[161]

In the wake of the events in Rwanda, the UN Secretary General proposed three alternatives to the Security Council. The first was an immediate and massive reinforcement of UNAMIR, capped with a Chapter VII authority to coerce the opposing forces into a ceasefire, restore law and order, and put an end to the killings. The second consisted of maintaining a small group of 270 persons (military and civilian) to act as an intermediary between the parties in an attempt to broker a ceasefire and the withdraw of all the remaining personnel; while the third called for a complete withdrawal, which was not favoured by the Secretary General.

On 21 April 1994 the UN Security Council decided to proceed with the second alternative, despite intensive efforts by members of the non-aligned movement for a more engaging direct UN involvement. The Council authorized a drastically reduced UNAMIR force level of only 270, from an earlier force level of 2,486.[162] In the words of Anyidoho, UNAMIR's Deputy Commander, it was "the last straw that broke the camel's back".[163] The decision effectively terminated international presence in Rwanda permitting the organizers of the genocide to proceed virtually

159 Khan S M Learning the Lessons from Genocide in Rwanda, The East African, 9-15 February 1998.

160 Id.

161 OAU (2000) Report of the International Panel of Eminent Personalities, E.S. para. 23.

162 UN SC res. 912 (1994), UN Doc. S/1994/912 (1994), 21 April 1994; See also, Special Report of the Secretary-General on UNAMIR, UN Doc. S/1994/470, para. 7, 20 April 1994; 'the international community's diagnosis was faulty and the prescription that the Security Council provided was the traditional one for civil wars', Khan S M (2000) The Shallow Graves of Rwanda, p. 196.

163 Anyidoho H K (1999) Guns Over Kigali, p. 49.

unhindered.[164]As the events unfolded, the reaction of the Security Council was shocking; it merely followed the United States lead in denying the reality of the genocide.[165] US President Bill Clinton made his mea culpa in Kigali on 25 March 1998 in these words:

'We are all responsible for this failure. It is genocide. I failed. It is a scandal. We did not immediately call the crimes by their real name: genocide.'[166]

He formally apologized for the failure, and claimed it was a function of ignorance.[167]

For Annan the fundamental failure over Rwanda was not a shortage of information provided by the United Nations about the possibility of genocide, but rather the lack of political will on the part of UN Member States to provide the troops to stop it.[168] During his visit to Rwanda on 8 May 1998 while addressing the Rwandan Parliament he admitted that "signs were not recognized", and that the world had "failed" the people of Rwanda, and "must deeply regret this failure", but added that "the horror came from within" Rwanda and Rwandans had to change themselves if they wanted to restore trust.[169] He refused to personally apologize. The speech irked the Rwandan President Paster Bizimungu, Vice President Kagame, and the Prime Minster who all failed to show up at a dinner hosted in his honour following his speech which they considered arrogant, insensitive and insulting to the Rwandan people. Annan was snubbed by genocide survivors he was supposed to meet at the Don Bosco technical college in Kigali. On its part the Organization of African Unity concluded that the events constituted a colossal failure by itself , African Government, the United Nations, and the governments of the US, France and Belgium to call the full-blown genocide, its rightful name, and act decisively to repress it.[170]

Established in a diplomatic mode, and as a barebones peacekeeping mission,[171] UNAMIR could not do much in the wake of escalating massacres. In his testi-

---

164 Suhrke A (1999) UN Peacekeeping in Rwanda, pp. 2, 7.

165 Boutros-Ghali B (1999) Unvanquished: A US-UN Saga reprinted in Part II, The East African.

166 Le Monde 'Rwanda: enquête sur un génocide', 31 mars- 4 avril 1998; On US reaction see, Samatha P, By Stanfders to Genocide: Why the United States Let the Rwandan Tragegy Happen, The Atlanta Monthly, September 2001. It constituted "a carefully worded acknowledgement", Samatha P, Id.

167 Id.; See also, OAU (2000) Report of the International Panel of Eminent Personalities, E.S. para. 37.

168 Annan defends record on Rwanda, BBC, 4 May 1998.

169 UN Chief leaves Rwanda after unhappy visit, Reuters, 8 May 1998; Rwanda Stands up to UN, Tells Annan 'We Don't Need Help', The East African, 14-20 May 1998; Annan Visits Rwandan death sites, BBC, 8 May 1998; Rwanda's hostility towards UN justified, The Minnesota Daily, 12 May 1998.

170 OAU (2000) Report of the International Panel, E.S. para, 42 Id.

171 Suhrke A (1997) The UN Peacekeeping in Rwanda, p. 109, also by same author (1998) Dilemmas of Protection: The Log of the Kigali Battalion, International Peacekeeping, vol. 5/2, p. 15.

mony before the Rwanda Tribunal, General Delaire estimated that with strength of 5,000 troops UNAMIR might have halted the genocide.[172] In responding to the Rwandan crisis, the Security Council acted with indecision, indifference, incompetence and delay.[173] For the OAU Secretary General, Salim Ahmed Salim, the withdrawal of UNAMIR was a tremendous let down to the people of Rwanda.[174] For the Arusha Peace Accords facilitator, President Ali Hassan Mwinyi of Tanzania, it was the most unfortunate decision of the Security Council, and one in sharp contrast to UN peacekeeping efforts.[175] A decision that the UN belatedly lived to regret, and for which it had to admit certain responsibility. There was a persistent lack of political will by Member States to act, or to act with enough assertiveness.[176] The failure by the United Nations to prevent, and subsequently, to stop the genocide was a failure by the United Nations system as a whole.[177] In summary the UN by this failure acquiesced in the horrifying loss of human life[178]

Between April and May 1994 UNAMIR had daily meetings with the warring parties in order to broker a cease-fire, and to provide humanitarian assistance to victims of the conflict.[179] The Rwandan Armed Forces put as conditions, an immediate cease-fire, a return of RPF to the north sector and to their barracks, and the re-establishment of the weapons free zone.[180] The RPF, on the other hand, insisted that a number of conditions had to be fulfilled even before beginning negotiations. These included immediate control of the Presidential Guard and its identification as an entity that reported to the Rwandan authorities, an immediate stop to massacres, including a significant showing that they were indeed stopping, and that they would negotiate with the Crisis Committee and the interim Chief of Staff, but not the interim Government.[181] The only halt in armed confrontation that UNAMIR was able to obtain was a 24-48 hour cease-fire to allow the transfer of several thousand of soldiers behind lines.

An estimated 800,000 people were killed as a result of the Rwandan atrocity crimes, which took place between 7 April and end of July 1994. In a reversal of its decision the Security Council on 17 May 1994 decided that the situation in Rwanda constituted a threat to peace and security in the region, and acted under Chapter VII of the Charter to authorize the expansion of UNAMIR's force level to

---

172 Pillay N (1998) The Rwanda Tribunal and its relationship to national trials in Rwanda, Am. U. Int'l Law Review, vol. 13, p. 1479.

173 Des Forges A Face au genocide: une reponse désastreuse des Etats – Unis et des Nations Unies. In Guichaoua A (1995) p. 461.

174 United Nations (1996) The UN and Rwanda, p. 266; Uganda's President Yoweri Museveni appealed for UNAMIR's presence, See UN Doc. S/1994/479, 21 April 1994.

175 UN Doc. S/1994/527, 2 May 1994.

176 Report of the Independent Inquiry into the Actions of the UN.

177 Id.

178 Report of the Secretary-General on the situation in Rwanda, UN Doc. S/1994/924, 3 August 1994.

179 General R. Dellaire, Testimony, ICTR, Transcript, p. 149.

180 P. 149-150, Id.

181 P. 150, Id.

5,500 troops.[182] This was prompted by the non-cessation of armed hostilities, surfacing evidence of systematic and widespread atrocities, including possible acts of genocide, and an unprecedented humanitarian crisis that resulted in the abrupt flow of millions of refugees and displaced persons into neighbouring states and within Rwanda. Even with the Council decision being adopted, UNAMIR's authorized troop level was never significant. On 25 July 1994, less than 500 peacekeepers were on the ground, apart from a number of military observers.[183] The Secretary General attributed this to slow bureaucratic process in the UN Secretariat, the reluctance of governments possessing required resources to make them available, and the genocide itself, which constituted a strong disincentive against involvement.[184] Member States, particularly Security Council permanent members, were unwilling to reinforce, re-support or otherwise strengthen UNAMIR when faced with genocide.[185] Delays were the result of a macabre ballet between African countries providing troops, and states willing to provide resources and equipment.[186] In one instance it took five weeks for the UN to negotiate the rental of 50 tanks from the US government.[187]

Operation Turquoise

Delay in the deployment of an expanded UNAMIR, and the continued massacre of civilians in Rwanda, led to the offer by France to conduct a multinational operation under Chapter VII of the Charter to provide security and protection to civilians.[188] On 22 June 1994 the Security Council acting under Chapter VII authorized the establishment of a temporary operation, limited to a period of two months, and under national command and control, aimed at contributing in an impartial way, to the security and protection of displaced persons, refugees and civilians at risk.[189] It should be noted that the decision to authorize a force under national, rather than that of the United Nations command was not unanimously adopted.[190]

---

182 UN SC res. 918 (1994) UN Doc. S/RES/918(1994), 17 May 1994, para. 3. By 25 July, over two months after resolution 918 (1994) was adopted, UNAMIR still only had 550 troops, a tenth of the authorized force, Report of Independent Inquiry into the Actions of the UN.

183 UN Doc. S/1944/923, 3 August 1994.Ghana. Ethiopia, Zambia, Tunisia, Nigeria, Mali and Mali had made offers for troops, and Canada, UK, Australia, and Mali for specialized units totalling 5,760 troops.

184 Id.

185 Suhrke A (1998) p. 15.

186 Des Forges A Face au génocide,: une reponse desastreuse des Etats-Unis et des Nations Unies. In Guichaoua A (1995) p. 461.

187 P. 461, Id.

188 Letter dated 20 June 1994 from the Permanent Representative of France to the UN, UN Doc. S/1994/734, 21 June 1994.

189 UN SC res.929 (1994), UN Doc. S/RES/929, 22 June 1994.

190 Adopted by 10 in favour, five abstentions (Brazil, China, New Zealand, Nigeria and Pakistan), and none against.

Operation Turquoise played a significant role in the southwest sector in stabilizing the situation, allowing humanitarian agencies to penetrate the region, and in particular it was able to convince the almost one and a half million displaced persons in the area not to create a second Goma in the Bukavu sector of the Democratic Republic of Congo.[191] It was instrumental in convincing the tidal wave of humans, not to continue moving towards the West.[192] Braeckman has advanced that although the operation directly saved 10,000-15,000 Tutsi survivors in Cyangugu and Bisesero areas, it was a public relations exercise that represented the summit of humanitarian manipulation.[193] She suggests that the real objective of France was military, that is to assist the Rwandan Armed Forces not to founder, to bar the route to RPF, and force them to negotiate in order to create a Hutu territory on the ground, as well as to collect any military assets it may have provided to the Rwandan Armed Forces.[194] The Operation permitted the escape of the planners and authors of the genocide, particularly to the Democratic Republic of the Congo, where they were able to re-launch a genocide insurgency into Rwandan territory.[195] The Operation did not stop RTLM from broadcasting from the zone it had set up.[196] In May the Pentagon had rejected a proposal to jam the radio station considering it ineffective and an expensive option that would have required a special plane costing USD $ 8,500 an hour to operate.[197] Instead it proposed delivering blankets and plastic sheeting to Rwandan refugees in neighbouring states.[198] With regard to Operation Turquiose, another author has suggested that France's military intentions can be deciphered from the excessive use of Special Forces deployed for the operation, whose political motive was also to assure African States of France's intervention capacity.[199]

RPF forces took full control of Kigali on 4 July 1994, of Butare on 5 July, of Ruhengeri on 14 July, and of Gisenyi, the last government stronghold on 17 July. On 18 July it unilaterally declared a cease-fire, effectively ending the conflict and the genocide. On 19 July 1994 a new government of national unity (which excluded the MRND and CDR political parties) was installed by RPF. The genocide and the armed conflict triggered a massive exodus of refugees to Goma and south Kivu (DR Congo), Tanzania, and Burundi estimated in mid July 1994 at 2.5 mil-

---

191 General General R. Dellaire, Testimony, ICTR, Transcript, pp. 187-188.

192 P. 188, Id.

193 Braekmann C (1994) pp. 296, 300.

194 Pp. 296-299, Id.

195 Rep. of Rwanda, Ad hoc Working Group on Conflict Prevention and Resolution in Africa, The Situation in Africa, para. 40, UN Doc. S/PV.4538, 22 May 2002; Martin I, Justice and Reconciliation: Responsibilities and Dilemmas of Peace-Keepers and Peace-builders. In Hankin A H (2002) p. 84.

196 Braeckmann C (1994) pp. 300-301.

197 Memos reveal Rwanda Delay, The Washington Post, 23 August 2001; See also Metzl J F (1997) Rwandan Genocide and the International Law of Radio Jamming, A.J.I.L. vol. 91, pp. 628-651.

198 Id.

199 Verschave F-X (1994) Complicité de Genocide.La politique de la France au Rwanda, Editions La Découverte, Paris, pp. 125-126.

lion. In Goma alone, the hourly rate of refugee arrivals was between 12,000 and 20,000 refugees.[200]

Violence: An Inquiry

In *P. v. J. P. Akeyesu*, the Trial Chamber held that genocide was indeed committed in Rwanda in 1994 against the Tutsi as a group, the crime itself meticulously organized.[201] Several plausible causes, rather than a single reason, explain the genocide.[202] Among them is the colonial ideology of ethnic and racial division, the economic and social crisis of the 1980s and 1990s, the very highly organized nature of Rwandan society, the use of sophisticated propaganda techniques, the escalating cycle of internal violence, and the fragile regional class base of a political faction determined to hold on to state power at any cost.[203] The essential motive of the genocide was to retain political power and all that went with it.[204] Its initial goal was regime survival.[205] It was the result of a calculated, conscious, and planned action on the part of a political elite who feared losing their positions of privilege, used the machinery of the state.[206] A small group of extremist politicians organized and implemented the genocide using every means possible to hold onto power.[207] The Hutu ruling clique from the northwest sought to exploit residual anger towards the remnants of the former oppressors to legitimatize their own predatory rule.[208] The former Government considered persecution of the Tutsi as the necessary price for Hutu emancipation.[209]

It has seen submitted that the events in Rwanda in 1994 took place under the aegis of the Rwanda state, and the cause was political not social.[210] For one, killings on such a massive scale presuppose a key role for the state.[211] As suggested by Des Forges

[200] Rapport sur la situation des droits des l'homme au Rwanda, UN Doc. E/CN.4/1995/71, 24 Janvier 1995, para. 42.

[201] *Akayesu* Judgement, T.C, para. 126.

[202] Hintjens H M (1999) Explaining the 1994 Genocide in Rwanda, The Journal of Modern African Studies, vol.32/2, p. 280.

[203] P. 280, Id.

[204] Surkhe A (1997) UN Peace-Keeping in Rwanda, p. 101, Cf. "The genocide represented a last ditch effort by an increasingly autocratic and unpopular regime to cling to state power, whatever the cost for the population at large", Hintjens H M (1999) p. 247.

[205] Hintjens H M (1999) p. 248.

[206] Newbury C, Newbury D (1999) p. 296.

[207] Berry C P, Berry J A (1999) p. 3.

[208] Smith D N Post Colonial Genocide. In Dobkowski M N, Wallimann I (eds.) (1998) The Coming Age of Scarcity. Preventing Mass Death and Genocide in the Twenty-First Century, Syracuse Univ. Press, p. 277.

[209] Berry C P, Berry J A (1999) p. 4.

[210] Hintjens H M (1999) pp. 244, 281 "It was an armed political struggle for the state apparatus and concerned socio-cultural prestige or hegemony over the civil society", Lema A Causes of Civil War in Rwanda. In Braathen E, Boas M, Saether G (2000) p. 81.

[211] Newbury C, Newbury D A (1999) p. 317.

"The genocide was remarkably modern in its organisation. It made use of the administrative network of the State. The Rwandan society, even from pre-colonial days, was a highly organised, a very intensively controlled and controlling State. That mechanism was used by the organisers of the genocide who took control of the State, essentially effecting a *coup d'etat,* and who then were able to use the military, the administrative, the political party structure, the radio, and a network of personal contacts to organise a genocide throughout the country".[212]

The atrocities were the culmination of a historical, structural and socio-cultural conflict between two groups struggling for social justice by means of securing political power and social prestige within the socio-cultural framework of Rwandan society.[213] The genocide was not a killing machine that rolled inexorably forward, but rather a campaign to which participants were recruited over time by use of threats, and incentives.[214] Both in its conduct and planning, the genocide was not spontaneous; it resulted from an organized programme of violence that was planned, calculated, orchestrated, and encouraged by political authorities.[215] The conflict offered the pretext, the occasion to execute the final solution.[216]It was engineered meticulously by a state that hoped to profit from fear and anger of its citizens.[217] The genocide involved the use of the state apparatus to carry out the conscious policy of a faction within the Government.[218] For Goldstone, the Rwanda Tribunal's first Prosecutor genocide was planned, and executed openly and even boastfully by Government leaders.[219]

In discussing the causes of the atrocity crimes in Rwanda it is misleading to attribute responsibility for them to the Rwandan state. At least not in international law. The preferred reference should be the Rwandan Government. In international law a state is a recognized legal person and the criteria for statehood is laid by law, such as a permanent population, a defined territory, an effective or stable government, capacity to enter into relations with other states, and willingness to observe international law.[220] It was basically the Interim Government that was responsible for the genocide, not the Rwandan State as such. The UN Independent

212 Des Forges A (2001) Justice in the Balance, p. 1.

213 Lema A in Braathen E, Boas M, Saether G (2000) p. 83, "To label the Rwanda civil war as 'tribal' or 'ethnic' is to miss the point, merely giving it a colonial epithet', at p. 72.

214 Human Rights Watch/FILDH (1999) Leave None to Tell the Story, p. 6.

215 Newbury C, Newbury D (1999) p. 318.

216 Verwimp P (2000) Development Ideology, the Peasantry and genocide: Rwanda represented in Habyarimana's Speeches, Journal of Genocide Research, vol. 2/3, p. 327.

217 Smith D N (1998) Post Colonial Genocide. In Dobkowski M N, Wallimann, I (eds.) (1998) The Coming Age of Scarcity Preventing Mass Death and Genocide in the Twenty-first Century, Syracuse University Press, p. 229.

218 Newbury C, Newbury D (2003) The Genocide in Rwanda and the Holocaust in Germany: Parallels and Pitfalls, Journal of Genocide Research, vol.5/1 pp. 130, 139.

219 Goldstone R J (1998) Healing Wounded People-War crimes and Truth Commissions, C.F. Muller Verlag, Heidelberg, p. 18.

220 See, Brownlie A (1998) Principles of Public International Law, 5th Edition, Clarendon Press, Oxford, pp. 70-84.

Commission of Experts opined that the extermination of Tutsi by Hutu had been planned months in advance of its actual execution.[221] It concluded that mass extermination of Tutsi was carried out principally by Hutu elements in a concerted, planned, and methodical way, and that it was motivated out of ethnic hatred, and carried out with intent to destroy the Tutsi group as such, within the definition of the Genocide Convention.[222]

As we shall detail in our analysis of accountability for the Rwandan atrocity crimes, it is not the dual ethnic character of Rwandan society that caused the genocide, but the political manipulation and design by extremists within the political parties, the military, the government, civil administration, and the media. Ethnic identity was the means used for rallying hatred, fuelling fear, selecting, targeting and eliminating the enemy identified beforehand as Tutsi and moderate Hutu. Ethnicity served as a language through which fears and ambitions were expressed, but it was not ethnicity that caused the violence.[223] The thinking that led to genocide was not the invention of ethnicity, but the apotheosis of ethnicity: putting ethnic policy into action.[224] Agreed it is politics which makes ethnicity significant (or insignificant), and not ethnicity that defines politics.[225]

Missionaries and the church also played a primary role in creating ethnic myths and in interpreting Rwandan social organization as one of defined and inflexible ethnic groups, concepts that fuelled ethnic killings.[226] Notwithstanding the fact that 89.8 % of the population claimed membership in a Christian church,[227] the Church was complicit since it helped create and maintain the authoritarian and divided society that made the genocide possible, and because the entanglement of the churches with the state made the churches partners in state policy.[228] In what represents an example of the involvement of a priest in atrocities, *In P. v. Elizaphan and Gerald Ntakirutimana*,[229] the ICTR Trial Chamber found out that the

---

221 Final Report of the Commission of Experts established pursuant to SC res. 935 (1994), UN Doc. S/19994/1405, 9 Dec.1994, paras. 58, 184.

222 Paras. 58, 184, Id.

223 Newbury C, Newbury D (1999) p. 316.

224 P. 315, Id.

225 Id.

226 Longman T Christian Churches and Genocide in Rwanda. In Burtov D, Mack P (2001) In God's Name. Genocide and Religion in the Twentieth Century, Berghahn Books, N.Y. and Oxford, pp. 114-145; see also De Lespinay C The Churches and the Genocide in the East African Great lake Region. In Burtov D and Mack P (2001) pp. 161-179; On the Vatican's complicity in the Congo, see, Weisbord R G (2003) The King, the Cardinal and the Pope: Leopold II's genocide in the Congo and the Vatican, Journal of Genocide Research, vol.5/1, pp. 35-46.

227 Of this percentage 62.6 % (Catholic), 18.8 % (Protestant), 8.45 (Seventh Day Adventist), Government Rwanda (1994) Recensement General de la Population et de L' Habitant au 15 Aout 1991: Analyse des Resultat Definitifs, Kigali, pp. 126-128.

228 Longman T Christian Churches and Genocide in Rwanda. In Burtov D, Mack P (2001) In God's Name: Genocide and Religion, p. 157.

229 *P. v. Elizaphan and Gerard Ntakirutimana*, Judgement and Sentence, T.C, Cases No. ICTR-96-10 & ICTR-96-17-T, 21 February 2003. The findings are in paras. 788- 790, 828- 831.

former conveyed armed attackers to Mugonero Complex in his personal vehicle on the morning of 16 April 1994, where the attackers proceeded to kill Tutsi refugees at the Complex. On the eve of that attack he received a letter from Tutsi Pastors in which they plead for his assistance adding: "tomorrow we shall die with our families". Considering his position of authority in the community as a senior pastor, the fact that he personally drove armed attackers in his own vehicle to the Complex, his association with the armed attackers, and presence at the scene of the attack, the Chamber held that his deeds constituted practical assistance and encouragement to the attackers, which substantially contributed to the commission of the crime of genocide by them. It found him individually criminally responsible for aiding and abetting in the killing and causing of serious bodily or mental harm to the Tutsi refugees pursuant to Article 6(1) of the Statute and convicted him of guilty of genocide as charged.

That apart, sometime between 17 April and early May 1994, Elizaphan Ntakirutimana conveyed attackers to Murambi Church, Bisesero and ordered the removal of the church roof so that it could no longer be used as a hiding place for the Tutsi. In doing so, he facilitated the hunting down and the killing of the Tutsi refugees hiding in the Church. In mid May 1994, he brought armed attackers in the rear hold of his vehicle to Nyarutovu Hill. The group was searched for Tutsi refugees and chased them. He pointed out the fleeing refugees to the attackers who then chased these refugees singing: "Exterminate them; look for them everywhere; kill them; and get it over with, in all the forests". Again the same month he joined in a convoy of vehicles carrying armed attackers to Kabatwa Hill, and later the same day, at neighbouring Gitwa Hill, he pointed out the whereabouts of Tutsi refugees to attackers who attacked them. That same month he was present in the midst of the killing of Tutsi individuals at Mubuga. At that occasion he was in his vehicle transporting armed attackers as part of a convoy which included two buses, all carrying armed attackers, who sang "Let us exterminate them" and proceeded to kill people until the evening. One day in May or June 1994 he yet again transported armed attackers who were chasing Tutsi survivors at Murambi Hill. The Chamber equally held him criminally responsible for adding and abetting the killings.

East Timor

Turning now to East Timor, a brief recital of historical and political developments that transcended into atrocity crimes in 1999 is also warranted. This offers a better appreciation of the complexity of the age old conflict, the extent of the involvement of de jure and de facto organs of the Indonesian Government, and the response of the international community towards East Timor's decolonisation process. It also provides an informed understanding of the urge for accountability, and the corresponding arrangements promulgated both in East Timor and Indonesia.

It is not within the remit of this book to detail the colonial history of East Timor, nor its struggle for self determination. This has been thoroughly done elsewhere.[230] East Timor, a former Portuguese colony for over 450 years, traces its colonial past to the early 16th Century when Portugal first made contact and set up settlement. The seat of the colonial government was established in the island of Timor in the 18th Century, and the first Portuguese Governor nominated in 1710. By the 1900s the Portuguese flag and the Church were presented as symbols of the temporal and spiritual majesty of Portuguese civilization.[231] So remote was East Timor, as a colonial holding that it was visited only twice by a Portuguese minister throughout Portugal's entire rule. The 25 April 1974 *coup d'etat* in the metropolis ("Carnation Revolution") ushered in, a wave for the dispossession of overseas territories. The new Government enacted a law on 27 July 1974, acknowledging that all non-self governing entities under Portugal's administration had a right to self-determination. Already in June 1974 Portugal had spelt out three options for East Timor; namely, continued association under Portugal, independence, or integration with Indonesia. This to be decided through a ballot process.

Political differences on the future status of the territory, as well as on the mode of expression of the options offered by Portugal between hastily formed political parties led to open hostilities and civil war on 11 August 1975. Among the major parties, the UDT (Uniao Democratica Timorense or Timorese Democratic Union) advocated federation with Portugal as an intermediary step towards ultimate independence. The ASDT (Associacao Social Democratica Timor or Timorese Social Democratic Association), which later changed its name to FRETILIN (Frente Revolutionaria de Timor –Leste Independente or Devolutionary front for an Independent East Timor) urged immediate independence. Jose Ramos Horta, then Secretary for International Affairs put it thus: 'one dos not ask a slave whether he wants to be free'.[232] The APODETI (Assiciacao Popular Democratica Timorense or Timorese Popular Democratic Association) favoured an autonomous integration into Indonesia. Hostilities led the Portuguese Governor to abandon his post in Dili on 26 August 1975. He fled to nearby Atauro Island, and later left the territory leaving behind a political vacuum. On 28 November 1975 FRETILIN unilaterally issued a Declaration of Independence, and announced the founding of the Democratic Republic of East Timor. On 30 November UDT and APODETI also proclaimed independence and its integration with Indonesia. On 7 December, Indonesia launched a naval, air and land invasion of East Timor. On the eve of the invasion, on 6 December President Gerald Ford and Secretary of State Henry Kissenger had stopped in Jakarta enroute from China, and President Suharto had informed them of Indonesia's intention. Ford's response, " we will understand and not press on the issue", and advice that " it is important that whatever you do succeeds quickly", and further that " if you have made plans, we will do our best to keep everyone quiet until the president returns home", makes them privy to Indo-

230 See, Dunn J (1996) Timor. A People Betrayed, ABC Books, Sydney.
231 P. 45, Id.
232 P. 82, Id.

nesia's illegal occupation of East Timor.[233] On 17 July 1976 Indonesia legislatively incorporated East Timor as its 27th Province.

On 22 December 1975 the UN Security Council called upon Indonesia to withdraw without delay all its forces from the territory, and called upon all states to respect the territorial integrity of East Timor.[234] This request went unheeded. Subsequent General Assembly resolutions unanimously condemned Indonesia's invasion, rejected the incorporation of East Timor into Indonesia, and reiterated the inalienable right of East Timorese to self-determination.[235] The forced occupation and annexation denied East Timor its rights and privileges under Article 73 of the UN Charter, as a non-self governing territory. From 8 December 1975 East Timor came under Indonesian occupation within the meaning of both common Article 2 of the Four Geneva Conventions of 1949, and customary international law.[236] This is an important legal submission in that the question of prosecution of war crimes committed in East Timor at the relevant times rests, to a decisive extent, on the question of Indonesia's presence in East Timor as an occupation under international humanitarian law.[237] Both armed resistance and peaceful protest punctuated the occupation.

The turning point in East Timor's struggle for independence took place on 27 January 1999 when President B. J. Habibie of Indonesia announced that the East

233 Embassy of Jakarta Telegram 1579 to Secretary of State, 6 December 1975, see, details, http://www.gwu.edu/~narchives/NSAEBB/NSAEBB62; See, Davies M (1996) East Timor, Genocide, and the "Emperor". In Alfredsson G, Macalister-Smith P (1996) The Living Law of Nations, N.P. Engel Publishers, Kehl, pp. 269-278.

234 UN SC resolution 384 (1975), 22 December 1975; UN SC resolution 389 (1976), 22 April 1976; On East Timor decolonisation process see, Klein N S (1966) Multilateral Disputes and the Doctrine of Necessary parties in the East Timor case, Yale Journal of International law, pp. 305 *et seq.*; Grant T D (2000) East Timor, the U.N. System, and Reinforcing Non-Recognition in International Law, Vand, J, Transnat'l L. vol. 33, pp. 273 *et seq.*

235 UN GA resolution 3485, U.N. GAOR, 30th Session, Supp. no: 34, U.N. Doc. A/10034 (1976); G.A. resolution 31/35, U.N. GAOR, 31 Sess. Supp. no: 39, U.N.Doc. A/31/39 (1977); G.A Res. 32/34, U.N. GAOR, 32 Sess. Sup. No. 45, U.N. Doc. A/32/45 (1978); G.A resolution 37/30, U.N. GAOR, 37th Sess. Supp. No.51, U.N. Doc.A/37/51 (1983).

236 See, Kress C (2002) The 1999 Crisis in East Timor and the Threshold on the Law of War Crimes, Criminal Law Forum, vol.13, pp. 409-470; For text of the Four Geneva Conventions and Additional Protocols, see, Convention for the Amelioration of the Condition of the Wounded and the Sick in Armed Forces in the Field (GCI), 12 August 1949, 75 U.N.T.S. 31; Convention for the Amelioration of the Condition of the Wounded, Sick and Shipwrecked members of the Armed Forces at Sea,(GCIII), 75 U.N.T.S. 85; Convention Relative to the Treatment of Prisoners of War, 75 U.N.T.S 135; Convention Relative to the Protection of Civilian persons in Times of War (GCIV), 75 U.N.T.S. 28; Protocol I Additional to the Geneva Conventions of August 12, 1949 and Relating to the Protection of Victims of International Armed Conflicts, 12 December 1977, UN Doc. A/32/44, Annex I, reprinted in 16 I.L.M 1391, Protocol II Additional to the Geneva Conventions of August 12, 1949 and Relating to the Protection of Victims of Non-International Armed Conflicts, December 12, 1977, UN Doc. A/32/144, Annex II, reprinted in 16 I.L.M 1391.

237 Kress C (2002), pp 410-411.

Timorese would be allowed, through a popular referendum to choose whether they accepted or rejected the Indonesian Governments' proposal for autonomy. On 5 May 1999 Indonesia, Portugal, and the UN Secretary General signed an agreement in New York laying out a constitutional framework for the future status of East Timor and establishing modalities for a popular consultation.[238] The agreement charged the UN with the responsibility to organize the ballot. It also stipulated that the responsibility for ensuring a secure environment devoid of violence and intimidation and conducive to the popular consultation would rest with the appropriate Indonesian security authorities. It further stressed that the absolute neutrality and impartiality of the Indonesia Armed Forces (TNI), and the Indonesian Police would be essential in that regard.

During the negotiations a number of proposals, including the disarmament of all paramilitary groups and the withdrawal of some Indonesian forces from East Timor in the period leading up to the consultation, were put forward, but were rejected by Indonesia. The UN Secretary General had identified six pre conditions for the implementation of the consultation process. Namely bringing armed civilian groups under strict control, prompt arrest and prosecution of those who incite or threaten to use violence, a ban of rallies organized by armed groups, ensuring freedom of association and expression of all political forces and tendencies, redeployment of Indonesian military forces, and immediate institution of a process of laying down arms by all armed groups to be completed well in advance of the ballot.[239] Indonesia, on its part, insisted that it could not accept any dilution of its overall responsibility for security.[240] In furtherance of the agreements, the Security Council on 11 June 1999 established UNAMET, with the specific mandate to organize and conduct a popular consultation in order to ascertain whether the East Timorese people accept the proposed constitutional framework providing for special autonomy for East Timor within the unitary Republic of Indonesia or reject the proposed special autonomy for East Timor.[241]

From January to September 1999, Indonesian authorities and the pro-autonomy civil administration in East Timor not only engineered violence by militia, but they also condoned public discourse on violence. On 17 April 1999 Eurico Guterres, the Commander of *Aitarak* (Thorn) militia, whom Sergio Vierra de Mello,

---

[238] Three agreements were signed. A man, overall agreement between Indonesia and Portugal on the question of East Timor, to which was annexed the constitutional framework for autonomy, an agreement on modalities for the popular consultation of the East Timorese through a direct, secret ballot, and a broad agreement on security arrangements. Both parties and the Secretary General signed the later two. For text See, UN Doc A/53/951_S/1999/513, 5 May 1999.

[239] Question of East Timor, Report of the Secretary General, UN Doc. S/1999/513, 5 May 1999, para. 6.

[240] Question of East Timor, Progress Report of the Secretary-General, para. 11, UN Doc. A/54/654, 13 December 1999.

[241] UN SC resolution 1246(1999), 11 June 1999; On the popular consultation process, See, Martin I (2001) Self-Determination in East Timor, The United Nations, the Ballot and International Intervention, International Peace Academy Occasional paper Series, Lynne Reinner Publishers Inc., London.

UNTAET's Transitional Administrator had labelled, "a thug",[242] made an incendiary speech at a well attended militia rally in front of the Governor's office, which was attended by senior Indonesian military and Police authorities, including the Governor of East Timor. Guterres threatened:

"Be it white, be it red, as long as you betray the integration, you are, my enemy. In this opportunity, I instruct all the soldiers, be representatives (from other militia groups) or Aitarak Militia Command, from 14 April onward, to find and arrest them. Arrest them and bring them to the International Tribunal. And this is the business of integration. I, Eurico Guterres and my entire forces would launch a cleansing operation in all the government's offices. And this, (for) this action, I, Eurico Guterres would take responsibility."

The violence led to between 40,000-60,000 internally displaced persons (IDPs). This was the direct result of a campaign by militia to intimidate, threaten, and coerce pro-independence communities to vote against independence.[243] Although there were several incidents of violence, threats and intimidation, largely committed by pro-integration militia, the popular consultation went ahead on 30 August 1999. A total of 446,953 East Timorese, representing 98.6 % of registered voters cast their ballots within and outside the Territory.[244] On 4 September 1999 the UN Secretary General announced that 344, 580 individuals or 78.5 % of East Timorese, had voted to reject the Indonesian Government's proposal for special autonomy, while 94, 388 people or 21.5%, had voted in support of it.[245] These unequivocal results were certified by the Independent Electoral Commission, and represented a firm desire by East Timorese for independence.

Immediately after the announcement, unprecedented violence erupted. Pro-integration militia groups and elements of the Indonesian security forces unleashed a wave of violence in which pro-independence supporters were targeted, terrorized, and killed.[246] Militia conducted organized, coordinated, operations through population centres, ransacking towns and forcibly displacing hundreds of thousands of

---

242 Open Briefing to the UN Security Council on East Timor by Sergio Vieira de Mello, SRSG & Transitional Administrator, 29 September 2000, N.Y; De Mello, Special Representative of the Secretary General in Iraq together with at least 20 other UN staff were killed in Baghdad on 19 August 2003 in a terrorist bomb attack on the Headquarters of the UN Mission in Iraq. As of 6 October 2003, 1837 UN Staff (80 civilians and 1, 555 military personnel) had died in action, 'UN unveils memorial for more than 1,800 staff who died on duty', AFP, 24 October 2003.

243 Martin I (2001) Self-Determination in East Timor, The United Nations, the Ballot, and International Intervention International Peace Academy Occasional Paper Series, Lynne Rienner Publishers, London, p 45; United Nations (2000) The United Nations and East Timor, Self-determination through popular consultation, Dept. of Pubic Information, N.Y, p. 23.

244 Question of East Timor, Progress Report of the Secretary-General, para. 30.

245 para. 31 Id.

246 Report on the Joint mission to East Timor undertaken by the Special Rapporteur on extra judicial, summary or arbitrary executions, the Special Rapporteur on the question of torture and the Special Rapporteur on violence against women, its causes and consequences, UN Doc. A/54/660, 10 December 1999, para 20.

East Timorese to the hinterland and to West Timor, Indonesia.[247] Acts of violence forced UNAMET to evacuate its staff from East Timor on 14 September 1999. As a result of the violence an estimated 250,000 people were displaced or forcibly deported to West Timor.[248] This evacuation was pre planned.[249] What actually took place was nothing less than a systematic implementation of a "scorched earth" policy in East Timor under the direction of the Indonesian military.[250]

The pattern of violence and breaches of International Humanitarian Law took the form of systematic and widespread intimidation, humiliation, and terror, killings and massacres, torture, violence against women, that included humiliation, harassment, stripping and sexual slavery, and large scale destruction of property.[251] Most hospitals, health centres, schools and public offices were completely destroyed. Damage to private and public property raged from 60 to 80% throughout the whole country.[252] The widespread and systematic nature of the destruction indicated that it was planned and coordinated.[253] As the events were unfolding in East Timor, the Security Council dispatched a Mission to Jakarta and Dili from 8-12 September 1999, in order to discuss with the Government of Indonesia concrete steps for the peaceful implementation of the 5 May Agreement. In discussions with General Wiranto, Indonesia's Minister of Defence, in Jakarta on 9 September 1999, the General stated that the TNI was committed to handling the situation, however complex, and he had full confidence that martial law would allow his forces to stabilize the situation. Following the Mission's visit to Dili, it opined that the violence perpetrated by pro autonomy militias could not have occurred without the involvement of large elements of the Indonesian military and police.[254] It found that the lack of adequate response to militia violence, despite the overwhelming superiority of TNI and police, supported the view that militia activities were organized and supported by parts of TNI.[255]

The violence against UNAMET, humanitarian workers, and the media was aimed at ridding the territory of any international presence, thereby limiting outside observation.[256] Hutu extremists in Rwanda had adopted a similar strategy in 1994, to provoke through anti-Belgium and anti UNAMIR propaganda, the depar-

---

247 Question of East Timor, Progress Report of the General-General, para. 32.

248 United Nations (2000) The United Nations and East Timor, p. 54, ibid; UN, Question of East Timor, Progress Report of the Secretary General, para 35, ibid; Report of the International Commission on Inquiry on East Timor, UN Doc. A/54/726, S/2000/59, para. 93.

249 Report of the International Commission of Inquiry on East Timor, paras. 93, 131-133, Id.

250 Report prepared by UNAMET on 11 Sepet.1999, 'The destruction of East Timor since 4 September 1999, Annex to UN Doc. S/1999/976, 14 Sept.1999, para. 1.

251 Report of the International Commission of Inquiry, paras. 123-127, 142.

252 Para. 130 Id.

253 Id.

254 Report of the Security Council Mission to Jakarta and Dili, UN Doc. S/1999/976, 14 September 1999, para 14.

255 Id.

256 Id.

ture of the Belgium UNAMIR contingent and UNAMIR itself. The Security Council Mission concluded that the involvement of large elements of the Indonesian military and police in East Timor in organizing and backing the unacceptably violent actions of the militia had indeed taken place, and that the TNI's failure, inspite of their undoubted capacity, to carry out the Government's obligations and assurances to provide security to UNAMET, international organizations, and the population as a whole meant that the Indonesian authorities were either unable or unwilling to provide a proper environment for the peaceful implementation of the 5 May Agreement.[257]

The Mission also found that there was strong prima facie evidence of abuses of International Humanitarian Law committed since the announcement of the ballot results on 4 September 1999.[258] It recommended that the Security Council initiate action for the investigation of apparent abuses of international humanitarian law.[259] This was also echoed by the UNHCHR, who also called for facts to be gathered with a view to shed light on what had taken place, and with a view to bring to justice those responsible.[260] On their part the thematic Special Rapporteurs of the UN Commission on Human Rights concluded that the violence, which included murder, torture, sexual violence, forcible transfer of the population and other persecution, and inhuman acts had taken place in the context of an attack against the East Timorese population whom overwhelmingly supported independence from Indonesia.[261] It also found out that the scale of violence was widespread or systematic or both.[262]

The International Commission of Inquiry on East Timor, which was tasked by the UN Commission on Human Rights to gather and compile systematic information on human rights violations which constituted breaches of international humanitarian law, found out that the TNI began engaging militia in the beginning of 1999 in a strategy to intimidate the population in order to influence the outcome of the popular consultation in favour of autonomy within the Unitary State of Indonesia.[263] Intimidation and terror were systematically used to prevent the people from freely exercising their political choice.[264] The Commission found that this policy of engaging militias was implemented by KOPASSUS (Special Forces Command of the TNI), and other intelligence agencies of the Indonesian army.[265] It manifested itself in the form of active recruitment, funding, arming, guiding, and providing logistic means to support the militias in intimidation and terror.[266] In

[257] Para 149, Id.

[258] Para. 21, Id.

[259] Paras. 21, 27, Id.

[260] Report of the High Commissioner for Human Rights on the human rights situation in East Timor, UN Doc.E/CN.4/S-4/CRP. 1, 17 September 1999. para. 4.

[261] Report of Special Rapporteurs, para. 71.

[262] Id.

[263] Report of the International Commission on Inquiry on East Timor, UN Doc. A/54/726, S/2000/59, 31 January 2000, paras. 46, 136.

[264] Para 124, Id.

[265] Para. 137, Id.

[266] Id.

addition to directing militias, in certain cases, Indonesian army personnel, were directly involved.[267] It concluded that ultimately the Indonesian army was responsible for the intimidation, terror, killings and other acts of violence experienced by the people of East Timor before and after the popular consultation.[268]

On 20 September 1999 the UN Security Council authorized, under Chapter VII of the Charter, the deployment of an international force (INTERFET) and tasked it to provide security, facilitate distribution of humanitarian aid, and re-establish law and order. Prior to that, on 12 September, the President of Indonesia had informed the Secretary-General that he was inviting an international peacekeeping force to cooperate with Indonesia in restoring peace and security. Speaking at the Asia and Pacific Forum (APEC), in Auckland, New Zealand, United States President Clinton had this to say:[269]

"The Indonesian military has aided and abetted militia violence in East Timor, in violations of the commitment of its leaders to the international community. This has allowed the militias to murder innocent people, to send thousands fleeing for their lives, [and] to attack the United Nations compound. The Indonesian Government and military must not only stop what they are doing but reverse course. They must halt the violence not just in Dili but throughout the nation".

Acting under Chapter VII of the UN Charter, the Security Council on 15 September authorized the establishment of a multinational force empowered to use all necessary measures to restore peace and security in East Timor.[270] INTERFET, under Australia's Command, began deployment on 20 September 1999. At its peak it comprised forces from 22 countries. It moved quickly, and succeeded in restoring peace and security within a matter of weeks. On 19 October 1999 the Indonesia's People Consultative Assembly (MPR) agreed by consensus to revoke its 1976 Decree that had incorporated East Timor as Indonesia's 27th Province. On 22 October Xanana Gusmao, President of CNRT, who had served seven years of a life imprisonment term, but later reduced to 20 years, was freed and returned to East Timor. By 31 October all elements of the Indonesian Armed Forces had withdrawn from East Timor.

On 25 October 1999 the Security Council decided to establish a United Nations Transitional Administration for East Timor (UNTAET). It had several urgent simultaneous tasks: to build the foundations for a democratic and stable state, to prepare East Timorese for governance, to facilitate the drafting of a constitution, and to build a legal system, a judiciary, a police force and a civil service. The role of UNTAET was not to administer East Timor on its own; East Timorese were to play an integral part. This in fulfilment of a trusteeship relation that UNTAET had with East Timor, on behalf of the United Nations. In the wake of the post ballot violence, the civil administration in East Timor was no longer functioning, the ju-

267 Para.138, Id.

268 Para. 140, Id.

269 Extract of speech cited in A.J.I.L. (2000) Contemporary Practice of the United States, vol.94, A.J.I.L, fn.11, 2000, p. 106, fn. 11.

270 UN SC res. 1264 (1999) 15 Sept. 1999.

diciary and court systems had ceased to exist, and essential services were on the brink of collapse.[271]

The thematic Special Rapporters of the UN Commission of Human Rights opined that while atrocities committed could be clearly attributed to pro-integration militia elements, the information collected and testimonies heard left little doubt as to the direct and indirect involvement of the TNI and police in supporting, planning, assisting, and organizing the pro-integration militia groups.[272] They went on to add:

> "Even applying the strict standards of the International Court of Justice to establish State responsibility for the acts of armed groups in a context of external intervention (dependency of the group on the state) and the exercise of effective control of the group by the State-a standard which cannot reasonably be applied to a State's own acts and omissions of governance of its own people-there is already evidence that TNI was sufficiently involved in the operational activities of the militia, which for the most part were the direct perpetrators of the crimes, to incur the responsibility of the Government of Indonesia. What still remains to be determined is how much of TNI and to what level in the hierarchy was there either active involvement or, at least, culpable tolerance of the activities".[273]

For the UN Secretary-General Kofi Annan accounting for the violations of human rights that occurred in the aftermath of the popular consultation process was vital to ensure a lasting resolution of the conflict, and the establishment of the rule of law in East Timor.[274]

On 20 May 2002 East Timor joined the community of nations as the newest independent state, and the world's 192nd nation. Under international law this sovereign independence did not represent a secession of territory from Indonesia, but the release of a colony from a metropolitan power.[275] Prior to that date, on 17 May 2002, the UN Security Council established under Chapter VII of the Charter, a United Nations Mission of Support in East Timor (UNMISET).[276] It mandated the successor mission to provide assistance to core administrative structures critical to the viability and political stability of East Timor; to provide interim law enforcement and public security, and to assist in the development of East Timor Police Service, a new law enforcement agency; and to contribute to the maintenance of external and internal security of East Timor. With regard to accountability, it foresaw as one of the civilian components of the mission, a Serious Crimes Unit.

271 Question of East Timor, Progress Report of the Secretary-General, para. 37.

272 Report of Special rapporteurs, para. 59.

273 Para. 72, Id.

274 Question of East Timor, Progress Report of the Secretary-General, para. 42.

275 Richardson H J (2000) Recent Developments in East Timor: A Critical Thought on Self Determination For East Timor and Kosovo (Symposium), Temp. Int'l & Comparative L. J. vol 14, pp 101 et seq.

276 UN SC resolution 1410 (2002), UN Doc. S/RES/1410(2002). 17 May 2002.

Conclusion

This chapter narrated significant socio-political and other developments that took place in Rwanda and East Timor before during and immediately after the violence. It outlined the sequence of events intended to provide an informed understanding of legal and policy issues of accountability. As regards Rwanda, the chapter detailed the bitter political divide that surfaced prior to, and after, independence, the Arusha Peace Agreement, the multi-party process, the UNMIR presence in Rwanda, the armed conflict that commenced on 1 October 1990, and the subsequent atrocity crimes of 1994. In the case of East Timor readers were provided with a resume of Indonesia's occupation of East Timor, the popular consultation process, the UN presence, and the involvement of de jure and de facto Indonesian entities in the ensuing violence of 1999. The underlying message being that atrocity crimes have political origin, which when analyzed provides the right entry point for criminal investigations, and accountability for atrocity crimes.

In this regard one should mention the importance of triggering events for an explanation of the truth behind the commission of such crimes. In Rwanda it is accepted by all, the Prosecution and the Defence, that it was the shooting down of the Presidential plane on 6 April 1994 that marked the commencement of the atrocity crimes. The search for accountability, truth, and national reconciliation requires its investigation by an independent and impartial body. Much as it was the ignition of atrocity crimes in Rwanda, it has not been part of the prosecution's priority for acceptable reasons, such as lack of financial resources, technical know how, and expertise. But this does not rule out a consideration to contracting or sourcing out such an investigation, or to handle it within the ICTR as a once off, specially funded and technically assisted, project. This with the caveat that such an investigation is not the monopoly of the ICTR. Other concerned states acting jointly may have a genuine interest in pursuing this issue, and its outcome.[277]

In relation to East Timor, initial violence by pro autonomy militia began in January 1999. However it was the announcement of the results of the popular consultation on 4 September 1999 that unleashed unprecedented violence that led to the near total destruction, if not substantial collapse of East Timor. With regard to both triggering events, we stress one essential factor. It is only a gestational prosecution and investigation strategy that can lead to the detection of those ultimately responsible, and to effective accountability for atrocity crimes.

In this chapter, the author examined various reports by the United Nations Security Council Missions, the UN Special Rapporteurs, and officially mandated Commissions of Inquiry into atrocity crimes. They all provide an instructive reference to the events, and towards the deciphering of the pattern of violence. In the

[277] "It is therefore nonsensical to hold me or the RPF responsible for the tragedy. The issue who killed Habyarimana should not be linked to the current government in Kigali…It is not me….! To date I don't know who killed him." P. Kagame, President of Rwanda, in Kagame denies part in shooting of Habyarimana's place, The Guardian, 28 June 2000.

two comparative situations studied, the violence was organised, planned[278] and orchestrated with the active involvement of Governmental authorities, including the military, the civil administration, and other organisations or entities, such as Political parties, the media, para-military and militia groups, and even private individuals. At times authorities purposely omitted to take remedial action to prevent or immediately restore law and order. The pattern of criminality that resulted was widespread and systematic. It was directed against an unarmed civilian population. Most of it was synchronized, and methodically executed. In the case of East Timor, the forceful deportation of 250,000 East Timorese to West Timor, Indonesia, was part of the policy of destruction. This provides some indication of preplanning or at least common design. Factors important in the matrix of accountability developed later.

[278] United Nations (1996) The UN and Rwanda, p. 266; Uganda's President Yoweri Museveni appealed for UNAMIR's presence, see UN Doc. S/1994/479, 21 April 1994.

Chapter 3
Accountability Arrangements: Rwanda

Chapter 3 examines the major reasons put forward by the United Nations and its Member States for the establishment of the International Criminal Tribunal for Rwanda, the validity of those reasons, and the essentials of its institutional arrangements. This is crucial to an appreciation of the international community's demand for accountability for the events in Rwanda, and assessment of the satisfaction, if any, of that demand. The precedent set by the establishment of the ICTR is that it was the first time in history that a failure to respect the principles of International Humanitarian Law in an internal conflict had been internationally criminalized.[1] The issues that will be pinpointed in this chapter are directly related to the legal and policy debate on the targets of accountable. Some of these considerations explain the particular institutional design that was finally adopted for the ICTR. Yet others explain the role expected of it. In inquiring into the reasons for its establishment, a revisit will be made of the attitude of Rwanda, which formally called for its creation on 28 September 1994,[2] but eventually voted in the Security Council against its very establishment.

This preview is important given that Rwanda is at the epicentre on which the whole accountability and judicial process related to the 1994 atrocity crimes rotates. The Statute of the ICTR refers to Rwanda 53 times. As we shall see later, the attitude of Rwandan Government authorities is linked to cooperation with the Tribunal, the exercise of concurrent jurisdiction with other states, the continuity of accountability, the Completion Strategy, and, in the finality, justice. Without connective tissue between national and international criminal jurisdictions, efforts to enhance accountability against those responsible for atrocity crimes are bound to have gaps.[3] As explained earlier, our analysis will also comment on the reasons for

---

1 Speech by Judge Laity Kama President of the ICTR before the UN General Assembly, 10 December 1996, ICTR Yearbook, 1994-1996, Arusha, p. 5.

2 Letter dated 28 September 1994 from the Permanent Representative of Rwanda to the United Nations addressed to the President of the Security Council, transmitting a statement dated 28 September 1994 of the Govt. of Rwanda on the establishment of an International Tribunal for the prosecution of persons responsible for genocide and other serious violations of international humanitarian law in relation to Rwanda, U.N.Doc S/1994/1115, 29 September 1994.

3 Cf. "The ICC is not a perfect model of symmetrical enforcement. The Treaty Statute preserves pockets of immunity and elements of asymmetrical enforcement", Meyerfeld

the establishment of the ICTR as against the institutional arrangements (i.e. the organizational framework) agreed upon for the accountability of persons alleged to have been responsible for the atrocity crimes committed in Rwanda. It is inevitable that one discusses the merits and demerits of a single Prosecutor for both the two UN ad hoc Tribunals. This chapter further discusses the 'special investigations' related to Rwanda Patriotic Army (RPA) soldiers, and their eventual accountability by the ICTR and/or Rwanda for violations of crimes under its Statute. This thorny issue remains at the drawing board. Its satisfactory resolution will be the measuring rod of the effectiveness of the rule of law, both nationally and internationally, the comprehensiveness of accountability as mandated to the ICTR by the Security Council, and the promotion of national reconciliation in Rwanda.

Accountability Demand

The central debate on the establishment of the ICTR is directly connected with the adoption of **UNSC resolution 955 (1994)**, on 8 November 1994 over three and a half months (113 days) following the RPF unilateral declaration of ceasefire on 18 July 1994, which effectively brought an end to the genocide in Rwanda. Five major reasons can be traced for its establishment. Some are clear-cut, while others are a distant wish. The Rwanda Tribunal was set up primarily, (a) to bring perpetrators of crimes to justice, (b) to put a stop to impunity, (c) to re-establish the rule of law, (d) to promote national reconciliation, and (e) to restore peace and security.

The unprecedented scale of atrocities, the failure of the international community, in particular the Security Council, to effectively intervene, and solve the crisis, the earlier establishment of a twin Tribunal (i.e. the ICTY), were all contributory factors behind the demand for judicial accountability by the Security Council for the atrocity crimes committed in Rwanda.[4] After witnessing the genocide in Rwanda, on a scale reminiscent of that which occurred during the Second World War, the response could be no less that it was in Nuremberg or Tokyo decades ago, or in respect of war crimes committed in the former Yugoslavia a year earlier.[5] In the case of the ICTY, as in that of the ICTR, the decision to establish the ad hoc international tribunals was a political expression of the Security Council's condemnation of atrocities,[6] and a response to the cry for justice that had echoed in that Council.[7]

J Who Shall be Judge?: The US, the ICC, and the Global Enforcement of Human Rights, Human Rights Quarterly, vol. 25, p. 123.

4 "The international legal community responded to atrocity in Rwanda simply by using as boiler plate the statutes of ICTY", Drumble M A (2000) Punishment, Post Genocide: From Guilt to Ham to Civil in Rwanda, vol. 75/II, Yale Law Journal, p. 1231.

5 Statement Rep. of New Zealand, UN Doc. S/PV. 3453, 3453rd Meeting, 8 November 1000, p. 4.

6 Statement Rep. of Brazil, p. 9 Id.

7 Statement Rep. of Brazil on adoption of UN S.C. res 827 (1999) relating to ICTY. In Morris V, Scarf P M (1998) An Insider's Guide to the International Criminal Tribunal

The prime reason for the establishment of the ICTR was to hold persons individually accountable for serious international humanitarian law violations. This required that perpetrators of crimes be investigated, tried, and if convicted, be sentenced. Its establishment was meant to be an eloquent message that the international community was not prepared to leave unpunished the grave crimes committed in Rwanda.[8] It was a signal of its determination that offenders must promptly and properly be brought to justice.[9] Individuals, regardless of the community to which they belong, must be brought to trial and jailed if they have violated the most fundamental rules of war, if they have committed crimes against humanity and, above all, if they have orchestrated attempts to destroy all or part of an ethnic group; that is to say, genocide.[10] Murder, let alone genocide, had to be punished for a sense of right, a sense of law and order, to be restored in a society that has seen all norms of life shattered.[11]

As stated by the Representative of the Russian Federation during the debate on the establishment of the ICTY:

> "Those guilty of mass crimes covered by the 1949 Geneva Protocols, violations of the laws and customs of war, crimes of genocide and crimes against humanity must be duly punished. It is of particular importance that for the first time in history, it is not the victors who are judging the vanquished, but the entire international community that, through the Tribunal, will be passing sentence on those who are grossly violating not only the norms of international law but also even quite simply our human concepts of morality and humanity. We favour the establishment of the International Tribunal because we see in it not a place for summary justice or a place for settling scores or for seeking vengeance, but an instrument of justice which is called upon to restore international legality and faith of the world community in the triumph of justice over reason".[12]

Secondly the establishment of the ICTR was also meant to curb impunity through justice. It was considered especially necessary for Rwanda, which for decades had lived in a culture of impunity, a culture where massacres, which had gone unpunished, constituted a part of its contemporary history.[13] Those culpable of massacres had even become national heroes.[14] Serial massacres had been committed in Rwanda and in particular in 1959, 1963, 1966, 1973, and from 1990 to 1994. The genocide, which awakened, shocked, and saddened universal conscience was the

for Rwanda, A Documentary History and Analysis, vol. 2, Transitional Pub. Inc., p. 200.

8 Statement Rep. of Argentina, UN Doc. S/PV. 3453, 3453rd Meeting, 8 November 1000, p. 8.

9 Statement Rep. of UK, p. 6; Rep. of Brazil, p. 9.

10 Statement Rep. of France, p. 3; See also Statement Rep. of Oman, p. 16.

11 Statement Rep. of Czeck, p. 7.

12 Statement of Rep. Russian Federation, UNSC debate on the adoption of UNSC res. 827 (1993) on the establishment of ICTY. In Morris V, Scharf M P (1995), An Insider's Guide to the International Criminal Tribunal for the Former Yugoslavia, Transitional Publishers, Inc., N.Y., p. 206.

13 Statement of Rep. of Czech, p. 7.

14 Guichaoua A (1995) p. 45.

direct result of the culture of impunity, which had characterized Rwandan society.[15] Simply stated, getting away with murder is precisely what the international community wanted to help prevent by way of an international tribunal.[16]

The third reason advanced by the Security Council was the restoration of the rule of law, both domestic, and international.[17] The Tribunal was meant to be an instrument for ending a state of lawlessness. The gravity of the crimes committed extended far beyond Rwanda; they concerned the international community as a whole, and justice was a matter of deterrence.[18] The evolution of international society had revealed the need to create a corrective and punitive forum, in cases of crimes affecting the very essence of the civilized conscience.[19] Criminal acts against humanity had to be collectively punished, by the international community since they entail global accountability.[20]

The establishment of an international tribunal was a resounding expression by the United Nations of its common resolve not to tolerate infamy, and to assert the rule of law.[21] The rule of law requires a system of criminal justice that deters and punishes banditry and acts of violence, allowing the citizenry to live with a sense of security.[22] It implies that no individual is above the law, and that government decision-making is accountable to pre-determined legal standards applied by an independent and impartial judicial body.[23] It protects the rights of all members of society and establishes rules and procedures that constrain the power of all parties, and hold all of them accountable for their actions.[24]

The fourth aim, which remains controversial and debatable and to a large measure still quantifiably unfulfilled, was that the Tribunal was expected to promote national reconciliation. That it would restore 'civil peace' in Rwanda.[25] The Security Council was convinced of that.[26] A belief was shared that the smooth, and expeditious functioning of the Tribunal would, apart from dispensing justice, help in the attainment of the larger objective of national reconciliation, and in restoring

15 Statement of the Rep. of Rwanda, p. 14.

16 Statement of the Rep. of Czech, p. 14.

17 Statement of Rep. of Spain, p. 12; "we are convinced that the international tribunal will promote the justice which we all aspire and will strengthen the rule of law in international relations". Statement of the Rep. of Morocco. In Morris V, Scharf P M (1995) p. 196.

18 Statement Rep. of UK, p. 6, Id.

19 Statement of the Rep. of Venezuela on adoption by UNSC res. 827 (1993) relating to ICTY, in Morris V and Scharf M P (1995) p. 182, Id.

20 Statement Rep. of Nigeria, p. 13, Id.

21 Statement Rep. of France, p. 185, Id.

22 Kritz N J The Rule of Law in the Post Conflict Phase. In Crocker C A *et all.* (1996) Managing Global Chaos, Sources of and Responses to International Conflict, U.S.I.P. Press, Washington D.C, p. 591.

23 Whitford W C (2000) The Rule of law: New Reflections on an old Doctrine, East African Journal of Peace and Human Rights, vol.6/2, p. 158.

24 Kritz N J in Crocker C A *et all.* (1996) p. 588.

25 Statements Reps. Of Russian Fed, p. 2; France, p. 3 Oman, p. 16; Brazil, p. 10.

26 UN SC res.955 (19994), 8 Nov.19994, UN Doc. S/RES/944 (19994), vote: 13-1-1.

confidence in all sections of the Rwandese polity.[27] For the purposes of long-term reconciliation, accountability underscores that specific individuals-not entire ethnical, religious or political groups committed atrocities for which they need to be held accountable.[28] The way in which it would contribute to the process of reconciliation was that, on one hand it would show the people, both victims and those responsible, that justice exists, and, on the other hand, that justice will be applied with impartiality and independence.[29] Rwanda itself considered that the Tribunal would help the national reconciliation process, and the construction of a new society based on social justice and respect for the fundamental rights of the human persons, all of which would be possible only if those responsible for the tragedy were brought to justice.[30]

This role of the ICTR in facilitating the national reconciliation process in Rwanda has been commented upon on a number of occasions. Judge Shahabuddeen expressed it thus:

> "The interest of the international community in organizing prosecutions is only half of its interest. The other half is this: such prosecutions are regarded by the international community as also designed to promote reconciliation and the restoration of and maintenance of peace, but this is possible only if the proceedings are seen as transparently conforming to internationally recognized tenets of justice. The Tribunal is penal; it is not simply punitive".[31]

As mentioned earlier, the role of the Tribunal in the promotion of national reconciliation though advocated for by most is not without its critics. Voicing a contrary view, the Representative of the Czech Republic considered that:

> "Justice is one thing; reconciliation however is another. The Tribunal might become a vehicle for justice, but it is hardly designed as a vehicle for reconciliation. Justice treats criminals whether or not they see the errors of their ways; but reconciliation is much more complicated, and it is certainly impossible until and unless the criminals repent and show remorse. Only then can they even beg their victims for forgiveness, and only then can reconciliation possibly be attained......we have seen few if any signs of remorse and repentance-let alone apology- from those responsible for the genocide".[32]

The final reason advanced by the Security Council for the establishment of the Rwanda Tribunal was that it would promote peace and security in, and beyond, Rwanda. The serious international humanitarian law violations committed were a threat to international peace and security, and had compelled the Security Council in the discharge of its responsibility in the maintenance of peace and security to invoke Chapter VII of the Charter. It was submitted that the Council was acting

---

27 Statement of the Rep. of Pakistan, p. 10.

28 Kritz N J in Crocker C A *et all.* (1996) p. 595.

29 Statement of Rep. of Argentina, p. 8.

30 Statement of the Rep. of Rwanda, p. 14.

31 Separate Opinion of Judge Shahabuddeen, *P. v. J.B. Barayagwiza*, Case no. ICTR-19-AR72, Arret, 31 mars 2000, para. 71.

32 Statement of Rep. of Czech Republic, p. 7.

within the framework of international law when it used its authority under that Charter to respond, as it had done, in establishing the Tribunal.[33]

The Rwanda Tribunal's contribution to the realization of this objective needs to be examined at a number of levels; including that of promoting peace and security inside, and outside Rwanda. The arrest, detention, and trial by the Tribunal of a number of accused alleged to have played a significant role in the commission of genocide in Rwanda has meant that they have been prevented from directly taking part in the conflict in the Democratic Republic of Congo or elsewhere.[34] On the other hand the presence from 1994 to about 2003 of interahamwe and other Rwandan militia in the DR Congo was one of the fuels that ignited the armed conflict there; in which six regional sates, and over twenty warring parties are involved, and which has resulted in egregious human rights violations.[35]

While we have indicated the major reasons behind the urge for accountability that led to the establishment of the ICTR, it is worth observing that there are a number of residual expectations as well. It was thought that the Rwanda Tribunal would provide penal experience which will be useful for the establishment of the future permanent International Criminal Court.[36] Furthermore it would assist in the return of millions of refugees, scattered across Burundi, DR Congo, and Tanzania.[37] The genocide and armed conflict had caused an estimated 1.2 million people to flee Rwanda over a four-day period in mid July 1994, to the Kivu region of the DR Congo, in one of the largest and most sudden movements of refugees in modern history.[38] It had forced almost half the population to take to the road.[39]

It is evident that the experiences of both the ICTY and the ICTR have positively contributed to the establishment of the ICC. It is hard, however, to see how

---

33 Statement Rep. of New Zealand, p. 4; Statement Rep. of Spain, p. 12; Cf. contrary views, "The Security Council's responsibilities lie not in the judicial or institutional-building field, but in the maintenance of international peace and security. Therefore, the invocation of Chapter VII of the Charter for the purpose of establishing an international tribunal goes, in our view, beyond the competence of the Council as clearly defined in the Charter", Statement of Rep. Brazil, p. 9.

34 General Augustine Bizimungu, former Minister of Defence of the Interim Government of Rwanda was arrested in Angola on 13 August 2002, following the demobilization of UNITA (National Union for the Total Independence of Angola). The Rwanda Government claims that he was arrested in the DRG and then transferred to Angola. See, Le general Bizumungu arête en RD Congo, AFP, 29 August 2002.

35 See, Human Rights Watch (2003) Covered in Blood: Ethnically Targeted Violence in Northern Democratic Republic of Congo, Human Rights Watch, N.Y.; Human Rights Watch (2002) The War Within the War: Sexual Violence Against Women and Girls in Eastern Congo, Human Rights Watch, N.Y.

36 Statement Rep. of France, p. 4.

37 Statement Rep. of Russian Federation, p. 2.

38 Report of the UN Secretary-General outlining three options for a possible Peace-keeping Operation to enhance security in camps for Rwandan Refugees, UN Doc. S/1994/1308, 18 Nov. 1994, para. 6.

39 Opening Address by the UN Secretary - General launching the United Nations Inter-Agency Appeal for Victims of the Crisis in Rwanda, UN Press Release SG/SM/5375-IHA/528, 22 July 1994.

the ICTR, an international judicial institution, could have contributed to the voluntary return of refugees who were at that time under the control of former Rwandan political leaders, ex Rwandan Armed Forces soldiers, and the militia. The latter controlled access into and out of camps. They openly resorted to a campaign of incitement, intimidation, and threat. Even though the protection of refugees, and their voluntary repatriation, are governed by customary and convention norms, the return of refugees as a judicial outcome of the Rwanda Tribunal seem a far-fetched objective.

Our analysis of accountability will not be complete without reference to the basic reasons that initially led Rwanda to seek, in the first place an international tribunal. In requesting a tribunal, Rwanda wanted "a toll for justice that knows no borders".[40] It advanced five reasons for requesting such an institution.[41] First by involving the international community, which was also harmed by the atrocity crimes it wanted to enhance the exemplary nature of a justice that would be seen to be completely neutral and fair. Second, in order to avoid any suspicious of it wanting to organize a speedy and vengeful justice. Third, to make it easier to obtain accused who had sought refuge in third states. Fourth, that the crimes committed could only be suppressed by the international community as a whole, and fifth, that it would assist in national reconciliation and the construction of a new society based on social justice and respect for the fundamental rights of the human person.

Former Rwandan President Pasteur Bizimungu firmly linked the imperative for justice with that of the national reconciliation process in this way:

"Political and social stabilization in Rwanda depends on whether all citizens, regardless of their ethnic origin, can be reconciled. Such national reconciliation would imply the due administration of justice, first of all to ensure that the guilty parties no longer feel they can act with impunity, which would act as a deterrent. Secondly, it would enable victims and their families to feel that justice was being done and that the real perpetrators were being punished, which would dampen any feelings of revenge. If justice is not done, there may be no end to hatred, and atrocities could go on and on, with executioners believing they were immune to prosecution and the victim's thirst for revenge fuelled by a sense of injustice and the ideal that an entire ethnic group was responsible for the atrocities committed against them. In this regard it is of paramount importance that justice be done, because this will help replace the idea of collective political responsibility with the idea of individual criminal responsibility."[42]

While Rwanda had earlier sought accountability through an international tribunal, in the final hours it voted against the Security Council resolution establishing it.[43] An examination of the reasons is compelling. They better explain the relationship,

---

40 Statement of Pasteur Bizimungu, President of Rwanda to U.N. General Assembly, UN. GAOR, 49 Session, 21st Plenary Meeting, UN Doc. A/49/PV.21, pp. 3 and 5.

41 Statement of the Rep. of Rwanda, p. 14.

42 Statement of President of Rwanda, P. Bizimungu to UNGA, U.N. GAOR, 51st Session. U.N. Doc. A/51/PV.78 (1996), p. 5.

43 Statement of Rep. of Rwanda, pp. 14-16; " greater sensitivity towards Rwanda would certainly have led to Rwanda abstaining, if not voting in favour of Resolution 955 setting up ICTR", Khan S M (2000) The Shallow Graves of Rwanda, p. 60.

and cooperation dynamics between Rwanda and the ICTR. Notwithstanding the binding character of the obligation of states, including Rwanda, to cooperate with it,[44] this relationship has at times been volatile. As we shall highlight, there has been tension, friction, and divergence of opinion on key issues relating to accountability, including on the prosecution strategy, investigation priorities, and Rwanda's compliance obligations.

Rwanda's dissatisfaction with the founding resolution and its annexed Statute, first stems from the limited temporal jurisdiction of the ICTR (i.e. 1 January 1994 to 31 December 1994), whose time frame neither covers previous occasions in which "pilot projects" for extermination were successfully tested, nor the planning and preparation phases of the genocide. Secondly it viewed the composition of judges, an Appeal Chamber, and a common Prosecutor with the ICTY, inappropriate and ineffective. Rwanda pleaded for the tribunal to be given its own Appeal Chamber, and Prosecutor. Thirdly Rwanda claimed that nothing in the Statute indicated the order of priority of crimes for which the Tribunal had jurisdiction, leaving a possibility for genocide, "the crime of crimes"[45] to be relegated to a secondary level during investigation and prosecution. Fourthly Rwanda was concerned that judges would be appointed from countries which took a very active part in the conflict. Fifthly it was difficulty, for it to accept that imprisonment of accused would be served outside Rwanda. For Simeone Rwegasore, Rwanda's former Chief Justice, this amounted to "excessive mistrust", and was "contemptuous" of Rwanda.[46] Sixthly it felt that the exclusion of capital punishment, in the Tribunal's Statute, would result in disparity in sentencing between planners and organizers of the genocide tried by an international tribunal who would escape capital punishment, and executors who, if tried in Rwanda may receive such a punishment, given its continued application in Rwanda.[47] In relation to its own national trials, on 28 April 1998, Rwanda executed in public and by firing squad 22 accused convicted of genocide and crimes against humanity.[48] It did not heed Pope John Paul II's clemency plea, claiming that the executions were legally and mor-

---

44 Art. 28 'Cooperation and judicial assistance', ICTR Statute; Art. 29, ICTY Statute.

45 Reference to genocide as "crimes of crimes" was first uttered by Rwanda's representative during the Security Council debate on the adoption on UN SC res. 955 (1994) on the establishment of the Rwanda Tribunal. In relation to the Tribunal Statute, he retorted, that his "delegation was surprised to see in the draft statute that the International Tribunal, instead of developing its meagre human resources, and probably equally meagre financial ones, to trying, the *crime of crimes*, genocide, intends to disperse its energy by prosecuting crimes that come under the jurisdiction of internal tribunals", UN Doc. S/PV.3453, p15, 8 November 1994. The term "*crimes of crimes*" for genocide was also coined by the ICTR in its judgements, See, e.g. *P. v. J. Kambanda,* Judgement and Sentence, Case no: ICTR-97-23-S, 4 September 1998, para 16; *P. v. O. Serushago*, Judgement, T.C, Case no: ICTR 98-39-S, 5 February 1999, para. 27.

46 Interview with Author, Kigali, 11 December 2002.

47 C.f. "New Zealand could never support an international tribunal that could impose the death penalty. For over three decades the United Nations has been trying progressively to eliminate the death penalty. It would be entire unacceptable-and indeed a dreadful step backwards-to introduce it here", Statement of Rep. of New Zealand, p. 5.

48 Was Firing Squad in Rwanda a solution? The New Vision, 30 April 1998.

ally necessary and constituted a key element to eradicate impunity.[49] Finally Rwanda was also dissatisfied that the seat of the Tribunal would not be in Rwanda, but in a third country.[50]

In deciphering the basis for accountability under the United Nations, it is worth recalling that as an independent and impartial judicial institution, the ICTR, was not considered a legal instrument of revenge,[51] nor one which would apply the principle of "an eye for an eye" no matter how horrendous the crimes individuals may have been committed.[52] As emphasized by former US Secretary of State, Madeleine Albright:

> "This will be no victors' tribunal. The only victor that will prevail in this endeavour is the truth".[53] Truth is the corner stone of the rule of law, and it will point towards individuals, not peoples, as perpetrators of crimes."[54]

Similarly, the Representative of the Russian Federation stated that:

> "The international Tribunal...is not a place for summary justice, nor a place for settling scores or for seeking revenge, but an instrument of justice which is called upon to restore international legality and the faith of the world community in the triumph of justice and reason."[55]

The author has flagged these observations since they have an influence on the accomplishment of the mandates of the ad hoc international criminal tribunals, as well as on prosecution strategies, and policies that we shall refer to. The Tribunal was meant to spare no one; no matter which side of the conflict he or she belonged and irrespective of position in society, rank or official status, from criminal accountability.

On this issue one is compelled to address a more pertinent question; namely, that of victor's justice and the ICTR. An issue if not well resolved will bring an ir-

---

49 Go on, shot them all; Genocide: Rwanda executes 22, The New Vision, 25 April 1998.

50 C.f. "the best location for the Tribunal's work would be Kigali, provided that all the necessary arrangements could be made for its efficient functioning there", Statement Rep. of Pakistan, p. 10. The seat of the Tribunal, Arusha, Tanzania was decided by the UN Security Council subsequent to the adoption of UNSC res. 955 (19994) taking into account considerations of justice, fairness, administrative efficiency, including access to witnesses, economy and appropriate arrangements between the UN and the host State. UN Secretary-General, Boutros-Boutros Ghali was guided by the preference for "an African seat", United Nations (1996) The UN and Rwanda (1993-1996), UN Blue Book Series, Dept. of Public Information, N. Y, p. 65; Arusha, the seat of the Tribunal was decided upon by the UN SC on 22 Feb.1995, See, SC res.977 (1995), UN Doc. S/RES/977 (1995), 22 February 1995.

51 Statement of Rep. of Oman, p. 16.

52 Statement of Rep. of New Zealand, p. 5.

53 UN Doc. S/PV.3175, p. 11.

54 Statement of M. Albright. In Morris V, Scharf P M (1998) p. 185.

55 Statement of Rep. of Russian Federation, (also President of Security Council session), p. 208.

reconcilable divide between Rwanda and the ICTR. In so far as the UN ad hoc tribunals were an inspiration of the Nuremberg Tribunal in terms of a number of legal principles, such as superior orders and individual criminal responsibility, a common criticism of the latter is that it represented victor's justice.[56] That it was set up by the four victors of World War II (Great Britain, USA, France and the Soviet Union); that only nationals of those States served as Judges or Prosecutors; that both participated in the collection of evidence and the drafting of Indictments, and that only vanquished accused (i.e. 22 Germans) were held accountable before it. At the Tokyo Tribunal, the assignment of Judges from victor nations, to sit in judgement over the accused from defeated nations, was bitterly criticised by Judge Radhabinod Pal (India), thus:

> "It has been said that a victor can dispense to the vanquished everything from mercy to vindictiveness; but the one thing the victor cannot give to the vanquished is justice. At least, if a tribunal be rooted in politics as opposed to law, no matter, what its form and pretences, the apprehension thus expressed would be real, unless justice is really nothing else than the interest of the strongest".[57]

Morris and Scharf have submitted that this criticism of the Nuremberg Tribunal as victor's justice is without any foundation in terms of international law, then applicable, which gave the Powers competence to prosecute those who violated the laws and customs of war, and that the alternative that was considered, summary execution, would have amounted to victor's revenge.[58]

This issue has central relevance to the prosecution strategy. It concerns the question of who should be the subject of international accountability. It is related to the setting of investigation and prosecution priorities, and of the timing and opportunity for prosecution. Is there an obligation for the ICTR, which is dispensing justice in the name of the international community and Rwanda, to investigate and try both the implicated members of the former Government or its armed forces, as well as individuals from the Rwandan Patriotic Army (RPA) suspected of having committed atrocity crimes? If so, which forum, domestic or international is better situated to adjudicate such abuses? What is in the public interest? What serves most, with respect to justice and national reconciliation? And whose interests are best served by such an approach, Rwandans or that of the international community'?

---

56 See, Finch G A (1947) The Nuremberg Trial in International Law, vol.41, A.J.I.L, pp. 20-37; See also Cooper B (ed.) (1999) War crimes and The Legacy of Nuremberg, T.V. Books, N.Y.

57 Judge Pal's Dissenting Opinion cited in Brook T (ed.) (1999) Documents on the Rape of Nanking, University of Michigan Press, Ann Arbor, p. 294.

58 Morris V, Scharf M (1998) p. 11.

Genocide

It has been established by judicial decisions, international inquiries by the United Nations and the organization of African Unity that the events that took place in Rwanda in 1994, including between April and July 1994 constituted genocide.[59] In P. v. Niyitegeka, the Trial Chamber also opined that there was genocide in Rwanda during the same period at specific localities, and massacres were committed by Hutu against the Tutsi.[60] In P. v. Omar Sherushago the Appeal Chamber considered it common ground that the acts of violence in the order of genocide and crimes against humanity, with Tutsis and moderate Hutus as the victims took place in Rwanda in 1994.[61]

The fact that genocide took place, that it was committed against the Tutsi population and that widespread or systematic attacks directed against the civilian population on the grounds of political persuasion, ethnic affiliation, or racial origin has also been admitted by a number of accused.[62] As stated by the UN Independent Commission of Experts, mass exterminations perpetrated by Hutu elements against the Tutsi group as such, took place in Rwanda and constituted Genocide within the meaning of Article 1 of the Convention on the Prevention and Punishment of the Crime of Genocide.[63] Furthermore overwhelming evidence existed to prove that 'acts of genocide' against the Tutsi group were perpetrated by Hutu elements in a concerted, planned, systematic and methodical way.[64] On the other hand, the Commission stated that at time of their inquiry there was no evidence to indicate that Tutsi elements, who were the majority of the victims, perpetrated acts with intent to destroy the Hutu ethnic group, as such, during the same period in Rwanda.[65] It did not find evidence to indicate that killings of Hutu perpetrated by a number of individual RPF soldiers were systematic, or were sponsored or even approved by Government officials or army commanders.[66]

Serious violations of international humanitarian law were committed in Rwanda by both Hutu and Tutsi. The conclusion reached by the UN Independent Commission of Experts was that "ample" evidence indicated that individuals from both sides of the armed conflict perpetrated crimes against humanity in Rwanda.[67] In relation to RPF the UN Secretary General also received reports concerning summary or arbitrary executions carried out by RPF Forces, in what was described

---

59 *P. v. J. P Akayesu*, Judgement, T.C. Case no: ICTR-96-4-T, 2 Sept. 1998, para. 126.

60 *P. v. E. Niyitegeka*, Case no: ICTR-96-14-T, 16 May 2003, para. 396.

61 *P. v. O. Serushago,* A.C, Case no: ICTR-98-39-A, 6 April 2000.

62 *P. v. A. Musema*, Judgement and Sentence, ICTR-96-13-T, 27 January 2000, paras. 310, 316.

63 Preliminary Report of the Independent Commission of Experts established in accor dance with SC res. 935 (1994), UN Doc. S/1994/1125, para.148.

64 Final Report of the Independent Commission of Experts, para. 183, UN Doc. S/1994/1405, 9 December 1994.

65 Preliminary Report, para. 148.

66 Final Report, Independent Commission of Experts, para. 98.

67 Preliminary Report, para. 147.

as acts of revenge.[68] General Paul Kagame, then Vice President and Minister of Defence of the new Government of Rwanda, informed the Independent Commission of Inquiry that 70 RPA soldiers, including three Majors had been detained after the conflict, that the government intended to try them for private acts of revenge exacted against Hutus, that these acts were not only unauthorised, but also subject to heavy military discipline and punishment, and that he intended to bring to a halt any such breaches of military discipline in his own ranks.[69] On 17 January 1998 an RPA soldier was executed in public at Ruhengeri Stadium before 2000-3000 people for having killed a veterinarian of Kigombe commune, Ruhengeri Prefecture.

As such the establishment of the ad hoc international criminal tribunals at that particular time was a breakthrough when compared with the Cinderella process of the codification of international law.[70] The decisions to create them, propelled by political and community interest were special steps taken to decisively deal with the exceptional circumstances, that of gruesome armed conflicts, crimes against humanity and genocide. As it now stands international law, through both human rights and international humanitarian law, is moving towards an increased notion of individual accountability and punishment, during and after conflict, in cases of both non international and international armed conflicts.[71]

As mentioned earlier, this chapter will reflect on the institutional framework of the ICTR. This provides an informed appreciation of the legal and policy issues related to accountability. What is needed is to highlight three areas essential to any reading of the framework. That is the Tribunal's jurisdiction; its organizational structure and its relationship with the Security Council and States.

Jurisdiction

The institutional framework of the ICTR is regulated by its Statute, annexed to UN SC resolution 955 (1994), and by its Rules of procedure and evidence, adopted and periodically amended by its Judges.[72] The Statute grants the Tribunal authority and competence to prosecute persons responsible for serious international humanitarian law violations committed in the territory of Rwanda, as well as Rwandan citizens who are natural persons responsible for such violations committed in the territory of neighbouring States.[73] The temporal jurisdiction of

---

68 Report of the Secretary-General on the investigation of serious violations of international violations of international humanitarian law committed in Rwanda during the conflict, para. 9 - 10, UN Doc. S/1994/867, 25 July 1994.

69 Final Report, Independent Commission of Experts, para. 99.

70 Statement of the Rep. of Czech, p. 6.

71 Bell C (2000), Peace Agreements and Human Rights, Oxford University Press, Oxford, p. 285.

72 Art.14, Statute, ICTR. The first Rules of procedure and evidence were adopted on 5 July 1995. They have been regularly updated and amended.

73 Art.1, Statute, ICTR.

Tribunal is from 1 January 1994 to 31 December 1994.[74] Its territorial jurisdiction extends to the territory of Rwanda, including its land surface and air space, as well as to the territory of neighbouring States in respect of serious violations of international humanitarian law committed by Rwandan citizens.[75] The Tribunal has personal jurisdiction over natural persons only.[76] This is the crystallization of a sacrosanct legal principle. That of individual criminal responsibility recognized by customary and conventional international law.[77] It squarely incorporates the Nuremberg Tribunal's conclusion that "crimes against international law are committed by men, not abstract entities, and only by punishing individuals who commit such crimes can the provisions of international law be enforced".[78]

The scope of the ICTR's subject matter jurisdiction[79] covers the following crimes:

Article 2: Genocide

1. The International Tribunal for Rwanda shall have the power to prosecute persons committing genocide as defined in paragraph 2 of this article or of committing any of the other acts enumerated in paragraph 3 of this article.

2. Genocide means any of the following acts committed with intent to destroy, in whole or in part, a national, ethnic, racial or religious group, as such:
   (a) Killing members of the group;
   (b) Causing serious bodily or mental harm to members of the group;
   (c) Deliberately inflicting on the group conditions of life calculated to bring about its physical destruction in whole or in part;
   (d) Imposing measures intended to prevent births within the group;
   (e) Forcibly transferring children on the group to another group.

3. The following acts shall be punishable:
   (a) Genocide;
   (b) Conspiracy to commit genocide;
   (c) Direct and public incitement to commit genocide;
   (d) Attempt to commit genocide;
   (e) Complicity to genocide.

---

74 Art. 7, Statute, ICTR. C.f. There is no temporal limitation for the ICTY, which has the power to prosecute persons for serious international humanitarian law violations committed in the territory of the former Yugoslavia since 1991, Art. 1, ICTY Statute.

75 Art.7, Id.

76 Art 5, Id.

77 Art. 5, Id. C.f. Under Art. 9 and 10 of the Nuremberg Charter criminal organizations were prosecuted.

78 Nuremberg Judgement, at 447.

79 Cf. Cassese A (1999) The Statute of the International Criminal Court: Some Preliminary Reflections, E.J.I.L, vol. 10, pp. 144-171.

Article 3: Crimes against Humanity

The International Tribunal for Rwanda shall have the power to prosecute persons responsible for the following crimes when committed as part of a widespread or systematic attack against any civilian population on national, political, ethnic, racial or religious grounds:
(a) Murder
(b) Extermination
(c) Enslavement
(d) Deportation
(e) Imprisonment
(f) Torture
(g) Rape
(h) Persecutions on political, racial and religious grounds
(i) Other inhuman acts

Article 3: Violations of Article 3 Common to the Geneva Conventions and of Additional Protocol II

The International Tribunal for Rwanda shall have the power to persecute persons committing or ordering to be committed serious violations of Article 3 common to the Geneva Conventions of 12 August 1945 for the Protection of War Victims, and of Additional Protocol II Thereof of 8 June 1977.These violations shall include, but shall not be limited to:
(a) Violence to life, health and physical or mental well-being of persons, in particular murder as well as cruel treatment such as torture, mutilation or any form of corporal punishment
(b) Collective punishment
(c) Taking of hostages
(d) Acts of Terrorism
(e) Outrages upon personal dignity, in particular humiliating and degrading treatment, rape, enforced prostitution and any form of indecent assault
(f) Pillage
(g) The passing of sentences and the carrying out of executions without previous judgement pronounced by a regularly constituted court, affording all the judicial guarantees which are recognized as indispensable by civilised peoples
(h) Threats to commit any of the foregoing acts

A fundamental and distinctive feature of the ICTR relates to concurrent jurisdiction. Both ICTR and State national courts have concurrent jurisdiction to prosecute persons for serious international humanitarian law committed in the territory of Rwanda and Rwandan citizens for such violations committed in the territory of neighbouring States, between 1 January 1994 and 31 December 1994. [80] Belgium, France and Switzerland have exercised such jurisdiction in relation to accused that

[80] Art.8.1 & Art 9.1 Statute ICTR.

could also have been held accountable by the ICTR or Rwanda. Although this has been a matter of mutual consultation between the Prosecutor and the states concerned, at least in one instance (i.e. the only case of a dismissal of an indictment during a confirmation hearing before a Judge) it may have been due to other pressing prosecutorial priorities that led to the suspect's eventual trial by Belgium Courts.

In August 1996 the Prosecutor sought confirmation before a judge of the Tribunal, of an indictment against Alphone Higaniro, former General Manager of SORWAL (Societe Rwandaise des Allumettess) the Government owned Matchbox Company located in Butare Prefecture. Higaniro a prominent MRND member, closely related to President Habyarimana, had served in 1991 as Minister for Transport and Communications. The indictment issued on 9th August 1996 alleged that he had used the factory as a base and a depot for the criminal activities of the military and interahamwe; that he allowed the use of factory vehicles by interahamwe in the hunt and subsequent killing of Tutsi, and that while in Gisenyi he had directed and ordered the commission of crimes. It charged him with direct individual responsibility for three offences, namely genocide, complicity in genocide, and crimes against humanity (extermination). The confirming Judge, William Sekule, dismissed the indictment for insufficiency of evidence linking the accused to the criminal acts that took place at the match box factory while he was in Gisenyi. Belgium, which had also commenced investigations against Higaniro, pursued the case. He was tried and on 8 June 2001 convicted by the cour d'Assises of Brussels and sentenced to a term of 20 years imprisonment. His appeal was dismissed on 9 January 2002 by the Belgium Court of Criminal Appeals (cour de Cassataion).

Furthermore under Article 8.2 of the Statute, the ICTR has primacy over the national courts of all states. It may at any stage of the procedure (i.e. during investigation or prosecution) formally request national courts to defer to its competence. Rule 9 of the Tribunal's rules of procedure and evidence provides that where it appears to the Prosecutor that crimes which are the subject of investigation or criminal proceedings instituted in the courts of state; (a) are the subject of an investigation by the Prosecutor, or (b) should be the subject of an investigation by the Prosecutor due to the seriousness of the offence, the status of the accused at the time of the alleged offences, or the general importance of the legal questions involved in the case, or (c) are the subject of indictment in the Tribunal, the Prosecutor may apply to the Trial Chamber to issue a formal request that such court defer to the competence of the Tribunal. [81]States are required to comply to deferral requests without undue delay in accordance with their obligations to provide assistance and cooperate with the Tribunal, under Article 28 of the Statute. [82] Non-respect of a Trial Chamber's request for deferral may lead to a formal complaint by the President of the Tribunal to the Security Council.[83]

81 See, Decision on the Formal Request for Deferral presented by the Prosecutor in the Radio Television Libre des Milles Collines, SARL, IT-96-6-D, 12 March 1996.

82 Rule 10 (c).

83 Rule 11.

As stated by Judge Sidhwa in his separate opinion to the ICTY Appeals Chamber's *Decision on the Defence Motion for Interlocutory Appeal on Jurisdiction*:

"The rule obliges States to accede to and accept requests for deferral on the ground of suspension of their sovereign rights to try the accused themselves and compels States to accept the fact that certain domestic crimes are really international in character and endanger international peace and that such international crimes should be tried by an international tribunal, that being appropriate and competent body duly established for this purpose by law. The rule cuts national borders to bring to justice persons guilty of serious international crimes, as they concern all States and require to be dealt with for the benefit of all civilized nations. Last but not least, the rule recognizes the rights of all nations to ensure the prevention of such violations by establishing international tribunals appropriately empowered to deal with these matters, or else international crimes would be dealt with as ordinary crimes and the guilty would not be adequately punished."[84]

The ICTR's primacy of jurisdiction is an entitlement, not an obligation, and is definitely not exclusivity of jurisdiction. [85] The objective of proving concurrent jurisdiction was to allow a wider possibility of accountability by other states, including Rwanda. It was foreseen that numerically an international tribunal could not single-handed cope with the responsibility of trying everyone involved. Primacy is a specific and distinctive feature of the UN ad hoc Tribunals. This principle has not been retained by the International Criminal Court (ICC), which is complementary to national criminal jurisdictions.[86] Another jurisdictional feature of the ICTR relates to the transfer of cases to national courts for prosecution. Under Rule 11 *bis* of the Rules of Procedure and Evidence a Trial Chamber can transfer a case on application by the Prosecutor, or by its own decision, where it appears that: (i) the authorities of the country in which the accused was arrested (the arresting state) are prepared to prosecute the accused in their courts; or (ii) the authorities of another country (the receiving state) are prepared to do so, and the authorities of the arresting state do not object; and (iii) it is appropriate in the circumstances for the courts of the arresting or receiving state to exercise jurisdiction over the accused.

84 *P. v. D. Tadic*, Case no:IT-04-T, Decision of 2 October 1995.

85 See, Othman M C (2002) Concurrent Jurisdiction: Legal and Policy Considerations. In OPCW (2002) The Chemical Weapons Convention and International Cooperation, The Hague, 2002.

86 "Under the proposed system [ICC] we are simply re-arranging the chairs on the deck of the Titanic", Arbour L (1998) History and Future of the International Criminal Tribunals for the Former Yugoslavia and Rwanda, Am.U. Int'l Rev., vol.13, p. 1500.

Institutional Organs

The organic structure of the ICTR consists of three organs. The Chambers comprising Trial Chambers and an Appeals Chamber; the Prosecutor, and a Registry.[87] The Chambers are composed of sixteen permanent judges and a maximum at any one time of four ad litem independent judges.[88] Each Trial Chamber is to be served by three judges composed of permanent and ad litem judges.[89] Each appeal is heard by five Appeal Judges.[90] Members of the Appeal Chamber of the ICTY also serve as members of the Appeal Chamber of the ICTR.[91] The President of the Tribunal is elected by and amongst the permanent Judges.[92] The President after consultation with Judges, assign Judges to Trial Chambers, and once assigned, they only serve in the Chamber to which they are assigned.[93] The President is also a member of one of the Trial Chambers.[94] Judges of each Trial Chamber elect a Presiding Judge, who has the responsibility of overseeing the work of that Trial Chamber as a whole.[95] The President of the Tribunal has a number of statutory responsibilities, important among them is the submission of an annual report to the Security Council and to the General Assembly,[96] presiding over all plenary meetings of the Judges, co-coordinating the work of the Chambers, supervising the activities of the Registry, and that of notification to the Security Council of a State's non compliance with mandatory obligations under the Statute.[97]

The other organ of the Tribunal consists of the Prosecutor. The Prosecutor has the sole responsibility for investigation and prosecution, and acts independently as a separate organ of the Tribunal.[98] He or she is required not to seek or receive instructions from any Government or from any other source.[99] In the original Statute

87 Art.10 Statute ICTR, The Statute of ICTR and ICTY was amended by the UN Security Council on 14 August 2002 in order to establish a pool of *ad litem* judges to expedite the conclusion of its work at the earliest possible date. See Annex I (ICTR) and II (ICTY) of UNSC res. 1431 (2002), UN SC Doc. S/RES/1431(2002), 14 August 2002.

88 Art.11.1, as amended.

89 Art.11.2, Id.

90 Art.11. 3, Id.

91 Art.13.4, Id.

92 Art. 13.1, Id.

93 Art. 13.5 & 13.6, Id.

94 Art. 13.2, Id.

95 Art.13.7, Id.

96 Art. 31, Id.

97 Rules 7*bis*, 11, 19, & 30.

98 Article 15.1 –15.2. Richard Goldstone was appointed by the Security Council to serve as Prosecutor for ICTY and ICTR on 8 July 1994, UN SC res.936 (1994), UN SCOR, 49th session, p. 44, UN Doc. S/INF/50 (1996). He was succeed by Louise Arbour appointed by the Security Council on 29 February 1966 (took up position on 1 October 1966), SC res.1047 (1966), U.N. SCOR, 51st session, UN Doc. S/INF/52. The others subsequently in office; Carla del Ponte, and Hassan Jallow appointed on 4 September 2003.

99 Art. 15, Statute.

it was provided for in Article 15.3 that the Prosecutor of the ICTY shall also serve as the Prosecutor of the ICTR. The Prosecutor at the ICTR is seconded by a Deputy Prosecutor, who is appointed by the Secretary General on the former's recommendation.[100] It was intended that the Deputy Prosecutor exercise major responsibility in investigation and prosecution, and that he serve as a special deputy for Rwandan affairs[101]. The position of a Deputy Prosecutor, the secondd in command, was incorporated into the ICTR Statute to accommodate Rwanda's distaste for a common Prosecutor for both Tribunals.[102] Rule 30 of the Tribunal's Rules of Procedure and Evidence empowers the Deputy Prosecutor to exercise the functions of the Prosecutor in the latter's absence or inability to act, or upon his or her express instructions.

The post of a shared and common Prosecutor for both the ICTR and the ICTY has been one of conflicting and divergent views.[103] It represented an initial faulty design. It was a curious formula for two separate ad hoc Tribunals established separately by the Security Council through two unrelated resolutions.[104] As we shall see the existence of this common office has to some extent, contributed to automatic copycat accountability policies and procedures. It also deprived the ICTR of the advantages of full–time attention, on the spot duty, intra office diligence, and the absence of a permanent interlocutor at the seat of the Tribunal in Arusha. It contributed to long-distance management, or rather remote control supervision, of the Office of the Prosecutor. Goldstone visited Rwanda a total of less than a month throughout his tenure; Louis Arbour who was most instrumental in the development of the conspiracy strategy also visited her Office in Kigali less than 45 days a year when she served as Prosecutor. It is not out of disinterest, but the reality of the geography that separates the office of a common Prosecutor with the ICTY that makes it a physically Herculean task for a single individual to be a twin-prosecutor. For Bassiouni the choice of a single prosecutor was ill advised because no person, no matter how talented, could oversee two major sets of prosecutions separated by 10,000 miles.[105] The idea that one can shuttle between The Hague in the Netherlands and Arusha, Tanzania, as part of a normal work schedule, is nothing short of absurd.[106]

It is worth noting that the existence of a common Prosecutor was initially objected to by Rwanda, during the adoption of UN SC resolution 955 (1994). After that, it continued to be an issue of serious misgiving by Rwanda. The earlier determination of the organizational structure and functions of the Prosecutor for the ICTY influenced the subsequent formula adopted for the Prosecutor of the ICTR.

---

[100] Art. 15.3, Id, Rule 38, Id.

[101] Statements of the Rep. of France, Argentine and USA, pp. 4, 8 & 17.

[102] Morris M, Scharf M (1998) p. 390.

[103] Cf. "The explanation that having one Prosecutor would ensure consistency in prosecutorial approaches is less than convincing", Morris M The Trial of Concurrent Jurisdiction: The Case of Rwanda, p. 571 in Bassiouni (1999) M.C, International Criminal Law, (Enforcement) Vol. III, Transnational Pub. Inc, Ardsley, N.Y.

[104] Bassiouni M C (1999) p. 60.

[105] P. 60, Id.

[106] Pp. 60-61, Id.

The Security Council opted for that function to be performed by a single individual rather than a collegial body of Prosecutors, as was the case for the Nuremberg Tribunal or for that matter, for judges to play an investigative role as in an inquisitorial system.[107] The reasons offered for a common Prosecutor for the two UN ad hoc Tribunals was to allow the ICTR to have an early jump-start; for it to take advantage of the mileage already gained by the Prosecutor of the ICTY who was already in office; to cater for uniformity of approach in investigations and prosecutions, and to benefit from economy and efficiency of resources.[108]

While these represent understandable considerations, they fell short of tangible gains of a full-time Arusha based independent Prosecutor for the Rwanda Tribunal. Louise Arbour Prosecutor, from 1996-1999, for both the ICTY and the ICTR considered that separation of the two was not in the interest of the ICTR, although she recognized that the latter was short-changed in the allocation of the Prosecutor's time as one could not simultaneously be in two places at the same time.[109] Morris and Scharf have observed that by having a common Prosecutor an "immense burden" was imposed on an individual, particularly in view of the distance that separates the investigations of crimes committed in the territory of the Former Yugoslavia, the investigations conducted in Rwanda, and the presentation of cases in The Hague and Arusha.[110] Since our analysis will deal with pertinent legal and policy issues concerning accountability for "big, medium and small fish" (i.e. all levels of perpetrators), it is of essence that we also discuss the initial concept of a common Prosecutor has for both the ICTR and the ICTY. If one is to be guided by past record, it is certain that this detectable cancer in the ICTR's initial institutional framework would have compounded the malaise in enhanced accountability, and in particular, the effective and efficient functioning of the Prosecution as the Tribunal embarks on its Completion Strategy, which requires that it complete all its work by 2010. The two things the common post led to, in the words of Andre Guichaoua, were unfamiliarity with Rwanda, and remote control management (*"gestion a la petit semaine")*.[111]

In a turn of events, prompted by new thinking by United States and United Kingdom concerning the merits and demerits of a common Prosecutor for both the UN ad hoc Tribunals, the UN Secretary-General on 28 July 2003, informed Security Council Member States that it was now time to split the positions of the Prosecutor for the ICTY and the ICTR so that different people occupy each post.[112] He submitted that as the two tribunals were moving towards implementing

---

[107] Morris M, Scharf M (1998) pp. 380-381.

[108] Statement of the Rep. of France, p. 4; of Rep. of USA, p. 17; see also Report of the Secretary General pursuant to Para 5 of S.C resolution 935 (1994), para 9, UN SCOR, 50th Sess. UN. Doc. S/1995/134 (1995).

[109] Arbour L (2004) The Crucial Years, Journal of International Criminal Law vol. 2 p. 396.

[110] Statement of the Representative of France, p. 383-384.

[111] Guichaoua A The International Tribunal for Rwanda: from crisis to failure, Le Monde, 4 September 2002.

[112] Letter dates 28 July from the Secretary-General addressed to the President of the Security Council, UN Doc.S/2003/766, 29 July 2003.

their respective Completion Strategies, it was of essential and in the interest of efficiency and effectiveness that each Tribunal is allocated its own Prosecutor.[113] A person who can devote his or her entire energy and attention to the organization, oversight, management, and conduct of the outstanding investigations and prosecutions before that Tribunal.[114]

Invited to share her experiences as Prosecutor of both Tribunals, former Prosecutor Carla Del Ponte on 8 August 2003 argued before the Security Council that separation would have a detrimental effect in the smooth implementation of the Completion Strategy; that it would create a leadership vacuum in the Prosecutor's Office; result in additional costs to hire another full time Prosecutor, and disrupt the coherency of the practice, strategies, and policies of the two Tribunals that had hitherto been ensured by a common Prosecutor. She also advanced that separation might undermine the independence of the Prosecutor, and asked what kind of signal would be sent to those who tried to exert pressure on the Prosecutor, and whether separation would result in undermining investigations of members of the Rwanda Patriotic Army (RPA), and of persons associated with the current Rwandan leadership?

In a statement submitted to the Security Council on 5 August 2003, Rwanda welcomed the Secretary-General's recommendation on the separation, a proposal that vindicated Rwanda, which had advocated the establishment of separate Prosecutors since 1994.[115] As regards the Office of the Prosecutor, Rwanda expressed concern about inefficiency and ineffectiveness arising from the separate geographical locations of the various branches of that Office and general neglect of the Rwanda aspect of the mandate, illustrated by the fact that the Prosecutor spends no more than 30 days or so in Kigali or Arusha in any one year, and devoted most of her time and attention to he ICTY. Rwanda called upon the Council not only to approve the Secretary General's recommendation, but also to consider additional reforms, including that of transferring ICTR into a "Sierra Leone" type court, or transferring cases of indictees and persons not yet indicted to the special chambers of Rwanda's domestic courts.

Expressing its views on the issue, the United States supported the Secretary General's proposal and pointed out that the object of the separation was neither "punishment for non-performance",[116] nor part of the problem that the Government of Rwanda had with the ICTR. For United Kingdom there was no question of a "political sell out" to any Government. It was of the opinion that to accept the Prosecutor's financial argument would be in defence of the status quo, and would deprive the Council of the advantages of dedicated Prosecutors working in each Tribunal. On its part, China supported any measures that would enhance the effi-

[113] Id.

[114] Id.

[115] Letter dated 5 August 2003 from the Permanent Representative of Rwanda to the UN addressed to the President of the Security Council, UN Doc. S/2003/794, 5 August 2003.

[116] Cf. Rwandan Civil Society Groups Deeply Concerned About Renewal of ICTR Prosecutor, A Petition from 40 Rwandan Groups to the UN Security Council, July 2003.

ciency of the Tribunals whose combined costs represented almost one-tenth of the United Nation's regular budget. Russia emphasized that it was the job of the Council to ensure that it was not trying to stop investigations or interfere with the Prosecutor's work.

Finality to this question was reached on 28 August 2003, with the Council's unanimous adoption of resolution 1503(2003) that amended Article of the Statute of the ICTR, for it to have an independent separate Prosecutor.[117] The Council was convinced that both the UN ad hoc Tribunals can most efficiently and expeditiously meet their respective responsibilities if each had its own Prosecutor. Rwandan Foreign Minister Charles Muligande hailed the decision, stating, "No tears would be shed" with the departure of the common Prosecutor. On her part the Prosecutor claimed that it was political pressure from the Rwandan President Paul Kagame that had contributed to the non-renewal of her term of office at the ICTR.[118] On 4 September 2003 the Security Council, on nomination by the Secretary-General, appointed Hassan Bubacar Jallow for a four-year term as Prosecutor for the ICTR. In its Ninth Annual Report (2004) to the United Nations Security Council and General Assembly, the ICTR opined that a full-time Prosecutor since September 2003 has enabled a more frequent or constant presence in Rwanda, the location of the crimes, the possibility to attend to problems on the spot as they emerge, and an in depth discussion with Rwandan authorities on the transfer of cases to Rwanda.[119]

The other organ of the ICTR is the Registry. Its primary responsibility is the administration and servicing of the Tribunal. [120] A Registrar, who is appointed for a four-year term by the UN Secretary-General after consultation with the President of the Tribunal, heads the registry. [121] He is under the authority of the President, and serves as the Tribunal's channel of communication.[122] The functions of the Registry include that of assisting the Trial and Appeal Chambers, the plenary meeting of Tribunal, Judges and the Prosecutor in the performance of their functions. He has direct responsibility over court management services, the management of a legal aid scheme involving the assignment of defence counsel to indigent suspects or accused, superintending the UN Detention Facility, management of the witnesses and victims support services, and conduct of relations with the host State, Tanzania.

---

[117] SC resolution 1503 (2003), UN Doc.S/RES/1503 (2003), 28 August 2003. Adopted (15-0-0). See also UN Doc. S/PV.4817, 28 August 2003.

[118] I was sacked as Rwanda genocide prosecutor for challenging President, says Del Ponte, The Guardian, 13 September 2003; Del Ponte says UN caved to Rwandan pressure: Former Chief Prosecutor speaks out about forced exit, National Post, 17 September 2003.

[119] Report of the ICTR to the Security Council and the UN General Assembly, UN Doc. A/59/183-S/2004/601, 27 July 2004, p. 3.

[120] Art. 16, ICTR Statute.

[121] Art.16.3, Id.

[122] Rule 33.

Accountability: Start up to Completion

Much as recounting the detailed history of the ICTR is not with the mainstream of our study, a brief recital of its early beginnings and its first judicial activities will assist in better appreciating its difficult beginnings, the question of accountability addressed in this book, and the legal and policy issues that will be discussed. To jumpstart accountability for atrocity crimes one requires more than just appropriate legal instruments. As we shall vividly see, it is also a question of having adequate infrastructure, technical equipment, financial means and human resources. Although the ICTR was established by the Security Council on 8 November 1994, it was obliged to wait for a full year for a headquarters.[123] The first group of Trial Judges was elected by the General Assembly on 24 and 25 May 1995, and the first plenary meeting of Trial and Appeal Judges was held at The Hague from 26 to 30 June 1995.[124] This meeting took place in The Hague, because the Headquarters of the Rwanda Tribunal was not ready. On 22 February 1995 the General Assembly decided, subject to appropriate arrangements between the United Nations and Tanzania, that the ICTR will have its seat at Arusha.[125] The Headquarters Agreement between the two parties was signed on 31 August 1995.[126]

The Tribunal officially started functioning at its headquarters in Arusha on 27 November 1995. The first indictment against Clement Kayishema and 7 other accused was confirmed by Judge Pillay on 28 November 1995.[127] The first 12 cells for holding detainees were completed in May 1996, and the first detainees, (Clement Kayishema, Jean Paul Akayesu and Georges Rutaganda) were transferred from Lusaka, Zambia to the Tribunal's custody and detention facilities on 26 May 1996. The first public hearing took place on 11 January 1996, when a Trial Chamber considered the Prosecutor's request seeking a deferral of investigations and prosecutions instituted in Belgian Courts in respect of 3 suspects, all of whom had been detained by the Belgian authorities.

The other factors that compounded effective early start up were the geographic disparity of the organs and officials of the Tribunal, with the Prosecutor and the Appeal Judges located in The Hague, the Office of the Prosecutor located in Kigali, Rwanda, and in The Hague, and the Trial Judges, and the Registry based in Arusha. Administrative and Court infrastructure was not immediately available, the financial situation was precarious, and the organization did not enjoy the support of the United Nations administration that it had expected.[128] In terms of staffing by 31 December 1996, out of 311 total staff (local and international) of all

---

[123] Speech by Judge L. Kama President of the ICTR before the UN General Assembly, 10 December 1996, ICTR Yearbook, 1994-1996, ICTR, Arusha, p. 7

[124] UN G.A. resolution 49/324, 25 May 1995.

[125] UN G.A. resolution 977 (1995), 22 February 1995.

[126] For text see, Agreement between the United Nations and the United Republic of Tanzania concerning the Headquarters of the International Tribunal for Rwanda, 31 August 1995, Annex to Un Doc 96-25167 (E), also in ICTR Yearbook 1994-1996, pp. 277-315.

[127] *P. v. C. Kayishema et all.*, Indictment, Case no: ICTR-95-1-I, 28 November 1995.

[128] Speech by Judge L. Kama President of the ICTR, ICTR Yearbook, 1994-1996, p. 15.

categories (i.e., professional, field and general services), the Office of the Prosecutor had 159, of which 32 were seconded from 9 Governments.[129] This represented about 33 % of its 2004 authorized staffing level of 1, 039.[130] The early teething problems of the ICTR included serious budget deficiencies, lack of administrative support to the Office of the Prosecutor in Kigali, the absence of internal United Nations rules suitable for criminal investigations, and inter department conflicts.[131] There was also lack of measures to ensure effective witness support and protection.[132] The ICTY was also not spared of the same. There gender and racial discrimination led to the appointment of a senior member of the Office of the Prosecutor with full authority from the Prosecutor to investigate any allegations on his behalf and authority.[133]

We have purposely referred to the start up phase of the ICTR, to allow a comparative reading of the setting up of the accountability framework with that established in East Timor. As of 1 September 2003, out of 81 indictees, 66 accused had been apprehended and detained at the ICTR Detention Facility. In 79 months of judicial activities, beginning from January 1997, the ICTR delivered 11 judgements involving 13 accused, 18 accused were on trial, and the rest were awaiting trial.[134] On average it had rendered one judgement every 7 months.[135] In the first 10 years of its tenure, and as of 1 January 2005, 23 accused had been tried, of which 20 were convicted (in 17 judgements) and 3 acquitted, 25 were undergoing trial, and 18 others awaiting trials. 14 other accused were still at large. The Tribunal's Completion Strategy foresees that new indictments against 26 accused will be issued by the Prosecutor come July 2005, that it will arrest and try about 17 accused already indicted but at large, and that the cases of 40 accused will be transferred to national jurisdictions, including Rwanda. Among the fugitives is Felicien Kabuga, an alleged member of the Akazu and financer of R.T.L.M, and the genocide, whom the United States Government has offered a reward of USD $ 5 million for information leading to his arrest.[136]

---

129 For staffing details see, ICTR Yearbook 1994-1996, Annex to Volume 1, pp 213-221.

130 Ninth Annual Report of the ICTR to the SC and the GA, UN Doc. A/59/13-S/2004/601, 27 July 2004, p. 18.

131 Cf. "Getting the ICTR on its feet was a chaotic process. A new judiciary structure had to be set up practically ex nihilio", International Crisis Group (1999), Five Years After The Genocide in Rwanda, Justice in Question, 7 April 1999, p. 3.

132 See, Othman M C (2002) The Protection of Refugee Witnesses before the International Criminal Tribunal for Rwanda, International Journal of refugee Law, vol. 14/4, pp. 495-508.

133 Goldstone R (2003) Comments on the Office of the Prosecutor, Expert Consultation Process on General Issues relevant to the ICC Office of the Prosecutor, ICC-OTP, The Hague, at www.icc-cpi.org.

134 ICTR Judicial Performance and Achievements from January 1997 to August 2003, ICTR Newsletter, vol. 1/3, September 2003, p. 2.

135 Id.

136 Revelations sur l'accusation de Felicien Kabuga, Le fugitif aux doights d'or, Ubutabera, No. 70, 13 September 1999, pp. 1-3.

State Cooperation and ICTR's Mandate

An essential characteristic of the ICTR, and for which a revisit will be made as regards accountability for atrocity crimes committed in Rwanda and East Timor, is that related to State cooperation and compliance. Article 28 of the its Statute requires States, as a mandatory obligation to cooperate with the Tribunal in the investigation and prosecution of accused, and must comply without undue delay with any request for assistance or an order issued by a Trial Chamber, including but not limited to those relating to the identification and location of persons, the taking of testimony and the production of evidence, the service of documents, the arrest and detention of suspects or accused, and the surrender or transfer of accused to the Tribunal.[137] Non-cooperation with the Tribunal is a breach of an international legal obligation imposed by the Statute.[138]

In practice state cooperation is not just a matter of compliance with UN Security Council obligations. Slobodan Milosevic's transfer to The Hague had a little to do with Serbia's mandatory obligations to cooperate with the ICTY. It was the product of Western pressure, domestic political calculation and cold hard cash.[139] The United States and European Union promised the Serbian Government USD $ 1.28 billion as "reward" n the form of economic assistance for that transfer. There was bitter disagreement internally between those who considered transfer a humiliation, national disgrace and an assault on Yugoslavia's dignity, and others who considered it a price to that had to be paid rather than a move necessary for reasons of justice.[140] Serbia's Prime Minister Zoran Djindjic was in favour; President Vojislan Kostunica loudly protested, but was outvoted.[141] Political pragmatism dictated the willingness to cooperate, rather than any insight into the moral necessity of coming to terms with War Crimes.[142]

We have focused on judicial assistance and cooperation because it impacts on the continued effective functioning of the ICTR. In many vital areas of its administration of justice an international judicial institution, like the Rwanda Tribunal must depend on the cooperation of states. It must turn to states if it is effectively to

---

137 Arts. 28.1 and 28.2, ICTR Statute; Arts. 29.1 and 29.2, ICTY Statute.

138 Cf. "There is no question that we tend to get, although it is not always true of all, the very best cooperation when what we ask is in the self-interest of that government", L. Arbour (1998) History and Future of the International Criminal Tribunals', Am. U. Int'l Rev. vol.13, p. 1507.

139 The End of the Line, Time, 9 July 2001; The War Crimes Issue has turned into a financial Issue, Times, Id.

140 The End of the Line, Times, 9 July 2001; Milosevic's transfer was the price that had to be paid, The Guardian, UK, 6 July 2001; Serb Leaders Hand over Milosevic For Trial by War Crimes Tribunal, The Washington Post, 29 June 2001; Serb Leader tells of Milosevic gamble, The Times, 6 July 2001.

141 End of the Road: Ethnic Cleansing on trial, The Statesman (India), 30 June 2001; Extradition Causes Rift in Belgrade, The Washington Post, 30 June 2001.

142 Justice and Injustice in the Balkans, 7 August 2001, www.nz.ch/enlir; D. Djindjic was shot and killed as he walked of his armoured vehicle outside a Serbian government building on 12 March 2003.

investigate crimes, collect evidence, summon witnesses and have indictees arrested and surrendered to the International Tribunal.[143] As stated by Judge Shahabuddeen:

"The Tribunal has no coercive machinery of its own. The Security Council sought to fill the gap by introducing a legal requirement for States to co-operate with the Tribunal. That obligation should not be construed so broadly as to constitute an unacceptable encroachment on the sovereignty of States; but should certainly be interpreted in a manner which gives effect to the purposes of the Statute".[144]

Article 28 of the Statute referred to above, provides a general obligation incumbent on all states, but the Rwandan Government is specially obliged, because the Tribunal was established "for the sole purpose of prosecuting persons responsible for genocide and other serious violations of International Humanitarian Law committed in the territory of Rwanda", and being the territory in which most of the alleged crimes took place, the cooperation of that government in the fulfilling of its obligations is paramount.[145] This obligation of the Rwandan government is absolute, and is one that cannot be overridden in particular circumstances by considerations of convenience or politics.[146]

The Rwanda Tribunal's relationship with the Government of Rwanda as we have just observed, has at times been very fruitful and friendly, and at other strained. Once at a press conference on 23 November 1999 Kagame then Vice President announced that "cooperation is better than confrontation". In the early years of its establishment, there was competition between the ICTR and Rwanda over the arrest and transfer of suspects by national authorities. On one occasion, on 7 April 1997, members of IBUKA, the Rwandan association of genocide survivors chanted anti-Prosecutor slogans during a peaceful demonstration at the office of the Prosecutor in Kigali. That office as the face of ICTR in Rwanda bore the blunt of Rwandan dissatisfaction. A few years later in February 1999, the Prosecutor was invited to the installation of the new Rwandan Government in Kigali.[147] In another development there was serious delay in the issuance of a visa for the Prosecutor, Del Ponte. Cooperation was also once suspended, if not temporarily withdrawn. This occurred on 3 November 1999 when the Appeal Chamber dismissed with prejudice, the indictment against J. B. Barayagwiza. On precisely this occasion Judge Raphael Nieto-Novia, warned that the Rwanda Tribunal should be one whose decisions must be taken, solely with the intention of both implementing the law and guaranteeing justice to the case before it, and not as a result of politi-

---

143 *P. v. T. Blaskic*, Judgment on the Request of the Republic of Croatia for Review of the Decision of Trial Chamber II of 18 July 1997, Case No. IT-95-14-AR108 *bis*, 29 October 1997, para. 26.

144 Separate Opinion of Judge Shahabudden, *P. v. J-B Barayawiza*, Arret (demande de Procureur en revision ou reexamen), ICTR-97-19-AR72, 31 mars 2000, para. 58.

145 Declaration of Judge Rafael Nieto-Navia, para 5, Id.

146 Para. 6, Id.

147 Fourth Annual Report of ICTR to the General Assembly for the Period 1 July 1998 - 30 June 1999, para. 64.

cal pressure and threats to withhold co-operation being exerted by an angry Government.[148]

Issues of controversy and divergence of opinion between the ICTR and Rwandan authorities have been manifold. These include the scramble over defendants during the early years of the ICTR's establishment. The imposition of travel documentation and procedures for witnesses required to attend trials in Arusha, and what one writer termed "witness based extortion" by Rwandan authorities,[149] the recruitment by the Tribunal of Rwandan suspects as investigators or translators in Defence Counsel teams, and of late, investigations by the Prosecutor against RPA soldiers who may have been implicated in war crimes or other crimes within the jurisdiction of the Tribunal. The latter is of certain significance in that it relates to the question of full accountability, of the prosecution strategy, and that of a fair, equitable, and transparent justice dispensed by an impartial international tribunal. In this regard on 23 July 2002 Del Ponte submitted for the first time since the establishment of the ICTR, a report to the Security Council alleging difficulties in obtaining full cooperation from Rwandan authorities as regards availability of witnesses, including detained witnesses for on-going trials, and in her investigations of crimes allegedly committed by members of the RPA in 1994. She informed the Council that Rwanda's position as regards cooperation had "hardened", and that it had no genuine political will to provide assistance in the RPA investigations, the consequence of which is her inability to effectively achieve the investigation of those crimes.[150] In specific reference to three on-going trials in which two Trials Chambers had issued decisions drawing the attention of the Rwandan Government's failure to issue travel documents in a timely manner so that witnesses could appear before the Tribunal, the Tribunal's President, Judge Pillay, also informed the Security Council on 29 July 2002, that it was "uncertain" that trials which were scheduled to resume would be able to do so without the Council's intervention.[151]

The Rwandan Government dismissed as "false and unfair" the Prosecutor's claims.[152] It counter-claimed against the Tribunal the lack of protective measures and harassment of witnesses; the employment of genocidaires as members of defence counsel teams; the slow pace of trials and recruitments, especially that of a replacement Deputy Prosecutor; the failure to indict and apprehend genocide suspects still at large in the DR Congo, and mismanagement. [153] As regards the travel and appearance of witnesses from Rwanda, it stated that no special requirement

---

148 Declaration of Judge R. Nieto-Novia, para. 7.

149 Guichaoua A The International Tribunal for Rwanda: from crisis to failure, Le Monde, 4 September 2002.

150 Report of the Prosecutor to the Security Council, August 2003.

151 Letter dated 26 July from the President of the ICTR addresses to the President of the Security Council, UN Doc.S/2002/847, 29 July 2002.

152 Letter dated 26 July 2002 from the Permanent Representative of Rwanda to the United Nations addressed to the President of the Security Council, UN Doc.2/2002/842, 26 July 2002. See also, Note by the ICTR on the Reply of the Govt. of Rwanda to the Report of the Prosecutor of the ICTR to the Security Council, ICTR, Arusha, 8 Aug. 2002.

153 Id.

had been established for them and that as a sovereign government it cannot be expected to issue travel documents to persons whose identity has not been clearly established.[154] While reiterating its general support for the Tribunal, Rwanda called upon the Security Council to amend the Statute to create an Office of the Prosecutor separate and distinct from that of the ICTY Prosecutor, to devise a plan to transfer the Tribunal to Rwanda, and for the establishment of a commission of inquiry by the Secretary General to investigate matters it has raised.[155]

On the thorny issue of investigations of persons within the ranks of the RPA, the Government admitted to having knowledge of the investigations, as well as of persons conducting those investigations, but questioned the very basis of for accountability for RPA soldiers by the ICTR. It put forward four reasons. First, that it did not believe that abuses committed by the RPA should be equated to the crimes committed by the perpetrators of genocide, in that RPA not only stopped the genocide, but also continues to defend Rwanda from genocide perpetrators in the region.[156] Secondly that these investigations were politically motivated following admission by the Prosecutor that she was under pressure from certain states to pursue those investigations.[157] That the proposed indictments of the RPA were intended to appease advocates of "ethnically balanced justice "and revisionism.[158] Thirdly that the most appropriate forum for such prosecution is the national courts of Rwanda which had already brought members of the RPA who had committed international humanitarian law violations in 1999 to justice, some of who had been sentenced to death and executed. Rwanda considered that the Tribunal's docket was full, in that it had been unable to conduct trials of 29 accused still awaiting trial. Furthermore, that the Tribunal still had hundreds of genocide suspects still at large, and was in fact scaling down the issuance of indictments from 250 to 130 for the remaining life of the Tribunal.[159] Finally that any such prosecution is non conducive to stability and national reconciliation.

The Statute of the Tribunal does not rank the various crimes falling under its jurisdiction.[160] In *P. V. Jean Kambanda* the Trial Chamber stated that it was "difficult" for it to rank genocide and crimes against humanity in terms of their respective gravity, and that the former already punished by the Nuremberg and Tokyo Tribunals, and genocide, a concept define later, were crimes which particularly

---

[154] Para. 1.3, Id. As of 31 August 2002, nearly 600 witnesses had testified before ICTR in 17 completed or part held trials of twenty-nine accused. Of these 400 witnesses, mostly from Rwanda testified for the Prosecution.

[155] Part 3, Conclusion, Id.

[156] Para. 1.5, f.n. 146; See also Kagame Criticizes ICTR's RPA investigations, Internews, 17 August 2002, Arusha, www.internews4@habari.co.tz.

[157] Id.

[158] Id.

[159] Id.

[160] *P. v. J. P. Akayesu*, Sentence, Case no. ICTR-96-4-T, Oct.1998, para 5; *P. v. A. Musema*, Judgment and Sentence, Case no. ICTR-96-13-T, 27 January 2000, para. 978.

shock the collective conscience.[161] In its sentencing decision in *P. v. J. P. Akayesu* the Trial Chamber stated:

"Regarding the crimes of genocide, in particular, the preamble to the Genocide Convention recognizes that at all periods of history, genocide has inflicted great losses on humanity and reiterates the need for international cooperation to liberate humanity from this scourge. The crime of genocide is unique because of its element of *dolus specialis* (special intent) which requires that the crime be committed with intent to" destroy in whole or in part, a national, ethnic, racial or religious group as such", as stipulated in Article 2 of the Statute; hence the Chamber is of the opinion that genocide constitutes the "crime of crimes".[162]

After an exhaustive consideration of the hierarchy of crimes stipulated in the Statute, the Appeal Chamber in *P. v. Dusko Tadic* was of the view that there is in law no distinction between the seriousness of a crime against humanity and that of a war crime, and that there is no basis for such a distinction in the Statute or the Rules of procedure and evidence of the international tribunal constructed in accordance with customary international law.[163] A crime against humanity may be viewed as the most heinous of all crimes; but as between it and a war crime the law of the Tribunal stipulates no ranking and provides for a common penalty.[164] A war crime can be very serious, extensive and as odious as a crime against humanity, all depending on the facts of a particular case.[165] Crimes against humanity are intended to protect a societal interest other than those visualised by the law relating to war crimes; but this fact does not make the former more serious than the latter.[166] International humanitarian law is not based on reciprocity, absolute and unconditional obligations[167] Under general principles of law; an accused does not exculpate himself from a crime by showing that another has committed a similar crime, either before or after the commission of the crime by the accused.[168]

The investigation initiatives, prosecution strategy, and policies of the Prosecutors of the ICTR have allocated priority to those suspected of having committed genocide, mostly Hutu elements. This is evidenced from the chronology of indictments issued, and the ethnicity of the accused. To date all accused are Hutu. This is not to say that other violations of international humanitarian law, such as those falling under common Article 3 of the Four Geneva Conventions, and of Additional Protocol II have not been investigated earlier on. From the point of

[161] *P. v. J. Kambanda*, Sentence, 4 September 1998; See also, *P. v. J. P. Akayesu*, Sentence, para. 7.

[162] *P. v. J. P. Akayesu*, Sentence, para 8; *P. v. A.Musena*, Sentence, para. 981.

[163] *P. v. D. Tadic*, Judgement in Sentencing Appeal, A.C, ICTY Case no: IT-94-I, 26 January 2000, para. 69.

[164] *P. v. D. Tadic*, Separate Opinion of Judge Shahabuddeen. Id.

[165] Id. See also, Separate and Dissenting Opinion of Judge Li, *P. v. D. Erdemovic*, Appeal Chamber, ICTY Case no: IT-96-22-A, 7 October 1997, paras. 20-22.

[166] *P. v. D. Tadic*, Separate Opinion of Judge Shahabuddeen.

[167] *P. v. Zoran Kupreskic et all,* Judgement, ICTY Case no: IT-95-16-T, 14 January 2000, para. 517.

[168] *US v. von Leeb et all.* (The High Command case), Law Reports of the Trial of War Criminals, US Military Tribunal, Nuremberg, vol. 12, p. 1, at p. 64.

view of accountability, it was essential as directed by the Security Council, that organizers, planners and architects of the genocide in Rwanda be pursued first, and once indicted efforts be made to apprehend and try them. It remains imperative that this succeeds. From the perspective of full accountability, however, all crimes, the subject matter of the Tribunal's jurisdiction have to be investigated, no matter the ethnic affiliation, rank, position or status of a suspect. The reestablishment of the rule of law in Rwanda requires the prosecution of perpetrators, both Hutu and Tutsi. The tribunal's fundamental aim is to vindicate the highest standards of international criminal justice, in providing an impartial and equitable system of justice.[169]

The objectives of the ICTR, as originally envisaged, should remain sincere to the Security Council's intentions. The ethnic designation by the Tribunal of who are the "bad" and "good" guys of the genocide in Rwanda is not a valid exercise of discretion conferred by the Statutes upon the Prosecutor. Judicial discretion must be exercised reasonably and judiciously. The Prosecutor of the Rwanda Tribunal is not required to be neutral in a case; she is a party, not a partisan.[170] The thrust of investigation and prosecution should continue to unearth those with greatest responsibility for the genocide, crimes against humanity, and violations of laws of war, not to attempt a judicial balance of ethnicity. Ethnically balanced justice is not a courtroom affair.

It is also of concern if political pressure from a few States or other entities is currently the determining consideration for the re-launching, and acceleration of investigations against RPA soldiers. It ought not to be so.[171] Any form of pressure is unwarranted interference in the independence of the judiciary, and the independent exercise of the functioning of the Office of Prosecutor. The principle of independence of the judiciary is overriding and should at all times take precedence faced with any conflict, political pressure or interference.[172]Actions by the Prosecutor should not contain a suggestion that the Prosecution is merely responsive to political pressures or an advancement of political interests.[173] Justice in the name of the international community must not be dispensed to favour the wishes of any political group, or state no matter its role in financing or supporting the Tribunal. As a way to safeguard the ICC from politically motivated prosecutions, Article, 54 (2) (c) permits the Prosecutor, subject to review by a Pre Trial Chamber, not to proceed where a prosecution is not in the interest of justice, taking into account all the circumstances, including the gravity of the crimes, the interests of victims and

---

169 Declaration of Judge Raphael Nieto-Novia, *P. v. J.B. Barayagwiza*, Arret, para. 15.

170 Separate Opinion of Judge M. Shahabuddeen, *P. V. J.B. Barayagwiza*, Arret, para. 66, Id.

171 Cf. "The proposition put forward by the Prosecutor that political considerations can play a role in the Appeal Chamber's decision making and actions is not acceptable", Declaration of R. Nieto-Novia, para. 11.

172 Para. 11, Id.

173 L. Arbour (1998) History and Future of the International Tribunals, p. 1505.

the age or infirmity of the alleged perpetrator, and his or her role in the alleged crimes.[174]

In May 2003, in Washington D.C, the Office of the Ambassador at Large for War Crimes Issues at the United States Department of State attempted to broker an agreement between the Government of Rwanda, and the Prosecutor with regard to RPA investigations and prosecutions. It appears that both parties had reaffirmed their commitment to accountability for serious international humanitarian law violations that took place in Rwanda and to the principles of both concurrent and primacy of jurisdictions. The compromise considered was for the Government of Rwanda to have a first option to prosecute RPA cases, which would require it completing those investigations by 2004; the Prosecutor reserving an opportunity to review the trials once completed, including an opportunity to review all cases, which Rwanda had determined that no prosecution was warranted. Under the arrangements discussed the Prosecutor was not to seek an indictment or otherwise bring a case before the ICTR unless it was determined that the investigation or prosecution by the Government of Rwanda was not genuine. Although it has been confirmed that the consultations did take place along the lines detailed above, no formal agreement has so far been concluded. While the Washington formula is one option it requires strengthening. If pursued and agreed upon, it must incorporate fully the requirements contained in Article 17 of the ICC Statute. Apart from the test of 'genuineness' which was provided for in the Washington framework, other tests and criteria such as 'unwillingness' and fundamental respect of due process in the RPA accountability process in Rwanda should also been part of the arrangement.

It is perhaps worth observing that in the Security Council debate related to the separation of the post of Prosecutor, Council Members had stressed the importance of punishing crimes, regardless of the persons committing the crimes; that crimes against humanity and war crimes committed in Rwanda should not go unpunished; that the two UN ad hoc Tribunals should remain free from politically motivated pressures, and that the role of the Prosecutor should remain independent. In relation to accountability for crimes committed by RPA when addressing British Parliamentarians on 22 November 2002, the Prosecutor explained her position thus:[175]

> "For me, a victim is a victim, a crime falling within my mandate as the ICTR Prosecutor is a crime, irrespective of the identity or ethnicity or the political ideas of the person who committed the said crime. Justice does not accommodate political opportunism. No one should remain immune from prosecutions for the worst crimes. The political and military leadership of Rwanda has to accept that it needs to respond to the allegations of crimes that may have been committed by their own side. If they are genuinely interested to foster true peace and reconciliation in their country, and in the Great Lakes Region, they should fully and unconditionally co-operate with the ICTR".

---

174 Article 54 (3) (a) & (b); See also, Barboza J (1999) International Criminal Law, Academie de Droit International, Recueil des Cours, Collected Courses, T. 278, p. 162.

175 Speech by C. Del Ponte to the All Parliamentary Group on the Great Lake Region and Genocide Prevention, London, 25 November 2002, p. 7.

For Rwanda's former Chief Justice, Simeone Rwegasore, it is otherwise. He considered the address to the Parliamentarians "political activism" by the Prosecutor; that it was "imprudent" to ask them to put pressure on Rwanda, and that the investigations against RPA soldiers was not "an official act of office" by the Prosecutor, but that of pressure from some Western powers.[176] On 8 August 2003 De Ponte claimed before the Security Council that while she had been guided by the fundamental principles of independence and criminal justice, undue pressure had taken place to push her to abandon certain investigations. Not directly interfering into this matter the Council, in Resolution 1503(2003), adopted on 28 August 2002, specifically called upon Rwanda, Kenya, DR Congo and the Republic of Congo to intensify cooperation with and render all necessary assistance to the ICTR, including on investigations of the RPA.[177] By implication therefore such investigations continue to be part of the Prosecutor's portfolio, and an inherent part of the completion strategy, whatever the final forum of accountability decided upon.

For Alain Destexhe to compare the RPA with the FAR is at best a display of ignorance, at worst propaganda, and to suggest that both parties have committed atrocities can often be seen as an underhand way of giving them the same status.[178] He argues that:[179]

"The FAR have committed genocide and the RPF have carried out exactions: the two things cannot be compared. If a distinction is not made, then genocide is reduced to the status of common murder-but murder is *not* the same as genocide. They differ both in nature and in degree, a fact that needs to be constantly emphasized if the crimes committed in Rwanda are not to be pushed to the back of international consciousness".

In his *Separate Opinion Concerning Serious Violations of Articles 3 Common to the Geneva Conventions and Additional Protocol II*, Judge Yakov Ostrovsky, could not have been more explicit. He opined:

"Having started the war in 1990, the RPF did not target any ethnicity. It was a war for power in the country. There is no evidence that there was genocide in 1990, 1991, 1992, and 1993. The policy of genocide was unleashed only after 6 April 1994, and not by the RPF, and not against the RPF and its members. The evidence shows that this policy of genocide was unleashed by the Rwandan authorities against their own civilian population of a particular ethnicity. This crime was parallel to the armed conflict, but never intersected with it".[180]

---

176 Interview by author, Kigali, 11 December 2002.

177 SC resolution 1503(2003), operative para.3, UN Doc. S/RES/1503 (2003), 28 August 2003.

178 Destexhe A (1995) Rwanda and Genocide in the Twentieth Century, Pluto Press Ltd., London, East Haven, CT, p. 61.

179 Destexhe A (1995), p. 61, Id.

180 Judgement and Sentence, Separate Opinion of Judge Y. Ostrovsky, *P. v. L. Semanza*, Case no: ICTR-97-20-T, 15 May 2003, paras. 31-31.

Human Rights Watch has submitted that international efforts at justice will gain full credibility only if the victors in 1994 are held accountable for their alleged violations of international humanitarian law just as the losers are brought to justice for the genocide they executed.[181] To Guichaoua the ICTR's "second mandate", namely, the non accountability for war crimes and crimes against humanity attributed to the "victors" or "liberators" amounts to the trading of one silence for another, concerning the crimes committed, respectively by Rwanda's two opposing military blocks that have dominated the Rwandan political landscape since the 1990s.[182].

If the ICTR operates on the mindset of the international criminal order of 1994, that ranks primacy of jurisdiction over national courts, then RPA indictees should be in the docket of the ICTR. That of 1994 was exclusive of Rwanda, in that Rwandans were barred to serve as Judges and Prosecutors. Another signal of remoteness of that process is the fact live broadcast of trials to the Rwandan public is very limited. As of 8 November 2003 nine years after the establishment of ICTR, none of Rwanda's Justice Ministers has ever officially visited the Tribunal. As submitted by Gouichaoua, the principle disappointment of the ICTR is its failure to engage the Rwandan populace, to mobilise it around the values embodied in the Tribunal, or for it to serve as a dynamic point of reference in spurring the domestic wheels of justice or in propagating the official legitimacy conferred upon it.[183] The mindset we have just descried is similar to the one that led, in 1999, to the recommendation by the UN Group on Experts for Cambodia that trials of senior Khmer Rouge leaders be conducted outside Cambodia; a recommendation which Cambodian Prime Minister Hun Sen remarked would have meant that the only accountability job given to Cambodians by the UN Secretary-General would be to "go to the jungle to capture the tiger".[184] In 1994 it was inconceivable that there would be referral of cases from the ICTR to Rwanda. Such a possibility was only incorporated in the ICTR Statute in July 2002.[185] If, however, the ICTR operates on the mindset of the new international criminal order as envisioned by the ICC, which recognizes the primary responsibility of states to exercise criminal jurisdiction, and in which, states have priority in case of concurrent jurisdiction, then prosecution by Rwanda, and for that matter other states is most appropriate for RPA soldiers. As stated by the ICC Prosecutor in his prosecutorial policy statement:

---

181 Human Rights Watch/FILDH (1999) Leave None to Tell the Story, p. 737.

182 Guichaoua A The International Criminal Tribunal for Rwanda: from crisis to failure? Le Monde, 4 September 2002.

183 Id.

184 Sok An, Paper presented at Conference on The Rule of Law and the Legacy of Conflict, Gabarone, Botswana, 16-19 January 2003, United Nations Association of the USA; For the Report of the UN Group of Experts, see, Report of the Group of Experts for Cambodia established pursuant to General Assembly resolution 52/135, UN Doc. A/53/850, S/1999/231, 16 March 1999.

185 Rule 11 *bis*: Suspension of Indictment in Case of Proceedings before National Courts

"The effect of the ICC should not be measured only by the number of cases that reach the Court on the contrary the absence of trials by the ICC as a consequence of the effective functioning of national systems, would be a major success".[186]

This specific process of accountability for RPA soldiers, if done in Rwanda according to the required standards of international justice should not be perceived as the mortgaging of the Tribunal's primacy, the abdication of its responsibilities or the melting of accountability, but part of the fulfilment by Rwanda of its obligations. It would also require stringent legal and judicial oversight by the Prosecutor and the Tribunal.

In its report on the ICTR the International Crisis Group has recommended that the Prosecutor re-launch discreetly outside Rwanda the investigations into crimes alleged to have been committed by RPA; keep the cases open after the end of 2004, the Tribunal's Completion Strategy's envisaged end date of investigations, and be ready, if necessary, to bring indictments.[187] It specifically recommends that the responsibility for the accountability of RPA soldiers allegedly implicated in crimes against humanity and war crimes be given, in the first instance, to Rwanda on the basis of the Washington formula, and Rwanda's inherent obligation to punish such crimes seriously.[188] That apart it suggests as part of this arrangement the setting up of an effective monitoring and verification procedures by the Tribunal. It equally called upon the Security Council to ensure that crimes committed by RPA in 1994 are effectively prosecuted, whether left in the first instance to the Rwandan authorities or remaining within the mandate of the ICTR.[189]

Much as the sensitivity and complexity of the issue we have raised is different from that dealt with in East Timor, it is worth noting that one of the first prosecutions to take place before the Special Panel for Serious Crimes of the Dili District Court was the trial of Julio Fernandez, indicted on 16 November 2000, for murder under Section 8 of UNTAET Regulation 2000/15 and Article 340 of the Penal Code of Indonesia, committed immediately after the popular consultation.[190] He had been arrested by CIVPOL on 5 May 2000. Fernandez, a member of FALATIN (Armed Forces for the National Liberation of East Timor) since 1991, and a platoon commander in 1999, returned to Ermera on 26 September 1999. He had fled to the mountains to avoid militia attacks, and forced deportation to West Timor under the hands of Darah Merah (Red Blood) Militia that had taken place immediately after the announcement of the results of the popular consultation. When he arrived in Gleno village, unidentified villagers had captured a militia Americo de Jesus Martins, placed him on a chair with his hands tied behind his

---

[186] ICC, Paper on Some Policy Issues before the Office of the Prosecutor, ICC Doc.111-OT, 2003, at www.icc-cpi.int/otp/policy/php.

[187] International Crisis Group (ICG) The International Criminal Tribunal for Rwanda: Time for Pragmatism, recommendation no: 5, ICG Africa Report no: 69, Nairobi and Brussels, 26 September 2003.

[188] Recommendation no: 6 and 8, Id.

[189] Recommendation no: 10 Id.

[190] *P. v. J. Fernandes*, Judgement, Case no: 02 C.G.2000, 27 February 2001, Special Panel for Serious Crimes, Dili District Court.

back, and had seriously maltreated him. Both his eyes had been cut out, and he had been struck with a machete on one arm. Martins was surrounded by a crowd screaming that he was a militia and should be killed. After questioning as to whether he was militia, and Martins admission that he was a member of Darah Merah, Fernandez stabbed him twice with a knife; on the right side of the chest and on the back, near his neck bone. Martins fell off the chair and died. Fernandez then ordered the villagers to bury him. Post mortem reports revealed that he had died of sharp force injury of the trunk and right upper extremity. The Special Panel for Serious Crimes held that Fernandez had killed the militia with premeditation, and sentenced him to 7 years imprisonment. They found as aggravating circumstances the fact that the victim was defenceless, bleeding, and suffering from serious maltreatment, and the fact that as FALANTIL platoon commander he knew that there was an order from FALANTIL Command not to kill militia members.

Conclusion

The demand for accountability by the Security Council in the case of atrocity crimes committed in Rwanda in 1994 was aimed at bringing perpetrators to justice, an anti-impunity measurement, to re-establish and reassert the rule of law, promote national reconciliation, and foster peace. For decades impunity had flourished in spite of serial atrocities between 1959 and 1990. The gravity of the crimes concerned not just Rwanda, but extended to the Great Lakes Region and to the international community. International justice therefore had to be a visible part of the solution. Justice was also meant to be a confidence building measure to a community divided along entrenched ethnic lines.

Although the initiative to establish the Tribunal was Rwanda's, it did not subscribe to its official establishment by the Council. It voted against SC resolution 955 (1994) which created the institution. Rwanda was dissatisfied with the Tribunal's one year temporal jurisdiction, its internal organization, including a common Prosecutor and Appeal Chamber for both the ICTY and the ICTR, non ranking of the three crimes subject to the Tribunal's jurisdiction, the imprisonment of accused outside Rwanda and disparity in sentencing between those with the greatest responsibility, who were outside Rwanda and who were likely to be tried by the Tribunal and the "small fish" who were to be prosecuted in Rwanda, and finally the non application of the death penalty. Some of these reservations continue to hold ground in the relationship between Rwanda and the ICTR, and in particular as regards assistance and cooperation that the later is statutorily bound, like all other states, to provide to the Tribunal.

In this chapter we detailed the organizational framework of the ICTR. One that operates on the basis of concurrent jurisdiction and the Tribunal's primacy of jurisdiction over national courts of all states. With regard to the organs of the Tribunal, after 8 years of operation the Security Council has now corrected an original defect of a common Prosecutor for both the ICTY and the ICTR. As of 4 September 2003 each of these institutions has been statutorily allocated its own full time Prosecutor for a term of four years. The task ahead for both is the efficient and expeditious implementation of the Completion Strategy, a voluntary winding up petition, fully endorsed by the Security Council.

That, however, is not all. A prosecution strategy must answer a number of questions. Who is to be investigated and prosecuted? What category of perpetrator should be indicted: "big, medium or small fish"? What are the valid criteria for the establishing priorities and accountability? Who should be investigated first? In the case of Rwanda, as we had observed the International Commission of Inquiry found out that serious international humanitarian law violations had been committed by both Hutu and Tutsi; that there was evidence that individuals from both sides of the armed conflict had perpetrated crimes; that there was overwhelming evidence to prove that acts of genocide against the Tutsi group were perpetuated by Hutu elements in a concerted, planned, systematic, and methodical way; that abundant evidence shows that these mass exterminations constitute genocide within the terms of the Genocide Convention; and that there were ongoing reports of violence committed by some RPF soldiers, which ought to be investigated.[191]

A central issue that remains unresolved, that borders on victor's justice, impartiality, and unequal judicial treatment, is that of the investigation and prosecution of RPA soldiers implicated in atrocity crimes. There is no question that crimes within the jurisdiction of the Tribunal committed by all the parties to the conflict are subject to its order. The Statute does not rank or prescribe a hierarchy of crimes. A prosecution strategy must however allocate investigation priorities. This is within the discretion of the Prosecutor. It is part of the exercise of the principle of independence. In the Rwandan situation, genocide, the "crime of crimes" must rank first. It is also the logic of the victimization of the genocide. That said this does not entail the exclusion of investigations of other crimes of comparable gravity. What the Tribunal cannot achieve is engineer a judicial balance of ethnicity. This is a political process, not a courtroom or judicial function. The forum of prosecution for RPA soldiers, "big, medium or small fish", can only find a satisfactory answer within the framework of concurrent, complement, and primacy of jurisdiction. In matters of strategy, the opportunity of prosecution performs a critical function.

[191] Report of the Commission of Experts established pursuant to Security Council resolution 935 (1994), paras. 181- 186, UN Doc. S/1994/1405, 9 December 1994; see also, Human Rights Watch/FILDH (1999) Leave None to Tell the Story, pp. 692 –735.

Chapter 4
Accountability Arrangements: East Timor

This chapter reviews the legal framework for the investigation and prosecution of atrocity crimes committed in East Timor in 1999. It examines the accountability system as set up by UNTAET, and followed up by the United Nations Mission of Support in East Timor (UNMISET). A successor mission tasked by the Security Council to provide post independence assistance in the development and strengthening of East Timor's infrastructure, public administration, law enforcement, and defense capacities. The chapter also critically looks at the arrangements for accountability by Indonesia for the atrocity crimes committed in East Timor. Since the model of accountability is one anchored on the domestic legal system in both states, an inquiry will first be made of the legal instruments and the corresponding judicial institutions. In East Timor the specificity of accountability is that it was established under a peacekeeping framework; that of a United Nations transitional administration. It is based on the exercise of concurrent jurisdiction by both East Timor and Indonesia. It is also dependent on effective complimentarity. In this respect the accountability demanded by the Security Council differs from that prescribed for the two UN Ad hoc Tribunals, which function on the basis of primacy of jurisdiction over national courts of all states.

Secondly the chapter examines serious crimes investigations. The lessons learnt are important given that investigations were conducted under the umbrella of a transitional administration, a peacekeeping modus operandi, and a collapsed or substantially collapsed territorial environment. The violence that erupted after 4th September 1999 left East Timor a charred ruin.[1] Thirdly the chapter details two complex issues that surfaced in the accountability process. The pre-trial detention of low-level perpetrators (i.e. the small fish), and accountability for militia suspects. Issues that are bound to resurface in post conflict situations engulfed by atrocity crimes. Fourthly the chapter will highlight the prosecution strategy. This will involve a discussion of policy directives related to accountability for all categories of perpetrators; the "big, medium and small fish". Fifthly a study on accountability for the East Timor violence is incomplete without detailing the framework of investigations and prosecutions in Indonesia, cooperation between it, UNTAET, UNMISET, and East Timor, and the outcome of the Jakarta Human Rights Court process. Finally, conclusions will be drawn on the accountability

---

1 See, Human Rights Watch (2001) World Report, http://www.hrw.org/wr2kl/asia/etimor.html; Cahin G (2000) L'action Internationale au Timor Oriental, Anuaire Francais de Droit International, Vol. XLV1, pp. 139-175.

process as a whole, its achievements and drawbacks in bringing to justice those with the greatest responsibility for the atrocity crimes committed in East Timor in 1999.

I. Institutional Arrangements: East Timor

A direct result of the September 1999 violence in East Timor was the total destruction of the court infrastructure and the collapse of the system for the administration of justice. Court records were littered and burnt to ashes. The implementation by UNTAET of UN SC Resolution 1272 (1999), that called for accountability, and the establishment of law and order, required a reengineering of the entire judicial sector. Given the substantial collapse of the past regime's civil administration, the judicial system had to be built before it could be administered.[2]

It thus became essential for accountability to be established, not only for past crimes, but also for current and future crimes. This was part of UNTAET's assignment as East Timor's transitional authority. The simultaneous creation in East Timor of a legal framework to deal with accountability for atrocity crimes, and those committed post-UNTAET, heavily burdened the newly created machinery for the administration of justice. It was like laying layers of a brick wall before the cement in between the bricks could harden. Given the need to start afresh, and before the relevant institutions for accountability were officially established, UNTAET, on 27th November 1999, promulgated Regulation 1999/1 dealing with the application of laws in East Timor.[3]

This Regulation, equivalent in many jurisdictions to the 'Interpretation of Laws Ordinances', provided in Section 3.1 that the laws which applied in East Timor prior to 25 October 1999 were to be applied, in so far as they did not conflict with internationally recognized human rights standards, the fulfilment of UNTAET's mandate or any other regulation issued by the Transitional Administrator. Section 3.2 of the Regulation specifically abrogated a series of Indonesian laws considered incompatible with the transitional status of East Timor, and recognized human rights standards, such as the laws related to mobilization and demobilization, anti-subversion, defence and security. By virtue of the recognition under Regulation

---

2 Strohmeyer H (2000) Building a New Judiciary for East Timor: Challenges of a Fledging Nation, Criminal Law Forum, vol.11, p. 262; Collapse and Reconstruction of a Judicial System: The United Nations Mission in Kosovo and East Timor, A.J.I.L, vol.95, p. 50; See also, Egonda-Ntende F (2001) Building a new Judiciary in East Timor: The first steps and missteps, Commonwealth Juridical Journal, vol. 14/1, p. 22 et seq.; Linton S (2001) Rising from the Ashes: The Creation of a Viable Criminal Justice System in East Timor, Melbourne University Law Review, vol. 25, pp. 122-180; Linton S (2001) Prosecuting Atrocities at the District Court of Dili, Melbourne Journal of International Law, vol. 2, pp. 301-345; Othman M C (2003) East Timor: A Critique of the Model of Accountability for serious Human Rights and International Humanitarian Law Violations, vol. 72, no: 4, pp. 449-482.

3 UNTAET Regulation 1999/1, 27 November 1999.

1999/1 of the application of Indonesian laws, the Penal Code of Indonesia was deemed applicable in East Timor.

In a twist of events that complicated the application of laws in East Timor, the post independence Court of Appeal, composed in the majority by Portuguese judges, on 15 July 2003 interpreted Section 3.1 of UNTAET Regulation 1999/1 as providing that the law applicable before 25 October 1999 was Portuguese law and not Indonesian law.[4] It decided that from a legal perspective, the Indonesian administration, as well as Indonesian law, had never been validly in force in the territory of East Timor because the Indonesian occupation was in breach of international law.[5] The Special Panel for Serious Crimes (SPSC), in *P. v. J. Sermento & D. Mendonca* decided not to follow that decision on the ground that the Court of Appeal had violated the Constitution, the laws of East Timor, and international human rights standards.[6] In a subsequent decision the Appeal Court stood by its decision.[7] This judge made crisis on the applicable legal regime in East Timor has led, on one hand, to the Special Panel for Serious Crimes applying Portuguese law and the Court of Appeal applying another.

It is incomprehensible how the Court of Appeal could have come to that decision without an iota of reference to its own previous decisions which had recognized the application of Indonesian law during UNTAET's mandate. The need for certainty in criminal law requires a Court of Appeal to depart from its previous decisions with reason and caution, and only when justified by the interests of justice, not nostalgia. Furthermore, the Court did not mention a word on the canons of statutory interpretation it used, and dismissed the specific references to five Indonesian legislations that had been named and abrogated under Section 3.2 of Regulation 1999/1. In also never cited Executive Order No. 2000/2 on the Decriminalization of Defamation, and Executive Order No.2001/16 on the Decriminalization of Adultery promulgated on 7 September 2000 and 23 August 2001 respectively by UNTAET's Transitional Administrator, which abrogated specific provisions of the Indonesian Penal Code. By these Executive Orders the specific provisions in the Indonesian law related to the above offences were declared of a non-criminal nature in East Timor, and no criminal charges could be brought by the Public Prosecutor for those offences. If UNTAET had deemed Portuguese laws applicable, why then abrogate provisions of the Indonesian Penal Code? The Appeal Decision clearly exceeded the authority of that Court to interpret the law. It was tantamount to judicial legislation. In its unconvincing decision it created more uncertainty in the applicable law. This retards the administration of justice. The solution, much as it is not in the interest of separation of powers, is Parliamentary intervention to correct that Appeal decision, which is bad in law.

---

4 *P. v. Armando do Santos*, p. 4, Court of Appeal, Case No: 16/PID.C.G/2001/PD.DIL, 15 July 2003. Two Portuguese Judges were in the majority, and one East Timorese Judge in the minority.

5 P. 4, Id.

6 *P. v. J. Sermento & D. Mendonca*, SPSC, Dili District Court, Case no: 18a/2001, 24 July 2003.

7 See also, *Augustinho. da Costa v. P*, Appeal Court, Case no: 3/2002, 18 July 2003; *P. v. Pascoal Mean da Costa v. P*, Case no: 11/2002, 23 July 2003.

In a move towards that direction a group of Parliamentarians introduced a draft legislation, the effect of which would be to recognize that the applicable law in East Timor means "all Indonesian laws applied and those which were in force 'de facto' in East Timor, prior to 25 October 1999, as provided for by UNTAET Regulation No.1/1999".[8] The bill also rebukes the Court of Appeal, in its observation that 'to interpret a law literally, outside its context and system, aloof from reality, and in violation of the most elementary rules of legal hermeneutics, leads to an absurdity, which may undermine East Timor's stability, as it tends to bring out a situation of institutional crisis that would otherwise not exist'.[9]

Subject Matter Jurisdiction

Apart from this Code, UNTAET on 6 June 2000 promulgated Regulation 2000/15 on the establishment of Panels with exclusive jurisdiction over serious criminal offences. The Regulation incorporated into the domestic law of East Timor a number of key provisions of the Rome Statute of the International Criminal Court. The definitions of genocide, crimes against humanity, and war crimes provided for in Sec. 4, 5 and 6 of UNTAET Regulation 2000/15 are identical to those in Sec. 6, 7 and 8 of the International Criminal Court Statute. The Regulation also adopted in its entirety the provisions of the ICC Statute on the essential principles of criminal law, such as the *Ne bis in idem*, *Nulla poena sine lege*, mistake of fact or of law, the mental element for crimes, the grounds for exclusion of criminal responsibility, and the irrelevancy of official position in the commission of these crimes. Section 14 of Regulation 2000/15, as that of the ICC Statute (Sec. 25) stipulates that jurisdiction over serious international humanitarian law violations in East Timor is to be over natural persons only, and that a person who commits such a crime is individually responsible. Modes for the commission of criminal offences are also similar in the two instruments. The significant imprint of the ICC Statute into the domestic laws of East Timor had the merit of assimilating in East Timor the ICC's legal provisions that had represented a progressive codification of international humanitarian law[10]

Apart from the above-mentioned crimes, the crime of torture is provided for in three different sections in Regulation 2000/15. As a crime against humanity under Sections 5.1 (f) and 5.2 (d); as a war crime under Section 6.1. (a) (ii); and as a distinct crime under Section 7. While the definition of torture as a crime against humanity and as a war crime is similar to that in Articles 7.1 (f), 7.1 (e), and 8.2 (a) (ii) respectively of the ICC Statute, on the other hand, the definition of torture under Section 7 is almost the same as that prescribed in Article 1 of the UN Conven-

8 See Draft Legislation, Section 1, 'Authentic Interpretation', Interpretation of Section 1 of Law No.2/2002, if 7 August, and Sources of Law, 20 May 2002.

9 Id.

10 Cf. It has been submitted that certain provisions of the ICC Statutes, such as Art 33 marks a regression from existing customary international law, See, Cassese A (1999) The Statute of the International Criminal Court: Some Preliminary Reflections, E.J.I.L., vol.10, pp. 144-171.

tion against Torture[11]. Under it torture is defined as any act which intentionally inflicts severe mental or physical pain on a victim for the purpose of obtaining information or a confession or for punishing the victim.

The ICTY and ICTR Statues do not contain a definition of torture. The UN ad hoc Tribunals have however developed an extensive jurisprudence on torture both as a crime against humanity and as a war crime[12]. They have given torture a relatively strict interpretation, by requiring that the perpetrator's acts be in the pursuit of a certain purpose or objective, such as obtaining information or confession, punishing, intimidating, coercing or discriminating the victim[13]. In their jurisprudence, torture as a criminal offence under international humanitarian law is much narrower than that defined under international human rights law, as the two bodies of law address two different subjects; the former to individuals, the latter to states[14].

In considering torture as a crime against humanity under Section 5 of Regulation 2000/15, the Court responsible for accountability for atrocity crimes, namely, the Special Panels for Serious Crimes of the Dili District Court opined that the section embodied words contained in Art. 7 of the Finalized Draft Text of the Elements of Crimes of the Preparatory Commission for the International Criminal Court[15]. To date the Special Panels have followed the jurisprudence of the UN ad hoc Tribunals, by taking into account the unlawful purpose pursued by the accused[16]. Indirectly this has limited the scope of application of Section 5. In requiring the added element of a purpose for the crime of torture, the Special Panels for Serious Crimes crossed the distinctive line drawn by the legislator between these sections of the Regulation, and took into consideration the purpose requirement of torture specified in Section 7. The inevitable result of this is a jigsaw prescription of torture as a serious crime in East Timor. On this, Rodley has submitted that no clear explanation emerges from the travaux preparatoire of the ICC Statute to

11 Convention against Torture and Other Cruel, Inhuman or Degrading Treatment or Punishment, GA Res. 39/46, Dec.10, 1984, 23 I.L.M. 1027 (1984), 24 I.L.M. 535 (1985); Ambos K, Wirth S (2002) The Current Law of Crimes Against Humanity. An Analysis of UNTAET Regulation 15/2000, Criminal Law Forum, 13: 1-90.

12 Cf. *P. v. M. Krnojelac*, Judgment, T.C, Case No.IT-97-25-T, 15 March 2002, "The Tribunal defines the elements of the crime as follows: the infliction, by act or omission, of severe pain or suffering, whether physical or mental; the act or omission must be deliberate, the act or omission must have occurred to obtain information or a confession, or to punish, intimidate or coerce the victim or a third person, or to discriminate on any ground against the victim or a third person", para. 179; *P. v. J. P. Akayesu*, Judgement, Case No.96-4-T, 2 September 1998, paras. 593-594.

13 *P. v. M. Krnojelac*, para. 179; It should be noted that the ICC Elements of Crime of Torture as a Crime against Humanity do not require that the act to be committed with a specific purpose.

14 *P. v. M. Krnojelac*, para. 181.

15 *P. v. Joni Marques et all.* Judgment, Case no: 09/2000, SPSC, 11 December 2001, para. 634.

16 See, *P. v. Joni Marques and Others*; "maltreatments inflicted to obtain information from the victim" (at para.707); "his conduct and his purpose were unlawful" (at para. 713), Id.

abandon the purposive element which is *the* central component of the concept of torture[17].

A few more words on the purpose element for the international crime of torture. As mentioned earlier, Article 7 (2) of the ICC Statute defines torture as a Crime against Humanity as an "intentional infliction of sever pain or suffering, whether physical or mental, upon a person in custody or under the control of the accused, except that it shall not include pain or suffering arising only from, inherent in or incidental to, lawful sanctions". On the other hand according to Article 1 (1) of the Torture Convention, torture is defined as "any act by which severe pain or suffering, whether physical or mental, is intentionally inflicted on a person for such purposes as obtaining from him or a third person information or a confession, punishing for an act he or a third person has committed or is suspected of having committed, or intimidating or coercing him or a third person, or for any reason based on discrimination of any kind". Thus unlike the Torture Convention, the ICC Statute omits the purpose requirement as an element of that crime. It should be noted that the jurisprudence of the UN Ad hoc Tribunals however considers the purpose requirement as part of the definition of torture under international customary law, and considers it a prerequisite for that offence.[18] Purposes considered valid include those used to obtain information or a confession, punishing, intimidating or coercing the victim or a third person, and discriminating on any ground against the victim or a third person.

Ambos and Wirth have questioned whether the purpose element ought to be a constitutive element of torture, as the ICC Statute introduces a control requirement to distinguish torture from other attacks on the victim's physical or mental integrity, which is an element absent in the Torture Convention.[19] It is their submission that the requirement that the victim must be in the custody or under the control of the perpetrator suffices, the rationale for the criteria being the particular helplessness of such victim, and lack of any possibility of escape. They argue that torture under international law requires either a custody or control over the victim; and that they should be alternative and not cumulative. They subscribe to what has been provided for in Article 7 (2) of the ICC Statute, and a similar provision in Sections 5.1 (f) and 5.2 (d) of UNTAET Regulation 15/2000 as it enlarges the scope of protection of a torture victim rather than by subscribing to a purpose re-

---

17 Rodley N (2002) The Definitions(s) of Torture in International Law, vol. 55, Current Legal Problems, p. 491.

18 For ICTY jurisprudence see, *P. v. Kvoska et all.*, Judgement, A.C, Case no: IT-98-30-A, 25 February 2005, paras. 278 et seq.; *P. v. Radoslav Brdanin*, Judgement, T.C, Case no: IT-99-36-T, 1 September 2004; *P. v. Naletilic and Martinovic*, Judgement, T.C, Case no: IT-98-34-T, 18 March 2003; *P. v. Delalic et all.* (*Celebici*), Judgement, T.C, Case no: IT-96-21-T, 16 November 1998; *P. v. Delalic et all.* (*Celebici*) Judgement, A.C, Case no: IT-96-21-A, 20 February 2001; *P. v. Furundvija*, Judgement, T.C, Case no: IT-95-17/1-T, 10 December 1998; *P. v. Kunarac et all.*, Judgement, T.C, Case no: IT-96-23-T & IT-96-23/1-T, 22 February 2001, para. 485 et seq.; *P. v. Kunarac et all.*, Judgement, A.C, Case no: IT-96-23, IT-96-23/1-A, 12 June 2002; *P. v. v. Kvoska et all.*, Judgement, T.C, Case no: IT-98-30-PT, 2 November 2001.

19 For detailed submissions See, Ambos K, Wirth S (2002), pp. 1-90.

quirement which contemplates the victim as a mere object of information or a confession. While it is definitely most desirable, and in the interests of international humanitarian law that the ambit of protection for potential victims of torture be enlarged, it would appear that with the removal of both the purpose requirement, and the public agent test, what is left behind are two other penalized offences, namely, serious physical or mental harm, or inhuman acts, since these can be committed no matter whether the victim is in or out of custody or control of an accused.

Judicial Institutions

An appreciation of accountability for atrocity crimes in East Timor necessitates an expose of the organization and structure of the judiciary and the criminal law regime.[20] As noted earlier, the total collapse of the Indonesian administration, as a direct result of the events of 1999, led to the establishment of a completely new judiciary. The first East Timorese judges, prosecutors and public defenders were sworn in on 7 January 2000. No succession was provided to the colonial Court arrangements under Portuguese rule, or to the Court system that existed during Indonesian occupation of East Timor. In Rwanda, too the atrocity crimes had completely eroded the Courts of its officers. The result was that in 1994 only around 2 % or, 15 out of 800, of the magistrates had a law degree, while most of the remaining magistrates had received only three or six months of training.[21]For the judiciary, a two-tier court system made up of District Courts and one Court of Appeal has been set up[22]. District Courts, which are competent in criminal and civil matters of first instance, have territorial jurisdiction covering a particular geographic area[23]. Each of the District Courts has at least one judge specially appointed to act as an Investigating Judge, a judicial function that did not exist under the previous Indonesian court system. Investigating Judges have no responsibility in directing criminal investigations. This remains the exclusive competence of Prosecutors.[24] Investigating Judges are empowered to ensure respect of the rights of any person subject to a criminal investigation and the rights of any alleged victim[25]. They have the power to issue warrants or orders lawfully requested by Prosecutors. They deal mostly with pre-indictment criminal litigation, such as the

20 See also, Othman M C The Framework of Prosecutions and the Court System in East Timor, in Ambos K, Othman M C (eds.) (2000) New Approaches in International Criminal Justice: Kosovo, East Timor, Sierra Leone and Cambodia, Max Planck Institute for Foreign and International Criminal Law, Freiburg im Breisgau, pp. 85-112.

21 Report on the Situation of Human Rights in Rwanda submitted by the Special Representative, UN Doc. E/CN.4/1999/33, January 1999, para. 39.

22 Section 4, UNTAET Reg.2001/25, 14 Sept.2001.

23 Section 7 and 9 Id.; Currently four District Courts have been established covering East Timor's thirteen districts.

24 Sections 7, 9.6, Id.

25 Section 9.1, Id.

issuance of warrants or orders concerning arrest, initial or continued detention of suspects or accused, search and seizure, exhumation, and forensic examination.

Furthermore, each District Court has a judge appointed by the President of the Court of Appeal, to act as Judge Administrator with responsibility over all administrative matters of that court[26]. The organization of the Courts also provides for a Registry at each District Court with responsibility for the organization of the filing of judicial pleadings, organization of court documents, and security of the premises. Staffs, of the Registry exercise their responsibilities under the direction of the Judge Administrator or the President of the Court of Appeal[27]. District Courts are composed of East Timorese and international judges, who sit individually or in panels of three in criminal matters that carry a penalty of imprisonment exceeding five years, if the Public Prosecutor in the indictment or the accused or his counsel so requests[28].

Panels with Exclusive Jurisdiction over Serious Criminal Offences

The distinctive feature of the system of accountability set up in East Timor is the Special Panels for Serious Crimes (SPSC) established only within the District Court of Dili, and composed of a panel of judges, international and national, designated exclusively with jurisdiction over serious criminal offences.[29] Serious offences are defined as: [30]

(a) Genocide,
(b) War crimes,
(c) Crimes against humanity,
(d) Torture,
(e) Murder, and
(f) Sexual offences.

The Dili District Court has jurisdictional monopoly over all serious crimes. Furthermore similar panels within the Court of Appeal, based in Dili, determine appeals on all serious crime matters.[31] With regard to the first four serious crimes mentioned above, the SPSC exercises universal jurisdiction[32]. This is defined as jurisdiction irrespective of whether the serious criminal offence at issue was committed within the territory of East Timor, or was committed by an East Timorese citizen, or the victim of the serious criminal offence was an East Timorese[33]. For murder and sexual offences, the Special Panels have exclusive jurisdiction only in so far as the offence was committed between 1 January and 25

26 Section 6A, Id.
27 Section 21, Id.
28 Section 12.1, UNTAET Regulation 2001/25.
29 Section 1.1, Id.
30 Section 1.3, Id.
31 Section 1.2, Id.
32 Section 2.1, Id.
33 Section 2.2, Id.

October 1999.[34] The Special Panels also has jurisdiction in respect to crimes committed in East Timor prior to 25 October 1999, only in so far as the law on which the serious offences is based is consistent with international human rights standards as set out in International Human Rights Conventions[35]. The Special Panels for serious crimes have jurisdiction (*ratione loci*) throughout the territory of East Timor[36].

The 'mixed' and 'hybrid' character of the Special Panels is marked by the international and national composition of its judges. Each Panel is composed of three judges (i.e. one East Timorese and two international judges).[37].In the Appeal Chamber the composition is the same. The participation of East Timorese judges in the Special Panels, both at the trial and Appeal Chambers has the added value of facilitating a better understanding of socio-cultural factors, the interpretation of the demeanour of witnesses and the evaluation of the credibility of the evidence. The mixed composition of judges has the merit of allowing the conscious input in the accountability process of non-East Timorese experienced judges. The internationalised composition of the Special Panels however, does not water down the fact that the system for administration of justice in East Timor, other judicial institutions, including the Judicial Service Commission, and the applicable laws, are anchored on domestic promulgated laws rather than by authoritative United Nations Security Council resolutions as in the case of the two UN Ad hoc Tribunals, or by a Special Agreement between the United Nations and the State concerned, as is the case with the Special Court for Sierra Leone. It is worth observing that the establishment of the Special Panels for Serious Crimes does not preclude the jurisdiction of an international tribunal for East Timor over these offences, if such a tribunal is established.[38]

In exercising jurisdiction it is mandatory for the Special Panels to apply, (a) the laws of East Timor, past or future, recognized as applicable by relevant UNTAET regulations, and (b) where appropriate applicable treaties and recognized principle, and norms of international law, including the established principles of the international law of armed conflict[39]. The law also recognizes that in the event of a change in the law applicable to a given case prior to a final judgment, the law more favourable to the person being investigated, prosecuted or convicted, shall apply. This is in line with recognized criminal law principles.

Although accountability was, in the first place, called for by the Security Council, it was initially an integral part of the transitional administration. It is now a connected part of the post independence judicial system. East Timor's new Constitution provides in Section 160, that the judiciary existing in East Timor on the day East Timor's constitution enters into force (i.e. 20 May 2002), remains operational until such times as the new judicial system is established and begins to function.

---

34 Section 2.3, Id.
35 Section 2.4, Id.
36 Section 2.5, Id.
37 Section 12.3, Id.
38 Section 9.4, Id.
39 Sections 3.1 and 3.2, UNTAET Regulation 1999/15.

Section 163 further stipulates that the existing collective judicial institutions, comprising of national and international judges with competence to judge serious crimes committed between 1 January and 25 October 1999, shall remain operational for the time necessary to conclude cases under investigations. This is a value added to the consolidation of the accountability process as initiated and set up by UNTAET.

In the design of the legal framework for the investigation and prosecution of crimes, UNTAET opted for a single prosecution authority, headed by a General Prosecutor, and hierarchically seconded by two Deputy Prosecutor Generals, one in charge of the Department of Ordinary Crimes and the other the Department of Serious Crimes[40]. The Prosecution Service is a constituent organ of the civil administration of East Timor. It is specifically mandated to exercise criminal investigation functions, and to bring criminal action in the courts of East Timor[41]. The Public Prosecutor is the only authority empowered to issue an Indictment (Sec.7.1, TRCP), and to keep the files of the case during investigations (Sec.77 TRCP). He or she is by law required to investigate incriminating and exonerating circumstances equally (Sec.7. 2, TRCP).

Ordinary Crimes

The Department of Ordinary Crimes is the "classical" national prosecution service within a territorial organization, similar to the Directorate of Public Prosecutions (DPP) in 'common law' jurisdictions, the Ministère Public in France, or the Staatsanwaltschaft in Germany. It forms the backbone of the prosecution of ordinary crimes. A District Prosecutor is assigned to each of the district courts as head of the prosecution office at that Court[42] He or she exercises prosecutorial authority in the districts, but reports to the Deputy Prosecutor General for Ordinary Crimes, who is the principal prosecution official for that category of crimes. Criminal Investigations for ordinary crimes are undertaken jointly by UN Civilian Police (CIVPOL), and by the newly established East Timorese Police Force (TLPS). It is envisioned that the latter will take over full policing responsibilities in the near future. As of 31 July 2001 the department dealt with 593 ordinary crimes that included 32 murders, 24 attempted murders, 20 rapes, 33 sexual assault, 58 thefts and extortion, and 176 cases of serious and minor maltreatment. These offences were committed after 25 October 1999.

---

40 UNTAET Regulation No. 2001/16, On the Organization of the Public Prosecution Service in East Timor, UNTAET/REG/2000/16,6 June 2000.

41 Section 1.2 and 3, Id.

42 C.f. Section 5.1.b and 16, Reg. 2000/16; Sec.24, Reg. 2001/25, 14 Sept. 2001.

Serious Crimes

The Department of Serious Crimes of the General Prosecutor's Office is vested with responsibility for the investigation and the prosecution of serious crimes. The Deputy Prosecutor General for Serious Crimes serves as the principal official, and has the exclusive prosecutorial authority to direct and supervise the investigation and prosecution of such offences[43]. Like his counterpart for Ordinary Crimes, he directly reports to and is supervised by the General Prosecutor[44]. Attached to the Department is a Serious Crimes Investigation Unit (SCIU), staffed by UN criminal investigators, as well as a skeleton forensic team[45].

II. Serious Crimes Investigations

The first official agency in East Timor to be responsible for the investigation of atrocity crimes was the United Nations Civilian Police (CIVPOL). From November 1999 to March 2000 CIVPOL was responsible for criminal investigations relating to both the 1999 violence, as well as on-going crimes. On 22 March 2000 the Transitional Administrator placed authority for all investigations into atrocity crimes committed in East Timor under the UNTAET Human Rights/War Crimes Investigation Unit. The Head of the Unit, who was responsible for prioritizing serious crimes investigations and providing strategic directions to these investigations, reported directly to the Head of the Human Rights Unit; who was designated the lead person within the Office of the Transitional Administrator on issues related to serious human rights and international humanitarian law violations committed in East Timor between January and October 1999. In March 2000 this Unit had one UN contracted staff, one seconded staff, and a small forensic team. Soon thereafter its staff strength was increased with the addition of specially designated CIVPOL investigators, UN direct-hired investigators, staff from UNTAET's Judicial Affairs Department and the Office of Legal Affairs, crime scene investigators from the military police section of PKF, and seconded forensic experts from the Canadian Government. The latter were required to attend to the exhumation and autopsy of human corpses related to both human rights/war crimes investigations, and homicide cases. The custody of witness statements and other evidential material was placed into the hands of CIVPOL.

While this potpourri staffing arrangement was meant to booster this single coordinating agency (i.e. the Human Rights/War Crimes Investigation Unit) for atrocity crimes investigations in East Timor, inter-agency cooperation between the various agencies within UNTAET proved a gigantic task.[46] UNTAET's six differ-

---

43 Section 14.3 and 14.4, UNTAET Reg. 2000/16.

44 Section 14.2, Id.

45 Administrative Directive on the SCIU, UNTAET, October 2000.

46 "The change was only on paper; the new unit had no investigators other than civpol", See, Human Rights Watch (2001) World Report. http://www.hrw.org/wr2kl/asia/etimor.html.

ent agencies concerned with accountability for the 1999 crimes-judicial affairs, human rights, political affairs, legal affairs, CIVPOL and the East Timorese Courts went ahead with their own efforts, sometimes tripping over each other in the process.[47]

The most mature step into setting up, on more sustainable basis, institutional arrangements for accountability was the creation, 9 months after UNTEAT's establishment by the Security Council, of a Prosecution Service. Regulation 2000/16 on the Organization of the Public Prosecution Service in East Timor, promulgated on 6 June 2000, created a national prosecution service, responsible for directing criminal investigations and bringing criminal action before East Timor Courts.[48]

Investigation Capacity

As we have stated earlier, the initial conduct of criminal investigations related to atrocity crimes in East Timor was assigned to CIVPOL. This force was made up, at its peak of 1,485 police personnel from over 30 UN Member States.[49] Most CIVPOL had a tour of duty in East Timor of between 3 to 6 months. Hardly any had experience or prior training in atrocity crimes investigations. Moreover there was a serious lack of women investigators. In the whole force, less than a handful had expertise in sexual violence investigations. In March 2001 the Serious Crimes Investigation Unit (SCIU) had only three gender crimes investigators to cover sexual violence investigations committed in East Timor in 1999.

With regard to the effectiveness of atrocity crimes investigations, CIVPOL investigators treated each serious crimes case as a routine homicide investigation. No attention was paid to the role or participation of the Indonesian security forces, or for that matter the linkage of the suspect in the interconnected violence that took place.[50] For example, in the investigation of the Los Palos Case related to the killing by members of *Tim Alfa* militia of the clergy on 25 September 1999, nearly all the witness statements initially taken by investigators concentrated on the recital by witnesses only of that day's events. There were hardly any questions asked to witnesses on the past criminal conduct of *Tim Alfa* members, who had been engaged in an orgy of violence in Lautem District since April 1999, in concert with elements of the Indonesian Armed Forces, and with the knowledge of the District's Civil Administrator, the Bupati of Los Palos.

Furthermore most CIVPOL investigators operated on a false assumption that the widespread and systematic violence that occurred in East Timor, was a post ballot occurrence. That it took place only from 4 September 1999, when in fact the victimization of pro- independence supporters, by pro-integration militiamen with the encouragement and direct support of the Indonesian security forces had inten-

47 Id.

48 UNTAET/REG/2000/16, 6 June 2000.

49 Report of the Secretary-General on the United Nations Transitional Mission in East Timor, UN Doc. S/2001/983.

50 Human Rights Watch (2001) World Report.

sified, immediately after the announcement on 27 January 1999 by Indonesian President B.J. Habibie that East Timorese would be allowed to choose their political future through a popular consultation process.[51] UNAMET had estimated that by May 1999 some 60,000 East Timorese had been internally displaced as a result of generalized intimidation and threats.[52] In summary many investigators had difficulty in appreciating the proof requirements of atrocity crimes, including the legal elements constituting crimes against humanity. An estimate put it that out of the 1485 deployed, only 10-12 investigators had the necessary skills for deployment to the SCIU.[53]

CIVPOL's deployment policy, in particular the rotational nature of the duty tour of its investigators, brought about problems of continuity and the preservation of an institutional memory in serious crimes investigations. Of 24 CIVPOL investigators deployed to the Serious Crimes Investigation Unit in March 2001, 14 left UNTAET by June 2001. Repeated questioning of witnesses by different investigators, at different times compounded the problem of evidence gathering.

When the SCIU was finally tasked with handling atrocity crimes investigations in East Timor, the configuration of investigators was heavily CIVPOL dominated. It then provided the backbone of serious crimes investigators. In September 2000 the SCIU had 23 CIVPOL investigators, and six UN hired experienced investigators. Between 2000-2002, the Unit had approximately 50-65 % of its investigators composed of CIVPOL staff. The original agreement between the SCIU and the CIVPOL Commissioner was that up to 30 individuals would be deployed at any one point in time. This was reduced to 18 following the East Timor Consultative Assembly elections, and the adoption by CIVPOL of communal policing as a policy in East Timor. Gradually as more resources were allocated through the UNTAET and UNMISET assessed budgets, the direct recruitment under UN contracts of experienced international investigators was effected. With regard to gender-based crimes, as we have already mentioned, the number of serious crimes investigators was also minimum. It remained so throughout UNTAET's tenure. In October 2000, one year after the cessation of violence in East Timor, the Serious Crimes Investigation Unit had a team of only 2 investigators working on 12 sexual violence investigations that had identified about 50 perpetrators. At times the same investigators were often loaned to the Office of the Deputy Prosecutor General for Ordinary Crimes to deal with complicated gender crimes such as alleged sexual violence committed by members of a PKF Battalion stationed in the Oecussi enclave of East Timor.

---

51 See, *P. v. Joni Marques and Others* Indictment; para. 1, Id.; *P. v. Joao Franca Da Silve aka Jhoni Franca and Others*, Indictment, 6 February 2001, para. 1.

52 UN (2000) The United Nations and East Timor, Self Determination through popular consultation, UN Dept. of Public Information, N.Y, p. 23.

53 For details, see, Olsen O H Investigation of Serious Crimes in East Timor, in Ambos K, Othman M C (eds.) (2003), pp. 113-128.

Financing of Investigations

The effectiveness of accountability for atrocity crimes is also dependent on the availability of adequate financial allocation. The experience of the UN Ad Hoc Tribunals, and that of the Special Court for Sierra Leone, demonstrates that *the more international the model of accountability, the more costly the investigation and prosecution of atrocity crimes.* As of the end of 2003 both the ICTR and the ICTY had received a budgetary allocation of USD $ 1 billion from the United Nations. The net budget for 2004-2005 for the ICTY is USD $ 255.91 million and that for the ICTR is USD $ 231.51 million for the ICTY. The three-year budget of the Special Court for Sierra Leone, a mixed judicial arrangement sanctioned by the UN Security Council and recognized under Sierra Leone law, has been set at USD $ 57 million. The 2002 UN allocated budget for the accountability process in East Timor was, however, a meagre USD $ 6.3 million, $ 6 million of which was allocated to the Prosecution, and the balance to the Special Panels for Serious Crimes to meet the salary of international judges.[54]

In the early part of UNTAETs life span the cost implication of financing the accountability for atrocity crimes, and the cost of the expertise needed for effective investigation and prosecution of such crimes, was misinterpreted. The international community also paid lip service to the repeated demands for additional resources relayed to it by UNTAET, even though the Security Council had in the first place demanded accountability. An example, the ideal of deploying "SWAT" teams put forward by United States and United Kingdom delegations during the visit of the Security Council Mission to East Timor in September 2000, and accepted by UNTAET, never materialized. Accountability on a shoestring budget never works. Neither does it make sense in a situation that emerges out of the egregious commission of atrocity crimes, as in East Timor where accountability was a declared part of UNTAET responsibility as East Timor's Transitional Administration.

UNTAET's original 2001 budget submitted to the UN Headquarters in New York only made provision for a limited number of UN Volunteers to serve as Forensic Pathologist, Forensic Anthropologist and the Head of Witness Protection Office, when similar positions in the UN Ad hoc Tribunals were held by professionals (i.e. at least, P3 to P5 levels). It requested 8 UN Volunteers to serve as serious crimes investigators, when those at the two UN Ad hoc tribunals are at UN professional categories. While the overall requirement was estimated at seventy (70) investigators to enable serious crimes investigations to be completed by the time East Timor gained independence on 20 May 2002, that budget request was for only a dozen investigators. No provision was made for the recruitment of any local staff or for interpreters for the Office of the General Prosecutor. In spite of internal bureaucratic opposition, the budget which had already been sent to UN New York for processing was ultimately revised following sympathetic last minute intervention by UNTAET's Transitional Administrator Sergio Vieira de Mello.

[54] Cohen D (2002) Seeking Justice on the Cheap: Is the East Timor Tribunal Really a Model for the Future?, Asia Pacific Issue, No.61, East-West Center, p. 1.

The resources for international Defence Counsel services were also marginal. In fact they were non-existent. In 2001 the most senior practicing Defence Counsel was an energetic P2 UN professional. Defense Counsel to persons accused of ordinary or serious crimes were provided by two UNTAET professional staff, two UNV Public Defenders, and a team of 11 East Timorese public defenders. The budget for this service was neither sufficient nor autonomous. It was catered for within the Department of Justice. The reason for this being the need to create and support a public defender service in East Timor, which in turn would be available equally to all suspects and persons accused of ordinary or serious crimes in East Timor. It had ignored the imperative of having experienced Counsel in complex criminal litigation to defend persons accused of serious crimes at the word go. Furthermore there was all along a disproportionate allocation of resources between the Prosecution and those for Defence Counsel. Those for the former dwarfed those allocated to the SCIU.

There are two reasons attributable to this development. First was the decision by UNTAET to establish a salaried Public Defender System as the most economic and viable way of ensuring, on a long-term basis, access to justice. With hardly any experienced East Timorese Defence Counsellors in private practice, a Bar Association did not exist when UNTAET assumed responsibility for the transitional administration of East Timor. The budget for Public Defenders Services was thus incorporated within the Department of Justice. While Public Defender System can be made to work, it is often seen as "factory line justice" in that it is invariably under-resourced, inexperienced and propelled by overworked Counsellors.[55] In East Timor, too, inexperienced Public Defenders have been called upon to defend those accused of serious crimes. The second was the failure to regard the accountability for serious crimes as combined process that requires a holistic approach. Recognition of this would have imperatively necessitated the prioritization of this service, and the allocation of at least sufficient resources for it to function effectively. In the absence of that, one is justified in questioning whether suspects and accused have received or are receiving effective assistance of Counsel. This is an entitlement not a privilege.

That apart insufficient resources also plagued the Special Panels for Serious Crimes. Judges functioned without law clerks or assistants. And to sour matters, the Appeals Court never met in 2002.[56] While the law provides that the Court is responsible for ensuring that in each hearing, a transcript of proceedings is taken and made available to all the parties, including Defence Counsel,[57] in reality trial proceedings before the Special Panels have only been recorded by way of an amateur video recording camera. The user-friendliest method, that is, transcribing facilities have never been made available. There has generally been minimum provision for covering transcription costs for trials. Section 36 of UNTAET regulation 2000/11 stipulates that the four working languages of the Courts in East Timor

---

[55] Pitfalls of the public defender system, The Times, 24 July 2001.

[56] Situation of Human Rights in Timor-Leste, Report of the UN High Commissioner for Human Rights, UN Doc. E/CN.4/2003/37, 4 March 2003, para. 47.

[57] Section 26 (Transcripts of proceedings), Regulation 200/11.

during the transitional period shall be Tetum, Portugeuse, Bahasa Indonesia, and English. The right to effective assistance of counsel, and for the Judges of the Special Panels to communicate among themselves, fairly conduct proceedings, as well as render oral and written decisions can only be exercised by the availability of appropriate language and transcription facilities. It was much later during the mandate of UNMIET, that additional funding was provided; at least for the Prosecution to complete investigations by May 2004, as a once–off project. In August 2003 the SCIU had 111 staff members, including 41 UN professional staff, 19 CIVPOL, 35 UN national staff, and 6 East Timorese Police investigators.[58] Even then other needs for Defence Counsel and the Special Panels remained unsatisfied. This included resources needed to complete serious crimes trials at trial and appeal levels, before the expiry of UNMIET's mandate currently set at May 2004. 'Justice on the cheap', aimed at avoiding the exorbitant expenditures of the ICTR and the ICTY, is not the way the UN should proceed when it comes to accountability.[59]

Equipment and Material Support

Apart from the lack of financial resources for accountability in East Timor, there were also limited material resources made available to jump-start, consolidate, and sustain the overall accountability process. Almost one year after UNTAET's establishment in September 2000, the office directly in charge of the investigation and prosecution of atrocity crimes, the SCIU, had one borrowed vehicle. There was no technical equipment for investigators to view audio or video evidence, including crime scene footage of exhumations conducted by INTERFET. There was no "strong room" to preserve and store evidence. Often the questioning of witnesses had to be interrupted due to the unavailability of English-Tetum or English-Bahasa Indonesia interpreters. There were insufficient translators to handle the two container loads of documentary evidence collected and preserved by INTERFET and CIVPOL. While there was official talk of the importance of accountability, in reality rehabilitation, reconstruction, peacekeeping, and other transitional priorities superseded those of justice. Priority elsewhere it took over 4 months for administration to honour a request for coffins to enable the Serious Crimes Forensic Service to arrange the return of exhumed and autopsied human bodies to the communities in which they belonged.

Six brand new vehicles donated by USAID in late August 2000 could not be immediately used by the SCIU due to the unwillingness of UNTAET Administration to receive the donation before the problem of their registration and integration into the UNTAET fleet of vehicles had been technically and legally resolved. UNTAET's Administration insisted that the vehicles be donated un-earmarked for the SCIU, in order to consider such assistance an integral part of UNTAET's

---

[58] Serious Crimes Unit Update VII/03, UNMIET, 5 August 2003.

[59] Cohen D (2002) Seeking Justice on the Cheap, p. 7.

property, and thus justify the eventual supply of fuel and spare parts for eventual repair. A lot of investigation time was lost resolving this bureaucratic requirement.

Information and Evidence Gathering

UNAMET was a source of information on human rights violations committed in 1999, especially that before and immediately after the popular consultation. Its staff covered all the districts of East Timor. It had dealt with the various Indonesian Military and Police officers, including senior commanders, as well as those of pro-integration militia groups. It had information on the pattern of violations that had been committed during the pre-ballot interim. The Military Liaison Officers (MLO) also had close coöperation with the Indonesian military and had collected information on their organization and structure. This information was passed on to the SCIU, and provided the initial basis for deciphering the pattern of criminality associated with the popular consultation process. That apart, the media was also a source of information, and recollection of events, since a number of foreign correspondents and independent journalists had lived though the 1999 violence. Their value added is best exemplified by the fact that in the case of the ICTY, the first time Goldstone knew of the 5 July 1995 Srebrenica massacre was when he revived a call from ABC Television informing him that they had sent a crew to interview Erdemovic, a former member of the Bosnian Serb Army, who was living in the Federal Republic of Yugoslavia (Serbia and Montenegro), and who had fall out with his Platoon Commander.[60] Erdemovic provided information not only on his participation, but also provided a rough map where the executions had been carried out.[61]

Following UNTAET's request some of the potential evidentiary materials submitted by individuals and NGOs to the International Commission of Inquiry for East Timor (ICET) were handed over by the UN High Commissioner for Human Rights to the SCIU in May 2001.They included reports from a number of human rights NGOs, such as Human Rights Watch (HRW), on Maliana atrocities and the Suai Church massacre, confidential reports by various witnesses, reports from Medicines Sans Frontiers (Doctors Without Border) on deportations from East to West Timor, Indonesia, and reports complied by UNAMET.

It should be noted that at times the *unregulated and haphazard gathering of evidence by various interest groups in post conflict situations undermines the authenticity of potential evidence and its admission in a court of law*. In East Timor those who gathered evidence on the violence and on perpetrators were varied. It included UNAMET, NGOs, and vocal East Timorese human rights groups, such as a Yayasan Huk, journalists, as well as individuals. The handling of the so-called Ganardi Document is one example of how it can go wrong. The discovery of this document illustrates the damaging effect of many hands in evidence collection.

---

60 Goldstone R J (1998) Healing Wounded People- War Crimes and Truth Commissions, p. 12.

61 p. 12, Id.

The document dated 3 July 1999 titled "General Picture if First Option Fails" and marked secret, was signed by H. R. Ganardi and addressed to Feisal Tanjung, Indonesia's Minister for Politics and Security Coordination.

The document first spoke of the positive development of East Timor after 23 years of integration with Indonesia, which had not been accompanied with the spiritual and mental acceptance by East Timorese. It mentioned that armed resistance was gaining momentum, and that the TNI had been forced into a corner. That there was no more profit for Indonesia to keep East Timor, and that UNAMET was dominated by anti-integration parties. To win special autonomy, Ganardi suggested offering East Timorese a floating mass (rakyat mengambang) of food and medicine as a strategy for buying sympathy. The document then forecasted what would happen if the first option (i.e. autonomy) were rejected. It predicted that if independence was chosen pro-integrationist would continue to resist, and that most civil servants would move with their families to West Timor, Indonesia. In the last part the document called upon Indonesia to stick to the commitment to win autonomy, and to prepare a contingency plan; a plan for the evacuation of Indonesian civil servants. The plan would require alerting all parts of the TNI so that personnel and equipment can be evacuated, preparing West Timor to accept a large number of refugees and guarantee their safety, and securing if need be vital facilities and objects which will be destroyed. While a lot of interpretation has been given to the contents of this document, it remains a fairly innocuous one. It is definitely not the smoking gun on the planned post ballot destruction of East Timor in September 1999. Its best use would have been to prove that Indonesian authorities at the Cabinet level, and those in the upper hierarchy of the Indonesian Armed Forces General Staff, were at least aware of the likelihood of imminent violence in the event of a pro-independence victory.

It suffices to add that the Ganardi Document was first sighted by a civil servant working in the District Military Command (Kodim) in Dili in 1999. It was copied, and passed on to UNAMET. Its weakness as a piece of admissible documentary evidence arises from the lack of a chain of custody. The name of the civil servant that first discovered the original and made the photocopy remains unknown, and the SCIU does not posses an original. Although there is information that that the Office of the Attorney General of Indonesia, the Indonesian Human Rights Commission, and a number of journalists also have copies, they are of limited evidential utility.

Forensic Investigations

An important tool for accountability of atrocity crimes that ought to be taken into account, at an early stage of intervention, is forensic evidence. In East Timor, following the deployment of INTERFET and as soon as the security situation permitted, the post mortem or forensic investigation of human deaths due to the East Timor violence commenced. This led to an early assignment of forensic experts in serious crimes investigations, and the integration of forensic investigations into the overall prosecution efforts. Morgue facilities were operational in Dili as of February 2000.

During INTERFET's deployment its Military Police (MP) handled crime scene investigations. They collaborated with CIVPOL, INTERFET Medical personnel, and the International Committee of the Red Cross (ICRC) in handling deceased persons. INTERFET issued specific procedures for the processing of deceased persons other than its own personnel. These procedures were intended to ensure that account was taken of legal, intelligence, health, cultural, customary and religious considerations in carrying out appropriate action.[62] This function was transferred to CIVPOL crime scene investigators, and later on taken over by the SCIU's forensic service, which had internationally UN staff for this purpose.

That apart the objectives of the forensic program in East Timor were:

1. Determination of personal identification of the dead body.
2. Determination of cause of death.
3. Determination of manner of death (natural, accident, suicide, homicide, or undetermined).
4. Collection of physical evidence for investigation (e.g. projectile).

East Timor's forensic investigations reached important conclusions regarding the pattern of homicide that occurred in East Timor in 1999. Although lethal injuries committed during the violence were due to sharp force trauma, there were also cases of gunshot wounds, unarmed incinerated human bodies, ritualized ligature strangulation ('incaprettamento') and the use of 'rikatans' (home made shotguns). In one discovery at the barracks of Battalion 747 of the Indonesian Armed Forces, in Los Palos, Leutem District, the exhumation of a dry ground water well used as a clandestine grave to conceal many homicide victims was unveiled through forensic investigations. The forensic services enabled the identification of some bodies, including human remains by presumptive identification through items such as wallets and identification papers found with the bodies or tattoo marks, which family and relatives knew to have belonged to the deceased.

The Forensic Service in East Timor was attached to the SCIU. Functioning as a coroner's service it catered for the needs of both ordinary and serious crimes. From the end of 1999 to end of February 2001, over 95 % of exhumations and 75% of autopsies performed by this Unit related to serious crimes investigations. Among the important ordinary crimes cases handled were those relating to the killing by UN Peacekeeping Forces of suspected militia, and those related to the killing by militiamen on 6 September 2000, of three UNHCR staff by militiamen in Atambua, West Timor, Indonesia. Instead of being attached to a hospital or health facility, as is the conventional practice, operational imperatives and the near complete destruction of the health infrastructure in East Timor led the Unit's attachment to the SCIU.

From the time the SCUI was officially establishment by UNTAET to February 2002, 12 forensic pathologists served in East Timor for contract periods of be-

---

62 COMINTERFET Directive, Procedures for Processing Deceased Persons (Other than INTERFET Personnel), 15 October 1999.

tween 8 days and 3 months. The frequent turn over of forensic experts delayed investigations and contributed to the lack of continuity in forensic data collection. Staff turnover was not peculiar to atrocity crimes investigations and prosecution in East Timor. It was also UNTAET's chronic illness. Other associated problems of forensic investigations in East Timor included the unavailability of forensic pathologists on the open market, and the unwilling of many to take up long-term assignment in East Timor. According to the North South Wales Institute of Forensic Medicine, which supported forensic investigations in East Timor, the international forensic pathology community was relatively small, and the group within it interested in doing the kind of work that was required to be done in the event of atrocity crimes was even much smaller. The most qualified and experienced forensic pathologists had full time employment elsewhere, had legally binding court appearances, and academic teaching engagements, which made it difficult for them to be available for long term UN assignments. To this one must add the financial difficulty of matching their lucrative remuneration in the private sector. Full-time salary forensic pathologists in Canada earn approximately CAD $200,000 per annum, and in the United States the annual salaries range from approximately USD $150,000 to over USD $250,000 for senior experienced experts. This surpasses by far the UN equivalent professional pay.

A system for the prompt recruitment of forensic pathologists hardly existed in East Timor. There were significant periods, some time up to 6 months, in which the SCIU found itself without full staffing by forensic expertise. At one point, in April 2001, with no forensic experts on hand, thirty deceased awaited autopsy and 57 exhumation requests were pending. Delays in forensic investigations lead to progressive deterioration of the human body due to climatic conditions. It is worth noting that the rate of human decomposition depends on environmental factors, such as climate and weather, and the location of the bodies and tissues.[63]These inevitably minimize the prospects for the presumptive identification of the human remains and adversely affect autopsies. That apart, at the beginning, UNTAET's administration had limited appreciation of the forensic expertise required for effective atrocity crimes investigations. For example the initial 2001 budget for the SCIU had foreseen a UN Volunteer forensic pathologist to head the Unit. It took the General Prosecution's voice of concern, and the intervention of Sergio V. de Mello, the Transitional Administrator, for the budget to be amended and to incorporate instead a P4 Forensic Pathologist. The UN professional level of such expertise determined in the 2003-2004 for the Office of the Prosecutor of the International Criminal Court was P5.

Despite some of the hardships encountered, including that of the lack of consumables (i.e. rubber gloves, mortuary cleaning supplies, and body bags) for the SCIU's Forensic Service, it was able between September 1999 and 4 June 2001, a period of 21 months, to carry-out 230 serious crimes autopsies. By 20 July 2001 the Forensic Unit had conducted 341 autopsies for all crimes, out of which 252 related only to serious crimes investigations.

---

63 Now, Doctors Must Identify the Dead Among the Trade Centre Rubble, The New York Times, 25 September 2001.

III. Specific Accountability Issues

(a) Arrest and Pre-trial Detention

Between 15 September 1999, when the Security Council authorized the deployment of INTERFET, and the establishment of the Serious Crimes Investigation Unit, there was no structured entity or organization to methodically investigate and effectively prosecute INTERFET, and later CIVPOL, arrested militia suspected of involvement in atrocity crimes. Neither the laws nor the court system existed. In the course of the fulfilment of the mandate entrusted to it by SC res. 1264 (1999), which included the restoration of peace and security, protection and support to UNAMET, and facilitation of humanitarian assistance, INTERFET apprehended and disarmed a number of East Timorese. They were kept in custody as "security" detainee pursuant to a Detention Ordinance issued by COMINTERFET on 21 October 1999.[64] Some were militiamen who had been arrested and detained by INTEEFET and CIVPOL for allegedly having committed serious crimes or for security or public order concerns. It is worth noting that the COMINFRET detention and disarmament policy spoke of 'apprehension' rather than arrest. Under that policy any member of INTERFET could apprehend, and/or disarm any person in the following circumstances:

(a) Where there was reasonable grounds to suspect that any person has committed a serious offence;
(b) Where a reasonable belief exists that any person is interfering with the accomplishment of the mission;
(c) Where a reasonable belief exists that any person is acting suspiciously;
(d) Any person who is outside the criteria set above, but who is carrying a weapon.

The Detention and Disarmament Policy defined serious offences as murder, manslaughter, grievance bodily harm, rape, and/or sexual assault, possession of a weapon with intent to injure, carrying a weapon with criminal intent, causing explosions likely to endanger life or property, kidnapping, looting, burglary, and theft.

The acceptable international human rights standard for triggering an arrest is reasonable suspicion, not 'acting suspiciously'. The former is suspicion based on honest belief founded on grounds which would lead an ordinary cautious person to the conclusion that the person arrested was guilty.[65] It need not amount to prima facie proof; it need only be based on definite facts that throw suspicion on the person arrested. The legal requirement is definitely not the mere finger pointing of an alleged suspect. What is essential is the factual and evidential material on which the reasonable suspicion is to be based upon.

---

64 See also, Oswald B M (2000) The Interfet Detainee Management Unit in East Timor, Yearbook of International Humanitarian Law, 2000, T.M.C. Asser Press, The Hague, pp. 347-361.

65 Cf. Section 42, Criminal Procedure Act, England.

During INTERFET's deployment, a Force Detention Centre was established as a holding facility for apprehended and detained persons. Apprehended persons could be questioned by INTERFET members on issues relating to the security of INTERFET, UNAMET, and humanitarian relief operations as long as the questioning did not jeopardize INTERFET police investigations. The International Committee of the Red Cross was granted unlimited access to all detainees wherever held, unless the security situation did not permit the same. Within 48 hours of apprehension INTERFET investigators were required to finalize a preliminary assessment of the incident and to forward the report to COMINTERFET's Senior Legal Adviser (CSLA). Within 72 hours of a detainee's arrival at the Force Detention Centre the CSLA was required to review the preliminary assessment and determine whether legal grounds existed so as to warrant further detention. Where no grounds existed for continued detention, the detainee, subject to his consent, was to be released in the locality of the Detention Centre to the Indonesian Armed Forces or Police, to the place of his apprehension, or subject to the agreement of INTERFET Headquarters to a place of his choice. If it was determined that grounds for continued detention existed, the detainee could be further detained. A detainee was not to be detained for longer than 96 hours after apprehension without the consent of COMINTERFET. Where COMINTERFET has agreed to the continued detention of a detainee after 96 hours from the time of apprehension, that decision had to be reviewed again by the COMINTERFET every 7 days thereafter.

The above best explains the reasons behind the inheritance by the SCIU of a significant caseload of detained low-level suspects after the end of the multinational operation commanded by INTERFET. As observed earlier the legal and evidential thresholds for arrest under INTERFET was lower that than under the Indonesian criminal procedure code. That code provided that an order of arrest shall be carried out against a person who is strongly presumed to have committed a criminal act on the basis of initial evidence.[66] The COMINTERFET Detention and Disarmament Policy permitted the arrest of persons on the basis of a reasonable belief that a person was acting "suspiciously" or was interfering with the accomplishment of its mandate in East Timor. Equally its definition of a serious offence was more extensive, and included offences such as looting and theft that did not constitute serious crimes under UNTAET Regulation 2000/15.

In East Timor Section 19.4 of Regulation 2000/30, on the Transitional Rules of Criminal Procedure empowered the police to arrest a suspect without a warrant when in the course of ordinary law enforcement activities, (a) the suspect is found in an act of committing a crime; or (b) there are reasonable grounds to believe that the suspect has committed a crime and that there is an immediate likelihood that before a warrant could be obtained the suspect will flee or destroy, falsify or taint evidence, or endanger public safety, or integrity of the victims or witnesses; or (c) the police are in hot pursuit of a suspect immediately after the commission of a crimes and evidence of the suspect's participation in the crime is found in the sus-

---

66 Article 17, Indonesia Code of Criminal Procedure, Act No.8/1981, Dept. of Information, Indonesia.

pect's possession.[67] The police are required to immediately inform the public prosecutor of all circumstances of the arrest and of any restrictive measures applied.[68] Upon receipt of the Police Report the public prosecutor may apply to an investigating judge to request a warrant of arrest, continue the investigation, but order the suspect to be released from custody, or dismiss the case and order the suspect to be released from custody.[69] An investigating judge may issue a warrant of arrest if there are reasonable grounds to believe that a person had committed a crime.[70] Where a suspect is arrested and detained after a warrant has been issued, the public prosecutor may dismiss the case and request an investigating judge to order the release of the suspect where there is insufficient evidence that a crime has been committed; or the acts under investigation are found to be non criminal; or the period of limitation has extinguished the criminal action; or there is sufficient evidence that a crime has been committed, but the evidence against the accused is not sufficient and there is no reasonable possibility to bring additional evidence into the case.[71]

The investigating judge is required to hold a review hearing within 72 hours of arrest to examine the lawfulness of arrest and detention of the suspect. This hearing requires the presence of the suspect together with his or her legal representative, if such a person has been retained or appointed.[72] At the conclusion of the hearing, the investigating judge may confirm the arrest and order the detention of the suspect; order substitute restrictive measures instead of detention; or order release.[73] Substitute restrictive measures such as house detention, a regime of period visits by the suspect to an agency or authority designated by the judge, prohibition from leaving the designated area, or appearing at identified places or meeting a named individual.[74] An investigating judge may confirm the arrest and order detention of a suspect when, (a) there are reasons to believe that a crime has been committed, or (b) there is sufficient evidence to support a reasonable belief that the suspect was the perpetrator, or (c) there are reasonable grounds to believe that such detention is necessary.[75] Reasonable grounds for detention exists when there are reasons to believe that the suspect will flee to avoid criminal proceedings; or there is the risk that evidence may be tainted, lost, destroyed or falsified, or there are reasons to believe that witnesses or victims may be pressured or manipulated or their safety endangered; or there are reasons to believe that the suspect will continue to commit offences or poses a danger to public safety or security.[76] The investigating judge is required to review the detention of a suspect every 30 days,

---

67 UNTAET Regulation 2000/30, On Transitional Rules of Criminal Procedure, 25 September 2000.
68 Section, 19.5, Id.
69 Section 19.6, Id.
70 Section 19.1, Id.
71 Section, 19.7, Id.
72 Section 20.1, Id.
73 Section 20.6, Id.
74 Section 21.1, Id.
75 Section 20.7, Id.
76 Section 20.8, Id.

and may issue orders for further detention or substitute restrictive measures or release.

By virtue of Section 20.11 of UNTAET Regulation 2000/30, it is only the Special Panel for Serious Crimes of the Dili District Court that is permitted to extend for an additional three months period the detention of persons who have already been held in pre-trial detention for six months, in the case of a crime carrying a penalty of more than 5 years, and if the interest of justice so requires based on compelling grounds. On exceptional grounds, and taking into consideration the prevailing circumstances in East Timor, for complex cases of crimes carrying imprisonment of ten years or more under the law, a Panel of the Dili District Court may, at the request of the Public Prosecutor, order the continued detention of a suspect, if the interest of justice so requires, and as long as the length of pre-trial detention is reasonable in the circumstances, and having regard to international standards of fair trial (Section 20.2). An arrest in the above circumstances requires the police to immediately inform the public prosecutor, including any restrictive measures applied.[77] Upon receipt of a report on the above, the public prosecutor may apply to an investigating judge to request the issuance of a warrant of arrest.[78] These warrants are issued if there are reasonable grounds to believe that a person has committed a crime.

The pre-trial detention of low-level perpetrators took a heavy toll on atrocity crimes investigations in East Timor. By July 2000 74 such non-indicted suspects had been detained without charges by UNTAET.[79] On 20 March 2001 of 41 serious crimes suspects detained, 9 had been held in custody for more than 9 months without charges. This infringed universally recognized human rights standards. If it were not for the specific prosecution policy adopted for the handling of such a caseload, it would have caused a fatal blow to accountability, and to the reestablishment of the rule of law. The investigation of low-level perpetrators, most of whom had been detained by the time the Prosecution Service was established on 6 June 2000, consumed an enormous amount of investigative resources. In order to expedite the pending investigation of 50 non-indicted detained militiamen, in March 2001, over 50% of serious crimes investigators were assigned to speedy up and complete the investigation files of detained militiamen.

Given the urgent need to accelerate the prosecution of numerous low-level detained suspects, a pragmatic prosecution policy was adopted in October 2000, to charge suspected and detained "small fish" with offences under the Penal Code of Indonesia. A number of considerations had to be taken into account whether or not to charge under that Penal Code or in the alternative to indict for Crimes against Humanity. This included the leadership or command position of the suspect; whether the suspect acted alone or with other non detained suspects who were at large; the gravity of the offences; the notoriety of the acts of the suspect; whether the criminal conduct constituted a single offence or a series of criminal offences

77 Section 19.5, Id.

78 Section 19.6 Id.

79 See, Olsen O Investigation of Serious Crimes in East Timor. In Ambos K, Othman M. C (eds.) (2003) New Approaches in International Criminal Law.

committed over a considerable period of time taking into account the jurisdiction of the Special Panel for Serious Crimes; the sufficiency of evidence for immediate trial; the existence of linkages with other potential suspects in superior or command positions, admission of guilt, the willingness of a suspect to cooperate with the Prosecution, and the probative value of any future testimony offered by such person. Adherence to this policy led to the indictment of 29 detained persons for murder under Section 340 of the Penal Code of Indonesia by 21 March 2001, thus remedying the abuse of the judicial process caused by prolonged pre trial detention of non-indicted suspects.

(b) Accountability for Militia Refugees

The 1999 violence in East Timor led to the forcible deportation of an estimated 250,000 East Timorese to West Timor, Indonesia. In 2001 more than 100,000 still remained there. Most of those who stayed behind remained under the control of pro integration leaders and militia commanders whom Indonesian authorities chose not to disarm or in any way challenge. This control was particularly strong in camps such as those of Tuabakan and Noelbaki, which housed a number of ex-Timorese members of the Indonesian Army and the Police. The level of intimidation was also high. It was directed not just against refugees wishing to return to East Timor, but also against UNHCR staff.[80] On 6 September 2001 three UNHCR staff members were killed in an attack by a mob that gathered for the funeral of a notorious pro- integration militia member, Olivio Mendonca Moruk, Commander of the *Laksaur* Militia.

The presence of armed militia in West Timor, Indonesia has been a major source of security concern for East Timor. In the wake of atrocity crimes in Rwanda in July 1994, interahamwe and other perpetrators in their flight across Rwanda's border in the Kivu region of the Democratic Republic of Congo brought with them a significant "hostage" population that they controlled in refugee camps. It was from this complex and volatile situation in the Kivu region that the rebellion arose which led to the overthrow of President Mobutu's regime in Zaire (i.e. DR Congo), and the advent of Laurent-desire Kabila to power in the newly remained Democratic Republic of the Congo.[81]

In East Timor militia based in West Timor had undertaken hostile incursions into its territory, in particular the border districts. This prompted a robust posture by UN peacekeeping forces. In September 2000 the PKF launched 'Operation Cobra', aimed at inducing the surrender, capture, or elimination of militia in Manufahi, the district with the most significant militia incursions. Private Devi Ram Jaisi, a Nepalese PKF Soldier, was a killed in Suai District, East Timor on 10 August 2000 by members of *Ablai* Militia (Aku Berjuang Lestikaran Amanat Intergrasi) (I will Fight to Preserve the Mandate for Integration). He was shot dead and

80 See, Human Rights Watch (2001) Report.

81 Report on the Situation of Human Rights in Rwanda submitted by the Special Representative, UN Doc. E/CN. 4/1999/33, January 1999, para. 18.

some of his colleagues were injured during armed confrontation with *Ablai* militia, some of whom escaped into West Timor, Indonesia. There they remain at large. On 25 October 2000 UNTAET called upon Indonesia to conduct investigations into this crime, the alleged suspects of which included the Commander of the *Ablai* militia group and others known to be in Indonesia. This call remains unheeded.

The framework of accountability in East Timor had to take into account the particular circumstances of East Timor. One in which the violence had caused the forced deportation of almost one-third of the population of East Timor into West Timor, Indonesia, as a result of the violence that was unleashed following the announcement on 4 September 1999 of the results of the popular consultation. Militia groups, with the support of the TNI, were largely responsible for the forced deportation of the East Timorese population. Refugees in camps in West Timor thus found themselves under intimidation, threat and control of militiamen, often from their own districts and communities. The sensitive and thorny issue of East Timorese militia presence in West Timor preoccupied both UNTAET and UNHCR. Among the refugee community there were many low-level perpetrators, as well as the majority of the senior commanders and the intermediate company, or unit commanders, of the East Timor militia groups.

Cancio Lopes de Carvalho, Commander of the *Mahidi* (Mati Hidup Demi Integrasi) (Dead or Alive for Indonesia) militia group, indicated on a number of occasions to UNATET officials in Kupang, West Timor in 2000-2001, and personally to Xanana Gusmao when they met in Kupang in November 2001 and at Salele, Covalima District, East Timor that he was ready to return to East Timor and to face justice.[82] He was also conscious that he would be subjected to arrest and detention as soon as he set foot into East Timor. The only condition he posed was to be assigned a Defence Counsel of his choice. This he did on 29 November 2001. His younger brother, the Deputy Commander of *Mahidi* militia group, Nemecio Lopes de Carvalho, had returned together with 378 refugees, under Operation Ainaro II, organized by UNTAET on 17 October 2001.[83] On that day, by prior agreement between UNTAET officials and the *Mahidi* Commander and Deputy Commander, Mahidi made a public demonstration at the Salele border by handing over to Xanana Gusmao a *Mahidi* T-shirt, as a token of the disbanding of the militia group. Also present at the border were the President of the East Timor Constituent Assembly, Francisco Guterres, Brigadier General Taur Matan Ruak, Chief of Staff of the East Timor Defence Forces, UNTAET's Chief of Staff, Malaysian veteran diplomat, Datuk N. Parameswaran, East Timor's General Prosecutor, Major General William T. da Costa, Indonesian Armed Forces Udayana Military Commander and East Nusa Tenggara (NTT) Governor, Piet A. Tallo.[84] It was believed that Cancio Lopes de Carvalho's return would also trigger the inevitable re-

---

[82] East Timor: Ex Militia Leader Too Afraid to Return Home, *Lusa*, 8 January 2002; Hundreds of East Timor Refugees cancel planned trip home, Associated Press, 9 January 2002.

[83] Militia Boss back, East Timor Sun, October 25-November 1, 2001.

[84] Xanana greets 800 ex-militia and families, The Jakarta Post, 18 October 2001; Sluggish Train of Justice Moves Some Only to Tears, Sydney Morning Herald, 5 January 2002.

turn of the remaining refugees under his control in Betun camp, West Timor, as well as dozens of suspected *Mahidi* militia. De Carvalho was indicted on 28 February 2003, and he together with all the other 22 indictees continues to remain in at large in West Timor, Indonesia.

UNTAET considered that it was its responsibility to facilitate the return of East Timor refugees in a manner that was coordinated, safe, and dignified, while at the same time ensure that the mandate of the UN to prosecute those responsible for atrocity crimes is accomplished while ensuring uniform application of the law with due regard to security, and law and order in East Timor. A common policy had to be worked out between the Office of the General Prosecutor, PKF, CIVPOL, the Justice Department and Human Rights Unit of UNTAET and UNHCR, the UN's lead agency on refugee matters, as to the most accommodating action to be taken when individuals suspected of committing serious crimes were among a group of returnees.

The policy and procedural guidelines agreed upon by all concerned UN parties, and endorsed by the Transitional Administrator on 17 October 2001, was that indicted returnees, for whom warrants of arrest had been issued, would be subject to arrest when they entered East Timor. In this regard the suggestion in the Review of Peacekeeping Operations by King's College's Security and Development Group, that early arrest warrants that were issued by the Serious Crimes Prosecutors against key militia leaders were never executed due to informal agreements between the General Prosecutor and UNTAET's Chief of Staff who was negotiating with those same figures for return from West Timor, is incorrect.[85] First it is not Prosecutors who issue arrest warrants. Under Section 19.1 of UNTAET Regulation 2000/30 of the Transitional Rules of Criminal Procedure arrest warrants for suspects are issued by investigating judges. Those for accused may be issued by District Court judges. It would have been an abuse of process for the law in East Timor to empower Prosecutors to issue arrest warrants. Secondly no valid arrest warrants duly issued by a competent judge for a serious crime suspect or accused was unexecuted by CIVPOL or any other authority during UNTAET's tenure. To do would not only have been against the agreed upon policy guidelines signed approved by the Transitional Administrator, but also against the law. It would have been considered unacceptable by the courts, since such warrants are court orders; their non-execution is not a matter of discretion. Non-respect of Court order can amount to contempt of court. On this issue the policy guidelines adopted in East Timor were most respectful of the law. No exception was made for the non-arrest of an indicted accused.

According to the joint policy adopted by all concerned agencies, for non-indicted suspects, a determination had to be made by the Office of the General Prosecutor whether or not to seek an arrest warrant from the court. Under Section 19.1 UNTAET Regulation 2000/30, an arrest warrant may be sought if there are reasonable grounds for believing that a crime has been committed and that an in-

85 A Review of Peace Operations. A Case for Change, East Timor Report, Conflict Security and Development Group, IPI, Kings College, London, 28 February 2003, para. 280, http:/ipi.sspp. kcl.ac.uk/rep006/index.html.

dividual is criminally responsible for that crime. It was expressly laid down in the policy guidelines that arrests at the border or elsewhere, if any, were only to be executed by CIVPOL. The guidelines laid down that an arrest was to be effected in a manner that will ensure the safety of the suspect and the community, and to be undertaken in a manner that did not jeopardize the safe and timely return of refugees in a dignified manner. No arrests were to be carried out by PKF in the context of organized refugee return-movements through legal border crossing points. Where the return was spontaneous, and PKF identified a suspect, it had to notify a Public Prosecutor or CIVPOL. This provision was a return to sound transitional governance. It departed from the early days of INTERFET, when persons could be detained by the robust multinational forces, on much lower threshold evidence, such as acting suspiciously. This also avoided the manhandling of refugee suspects at frontier crossing points.

The guidelines provided that as a rule arrests were not to be made at the border or at the transit centre where UNHCR was conducting its mandated protection interviews of returnees. Arrests were to be effectuated at a time to be determined by the Prosecution, at the place where the indictee or suspect returns or on a different manner to be determined by the competent Prosecutor with due regard to local sensitivities; and bearing in mind the overall goal of promoting further returns. When an arrest is made it was required that the accused or suspect be made to appear before the Special Panel for Serious Crimes, or an investigating judge, respectively within 72 hours as required by law. At that hearing, the Panel or investigating judge had authority to, (a) confirm the arrest and order the detention of the individual; (b) order the provisional release of the person with restrictive measure; or (c) order the release of the individual. UNTAET also agreed to provide Defence Counsel to ensure respect of the rights of arrested persons.

A significant issue on refugees, which also touched on accountability, was the arrangements for reconciliation meetings in East Timor between East Timor leaders and their communities and Indonesia-based Timor pro-integration leaders and their supporters, some of whom were suspected of having committed atrocity crimes in 1999. On a number of occasions the Prosecution had indicated to senior UNTAET and UNHCR officials that the entry into East Timor for reconciliation meetings, for whom the prosecution had arrest level evidence or that sufficient to indict, would trigger their arrest. A 'grand' reconciliation meeting between the National Council of Timorese Resistance (CNRT) and pro-autonomy leaders, brokered by UNTAET and scheduled for 17-19 April 2001, had foreseen the participation of Joao Da Silva Tavares, the Supreme Commander of the umbrella East Timor militia organization, Integration Fighting Forces (PPI), Edmundo da Conceicao, the Bupati of Leutem District, and Leonito Martins, the Bupati of Liquica. The former was eventually indicted on 10 July 2003 together with 57 other accused in connected with crimes against humanity committed in Bobonaro sub district. Da Conceicao who is alleged to have been implicated in the killing of the Liurai (King) of Los Palos has also been indicted,[86] as has been Martins who was

[86] Case no: 12/2003, SPSC, Dili District Court.

charged together with 22 other accused on 22 November 2001 in relation to the 6 April 1999 Liquica Church massacre.

On 7 December 2001 UNTAET formulated an additional set of procedures agreed upon by the Transitional Administrator, governing the convocation and conduct of reconciliation meetings at or near the border between East Timor and West Timor, Indonesia. These reconciliation meetings had as their objective the creation of conditions whereby separated communities in East and West Timor could meet face to face, and work out arrangements prior to an eventual voluntary return to East Timor. For such reconciliation meetings it was agreed that there would be no arrest made of any serious crimes suspect whilst travelling to, or attending such a meeting held within the jurisdiction of East Timor, provided the following conditions were met:

(i) The reconciliation meeting is arranged, managed and facilitated by UNHCR
(ii) UNHCR provides 48 hours notice of the meeting to all relevant agencies, including PKF, District CIVPOL, District Administrators, Border Control Services, District Human Rights Officers and the Serious Crimes Unit
(iii) The notices includes the date of the intended reconciliation meeting; the anticipated time of commencement of the meeting, and a list of participants
(iv) The reconciliation meeting is conducted at or near the border within a secure and defined venue and it is held on a weekday during daylight hours
(v) Participants carry some means of identification and
(vi) The identified suspects remain within the venue notified for the meeting.

As noted the above provisions did not apply to indicted accused. For them the strict provisions of the law were applicable. The procedures that were adopted were meant to promote the voluntary return of refugees, and facilitate longer-term national reconciliation goals. This UNTAET was entrusted to encourage as part of its transitional responsibilities.

The arrest, detention, and subsequent conditional release of Joao Mendonca de Araujo demonstrated the sensitivity of border arrests of militiamen by PKF and CIVPOL, as well as conditional release of suspects, much as the law provides that for. De Araujo a pro-autonomy supporter who was arrested by PKF at Salele, known as Junction Point Foxtrot, on 21 March 2001, when he crossed into East Timor with a large group of refuges from Betun in West Timor. Some Covalima residents identified him, at the time of crossing, as one of the militia leaders who had directed the massacre at Suai Church on 6 September 1999. De Araujo was immediately transferred to Dili. He was made to appear before an investigating judge who ordered his pre trial detention for a month. This demonstrated impartiality on the part of the investigating judge. Mendonca's younger sister was a judge at the Dili District Court. That apart his arrest almost triggered a halt in the return of refugees, and, in the reconciliation efforts that were being ushered by UNTAET.

When the initial detention period expired, there was insufficient evidence to charge the accused. The progress of investigations into the Suai Church massacres indicated that it would take months to complete. Two options surfaced for the Prosecution. To seek repeated extension of pre-trial detention periods until an indictment could be brought up or to order a conditional release. Motivated by the desire to avoid, yet again, the long-term detention of a non-indicted suspect, and to uphold a higher threshold of evidence for the further detention of suspects, on the General Prosecutor's instruction, the prosecution sought conditional release. This was granted. The investigating judge ordered the suspect to report to CIVPOL every 15 days and confined his movement.

In relation to another three long-term detained suspected militiamen, it had taken 14 months for the SCIU to muster sufficient investigative recourses to enable a comprehensive investigation on the suspects who it was alleged had been involved in a murder in Covalima District in 1999. They were arrested on the basis of identification by a single witness. When that witness was re-interviewed by the SCIU, in May 2001 that very witness stated that he had learnt of the identity of militiamen while he was in a refugee camp in West Timor. The SCIU found that there was no direct evidence that they had participated in the crime. Prosecutors then sought their release, but this occurred only after they had spent a considerable amount of time in pre trial detention.

As regards the conditional release of De Araujo, CIVPOL expressed concern. It wished that the court had taken into account the impact of the suspect's release, especially public tranquillity in Covalima, which was bound to be disturbed by the suspect's reinsertion into the community. Past events had shown that even the definite release, by the Special Panels for Serious Crimes, of long term detained suspects for whom the prosecution had no evidence, was problematic given the social stigma of labelling a person a "criminal" once arrested and detained. East Timor's main prison, in Becora, Dili, had been destroyed as a result of the violence, and was only rehabilitated around May 2000.

On its part the UN Peacekeeping Force was most concerned about the fulfilment of its security mandate. For UNHCR arrests at the border negated the momentum of voluntary return of refugees. To UNTAET's Chief of Staff Ambassador Nagalingam Parameswaran tasked to facilitate reconciliation between East Timorese in East Timor and those in West Timor, Indonesia, the tendency of various departments of UNTAET to play "cops" on refugee return also delayed reconciliation. Whatever the case, the return of even 100 suspected militiamen would have thrown the whole system of accountability, and the fragile judiciary, in total disarray. UNTAET simply had no investigation or detention capacity to cope with such an eventuality. At one point CIVPOL stopped making any arrest of suspected ordinary crimes criminals, including those involved in the 1999 violence, because it had no place to put them; the only detention centre in the entire territory being a former Ministry of Tourism building that had long since exceeded capacity.[87]

Considerations of public commotion alone cannot override the entitlement of suspects for conditional release, when the prosecution has marginal evidence and is hardly ready to proffer an indictment within a reasonable period. The other factors that weighed in the decision to seek conditional release of De Araujo included the policy directive to seek detention only where there was a higher threshold of evidence against a suspect, and to avoid new detainees queuing up for investiga-

---

87 See, Human Rights Watch World (2001) Report.

tion. It was considered that the need for the SCIU to carry on further investigations per se, against a suspect, should not by that reason alone justify indefinite pre trial detention of suspects. Other judicial consideration came into play in a decision to seek detention or conditional release, including the likelihood of witness intimidation and the possibility of absconding from trial by the suspect. When the Prosecution on 28 February 2003 filed the Indictment on the Suai Church massacre and other crimes committed in Covalima District, it charged the Deputy Commander of *Laksaur* militia, four sub district commanders, and 9 other militiamen for the crimes. De Araujo was not charged. Had he been further detained, it would have meant that he would have been in custody without charges for 19 months. An unacceptable violation of international human rights norms, and an abuse of due process by the standards set by the ICTR Appeals Chamber in *J.B. Barayagwiza v. P.* [88] There it was held that it is well-established under international human rights law that pre-trial detention of suspects is lawful, as long as such pre-trial detention does not extend beyond a reasonable period of time, and that a detained suspect has a right to be promptly charged pursuant to international standards.[89]

IV. Prosecution Strategy and Policies

A sound prosecution strategy is one that is based on an analysis of the pattern of violence. It is borne out of a review of policies and practices of implicated entities, agencies whether governmental, civilian, military, para-military, economic, financial or the media. In encompasses investigations into the planning, organization, sponsorship, and commission of atrocity crimes. It is crafted on the basis of a preliminary identification of individuals behind its orchestration. The report of the UN International Commission of Inquiry, that of the three thematic Special rapporteurs of the UN Commission on Human Rights that of KPP-HAM, and that of the initial serious crimes investigations in East Timor suggested that the commission of atrocity crimes was part of an orchestrated, widespread, and systematic campaign of violence directed against the civilian population. That the central feature of individual criminal responsibility was one of co-perpetration involving members of the Indonesian security forces, senior civil administrators and militia groups in the organization, planning and execution of the crimes. Co-perpetration requires a plurality of persons, the existence of a common plan, design or purpose, which amounts to or involves the commission of a crime provided for in the law and participation of the accused in the common design.[90] As far as *mens rea* is concerned, what is required is the intention to perpetrate a certain crime as the

[88] *J.B. Barayagwiza v. P*, Decision, Appeal Chamber, Case no: ICTR-97-19-A, 3 November 1999; See also Prosecutor's Request for Review and /or Reconsideration, Appeal Chamber, Case no: ICTR- 97-19-AR72, 31 March 2000.

[89] Paras. 63, 100, Id.

[90] *P. v. Z, Kupreskic, D. Josipovic, D. Papic and V. Santic*, Judgement, Case no: IT-95-16-T, 14 January 2000, para. 772.

shared intent on the part of all co-conspirators.[91] Acts of violence were also encouraged by omission or by a failure of the military, police and civilian authorities to intervene in order to protect victims or to restore public order. Serious human rights abuses, which particularly targeted adolescents, young adults, and women, took place throughout East Timor, and occurred over an extended period. Between January and October 1999 women were the specific target of sexual violence, torture, arbitrary detention, and other inhuman acts.

The prosecution strategy and investigation plan that was adopted in mid 2000, in East Timor, first and foremost cantered on the major incidents of mass killings committed throughout the major part of 1999. The time frame for investigation of atrocity crimes also covered both the pre and post-ballot periods of violence. This was designed to investigate at one pace, all levels of perpetrators, the "big, medium and small", both in the districts and at national level connected with atrocity crimes. At the same time it was meant to hold answerable those with the greatest responsibility for the resulting campaign of persecution, deportation, or forcible transfer of the civilian population from East Timor to West Timor that took place in 1999.

Second, the prosecution strategy aimed at *full*, rather than *partial* accountability. While resources and other constraints slowed the pace of investigations, it was made clear, at least as of July 2000, that the public outcry to hold accountable those involved in atrocity crimes necessitated full accountability for all level of actors. This was grounded on the communal nature of the East Timor violence, the identifiable character of perpetrators, the domestic nature of the model of accountability, the need to establish the rule of law, and to create a viable system of administration of justice in East Timor. If the system of accountability had been of the enforcement kind, modelled on the two UN Ad Hoc tribunals, full accountability would not have been required. The prosecution of only a handful of perpetrators, not all or even a significant number can allow them to fulfil their mandate. ICTR, which envisions the conclusion of investigations by 2004, foresees the prosecution of only about 106 accused by the time it is expected to wind up all its work in 2011. This aspect of the prosecution strategy, although all encompassing, was overly ambitious. In the context of East Timor, where the thirst for justice among the population was intense, the policy option to hold accountable, perpetrators at all levels, was inevitable. The locally rooted arrangements for accountability, and the acute demand for justice by the community, did not warrant the exclusion of any category of perpetrator, be it with greatest responsibility, intermediate, or low level.

A third factor that the prosecution strategy had to address, as a matter of urgency, was the criminal fate of numerous low-level perpetrators. The situation in East Timor in 1999 differed little from that of Rwanda as concerns the participation of militia in the atrocity crimes. UNTAET's SCIU inherited from both INTERFET and CIVPOL a caseload of 74 non-indicted low-level suspects, mostly militiamen, arrested and detained on suspicion of having committed atrocity crimes. The policy option adopted by the prosecution aimed at investigating and

[91] Para. 772, Id.

prosecuting such persons together with others in superior or command positions, where criminal participation involved a common criminal enterprise or was part of a common transaction. Their prosecution was seen as accumulative of evidence against middle and leadership targets. Additionally those who committed particularly egregious criminal acts or pursued such acts in a particularly zealous fashion were also the objects of accountability.

When the UN Security Council Mission visited East Timor in September 2000 most of the 56 militiamen detained at Becora or Gleno prison had been indicted; about 36 had been provisionally or definitely released for lack of evidence or any reasonable prospects of gathering any evidence at all, and 800 non–indexed investigation case files opened by CIVPOL were being sorted out by the SCIU. By March 2001 29 serious crimes detainees had been indicted, most with murder, under Section 340 of the Penal Code of Indonesia, deemed applicable in East Timor under UNTAET. It is worth noting that the non-indexed investigation files related to serious crimes alleged to have been committed in East Timor in 1999. The records in some of these files were flimsy. In a number the only information contained in the file was that a body has been located and buried, with no indication of the name of the victim, witness or any potential suspect. Other investigation files only contained sketches of crime scenes, or photographs of a decomposed human body or a skeleton.

The prosecution policies relating to atrocity crimes in East Timor had to be dictated by, among other factors, the human rights of detained militia. This had not been the case with the UN Ad hoc Tribunals or the Special Court for Sierra Leone. In East Timor as we had said, a sizeable caseload had spent considerable time in pre trial detention without charges. In this group were *Tim Alfa* militia members who had been arrested and detained by INTERFET as early as October 1999. They were finally indicted with crimes against humanity offences on 11 December 2000, 15 months after their arrest and detention. This is the hard reality of atrocity crimes when accountability is domestic, and part of the national system of justice. The situation is exemplified in the case of the genocide in Rwanda where the justice system has been strenuously coping over 9 years (i.e. 1994-2003) with the astronomical caseload of some 115,000 suspected *genocidaires*. Between July 1994 and September 1998 the arrest and incarceration rate persons suspected of participation in massacres was between one and 3,000 per month, and at its peak reached 123,000 detainees.[92] While in East Timor the caseload of low-level perpetrators had to be attended to, it was realized that the accountability requirement of UN SC res. 1272 (1999) would not be met only through the prosecution of lower level perpetrators. Neither would the East Timorese lust for justice be fulfilled by trials of such perpetrators. To paraphrase the headlines in the German daily, Frankfurter Allgemeine Zeitung the "big fish in uniform" needed to stand under the "fans of the Dili District Court".[93]

---

92 Five Years After The Genocide in Rwanda, Justice in Question, International Crisis Group, 7 April 1999, p. 9.

93 Die grossen Fische wird Othman nicht erwischen, Franfurter Allgemeine Zeitung, no: 198, 27 August 2001.

Fourth, the prosecution strategy also foresaw the need to welcome the cooperation of suspects or accused with the prosecution. The criminal laws of all major legal systems of the world recognize the judicial value of substantial cooperation of accused persons with investigation authorities, and in the voluntary, informed, and unequivocal admission of guilt. This possibility of admission of guilt and co-operation by accused persons was incorporated in the plans of the SCIU. The legal parameters of admission of guilt were spelled out in the Penal Code of Indonesia and the Transitional Rules of Criminal Procedure. These will be discussed in Chapter VII.

Fifthly the Prosecution set for itself a higher evidential barometer, namely, to indict accused on the basis of trial ready evidence rather than prima facie evidence of the kind required to indict an accused under Article 17 (4) and 18(1) of the Statute and Rule 47 of the Rules of Procedure and Evidence of the ICTR. Proceeding by way of prima facie evidence would have resulted in considerable trial postponements and delays. It would have led to a constant amendment of indictments, as had been the case at the two UN ad hoc Tribunals in their formative years. A valid reason for this approach was the conscious decision by the Office of the General Prosecutor to leave behind, following East Timor's independence, well investigated cases that could withstand any international judicial scrutiny. This was also judicially called for, and remains a legal requirement of the Transitional Rules of Criminal Procedure. As ambitious as it was, it also squeezed the under resourced SCIU of the oxygen needed to simultaneously embark on other priority investigations, including that of leadership targets.

Sixth the prosecution strategy and investigation plan was in many aspects prosecution driven. It was instructional. It was also meant to avoid non essential evidence gathering, and to maximize investigation results through the assignment of investigators to identifiable targets or "*priority cases*" where evidence of the participation of medium level perpetrators, especially Militia Commanders, District and Sub District Military and Police Commanders, as well as District Administrators (Bupati) had emerged. Co-perpetration of crimes as we have indicated was an essential feature of the pattern of atrocity crimes in East Timor.

The above-mentioned strategic directions led to the identification by mid 2000, of what came to be known as East Timor's ten or so "*priority cases*". These cases cantered on major incidents of atrocities that had caused the death of hundreds of unarmed civilians, the victimization of thousands, and where initial evidence had revealed the names of identifiable perpetrators. The identified priority cases included:

- the Liquica Church massacre of 6 April 1999
- the killings at the house of Manual Carrascalao, in Dili, on 17 April 1999
- the violence and murders in and around Kailako in April 1999, and the Maliana Police Station, from 2-8 September 1999
- sexual violence investigations in Lolotoe sub District between 2 May and 16 September 1999
- investigations involving the killing of UNAMET local East Timorese Staff
- the Suai Church massacre of 6 September 1999

- the Passabe and Makeleb (Oecussi) massacres in September and October 1999,
- the Los Palos Case and violence in Leutem District from April- September 1999
- the attack and killings at the Dili Diocese, and at Bishop Carlos Belo's compound in Dili ion 5-6 September 1999
- the crimes committed by TNI Battalion 745 between April and September 1999, including the murder of a Dutch Journalist Sander Thoenes in Dili, on 21 September 1999 and
- a special investigation that targeted a selected group of 15 high ranking TNI and Indonesian Police officials as well as Civilian administrators, including the former Governor of East Timor, on the campaign of persecution and the massive deportation of the civilian population from East Timor to West Timor. It was then believed by the Prosecution that this group consisted of persons who had the greatest responsibility for the atrocity crimes committed in East Timor in 1999. Of this group, East Timor's Deputy Prosecutor General for Serious Crimes indicted 7 accused on 24 February 2003.[94] Among those charged was General Wiranto, the former Indonesian Minister of Defence and Security (Menteri Pertahan dan Keamanan, Menhankam) and Commander of the Armed Forces of Indonesian (Panglima Angkatan Bersenjata Republik Indonesia/ Panglima Tentara Nasional Indonesia); Major General Zacky Anwar Makarim, member of the Indonesian Task Force to oversee the popular consultation in East Timor; Major General Adam Rachmat Damiri, Commander of the Udayana Regional Military Command IX Major General Kiki Syahnakri, Commander of the Martial Law Operations Command in East Timor; Brigadier Suhartono (Tono) Suratman, Commander of the Sub Regional Military Command 164 (East Timor); Colonel Mohamed Noer Muis, Commander of the Sub Regional Military Command 164; Lt. Colonel Yayat Sudrajat, Commander of the Intelligence Task Force, of Sub Regional Military Command 164; and Abilio Jose Osorio Soares, the former Governor of East Timor.

At the ICTR conspiracy to commit genocide was the main thrust of the prosecution strategy. At the ICTY persecution as a crime against humanity, is the umbrella charge for crimes committed by accused in the former Yugoslavia. It is also the bargaining chip for guilty pleas. In East Timor the prosecution strategy counted on (a) massacres, in particular those forming part of the priority cases, (b) the 9 months campaign of persecution (i.e. January to September 1999), and (c) forced deportation of an estimated 250,000 civilians to West Timor, Indonesia, in September 1999 as the "dragnet"; to hold accountable those with the greatest responsibility for the East Timor atrocity crimes.

The ascending nature of the issuance of indictments in East Timor demonstrates the determined attempt of the Prosecution to shorten any impunity gap that might have arisen through the exclusive pursuit of one category of perpetrators over the others. As of 19 March 2001, 20 indictments had been filed with the Special Penal

---

[94] *P. v. Wiranto, Zacky Anwar Makarim, Kiki Syahnakri, Adam Rachmat Damiri, Suhartibi Suratman, Mohamed Noer Muis, Yayat Sudrajat and Abilio Jose Osorio Soares,* Case no: 5/2003, SPSC, Dili District Court, 24 February 2003.

for serious crimes of the Dili District Court; and by almost a year later, on 31 March 2002, 35 serious crimes indictments against 101 individuals, of whom 77 had been accused of crimes against humanity had been accused. As of 1 August 2003, 65 serious crimes indictments against 301 accused have been filed.[95] Of these 183 accused have been charged with crimes against humanity in the ten priority cases referred to earlier. Others have been charged with offences under the Penal Code of Indonesia. By 9 December 2003 trials against 42 accused had been completed.

The first indictment in East Timor alleging crimes against humanity was filed on 11 December 2000.[96] It charged Joni Marques, Commander of *Tim Alfa* militia, also known as Jati Merah Putih (Authentic Red and White) and ten other accused for having committed crimes against humanity (murder, torture, and the deportation or forcible transfer of the civilian population) in Los Palos, Lautem District, between 21 April and 25 September 1999. Among those indicted was an Indonesian Army Officer, the Deputy Commander of the Special Forces of the Indonesian Armed Forces (KOPASSUS) stationed in Los Palos, Leutum District in 1999, with the mutilation, torture, and killing of Averisto Lopes on 21 April 1999 at the *Tim Alfa* base. It was alleged that the team had been involved in an orgy of killings, the most atrocious being the ambush and killing on 25 September of a group of clergy (5 priests and nuns), two Church workers, an Indonesian journalist, and a youth near the village of Verokoco, Los Palos, Lautem District. They were also charged with deportation and forcible transfer of the civilian population of Leuro village to the barracks of TNI battalion 745, and then to the port of Com, and some to West Timor. Trial before the Special Panel commenced on 3 July 2001, and Judgment was delivered on 25 January 2001. Joni Marques was sentenced to 33 years and 4 months imprisonment while the other co-accused received sentences between 4 and 33 years.

On 6 February 2001 the Office of the General Prosecutor filed a second crime against humanity indictment, *P. v. Joan Franca Da Silva, aka Jhoni Franca et all.*.[97] In it five accused were charged with murder, rape, torture, unlawful deprivation of liberty, inhuman and degrading treatment, and persecution committed in Lolotoe sub-district, Bobonaro district. Those indicted included the Commander and Deputy Commander of the *Kaer Metin Merah Putih* militia (Firmly Hold on the Red and White), an Indonesian army officer, the Commander (Danramil) of the TNI in Lolotue sub- District, and two other militiamen.

The issuance of the indictment against General Wiranto and other senior Indonesian officials on 24 February 2003 caught by surprise, East Timor's President, Xanana Gusmao, who was attending the XII Summit of the Non-Aligned Movement (NAM) in Kuala Lumpur, Malaysia. He had not been pre-warned by the General Prosecutor, and had learnt of the indictment through the media. In a statement issued on 28 February 2003, the President plainly reiterated his position

---

95 See, Serious Crimes Update, VII/03, UNMIET, 5 August 2003.

96 *P. v J. Markos et all.*, Case no: LA-5-99-SC, SRSC, Dili District Court.

97 Case no: 4/2001, SPSC, Dili.

as regards accountability for the atrocity crimes committed in East Timor.[98] He bluntly stated that given the reconstruction problems facing East Timor, an international tribunal was not a priority, least of all, in Timor-Leste. In full respect of the East Timor constitution, which enshrines the independent nature of the courts and the judiciary, as an organ of sovereignty, he respected the decision of the Prosecution to indict. However, he was displeased with the methodology adopted. He regretted that the Office of the General Prosecutor, whilst, the General Prosecutor was abroad, did not postpone this matter until the President's return to East Timor.

President Gusmao considered that it was not in the national interest to hold a legal process against the Indictees in East Timor. He cited three reasons. First that East Timor must pursue the process of national reconciliation taking into account successive acts of violence perpetrated as far back as 29 years (i.e. from 1974 rather than 1999). It should be noted that the temporal jurisdiction of the Special Panels for Serious Crimes is for offences committed between 1 January up to 25 October 1999. He was of the conviction that it was time to put an end to the past and to start building a new environment for the future, and that political reconciliation rather than justice is what will satisfy the social and economic needs of East Timorese[99]

Secondly the international community, via the Security Council, had endowed UNTAET and UNMISET with a mandate to bring to justice those responsible for the 1999 violence and the destruction of East Timor. Stemming from that, he was of the view that the international community should have the responsibility for administering that justice, and organizing the structures and mechanisms to put it into effect. Third, that Indonesia under the Government of former President Abduhrraman Wahid, and that of President Megawati Soekarnoputri, and the Indonesian Armed Forces (TNI) as an institution, had been an example of state effort to build with East Timor a good neighbourly relationship. That peace, stability, and progress in East Timor depends on the relationship it will forge with the Republic of Indonesia. In a move intended to mend any shift in the evolving positive relations between the two states, and to make clear that East Timor's relations with Indonesia are too important to be undermined by the indictment, Gusmao in early March 2003 sent his Foreign Minister Jose Ramos Horta to Jakarta.[100] On their part, East Timor human rights groups strongly deplored the behind-the-scene interference by politicians in the justice process when it was alleged that President

---

98 See, Statement by His Excellence Kay Rala Xanana Gusmao, President of the Democratic Republic of Timor-Leste, On the Indictment by the Deputy General Prosecutor for Serious Crimes of Indonesian Officers for Events in Timor –Leste during 1999, 23 February 2003.

99 Ravished East Timor still struggles to find justice, The Age, 28 September 2001; Xanana Gusmao: International Court Not Priority for Timorese People, Suara Timor Lorosae, 6 April 2001.

100 Timor Distances itself from Indonesian Indictments, Reuters; Xanana worried Indictments may damage relations with Jakarta, UNMISET Daily News Review, 3 March 2003.

Gusmao and other East Timor high officials had secretly met Wiranto at the Oberoi Hotel in Seminyak, Bali on the 31 January or 1 February 2004.[101]

The filing of the indictment against some of the most senior Indonesian Military Commanders alleged to have been criminally responsible for the East Timor violence also caused a mild sandstorm within the UN, in particular UNMISET and the UN Headquarters. They regrettably tried to distant themselves from the maturing of the accountability process that the indictments represented. In Dili UNMISET issued a statement stating that the UN did not have any legal authority to issue indictments, and that they were issued under the legal authority of the East Timorese Prosecutor General. In New York the UN Spokesman stated that the United Nations hoped that in the future, one would refer to the indictments as "*East Timor indicts*", and not "*United Nations indicts*".[102]

It is of concern that the UN, a robust advocate of accountability for serious international humanitarian law violations, and a frontrunner in combating impunity, chose to distant itself and marginalize its portion of responsibility in the East Timor serious crimes process. On 31 January 2000 the UN Secretary-General, in simultaneously transmitting to the General Assembly, the Security Council, and the Commission of Human rights the report of the International Commission of Inquiry on East Timor, had expressed his intention to strengthen the capacity of UNTAET to conduct investigations with a view to bringing to justice those responsible for serious international humanitarian law violations.[103] In his words the United Nations had an important role to play investigating violations, establishing responsibility, punishing those responsible and promoting reconciliation.[104] That the UN is also the "alfa and omega" of the accountability process stems from the wanton disregard of the UN Security Council decision endorsing the popular consultation process. As remarked by the International Commission of Inquiry:

"The actions violating human rights and international humanitarian law in East Timor were directed against a decision of the United Nations Security Council acting under Charter VII of the Charter and were contrary to agreements reached by Indonesia with the United Nations to carry out that Security Council decision. Under Article 25 of the Charter, Member States agree to accept and carry out the decisions of the Security Council. The organized opposition in East Timor to the Security Council decision requires specific international attention and response. That United Nations, as an organization has a vested interest in participating in the entire process of investigation, establishing responsibility and punishing those responsible and in promoting reconciliation. Effectively dealing with this issue will be important for ensuring that future Security Council decisions are respected."[105]

---

101 East Timor National Alliance for an International Tribunal (ETAN), East Timor Political Leaders Must Not Interfere with Justice, Press Release, 15 February 2002, http://www.etan.org/1h.

102 Timor-Leste, not UN, Indicts Indonesian general for War Crimes, UN Wire, 26 Feb. 2003; See also criticism of the UN position by Mari Alkatiri Prime Minister of East Timor in Timor PM Slams UN on War Criminals, Asia Times, 15 May 2003.

103 UN Doc. A/54/726, S/2000/59, 31 January 2001.

104 Id.

105 Report of the International Commission of Inquiry on East Timor, UN Doc. A/54/726, S/2000/59, 31 Jan.2001, para. 147.

The demand for accountability for the 1999 East Timor atrocity crimes as we have stated, firmly originated from the UN Security. The establishment of the legal framework for investigation and prosecution was initiated and legislated by UNTAET. Human, financial, and material resources to carry forward that process continue to be provided by UNMISET. Indeed SC res. 1410 (2002)[106] goes even further. In deciding to establish a successor mission in East Timor, it stipulated that UNMISET should, among its civilian components, have a Serious Crimes Unit.

On 10 May 2004 less than 3 months after Wiranto was indicted a Judge of the Special Panel issued an arrest warrant against him.[107] It was based on a request by Serious Crimes Prosecutors and on a judicial finding of the existence of a reasonable basis for its issuance under section 19A.1 of UNTAET Regulation 2001/25. Subsequent to the filling of the indictment Serious Crimes Prosecutors had presented to the Panel, 21 volumes off documents arranged in 39 binders amounting to over 15,000 pages including statements from 1,500 witnesses.

The East Timorese Prosecutor General Longuinhos Monteiro who had not been informed by his deputy of the arrest warrant request compared his move as that of "a soldier who fired a shot from behind' without telling him", as non-respect of his strategy and of East Timor's interest.[108] On 11 May, he filed a motion under section 27.1 and 32.1 of UNTAET's Transitional Rules of Criminal Procedure seeking a review and amendment of the Indictment. That action was supported by Gusmao who considered that he was acting "in the interest of the State."[109] On 17 May 2004 the Serious Crimes Panel denied the request on the grounds that it was insufficient in it form, and did not allege what defects, if any were present in the indictment, that it did not describe the specific proposed amendments for which court approval was sought.[110]

Indonesia considered that the Special Panel had no jurisdiction, including on Indonesia and decided not to make "a fuss" about it.[111] The indictment issued at a time when Wiranto was one of the key contenders in Indonesia's Presidential elections led the United States Ambassador to Indonesia to remark: "we can work with anybody that comes out of a free [election] process",[112] reflecting potential political accommodation over justice. Gusmao on his part had this to say:

"This is a legal matter. So I cannot comment on it. According to procedures, as a head of State I do not get such reports……In East Timor, the institution of the Serious Crimes Unit

---

106 UN Doc. S/RES/1410(2002), 17 May 2002.

107 Timorese Prosecutors Urge Arrest of Indonesia's Wiranto, Associated Press, 29 January 2004.

108 E. Timor Prosecutor regrets Wiranto Warrant, Wiranto blames enemies, AFP, 12 May 2004.

109 Interview with Kay Xanana Gusmao: "Its Easy To Shout Arrest Wiranto", Tempo, 15-21 June 2004.

110 Decision on the Motion of the Prosecutor General to Review and Amend the Indictment, Case no: 05/2003, 17 May 2004.

111 FM Plays down arrest warrant for Wiranto, The Jakarta Post, 12 May 2004.

112 The Wiranto Surprise, The Asia Wall Street Journal, 23-24 April 2004.

operates independently. There is no foreign intervention. As head of State, I cannot intervene in the Serious Crimes Unit. I am also unable to intervene with the courts. If there are errors, I can only say that is wrong, but I cannot intervene".[113]

Continued Accountability

The pursuit of accountability through the serious crimes process continued, and on 28 February 2003 the Office of the Deputy Prosecutor General for Serious Crimes issued another 8 indictments against a total of 48 accused. These included an indictment against Egidio Manek and 10 other *Laksaur* militiamen in relation to the massacre at Suai Church on 6 September 1999, as well as other crimes committed in Covalima District in 1999. Manek had been Deputy Commander (Danyon) of the *Laksuar* militia group and a member of Gadapaksi. Also on the same day, the former Commander of the *Mahidi* Militia group, Cancio Lopes de Carvalho, was indicted together with 21 other militiamen.[114] Another indictment against the Indonesian ex-Chief of Police of East Timor, Brigadier General Timbul Silaen, and Eurico Guterres, the former Commander of *Aitarak* milita was also issued; alleging responsibility for the militia attack and killings at the Dili Diocese and at Bishop Carlo Belo's residence, as well as the deportation and forcible transfer of some 25,000 civilians from Dili into West Timor between 5 and 9 September 1999.

Prospects for the arrest and transfer to East Timor of indictees who have sought refuge in Indonesia are non-existent. They have benefited from an impunity gap. As of 9 December 2003 281 accused consisting of 37 Indonesian Armed Forces (TNI) officers, 60 East Timorese TNI members, 4 Indonesian Police Officers, dozens of militia Commanders and numerous militiamen were alleged to be in Indonesia, outside East Timor 's jurisdiction. Of 183 accused charged in the ten priority cases, 168 were at large in Indonesia. All in all by 31 December 2004 about 300 serious crimes accused were reliably believed to be in Indonesia, the vast majority in West Timor, outside East Timor's jurisdiction. Under the Indonesian Human Rights Court Act, the court has personal jurisdiction only over Indonesian citizens, and not East Timorese. Secondly as stated by President Megawati Soekarnoputri in relation to the Indictment against General Wiranto and six others, Indonesia is not obliged to send the General to East Timor because East Timor and Indonesia do not have an extradition treaty. Thirdly a manifest unwillingness by Indonesia to cooperate with East Timor has long characterized judicial assistance and cooperation between these two states. Fourth, the attitude of East Timor political leaders, such as President Gusmao who strongly prefers that East Timor skip the page on accountability for atrocity crimes, undermines the moral force for the international community to insist upon Indonesia to fulfil its responsibility and

---

[113] Interview with Kay Xanana Gusmao: "Its Easy To Shout Arrest Wiranto", Tempo, 15-21 June 2004.

[114] *P. v. C. L de Carvalho and others*, Case no: 6/2003, SPSC, Dili District Court, 28 February 2003.

commitment. [115] Finally the lack of affirmative action by UN Security Council has gradually eroded the passion for accountability that characterized the earlier establishment of the two UN Ad hoc Tribunals in 1993 and 1994.

With the above in mind, it is predictable that an overwhelming majority of accused who allegedly committed serious crimes and who are in Indonesia will certainly not face justice either in East Timor or Indonesia. This is a clear defect of the intentions of the Security Council, UNTAET, and UNMISET to hold accountable perpetrators of serious international humanitarian law violations committed in East Timor. It is also a rebuff of the repeated demands of the UN Security Council for Indonesia to respect its express commitment to curb impunity in relation to the East Timor violence. The question that comes to mind is what purposes does an unenforceable accountability process serve, if the only thing it is capable of doing is merely to investigate but not prosecute? This is the unfortunate demise of the East Timor serious crimes process in which 90% of accused charged with crimes against humanity remain in Indonesia, outside the reach of the Special Panels for Serious Crimes.[116] Those with the greatest responsibility, among whom are top Indonesian military officers, militia Commanders, and senior civil administrators, will most probably not have to answer for their criminal misdeeds in any jurisdiction, be in East Timor or Indonesia.

V. Indonesia: Accountability and the Legal Framework

East Timor and Indonesia exercise concurrent and independent jurisdiction for the prosecution of persons responsible for atrocity crimes committed in East Timor in 1999. As the violence unfolded the UN Security Council promptly demanded that those responsible for such violence be brought to justice.[117] The accountability favoured by the Security Council in resolutions 1272 (1999), 1319 (2000) and 1410(2002) is domestic prosecutions in each of the two states. This was an amplification of the stand of some members of the Security Council such as Norway. It had clearly stated that prosecutions by national courts were a far better approach than the setting up of an international tribunal, which should always be the very last resort.[118] This trend is a reflection of the new criminal order emerging out of the ICC. Its Statute recalls in the preamble that it is the duty of every state to exercise its criminal jurisdiction over those responsible for international crimes. Fur-

---

[115] It should be noted that the issue of post conflict justice remains a vexing question among East Timorese. Among those opposed to Xanana Gusmao's view is Bishop Carlos Belo. See, Gusmao and Belo on collision course over justice' Sydney Morning Herald, 18 December 2000.

[116] Report of the Secretary-General on the UN Mission of Support in East Timor, 21 April 2003, para. 27.

[117] UNSC resolution 1264 (1999), UN Doc. S/RES/1264, 15 September 1999; UN SC resolution 1272 (1999), UN Doc. S/RES/1272, 25 October 1999, para. 16.

[118] UN Doc. S/PV.4351, 30 July 2001, p. 2.

ther under the Statute, the presumptive forum for the trial of international crimes is national, and the court is only meant to supplement national court proceedings[119].

As we have noted in responding to atrocity crimes committed in East Timor, the Security Council opted for serious crimes prosecutions to be on two parallel tracks; taking place in both East Timor and Indonesia. Under the framework of the 5 May Agreements concerning, among other issues, the popular consultation signed by the Government of Indonesia and Portugal and by the United Nations Secretary General, Indonesia's security authorities assumed responsibility for ensuring a secure environment devoid of violence or other forms of intimidation during this process[120]. Indonesia made it clear that it could not accept any dilution of its overall responsibility for security in East Timor[121]. This undertaking carried with it a collateral responsibility. To hold accountable those in positions of authority and control who had committed atrocity crimes.

Widespread and systematic attacks on the civilian population had been orchestrated by, and committed with the active involvement of elements of, the Indonesian Armed Forces (TNI) and the Indonesian Police Force (POLRI); and acts violating basic human rights to life were allowed to be carried out by the same authorities with impunity[122]. As observed by the three thematic Special Rapporteurs, the Indonesian Armed Forces was sufficiently involved in the operational activities of the direct perpetrators (i.e. militia) to incur the responsibility of the Government of Indonesia[123]. In addition UN Member States have accepted the principle that every state had a right to try its own nationals for war crimes and crimes against humanity[124]. In addressing this issue, the Secretary-General was encour-

[119] See, Wedgwood R National Courts and the prosecution of war crimes. In McDonald G K, Swaak-Goldman O (ed.) (2000) Aspects of the International Criminal Law, vol.1, Kluwer Law Int., The Hague, pp. 389-413.

[120] Question of East Timor, Progress Report of the Secretary General, UN Doc. A/54/654, 13 Dec. 1999, paras. 4, 9 – 13. On 5 May 1999, three agreements were signed, a main overall agreement between the Rep. of Indonesia and the Republic of Portugal on the question of East Timor, to which was annexed the constitutional framework for autonomy, an agreement regarding the modalities for the popular consultation of the East Timor through a direct, secret ballot, and a broad agreement on security arrangements. Both parties and the UNSG signed the later. For texts see, UN Doc. A/53/951-S/1999/513.

[121] Question of East Timor, Progress Report of the Secretary General, 13 December 1999, para. 11.

[122] Report of the Security Council Mission to Jakarta and Dill, UN SC Doc. S/1999/976, 14 Sept. 1999, para. 14; Report of the High Commissioner for Human Rights on the situation in East Timor, UN Doc. E/CN.4/S-4/CRP. 1, 17 Dept.1999; Report of the International Commission of Inquiry on East Timor, UN Doc. A/54/726, S/2000/59, 31 Jan. 2000.

[123] Report of the Special rapporteur on extra-judicial, summary or arbitrary executions, the Special rapporteur on the question of torture, the Special rapporteur on violence against women, UN Doc, A/54/660, 10 Dec. 1999.

[124] Principles of international cooperation in the detention, arrest, extradition and punishment of persons guilty of war crimes and crimes against humanity, adopted by UNGA

aged by the commitment of the President of Indonesia, Abdurrahman Wahid, to uphold the law, and to fully support the national investigation process under way in Indonesia.[125] He had also been strongly assured by Foreign Minister, Alwi Shihab, of Indonesia's determination that there will be no impunity for those responsible[126]. The Secretary General was of the view that Indonesia should be given the chance to demonstrate its capacity to do a credible and transparent job of holding people accountable for the crimes.[127] The UN Security Council relying on Indonesia's reaffirmation of commitment to pursuing investigation and prosecution as a matter of priority has continued to urge Indonesia to move ahead with appropriate urgency in the fulfilment of this undertaking[128].

Indonesia Ad Hoc Human Rights Court

Following the publication of the Report of the Indonesian Commission of Inquiry into Human Rights violations in East Timor,[129] known as KPP-HAM, a body appointed by the Indonesian National Commission of Human Rights, the first legislative framework for the prosecution of gross human rights violations was the adoption by the Indonesian legislative assembly (DPR) of the Human Rights Court Act[130]. The Act establishes procedures for the investigation and prosecution of gross human rights violations. These are defined as the crime of genocide and crimes against humanity.

A Human Rights Court is a special court within a Court of general jurisdiction (Art. 2), with the authority to hear and rule on cases of gross human rights perpetrated by an Indonesian citizen above eighteen years of age, living outside the territorial boundaries of the Republic of Indonesia (Art. 5 and 6). Judicial procedures for such cases are to be conducted according to the Indonesian criminal procedure

Res. 3074 (XXVIII), 3 Dec. 1973; Note The Penal Code of Indonesia recognizes the active national principle of jurisdiction in Art. 5.

125 Identical Letters Dated 31 January 2000 from the Secretary-General to the President of the General Assembly, the President of the Security Council and the Chairperson of the Commission on Human Rights, UN Doc. A/54/726, S/2000/59, 31 Jan. 2000.

126 Identical Letters Dated 31 January 2000 from the Secretary-General to the President of the General Assembly, the President of the Security Council and the Chairperson of the Commission on Human Rights, UN Doc. A/54/726, S/2000/59, 31 Jan. 2000.

127 The Secretary General's Briefing to the Security Council on Visit to Southeast Asia, New York, 29 February 2000; http://www.un.org/peace/etimor/docs/BSG.htm.

128 UNSC Meeting, The Situation in East Timor, UNSC Doc.S/PV.4236, p. 7.See also reports of the Security Council Mission to East Timor and Indonesia, para.30, 18 Nov.2000; 'All human rights violations in and outside East Timor should be brought to credible justice as soon as possible', Statement of the Rep. of Korea, The Situation in East Timor, UN Doc. S/PV. 4351, p. 17; c.f. 'Indonesia is committed to upholding justice', Statement of Indonesia, p. 20, Id.

129 For Executive Summary, See Embassy of Indonesia, Ottawa, Canada, Doc No. BB-451/DEP/030300,http://www.indonesia-ottawa.org/nes/Issues/HumanRights/ham-kpp-timtim-oi3i2000.htm, 10 March 2001.

130 Act 26/2000.

code (Art. 10). The start-up process for prosecuting a gross human rights violation is for inquiries into such situations to be conducted by the Indonesian National Commission on Human Rights, the sole body with competence to trigger a judicial process (Arts. 18-20). This is meant to preserve the objectivity of the inquiry findings since the National Commission of Human Rights is an independent non-state institution[131]. When an inquiry is initiated, the Commission is required to inform the Attorney General of Indonesia (Art. 19(2)). Following an inquiry, and where there is sufficient evidence that a gross violation of human rights has occurred, a summary of the findings must be submitted to the Attorney General, who is the exclusive and only designated investigator and prosecutor of such offences. (Articles 21 and 23). The legislation provides for a specific time frame for the conduct of investigations, and for the prosecution of cases before Ad Hoc Human Rights Courts. Cases are to be heard by an Ad hoc Human Rights Court, and each case is to be tried by a panel of five judges (two judges from the relevant Human Rights Court and three Ad Hoc judges), who are appointed for a period of five years, by the President of Indonesia upon the recommendation of the Chief Justice of the Supreme Court (Arts. 27 and 28). The prescribed penalty for genocide or crimes against humanity is capital punishment or life imprisonment, which is determined to be 25 years. The minimum sentence is a term of imprisonment of not less 10 years (Arts. 36 & 37).

Finally the establishment of an Ad Hoc Human Rights Court for a particular incident of gross human rights violations requires a recommendation of the Indonesia Lower House of Parliament (DPR), following the issuance of a Presidential Decree (Art. 43). With regard to East Timor, the DPR set the legal process in motion on 21 March 2001 when it formally requested the President of Indonesia to set up a special Ad Hoc Human Rights Tribunal to try those responsible for serious human rights violations in East Timor. The President, Abdulrahman Wahid, promulgated a Presidential Decree on the Establishment of Ad Hoc Human Rights Tribunal at the Central Jakarta District Court on 23 April 2001[132]. Article 1 of the Decree granted the Ad hoc Human Rights Tribunal authority to investigate and try cases of serious human rights violations that occurred in East Timor after the popular consultation (i.e. 30 August 1999). This jurisdictional limitation constituted a serious curtailment on the possibility of prosecuting cases related to the 1999 events in East Timor, and Indonesia was urged by the UNSC, UNTAET and the UNHCHR to expand the scope of this law. Recognizing the need to perfect this Presidential Decree, by clarifying the time and the place of criminal acts (locus and tempus delicti) constituting human rights violations in East Timor, the decree was amended by Indonesia's President Megawati Soekarnoputri on 1 August 2001, by conferring on the Ad Hoc Human Rights Court jurisdiction to investigate and deliver verdicts on cases of human rights violations committed in East Timor

[131] Notes to Act No 26/2000 on the Republic of Indonesia concerning Human Rights Courts, Art. 18.

[132] Act No.53/2001, State Gazette of the Rep. of Indonesia No. 38/2001, 23 April 2001.

in the districts of Dili, Liquica and Suai occurring in the months of April and September 1999.[133]

While on the surface the amended Decree appears more specific, it incorporates further temporal and territorial jurisdictional limitations, which fall short of full accountability for atrocity crimes. As highlighted by the KPP-HAM Report, and that of the International Commission of Inquiry, atrocities were committed not only in the months of April and September 1999, and not exclusively in just 3 of East Timor's 13 districts.[134]

The accountability process in Indonesia gained temporary momentum, when on 1 September 2000 the Attorney General of Indonesia announced a list of 21 suspects.[135] It included Abilio Soares, the former Governor of East Timor; the former Regional Military Commander (Dandem); the former Chief of Police (Kapolda); 2 Bupati; 3 District Military Commanders (Dandim); 3 District Police Chiefs (Kapolres), and a sub district military commander (Kasdim). With the exception of those with provincial portfolios, most of the named suspects held official functions in the 3 districts in which the Indonesian Human Rights Court has jurisdiction. That is Dili, Liquica, and Suai. The Indonesian Attorney General's list contained only 17 of the 31 names listed in the conclusion and recommendations of the KPP-HAM report.[136] Ultimately only 18 persons were indicted by the Attorney General, and answered charges before the Indonesian Human Rights Court.

VI. Cooperation in Legal, Judicial and Human Rights Matters

Accountability by UNTAET and Indonesia for the atrocity crimes was premised on a workable cooperative arrangement between UNTAET and the Government of Indonesia. It was conceived that there would be complementarity. UNSC res. 1272 (1999) called on all parties to cooperate in investigations related to the flagrant international humanitarian and human rights violations. To facilitate this process a Memorandum of Understanding (MOU) regarding cooperation in Legal, Judicial and Human Rights related fields was signed between UNTAET and Indonesia on 6 April 2000.[137] The MOU, which is modelled on the General Assembly Model

133 Decree of the President of the Republic of Indonesia No.90/2001 regarding Amendment on the Presidential Decree No.53/2001 regarding Formation of An Ad Hoc Tribunal for Human Rights Violations at the Central Jakarta Court, Art. 2, 1 August 2001, State Gazette of the Republic of Indonesia, No. 111/2001.

134 East Timor is administratively and territorially organized into thirteen districts, subdivided into 62 sub districts and 462 municipalities.

135 Indonesia names East Timor crimes suspect; Wiranto not indicted, Associated Press, 1 Sept. 2000. Ultimately only 18 have been charged and tried.

136 The Report has been published by the Sydney Morning Herald, http://www.smh.com/au/news/0104/29/etimor02.html-BD, 30 April 2001, See also, http://www.tip.net.au/~wildwood/01aprkppham.htm.

137 UNTAET, Official Gazette of East Timor, vol. 1/3, pp. 93–96.

Treaty on Mutual Assistance on Criminal Matters, was intended to be a temporary instrument of cooperation during East Timor's transitional period[138]. It was also meant to provide UNTAET and Indonesia with the highest possible measures of mutual assistance in investigations and court proceedings in respect to offences, the prosecution of which at the time of the request for assistance falls within the jurisdiction of the judicial authorities of the requested state (Art. 1). The fields of cooperation that were envisaged included ordinary, serious, and cross border crimes, and other areas of interest such as the taking of evidence or statements from persons, service of judicial documents, the execution of arrests, searches and seizures, the facilitation of forensic examinations, access to information, and facilitating the transfer of persons. The MOU, as noted earlier, is based on standard inter-state arrangements for cooperation in criminal matters.

Requests to Indonesia

On the basis of the Memorandum of Understanding between Indonesia and UNTAET, a number of requests were made to Indonesian authorities, mostly to the Attorney General's Office. These included requests:[139]

a. To question 22 persons of interest from the TNI, Indonesian Police, and former East Timor civil administration believed to be in Indonesia.
b. For a complete and an authenticated copy of the KPP HAM Report issued in January 2000.
c. For a copy of the written statement of Eurico Guterres, Commander of *Aitarak* militia to Prosecutors of the Office of the Attorney General of Indonesia.
d. To interview named members of Battalion 747 who served in East Timor in 1999.
e. To obtain written statements by the 21 named suspects under investigation by the Indonesian Attorney General.
f. For Indonesia to execute arrest warrants against Eurico Guterres, issued on 6 October 2000 by an Investigating Judge of the Dili District Court,[140] that

---

[138] U.N.G.A. Resolution 45/117, Model Treaty on Mutual Assistance in Criminal Matters, UNGA Doc.A/RES/45/117, 68th plenary meeting, 14 Dec.1990. C.f. European Convention on Mutual Assistance in Criminal Matters, 20 April 1959, entered into force on 12 June 1962, E.T.S. No. 30; On cooperation on criminal matters see also, Ambos K (1998) The International Criminal Court and The Traditional Principles of International Cooperation in Criminal Matters, Finnish Yearbook of International Law, vol. IX, pp. 413-426.

[139] See, Report of the Secretary General on the United Nations Transitional Administration in East Timor (for the period 27 July 2000 to 16 January 2001), UN. Doc. S/2001/42, 16 Jan.2001, para. 24; Indonesia Army Chief backs lawyers refusing UN probe over Timor, AFP, 12 Dec. 2000; Ex-Militia Leader refuses to be probed by UN over Timor atrocities, AF*P*, 23 Jan. 2001; 'East Timor militia leader refuses questioning by UNTAET, AFP, 13 March 2001; East Timor's militia leader refuses UNTAET questioning, The Jakarta Post, 14 March 2001.

against the KOPASSUS Deputy Commander stationed in Los Palos, Lautem District in 1999 issued by a Judge of the same Court on 9 February 2001; and that against the former TNI Sub District Military Commander of Lolotoe issued on 6 April 2001 by the Special Panel for Serious Crimes.

g. To open an investigation into the murder of 9 persons allegedly killed by members of Battalion 745 on or about 21 September 1999. UNTAET had evidence that the victims, were targeted by members of Battalion 747 who formed of the convoy that travelled from Los Palos to Dili on 20-21 September 1999 and
h. Further to the above, UNTAET on 25 October 2001 requested the Indonesian National HR Commission (KOMHASHAM) to conduct a preliminary investigation into the death on 16 October 1975 of five journalists, namely Gary Cunningham, Brian Peters, Malcolm Rennie, Gregory Shackleton and Antony Stewart); all alleged to have been killed by Indonesian Forces in Balibo, East Timor in 1975.

The above requests were officially transmitted according to the requirements of the MOU between UNTAET and Indonesia, to the Attorney General of Indonesia, via the Indonesian Mission in East Timor. None of the requests for cooperate have, to date been honoured. The request for an authenticated copy of the KPP-HAM Report was denied for reasons of strict interpretation of the Indonesian criminal procedure code. It provided, in Article 72, that at the request of a suspect (or his Counsel), copies of an investigation report or trial dossier, including the indictment, are to be given only to him in the interest of his defence[141]. The Indonesian Attorney General's Office used this clause to substantiate their inability to provide the report. It should also be noted that as an instrument of cooperation the MOU had also been challenged in Indonesia by a TNI Advocacy team on the grounds that it only constituted an initial legal agreement which required further formal agreement in the form of a treaty; that it constituted unwarranted interference in the judicial system of Indonesia, and that it was in violation of the Indonesian law governing international agreements between the Government of Indonesia and Foreign States or other Institutions[142].

Cooperation by UNTAET

On its part UNTAET's SCIU arranged for an investigation team from the Attorney General of Indonesia to record witness statements from 19 July to 2 August 2000, in East Timor, for cases under investigations by that Office. It also hosted 3 inves-

[140] Warrant of arrest No 598/ssp/ij/dcd/x/2000, issued on 6 October 2000, Dili District Court.

[141] The Code of Criminal Procedure, Act No.8/1981 (K.U.H.A.P.), State Gazette of the Republic of Indonesia, No.76/1981.

[142] Act of the Republic of Indonesia No.24/2000 Concerning International Agreements, State Gazette of the Republic of Indonesia, No. 4012/2000, 23 Oct. 2000.

tigators collecting evidence in relation to Sander Theones.[143] The Unit provided it, on 3 July 2000, with statements of witnesses and documentary materials related to the murder on 25 September 1999 of Sander Thoenes; on the Liquica Church massacre; on the attack on Bishop Belo's compound, and on the killings at Mario Carrascalao's house. UNTAET provided Indonesia with a post mortem report, as well as exhibits including an arm, ammunition and cartridges in connection with the trial at the Central Jakarta District Court, of Jakobus Bere and other militia involved in the killing on 24 July 2001, in Fatumea, East Timor, of Private Leonard William Manning, a New Zealand soldier, who was a member of the UN peacekeeping forces. The net result of the MOU between UNTAET and Indonesia is that cooperation resembles one-way traffic.

One of most sensitive issues on cooperation is the transfer of suspects or accused. Under Section 9 of the MOU (transfer of persons) Indonesia and UNTAET undertook to transfer to each other, all persons whom the competent authorities of the requesting party are prosecuting for a criminal offence or whom these authorities want for the purpose of serving a sentence (Section 9.1). The criminal offences for which a person may be transferred are those that are punishable under the laws of both parties by imprisonment or other deprivation of liberty for a maximum period of at least two years, or by a more severe penalty, as well as crimes against humanity (Section 9.2). Each party has a right to refuse a request for transfer if the carrying out of legal proceedings by authorities of the requesting party would not be in the interest of justice (Section 9.3), a non-defined term in the MOU. In reviewing a request for transfer, the parties are to be guided by the principle that individuals shall be generally held responsible in the jurisdiction where the crimes at issue was committed (Section 9.4), and if the requested party refuses to transfer a person, it has the mandatory obligation to submit the case to its own competent authorities for prosecution (Section 9.4). The transfer of suspects or accused is discretionary, and refusal more permissive than the arrangements under which the ICTY and ICTR operates. There is no treaty or Statute bound obligation between Indonesia and East Timor to surrender or transfer such persons whether national or non-national. This constitutes a major gap in the system of accountability as designed by the United Nations Security Council for the atrocity crimes committed in East Timor.

An in-depth appraisal of the current situation indicates that there are no prospects for the transfer of any serious crimes suspect or accused from Indonesia to East Timor; whether that person is an Indonesian or East Timorese national. In 2002 no response was received from Indonesia on UNTAET's request for arrest or transfer.[144] First this is borne out by the opposition of Indonesia's House of Representatives, the legislative body that would have to endorse any agreement to this effect under the applicable Indonesian law on international agreements between Indonesia and other states or international institutions. In relation to an 'ordinary

---

143 Report of the Secretary General on UNTAET, para. 36, UN Doc. S/20002/432, 17 April 2002.

144 Report of the Secretary General on the UNTAET, UN Doc.S/2002/432, 17 April 2002, para. 34.

crime' case, the Indonesian Government had also categorically refused to transfer to East Timor, Yakobus Bere, a member of Laksaur militia, accused with 3 others of murdering Private Leonard William Manning, a New Zealand UN Peacekeeping soldier. Private Manning was the first New Zealand soldier to die in combat since the Vietnam War. Manning was killed by a bullet, shot when his patrol was ambushed by militia at Foho Debululic, Covalima District, East Timor, on 24 July 2000. After his death his throat was slit, and both ears cut off with a machete. The militia also took his C9 minimi machine gun, pistol, and webbing. On 7 March 2003 the Central Jakarta District Court sentenced Bere to 6 years imprisonment.[145] On 22 March, the Court acquitted the other defendants. New Zealand Prime Minister Helen Clark, who had earlier put pressure on former Indonesian President Abdurrahman Wahid for justice to be done, considered the sentence "too light".[146] On its part UNMISET regarded the decision inadequate and disappointing.[147]

The result of the dual tract system of accountability, in East Timor and Indonesia is an incorrigible impunity gap. One that has been caused by lacunae in the relevant Indonesian laws, and an unwillingness to cooperate, we have referred to earlier. More denting is the non-transfer to East Timor of hundreds of East Timorese, accused before the Special Panels for Serious Crimes in Dili. As of 31 December 2004 80% of accused, indicted in East Timor of serious crimes committed in 1999, were presumed to be at large in Indonesia. They remain outside the reach of the East Timor justice system; and at the same time enjoy the impunity provided by the Indonesian Human Rights Act, which confers personal jurisdiction to its courts of only Indonesian citizens and not East Timorese. Indonesia has also not manifested any interest at all in investigating 32 Indonesians accused of serious crimes in East Timor. It has ignored the urgings of the Security Council for cooperation with UNAMET and UNMISET in order to ensure that those responsible are brought to justice.[148]

The credibility of the Indonesian judicial system may also be appraised through accountability involving the daylight murder of UNHCR staff members in Atambua. On 6 September 2000 six militia, together with hundreds of other militiamen, had escorted the remains of Olivio Mendonca Moruk, the Commander of *Laksaur* militia, from Betun refugee camp to Atambua, West Timor. Assailants had killed and mutilated his body. Upon arrival in Atambua, and following incitation from Igedio Manek, the group split into two parts; one proceeded to the Belu District People's Representative (DPRD) office while the other went to the UNHCR Office at No. 2, Jl Gatot Subroto, Atambua. They forced their way into the office, where they attacked and repeatedly stabbed to death three UNHCR international staff, Pero Simundza (Croatia), Carlos Caceres-Collazo (USA) and Samson Are-

[145] Para. 38, Id.

[146] Clark tells Wahid she wants justice for slain soldier, New Zealand Herald (NZH), 27 June 2001; Indonesian prosecutors appeal killers sentence, NZH, 23 March 2003; Indonesia militiaman found guilty of Private Manning's murder, NZH, 7 & 8 March 2003.

[147] Para 38, Report of the Secretary General on the UNTAET; Ambush on Timor jungle Trial, New Zealand Herald, 7 September 2002.

[148] UN SC res. 1410(2002), 17 May 2002, UN Doc. S/RES/1410 (2002), para. 12.

gahegn (Ethiopia).[149] Thereafter their bodies and the UNHCR offices were set ablaze. This gruesome incident occurred in broad daylight, and in the presence of ten Indonesian police officers.[150] As the mob attacked the office, one of the UNHCR workers managed to e-mail a plea; that militias were on their way and that they were sitting there as "bait".[151] Shocked by this incident, the UNHCR immediately suspended operations in West Timor.[152] Appalled by the "brutal murder" of UN Staff, which it termed an "outrageous and contemptible act", the Security Counsel on 8 November 2000 in SC Resolution 1319 (2000) called on the Indonesian authorities to take immediate and additional steps to disarm and disband the militia, ensure the safety and security of refugee camps, and stressed that those responsible must be brought to justice.[153]

For the crimes Indonesian authorities charged and tried, in two groups, six accused persons. The first group of three accused, who admitted to having stabbed the UNHCR staff, were charged as 'principles' for manslaughter under Article 338 of the Penal Code of Indonesia, an offence which carries a maximum sentence of 15 years. A subsidiary charge of maltreatment under Article 351 was also incorporated. The second group of three militia were charged with the lesser offence of collective participation in crimes against public order, under Article 170 (1) of the Penal Code of Indonesia, to wit, with unified force they openly committed violence against persons or property.

The North Jakarta District Court held that although some of the defendants had admitted to taking part in hacking the victims to death before the bodies were burnt, the three UNHCR workers had died in a "mob attack", and therefore could not be charged with manslaughter.[154] The Court ruled that the killings could not be directly linked to any of the defendants because of the rampaging mob. It further opined that in such a situation, of mob attack, it was difficult to determine who was the exact perpetrator of the death and reduced the charges to 'conspiracy to foment violence'.[155] The Court imposed sentences of between 16-20 months for the first group of accused, and that of between 10-15 months for the second group.

---

[149] See, Summary Report of the Inquiry into the death of three UNHCR staff workers in Atambua, Indonesia on 6 September 2000, Inspector General's Office, UNHCR, 8 December 2000, at www.unhcr.ch.

[150] Open Briefing to the UN Security Council on East Timor by Sergio Vieira de Mello, SRSG and Transitional Administrator, 29 September 2000, N.Y.

[151] See, US Senate Resolution 91, 21 May 2001.

[152] UNHCR confirms three staff killed in West Timor attack, UNHCR Press Release, 6 September 2000,http://www.unhcr.ch/news/pr/pr000906.htm; UNHCR Staff worldwide demand end to killings, UNHCR Press Release, 21 September 2000, http://www.unhcr.ch/news/pr/pr000921.htm.

[153] Council condemns 'outrageous and contemptible' killing of three UN staff in West Timor; Insists Indonesia disarm, disband Militia, UN Press Release, SC/6929, 8 September 2000.

[154] Indonesian prosecutors consider appealing UN murder verdicts, AFP, Jakarta, 5 May 2001; Outrage at Indonesia court's Timor murder sentences, Reuters, Jakarta, 4 May 2001.

[155] Cf. In case of death arising from mob attach, since death or grievous body harm was a probably cause of the attack upon the deceased and the attackers acted with a common

The UN Secretary-General on 4 May 2001 expressed shock with regard to the light sentences imposed by the Court. He considered the sentences incommensurate with what was known to have been deliberate and brutal killing of the UNHCR staff, and an unacceptable response to the ultimate sacrifice that the staff had made in humanitarian service.[156] On its part UNHCR branded the sentences a mockery of the international community's insistence that justice be done in this horrific case.[157] The US State Department was also extremely disappointed at the verdict. It expressed the view that the light sentences called into question Indonesia's commitment to the principle of accountability, and its commitment to the international community to bring to justice the perpetrators of this and other crimes committed in East and West Timor, especially given the defendants' admitted participation in the brutal slaying of the unarmed humanitarian workers.[158] On its part the US Senate decried the "token" sentences as inadequate for the self confessed killers of the UNHCR workers.[159] In resolution 91, of 21 May 2001, it called upon the President, at every appropriate meeting with officials of the Government of Indonesia, to stress the importance of ending the climate of impunity which shielded those individuals, especially senior members of the Indonesian military, suspected of perpetrating, collaborating in, or covering up extra judicial killings, torture and other abuses of human rights.[160]

On July 23, 2001 the High Court of Jakarta "affirmed" the verdicts of the North Jakarta District Court.[161] This further incensed the UNHCR and others concerned with accountability for the crimes. On 15 November 2002 the Indonesia Supreme Court overturned the decisions of the lower Courts, and increased the sentences of the three principal accused, to sentences ranging between 5 to 7 years.[162] The Su-

---

purpose, the accused is liable for the death even though he may not have struck the fatal blow. *R v. Usumau s/o Mpangani* 1967 High Court Digest (Tanzania) 390.

156 Secretary General shocked by light sentences handed down in Indonesian Court case concerning killing of UNHCR staff, Press Release SG/SM/7793, 4 May 2001.

157 UN refuge body blasts Timor verdicts as "mockery", Reuters, 4 May 2001.

158 US State Department on Indonesia Trial Verdict, Office of International Programs, U.S. Department of State, W.D.C, 4 May 2001.

159 S. Res. 91, 'Condemning the murder of a US Citizen and other civilians, and expressing the sense of the Senate regarding the failure of the Indonesian Judicial system to hold accountable those responsible for the killing', 107th Congress, 1st session, 147 Cong. Rec. S 5278, vol. 147, no: 70, 21 May 2001.

160 S. Res.91, 'Condemning the murder of a US Citizen and other civilians, and expressing the sense of the Senate regarding the failure of the Indonesian Judicial system to hold accountable those responsible for the killing', 107th Congress, 1st session, 147 Cong Rec. S 5278, Vol. 147, No. 70, 21 May 2001.

161 High Court (Courts of Appeals), Jakarta, Verdict No. 100/PID/2001/PT.DKI, In the Criminal Appeals Case, Julius Naisama, Jose Francisco and Joao Alves da Cruz, 23 July 2001.

162 Indonesia increases jail term of UNHCR staff killers, AFP, Jakarta, 18 January 2003.

preme Court, presided by Chief Justice Bagir Manan, ruled that the defendant's actions had clearly led to the death of the UN Staff.[163]

This case is a reflection of lack of clarity in the law and on charging deficiencies. Without international indignation and pressure from the UN, UNHCR, and the US Senate, for Indonesian authorities to correct the injustice arising out of the verdicts of District and High Court no corrective measures would have been undertaken. It is no mystery that the judicial system in Indonesia lacks credibility. This was admitted by Indonesia's former Attorney General Buharuddin Lopa on 3 July 2001, when he estimated that Indonesia would need more than two decades to combat corruption institutionalized within the judiciary, and called the network of corruption within the judiciary system a 'mafia' entangling all levels of the country's legal system.[164]

VII. Human Rights Trials: Indonesia

The outcome of trials held under the Human Rights Court Act, which began in Indonesia in March 2002, is one laden with acquittals of a significant number of senior Indonesian military and police officers. In mid August 2002 Timbul Silean, the former East Timor Chief of Police, was acquitted. Also in mid August 2002 five accused, namely, Colonel Herman Sedyono, the former Bupati of Covalima; the District Military Commander (Dandim) of Kodim 1635, the Chief of Staff of Kodim, the sub district Military Commander (Danramil) of Suai, and the District Police Commander (Kapolres) were also all acquitted of Suai Church massacre that took place on 6 September 1999.[165]

The judicial process that led to this acquittal reflected fundamental flaws in the way the prosecution was conducted. To prove its case beyond reasonable doubt, of the 16 witnesses called by the Prosecution in the Suai Church case, only 2 witnesses where direct witnesses who had been present at the church during the massacre. The violence that took place immediately before the Church attack had led to the displacement of an estimated 2000 Suai inhabitants, who were in the Church compound or in the Church on 6 September 1999. *Laksaur*, *Mahidi*, and the TNI, including the Suai sub-District Military Commander (Danramil) participated in the ensuing violence.[166] The latter was present at the Church at the time of the massacre, and assisted in ferrying and clandestinely burning the corpses across the bor-

[163] Convicted UN staff killers get heavier sentences, The Jakarta Post, 19 January 2002; Indonesia increases jail terms of UN staff killers, AFP, 18 January 2002; Jakarta Court toughens sentence on W. Timor murders, Reuters W. Ser., 17 January 2002.

[164] The Jakarta Post, 6 June 2001, cited in Rights trials still a distant dream, TOPAL, Topal Bulettin No. 162, The Indonesia Human Rights Campaign, July/August 2001.

[165] *P. V. H. Sedyono, L. Koeshadianto, G. Subiyakto, A. Syamsudin and Sugito*, Jakarta, August 2002.

[166] Report of the Indonesian Commission on Human rights Violations in East Timor, Executive Summary, par. 42, 31 January 2000 (hereinafter referred to as KPP-HAM Report).

der in West Timor.[167] It is odd that the Prosecution chose not to rely on the evidence of survivors or victims. Instead it opted to call, as the majority of prosecution witnesses, members of Kodim 1635 and policemen stationed in Suai. In a departure from internationally accepted criminal procedure, the Court also decided to consider the written deposition of 3 East Timorese witnesses who could not attend due to security concerns, and who were to appear for the Prosecution as exculpatory of the accused.

In its judgment, the Court held that the militia groups involved in the attack (i.e. *Laksaur* and *Mahidi*) were "community groups" that surfaced in East Timor on their own, and as a result of an individual desire to volunteer in order to support a pro-integration victory in the popular consultations. It further opined that these groups were independent groups that existed outside the structure of the government. These finding are not borne out by hard facts on the formation of the militia groups in East Timor, including the credible findings by the UN International Commission of Inquiry, and that of the Indonesian Commission of Human Rights Violations in East Timor (KPP-HAM). In its report issued on 31 January 2000, KPP-HAM found evidence of a strong relationship and linkages between the TNI, the Police, the Civil Administration and the militia, and that a massive program of support was launched involving the military apparatus at various levels.[168] Militia groups in East Timor were the brainchild of the Indonesian military, which trained, armed and provided logistic means. The militia groups were the direct coordination of the TNI.[169] These groups also had the support of the Government authorities, and received funding in the name of 'socialization' for autonomy. In Covalima District, between 7 and 12 September 1999 *Laksaur* and *Mahidi* were involved in joint operations with the TNI and the Indonesian Police, which resulted in death of 25 civilians.[170] In *P. v. Joni Marques et all.*, the Special Panel for Serious Crimes was of the view that widespread and systematic attacks against the civilian population, namely against known and alleged pro-independence supporters, took place in East Timor at least since January 1999, and aimed to press the population to vote for autonomy within Indonesia in the referendum of 30 August 1999, and after the announcement of the results on 4 September, to punish the population for its vote against the autonomy status, which led to the independence of the territory.[171]

With regard to the popular consultation, the Court held that there were acts of "fraud" committed by UNAMET in the voting process. It ruled that the popular consultation involved "dishonesty" both with regard to UNAMET staff that supervised the vote' and with regard to the counting of the vote, which was only witnessed by pro independence supporters. The judgment it would seem supported the claim by General Wiranto and the TNI that the post-ballot violence had been

---

[167] Id.

[168] Paras. 18 & 21, Id.

[169] Para. 29, id.

[170] See, *P. v. Wiranto et all.*, SPSC, Dili, 22 February 2003, paras. 79-96.

[171] *P. v. Joni Maques & Others*, para. 686, Id.

the result of "vulgar fraud" by the United Nations.[172] In a statement issued by the United Nations Headquarters in New York, the Organization stated that the allegations of irregularities by UNAMET were false and that not a single ballot was unaccounted for.[173] The United Nations insisted that it could not be concluded that the large scale, organized, and coordinated violence of September and October 1999, following the announcement of the results of the popular consultation, was a consequence of any irregularities in the ballot, bias or abdication of the security responsibility on the part of UNAMET.[174] The popular consultation was serviced by 400 UNV District Electoral Officers, 280 election observers from IFET, independent observers from various organizations and agencies, such as the EU and the Carter Centre, and an Independent Electoral Commission.[175] Security under the 5 May 1999 Agreements between Indonesia, Portugal and the UN was the sole responsibility of Indonesian security forces. The United Nations reiterated its offer to make available to the Indonesian Human Rights Court, upon request by Indonesian authorities, evidence in connection with the above and any other relevant issue before the Court. This offer was not taken up.

In its judgement the Indonesia Human Rights Court defined a widespread attack as "an action that has a national and international effect; an action that results in great losses both in a material and immaterial sense, an action that is horrifying; a brutal action designed to force a political end; an action that creates a sense of insecurity in individuals and the community; an action that involves a number of groups or parties and results in a pattern of similar incidents".[176] It defined systematic as "something that is planned in that it is a well organized policy or the continuation of a policy that may occur directly or indirectly. If an act is systematic in the direct sense, then the person who carries out the action directly realizes or makes happen whatever it is that is sought or desired. If an act is systematic in the indirect sense it may involve, for example, allowing someone to do something, or agreeing to it, intending that that act should happen, tolerating certain acts or activities, assisting or making it easier for the perpetrator to realize his or her intentions. These things may be achieved by working together; or conspiring together in a common policy already agreed upon in advance; or by allowing something to happen so that the actual perpetrator of the act can carry out his or her intentions without any obstacles; by only acting after the perpetrator has carried out his or her act, that is by not taking immediate steps to stop the perpetrator until the consequences have already occurred". Although the Court did find that the East Timor violence was part of a widespread and systematic attack directed against a civilian population, the above definitions of widespread and systematic attacks

[172] Wiranto scorns bid to prosecute his 'best men', Sydney Morning Herald, 11 October 2000.

[173] Secretary General Endorses Human Rights Commissioner's Concern over Indonesia Tribunal, Press Release No. SG/SM/8338, UN News Service, 14 August 2002; Military Innocent: UN to blame for Timor atrocities, Sydney Morning Herald, 17 August 2002.

[174] Id.

[175] Martikus J (2001) A Dirty Little War, pp. 270-271.

[176] *P. v. H. Sedyono et all.*

largely departed from those established by the jurisprudence of the two UN Ad hoc Tribunals.

The string of acquittals by the Indonesian Human Rights Court include that on 29 November 2002, of three accused, the Butapi of Liquica, the District Military Commander and the District Police Commander in relation to the Liquica Church massacre of 6 April 1999; and that of Brigadier General Suhartono (Tono) Suraman, on 22 May 2003, in connection with the Liquica Church massacre and the attack on the house of Manuel Carrascalao in Dili on 17 April 1999. Suratman's indictment did not contain ant allegation that when Carrascalao approached him for assistance immediately before the attack, he laughed at it, and suggested that the Carrascalao gets help from CNRT.[177] Suratman had served as the Commander of the Sub Regional Military Command 164 from June 1998 until 13 August 1999.

Commenting on the human rights trials, the UNHCHR's Special Rapporteur on the Independence of Judges and Lawyers had this to say:

"The several acquittals before the Ad Hoc Human Rights Court of East Timor are not surprising. The insufficient investigations and the failure to produce material evidence contributed to such acquittals. The Judges had to base their decisions on the evidence before the Court may not be faulted".[178]

As of 31 December 2003 of the 18 accused, charged under the Indonesian Human Rights Court Act, 12 have been acquitted and 6 convicted and sentenced to terms of imprisonment that range from 3 to 10 years. Those convicted include Abilio Soares, the former Governor of East Timor, who was sentenced to 3 years imprisonment in August 2003.[179] This sentence was below the minimum ten years sentence provided for by the law applicable. The Court, following a call for leniency by Gusmao handed down the light sentence. He had written to the Presiding Judge to plead for Soares, stating that the accused's self – imposed exile in Indonesia should be considered as punishment, and that any term of imprisonment would be double punishment.[180] This inappropriate sentence hardly takes into account the gravity of the offence and the accused's position as Indonesia's highest civilian official in East Timor. Also convicted was Lt. Colonel Soejarwo, former Dili Military Commander, sentence to 5 years imprisonment and Hulman Gultom, former Dili Police Chief, sentenced to 3 years imprisonment.

Two other accused in leadership positions have also been convicted. They are Eurico Guterres, the Commander of *Aitarak* Militia and Deputy Commander of the Pro Integration Forces (PPI), who was sentenced on 27 November 2003 to 10 years for involvement in the 17th April 1999 militia attack on the house of Manuel

---

177 See, *P. v. Waranto et all.*, Indictment, paras. 97-102.

178 Report of the Special rapporteur on the Independence of Judges and Lawyers, para. 100, UN Doc. E/CN.4/2003/65/Add.2, 13 January 2003.

179 Ex-Governor of East Timor Gets 3 years in Army killings, New York Times, 14 August 2002; Abilio gets three years in jail for Rights Violations, The Jakarta Post, 15 August 2002.Jakarta's Two Steps forward and one back, The Age, 16 August 2002.

180 Gusmao defends his Court plea for former Governor, Sydney Morning Herald, 14 August 2002.

Carasscalao, in which 12 persons were killed. The other is Brigadier General Mohamed Noer Muis, former Commander of the Sub-regional Military Command 164 (Komadan Korem 164/Wira Dharma), who on 12 March 2003 was convicted and sentenced to 5 years imprisonment. Muis had taken over command of Indonesian Armed Forces in East Timor on 13 August 1999 two weeks before the popular consultation. On 6 August 2003 in a surprise verdict, the Human Rights Court convicted Major General Adam Damiri, the highest ranking of the 18 accused, former Commander of the Regional Military Command IX, and sentenced him to 3 years imprisonment.[181] Earlier during the trial, the Prosecution in an "extremely unusual conduct" had sought an acquittal.[182] For one judicial monitoring group, this marked the completion of Indonesia's "theatrical performance" on accountability for the East Timor atrocity crimes.[183] All persons convicted have appealed to the Supreme Court.

The above reflects the shielding by the judicial process of top military and police officers for the East Timor violence. In a statement issued by the European Union, it expressed disappointment at the human rights trials, which it said has not been presented with all the evidence and had only passed on a few light sentences in a process that had not permitted that justice be done.[184] New Zealand, co- signatory to the EU statement, declared the process "deficient".[185] Only a few victims from East Timor were called to testify and no UNAMET officer or any member of the international election observer mission was called. These deficiencies had jeopardized the credibility of the verdicts, where few convictions were achieved, and where sentences for convictions failed to match the seriousness of the crimes committed.[186]

Furthermore, it has been submitted that the two convicted ethnic East Timorese (i.e. Abilio Soares and Eurico Guterres) had been purposely chosen as scapegoats.[187] The latter, a civilian militia Commander, had received the severest sentence of 10 years imprisonment. The few Indonesian officials convicted, including Major General Damiri and Brigadier General Muis, seem to have also been scapegoats to appease the international outcry on the human rights process and to defuse an international drive to set up an International Tribunal for East Timor under UN auspices. The political underpinning of Muis's verdict can be deciphered from the ruling of the Presiding Judge that, "the defendant's action has resulted in many

[181] Jakarta jails general over East Timor, The Age; Court jails top officer for Timor violence, Sydney Morning Herald; US disappointed with Indonesian Rights Tribunal, Timor Activists rage, AFP, 6 August 2003.

[182] Cohen, D, Intended to Fail, The Trials Before the Ad Hoc Human Rights Court in Jakarta, International Center for Transitional Justice, http://www.ictj.org/downloads? Intended_to_Fail--Final.pfd, 2003.

[183] Indonesia completes theatrical performance, Judicial System Monitoring Programme, http://www.jsmp. minihub.orgs/News06_8_3.htm.

[184] EU, rights group denounce Jakarta's flimsy human rights trials, LUSA, 6 August 2003.

[185] East Timor Tribunal has not delivered Justice, Press Release, New Zealand Government, 7 August 2003.

[186] Id.

[187] Civilians remain scapegoats in human rights abuses, The Jakarta Post, 20 August 2002.

victims and has created a negative image of Indonesia in the eyes of the world".[188] Currently serving as Deputy Head of the Indonesia's Land Forces Academy, he was politically expendable since he is no longer in the centre of power.[189] Damiri and Muis who had been held responsible under command responsibility were convicted of events in connection with the Suai Church massacre, when all the other Suai based military and police commanders, including the District Military Commander (Dandim) as well as the Suai sub-District Military Commander who had been on the spot during the massacre,[190] had earlier been acquitted by the Court.

In his Report to the 59th Session of the UN Commission on Human Rights, the UN High Commissioner for Human Rights, Sergio Vieira de Mello, pinpointed three areas of concern identified by informed observers of the Indonesian human rights process.[191] The first was the insufficiency of investigations conducted by the Office of the Attorney General of Indonesia, which had not taken into account the voluminous information placed before him by KPP-HAM, and the Serious Crimes Investigation Unit.[192] In the trials before the Court the Prosecution has made a half-hearted use of the raft of evidence compiled by the KPP-HAM or that available by the UN.[193] Moreover the conclusions and recommendations of the KPP-HAM report had stated that the Attorney General investigate 31 individuals, whom it named and which it suspected of involvement in the violence.[194] Of the 31 named suspects only 17 have been charged.

The second area of concern was weakness in the indictment themselves. With the exception of Eurico Guterres, who had been charged with both individual and command responsibility, all the remaining defendants were charged either as accomplices to the crimes committed by others or on a theory of command responsibility.[195] The indictments also failed to allege an organized or coordinated effort on the part of the Indonesian security forces or the Civil Administration to commit serious human rights violations, a confirmed finding of KPP-HAM and judgments delivered by the Special Panels for Serious Crimes.[196] The third area of critique concerned the absence of witness protection measures, which had led to the reluctance of witnesses from East Timor to appear before the Court, which in turn had weakened the prosecution cases.[197]

---

188 General gets jail for East Timor bloodshed, Associated Press, Jakarta, 12 March 2003.

189 Id.

190 *P. v. Wiranto et all.*, Indictment, para. 77.

191 Report of the UNHCHR, Situation of Human Rights in Timor-Leste, UN Doc. E/CN.4/2003/37, 4 March 2003, para. 53.

192 Paras. 53-54, Id.

193 A Fighting Cock finally realizes he has been shafted, Sydney Morning Herald, 30 November 2002; Guterres; the one that didn't get away, The Age, 30 November 2002.

194 See, Chapter VI, Conclusions and Recommendations, KPP –HAM Report, http://www.tip.net.au/~wildwoood/01aprkppham.htm;http://www.minihub.org/Reports/KPP%20Ham.htm.

195 Para. 55, Id.

196 Para. 55, Id.

197 Para. 56, Id.

The attitude of the Court that command or superior-subordinates relationship is one that only involves a de jure relationship is extremely restrictive. In one of its decisions the Court had considered only policemen as subordinates of the former Chief of Police of East Timor, and not those who served in public order functions as an extension of the Indonesian security forces. [198] Other weaknesses of the process include the non-use by Prosecutors of evidence made available to them by the UNTAET,[199] the appearance of only limited number of victims as witnesses, the absence of UNAMET witnesses, and those who had served as Independent election observers in East Timor.[200] Opportunity to correct the process and to effectively beef up prosecution evidence has been lost. Commenting on the human rights trials, the UNHCHR's Special Rapporteur on the Independence of Judges and Lawyers, had this to say:

> "The several acquittals before the Ad Hoc Human Rights Court of East Timor are not surprising. The insufficient investigations and the failure to produce material evidence contributed to such acquittals. The Judges had to base their decisions on the evidence before the Court may not be faulted".[201]

In a special report commissioned by the International Centre for Transitional Justice on the trials before the Ad Hoc Human Rights Court David Cohen attributes six reasons for the fundamental flaws in that process; namely, (i) that prosecution failed in almost all trials to press its case with professional commitment and to produce sufficient inculpating testimony, despite the ready availability of that evidence; (ii) the failure of the prosecution to present a coherent and credible account of the violence in East Timor sufficiently to justify convictions for crimes against humanity; (iii) the failure of political will in the Attorney General's Office and the highest levels of the Indonesian Government to encourage or even permit a serious attempt to establish the identity and guilt of those most responsible; (iv) the objective of the trials were to establish clear command responsibility at the institutional level, not just individual culpability and the concomitant failure to indict individuals at the highest level of the TNI, as recommend by KPP HAM; (v) the failure of trials to fulfill the "truth function", and (vi) the politicization of the prosecution that did not permit an independent prosecution of the human rights cases.[202]

The question whether international standards of fair trial and due process of law were met or not in the trials held by the Human Rights Court in Jakarta has also been the subject of a study by Bernd Hausler, Vice President of the Bar Associa-

---

[198] East Timor Police Chief Acquitted, BBC, 15 August 2002.

[199] Terror Acquittals Imperil US-Indonesia Trials, South China Morning Post, 21 August 2002; US critical of weak evidence in War Crimes Tribunal, Sydney Morning Herald, 21 August 2002.

[200] European Union Declaration on East Timor Trials, Press Release No. P/116/02, Brussels, 21 August 2002.

[201] Report of the Special rapporteur on the Independence of Judges and Lawyers, UN Doc. E/CN.4/2003/65/Add.2, 13 January 2003, para. 100.

[202] Cohen D (2003) Intended to Fail, The Trials Before the Ad Hoc Human Rights Court in Jakarta.

tion of Berlin and its Human Rights Commissioner, commissioned by Indonesia Watch and the German Commission on Justice and Peace [203] Based on an informed observation of 3 trials of 7 accused, it found that the weakness of the trials lay in the inadequate case files presented by the office of the Attorney General (i.e. prosecution), the non accessibility of documentary evidence on the Indonesian military's command and reporting structure and of its civil administration in East Timor, and the insufficiency of the case files and indictments themselves.[204] It opined that with the above, the verdicts were of no surprise.[205]

The above assessments of the Indonesia human rights process on the East Timor atrocity crimes indicate that there has been a manifest unwillingness, if not inability on the part of Indonesia to fulfil its repeated commitments on accountability for the atrocity crimes committed in East Timor.[206] While informed observers have now called for an international tribunal for East Timor, it is very doubtful that there will be unanimity among Security Council Member States given the political and financial implications of such an exercise. A stop gap measure is the appointment by the UN Secretary General of an independent commission of experts to assess why accountability has failed. Whatever the outcome, the lack of support for it by East Timor political leaders, and Indonesia's negative attitude towards any UN Security Council driven process seriously weakens prospects for any future effective accountability for the 1999 East Timor violence.[207]

In an endeavour to settle for an alternative, Gusmao and Indonesia's former President, Megawati Sukarnoputri had agreed in principle, on 14 December 2004, in Bali, Indonesia to establish a joint Commission of Truth and Friendship. [208] On 9 March 2005, Gumao, Mari Alkatiri East Timor's Prime Minister Mari and President Susilo Bambang Yudhyono of Indonesia signed the Commission's Terms of Reference.[209] These provide in its preamble that the establishment of the commission is motivated by the desire for both states to resolve "residual problems" of the past, deepen bilateral relations based on "forward looking" and reconciliatory approaches, and adherence to bring a "definite closure" of issues of the past. Furthermore, the past was to be looked at as a lesson and the future embraced with optimism. It is also specified that establishment of the Commission neither

---

203 Hausler B (2004) A Legal Opinion on the Indonesian Human Rights Trials Concerning the Crimes Committed in East Timor in 1999, Watch Indonesia and Deutsche Kommission Justitia et Pax.

204 Pp. 82-88, Id.

205 P. 86, Id.

206 See also, Martin I, No Justice in Jakarta, The Washington Post, 27 August 2002; Time has come for International Tribunal, Sydney Morning Herald, 17 August 2002; UN's Robinson to take Timor concerns to Security Council, Reuters, Dili, 23 August 2002; Impunity may reign after East Timor verdicts, The Jakarta Post, 20 August 2002; Activists call for Int'l human rights tribunals on East Timor, The Jakarta Post, 20 August 2002.

207 Indonesia says UN's East Timor Inquiry "Redundant"- Report, Reuter, 19Feb. 2005.

208 Timorese Church Opposes Indonesian deal on War Crimes, AFP, 7 February 2005.

209 Indonesia, East Timor seal deal on atrocities despite UN opposition, A F P, 9 March 2005.

prejudices the on-going judicial processes in both states, on the 1999 Human Rights violations in East Timor, nor does it recommend the establishment of any other judicial body.

As currently conceived the Commission's main objective is the establishment of the conclusive truth as regards the events prior to, and immediately after the popular consultation. It also aims at ensuring future non occurrence of similar events. One of its other objectives is to recommend amnesty. The Commission which is to be co-chaired is to be composed of 10 members, five appointed by the President of each state. The members are to be nominated from high standing and competent individuals from human rights fields, academia, religious and community leaders. The Commission is to have a one year renewable term, and is to submit its final report to the respective Heads of State of East Timor and Indonesia.

Explaining the process Jose Ramos Horta the Foreign Minister of East Timor had this to say to: "There will be no further trial process, but the process will be closed; these are the politics of our President and government".[210] The establishment of the Commission has been opposed by Bishop Alberto Ricardo da Silva, Dili's new Catholic Bishop, and East Timorese Human Rights groups.[211] It remains a divided issue in that newly independent nation. For Gusmao however, if East Timor "keeps digging the past", it would have no time building anything; "the past was the past", while the future is their destination.[212] This is an echo of what Prime Minister Hun Sen once told Cambodians on the atrocities committed during the period of the Khmer Rouge (1975-1979): "dig a hole and bury the past".[213] A democratic society cannot be built on falsehood or disregard for a criminal past; justice does not excuse forgiveness, yet one can only forgive with full knowledge of the facts or truth and rendering justice against the main perpetrators of crimes against humanity.[214]

---

210 Horta, J R, The Trial Process for 1999 Crimes is Now Closed, Timor Post, 7 February 2005.

211 See, The Indonesia-East Timor 'Truth and Friendship Commission': More Friendship, Less Truth, Impunity for the Law, www.jsmp. minihub.org/Press%20Release/a4Jano5_jsmp-truth%20comm-e.pdf.

212 Interview with Kay Xanana Gusmao: Its Easy To Shout Arrest Wiranto, Tempo, 15-21 June 2004'; "I 'm not a Judge, I 'm not a human rights advocate or lawyer. We are not looking for defendants, we are looking for truth", X Gusmao, Indonesia, East Timor seal deal on atrocities despite UN opposition, AFP, 9 March 2005.

213 Facing a Grisly Past, Newsweek, 13 August 2001; On atrocities committed See, Kiernan B (1996) The Pol Pot Regime, Race, Power, and Genocide in Cambodia under the Khmer Rouge, 1975-1979, Silkworm Books, Thailand.

214 Badinter R International Criminal Justice: From Darkness to Light, (Chp. 51). In Cassese A *et all.*, (2002) The Rome Statute of the International Criminal Court: A Commentary, Oxford University Press, Oxford, p. 1933.

Conclusion

Under both UNTAET and UNMISET accountability for atrocity crimes was not a singular assignment. It was a part and parcel of the transitional and post independence support. That apart it was also modelled on a cooperative arrangement between East Timor and Indonesia. Dual track accountability in both states was then the most pragmatic way forward, given Indonesia's assurances that it would deny impunity to its citizens who may have been implicated in the violence. It was envisaged that the accountability would be complementary.

The regulatory framework for accountability in East Timor was ushered in by UNTAET through regulations that had the force of law, issued by the Transitional Administrator under the authority of the Security Council. UNTAET Regulation 2000/15 established Special Panels with exclusive jurisdiction over serious criminal offences, defined to include, genocide, crimes against humanity, war crimes, torture, murder, and sexual offences. The definitions of the first four listed crimes were a footprint of almost similar provisions of the ICC Statute. Equally deemed applicable by UNTAET under regulation 1999/1, but now interpreted otherwise by the Portuguese dominated East Timor Court of Appeal, was the Penal Code of Indonesia. A two-tier Court hierarchy was also set up nationally, consisting of District Courts and a Court of Appeal. For atrocity crimes only the Dili District Court has a jurisdictional monopoly. This is conferred on the Special Panels for Serious Crimes, a kind of separate Trial Chamber of the Court with exclusive jurisdiction over serious crimes. The institutional framework is a 'mixed' or 'hybrid' Court in that composition of judges in these panels and at the Court of Appeal is both international and national, the former in the majority in a ratio of 2:1. Additionally the applicable law is both domestic and international law, including international humanitarian law.

While initial responsibility for investigating atrocity crimes were kick-started by CIVPOL, it was the establishment of the Serious Crimes Investigation Unit, and later the National Prosecution Service, on 6 June 2000, over half a year after UNTAET's presence in East Timor began, that saw the birth of serious crimes litigation. The commencement of investigations were saddled with a lack of investigation expertise among CIVPOL, lack of inter-agency cooperation, competition for resource allocation among various sectors, gross denial of equipment and materials, absence of any meaningful financial support, and insufficient staffing. The same issues that had plagued the ICTR when it began operations in mid 1995. Many of these constraints were gradually overcome by UNTAET and later by UNMIET. *A lesson learnt is that full accountability of the kind inevitable in East Timor is not a piggy bank affair*. It is the availability of appropriate expertise and adequate means that can only ensure timely and effective accountability for atrocity crimes. This applies to all models of accountability, international tribunals or hybrid Courts. One positive element in the initial efforts at accountability was forensic investigations. Prosecutors were able to link its findings on the personal identification of human remains, the causes and manner of death with cases before the Special Panels for Serious Crimes.

Chapter 4 examined two other issues particular to the accountability process in East Timor. Both had to do with the fragility of the post-ballot situation, the need to re-establish the rule of law, and that of the facilitation of national reconciliation among East Timorese. The first prolonged pre-trial detention of suspects, mostly low-level militiamen, had a heavy toll on criminal investigations. In the early years of UNTAET's mandate many of these suspects had spent considerable time in detention, without charges and against established international human rights norms. In East Timor the desired full accountability was a necessary evil. The policy adopted, of charging a number of low-level perpetrators under the Penal Code of Indonesia, and on the basis of a set of objective criteria proved suited for the occasion. The second matter, accountability for militia refugees, had to be cushioned with the imperative of balancing on the one hand justice and the rule of law, while on the other hand the healing and national reconciliation process. With over 70% of indictees in West Timor, Indonesia, among whom, were nearly all the notorious militia Commanders, currently out of the reach of accountability in East Timor and Indonesia, the right combination of justice and community based reconciliation was required. This remains a divided issue among East Timorese, exemplified by the divergent views of Gusmao who emphatically favours national reconciliation and development of bilateral relations with Indonesia over justice, and on the other side Nobel Peace Laureate Bishop Carlos Belo and human rights organizations who remains firm advocates of justice.[215]

The prosecution strategy and policies adopted in East Timor were aimed at *full* accountability, not the highly selective kind of only those in leadership positions or high command. The imperative was not to charge a symbolic number with the greatest responsibility. It was to hold accountable the three classes of perpetrators: low-level, many of who were already in custody; intermediate; as well as those alleged to have had prime responsibility. As questioned by the only East Timorese Judge of the Court of Appeal: "Is it fair to prosecute the small Timorese, and not the big ones who gave them orders?[216]

The policies for accountability in East Timor were cantered on, (i) the investigation of mass killings and violence, both pre and post ballot; (ii) aimed at comprehensive accountability rather than segmental; (iii) judicially solving an inherited case load of pre trial detained perpetrators; (iv) enlisting the cooperation of suspects or accused with the prosecution; (v) ensuring a higher evidential threshold to ensure trial ready indictments; and (vi) conducting prosecution directed investigations. The ten or so "priority" cases, including the special investigation of persons presumed to have had the prime responsibility for atrocity crimes in East Timor, were geared to accountability to the maximum level of perpetration, as well as that which was responsible for the direct execution of orders. For those with the greatest responsibility the particular strategy of accountability counted on (a) massacres, in particular those forming part of the ten priority cases, (b) the 9

---

215 Gusmao and Belo on collision course over justice, Sydney Morning Herald, 18 December 2000.

216 Modest Beginnings for East Timor's Justice System, The New York Times, 4 March 2001.

months campaign of persecution (i.e. January to September 1999) and (c) forced deportation of an estimated 250,000 civilians to West Timor, Indonesia, in September 1999, as the dragnet to hold accountable that group of offenders.

An inquiry into accountability for atrocity crimes in East Timor is incomplete without reference to the arrangements under the Indonesian ad hoc Human Rights Court that was specially established for the serious human rights violations committed in East Timor. The atrocity crimes were also committed by elements of the Indonesian Armed Forces (TNI) and the Indonesian Police Force (POLRI), as well as its civilian administrators and militia proxies. As stated by the three thematic Special Rapporteurs of the UN Commission on Human Rights, the Indonesian Armed Forces was sufficiently involved in the operational activities of the direct perpetrators (i.e. militia), to incur the responsibility of the Government of Indonesia.[217] We noted that the limited temporal, territorial, and personal jurisdiction of the ad hoc Human Rights Court amounts to a half-baked framework and incomplete framework for accountability. Furthermore only 18 defendants faced trial, and of which 12 were acquitted. Among the causes for this development, was the complete lack of prosecutorial diligence. Many suspects named in the KPP HAM Report, and dozens of others indicted in East Timor, have not been called to account by the Indonesian process.

The net result is not just a flawed accountability process, but "inability" and "unwillingness", as defined in Article 17 of the ICC Statute, genuinely to account for the atrocity crimes committed in East Timor. To this one must add the absence of any discernable political will to do so. The conclusion is that the outcome so far of the dual track option favoured by the Security Council, of simultaneous accountability in East Timor and Indonesia, is limited impunity to a few with low and intermediate level responsibility, and complete impunity to those with the greatest responsibility. This, notwithstanding the fact that the East Timor accountability process has sufficiently indicted the top leadership echelon allegedly held responsible for the violence. The incompleteness of that process is measured by the fact that over 80% of accused in the 10 "priority cases" continue to enjoy absolute unaccountability.

217 Report of the Special rapporteur on extra-judicial, summary or arbitrary executions, the Special rapporteur on the question of torture, the Special rapporteur on violence against women, UN Doc. A/54/660, 10 Dec. 1999.

Chapter 5
Profiling Perpetrators

Chapter 5 examines the targets of accountability for atrocity crimes. It highlights considerations that ought to be taken into account in holding answerable those suspected of having committed serious international humanitarian law violations: the "big, medium and small fish". The demand to hold such persons accountable originates from both national and international constituencies. Within the former is the urge for justice by victims, survivors and civil advocacy groups. It has also been recognized by the international community that it is the prime responsibility of national authorities to hold accountable those presumed to have committed such crimes. The call for justice by that community is one that has been ushered in by the United Nations Security Council and the UN Commission for Human Rights. It also arises out of treaty or conventional obligations. In addressing this issue it is essential to underline a non-compromising principle of accountability. That criminal responsibility is individual. It is neither associative nor collective. The accountability that is to be deciphered through investigation and effective prosecution is that of individual guilt. The individualization of criminal responsibility guarantees that guilt is not collectivized. This is the beacon that must guide the gathering of evidence. In the finality a court of law is required to pronounce a verdict, guilty or not guilty, solely on the basis of whether there is or there is not sufficient evidence, beyond all reasonable doubt.

As an introduction, this chapter first presents a conceptual framework on the profiling of perpetrators, and discusses direct individual criminal responsibility. In many situations of atrocity crimes, this forms a significant mode of criminal participation by all categories of perpetrators. The other mode of participation, that is, indirect superior responsibility will be detailed in Chapter 7. Secondly the chapter closely examines the main targets of accountability, with particular focus on those with the greatest responsibility for atrocity crimes (i.e. the instigators, planners, and organizers). It inquires into the preferences of the Secretary General Annan for international and mixed arrangements for judicial accountability to book persons "*most responsible*", and on the other hand that of the Security Council for such institutions to hold answerable, as a priority, those with the "*greatest responsibility*". Thirdly an analysis will be made of the classification of perpetrators alleged to have committed atrocity crimes by the Rwandan judicial authorities and that by UNTAET and Indonesian authorities as concerns the international humanitarian law violations committed in East Timor. It shall also look at the practices of the ICTR; in particular the development of its prosecution and investigation strategies from its establishment in 1994 to full maturity. Fourthly this chapter examines two examples, one typified by the Ntuyahaga affair, which may arise in the profiling of a suspect or an accused for accountability when there is no structured or legal linkage between international and national accountability; and the other the Rusatira affair, which reflects premature profiling.

I. Conceptual Framework on Profiling Perpetrators and Individual Criminal Responsibility

At a conceptual level Bassiouni has suggested that for the deterrence of international humanitarian law violations, it is more important to bring about a higher level of responsibility on decision makers and senior executives than low-level executors.[1] To achieve that he advocates for a distinction to be drawn between high-level decision makers and executors and those at the lower end of the echelons of the chain of command.[2] Ambos suggests three levels of participation suitable to international criminal law, and capable of apportioning responsibility as: the first and highest level composed of main perpetrators who plan and organize the criminal events as a whole and as such belong to the leadership level; the second level also comprising yet the main perpetrators of at least the mid-level of hierarchy who exercise some form of control over a part of the organization; and the third level consisting of accomplices who merely execute the crimes.[3]

In discussing the urge for accountability by the United Nations Security Council for the atrocity crimes committed in Rwanda it was emphasized in chapter 3 that one of the Council's aims was to not to prosecute rank-and-file perpetrators. It was to concentrate on those in leadership and other positions of authority. In the Rwandan situation, we exposed the pivotal role of the interim Government and the role played by the armed forces, gendarmerie, civil administration, media and political parties in planning and orchestrating the violence. In the context of the East Timor, we also narrated the role played by the Indonesian armed forces, militia organization and the civil administration in the pre and post-ballot violence. The commission of genocide and crimes against humanity invariably involves state action, omission or policy, and it makes sense to hold accountable first and foremost those at the highest level of authority or command in the government or its agencies. State action or policy it had been said:

---

1 Bassiouni M C (1999) Crimes Against Humanity in International Criminal Law, Kluwer Law International, 2nd ed. The Hague, p. 264.

2 P. 264, Id.; For a critique see, Ambos, K (1999), Current Issues in International Criminal Law, Criminal Law Forum 13: pp. 237-238.

3 Ambos K Article 25, Individual Criminal Responsibility, *Draft*, p 105 In Treffterer O (ed.) Commentary on the Rome Statute of the International Criminal Court, forthcoming revised edition.

"can be based on a decision by the head of State, or a common design agreed to by senior officers, who rely on the State's powers and resources, in whole or in part, to carry out such a decision, or when the conduct of low-ranking public officials relying on State powers and resources is committed with the connivance or knowledge of higher-ranking public officials, or when such high-ranking officials fail to carry out their obligation to prevent the conduct in question or fail to punish the perpetrators when the conduct is discovered or reasonably discovered".[4]

As noted above, condemnation of atrocity crimes by the Security Council has often entailed an affirmation that persons who commit such crimes bear individual criminal responsibility.

As regards to the atrocity crimes committed in Rwanda, the Council on 30 April 1994 not only condemned all breaches of international humanitarian law that were taking place, but also affirmed that persons who instigate or participate in such acts are individually responsible.[5] Authors of atrocities cannot escape personal responsibility for criminal acts they carried out, ordered, or condoned.[6] The Council, also through resolution 935 (1994), further endorsed the individuality of criminal responsibility for those who instigate or participate in international humanitarian law breaches, particularly those committed against the civilian population.[7] This affirmation of individual criminal responsibility has also been repeatedly fortified by resolutions of the UN Commission on Human Rights[8] and the General Assembly.[9] The East Timor violence also provided another occasion in which the[10] Security Council yet again, stressed the principle of individual criminal responsibility for flagrant human rights and international humanitarian law violations.[11]

In the Rwandan events, the UN Commission of Experts, established under UNSC res. 935 (1994),[12] considered that the international legal norms providing

---

4 Pp. 257-258, Id.

5 Statement by the President of the Security Council condemning the slaughter of civilians in Kigali and other parts of Rwanda, UN Doc. S/PRST/1994/21, 30 April 1994.

6 Report of the United Nations High Commissioner for Human Rights on his Mission to Rwanda of 11 –12 May 1994, UN Doc. ECN.4/S-3/3, 19 May 1994, para. 32.

7 Security Council resolution requesting the Secretary-General to establish a Commission of Experts to examine information on grave violations of international humanitarian law and possible acts of genocide in Rwanda, UN Doc. S/RES/935 (1994), 1 July 1994.

8 UNCHR Res. S-3/1, 25 May 1994, 22, Report to the Secretary –General on the investigation of serious violations of international humanitarian law committed in Rwanda during the conflict, UN Doc. S/1994/867, 25 July 1994, para. 22.

9 U.N.G.A. resolution on the situation of human rights in Rwanda, U.N.G.A. Doc. A/RES/49/206, 23 December 1994; UNGA resolution on the situation of human rights in Rwanda, UNGA Doc. A/RES/50/200, 22 December 1995.

10 UNCHR resolution 1999/S-4/1, Situation of human rights in East Timor, Report of the Commission on Human Rights on its Fourth Special Session, 23-24 September 1994, UN Doc. E/CN. 4/1999/167/Add.1, E/1999/23/Add.1, 20 October 1999.

11 UNSC resolution 1264 (1999), UN Doc. S/RES/1264, 15 September 1999; UNSC resolution 1272, UN Doc. S/RES/1272, 25 October 1999.

12 UN Doc. S/1994/935, 1 July 1994.

for individual responsibility for serious human rights violations had been breached in Rwanda between 6 April and 15 July 1994, and that certain individuals were responsible for breaches of (a) norms of international humanitarian law on a systematic, widespread, and flagrant basis; (b) norms prohibiting crimes against humanity; and (c) norms prohibiting acts of genocide. The Commission was of the view that the attribution of responsibility to the individual in propria personam was not entirely new, in that trials of individuals for having committed war crimes had taken place at least as far back as 1419, that legal norms for individual responsibility for slave trading, slave trafficking and piracy arose out of the Congress of Vienna (1815), and that the Nuremberg Trials had reinforced the principle in holding that any individual, regardless of office or rank, shall be held responsible in international law for war crimes, crimes against peace, or crimes against humanity.[13] Indeed as stated by the Nuremberg Tribunal, "crimes against international law are committed by men, not by abstract entities, and only by punishing individuals who commit such crimes, can the provisions of international law be enforced". [14]

In *P. v. D. Tadic*, the ICTY affirmed that there was a basis in customary international law for individual criminal responsibility derived from the practice of states, the Nuremberg Trial, the Military trials conducted under Control Council Law No. 10, international conventions, and national practice.[15] In reference to the trial of the major World War II criminals, it was understood from the outset that the trials would be limited, in accordance with the Moscow Declaration of October 30, 1946, signed on behalf of President Franklin Roosevelt, Prime Minister Wilson Churchill and Marshall Stalin, to a number of the highest ranking Nazi leaders and their principal accomplices.[16]

Article 6 (1) of the ICTR Statute provides for direct individual criminal responsibility:[17]

"A person who planned, instigated, ordered, committed or otherwise aided and abetted in the planning, preparation or execution of crimes referred to in articles 2 to 4 of the present statute, shall be individually responsible for the crimes".

In addition to responsibility as principal perpetrators, an accused can be held responsible for the criminal acts of others where he plans with them, instigates them, orders them, or aids and abets them to commit those acts.[18] In explaining the ambit

---

[13] Final Report of the Commission of Experts established pursuant to Security Council resolution 935 (1994), UN Doc. S/1994/1405, 9 December 1994, paras. 85, 102, 125-128, 169-172.

[14] Trial of the Major War Criminals Before the International Military Tribunal, vol.1, published at Nuremberg, Germany, 1947, p. 223.

[15] *P. v. D. Tadic*, Opinion and Judgement, Case no. ICTY-IT-94-1-T, 7 May 1997, paras. 633-669.

[16] Gross L (1999) The Punishment of War Criminals: The Nuremberg Trial, in Gross L Selected Essays on International Law and Organization, Transnational Publishers, Inc., Irvington-on-Hudson, N.Y., 1999, p. 160.

[17] Cf. Identical provision, Art 7 (1), ICTY Statute.

[18] *P. v. J-P. Akayesu*, Judgement, Case no: ICTR-.96-4-7, 2 September 1998, para. 472.

of this article, the Tribunal considered that the provision covered various stages of the commission of a crime, ranging from planning and organization to its execution.[19] It however qualified the scope of imputable acts, and opined that the principle of individual criminal responsibility, as provided for in Article 6 (1), implies that the planning or preparation of a crime must actually lead to its commission. As regards other forms of criminal participation, and in particular, those referred to in Article 6 (1), the tribunal was of the view that a perpetrator would incur criminal responsibility only if the offence were completed.[20]

For the purposes of this chapter only a brief restatement will be made on the scope of individual criminal responsibility, since detailed legal analysis of this liability is dealt with elsewhere.[21] Investigations into the five recognized forms of direct criminal participation often assist the prosecution in deciphering the role of each suspect or accused, and in allocating responsibility for the crime committed. *P. v J.P. Akayesu* provides a general account of the various forms of liability recognized in Article 6 (1) of the ICTR Statute, which had been consistently followed in other ICTR decisions.[22]

The first form of liability, recognized in article 6 (1) of the ICTR Statute is the *planning* of a crime. This occurs when one or several persons contemplated designing the commission of a crime at both the perpetrator and execution phases.[23] The second form of liability is *instigation*, which involves promoting another to commit an offence desired by the instigator to be committed, and which is in fact committed.[24] The third manner of liability is that of *ordering*. This implies a superior-subordinate relationship, between the person giving the order, who is in a position of authority, and the one executing it.[25] Under Article 91 of the Penal Code of Rwanda, ordering is also recognized as a mode of complicity through instructions given to the actual perpetrator of an offence.[26]

The fourth form of liability is that through *aiding* and *abetting*, a form of accomplice liability. Aiding means giving assistance to someone, while abetting in-

---

[19] Para. 473, Id.

[20] Para. 473, Id.

[21] For details see, Ambos K Individual Criminal Responsibility (Article 25). In Triffterer O (ed.) (1999) Commentary on the Rome Statute of the International Criminal Court, pp. 475-492; same author, Individual Criminal Responsibility in International Criminal Law: A Jurisprudential Analysis-From Nuremberg to The Hague. In McDonald G K, Swaak-Goldman O (eds.) (2000) Substantial and Procedural Aspects of International Criminal Law, vol. I, pp. 5-31; Eser A Individual Criminal Responsibility (Article 25). In Cassese A *et all* (eds.) (2000) The Rome Statute of the International Criminal Court: A Commentary pp. 767 et seq.

[22] *P. v. A. Musema*, Judgement and Sentence, Case no. ICTR- 96-13-T 27 January 2000, paras. 111-126.

[23] Para. 480, Id.

[24] Para. 481-483, Id.

[25] Para. 483, Id.

[26] For Penal Code of Rwanda, see, Decret-Loi Instituant Le Code Penal, Decree-Loi, No. 21/77 du 18 Aout 1977, Journal official de la Republique rwandaise, No. 13 *bis*, 1 Juillet 1998.

volves facilitating the commission of any act by being sympathetic thereto.[27] These separate definitions do not mean, however, that individual responsibility within the meaning of Article 6(1) of the ICTR Statute is only incurred if both forms of participation-aiding *and* abetting-have been realized; aiding *or* abetting is sufficient.[28] Aiding and abetting includes all acts of assistance by words or acts that lend encouragement or support, as long as the requisite intention is present.[29] Intangible assistance provided through moral support and encouragement could also qualify as aiding and abetting.[30] In *Tadic* it was held that the act in question must constitute a direct and substantial contribution to the commission of the crime.[31] Presence alone is not sufficient if it is an ignorant or unwilling presence; but knowing presence that has a direct and substantial effect on the commission of the illegal act can lead to a finding of participation and assignment of criminal culpability.[32] In *Furundzija* it was held that mere presence sufficed if it had "a significant legitimizing or encouraging effect on the principles".[33] With regard to participation, it is of importance to note that an accused may participate in the commission of crimes either through direct commission of an unlawful act or by omission, where he has a duty to act.[34] Summing up the case law of the ICTY and ICTR Ambos has submitted that aiding and abetting encompasses any assistance, physical or psychological, that has a substantial effect on the commission of the crime.[35]

The cardinal point in any system of coherent accountability is that anyone, or rather all, who commits serious human rights and international humanitarian law violations, should be held accountable for the commission of these criminal misdeeds. This irrespective of the position or rank of the individual. As advanced by Judge Pillay:

"The Statutes of the tribunal provides that individuals are not relieved of criminal responsibility for acting from official positions such as heads of state or government, or as superiors whose subordinates committed the acts, or as subordinates who acted under orders of a government or superior. From the perspective of deterrence of human rights violations it is as important, if not more important, to hold those in the highest levels of command responsible for the violations as it is to hold those who, acting under orders, commit the acts of violations. Ultimately, the understanding that every individual up and down the chain of

---

27 Para 484, ibid, Cf. "The Chamber is of the opinion that either aiding or abetting alone is sufficient to render the perpetrators criminally liable" at para. 484.

28 Ambos K (1999) Individual Criminal Responsibility, p. 482 and fn.37.

29 Para 689, *P. v. D. Tadic*, ibid.; P. *v. Z. Delalic, Z. Munic, H. Delic, E. Landzo (Celebici),* ICTY Case no: IT-96-21-T, 16 Nov. 1998, paras. 325-329; P. *v. Naletilic and Martinovic*, ICTY Case no: IT-98-34-T, 31 March 2003, para. 63.

30 Sliedregt V (2004) The Individual Criminal Responsibility of Individuals, p. 89.

31 *P. v. D. Tadic*, paras. 674, 688-692.

32 Paras. 689 & 692, Id.

33 *P. v. A. Furundzija*, ICTY Case no: IT-95-17/1-T, 10 Dec. 1998, paras. 190-233.

34 *P. v. A. Musema*, para. 123.

35 Ambos K Individual Criminal Responsibility, *Draft*, In Triffterer O (ed.), p. 14.

command will be held accountable will provide checks within the command structure on any attempt to violate international humanitarian law on any level."[36]

II. Profiling Perpetrators

As confirmed by a number of conflict situations, like those in Cambodia, Rwanda, East Timor, Sierra Leone, and Former Yugoslavia, it is common for such or similar situations to involve the participation of an arithmetically important number of perpetrators and accomplices. Those implicated include "the big, medium, and small fish". Proportionally, however, the vast majority are often "small fish" or low-level criminals. On the other hand, those responsible for the organization and planning of mass atrocities forming a much smaller crust of individuals at the top rung of the ladder. In the case of Rwanda, in 2003, the database of the Prosecutor General of Rwanda had a list of 571, 934 perpetrators.[37] The Rwanda Patriotic Army estimated that 2 million Rwandans participated one way or another (i.e. 30% of the country's population), in the 1994 atrocity crimes.[38] A question of choice and priority thus surfaces as to who should be the subject of national or international prosecution, and what prosecution strategy must be pursued in investigations and ultimately prosecution by international or mixed Tribunals.

For the 1994 events in Rwanda, the Security Council admitted that not all perpetrators could physically be accused before the ICTR, and that accountability had to be a shared responsibility with Rwanda, notwithstanding the primacy of jurisdiction of the former.[39] The ICTR on its own will not be able to take on the whole burden of prosecuting those responsible for the dreadful crimes.[40] That the Tribunal was to deal with principal perpetrators, the lesser ones to be handled by Rwandan authorities.[41] Furthermore all those individuals regardless of the community to which they belonged (i.e. Tutsi or Hutu) were to be brought before the Tribunal and judged if they had committed crimes against humanity or violated the most fundamental rules of war.[42] Individual were to be brought to justice regardless of their position in society.[43]

The Security Council foresaw that the ICTR would have easier access to those involved who were outside Rwanda, and thus it would be able to bring them to

---

36 Pillay N (1997) The Status of the International Criminal Tribunal for Rwanda, Conference paper, Securing State Cooperation and Compliance: The International Criminal Tribunal for Rwanda, Parliamentarians for Global Action, Cape Town, S. Africa, 24 February 1997, p. 4

37 Martin A Rwanda's Biggest Lesson from 1994 Genocide: Look After Yourself or Peril, The East African, 21-27 April 2003.

38 Rwanda: Enquete sur un genocide oblie, Le Monde, 1 avril 1998.

39 Statement of Rep. of France, p. 3; UK, p. 6, See Chapter 1.

40 Statement of Rep. of New Zealand, p. 6.

41 Statement of Rep. of New Zealand, p. 5.

42 Statement of the Rep. of France, p. 3, Rep. of USA, p. 18.

43 Statement of the Rep. of USA, p. 18.

justice in Arusha, than if Rwanda were to seek extradition. While these were meant to be indicators, it was left to the Prosecutor to determine the strategy to be adopted in fulfilling the mandate of the Security Council pursuant resolution 955 (1994). The presumption of the UN ad hoc Tribunals is that the leading perpetrators of the atrocity crimes will be prosecuted before those tribunals, whereas the middle and lower level perpetrators will be prosecuted either before competent domestic courts or handled through a non-judicial mechanism, such as a truth or reconciliation commission, set up at the national or local level.[44] It is in fact a matter of policy that international prosecutions should primarily be limited to leaders, policy makers, and senior executors.[45]

The first issue that needs to be addressed is determining who should be the main targets of prosecution. For the purpose of our analysis we define *profiling* to mean the process of determining, through indicators, the class or category of perpetrators that should be the subject of accountability. In so far as atrocity crimes are concerned such a process inevitably does not have genetic fingerprinting DNA accuracy of prediction. It is however, capable of offering structured parameters for identifying the plausible dens of perpetrators, and also suggesting avenues for the identification of individual suspects of significance. One word of caution; each situation engulfed by atrocity crimes is unique, and must be approached as such. Each event that culminates in egregious atrocities has its own smoking gun. There is, however, a possibility to reasonably match situations, through lessons learnt. This is what this chapter discusses.

A Prosecutor is required to be selective in bringing cases and, in principle, the most important cases are those which involve a consideration of factors such as the nature and seriousness of the crimes, the military or para-military rank or government position of an alleged perpetrator, the significance of legal issues involved in the case, the prospect of arresting the suspect, and the impact of the case on the resources of the office.[46] Various appellations have been employed to describe those who should be the key subject of accountability. It has been submitted that the priority of prosecutions should be the masterminds[47], arch criminals[48], top echelons[49], ringleaders,[50] supreme commanders, or high-ranking persons.[51]

---

44 Scheffer D J (2003) p. 418.

45 Bassiouni M C (1999) International Criminal Law, p. 23.

46 Bergsmo M, Cisse C, Stacker C The Prosecutors of the International Tribunals: The Case of the Nuremberg and Tokyo Tribunals, the ICTY and ICTR, and the ICC Compared. In Arbour L, Eser A, Ambos K, Sanders A (eds.) (2000) The Prosecutor of a Permanent International Criminal Court Max Planck Institute of Foreign and International Criminal Law, Freiburg im Breisgau, p. 68.

47 International Crisis Group, The Rwanda Tribunal: Justice Delayed, Recommendation No: 1 www.crisiweb.org /about/030/. Cfm.

48 Neier A (1999) Rethinking Truth, Justice and Guilt after Bosnia and Rwanda, in Human Rights in Political Transitions: Gettysburg to Bosnia, Zone Books, N.Y, pp 48-49.

49 Separate Opinion of Judge Sidhwa on the Defence Motion for Interlocutory Appeal on Jurisdiction, Case no: IICTY-94-1-AR72, 2 October 1995, para. 63.

In accounting for atrocity crimes by international tribunals, there are very valid reasons for the targeting of such individuals, and not each and every Tom, Dick or Harry-type perpetrator. Those who bear the greatest responsibility must be brought to trial for the sake of the victims, for having violated the moral order of the human race by attempting to destroy one of its members, and because of the political imperative that those responsible for the genocide should be punished.[52] For Pierre Prosper, US Ambassador-at-Large for War Crime Issues in the Bush Administration, it is essential to hold those in leadership positions accountable because they had an additional duty to prevent the commission of such crimes.[53] This also seem to be the official position of western governments. Criminal trials target a limited number of those with the highest level of guilt in that they deliberately implicated thousands of others in their egregious crimes.[54] It is also a demonstration to arch criminals that the most fundamental rules that make a civilized society may not be flouted with impunity.[55]

The essential reasons why the pursuit of those with greatest responsibility must be the priority of priorities, of international prosecuting authorities, include that of vindicating the victims and the law, and the discovery of the truth on the organization and planning of the campaign of violence, that underlie most atrocity crimes. Post atrocity denial, especially by leaders, is also a factor that makes the trial of those with the greatest responsibility an accountability imperative. Gerard Prunier classifies perpetrators of the Rwandan atrocity crimes into two groups; *the organizers* or those who actually carried out the organization of murder squads, distributed weapons, and who gave or relayed instructions at a high level, and *the killers* or the gun-and-machete totting actual killers, from entities such as the Presidential Guard, Military and Gendarmerie, and ordinary peasants.[56] He considers that 100 men locked up the whole nation into an airless sadomasochistic inferno.[57] On his part, Alain Destexhe suggests four levels of responsibility, namely, (a) those who instigated the genocide plot, (b) the level of administrative hierarchy, (c) those who profited from the climate of violence and apparent immunity to carry out particularly sadistic and odious acts, and (d) the thousands who represented the majority of the guilty, but who killed out of fear because they were ordered, or caught up in a situation of collective murder created by authorities. [58]

Our entry point on profiling the prime targets of international accountability is the serious debate that arose when consideration was being given by the Security

---

50 Sok An (2003) The Proceedings for the Trial of Senior Khmer Rouge Leaders, Paper presented at the Conference on The Rule of Law and Legacy of Conflict, USA-U.N. Association, Gabarone, Botswana, 16-19 January 2003, p. 2.

51 Forth Annual Report of the ICTR to the General Assembly of the United Nations for the period 1 July 1998 – 30 June 1999, at www.ictr.org, para. 27.

52 Destexhe A (1995) pp. 64-65.

53 Interview with Author, Washington D.C, 6 March 2003.

54 Neier A (1999) p. 51.

55 pp. 48-49, Id.

56 Prunier G (1997)p. 236.

57 P. 355, Id.

58 Destexhe A (1995) p. 65-66.

Council to the establishment of the Special Court for Sierra Leone. At that occasion the Secretary-General proposed the use of the more general term persons "*most responsible*", to designate the choice of persons that would be the subject of the Court's personal jurisdiction.[59] He was of the view that this would include the political or military leadership and others in command authority down the chain of command, judging by the severity of the crime or its massive scale. "Most responsible" denoted either a leadership or authority position of the accused, and a sense of gravity, seriousness or massive scale of the crime.[60] For the Secretary General that term would not necessarily exclude children between 15 and 18 years of age. He considered that while it is inconceivable that children could be in a political or military leadership position (although in Sierra Leone the rank of "Brigadier" was often granted to children as young as 11 years of age), the gravity and seriousness of the crimes they have allegedly committed would allow for their inclusion within the jurisdiction of the Court.[61] In proposing the use of the term "most responsible", the Secretary General was mindful that it be seen not as a test criterion or a distinct international threshold, but as guidance to the Prosecutor in the adoption of a prosecution strategy and in making decisions to prosecute individual cases.[62]

In that particular context the Council did not uphold the use of the Secretary General's term "most responsible". In Security Council resolution 1315 (2000), the Council recommended that the Court's personal jurisdiction should extend to those who bear "the greatest responsibility". This was understood as an indication of a limitation on the number by reference to their command authority and the gravity and scale of the crime.[63] Primarily it included those in political and military leadership positions, and others in command authority singled out by the gravity of the crime committed, or its massive scale or heinous nature.[64] Of course it was also recognized, that the specific determination of those who bear the greatest responsibility was finally a matter of prosecutorial discretion.[65] David Scheffer, then US Ambassador-at-Large for War Crime Issues in the Clinton Administration, considers that the Council insisted on that terminology (i.e."*greatest responsibility*") for three reasons; namely, to lay down an objective standard with respect to targeting of individuals for accountability, to purposely set a threshold that would 'knock out' minors since it was unlikely that they would meet that standard, and to ensure that the Court would hold accountable up to two dozen indictees,

59 Report of the Secretary General on the establishment of a Special Court for Sierra Leone, UN Doc. S/2000/915, 4 October 2000, para. 29.

60 Para. 30, Id.

61 Para. 31, "In view of the most horrific aspects of the child combatancy in Sierra Leone, the employment of this term (i.e "*the greatest responsibility*") would not necessarily exclude persons of young age from the jurisdiction of the Court"), at para. 36, Id.

62 Para. 30, Id.

63 Para. 29, Id.

64 Report of the Planning Mission on the Establishment of the Special Court for Sierra Leone, UN Doc. S/2002/246, 8 March 2002, para. 28.

65 Para. 28, Id.

thus containing financial costs.[66] As understood the reasoning behind that Court's limited number of eventual prosecution targets was twofold: the Court was specially designed to prosecute those few individuals who were in key positions of authority and power, and that it should complete its work quickly so that Sierra Leone can put its past behind it.[67]

Article 1 of the Agreement between the UN and the Government of Sierra Leone thus provides that the establishment of the Special Court is to prosecute persons who bear the "greatest responsibility" for serious violations of international humanitarian law, and Sierra Leonean law, committed in the territory of Sierra Leone. Article 1 (Competence) of the Court's Statute also provides in exact words the same, but adds that those to be prosecuted include leaders who, in committing such crimes, have threatened the establishment of and implementation of the peace process in Sierra Leone. Additionally Article 15 specifically tasks the Prosecutor with responsibility for the investigation and prosecution of persons who bear the "*greatest responsibility*". It should be noted that the Court's jurisdiction also covers peacekeepers, the primacy of jurisdiction of which rests with sending states,[68] and juveniles, under a special regime.

In Sierra Leone more than in any other conflict children had been used as child combatants. Of 47,000 combatants demobilized by United Nations Mission in Sierra Leone (UNAMSIL) almost 7,000 were child soldiers.[69] Initially abducted, forcibly recruited, sexually abused, reduced to slavery of all kinds, they were then trained, often under the influence of drugs, to kill, main and burn.[70] They had been transformed from victims into perpetrators through a process of psychological and physical abuse.[71] Article 7 of the Statute provides that the Court has no jurisdiction over any person under the age of 15 years at the time of the commission of the crimes, and persons who were between 15 and 18 years old at the time of alleged commission should be treated with dignity and a sense of worth, taking into account their young age, the desirability of rehabilitation, reintegration into and assumption of a constructive role in society in accordance with international human rights; in particular the rights of the child.[72]

In balancing the interests of judicial accountability for child combatants presumed responsible for crimes, and those of child care and rehabilitation, the Statute provides in Article 15, paragraph 5, that in the prosecution of juvenile offenders, the Prosecutor shall ensure that the child rehabilitation programme is not placed at risk, and that where appropriate, resort should be had to alternative truth and reconciliation mechanisms. Other provisions of the Statute also contain internationally recognized standards of juvenile justice, including the exclusion of im-

---

66 Interview with Author, New York, 5 March 2003.

67 The Special Court for Sierra Leone: Promises and Pitfalls of a "New Model", p. 3 and fn.17, International Crisis Group, 4 August 2003, www.intl-crisis-group. org.

68 Article 1 (2) & 3, Statute.

69 Adhoc Working Group on Conflict Prevention and Resolution in Africa, The situation in Africa, UN Doc. S/PV. 4577, 18 July 2002, p. 15.

70 Para 32, Id.

71 Para. 32, Id.

72 Article 7 (1), Id.

prisonment in the case of a juvenile offender, possibility for alternative options of a correctional or educational nature, as well as judicial and non-judicial guarantees.[73]

Rwanda

A practical attempt at a combined profiling of suspects responsible for atrocity crimes is the Rwanda Organic Law on the organization of prosecutions constituting the crimes of Genocide or War Crimes committed since 1 October 1990.[74] The law promulgated to deal with an astronomical number of perpetrators and accomplices, is a specially adopted measure intended at satisfy the need for justice, and to eradicate forever the culture of impunity that had reigned in Rwanda for decades.[75] The purpose of the law is the organization of criminal proceedings against persons accused of having, between 1 January 1990 and 31 December 1994, committed genocide or crimes against humanity.[76] The application of that Organic Law is in conjunction with the Penal Code of Rwanda.[77]

The Rwandan Organic Law on genocide and crimes against humanity groups alleged suspects into four categories.[78]

In Category 1 are:

(a) persons whose criminal acts or whose acts of criminal participation place them among the planners, organizers, instigators, supervisors, and leaders of the crimes of genocide or of crimes against humanity
(b) persons who acted in positions of authority at the national, prefectoral, communal, sector, or cell level, or in a political party, the army, religious organizations or in a militia and who perpetrated or fostered such crimes
(c) notorious murderers who by virtue of the zeal or excessive malice with which they committed atrocities, distinguished themselves in their areas of residence or where they passed
(d) persons who committed acts of sexual torture

In Category 2 are persons whose criminal acts or whose acts of criminal participation place them among perpetrators, conspirators or accomplices of intentional homicide or of serious assault against the person, causing death. For the purpose of this law an accomplice is defined as a person who provided essential assistance in the commission of the offence, or who by any means diverted criminal prosecution of persons in the categories referred in the organic law, or who failed to give information about them.[79] Category 3 consists of persons whose criminal

[73] See, Articles 7 (2), 15 (5) & 19.
[74] Organic Law No. 08/96, Official Gazette of the Republic of Rwanda, 35 Year, No.17, 1 Sept. 1996(hereinafter referred to as Organic Law on genocide), 30 August 1996.
[75] Preamble, Organic Law on Genocide, Id.
[76] Article 1, Id.
[77] Article 1, Id.
[78] Chapter II, Categorization, Article 2, Id.
[79] Art 3, Id.

acts or whose acts of criminal participation make them guilty of other serious assaults against the person, and in Category 4 are those individuals who committed offence against property. The law also prescribed penalties according to this categorization. Persons whose acts place them in Category I are liable to the death penalty.[80], For those in Category 2, the death penalty is replaced by life imprisonment. Those whose confession and guilty plea have been accepted by the Court to a range of imprisonment, [81] and those in Category 4 the penalty foreseen is only civil damages.

Pursuant to the Organic Law on Genocide, a list of Category I persons, containing the names of 1,940 suspects was issued by the Prosecutor General of the Supreme Court, on 25 November 1996.[82] As required under Article 9 of the Organic Law on Genocide, a revised list containing 2,133 names of persons in that Category was published on 31 December 1999[83]. A further updated list containing the names of 2,898 suspects and accused was issued on 19 March 2001.[84] The lists contain the names of those considered most responsible at the national, prefectoral, communal, and cell levels. Of the total number of suspects named in Category I, 110 are classed at the national level, and the rest at the Prefecture, Commune or Sector levels, or are suspects under the jurisdiction of military courts.

If one is to interpret the lists as containing an indication of those with the 'greatest responsibility' or 'most responsible', then it is of interest to note the professional background of those deemed accountable. Persons in Category I include Theodore Sindikubabwo, the former President of the April 9th 1994 Interim Government of Rwanda, who is presumed dead; Cabinet ministers, the Chiefs of Staff and Commanders of the Rwandan Armed Forces and the Gendarmerie, founders and leaders of political parties, Prefets, sub Prefets, Bourgmestres, municipal counsellors, cell leaders, servants, journalists, radio broadcasters, doctors, nurses, bishops, priests, teachers, mechanics, drivers, cultivators, carpenters, traders, businessmen, masons, interahamwe and impuzamugambe militia, magistrates, advocates, traders, school inspectors, tailors, barbers, accountants, watchmen, and messengers. This wide range of perpetrators is particular to the Rwandan atrocity crimes, in that the legal characterization of those in Category I include not only planners and organizers at the national level, but also those possessing authority at the prefectoral, communal and cell level, as well as notorious murderers, and the accused who committed acts of sexual torture. This classification is Rwanda specific. It is reflective of the widespread and territory-wide commission of atrocities,

80 Article 14 (a), Id.; The death penalty is also provided for in Article 26, Penal Code of Rwanda.

81 Articles 15 and 16, Organic Law on Genocide.

82 Publication of the List no.1 of the first category prescribed by article 9 of the organic law no 8/96 of 30 August 1996, Official Gazette of the Republic of Rwanda, 30 November 1996.

83 Publication of Updated List of the First Category prescribed by Article 9 of Organic Law No. 8/96 of 30 August 1996, Official Gazette of the Republic of Rwanda, 31 December 1999.

84 Updated List of the First Category prescribed by Article 9 of Organic Law No. 8/96 of 30 August 1996, Official Gazette of the Republic of Rwanda, 19 March 2001.

the cross- sectoral and extensive participation of the populace, and the need to include those who committed acts of sexual violence, in particular rape and sexual slavery.

Rwandan authorities recognized that the existing system of administration of justice would not be able to prosecute all those who should be prosecuted, and thus opted for such a categorization of offences and offenders.[85] It was a policy decision that took into account the complexity of the situation in which there was a high degree, indeed a very high degree, of criminal participation by the population. It also took into consideration the overwhelming size of the detention caseload. The acuteness of the problem was mirrored in this situation:[86]

In August 1994, authorities were arresting 800 suspects a day. By January 2003, Rwanda's 18 central prisons had 120,000 inmates-five times the capacity they were built for. Eighty percent of the inmates were incarcerated for involvement in the 1994 genocide (4-5 persons per square meter). In 1994 there were 14 central prisons and 230 dungeons (*cachot*). In Gitarama and Kibungo Central prisons overcrowding was so acute that 350 people were sharing one latrine. Kibuye prisons established to house 60 inmates had 2, 400 inmates on the day it closed; Kigali built for 2,000 held in April 2003 6,000 inmates.

By 1995 some 115,000 suspects had been detained by Rwandan authorities in fourteen prisons built to accommodate 11,500 detainees.[87] By 31 December 2002, that number had almost remained the same. In February 2003, by Presidential Decree, some 40,000 genocide suspects were provisionally released into re-education camps, decongesting prisons.[88] Of these, 22,000 were further released to their homes in May 2003.[89] Even with these positive human rights developments, around 80,000 genocide suspects remain in prisons, some detained without trial for eight years.[90]

Full trial of 90,000 defendants-more than one per cent of the total population-would not be feasible in even the wealthiest nation, and is emphatically not an option in Rwanda.[91] If the same atrocity crimes would have been committed in western democracies, it would have meant putting on trial 29 million suspects in USA, 8 million in Germany, and 6 million each in France and the United Kingdom. In order to accelerate and deal with the accountability of Category II and perpetrators

---

85 Rudasingwa T (1998) The Rwanda Tribunal and Its Relationship to National Trials in Rwanda, vol. 13, Am. U. Int'l L. Rev., p. 1486.

86 Rwanda Aims to Close Overpopulated Prisons by Year-End, The East African, April 28- May 4, 2003.

87 La Commission Governemental D'Information (CGI), Information generale et utile pour connaitre le Rwanda (Avec quelque chiffres et statistique), Kigali, 20 mars 1998, p. 8.

88 Building a New Foundation Through Democracy and Reconciliation', The East Africa, April 28-May 4, 2003.

89 Thousands of Genocide Suspects Released from Solidarity Camps, Hirondelle News Agency (Lausanne), 6 May 2003.

90 Id.

91 Morris M (1999) The Trials of Concurrent Jurisdiction: The Case of Rwanda, p. 7, American Diplomacy, at www.unc.edu/depts/diplomat/amdipl_6/morris.html.

at categories III and IV, Gacaca courts were introduced and set up in Rwanda. Gacaca (literary meaning "justice on the grass") Courts, estimated to hear cases of around 100,000 suspects, were inaugurated on 18 June 2002. The Courts involve extra judicial mediation, and re-integrative shaming under a restorative justice paradigm.[92] Gacaca needs to be seen as an instrument of reconciliation, an effective instrument of social cohesion, a form of consensual justice that brings people together to participate in the process of administration of justice with a view not only to facilitating reconciliation, but also alleviating the burden on the judicial system.[93] Much as gacaca's objectives are genuine, its application to complex and emotionally charged cases of genocide requires utmost care in ensuring the human rights of those concerned, fairness, integrity and impartiality of the tribunal members, particularly in relation to persons charged with crimes falling under Category II, who may be liable to receive a prison sentence of life, or in cases where a confession has been made, between 12 and 15 years.[94] The dualist nature of Rwandan society and widespread level of public participation calls for an accountability for genocide and deterrence of future inter-ethnic violence through effective restorative justice initiatives as opposed to retributive justice of the criminal trial.[95] Restorative justice initiatives, which emphasize the need for atonement, shamming and reintegration, might be well suited for such dualist post genocide societies.[96]

East Timor

Comparing the above with the atrocity crimes committed in East Timor, the Report of the Indonesian Commission of Investigation into Human Rights Violations in East Timor (KPP-HAM) identified three main categories of perpetrators as being those responsible for the crimes.[97] The *first* group was that which directly committed the crimes. It included militiamen and members of the Indonesian Armed Forces and the Indonesian Police. The *second* group comprised those who ran the field operations in the civil administration including the former Governor, the Bupati (i.e. District Administrators), local military and police officials. The *third* group consisted of those who held responsibility for superior policy, including high-level military officials who were involved and knew about the reign of violence, but failed to do anything to prevent it. It is of interest to note the pattern of violence, since this is also a beacon that can indicate accomplices involved in

---

92 Drumble M A (2000) Punishment, Post genocide: From Guilt to Shame to Civis in Rwanda, vol. 75, II, Yale Law Journal, p. 1226.

93 Report on the Human rights situation in Rwanda, submitted by the Special Representative, UN Doc. E/CN.4/1999/33, January 1999, para. 50.

94 Para. 51, Id.

95 Drumble M A (2000) p. 1323.

96 P. 1323, Id.

97 Report of the Indonesian Commission of Investigation into Human Rights Violations in East Timor, referred to as KPP-HAM Report), para.56 and 72, 31 January 2000; The report can be found at www.jsmp. minihub.org/Resources.htmmh.com.au/news/0104/29/etimor02.htm.

the commission of atrocity crimes. The KPP-HAM Report had concluded that civil authorities and the military, including the police, worked in cooperation with the militias to create conditions that supported crimes against humanity, and which were carried out by the civil authorities, the military, the police, and the militias.[98]

The KPP-HAM Report named 32 persons among whom were the former Governor of East Timor, Abilio Soares; five Bupati (Dili, Covalima, Liquica, Bobonaro and Las Palos); the Head of the Special Team/Adjutant General's Task Force for the Implementation of the Popular Consultation in East Timor, Major General Zacky Anwar Makarim; the Commander of the Regional Military Command IX, Udayana (Bali, East and West Nusa Tenggara and East Timor), Major General Adam Damiri; the Commanders of the Sub Regional Military Command 164 (East Timor), Brigadier General Suhartono (Tono) Suratman and Colonel Mohamed Noer Muis; the Chief of Police of East Timor, Brigadier General Timbul Silaen; 4 District Military Commanders (Bobonaro, Covalima, Dili, and Los Palos); the Commanders of Battalion 744 based in Dili, and Battalion 745 based in Los Palos; a number of sub district military Commanders and KOPASSUS/Intelligence Officers; the Commanders of 5 militia groups, *Aitarak*, *Laksaur*, *Tim Alfa*, *Besi Merah Putih*, and *Halilintir*, and 3 the *Tim Alfa* Militiamen.[99]

This selection of suspects was the outcome of the Commission's examination of the "primary cases" from which it sought information and evidence. These cases included the massacre at Liquica Church on 6 April 1999; the murder of Kailako villagers in Maliana in April; the attack on the home of Manuel Carrascalao on 17 April, immediately after the militia rally in front of the ex Governors' office commemorating Eurico Guterres's nomination of Commander of *Aitarak* militia; the attack on the Dili Diocese on 5 September 1999; the attack on Bishop Carlos Belo's compound in Dili on 6 September; the 4-8 September massive destructions and killings in Maliana; the Suai Church massacre of 6 September; the murder of a Dutch Journalist, Sander Thoenes in Dili on 21 September; the killings of members of the clergy in Los Palos on 25 September; and acts of violence against women.[100]

While the list involves a representative sampling of individuals from the civil administration, the military, the police and the militia, it does not by its composition suggest that enough consideration was given to identifying those with the greatest responsibility. It was restrained by the choice of the areas subject to the Commission's investigation. In any event the names cited represented an initial group of persons from the three categories of perpetrators whom the Commission suspected had been involved in serious human rights and international humanitarian law violations in East Timor

By way of contrast an examination of the profile of suspects named by the Attorney General of Indonesia, for serious human rights and international humanitarian law abuses that occurred in East Timor in 1999, shows the importance accorded to rank in the case of military Commanders, and to the function and posi-

---

98 KPP-HAM Report, para. 63, Id.

99 KPP-HAM Report, para. 73, Id.

100 KPP-HAM Report, paras. 32-51, Id.

tion of the individual in the case of civilians, for targeting those to be held accountable. With regard to profiling, the Attorney General of Indonesia made a further pruning of the suspects earlier named in the KPP-HAM Report. First, in January 2000, he named 21 persons as those he would investigate further and prosecute. This list dropped to 18 when criminal proceedings under the Human Rights Court Act were instituted at the Central Jakarta District Court in March 2002. It would appear that targeting choice was accorded to rank in the case of Commanders, and to position in the case of civilians. Left out were others; top militia Commanders, and most important the Commander in Chief of the Indonesian Armed Forces and Minister of Defence during the 1999 East Timor events, General Wiranto. The KPP-HAM Report had opined that:

"All crimes against humanity in East Timor, directly or indirectly occurred because of the failure of the Armed Forces Commander to guarantee security during the implementation of the announcement of the two options by the government. The police structure, which, at that time, was still under the command of the Defense Ministry, had already weakened the ability of the police force to carry out its security duties based on the New York Agreements. In view of this, Armed Forces General Wiranto as Armed Forces Commander is the party that must be asked to bear responsibility".[101]

On 22 February 2002 Prosecutors indicted General Wiranto for crimes against humanity, before the Special Panel for Serious Crimes of the Dili District Court. In Indonesia, the closest gesture of accountability was his questioning for seven hours by Prosecutors at the Attorney General's Office in May 2000.[102] With the end of the ad Hoc Human Rights Court process it is certain that he has eluded accountability in Indonesia, although he still stands accused in East Timor.

UN ad hoc Tribunals

The experience of the ICTY demonstrates that a coherent strategy to indict those with the greatest responsibility ("the big fish") was developed over time, and that its initial indictments contained more low-level perpetrators than those netted within a similar time period by the ICTR. Dusko Tadic, one of the former Tribunal's first indictees, was only "a small pawn" in the Bosnian Serb forces.[103] He had no official rank. Drazen Erdermovic, the first accused to plead guilty before that Tribunal, was a minor figure and a foot soldier although implicated in the killing of around 70 civilians at Srebrenica.[104] As observed by Judge Wald, the early indictments were notable for their vagueness, not to mention the relative insignifi-

---

101 KPP-HAM Report, para. 75, Id.

102 Former Indonesian Military Chief grilled over Timor Violence, Agence France Press, 16 May 2000.

103 Bass G J (2000) Stay the Hand of Vengeance. The Politics of the War Crimes Tribunals, Princeton University Press, N.J, p. 206.

104 Scharf M P (1997) Balkan Justice. The Story Behind the First International War crimes Trial since Nuremberg, Carolina Academic Press, Durham, N. Carolina, p. 85.

cance of those who were indicted.[105] The urge it had in its infancy to immediately issue indictments led to the focusing of investigations on the Prijedor region of the former Yugoslavia. This proved to be resource-intensive, and interfered with the efforts to conceive a throughout prosecution strategy from the outset. [106] Apart from accountability for sexual violence that had been committed at Foca, the ICTY decided not to prioritize theme cases or give priority to the didactic purposes of prosecution.[107] The reason behind this decision was mainly to avoid being perceived as "political" or to present "show trials".[108] The prosecutions that took place on the sexual violence at Foca were only levied against middle level officials and not senior officials who had directed the sexual assault policy as a weapon in the conflict in the Former Yugoslavia.[109]

Arbour dropped indictments against seventeen accused, at ICTY, for lack of sufficient evidence to obtain a conviction,[110] as well as the marginal position of the accused. Some of these earlier cases had rested on a small number of witnesses and were in fact unlikely to hold in Court.[111] The strategy of holding accountable lower-level perpetrators also swamped the Tribunal with minor cases and created a backlog of relatively petty defendants waiting trial.

Goldstone, the ICTY's first Prosecutor however justified the indictment of "small fish". His saw the prosecution strategy as including the investigation of lower level perpetrators directly involved in carrying out the crimes in order to build effective cases against the military and civilian leaders who were party to the overall planning and organization of those crimes.[112] Not all agreed. In an *in camera* meeting between Judges of the ICTY and the Prosecutor held on 20 January 1995, this 'pyramid strategy' in which investigations first targeted lower-level targets, and then gradually moved up to military commanders and political and military leaders was unanimously considered by all the Judges, from both civil law and common law tradition, to be flawed, because in their view, the role of the Tribunal was to immediately target the military and political leaders or the high-ranking commanders, based on the notion of command responsibility as laid down in Article 7 (3) of the Statute.[113] They insisted upon the Prosecutor to disregard minor perpetrators and, instead concentrate on the leaders or at least those who planned and ordered atrocities, including the top brass of the states and other par-

---

[105] Wald P M (2002) General Radislav Krstic: A War Crimes Case Study, Thomas F. Ryan Lecture, Georgetown University Law Centre, Washington D.C, 6 November 2002, fn. 15.

[106] Schrag M (2003) Lessons Learnt from ICTY Experience, Expert Consultation process on general issues relevant to the ICC Office of the Prosecutor, The Hague., www.icc-cpi.org.

[107] Id.

[108] Id.

[109] Id.

[110] Bass G J (2000) p. 233.

[111] Pp. 206, 233, Id.

[112] Scharf M P (1997) Balkan Justice, p. 85.

[113] Cassese A (2004) The Crucial Years, Journal of International Criminal Law vol. 2 p. 586-587.

ties to conflict, and those who masterminded large- scale crimes, but may perhaps not have directly killed anyone.[114]

For Cassese, former President of the ICTY this intervention was not contrary to judicial ethics or propriety as the judges who had acted collectively were the only body that could reorient prosecutorial action so as to keep it within the Statute's explicit or implied objectives, and that as long as they did not interfere with or make any pronouncement upon specific cases, their action was warranted.[115] It was only in 1996 when Arbour assumed office as Prosecutor that indictments against lower-level perpetrators were withdrawn, and the investigation strategy re-designed to focus systematically on the higher level echelons of leadership as the main targets of accountability.[116]

In Rwanda, when the Office of the Prosecutor commenced field investigations around May 1995 there was no strategy or a corresponding investigation plan. An in-house analysis of information that had been gathered or made available from a number of sources, including UNAMIR and Human Rights organizations, pin-pointed Kibuye Prefecture as one of the Prefectures where a large number of atrocities had been committed. A small team of investigators was deployed to Kibuye, and the Office of the Prosecutor's first official witness statement was taken. It is also worth mentioning that part of the initial drive to obtain investigation results was the pressure exerted upon investigators to come up with an indictment before the first anniversary of the establishment of the ICTR by the Security Council. As mentioned earlier, this indictment against 8 accused was confirmed on 28 November 1995 and contained allegations of atrocity crimes committed at a number of massacre sites in Kibuye.

Apart from the Kibuye investigations that commenced in the second half of 1995, the early strategy of the Office of the Prosecutor was to investigate in all communes of Rwanda in order to indict lower level perpetrators, and gradually move towards those with higher responsibility, such as Bourgmestres and Prefets. This copied the ICTY approach. Given the widespread and geographic character of the atrocities such a horizontal investigation plan was not sustainable due to the limited human and material resources available, as well as lack of experienced investigators. A number of investigation teams were organized along these lines. Investigators were also assigned to Prefectures to investigate named suspects. The Butare team was charged to investigate in Butare, and the Cyangugu team investigated in Cyangugu. This proved too laborious, and insufficient staffing meant that investigations into other Prefectures where atrocities had taken place, for example such as Gikongoro, could not be simultaneously carried out. Another factor that disturbed the focus of investigations was the arrest by other states, of suspects on the basis of requests for warrants of arrests and extradition made by Rwandan au-

[114] Pp. 586-587, 595, Id.

[115] Pp. 587-588; Cf. "One feature of the early days at the ICTY was the involvement of Judges in the work and policies of the Prosecutor", Goldstone R (2004) A view from the Prosecution, Journal of International Criminal Law vol. 2: 380 -384.

[116] Arbour L, (2004) The Crucial Years, Journal of International Criminal Law vol. 2 p. 198.

thorities. These suspects ended up at the ICTR following the refusal of some states, like Cameroon and Burkina Faso, to transfer such persons to Rwanda because of the application of the death sentence there, and for fear of that they might not receive a fair trial.

By way of comparison, at the ICTY the first investigations focused on atrocities that took place at five concentration camps, the Sucica camp (in eastern Bosnia), and the Omarska Camp, the Trnopolje camp, the Keratern camp, and the Luka camp in northern Bosnia; six Bosnian- Croatian cities (Bosnaski Samac in north-eastern Bosnia; Sarajevo, and Stupni, Do in central Bosnia; Srebrenica in East Bosnia; and Zagreb and Vukovar in Croatia), and two other areas (the Prijedor district in northern Bosnia and the Lasva valley in Central Bosnia.[117] The result by 1977 was that 75 indictments had been issued against 55 Serbs, 17 Croats, and 3 Muslims.[118]

On the targets of accountability in the first year of ICTR's operation (i.e. 1975), the Tribunals Annual Report to the General Assembly reported: [119]

> "Ever since the Tribunal was established the Prosecutor has made it clear that his strategy would be patterned on that of the Office of the Prosecutor for the International Criminal Tribunal for the Former Yugoslavia, and would give priority to investigations and prosecuting individuals who had held *important responsibilities* in the events which occurred in Rwanda in 1994. Given the financial and human resources available to it, the Office of the Prosecutor had no choice but to concentrate its efforts on individuals who had been in positions of responsibility". *[Emphasis added*]

"Important responsibilities" was not interpreted as the equivalent of "greatest responsibilities", and the ICTR's original arrestees and indictees included a number of lower level perpetrators. Among them were a communal counsellor, and even an accused that the Prosecutor's Office did not know whether he had occupied any official status or position, de jure or de facto at the time he committed the alleged offences. It should be added that there was also a conscious choice made to indict notorious perpetrators who committed heinous acts, as well as sexual violence, irrespective of the authority or position of the individual. *The pursuit of those with leadership responsibility is possible without recourse to lower level perpetrators as an inevitable stepping-stone to reach those with the greatest responsibility.* Analyzing the pattern of atrocity crimes, ante-natal investigations of events leading up to atrocities, an inquiry into the policies, pronouncements, and practices of Governmental authorities and other entities implicated, an examination of the participation of individuals in charge of the organs of the State, of the Government, including the military, the police, paramilitary groups, and the civil administration; plotting the contours of de jure and de facto responsibility of those in alleged positions of authority from warring parties and factions may well indicate to those with the higher responsibility.

---

[117] Scharf M P (1997) Balkan Justice, p. 85.

[118] P. 85, Id.

[119] First Annual Report of ICTR, Adopted by the General Assembly on 10 December 1996, UN Doc. 96-25167(E), p. 47.

It was much later that the ICTR focused on higher level targets; those who were in authority or in key political, administrative and military positions, as well as those involved in planning the atrocities or amplifying it through propaganda.[120] The major thrust by the Office of the Prosecutor on accountability for those with leadership responsibility was made from May 1997, following the belief by that office that the existence of a conspiracy to commit genocide was conceived much earlier than 1994. The ICTR's Fourth Annual Report to the General Assembly presented the strategy as thus:[121]

"This strategy is twofold: first, the targeting of investigations exclusively on persons who occupied positions of authority at the time of the genocide, more specifically, those who conspired to commit genocide, and secondly, the joinder of crimes in one indictment to reflect the various areas where such joinder applied at the level of the nation and prefectures. This "conspiracy theory" was given concrete expression by the joinder of accused, the arrest of key persons who were in power before and during the genocide and finally, by the guilty plea of Jean Kambanda and Omar Serushago."

It was subsequent to this conspiracy theory, of the prosecution, that many of those alleged to have had prime responsibility for atrocity crimes were indicted. Annex A provides a summary of the positions, ranks, or status of accused persons before the ICTR as of 31 December 2004. Those held accountable included the former Prime Minister of Rwanda, Cabinet Ministers, top leaders of political parties, the Chief of Staff of the Rwandan Armed Forces, the Chief of Staff of the Gendarmerie, various Battalion Commanders, Prefets, Bourgmesters, those directing the media (radio and press), heads of religious congregations, members of the liberal profession, businessmen, traders, and militiamen.

In relation to the Completion Strategy of ICTY, which foresees the completion of investigations by the end of 2004 and all trial activities at the first instance by the end of 2008 and all their work by 2010, the Security Council in endorsing such a strategy, called upon the Tribunal to concentrate on the prosecution and trial of "the most senior leaders suspected of being most responsible" for crimes within its jurisdiction.[122] It further specifically called for the transfer, to competent national jurisdictions, of cases involving intermediate and lower rank accused.[123] It emphasized that ICTY should concentrate in the prosecution of the civilian, military and paramilitary leaders suspected of being responsible for serious international humanitarian law violations committed in the former Yugoslavia since 1991 rather than on "minor actors".[124] When the Council on 28 August 2003 decided that each of the two UN ad hoc Tribunals should have its own separate Prosecutor, it reiter-

---

[120] Pillay N (1998) The Rwanda Tribunal and Its Relationship to National Trials in Rwanda, Am. J. Int'l Rev., vol.13, p. 1473.

[121] Fourth Annual Report of ICTR to the General Assembly and the Security Council, UN Doc. A/54/315, S/1999/943, 7 September 1999, para. 47.

[122] Statement by the President of the Security Council, UN Doc. S/PRST/2002/21, 23 July 2002; UN SC resolution1505 (2003), 28 August 2003, UN Doc. S/RES/1503 (2003).

[123] Id.

[124] Statement of the President of the Security Council, Id.

ated the same and called upon ICTR to follow suit. This was considered to be the best way in practice for the Tribunals to complete all trial activities at first instance by 2008, and to wind up all work by 2010.

To accomplish its Completion Strategy, the ICTR on its part has developed criteria that should enable it to determine the most senior leaders for the purposes of accountability. That choice would be made on the basis of, (a) the alleged status and extent of participation of the individual, (b) the alleged connection an individual may have with the other cases, (c) the need to cover the major geographical areas of Rwanda in which crimes were committed, (d) the availability of evidence with regard to that individual, (e) the concrete prospect of arresting the individual, and (f) the availability of investigative material for transmission to a state for national prosecution.[125]

An examination of the profile of accused indicted by the ICTR demonstrates that it is holding accountable all three level of accused mentioned earlier, namely, minor, intermediate, and those with the highest responsibility for the 1994 atrocity crimes. Such profiling has led to a criticism by Rwanda that the ICTR has indicted accused that in the first place should not be in Arusha. Furthermore, that it had not fully concentrated on those with the greatest responsibility. Judge Eric Mose, the President of the Tribunal, is also "not impressed" by some of the indictments issued in terms of the designation of those with the greatest responsibility.[126] All said the ICTR made a significant leap when it arrested and indicted the former Prime Minister of the Interim Government in 1997, and thereafter 11 former Ministers of his Cabinet. Among former senior FAR Commanders charged is the Chief of Staff, the Chief of Staff of the Gendarmerie, the Commander of G3 (Operations) at the Army Headquarters, the Commanders of the Para –Commando, and Reconnaissance Battalions, the Commander of the Presidential Guard, and a number of operational commanders (e.g. Cyangugu, Gisenyi, Ngoma). Indictees from political parties include the President of MRND, its Secretary General and a former National Vice President of the Interahamwe. Given the most vocal incendiary role of the media in the atrocity crimes, a number of initiators and journalists have also been held accountable. As of 31 December 2004 the civilians indicted include 5 Prefets, 11 Bourgmestres, senior Government civil servants, communal counsellors, businessmen, traders, and clergymen had also been indicted.

The ICTR was not meant to hold accountable each and every person suspected of having committed atrocity crimes in 1994. It was also recognized that both Rwanda and other states had jurisdiction. The principle adopted was that of concurrent jurisdiction. As advocated by the UN Security Council, intermediate and lower level accused must be transferred to national jurisdictions if the ICTR's Completion Strategy is to be achieved. As part of compliance to its own Completion Strategy the ICTY on 6 April 2004 adopted a new Rule 28(A). It provided that on receipt of an indictment for review from the Prosecutor, the President shall refer it to the Tribunal's Bureau, which shall determined whether the indictment, prima facie, concentrates on one or more of the most senior leaders suspected of

[125] ICTR Completion Strategy, 19 November 2004, at www.ictr.org, para. 12.
[126] Interview with Author, Arusha, 26 July 2003.

being "most responsible" for crimes within the jurisdiction of the Tribunal. If it determines that the indictment meets that standard, the President shall designate one of the permanent Trial Chamber judges for review under Rule 47. On the contrary if the Bureau determines that the indictment does not meet that standard, the President shall return the same to the Registrar to communicate this finding to the Prosecutor.

In so far profiling is concerned, it serves no added value for accountability by the ICTR to prosecute new or additional Bourgemestres. In fact, their transfer for trial by national jurisdictions as a part and parcel of the Completion Strategy should be expedited. This has precedent. In 1998 the Prosecutor did not seek from Switzerland the deferral of its investigations relating to Fulgence Niyonteze, the former Bourgmestres of Mushubati commune. He did not represent any particular interest in terms of greatest responsibility, and in any event Switzerland was willing and able to undertake prosecution. Of the 140 or so Bourgmestres who were in office between April and July 1994, 86 Bourgmestres have been classified as Category I suspects in the List of Suspects issued by the Prosecutor General of Rwanda under the Organic Law on Genocide and crimes against humanity (see Annex III). Of this figure the ICTR has indicted 11. This is only a fraction, and at best represents a more than sufficient sampling, of accountability at the international level for that level of communal governance or leadership responsibility. The right place to hold accountable any new Bourgmestres is in national jurisdictions.

Special Court for Sierra Leone (SCSL)

The Special Court for Sierra Leone is under instructions to hold accountable those with the 'greatest responsibility' for crimes committed since the Abidjan Peace Accord of 30 November 1996. The Court, established by agreement between the United Nations and the Government of Sierra Leone on 16 January 2002, began operations on 1 July 2002. In March 2003 its Prosecutor issued the first indictments against seven accused alleged to have had prime responsibility for war crimes, crimes against humanity, violations of common Article 3 to the Four Geneva Conventions and Additional Protocol II of 1977, and other serious violations of international humanitarian law, including the conscription and enlisting of children under 15 years of age in the armed conflict, and attacks against UNAMSIL personnel. Of those indicted five were arrested the same day in Freetown, Sierra Leone. Among those charged was Foday Saybana Sankoh, also known as Popay, Papa or Pa, leader of the Revolutionary United Front (RUF).[127] The indictment was the Court's premier, not because the accused was already under the custody of the Government of Sierra Leone, but rather because of the instrumental position of the accused, and his role in the bitter armed conflict and the peace processes brokered by ECOWAS with the participation of the United Nations. Sankoy had been

[127] *P. v. Foday Saybana Sankoh*, Indictment, Case no: SCSL-2003-02-I, 7 March 2003. Sankoy died on 29 July 2003.

signatory to both the Abidjan Peace Agreement of 30 November 1996 and the Lome Peace Agreement of 7 July 1999 with the Government of Sierra Leone. From the RUF, Issa Hassan Sesay, Battle Group Commander and Sam Bokarie (aka Mosquito, aka Maskita), Battle Field Commander respectively have been indicted.[128]

Among the other accused charged was Johny Paul Koroma, the Chairman and Head of the Armed Forces of Sierra Leone, who had been Sierra Leone's Head of State on 25 May 1977.[129] Also indicted by the Sierra Leone Special Court were Chief Sam Ninga Norman, the former National Coordinator of the Civil Defence Forces (CDF), Monina Fofana, the Director of War Operations of the Karamajor, and Allieu Kondewa, the former Karamajor High Priest.[130] A number of the principal leaders of the three warring factions, namely, the RUF, the AFRC and its splinter group the West Side Boys, and the Civil Defence Forces have been indicted. Also indicted by the Court, on 3 March 2003, but made public on 4 June 2003, was the President in exercise of Liberia, Charles Taylor. The Court had issued an arrest warrant for his arrest to Ghana, while the accused was on an official visit in that country. As of 1 September 2003 the Court had charged 12 persons. It is important to note that this highly selective accountability for atrocity crimes committed during the civil war in Sierra Leone is due not only to the conscious decision to limited the number of accused that would be held accountable by the Special Court, but also because of the decision of the main warring parties for Sierra Leone to have a Truth and Reconciliation Commission that would deal with other classes of perpetrators. Article XXVI of the Lome Peace Agreement provided for the establishment of such a commission, tasked to address impunity, break the cycle of violence, and provide a forum for both victims and perpetrators of serious human rights violations to tell their stories and to get a clear picture of the past so as to facilitate the healing and national reconciliation process.[131] The truth and reconciliation mechanism has enabled the non-judicial processing of many other classes of perpetrators, particularly, of intermediate and lower categories.

III. A Few Profiling Pitfalls

Ntuyahaga Affair

The Ntuyahaga Case before the ICTR demonstrates that a prosecution strategy is an ongoing process and a result of what an investigation reveals. Furthermore that

---

[128] *P. v. Issa H. Sesay*, Case no: SCSL-2003-05-01; *P. v. Sam Bokarie, aka Mosquito, aka Maskita*, Case no: SCSL-2003-004-0I.

[129] *P. v. Johny Paul Koroma*, Case no: SCSL-2003-03-I, Koroma is presumed dead by the SCSL; See, Accused of hiding War Crimes suspects, Liberia says it killed him, New York Times, 07/05/2003.

[130] *P. v. Sam Ninga Morman*, Case no: SCSL 2003 08 I.

[131] The Truth and Reconciliation Commission Act, 2000, established the Commission.

although determining who should or should not face prosecution before the Tribunal is subject to the Prosecutor's discretion in terms of initiating an indictment, that process is subject to the Trial Chamber's scrutiny once an Indictment is filed and an accused has appeared before the Tribunal. The affair is also a lesson learnt in terms of the profiling of an accused, since charges might not have been dropped against him if he had been earlier indicted together with the group of military accused, all alleged to have been responsible for the same set of acts.

Bernard Ntuyahaga, a former Major in the Rwandan Armed Forces, had served in April 1994 as a G4 officer (property and assets) based at the Kigali military camp. He voluntarily travelled to Arusha in June 1994 from Lusaka, Zambia where he had sought refugee status since June 1996 under the Zambia Refugee (Control) Act of 1970. There he feared abduction by Rwandan authorities, and having learnt of investigations by the Office of the Prosecutor against him, chose to present himself to the front desk of the Tribunal in Arusha on 14 June 1998. He was arrested by members of the Tanzanian Police Force on 18 June 1998 in Room 532 of the Novotel Mt. Meru Hotel, following a request made a day earlier by the Prosecutor to the Tanzania Government for his arrest and provisional measures, under Rule 40 of the Tribunal's Rules of Procedure and Evidence. On 10 July 1998 he was transferred into the custody of the Tribunal following an order by the Tribunal's President, the late Judge Laity Kama for his transfer and provisional detention under Rule 40 *bis* (B).

An indictment against him containing five counts, namely conspiracy to commit genocide (count 1), genocide (count 2), complicity in genocide (count 3), crimes against humanity (murder) (count 3), violation of Article 3 common to the Geneva Conventions and Additional Protocol II (violence to life and physical well being) (count 4) and crimes against humanity (murder) (count 5) against him was filed on 29 September 1998. The confirming judge Yakov Ostrovsky, dismissed counts 1, 2, and 4 of the indictment, ordered the Prosecutor to join count 5 with count 3, and confirmed count 3 of the indictment,[132] the same day the order for his provisional detention expired.[133] The outcome of the confirmed indictment was that Ntuyahaga was charged with only a single count of crimes against humanity for the murder of the former Prime Minister of Rwanda, Agathe Uwilingiyimana, and that of 10 Belgium peacekeeping soldiers.

The factual allegations[134] related to this were that at around 0930 hrs, on 7th April 1994, five Ghanaian UNAMIR peacekeeping soldiers who had assumed guard at the Prime Ministers residence in Kiyovu, Kigali, together with 10 Belgium peacekeeping soldiers who had been assigned the task of escorting the Prime Minister from her residence to Radio Rwanda so that she could reassure the popu-

[132] Decision on the Review of the Indictment, *P. v. B. Ntuyahaga*, Case no: ICTR-98-40-I, 29 September 1998.

[133] Extension of Provisional Detention, P. *v. B. Ntuyahaga*, Case no: ICTR -98-40-PD, 8 September 1998.

[134] *P. v. B. Ntuyahaga*, Indictment, Case no: ICTR- 98-40-I, 29 September 1998; See also, Rapport, Commission d'enquete parlementaire concernant les evenement de Rwanda, Senat de Belgique, Session de 1997-1998, 6 Dec.1977, pp. 401-401.

lation that her government was still in control, and appeal for calm, were disarmed, forcefully detained by members of the Rwandan Armed Forces, and taken by Ntuyahaga in his service vehicle, a VW mini van, to Kigali military camp in the pretext of driving them to a safe location or the UNAMIR base.[135] On their arrival at the camp, Ntuyahaga spread word that the Belgium soldiers were responsible for the shooting of the Presidential plane.[136] The uncontrollable reaction of the Rwandan soldiers was perhaps also conditioned by RTLM's anti Belgium propaganda.[137] Ntuyahaga ordered the peacekeeping soldiers to get out of the vehicle and sit down on the tarmac with hands above their heads.[138] They were beaten and physically manhandled by Rwandan soldiers. The "generalized lynching"[139] of the peacekeepers resulted in serious injury and death to four of the Belgium peacekeepers. The others sought refuge in the camp, resisted, and following separation of the Ghanaian from the Belgium soldiers, members of the Rwandan Armed forces killed the remaining six Belgium peacekeepers.

When the Belgium Peacekeepers were being attacked, UNAMIR's Commander General Delaire, on his way to a meeting of the Crisis Committee held at the Ecole Superieur Militaire 200 meters from Kigali Military camp, passed by the entrance of the camp and saw bodies of what appeared to be European UNAMIR soldiers on the ground.[140] Making inquiries he was informed they were not Belgium, but he could not enter into the compound due to the chaotic situation inside the camp. [141] Delaire proceeded to the meeting where his request to go back to the Camp was rebuffed by Bagosora, his main contact point with Rwandan authorities on the 6-7 April, and who chaired that meeting.[142] Later Dellaire had this to say of Bagasora, one of ICTR's principal accused: 'I know that God exists because I met the Devil'.[143]

While the confirming judge was convinced that a prima facie case against Ntuyahaga's had been established on his involvement in the murder of the former Prime Minister and the 10 Belgium peacekeeping soldiers, he considered that the indictment lacked a showing of the suspect's direct involvement in massacres or the extermination of the Tutsi, and in the conspiracy to commit genocide. On a legal issue concerning the application of common Article 3 to the Four Geneva Conventions of 1949 and Additional Protocol II (1977), the Judge considered that Belgium UN Peacekeeping Forces did not enjoy the protection accorded by those instruments, since there was no express provision in the texts of these instruments that guaranteed protection to UN Peacekeeping Forces. In dismissing this count he

---

135 Rapport, Commission d'enquete parlementaire, pp. 405-406, Id.

136 P. 405, Id.

137 Castonguay J (1998) p. 115.

138 Rapport, Commission d'enquete parlementaire, p. 405.

139 Id.

140 Suhrke A (1998) Dilemmas of Protection: The Log of the Kigali Battalion, International Peacekeeping, vol. 5/2, p. 8.

141 P. 8, Id.

142 Id.

143 L'ancien chef des forces de L'ONU au Rwanda reviendra devant le TPIR, Le Monde, 28 Fevrier 1998.

considered that common Article 3 and Protocol II protected only members of warring factions or parties to a conflict, that Belgium peacekeepers were not parties to the Rwandan conflict, were not victims of that conflict, and that their murder was not part of any military operations, but rather of crimes against humanity. Ntuyahaga made his initial appearance on 13 November 1998 and pleaded not guilty to the single count of murder as a crime against humanity.

The question of the application of international humanitarian law to UN Peacekeeping Forces was prematurely answered by the Judge at the confirmation hearing. Under the law of the Tribunal, the Prosecutor is not required to provide in the indictment its view of the applicable law. Questions of substantive law such as this are litigated at either the pre-trial stage under Rule 73 *bis* or during trial. Both the United Nations and the UN Peacekeeping Forces that operate under its mandate are bound by customary rules of international humanitarian law when engaged in hostilities.[144] Schindler has submitted that since the United Nations is bound by customary rules of international humanitarian law, states whose armed forces oppose UN forces are equally obliged to apply these rules.[145]

In the context of the UNMAIR it is worth recalling that Article 7 ((b) of the Agreement between the United Nations and the Government of the Republic of Rwanda on the status of the United Nations Mission for Rwanda (UNAMIR) signed, in New York on 5 November 1993, provided the following:

> "The Government undertakes to treat at all times the military personnel of UNAMIR with full respect for the principles and spirit of the general international conventions applicable to the treatment of military personnel. These international conventions include the Four Geneva Conventions of 12 August 1949 and their Additional Protocols of 8 June 1977".

UNAMIR and the Government shall therefore ensure that members of their respective military personnel are fully acquitted with the principles and spirit of the above mentioned international instruments."

The combined legal effect of the application of customary international law to the UN and peacekeeping forces; of the protection accorded under the Geneva Conventions in which parties are obliged not only to respect, but also to ensure respect for the Conventions in all circumstances (common Article 1 to the Four Geneva Conventions); of the extended scope of protection under Additional Protocol II; of the obligations of the Rwanda Government under the Forces Agreement with the UN, and of numerous Security Council resolutions recognizing the application of International humanitarian law to UN Peacekeeping Forces, leads to the conclu-

---

144 Schindler D United Nations forces and International Humanitarian Law, in Swinarski C (1994) Studies and Essays on International Humanitarian Law and Red Cross Principles in honour of Jean Pictet, ICTR, Martinus Nijhoff Pub., Geneva, p. 526.

145 Schindler D in Swinarski C (1994) p. 527; On the application of international humanitarian law to UN peacekeeping forces, See, Sandoz Y (1978) L'application du droit humanitarie par les forces armees de L'organisation des Nations Unies, International Review of the Red Cross, pp. 274-284; Bourloyannis C (1992) The Security Council of the UN and the Implementation of International Humanitarian Law, vol. 20, No. 2, Denver Journal of International Law and Policy, pp. 335-355.

sion that the ten Belgium peacekeeping soldiers enjoyed the protection of international humanitarian law. What remains contradictory in the confirmation decision is that a similar charge under common Article 3 and Additional Protocol II, and based on almost the same factual allegations concerning the killing of the ten Belgium soldiers as that contained in Ntuyahaga indictment, was confirmed as early as 5 August 1966 in the relation to Theoneste Bagosora.[146]

On 23 February 1999 the Prosecutor sought leave to withdraw the indictment against Ntuyahaga.[147] Although at the ICTY withdrawal of indictments, including for that matter insufficiency of evidence has been a feature of prosecutions, at the ICTR, this withdrawal was unprecedented. One explanation is the seriousness of genocide as a crime, and the fact that when an indictment is preferred it represents a confirmed desire to try the accused. In Ntuyahaga's case the motivation for the withdrawal of the indictment lie in strategic and policy considerations, rather than evidential insufficiency or legal technicalities. The withdrawal was aimed at promoting, under Article 8 (1) of the Statute, the exercise of concurrent jurisdiction by allowing national courts, in this case Belgium, to prosecute the accused. Furthermore, the Prosecutor submitted that a one count case limited to the sole incident of the murder of the former Prime Minister and the ten Belgium soldiers would be too myopic, and could no longer be placed within her strategy of showing the genocide as a conspiracy; that the decision of the confirming Judge had narrowed the scope of accountability, and deprived her of the opportunity to prosecute the accused for the totality of his criminal involvement; and that Belgium had already instituted criminal proceedings against Ntuyahaga. It was submitted that withdrawal would facilitate the judicial process given that the majority of witnesses and victims were already in Belgium. In Belgium Ntuyahaga was being charged under Articles 1 (3), 2, and 7 of the Belgium Law of 16 June 1993 (crimes de international) relating to the repression of serious breaches of the Geneva Conventions of 12 August 1949 and of Additional Protocol I and II of 8 June 1977.[148] The Prosecutor not only requested the Trial Chamber to grant leave for the indictment to be withdrawal, but also requested the Chamber to order Ntuyahaga's release from the Tribunal's custody to Tanzanian authorities,[149] which had meanwhile received an extradition request from the Belgium Government.

In order to clarify any ambiguity as to the motivations for the withdrawal, at the hearing on the motion to withdraw the indictment, the Prosecutor suggested to the Trial Chamber that should it have any doubt or certainty that the accused, if released, would evade justice through the non exercise of concurrent jurisdiction, then it was prepared to proceed with the indictment as it stood. The Prosecutor insisted that the reason for the withdrawal of the indictment was not lack of evi-

[146] Count No 4, *P. v. T. Bagosora*, Case no: ICTR-96-7-I, 5 August 1996.

[147] Prosecutor's Motion under Rules 51 & 73 to withdraw the Indictment against the accused, *P. v. B. Ntuyahaga*, Case no: ICTR- 98-40-I, 23 February 1999.

[148] See, Declaration Officielle de Procureur General, pres de la cour d'appel de Bruxelles a l'appiu de la demande de dessaisissement du T.P. I.R. en cause de Bernard Ntuyahaga, Annex 1, Expose d'*amicus curiae* de Governement belge.

[149] Addendum to Prosecutor's Motion to Withdraw the Indictment against the Accused, *P. v. B. Ntuyahaga*, Case no: I CTR- 98-40-1, 9 March 1999.

dence, but to permit the exercise of complementary jurisdiction with a national court (i.e. Belgium). To the Prosecutor and the Belgium Government, the motion to withdraw the indictment was pegged with conditionality; that Ntuyahaga should face prosecution. Rule 51 does not require the withdrawal of an indictment to be solely based on lack of evidence. The grant of leave to withdraw is at the discretion of a Judge or a Trial Chamber.

The Belgium Government which appeared as *amicus curiae*, in conformity with Rule 74, supported the Prosecutor's motion.[150] It argued that the cooperation provided for in Article 28 of the Statue, whereby all states must fully cooperate with the Tribunal implied necessarily a reciprocal cooperation of the Tribunal with states in order to facilitate due process of justice.[151] Belgium urged the Tribunal either to transfer and handover Ntuyahaga directly to its authorities or to obtain guarantees from Tanzania that Ntuyahaga would be extradited to Belgium.[152] It did not wish to see Ntuyahaga escape prosecution. Belgium further argued that a direct transfer from the Tribunal to Belgium would not interfere with Tanzania's sovereignty, and that such a procedure would avoid the consequences, in particular of Article XX (i.e. pertaining to the suspect or accused) of the Headquarters agreement between the United Nations and Tanzania.[153] This article provided:

1. The host country shall not exercise its criminal jurisdiction over any person present in its territory, who is to be or has been transferred as a suspect or an accused to the premises of the Tribunal pursuant to a request or an order of the Tribunal, in respect of acts, omissions or convictions prior to their entry into the territory of the host country.

2. The immunity provided for in this article shall cease when the person, having been acquitted or otherwise released by the Tribunal and having had for a period of 15 consecutive days from the date of his or her release an opportunity of leaving, has nevertheless remained in the territory of the host country, or having left it, has returned.

The Defence, on its part, counterclaimed and argued that the Prosecutor's motion was inadmissible, not well founded, and urged for its dismissal.[154] It further requested the Trial Chamber to make a finding of innocence, for the accused to be acquitted, and released.[155]

On 18 March 1999 the Trial Chamber ruled that the primacy of the Tribunal's jurisdiction meant that the Tribunal could request any national jurisdiction to defer

150 Expose *d'amicus curiae* du Governement belge sur la demande en dessaisissement du Procureur en l'affair Ntuyahaga, *P. v. B. Ntuyahaga*, Case no: ICTR- 98-40-I, 23 February 1999.

151 Expose *d'amicus curiae* de Governement belge, p. 4, Id.

152 Pp. 3 & 7, Id.

153 P. 63, Id.

154 See, Defence Brief in Reply including counter-claim, *P. v. B. Ntuyahaga*, Case no: ICTR- 98-40-1, 24 March 1999.

155 Id.

investigations or ongoing proceedings to it, and that the reverse, namely the deferral of investigations and proceedings by the Tribunal to any national jurisdiction was not provided for in the Statute.[156] As the indictment had been confirmed and the initial appearance had taken place, the question of concurrent jurisdiction could not be invoked in support of a request for the withdrawal of the indictment.[157] While stressing that it was the sole duty of the Prosecutor to devise the prosecution strategy of her office, and to decide even before instituting any proceedings, whether such action serves the interests of her mandate as Prosecutor, the Trial Chamber opined that it was not within its powers to consider the question as to whether or not the prosecution of a person on a single count relating to the murders of the former Prime Minister and ten Belgium soldiers enables the Prosecutor to "shed light" on the events that occurred in Rwanda in 1994.[158] The Trial Chamber stressed that all accused before the Tribunal were presumed innocent, were equal before the law, and that no distinction or ranking may be made among them on the basis of the number of counts with which they are charged.[159]

As regards the Defence submission, the Trial Chamber was of the view that in accordance with Rule 98 *bis*, an acquittal can only be considered at the stage where the Prosecutor has presented all her evidence and the Chamber finds that the evidence is insufficient to sustain a conviction on any one count.[160] Consequently the Chamber declared the Prosecutor's motion admissible and well founded under Rule 51 (A), and granted her leave to withdraw the indictment against Ntuyahaga.[161] It firmly held that the withdrawal of an indictment was tantamount to a termination of proceedings, and entailed the immediate and unconditional release of the accused.[162] To the Chamber, pursuant to general principles of law, a person who is no longer under indictment may not be deprived of his or her freedom and must therefore be released immediately if he or she is not held for any other cause.[163] It further opined that pursuant to both the Statutes and the Rules, it did not have jurisdiction to order the release of a person who is no longer under indictment into the custody of any given state, including the Host State; Tanzania.[164] The Chamber finally ordered, in the absence of any charges against Ntuyahaga, his immediate release from the Tribunal's Detention Facilities.[165] The Trial Chamber instructed the Registrar to take all the necessary measures to execute immediate release, if need be with the cooperation of the Tanzanian authori-

[156] Decision on the Prosecutor's Motion to Withdraw the Indictment, *P. v. B. Ntuyahaga*, Case no: ICTR- 98-40-I, 18 March 1999, p. 5.

[157] P. 5, Id.

[158] P. 6, Id.

[159] Id.

[160] P. 7, Id.

[161] Pp. 6 & 8, Id.

[162] Pp. 7, Id.

[163] Pp. 7, Cf. Decision on Motion by the Prosecutor for withdrawal of Indictment against Marinko Katava, *P. v. Zoran Kupresic et all.* Case no: ICTY-95-16-PT, 19 December 1997.

[164] Pp. 8, Id.

[165] Id.

ties.[166] An appeal by the Prosecutor, on 22 March 1999, against the Trial Chamber's decision led to a finding by the appeal Chamber that no right of appeal under Article 24(a) of the Statute or Rule 72 (D) lay against that decision.[167]

The Registrar released Ntuyahaga in Dar es Salaam on 29 March 1999,[168] having issued to him a "Safe Conduct" document,[169] of 15 days validity, corresponding to the 15 days grave period provided for in Article XX (2) of the Headquarters Agreement between the UN and Tanzania. Among other matters, the Safe Conduct document stated:

> "[Requested] Member States of the United Nations, other States, International Organizations and all other persons to whom it may concern, to accord safe conduct to Bernard Ntuyahaga and extend to him any necessary cooperation to enable him to move freely in or transit through, without let or hindrance, any country to his final destination, in accordance with the relevant provisions of international law".[170]

Tanzanian police rearrested Ntuyahaga on the same day of his release on charges that he violated immigration laws when he first entered Tanzania from Zambia in June 1998.[171] Bakari Mwapachu, Tanzania's Justice and Constitutional Affairs Minister also acknowledged that the arrest would provide enough time for Belgium and Rwanda to process their extradition requests.[172] In Dar es Salaam Ntuyahaga had unsuccessfully sought political asylum from the Danish Embassy.[173] On being informed that he had in his possession a safe conduct document, the Belgium Ministry of Justice strongly protested the attitude of the Registrar on the manner of Ntuyahaga's release.[174]

In an urgent request to the Trial Chamber, for an *ex-parte* hearing, the Prosecutor sought for the safe conduct document to be rescinded and declared null and void on the grounds, that first neither the Statute nor the Rules permitted the Registrar to issue such a document, and secondly that neither of those two instruments nor international law imposed on states and international organizations the obliga-

---

166 Id.

167 Decision rejecting Notice of Appeal, *P. v. B. Ntuyahaga*, Case no: ICTR- 98-40-A, 3 June 1999.

168 Decision by the Registrar in execution of the decisions by Trial Chamber I ordering the release of Mr. B. Ntuyahaga, *P. v. B. Ntuyahaga*, Case no: ICTR-98-40-I, 29 March 1999.

169 'Safe Conduct', The Registrar, ICTR, 29 March 1999: See also, ICTR Update, ICTR/UPD/015, ICTR, Arusha, 27 April 1999.

170 Id.

171 Dar Police arrest major Ntuyahaga freed by ICTR, The Guardian, 31 March 1999.

172 Id.

173 Rwandan Genocide suspect arrested, Associated Press, 31 Mach 1999.

174 Note Verbale from Embassy of Belgium to the Registrar, Dar es Salaam, 29 March 1999; See also Registrar's response addressed to the Embassy of Belgium, 30 March 1999.

tion to comply with a safe conduct document issued by the Registrar.[175] In a Declaration on a point of law, the Trial Chamber emphasized that Ntuyahaga's case was closed before the Tribunal, and ipso facto, the Prosecutor's motion was inadmissible, and that the motion was moot given that Tanzanian authorities had attached no weight to the safe conduct document.[176] However in the light of the significance of the issue raised by the Prosecutor, as to whether the Registrar had authority under the Statute and the Rules of Procedure and Evidence to issue a safe conduct document, the judges decided to issue a declaration on the status of such a document. They were of the view that neither the provisions of Security Council resolutions, nor those of the Statute, nor those of the Rules, nor any instructions rendered by the Trial Chamber, empowered the Registrar to issue that document, and that by issuing it to Ntuyahaga the Registrar had acted ultra vires, and declared it null and void.[177] They further stated that it was only a Trial Chamber that was empowered to issue such a safe conduct.[178]

Earlier, on 18 March 1999, Rwanda filed a request to Tanzania seeking Ntuyahaga's extradition.[179] With both Belgium and Rwanda seeking Ntuyahaga's extradition, the Government of Tanzania on 10 May 1999 turned down Belgium's request in favour of Rwanda apparently on the ground that the Tanzania-Rwanda Extradition Treaty took precedence over the Belgium Extradition Treaty in the event of concurring requests.[180] Following meetings between Belgium and Rwanda in which each state reiterated its desire and right to prosecute Ntuyahaga, Rwanda's Minister of Justice announced on 5 May 1999 that both countries had agreed to actively cooperate, whatever the jurisdiction he would finally appear.[181] Extradition proceedings to Rwanda, against Ntuyahaga took almost five years before the Kisutu Magistrate Court, in Dar es Salaam. The court ruled against extradition. On his release Ntuyahaga was granted entry into Belgium, and is currently facing charges in relation to the killing of the 10 Belgium Peacekeeping soldiers.

---

175 Prosecutor's Urgent Request to Rescind and Declare Null and Void document seeking to grant Safe Conduct issued by the Registrar, *P. v. B. Ntuyahaga*, Case no: ICTR- 98-40-I, 31 March 1999.

176 Declaration on a point of law, Trial Chamber I, ICTR, 22 April 1999, paras. 7 & 8.

177 Para. 17 (ii), Id.

178 Para. 16, Id. Cf. Decision on the Motion for release by the accused Slavko Dokmanovic, *P. v. M. Mrksic, M. Radic, V. Sljivancanin, S. Dokmanovic*, Case no: IT--95-13a-PT, 22 October 1997.

179 See, Declaration officielle du Governement Rwandais concernant la liberation du Major Ntuyahaga Bernard, Ministere des affairs etrangers et de la cooperation regionale, Kigali, 30 mars 1999; Press Statement, Office of the Vice President and Minister of Defence, Rep. Of Rwanda, 3 April 1999.

180 See, Belgium, Rwanda want re-arrest of genocide suspect, Daily News, 20 March 1999; Rwanda in tug of war for genocide suspect, Reuters, 10 May 1999.

181 Communiqué de Press, Mr. Jean de Dieu Mucyo, Ministre de la Justice, Kigali, 4 May 1999.

Rusatira Affair

The indictment against Leonidas Rusatira, a former colonel of the Rwandan Armed Forces, and ex-commander of the Ecole Superieur Militaire (ESO) or High Military School in the months leading to the events of 1994, was filed by the Office of the Prosecutor on 26 March 2002[182]. Rutasira had served at one time as *Directuer de cabinet* in the Ministry of Defence, a position that was held by Bagosora in April 1994. The indictment charged him with genocide, complicity in genocide, crimes against humanity (murder and extermination) and violations of Article 3 common to the Four Geneva Conventions of 1949 and of the Additional Protocol II of 1977. The indictment alleged that on or about 8 April 1994 he had supplied weapons to interehamwe leaders who had surrounded the Ecole Technique Officielle (ETO) or Official Technical School in Kicukiro sector, Kigali Rural Prefecture. There thousands of displaced Tutsi and numerous moderate Hutu had sought refuge, including Foreign Minister Boniface Ngulinzira. Ngulinzira had been targeted by the RTLM as an accomplice of the Tutsi for having signed the Arusha Peace Accords.

The indictment alleged that between 8 and 11 April 1994 Rusatira made frequent visits to ETO and on each occasion had asked the UNAMIR Belgian soldiers then providing protection to leave as security for the displaced would be assured by Rwandan Gendarmerie and FAR soldiers. It narrated that on 11 April in the afternoon, soon after the withdrawal of the Belgian contingent, interahamwe, soldiers and gendarmerie who had surrounded the school, attacked and killed about 100 persons including Ngulinzira. It further alleged that Rusatira had led the soldiers, while the interahamwe were led by Georges Rutaganda then vice president of the national committee of interahamwe.

The indictment additionally alleged that the about 2,000 remaining displaced persons were gathered together, led to SONATUBES, and following the arrival of reinforcements they were then taken to Nyanza. Along the way those identified as Hutu were separated from the others, and released, while Tutsi who tried to flee were immediately killed. At Nyanza more were further attacked, the result of which was thousands of death, most of the victims being Tutsi. The indictment also alleged that Rusatira had addressed the displaced at SONATUBES telling them to head for Nyanza where they would be safe. It stated that he had also supervised the soldiers and interehamwe who had led the displaced towards Nyanza. It finally alleged that soon after these killings he was promoted to the rank of General.

Criminal responsibility was imputed upon him by virtue of his affirmative acts in planning, instigating, ordering, committing or otherwise aiding and abetting the planning and execution of he crimes and in the alternatively as a superior for the acts of his subordinates (i.e. soldiers and gendarmerie), de jure or de facto, who acted under his authority and his failure to take reasonable measures to stop or prevent them or to discipline and punish them for their acts.

---

182 *P. v L. Rusatira*, Case no: ICTR-2002-80-I.

On 12 April 2002 Judge L. G. Williams confirmed the indictment and issued a warrant of arrest. On the basis of the warrant Rusatira who was publicly known to be in Belgium was arrested by Belgian authorities. He had earlier on cooperated with Belgium authorities in their investigations on the killing of the 10 Belgian peacekeeping soldiers, and had testified in the hearings of the Belgian Senate Commission on Rwanda. Four months later, on 12 August 2002 the Prosecutor sought to withdraw the indictment and related orders on the ground that there was insufficient evidence against him to proceed to trial; without prejudice to her right to pursue the same or other charges in the future based on on-going investigations.[183] On 14 August Judge Pillay granted leave to the Prosecutor to withdraw the indictment, and ordered the immediate withdrawal of the arrest warrant.[184]

Given his position and role during and after the April 1994 events in Rwanda the indictment against him surprised those most conversant, including the prosecution's own expert witnesses. One even considered he had been erroneously charged.[185] On the night of the 6-7 April 1994 during the meeting of officers of the Rwandan Armed Forces, Rusatira publicly told Bagosora that his self-proclamation at head of the crisis committee was unacceptable. Rusatira had been a signatory of the 12 April Communiqué calling for a stop of the massacres and hostilities in favour of the Arusha Accords. On 10th April he had evacuated the Public Prosecutor of Kigali to safety at the Hotel des Milles Collines, Kigali. On the day of the attack at ETO, on 11 April at 1200 hrs Rusatira and his armed escort had evacuated the family of Alexis Kanyarangwe President of the Rwanda Patriotic Front, and dozens of other persons in danger by accommodating them in his properties in Kigali and Kicukiro-Ribirizi, assisting them to reach Hotel Mille Collines, the International Committee of the Red Cross, the Belgium Red Cross and St Paul Parish. Actions that in the circumstances of extreme violence obtaining at that time exposed him to grave danger and personal risk. On 10th April the Commander of the 14th company UNAMIR Belgium contingent had asked him to arrange for Rwandan Gendarmerie to take over and assume protection, a request that he relayed on called General Ndindiyimana, former Chief of Staff of the Rwandan National Gendarmerie and which was not heeded to.

He was also the promoter of the 6 July Kigeme Declaration that called for the cessation of ethnic killings, and admitted that genocidal acts were being perpetrated in Rwanda. While the indictment may have been based on prima-facie evidence of his alleged implication in the events at ETO as can be inferred from the confirmation of the indictment, those conversant with the 1994 tragic events in Rwanda considered it incomprehensible, if not a error in the exercise of judicial discretion. In some quarters the indictment was termed "kidnapping", a new prosecution strategy aimed at inducing guilty pleas in default of wining the confidence of witnesses. It was fashioned upon a sampling of witness accounts inspired

---

183 Prosecutor's Application to Withdraw Indictment Against Leonidas Rusatira Without Prejudice, Case no: ICTR-2002-80-I, 12 August 2002.

184 Decision on the Prosecutors *Ex parte* Application For Leave to Withdraw the Indictment, Case no: ICTR- 2002-I, 14 August 2002.

185 Guichaoua A The ICTR: from crisis to failure? Le Monde, 4 Sept. 2002.

by self proclaimed auxiliaries of justice, which ICTR prosecutors adopted as said, without further inquiry.[186]

From the above it is possible to draw a number of lessons. That:

(a) it was premature to have indicted a "sitting" target with less than trial ready evidence, and without having interviewed key witnesses or closely examined the UNAMIR-Belgium log books. A prosecutor's charging decision it has been submitted, must be based on the belief that the individual is guilty; the prosecution case will result in a conviction; the effect made to prepare the case will result in conviction equal to the effort expended; and the influence of public opinion will be in the Prosecutor's favour.[187] The policy issues that have to be considered ought to include its *legal sufficiency* (i.e. the elements of crime are present), *system sufficient* (i.e. speedy and early disposal of cases), and *trial sufficiency* (i.e. strong evince to sustain a conviction).[188]

(b) it represented a complete misdirection on how military and gendarmerie officers were promoted within the Rwandan Armed Forces after the introduction of multi-party politics, and especially after 6 April 1994. It also misconstrued key considerations in promotions such as regionalism, party loyalty, the side-lining and bypassing of established rules on military promotions by the Interim Government, and the fact that some officers were Commanders in name, but had troops under their command.

(c) limited use was made by the Prosecution of investigation dossiers and the findings of various Belgium authorities;

(d) pressure, including that from Rwandan and external human rights organizations may have influenced the precipitated decision to indict,[189]

(e) lack of inter-office communications including those with The Hague where the decision to indict was made.[190]As observed by Goldstone a good esprit de corps in the Office of the Prosecutor is essential, and staff should be full partners in developing and articulating the strategy and agenda of the Office.[191]

(f) the indictment of an individual of his profile, and with his kind of itinerary required strategic and tactical considerations, not to mention evidential sufficiency.

---

186 Id.

187 Jacoby J E (1977) The Prosecutor's Charging Decision: A Policy Perspective, National Institute of Law Enforcement and Criminal Justice, US Dept. of Justice, W.D.C, p. 7.

188 Pp. 17-19, Id.

189 See, African Rights (2002) Left to Due at ETO and Nyanza: The Stories of Rwandan Civilians Abandoned by UN Troops on 11 April 1994, 'who will take responsibility for Rwanda's Serbrenica', 19 April 2002; ICTR Prosecutor to drop charges against genocide suspect, Internews, Arusha, 18 Aug. 2002.

190 ICTR Prosecutor seeks to drop charges, Id.

191 Goldstone R (2003) Comments on the Office of the Prosecutor, Expert Consultation process on general issues of relevance to the ICC Office of the Prosecutor, ICC-OTP, The Hague. On accountability Prosecutors, see, Ambos K (2000) The Status, Role and Accountability of the Prosecutor of the International Criminal Court: A Comparative Overview on the Basis of 33 National Reports, vol. 8/2, pp. 89-118.

In sum this represented prosecutorial misdirection in the appraisal and assessment of the April 1994 events, in deciding on one hand to prosecute a senior armed forces commander or on the other, to enlist him as a cooperating prosecution witness given his in-depth knowledge of the jure and defacto structure of the Rwandan Armed Forces through his prior position as the former *Directeur de Cabinet* of the Ministry of Defence, a position occupied by Bagosora, the alleged "mastermind" of the genocide.[192]

Conclusion

This chapter examined from a number of perspectives the targets of accountability. It first reviewed direct individual criminal responsibility and the varied forms of criminal liability provided for in Article 6 (1) of the Statute of the ICTR. These include the planning, instigation, ordering, aiding and abetting the commission of a crime. Direct individual responsibility is an acknowledged norm of criminal liability for atrocity crimes. One extensively resorted to by the UN ad hoc Tribunals for the prosecution of all categories of perpetrators.

A close inquiry was made on the profiling of targets of accountability. This is a function of prosecution strategy. Of determining by way of markers, the category or level of responsibility that is required to meet the demand for accountability and justice. It is also dependent on the gravity of the crimes, multi-facet participation of various actors, and in particular, the extend of involvement, direct or indirect, of those in charge of the organs of Governmental, other non State entities, the military establishment and the civil administration. To an extent it is also case specific. The chapter examined the two terminologies employed to describe those who ought to be the priority of priorities of accountability. Persons "*most responsible*" or those with the "*greatest responsibility*". While the UN Security Council opted for the latter, it is submitted that in reality the difference is a matter of semantics if not emphasis. All point almost towards the same prime targets. Those in governmental, military, political, civil, paramilitary, economic, financial, religious or community leadership positions, and who were behind the drawing board of atrocity crimes. That is, individuals at the highest echelon of national responsibility and leadership. International courts and tribunals, which can only provide symbolic justice, have no room at all to accommodate lower level perpetrators, and indeed very limited space, if any, for intermediary level culprits. Atrocity crimes are the product of a large-scale involvement of many perpetrators, and it is national jurisdictions that remain fundamentally responsible for accountability and the reestablishment of the rule of law.

---

192 Living under the Shadow of Genocide, Le Monde, published in The Guardian Weekly, UK, 12 April 1998.

The classification of suspects and accused by Rwandan authorities into Category I is a bold attempt at profiling in a situation of astronomical perpetration and unprecedented victimization. Only a national tribunal can dispense that kind of accountability involving huge numbers of suspects presumed to have had significant responsibility. International Tribunals are meant to focus and address themselves on the accountability of a few individuals of highest authority, command or position. As remarked by Judge Eric Mose, the ICTR's President, "if it was possible for the Nuremberg Tribunal to hold accountable and try 22 individuals, why not now?"[193]

A more selective approach is required by international tribunals on whom to hold accountable, and to determine the adequate level of responsibility. The author was critical that among the first group of accused before the UN ad hoc Tribunals were fairly marginal players, including foot soldiers or militia. Some had no significant position or rank in the Government, the Political Parties, the Army, the Civil Administration or even the community. The initial investigation strategy adopted by both Tribunals had in fact envisaged accountability for low-level perpetrators, the very category that the Security Council has now called upon to be transferred to competent national jurisdiction, as the best way of realizing their Completion Strategies.[194]

Lessons learnt has it that with the setting of marching orders on the level of responsibility desired for accountability (i.e. those with the "greatest responsibility"), as in the case of the Special Court for Sierra Leone, it is possible to indict those in senior leadership positions without first having recourse to minor perpetrators. The value, if any of lower rank accused for accountability before international tribunals, especially in cases of guilty pleas, is purely evidential. To generate evidence against those in senior leadership positions. The ICTR Completion Strategy, which envisions a transfer to national jurisdictions, including to Rwanda provided it abolishes the death penalty in respect of any transferred suspect or accused, of the investigations and prosecution of 40 suspects, 25 of which who did not occupy high positions of responsibility during the events of 1994, makes it imperative for the ICTR to shred of its jurisdiction cases involving intermediate and lower level perpetrators.[195] This should include Bourgmesters, Counsellors, pastors and priests, local militiamen, and private individuals of less than national leadership or political, military, social, economic or financial dominance.

At the ICTR, the classes of accused held accountable include persons who, if that Tribunal were to be re-enacted, would not have been before it. But, it also includes a significant number allegedly with senior leadership responsibility for the mayhem. This includes a former Prime Minster, 11 Cabinet Ministers, and top brass military commanders. In the situation of Rwanda, this is incomplete without those in the shadow of de facto authority who wielded parallel power. In this cate-

---

193 Interview with author, Arusha, 26 July 2003.

194 Statement of the President of the Security Council, UN Doc. S/PRST/2002/21, 23 July 2002.

195 Eight Annual Report of ICTR to the Security Council and the General Assembly, UN Doc. A/58/140-S/2003/707, 11 July 2003, para. 10.

gory is Felician Kabuga, share holder and financier of RTLM S.A, indicted by the Tribunal, but still at large in spite of a USD $ 5 million reward by the United States Government for information leading to his arrest.[196] It led Rwandan President, Paul Kagame, to retort: "Kabuga has become a mystery like Osama bin Laden because one day he is here and the other he is not".[197] On 28 August 2003 the Security Council directly called upon him to surrender, and asked Rwanda, Kenya, the Democratic Republic of the Congo and the Republic of Congo to intensify cooperation and render all necessary assistance to the ICTR in the efforts to bring the accused to account before the Tribunal.[198]

[196] *P. v. F. Kabuga*, Amended Indictment, Case no: ICTR-98-44-I, 21 November 2001.
[197] Rwanda, A Special Country Report, The East African, April 2- May 4, 2003.
[198] UN SC resolution 1503 (2003), 28 August 2003.

Chapter 6
Conspiracy to commit genocide

For atrocity crimes committed in Rwanda in 1994, conspiracy to commit genocide represents a unique tool for accountability. Prosecutions before the ICTR constitute the most extensive use of the crime of conspiracy as a charge by any international criminal tribunal. It surpasses, by far, the accusation of conspiracy as proffered in the Nuremberg and Tokyo Tribunals.[1] In a number of joint trials before the ICTR involving between 3 and 6 accused, namely the Cyangugu, Media, Butare, Military I and II and Government I and II Trials, over 28 accused have been charged with conspiracy to commit genocide, as well as the consummated offence, genocide. As of 1 September 2003 over 50% of indictees have been charged with conspiracy to commit genocide. Among those charged with that offence are the former Prime Minster of Rwanda, over 8 Cabinet Ministers of the Interim Government, senior military commanders, Prefets, and Bourgmestres. The pivotal character of that offence, in the context of the 1994 genocide in Rwanda, makes it an indispensable subject of any legal and policy inquiry on accountability. More so if the question of accountability for "big, medium and small fish" is to be comprehensively appreciated.

This chapter is divided into four parts. The first part traces the early development of the law of conspiracy. It details its legal characteristics and essentials. It examines evidential and procedural issues involved in prosecuting that crime. In the analysis offered, the judicial advantages, as well as the pitfalls, apparent or real, of conspiracy as an accountability tool are discussed. Secondly a revisit is made of the prosecution of conspiracy by the Nuremberg and Tokyo Tribunals;the historical and legal predecessors of the two UN Ad Hoc Tribunals. Third the author re-examines conspiracy to commit genocide as provided for in the UN Convention on the prevention and punishment of the crime of genocide (Genocide Convention). Specific reference will also be made to the ICC, including the distinctive omission of conspiracy to commit genocide in its Statute. Finally the chapter explores the process in which conspiracy to commit genocide became the arch strategy for the prosecution of atrocity crimes committed in Rwanda in 1994. This requires an examination of two issues. Establishing the conspiracy, and iden-

---

1 For the Nuremberg Tribunal, See, Agreement for the Establishment of an International Military Tribunal (IMT), 8 August 1945, and Charter of the IMT, in US Dept. of State, Trials of War Criminals, W.D.C. 1945, pp. 13-22;For the Tokyo Tribunal, See, Charter of the International Military Tribunal for the Far East, Trials of Japanese War Criminals, US Dept pf State, W.D.C. 1946, pp. 39-44.

tifying the dens of conspirators. As part of the analysis offered, the chapter will also discuss the legal and policy lessons that can be drawn from this experience. The overall aim being to determine the extent to which conspiracy to commit genocide can answer, in full, accountability for atrocity crimes;especially for those alleged to be in positions of authority and command.

I. Conspiracy: Law and Practice

The word conspiracy devolves from two Latin words, "*con*" and "*spirare*" meaning to "to breathe together".[2] Conspiracy, the "darling of the modern prosecutor's nursery",[3] was originally known to the law of England in a statutory form pursuant to the three ordinances of Edward I;the final one being the Ordinance of Conspirators (1305), which provided a remedy against "conspirators, inventors, and inciters of false quarrels and their abettors and supporters".[4] It was then aimed at preventing malicious prosecution.[5] A conception of conspiracy in the virgin soil of the common law ante dated the first Ordinance of Conspirators of 1293, and existed quite independent of these Edwardian Statutes.[6] This pre-Edwardian conspiracy law was limited to combinations whose object was to hinder or prevent the administration of justice.[7] During the 17th century it became established law that a combination to commit any crime was in itself a conspiracy, although such a crime may not have been committed.[8] By the 18th century the law of conspiracy assumed its current shape [9] a child of the law obtaining in England.[10] There has been

---

2 Per Dickson, J, in *Papalia v. R;R.V. Cotroni*, [1979] 2 S.C.R. 256 at 276, 7 C.R. (3d (185, 11 C.R. (3d) 150, 45 C.C.C. (2d) 1, 93 D.L.R. (3d) 161, 26 N.R. 133 (Canada);also Per Loffin, Cir. J, *US v. Spock*, U.S. Court of Appeals for First Circuit, 1969 416 F. 2d.165;Cf. "Etymologically the word "conspiracy" means a breathing together;and two people cannot breathe together unless they put their heads together", Williams G L (1961) Criminal Law. The General Part, 2nd Edition, The Law Book Company of Australia, Sydney, p. 677-668.

3 Per Leonard Hand, J, *Harrison v. U.S.* 7 F.2d 259, 263 (2d Cir.1925).

4 Gillies P (1990) The Law of Conspiracy, The Federation Press, 2nd Edition, Leichhardt, NSW, p. 1;For the Statutes, See, 20 Edw. I, (1292);28 Edw. I, Sta.3, C.10 (1300), and 33 Edwin, Stat. I (1305) in Bryan J W (1970) The Development of the English Law of Conspiracy, Da Capo Press, New York, fn18, p. 17, see also, Appendixes, Wright R S (1980) The Law of Criminal Conspiracies and Agreements, Wildy and Sons, London, pp. 89-90.

5 Hazel R (1974) Conspiracy and Civil Liberties, A Memorial Submitted to the Law Commission, A Lobden Trust Memorandum, Occasional Papers on Social Administration, Willmer Brother Ltd., Birkenhead, England, p. 11.

6 Bryan J W (1970) The Development of the English Law of Conspiracy, Da Capo Press, New York, p. 11.

7 P. 11, Id.

8 Harrison D (1924) Conspiracy as a Crime and as a Tort in English Law, Sweet and Maxwell, London, p. 16;See *Poulterer's Case* (1611) 9 Rep. 55.

9 Bryan J W (1970) p. 81.

no fundamental change in the essentials of the common law crime of conspiracy in the last 100 years.[11] In its stature and contents, conspiracy remains a 'common law' crime, even though in some jurisdictions like Australia, Canada, India, U.K. and USA, it is now codified.[12] This has given birth to what now known as statutory conspiracy.

In general, the concept of conspiracy as something punishable even where no crime has been committed is unknown in civil law systems.[13] Under civil law conspiracy or "complot" derogates from the principle that a person cannot be punished for mere criminal intent (resolution criminelle) or for preparatory acts committed.[14] Moreover conspiracy is viewed as entailing the punishment of an in-

---

10 Aiyar K J (1958) Law Relating to Criminal Conspiracy in India and Pakistan, Eastern Book Company, New Delhi, p. v.

11 Gillies P (1990) p. 261, Cf. "Conspiracy is a product of courts rather than legislatures", David A K (1993) The Movement Towards Statute-Based Conspiracy Law in the UK and the US, Vanderbilt Journal of Transnational Law, vol. 25, p. 951.

12 Cf. Section 120A," When two or more persons agree to do, or cause to be done- (1) an illegal act, or (2) an act, which is not illegal by illegal means, such agreement is designated a criminal conspiracy: provided that no agreement except an agreement to commit an offence shall amount to criminal conspiracy unless some act besides the agreement is done by one or more parties to such agreement in pursuance thereof", Penal Code of India Criminal Law Amendment Act, 1913 (VIII of 1913);On the Indian Penal Code, See, Gour H S (1968) The Penal Law of India, Vol. 1, 8th Edition, Law Publishers, Allah bad, 1968;Gaur K D (1992) A Textbook on the Indian Penal Code, Oxford and IBH Publishing Co. Pty Ltd, New Delhi, 1992;See also Section 1 (1), Criminal Law Act, 1977 (England);Section 423 (2), Canadian Criminal Code;See also Halbsury's Laws of England (1990), vol.11 (1) Criminal Law, 4th Edition, Butterworths, paras. 59-63; Holrord J (2000) The Reform of jurisdiction over International Conspiracy, The Journal of Criminal Law, pp. vol.64/2, pp. 323-331;"Statutory conspiracy occurs when two or more persons agree on a course of conduct which amounts to a criminal offence. Common law conspiracy differs from statutory conspiracy in allowing punishment where the course of conduct agreed will not necessarily amount to a criminal offence but will amount to an act involving (a) the corruption of public morals or outraging public decency, or (b) fraud. In both forms it is not necessary that each conspirator has agreed to commit the offence so long as the offence will be committed by at least one of the parties to the agreement", Wilson W (1998) Criminal Law, Doctrine and Theory, Longman, London, pp. 550-551;See also, David K A (1993) The Movement Towards Statute-based Conspiracy Law in the United Kingdom and the United States, Vanderbilt journal of Transnational Law, vol. 25, p. 951 et seq.

13 Hazel R (1974) Conspiracies and Civil Liberties, p. 101;Cf. "Except where the law provides otherwise, whenever two or more persons agree for the purposes of committing an offence, and it is not committed, none of them is punishable for the sole fact of making an agreement", Art. 115, para.1, Penal Code of Italy. The recognized exceptions are in relation to crimes against the international and internal personality of the State (Arts 302-7). For commentary of these Articles See, Lattanzi G, Lupo E (2000) Codice Penale, Dott A. Guiffre Editore, vol.111, pp. 217-221;See also, de Vabres Donnedieu (1947) Le Proces de Nuremberg devant les principes modernes du droit penal international, T. 70, I, Receiul des cours, Academie de Droit International, The Hague, pp. 529-530.

14 *P. v. A. Musema*, Judgment, T.C, Case no: ICTR- 96-13-T, 27 January 2000, para. 186.

dividual for an act of a group, when a crime could only be committed by an individual, since the will to commit a crime is that of an individual and guilt could only be an individual mater.[15] In these legal systems, where it exists, it is punishable only when its purpose is to commit certain crimes considered extremely serious, such as undermining the security of the state.[16] Most recently, it has been applied to organized crime.[17] In any event, where conspiracy is recognized in the civil law system there is a requirement of an overt act.[18] The rationale for that is that an idea not yet put into put into execution does not cause any trouble to society.[19]

The prosecution of conspiracy has two objectives. First it is a means of preventive intervention against persons who manifest a disposition to criminality.[20] It aims at deterring criminal conduct preparatory to the commission of a substantive offence.[21] Conspiracy is punishable because an agreement to commit a crime is a decisive act, fraught with potential dangers.[22] As an inchoate crime, which attacks potential criminal conduct, but at an earlier stage than attempt, the conspiratorial agreement derives its criminal character purely from criminal conduct that is the

---

[15] Woetzel R K (1960) The Nuremberg Trials and International Law, Stevens and Sons, London, p. 212.

[16] *P. v. A. Musema*, Judgment, T.C, para. 186.

[17] Cf. Article 450-1 Penal Code of France: "Constitue une association de malfaiteurs tout groupement formé ou entente établie en vue de la préparation, caractérisée par un ou plusieurs faits matériels, d'un ou plusieurs crimes ou d'un ou plusieurs délits punis d'au moins cinq ans d'emprisonnement";Conspiracy is any group formed or understanding reached with a view to the preparation, evidenced by one or more overt acts, of one or more felonies or of one or more misdemeanors punishable by ten years of imprisonment);Article 132-71 "Constitue une bande organisée au sens de la loi tout groupement formé ou toute entente établie en vue de la préparation, caractérisée par un ou plusieurs faits matériels, d'une ou de plusieurs infractions", An armed gang within the meaning of the law is any group formed and any understanding reached with a view to preparing, evidenced by one or more overt acts, one or more offences", See, The French Penal Code of 1994, in The American Series of French Penal Codes, 31, Fred B. Rothman and Co. Colorado, 1994.

[18] See, Article 450-1, French Pénal Code, 1994;Stefani G, Levasseur G, Bouloc B (1997) Droit Pénal Général, Dalloz, Paris, pp. 257, 317, 473, 653;Verny E (2002) Le Membre d'un Group en Droit Pénal, Librairie Général de Droit et de Jurisprudence, Paris, p. 334.

[19] Desportes F, Le Gunehec F (1998) Le Nouveau Droit Pénal, Tome I, Droit Pénal Général, Cinquième édition, Economica, Paris, pp. 358, 438.

[20] LaFave W R (1978) Principles of Criminal Law, Cases, Comments and Questions, West Publishing Company, St Paul, p. 43;Cf. "This is an opportunistic justification rather than one of principle, having regard to the approach of criminal law to individuals who alone form a criminal intention", Gillies P (1990) p. 7.

[21] Goode, M R (1975) Criminal Conspiracy in Canada, The Carswell Company Limited, Toronto, p. 82.

[22] Tewaru R B (1962) Conspiracy, Indian Law Institute, Essays on the Indian Penal Code, Published on the occasion of the centenary of the Indian Penal Code, N.M. Tripathi Private Company, Bombay, pp. 91-92.

[22] Gour H S (1968) p. 810.

object of the conspiracy.[23] As a prophylactic measure conspiracy is a more effective weapon than attempt since it is not restricted by the requirement of proximity.[24] Second, conspiracy is also a means of striking against the special danger inherent to group criminality.[25] It seeks to protect society from the dangers of concerted criminal activity.[26] It guards against partnership in criminal purpose.[27] Concert in criminal purpose is the salient factor in criminal conspiracy.[28] A joint resolution to commit a substantive crime or any other recognized wrong doing, is more likely to produce the substantive mischief than would be a resolution by a solitary individual to commit such an act.[29] Group association for criminal purposes often, if not normally, makes possible the attainment of ends more complex than those which one criminal could accomplish.[30] Collective criminal agreement, or partnership in crime, represents a greater potential threat to the public than individual delict;concerted action both increases the likelihood that the criminal object will be successfully attained and decreases the probability that the individuals involved will depart from the path of criminality.[31] A conspiracy poses a distinct danger quite apart from that of the substantive offence.[32] De facto it functions as a joint substantive offence of the most generic kind.[33] In discussing the basic reasons for subscribing to the offence of conspiracy, it is also worth mentioning that the rationale for the crime has also been criticised. It has been argued by LaFave and Gilles that two jointly resolved minds are not, as a matter of principle, more or less evil than a simple resolute mind;that it all depends on the strength of the resolution, and on the nature of the harm contemplated.[34] Ashworth on his part has cautioned that although the law of conspiracy may be defended as a vital tool against organized crimes, the difficulty is that it may bear oppressively on some of the individuals who are caught within its ample net.[35]

---

23 Hazel R (1974) p. 93.

24 P. 94, Id.

25 LaFave W R (1978) p. 43;Cf. "This argument is weak, too simplistic. The *mens rea* of two men committing an offence in combination will not usually be any different from that of a single offender, and there are no retributive reasons for punishing two men for conduct which if done by one man would not be punishable", Hazel R (1974) p. 98.

26 Johnson P C (2000) Criminal Law, Cases, Materials and Text, 6th Edition, West Group, St Paul, Minn, p. 607.

27 *U.S.A. v. Kissel*, (1910) 218 US 601, 608.

28 Dix G E, Sharlot M M (1973) Criminal Law, Cases and Materials, West Publishing Co., St Paul, Minn., p. 793.

29 Gillies P (1990) p. 4-5.

30 LaFave W R (1978) p. 496;Gillies P (1990) p. 264.

31 LaFave W R (1978) p. 496.

32 Id.

33 Gillies P (1990) p. 261.

34 LaFave W R (1978) p. 496;Gillies P (1990) p. 264.

35 Ashworth A (2003) p. 460.

Definition

The classic definition of common law conspiracy is that pronounced in a nineteenth century decision by the House of Lords in *Mulcahy v. R*, namely, that:

"[A] Conspiracy consists not merely in the intention of two or more, but in the agreement of two or more to do an unlawful act, or to do a lawful act by unlawful means. So long as such a design rests in intention only, it is not indictable. When two or more agree to carry it into effect, the very plot is an act in itself, and the act of each of the parties, promise against promise, actus contra actus, capable of being enforced if unlawful, punishable if for a criminal object or for the use of criminal means".[36]

The above definition may be regarded as constituting a "literal" definition of the crime pursuant to which "unlawful" not only denotes acts which are criminal, or a breach of the civil law, but as well as those which can only be viewed as being socially obnoxious according to broad considerations of public policy.[37] The truth is that the word "unlawful", when used as coextensive with criminal combination, now includes all criminal purposes and some purposes wrongful but not criminal apart from combination.[38] Guided by that settled definition, the Trial Chamber in *P. v. Musema,* defined conspiracy to commit genocide, under Article 2 (3) (b) of the Statute of the Tribunal, as "an agreement between two or more persons to commit the crime of genocide"[39].

---

36 *Mulcahy* (1868) LR 3 H.L 306, at 317;For the definition in the US, as *per* Shaw, C.J.: it "is a combination of two or more persons, by some concerted action, to accomplish some criminal or unlawful purpose, or to accomplish some purpose, not in itself criminal or unlawful, by criminal or unlawful means", *Commonwealth v. Hunt*, 45 Mass (4 Met) 111, 123 (1842).

37 Gillies P (1990) p. 1-2;Note, Common law recognizes the following heads of conspiracy, namely, conspiracy to commit a crime, conspiracy to defraud, conspiracy to corrupt public morals, conspiracy to commit a tort, and even conspiracy to cause economic loss, at p. 110-111;Halbury's Laws of England (1990) vol. 11 (1) paras. 60-63, See also House of Lords decisions, *Shaw v. DPP* (1962) AC 222 relating to conspiracy to corrupt public morals, and *Kamara v. DPP* (1974) AC 104 relating to conspiracy to commit a tort;"The doctrine that a combination to effect an admittedly illegal purpose by means not illegal per se is an indictable conspiracy is sound upon both reason and authority", Bryan J W (1970) p. 109;Cf. "Lord Denman did not himself intend so expansive a reading", Gillies P (1990) p. 71.

38 Wright R S (1980) p. 66;"The word "unlawful" in the first sentence means 'criminal' as shown in the later part of the definition", Harrison D (1924) pp. 64-67.

39 *P. v. A. Musema*, Judgement, Case no: ICTR- 96-13-T, 27 January 2000, para 192;*P. v. E. Niyitegeka*, Judgement and Sentence Case no: ICTR-96-14-T, 16 May 2003, para. 423.

Overt acts

Every act of conspiring with any person to effect that purpose, and every act done in furtherance of the purpose of any of the persons conspiring, is deemed to be an overt act manifesting the intention.[40] Generally under common law conspiracy no overt act is necessary to constitute the crime of conspiracy, unless changed or limited by Statute, as is the case with regard to statutory conspiracy.[41] The criminality of the conspiracy is independent of the criminality of the overt acts.[42] Courts have judicially endorsed this principle since the 18th century.[43] In common law conspiracy there need be no overt act beyond the making of the agreement.[44] An overt act being an outward act, done in pursuance of the crime and in manifestation of an intent or design, and looking forward to the accomplishment of the crime.[45] The function of the overact in a conspiracy prosecution is simply to manifest 'that conspiracy is at work', and is neither a project still resting solely in the minds of the conspirators nor a fully completed operation no longer in existence.[46]

On this, Brett J.A *R. v. Aspinall* stated:

> "Now, first, the crime of conspiracy is completely committed, if it is committed at all, the moment two or more have agreed that they will do, at once or at some future time, certain things. It is not necessary in order to complete the offence that any one thing should be done beyond the agreement. The conspirators may repent and stop, or may have no opportunity, or may be prevented, or may fail. Nevertheless, the crime is complete: it was completed when they agreed".[47]

It is worth recalling that common law conspiracy crimes are rather few, and in the U.K. conspiracy to defraud, to corrupt public morals, and to outrage public decency come within to this category. As we have pointed out statutory conspiracy crimes require an overt act. Ashworth has posed the question whether an agreement, without more, goes far enough to warrant criminalization?[48] The danger he sees is that it may lead to convictions based on inferences and mere association.[49] In so

---

40 Section 49, Penal Code of Tanzania, Cap 16 of the Laws.

41 Gour H S (1968) p. 800;Gillies P (1990) p. 1;Smith and Hogan (1988) Criminal Law, Butterworths, 6th ed., London, p. 258;Cf. In India the statutory requirement of an overact was opted for to provide an additional judicious safeguard, See, Gour H S (1968) p. 793;In the USA, the requirement of an overt act is that of the Statute, Dix G E, Sharlot, M M (1973) p. 809.

42 Gupta R L (1965) Law of Abetment, Criminal Conspiracy and Constructive Liability, Law Book Company, Allahabad, p. 242.

43 Bryan J W (1970) p. 86, See also, *O'Connell v. R* (1844) 11 Cl & F 155;*R.v. Boulton* (1871) 12 Cox 87.

44 Williams G L (1961) p. 663.

45 *Chavez v. US*, 9 Cir. 275 F.2d 813, 817.

46 *Yates v. US*, 394 U.S. 298, 77 S.Ct.1064, 1 L Ed. 2d 1356 (1957).

47 *Rex v. Aspinall* (1876) 2 Q.B. 48, 58 (C.A.).

48 Ashworth A (2003) Principles of Criminal Law, 4th ed., Oxford University Press, Oxford, p. 449-460.

49 Id.

far as accountability for atrocity crimes is concerned it is a rule of practice for the Prosecution to allege in the indictment and to prove as part of the evidence overt acts in order to demonstrate planning, knowledge, and the existence of concerted action as proof of a conspiracy. This reflects sound practice.

Merger: Conspiracy and the Substantive Offence

A conspiracy to commit an offence does not merge with the substantive offence when the latter is concluded.[50] In other words it does not sink into the consummated crime.[51] It is an offence separate and distinct from the offence in respect of which the parties conspired.[52] Conspiracy can be committed notwithstanding that the substantive crime to which it relates has not been committed.[53] This view was endorsed in *Pinkerton v. US*, where the US Supreme Court declared that: "it has been long and consistently recognized by the Court that commission of the substantive offence and a conspiracy to commit it are separate and distinct offences, and the power of the Court to separate the two and to affix to each a different penalty is well established".[54] Unlike attempt, conspiracy is not subsumed into the substantive crime. No consummation of the crime need be achieved or even attempted.[55] It is permissible to charge both a consummated crime and a conspiracy to commit it in one and the same indictment.[56] This practice of cumulative charging has been endorsed in the practice of both the two UN ad hoc Tribunals.

It has been suggested that a trial in which accused are charged with both conspiracy to commit an offence, and the substantive offence, in a sense offends the double jeopardy rule in that the same evidence is relied upon as proof of the two crimes. This objection is more by way of judicial self-defence than one motivated by a notion of injustice.[57] There is no prejudice in relying on the same evidence for multiple accusations, given that the evidence often forms part of the same criminal transaction. Additionally the supposed unfairness suggested is not borne out in the prosecution of atrocity crimes, which invariably are committed as part of a widespread or systematic attack directed against the civilian population.

---

[50] Ashworth A (2003) Principles of Criminal Law, Oxford University Press, 4th edition,Oxford, p. 458;See also, Card R (2001) Card, Cross and Jones Criminal Law, 15th Ed., Butterworths, U.K., para. 1734;*Brodie v. R.* [1936] S.C.R. 188 (Canada).

[51] Williams G L (1961) p. 683.

[52] In *Kravenia* [1955] S.C.R. 615, at 621 (Canada).

[53] Card R (2001) para 17.1.

[54] 328 US 640, 66 S. Ct.1180, 90 L. Ed. 1489 (1946).

[55] Gaur K D (1992) p. 186.

[56] Williams G L (1961) p. 684.

[57] Goode M R (1992) p. 182.

Legal Elements

The three legal ingredients of conspiracy are; (a) an agreement, (b) at least two persons by whom agreement is effected, and (c) a common object, which may either be the ultimate aim of the agreement or may constitute the means or one of the means, by which that aim is to be effected.[58]

a) Agreement

Criminal conspiracy is an offence of a technical nature, the essential requirement of which is the agreement to commit the offence.[59] Metaphorically put "conspiracy is nothing;agreement is the thing".[60] The gist of the offence of conspiracy lies not in doing the act, nor effecting the purpose, nor in inciting others to do them, but in the forming of the scheme or agreement between the parties.[61] The offence is complete as soon as there is agreement.[62] In view of the fact that genocide will usually be perpetrated by concerted action on the part of a group of persons, the mere fact or rather act of conspiring is punishable, even if no preparatory act has taken place.[63] Conspiracy is an agreement to work together towards a common objective.[64] The agreement to do the act is distinct from the doing of the act.[65] The *actus reus* in conspiracy is therefore the agreement to execute the unlawful conduct, not the execution of it.[66] The culpable doing, or *actus reus*, of the crime consists in the physical acts, words or gestures, by which the conspirators signify their mutual consent to the agreement or consensus.[67]

Conspiracy need not be proved by express agreement between conspirators to go forth and violate the law;it may be inferred from a collocation of circumstances.[68] The concept of agreement in conspiracy is not equivalent to contractual agreement;it has a wider meaning than in the law of contract, and cannot be analy-

---

58 Harrison D (1924) p. 64.

59 Gour H S (1968) p. 810;Desai D A, Jain M L, Menon N R D (1995) Ratanlal and Dhirajlal's Law of Crimes, Bharat Law House Put. Ltd., New Delhi, p. 381.

60 Per Lord Campbell, *Reg. v. Hamp*, (1852) 6 Cox C.C. 442, 445.

61 *State v. Carbone*, 10 NJ. 329, 91 A.2d. 571, 575 (S.C. New Jersey, US), cited in *Regle v. State*, C.A. Md., 1970, 9 Md. 346, 264 A. 2d 119.

62 Per Sulaiman, C.J. Meerut Conspiracy Case: *Jhabwala V. Emperor*, 1933 All 690;1933 ALJ 799;Gillies P (1990) p. 16.

63 Drost P N (1959) The Crime of State, II, Genocide, A.W. Sijhoff, Leyden, p. 12.

64 Colvin E (1991) Principles of Criminal Law, Thomson Professional Publishing Ltd, Canada, p. 347.

65 Dix G E, Sharlot M M (1973) p. 845.

66 Halbury's Laws of England (1990) vol. 11 (1), para 64," As far as the *actus reus* is concerned it is the agreement itself that is criminal", Mewett A W, Manning M S (1994) Mewett and Manning on Criminal Law, 3rd Edition, Butterworths, Toronto, p. 330.

67 Gillies R (1990) p. 16.

68 LaFave W R (1978) p. 433.

zed in terms of an offer and an acceptance.[69] A formal agreement need not be established;it is sufficient if the minds of the parties meet understandingly, so as to bring about an intelligent and deliberate agreement to do the acts contemplated.[70] Conspiratorial agreement is not mere acquiescence in or knowledge of the plan;it is not a formal agreement in any way;it may be tacit or express;it is less demanding than contractual agreement, and it is more than criminal negotiation.[71] Negotiations per se are not sufficient to convict for conspiracy;what is needed is an agreement.[72] Whether or not a person has agreed to something depends largely on his state of mind. It is nevertheless clear that even if the minds of several people can be said to be "agreed" on the furtherance of an unlawful objective there can be no conspiracy until the fact of such agreement is manifested by some form of physical communication between two or more parties.[73]

As regards the proof of conspiracy, the words of the Supreme Court of Canada in *Paradis v. R* are instructive:

> "No doubt the agreement.....is the gist of the offence [i.e. conspiracy], but only in very rare cases will it be possible to prove it by direct evidence. Ordinarily the evidence must proceed by steps. The actual agreement must be gathered from "several isolated doings" having possible little or no value taken by themselves, but the bearing of which one upon the other must be interpreted;and their cumulative effect, properly estimated in the light of all surrounding circumstances, may raise a presumption of concerted purpose entitling the jury to find the existence of the unlawful purpose." [74]

The existence of an agreement may be proven by either direct evidence that the parties actually met together and concluded it, and /or indirectly, usually by proof of the overacts done in the transaction of the agreement, where these acts are sufficient when taken with any relevant surrounding circumstance to justify the inference that their commission was the product of concert between the alleged parties.[75] The law does not require that the act of agreement take any particular form, and the fact of agreement may be communicated by words or conduct.[76] Any agreement by words or conduct to commit the wrong constitutes a conspiracy.[77]

The *mens rea* required for conspiracy is an intention to be a party to an agreement to do an unlawful act.[78] Conspiracy is a 'double intent' crime whose require-

---

69 Orchard G (1974) "Agreement" in Criminal Conspiracy, Crim.L.J. p. 299;Goode M R (1992) p. 10.

70 *Regle v. State*, 1970, 9 Md.App 346, 2643 A 2d. 119 (Court of Special App. Of Maryland).

71 Goode M R (1992) p. 16.

72 Williams G (1978) p. 351.

73 Orchard G (1974) p. 298.

74 *Paradis v. R*, Supreme Court of Canada, (1934) 61 CCC 184, 186.

75 Gillies P (1990) p. 16.

76 Orchard G (1974) p. 300.

77 Williams G L (1978) Textbook of Criminal Law, Stevens and Sons, U.K, London, p. 351.

78 Per Viscount Dilhorne, *Churchill v. Wilton* [1967] 2 A.C. 224, 237;Cf. *Per* Lord Scarman, "The *mens rea* of the offence is the intention to do the unlawful act, the *actus reus*

ment falls into two elements: (a) the intention to agree, or conspire, and (b) the intention to commit the offence which is the object of the conspiracy.[79] The agreement is the act while the intention to achieve the objective is the mental state.[80] There must be intention with respect to the material elements of the substantive offence[81] Two elements of conspiratorial *mens rea* are discernable: (i) the primary element (i.e. the intention) to agree upon the commission of the physical act consisting the criminal or other unlawful object of the crime;and (ii) the secondary elements of *mens rea* which is concerned with the degree of knowledge the conspirators must have as to the precise nature of this conspiratorial act, which knowledge will generally be concerned with the circumstances surrounding the prospective commission of this act and from which its criminal or other unlawful nature may be inferred.[82] If the object, adopted with full knowledge by the defendants is illegal, the guilty intent to accomplish it must be ascribed to the conspirator, although their individual desires may have been proper enough.[83]

A Continuing Crime

Conspiracy is a continuing offence, and it is not committed only at the point in time at which agreement is first reached.[84] The offence continues as long as the agreement exists, until the unlawful object is achieved or the agreement is otherwise terminated.[85] The fact that a conspirator is not present at, or does not participate in, the commission of any of the overt acts does not, by itself, exonerate him.[86] When a conspiracy is shown to exist, which in its nature is not ended merely by lapse of time, it continues to exist until consummated, abandoned, or otherwise terminated by some affirmative act;although no general rule of law can accurately be laid down as to when the conspiracy is at an end.[87] The withdrawal of some of the participants in a conspiracy and the joining of others does not interrupt the continuity of the conspiracy.[88]

There is reason to suggest that the genocide of the Tutsi in Rwanda was a continuous conspiracy, in which core conspirators, co-conspirators, and accomplices went on a criminal rampage not only in Rwanda between April and July 1994, but

is the fact of agreement", *D.P. P v.Nock*, [1978] 3 W.L.R- 57, 67 Cr.App. R. 116 [1978] 2 All E.R. 654 at 658 (H.L.).

79 LaFave W R (1978) p. 442.

80 LaFave W R (1978) pp. 442-444.

81 Colvin E (1991) p. 351.

82 Gillies P (1990) p. 20;Cf. " A dual mental state is required for conspiracy: (1) the intention required to commit the crime contemplated, and (2) the intention to act together in carrying out the common purpose", Charles E Torcia (ed.) (1996) Wharton's Criminal Law, vol. 4, 15th Edition, Clark Boardman Callaghan, Deerfield, p. 680.

83 Bryan J W (1970) p. 96.

84 Orchard G (1974) p. 302.

85 Id.

86 La Fave W R (1978) 432.

87 Gour H S (1968) 796.

88 Id.

also into neighbouring Democratic Republic of Congo subsequently after the fall of the Interim Government on 17 July 1994. In the commission of interconnected and synchronized atrocities in Rwanda, the overacts of one partner were often the continuation of those of the others, without there being an entirely new conspiratorial agreement, but rather only tactical alterations to the common object of exterminating the Tutsi and eliminating moderate Hutu.

b) Two or More Persons

There must be at least two persons involved for a crime of conspiracy to be legally constituted.[89] A person cannot be convicted of conspiracy with himself.[90] In the graphic metaphor of Howard, J, "one person cannot commit the crime of conspiracy any more than one pigeon can flock by itself in the corner".[91] If several conspirators are indicted jointly for conspiracy, the acquittal of all but one operates to free him also.[92] The reason being that a verdict of guilty against a single person would be inconsistent with the allegation of a concerted design.[93] The requirement is a community of purpose, a joint resolution of two or more parties that either one or more of the member should effect the object of each of them.[94] If two persons conspire together to commit an offence, each is regarded as the agent of the other and just as the principle is liable for the acts of his agent, so each of the agents is liable for what is done by his fellow conspirator, in furtherance of the common intention, which they both had entertained.[95]

A person may conspire with another although he does not know his identity and is not in direct communication with him, but he must at least know or believe that there is another who agrees with him.[96] There is no requirement that each party to a given conspiracy personally communicate to every other party his assent to the formation of the criminal agreement, and vice versa.[97]

A number of individuals may be held to be parties to the same conspiracy although they joined at different times.[98] And the original parties are not guilty of

---

[89] Cf. Article 416, of the Penal Code of Italy requires in the case of conspiracy for organized crimes (mafia) that there must be three or more persons joining together to commit more than one crime.

[90] Batra T S (1981) Criminal Law in India, Metropolitan Printing Press, Delhi, p. 557.

[91] *R. v. Segal* [1925] 4 D.L.R. 762, at 767 (Que. K.B.).

[92] Bryan J W (1970) p. 93;"The rule of law that the acquittal of one of the only two conspirators require the acquittal of the other is now not automatic but requires analysis of the basis for the accused's conviction. Thus, the conviction of one conspirator may survive the acquittal of the other conspirator", Eswaschuk E G (1996) Criminal Pleadings and Practice in Canada, 2nd Ed., Canada Law Book Co. Inc., Ontario, para 19:0040.

[93] Bryan J W (1970) p. 93.

[94] Gillies P (1990) p. 19.

[95] Aiyar K J (1958) p. 152.

[96] Orchard G (1974) p. 335.

[97] Gillies P (1990) p. 18.

[98] Orchard G (1974) p. 302

a new offence every time a new party joins.[99] A person may be held as a conspirator although he joins the criminal concert at a point in time far beyond the initial act of the conspirators.[100] If he joins later, knowing of the criminal design and acts in concert with the original conspirators, he may be held responsible not only for everything that may be done thereafter, but also for everything which has been done prior to his adherence to the criminal design.[101] A person who enters into a conspiratorial relationship is liable for every reasonable foreseeable crime committed by every other member of the conspiracy in furtherance of its objective, whether or not he knew of the crimes or aided in their commission.[102] Where the members of the conspiracy are members of different organizations it is not necessary to establish that the different organizations were connected with one another.[103] A defendant cannot escape criminal responsibility on the grounds that he did not join the conspiracy until well after its inception, or because he played only a minor role in the total scheme.[104] The addition of a new member does not create a new conspiracy;conversely the withdrawal of a conspirator does not create a new conspiracy nor does it change the status of the remaining members.[105]

Previous acquaintance between conspirators is unnecessary, nor is it necessary that each conspirator should have seen the other, or has knowledge, as to who all the members of the conspiracy are.[106] With regard to contact between co-conspirators, there is no need for proof of direct meetings or combinations;the agreement may be inferred from circumstances raising a presumption of a concerted plan to carry out the unlawful design.[107] Conspiracy implies concert of design, and not participation in every detail of execution, and it is not necessary that each conspirator should have taken part in every act or know the exact past performance or acts to be performed by the others in the furtherance of the conspiracy.[108] It is not the law that every conspirator must be present at every stage of the conspiracy.[109] As we have observed earlier, conspiracy is a continuing offence, and is committed not only when agreement is first reached, but also as long as the agreement to effect the unlawful object continues.[110]

---

99 Id.

100 LaFave W R (1978) p. 432.

101 P. 431, Id.

102 *Pinkerton v. U.S.*, 328 U.S. 640 (1946);*Callanan v. U.S*, 364 U.S. 587, 593 (1961).

103 Gupta R L (1965) p. 243, see also, *Jitewara Nath v. Emperor*, A.I.R. (1937) Cal. 99, 38 Cr.L.J. 818 (S.B.) 10 R.C. 69, 164 I.C. 977.

104 Johnson P C (2000) p. 615.

105 Wharton's Criminal Law, p. 679;LaFave WR (1978) p. 429, "But, a statement by one conspirator is not admissible against the others unless the existence of a conspiracy has been independently established", at p. 429.

106 Gour H S (1968) p. 798.

107 Aiyar K J (1958) p. 117.

108 Gour H S (1968) p. 798.

109 P. 810, Id.

110 *DPP v. Dott* [1973] 1 All E.R. 940 (House of Lords), Cf. "But a conspiracy does not end with the making of the agreement. It will continue so long as there are two or more

c) Common Object, Purpose or Plan

It is the 'common purpose or plan' between conspirators that forms the basis of conspiracy.[111] To constitute a single general conspiracy, there must be a common design and a common intention of all to work in furtherance of the common design.[112] Conspiracy is an offence of intention, and the conspirator is required to act with intention, or purpose, not only in relation to the formation of the agreement, but also in relation to the unlawful act or acts which are to be done pursuant to it.[113] A mere criminal intention formed in a man's mind is insufficient and that stage is never criminally cognizable.[114] To sustain a conviction for conspiracy to commit a particular offence, the prosecution must show not only that the conspirators intended to agree, but also that they intended to commit the elements of that offence.[115] As long as a design rests in intention only, it is not indictable.[116]

With regard to knowledge, a person cannot be a conspirator unless he at least knows what the unlawful object is, and must as a minimum know of the participation of other conspirators.[117] Proof of knowledge is a question of fact.[118] At the least a conspirator must be aware that he is participating in a "scheme".[119] A person cannot truly agree to something without knowing what he is supposed to be agreeing to.[120] He is not required to know the full extent of the scheme to which he attaches himself.[121] It is enough that he knows the essential nature of the conspiracy itself.[122]

Procedural Issues

Much of the debate between advocates and protagonists of the crime of conspiracy is centred not only on the extensive nature of the crime of conspiracy, but also the procedural advantages in favour of the prosecution.[123] In relation to the substantive offence, while the view that "the crime of conspiracy affords support for anyone

parties to it intending to carry out the design", per Viscount Dilhorne, *DPP v Dott*, at p. 947.

111 La Fave W R (1978) p. 43.
112 Desai D A *et all.*, (1995) p. 382.
113 Gillies P (1990) p. 22.
114 Tewaru R B (1962) p. 91.
115 LaFave W R (1978) p. 442.
116 Aiyar K J (1958) p. 18.
117 Orchard G (1974) p. 335.
118 La Fave W R (1978) p. 442.
119 *In Griffiths* [1965] 49 Crim.App. Rep. 279.
120 Orchard G (1974) p. 335.
121 P. 337, Id.;LaFave W R (1978) p. 432.
122 La Fave W R (1978) p. 432.
123 See, Abbate F J (1992) The Conspiracy Doctrine: A Critique, in Goor M J, Harwood S (1992) Controversies in Criminal Law, West View Press Inc., Boulders, Colorado, pp. 55-67;Klein S A (1957) Conspiracy-The Prosecutor's darling, Brooklyn Law Review, vol. XXIV, No.1, pp. 1-11.

who advances the proposition that criminal law is an instrument of government",[124] may have been valid when the crime was dominantly linked with offences against the security of the state, that submission is now outdated given the right to a fair trial engraved in regional and international human rights instruments, and the statues of international tribunals or courts.

There is no doubt that conspiracy prosecutions are most suitable in criminality associated with web-like organized crimes and in accountability for the top brass, not just lieutenants and foot soldiers of today's calculated globalization of criminality.[125] The effectiveness of conspiracy has been ably demonstrated in the prosecution of crimes involving illicit trafficking in drugs and narcotics,[126] money laundering, fraudulent accounting and securities fraud;traffic in human persons, and terrorism, where the criminal enterprise is extensive, multiple, pluralistic, resourceful, and often transnational.

In conspiracy the Prosecution is allowed to evade the rule prohibiting a duplicity or multiplicity of criminal allegations in a single count.[127] It has the ability to allege numerous crimes in one count.[128] Furthermore it can 'roll up' charges. This is the devise of charging a defendant with agreeing to do what he did, instead of charging him with doing it.[129] We have mentioned earlier that since conspiracy does not merge into the crime committed pursuant to it, the Prosecution is permitted to charge for both, the conspiracy and the consummated crime. This constitutes acceptable practice in the criminal procedure of the ICTR and ICTY. Cumulative charging is allowed in the light of the fact that, prior to the presentation of evidence, it is not possible to determine to a certainty which of the charges brought against an accused will be proved.[130] It is also legally possible for the accused to be found guilty of more than one crime on the basis of the same criminal conduct.[131]

It has been suggested that where there is an effective and sufficient charge of a substantive offence or offences, the addition of a conspiracy charge is undesirable in that it tends to prolong and complicate the trial.[132] This should not be considered a rule of law, or desirable practice in the prosecution of atrocity crimes. For such

124 Turner J W C (ed.) (1964) Russell on Crime, Vol. I, 12 Edition, Stevens and Sons, London, p. 200.

125 Gurule J (1996) Complex Criminal Litigation, Prosecuting Drug Enterprises and Organized Crimes, Michie Law Publishers, Charlottesville, Virginia, p. 4; See also, Ickler N L (1983) Conspiracy to Violate Rico. Expanding Traditional Conspiracy Law, 58 Notre Dame L. Rev. 587 et seq.

126 See, Bauman J (1994) Conspiring Drug Kingpins: Twice in Jeopardy? 61 *U.Chi. L. Rev*. 197.

127 Gillies P (1990) p. 11.

128 Id.

129 Hazel R (1974) 73.

130 *Celebici* Appeal Judgment, Case no: IT- 96-21, A.C, 20 February 2001, para. 400;*P. v. R. Kristic*, Decision on Defence Preliminary Motion on the Form of the Amended Indictment, Case no: IT-98-PT, 28 February 2000, paras. 4-7.

131 *P. v. R. Kristic*, Judgment, Case no: ICTY - IT-98-33, 29 November 2002, para. 660.

132 Card R (2001) para. 17.34.

crimes the charging of conspiracy to commit genocide and of the substantive crime of genocide is in the interest of justice. It elucidates full accountability, which may not be exposed through the charging only of the executed crime. The judicial truth of atrocity crimes cannot be deciphered through the accountability of the substantive offence only. It requires a criminal inquiry into conspiratorial acts as well. In addition the argument that it results in lengthy trials is not evidenced from the conduct of trials before the ICTR where accused have been charged with both offences, and where the Prosecution has relied on overt acts to prove simultaneously conspiracy to commit genocide, and the substantive crime genocide.

A penetrating critique on conspiracy is that of judicial fairness. It has been argues that in its zeal of making it easier to impose criminal punishment on members of groups that plot forbidden activities;conspiracy unavoidably increases the likelihood that persons will be punished for what they say rather than for what they do, or for associating with others who are found culpable.[133] It is further argued that it is difficult for an accused to make his own case stand on its own merits in the minds of jurors who are ready to believe that birds of a feather flock together: if he is silent, he is taken to admit it, and if, as often happens, co defendants can be prodded into accusing or contradicting each other, they convict each other.[134]

It has been forcefully submitted that an accused that must defend against a charge of conspiracy bears a particularly heavy burden.[135] In the words of Justice Jackson "a co-defendant in a conspiracy trial occupies an uneasy seat".[136] In *Krulewitch v. USA,* he further portrayed the overall effect of evidential rules in these terms: [137]

> "When the trial starts, the accused feels the full impact of the conspiracy strategy. Strictly, the prosecution should first establish prima facie the conspiracy and identify the conspirators, after which evidence of acts and declarations of each in the course of its execution are admissible against all. But the order of proof of so sprawling a charge is difficult for a judge to control. As a practical matter, the accused is often confronted with a hodgepodge of acts and statements by others, which he may never have authorized, or intended or even known about, but which help to persuade the jury of the existence of the conspiracy itself. In other words, a conspiracy often is proved by evidence that is admissible only upon assumption that the conspiracy existed."

Although conspiracy has been generally criticized in that it extends the radius of individual criminal responsibility there is hardly any merit in this argument when it comes to complex cross-frontier criminality such as international terrorism and money laundering. That rebuke is also at odds with accountability for atrocity crimes. First, culpability is not anchored on the criminality of organizations or as-

---

[133] Johnson P E (1973) The Unnecessary Crime of Conspiracy, California Law Journal, vol. 61/5, p. 1139.

[134] P. 620, Id.

[135] LaFave W R (1978) p. 428.

[136] (1949) 366 U.S. 440, 453-4.

[137] Id.

sociations. That was abandoned after the Nuremberg Trial. Secondly international courts and tribunals are required, to observe international standards of justice, the presumption of innocence, fairness and due process as mandatory obligations, which make it impossible that insinuate conduct or inferences will ever suffice to meet the standard of guilt required: proof beyond a reasonable doubt. Thirdly justice by the UN Ad Hoc Tribunals is dispensed by professional judges;not lay assessors or juries. Fourthly Rule 82 (B) of the Rules of Procedure and Evidence allows for severance if there is a conflict of interest that might cause serious prejudice to the accused in conducting his or her defense, and if it is necessary to protect the interests of justice.[138] Fifthly a sensible conduct of the trial by a Trial Chamber of an international tribunal or court should be able to remedy any procedural unfairness in a conspiracy charge.[139]

Conspiracy and Joinder

Because the existence of a common scheme is also the basis of a conspiracy count, the law of joinder of defendants is, to a large extent the law of conspiracy.[140] If a series of acts are so connected together by proximity of time, community of criminal intention, action and purpose, or from the relation of cause and effect as to constitute, in the opinion of the Court, one transaction, then the accused may be charged and tried in one trial for every offence committed in such series of acts, and if more persons than one are accused of different offences in a series of acts so connected they may also be tried together.[141] 'Transaction' does not necessarily mean proximity in time as much as continuity of progressive action and purpose towards a single object.[142] In *P. V. Kayishema, Ntakiritumana and Ruzindana* the Trial Chamber held that involvement in a same transaction must be connected to specific material elements which demonstrate on the one hand the existence of an offence, of a criminal act which is objectively punishable and specifically determine in time and space, and on the other hand prove the existence of a common scheme, strategy or plan, and that the accused therefore acted together and in concert.[143]

---

138 See, Decision on Prosecutor's Motion for Joinder of Accused and Prosecutor's Motion for Severance of accused, *P. v. M. Ngirumpatse, J. Nzizorera & J. Kageligeli*, Case no: ICTR-98-44-I, 29 June 2000.

139 Williams G (1978) pp. 354-5.

140 Johnson P E (1973) p. 1167, "Joint Trials exist to serve the convenience of the Prosecutor and the Courts, not the convenience of the defendant", at p. 1172; "Joinder is justified is the judge considers that the interests of justice demand it", Halbury's Laws of England (1990), vol. 11(1) para.67.

141 Aiyar K J (1958) p. 374.

142 P. 374, Id.

143 Decision on the Motion of the Prosecutor to Sever, to Join in a Superseding Indictment, and to Amend the Superseding Indictment, *P. v Kayisihema, Ntakiritumana & Ruzindana*, Case no: ICTR-95-1-T, 27 March 1997, p. 3.

The offence of conspiracy and offences committed in pursuance of that conspiracy form one and the same transaction.[144] That apart, the acts or omissions of the accused which are alleged to form the same transaction, necessary for joinder, need not be criminal or illegal in themselves.[145] It is however required that the acts of the accused, (a) be connected to material elements of a criminal act, (b) the criminal acts which the acts of the accused are connected to must be capable of specific determination in time and space, and (c), the criminal acts which the acts of the accused are connected to must illustrate the existence of a common scheme, strategy or plan.[146]

Rules 48 and 48 *bis* of the Tribunal's Rules of Procedure and Evidence confers upon Trial Chamber the authority to grant joinder of accused and joint trials, and Rule 82 (B) empowers it to order separate trials if it considers it necessary in order to avoid a conflict of interest that might cause serious prejudice to an accused. In *P. v. J. B. Barayagwiza* the Trial Chamber sustained the Prosecutor's motion for joinder and held that on the basis of the allegations linking the accused, with the other two accused in relation to both the media organizations and CDR, it was satisfied that a sufficient basis had been established to support the assertion that the accused, Nahimana, and Ngeze were involved in a number of acts or omissions being part of a common scheme, strategy or plan, committed in the course of the same transaction.[147] *In P. v. J. Kajelijeli et all.*, the Defence argued as inappropriate, unfair and unjust the Prosecutor's strategy of "bootstrapping" the accused, a Bourgmestre, to other Ministers using conspiracy law and against whom there may be more evidence.[148] The Trial Chamber held that the concurrent presentation of evidence of all the co-accused in that case would be unfair to the accused because most of the allegations in the indictment did not relate to him.[149] It noted that if the level of culpability of the accused was indeed lower than the rest of the co-accused, evidence brought against the co-accused could have a negative spill-over effect and unfairly magnify the responsibilities of the accused.[150] The Chamber accordingly ordered a separate trial. Joinder is not improper merely because the defendants did not participate in every act alleged in furtherance of the conspiracy or because the prosecution did not name the defendants in every count in the

---

144 Gupta R L (1965) p. 204.

145 Decision on the Prosecutor's motion for joinder and decision on Barayagwiza's extremely urgent motions for lack of jurisdiction and for waiver of the time limits under Rule 72 (a) and (f) of the Rules, *P. v. J. B. Barayagwiza*, Case no: ICTR-97-19-1, 6 June 2000, para. 8.

146 Decision on the Defence Motion Requesting an Order for Separate Trials, *P. v. G. Kabiligi*, Case no: ICTR-97-34-I, 30 September 1998, p. 2.

147 Decision on the Prosecutor's motion for joinder and decision on Barayagwiza's extremely urgent motions for lack of jurisdiction, *P. v. J. B. Barayagwiza*, paras. 17-18

148 *P. v. J. Kageligeli et all*, Decision on the Defence Motion in Opposition to the Joinder and Motion for severance and Separate Trial filled by the Accused J. Kajelijeli, Case no: ICTR-44-T, 6 July 2000, para. 34.

149 Para. 28, Id.

150 Para. 38, Id.

indictment.[151] It is proper if the indictment charges conspiracy even though the defendant is only named in the conspiracy count of a multi-count indictment.[152] In accordance with established national jurisprudence and in the interest of the good administration of justice co-conspirators should generally be tried together.[153]

Evidence of co-conspirators

The general rule in the case of conspiracy is the acceptance of the reception of the evidence of a co-conspirator;namely, when two or more persons conspire together to commit an offence, the acts and declarations of one made in pursuance of the conspiracy, may be admissible in evidence against the others, as well as against the defendant himself.[154] The rationale for this seems to be founded on *identity of interest* existing between the parties.[155] Sarkar has explained it in these terms:

"So far as one person is privy in obligation with another,, i.e. is liable to be affected in his obligation under the substantive law by the acts of the other, there is equal reason for receiving against him such admissions of the other as furnish evidence of the act which charges the equally".[156]

As mentioned, the evidence of one conspirator is admissible against all the conspirators, whether they were present or had authorized such acts or statements or not, provided that a foundation for the admission of such evidence is laid by independent proof of the conspiracy, and of the adherence to it by the actor and declarer.[157] The rationale advanced is that conspiracy is a plural crime, and can reasonably only be proved by reference to the words or acts of two or more persons, which need to be admitted against each of them to secure the conviction of that person.[158] It is further justified in terms of the concept of agency whereby recipro-

---

151 Gurule J (1996) 483-484.

152 Pp. 483-484, "The defendant need only be charged with committing an overt act in the conspiracy count to sustain joinder", at 484.

153 Decision on the Prosecutor's motion for joinder and decision on Barayagwiza's extremely urgent motions for lack of jurisdiction, *P. v. J. B. Barayagwiza*, p. 16.

154 Andrews J A, Hirst M (1997) Andrews and Hirst on Criminal Evidence, IIIrd Edition, Sweet & Maxwell, London, pp. 721-772;LaFave W R (1978) p. 429;See also, Levie J H (1954) Hearsay and Conspiracy, A Re-examination of the Co-Conspirators' Exception to the Hearsay Rule, vol.52/8, Michigan Law Review, pp. 1159-1178;For ICTR, Cf, " The Chamber notes that hearsay evidence is not inadmissible per se, even when it cannot be examined at its source or when it is not corroborated by direct evidence. Rather, the Chamber has considered such hearsay evidence, with caution, in accordance with Rule 89", *P. v. A. Musema*, Judgement and Sentence, T.C, Case no: ICTR-96-13-T, 27 January 2000, para. 51.

155 Sarkar S, Manohar V R (2003) Sarkar on Evidence, Wadhwa and Company Nagar, 15 th ed., p. 235 2074.

156 P. 235 Id.

157 Goode M R (1992) pp. 79, 185, 245, 250;Gillies P (1990) p. 185;Hazel R (1974) p. 79.

158 Gillies P (1990) p. 184.

cal relationships of principal and agent are imputed to each confederate in the conspiracy charged.[159] Another explanation offered is that such evidence is in itself a fact, and a part of the *res gestae* so combined and inseparable. In terms of judicial fairness however, all of the above has to be weighed against the potential risks in relying on evidence that may be prejudicial to the accused.

II. Nuremberg and Tokyo Tribunals: 'Common Plan or Conspiracy'

Accountability through the prosecution of conspiracy at the Nuremberg Tribunal constituted the first judicial consideration of the crime of conspiracy by an international criminal tribunal. Although the circumstances were different to those surrounding the establishment of the two UN Ad hoc Tribunals, an examination of the approach and the judgment of the Nuremberg Tribunal are of interest since the latter dealt with that crime in the context of egregious atrocity crimes. Article 6 of the Nuremberg Charter provided:[160]

"The following acts, or any of them, coming within the jurisdiction of the Tribunal for which there shall be individual responsibility:

(a) Crimes against peace;namely, planning, preparation, initiation or waging of a war of aggression, or a war in violation of international treaties, agreements or assurances, or participation in a common plan or conspiracy for the accomplishment of any of the foregoing.

Count one –'The Common Plan or Conspiracy' of the Nuremberg indictment alleged that "all the defendants, with divers other persons, during a period of years preceding 8 May, 1945 participated as leaders, organizers, instigators or accomplices in the formulation or execution of a common plan or conspiracy to commit, or which involved the commission of crimes against peace, war crimes, and crimes against humanity, as defined in the Charter".[161]

The Tribunal attributed individual responsibility to each for both his own acts and for acts committed by other persons in the execution of the common plan or conspiracy. That alleged that the defendants had planned, prepared, initiated, and waged wars of aggression in violation of international treaties, agreements and assurances. The prosecution case was that in the development and course of the conspiracy, it came to embrace the commission of war crimes as well as crimes a-

[159] La Fave W R (1978) p. 429;Gillies P (1990) p. 185;A criticism against that proposition is that it is not useful to co-opt principles of civil responsibility into criminal law, See, Goode M R (1992) p. 252.

[160] Article, 5, Charter of the International Military Tribunal for the Far East (Tokyo Tribunal), is almost identical, For text see, U.S. Dept. of State, The Trial of Japanese War Criminals, Documents, W.D.C., pp. 39-44;See also Sliedregt A (2004) The Criminal Responsibility of Individuals for Violations of International Humanitarian Law, T.M.C. Asser Press, The Hague, pp. 17- 34.

[161] For the Nuremberg Indictment, See, US Department of State, The Trial of War Criminals: Documents, US Dept. of State, W.D.C., 1945, pp. 23-63.

gainst humanity both within Germany and within occupied countries including murder, extermination, enslavement, deportation, and other inhuman acts against civilian populations before and during the war and persecution on political, racial or religious grounds in execution of the plan for aggressive war.[162]

The Nazi party (National Socialist German Workers Party) was presented as the central core of the conspiracy, the 'instrument of cohesion' among the defendants, and that of carrying out the aims and purposes of the conspiracy. These were to abrogate and overthrow the treaty of Versailles, to acquire the territories lost by Germany as a result of World War I (1914-1918) and other territories in Europe, and to acquire further territories in continental Europe. The pillars of the conspiracy were said to be in five groups of overacts whose character and magnitude were important considerations in proving that conspiracy.[163] These were (i) the seizure of power and subjugation of Germany to a Police State, (ii) the preparation and wagging of wars of aggression; (iii) warfare in disregard of international law, (iv) enslavement and plunder of populations in occupied countries, and (v) persecution and extermination of Jews, were all integrated into a common plan or conspiracy.[164] In essence the Nuremberg concept of a common plan or conspiracy represented conspiracy in an international context and the Prosecutor's submission in Counts III (*War Crimes*) and IV (*Crimes against Humanity*) was that war crimes and crimes against humanity had been committed in the course and furtherance of the common plan or conspiracy.

There is no question that the concept of conspiracy presented at the Nuremberg Trial was a 'grand' conspiracy. As stated by Jackson the US Chief Prosecutor:

"the aims of this conspiracy were open and notorious. It was far different from any other conspiracy ever unfolded before a Court of justice, not only because of the gigantic number of people involved, the period of time covered, the magnitude and audacity of it, but because unlike other criminal conspiracies, these conspirators often boastfully proclaimed to the world what they planned to do, before they did it".[165] The indictment against the major defendants was concerned with the Nazi master plan, not with individual barbarities and perversions, which occurred independently of any central plan.[166] This 'common plan or conspiracy' to seize the machinery of a State, to commit crimes against the peace of the world, to blot a race out of existence, to enslave and to subjugate and loot whole nations

[162] US Dept. of State, The Trial of War Criminals: Documents, p. 25;Jackson R H (1971) The Nuremberg Case as presented by Robert H. Jackson, Chief Counsel for the US, Cooper Square Pub. Inc, N.Y., pp. viii, xii;By common agreement between the four Prosecutors, the US dealt with Count 1, Britain with Crimes against peace, the USSR and France with war crimes and crimes against humanity in East and West respectively, Calvocoressi P (1947) Nuremberg, The Facts, the Law and the Consequences, Chatto and Windus, London, p. 24.

[163] Closing Address, cited in Jackson R H (1971) p. 125.

[164] P. 125, Id.

[165] Opening Statement of Jackson R H in Proceedings of the International Military Tribunal sitting in Nuremberg German, The Trial of German Major War Criminals, His Majesty's Stationery Office, London, 1946, pp. 101-102.

[166] Report of R.H. Jackson to the President in The Trial of War Criminals: Documents, US Dept of State, W.D.C., 1945, p. 5;Jackson R H (1971) p. 10.

could not be thought of in the same terms as the plotting of petty crimes, although the same underlying principles were applicable".[167]

On their part the defendants first argued that voluntary agreement the requirement of a conspiracy was impossible under a dictatorship and that Hitler's absolute powers precluded a conspiracy.[168] They submitted that no responsibility could be attached to anyone except him because all others were no more than the Dictator's henchmen without power to influence the course of events, without even a will of their own apart from the will to will what the Dictator willed.[169] The response of the prosecution was that the defendants may have been slaves of a dictator but he was their dictator, and his acts were their acts. Secondly the Defendants argued that they had belonged to different factions or cliques and had fought with each other, thus making conspiratorial agreement impossible. This was challenged by Jackson:

"It is not necessary that men should agree on everything in order to agree on enough things to make them liable for a criminal conspiracy. Unquestionably there were conspiracies within the conspiracy, and intrigues and rivalries and battles for power. Schacht and Goring disagreed, but over which of them should control the economy, not over whether the economy should be regimented for war...Rosenberg and Goring may have had some differences as to how stolen art should be distributed but they had none about how it should be stolen. Jodl and Goebbels may have disagreed about whether to denounce the Geneva Conventions, but they never disagreed about violating it. And so it goes through the whole long and sordid story. Nowhere do we find an instance where any one of the defendants stood up against the rest and said: "This thing is wrong and I will not go along with it". Whenever they differed, their differences were as to method or disputes over jurisdiction, but always within the framework of the common plan".[170]

In its judgment, the Tribunal had this to say:

"The argument that such common planning cannot exist where there is complete dictatorship is unsound. A plan in the execution of which a number of persons participated is still a plan, even though conceived by only one of them;and those who execute the plan do not avoid responsibility by showing that they acted under the direction of the man who conceived it".[171]

---

[167] Closing Address, Jackson R H (1971) p. 147.

[168] "Therefore, a conspiracy with a dictator at its head is a contradiction in itself. A dictator does not enter into a conspiracy with his follows, he does not make any agreement with them, he dictates", Final Argument of Dr Stahmer, Counsel for Goring, Tr.p. 12970 in Jackson R H (1971) p. 151;Appleman JA (1954), Military Tribunals and International Crimes, The Bobbs-Merrill Company, Inc., Indianapolis, p. 40.

[169] Calvocoressi P (1947) 42.

[170] Closing Address, Jackson R H (1971).

[171] Judgment, Nuremberg Tribunal, p. 482, Proceedings of the IMT sitting at Nuremberg Germany, The Trial of German Major War Criminals, Part 22, Published under the authority of the Attorney General of his Majesty's Stationery Office, London, 1950, p. 482.

The Tribunal held that Article 6 of the Nuremberg Charter did not create new and separate crimes of conspiracy to commit war crimes and crimes against humanity. It adopted a restrictive interpretation of the somewhat novel crime of conspiracy, and decided to disregard the charge of conspiracy to commit war crimes and crimes against humanity, and to consider punishable only common plan or conspiracy to prepare, initiate and wage aggressive war.[172] In this regard, it dealt with conspiracy, together with participation in a common plan, since for both the evidence submitted was the same.[173] The Tribunal was also of the view that the conspiracy could not be traced back to the early days of the Nazi power;it had to be judged only in close proximity to the war.[174]

As regard to the time frame of the Conspiracy, the Tribunal stated:

"Conspiracy is not defined in the Charter. But in the opinion of the Tribunal the conspiracy must be clearly defined in its criminal purpose. It must not be too far removed from the time of decision and of action. The planning, to be criminal, must not rest merely on the declaration of the party programme, such as are found in the twenty-five points of the Nazi Party, announced in 1920, or of the political affirmations expressed in *Mein Kampf* in later years".[175]

At the Tokyo Tribunal all the defendants who were tried were also charged under Count I-5, (*Crimes against Peace*) for having participated as leaders, organizers, instigators, or accomplices in the formulation or execution of a common plan or conspiracy, the object of which was to secure for Japan, the military, naval, political, economic domination of East Asia, the Pacific and Indian Oceans, and "all countries bordering thereon", including the Republic of China, by wagging declared or undeclared wars of aggression, and wars or wars in violation of international law, agreements and assurances.[176] Also charged in Count 5 was conspiracy the object of which was for Germany, Italy and Japan to secure the military, naval, political, and the economic domination of the whole world, each having specific domination in its own sphere, by the waging of declared or undeclared wars or wars of aggression, and wars in violation of international law.

On the criminal nature of the conspiracy, the Prosecution's Chief Counsel submitted:

"Under the usual law of conspiracy heretofore defined, it is always held that every member of the conspiracy is equally liable for every act committed by any member of the conspiracy in the furtherance of the common plan. When we add to this general rule the additional rule that every person is liable for the natural and probable consequences of his criminal acts, we find that these men, who held positions of power and influence in the Japanese

[172] Judgement Nuremberg Tribunal, p. 449;Gross L (1984) The Punishment of War Criminals: The Nuremberg Trial, in Essays in International Law and Organizations, Transnational Pub. Inc., Dobbs Ferry, New York, vol. 1, p. 350.

[173] Woetzel R K (1960) The Nuremberg Trials in International Law, Stevens and Sons, London, p. 204.

[174] Bloxham D (2001) Genocide on Trial, p. 20, fn. 14.

[175] Judgment, Nuremberg Tribunal, p. 448.

[176] For Indictment, See, US Dept. of State, Trial of Japanese War Criminals, pp. 45 – 63.

Government and by virtue of their positions conspired to, and planned, prepared, initiated, and waged illegal wars, are responsible for every single criminal act resulting there from."[177]

The defendants vigorously contended that persons operating in widely scattered theatres and with widely divergent responsibilities could not be considered to have conspired together, particularly when a number of the defendants had been violently opposed to enter the war.[178] On the other hand, the prosecution's view was that the acts in the various theatres were so similar in character as to show an overall understanding and methods of procedure in such instances.[179]

The Tokyo Tribunal did not take the view that the conspirators were seriously resolved in attempting to secure the domination of North and South America, and treated Count I of the Indictment as if the charge had been limited to East Asia, the Western and Southern Western Pacific Ocean and the Indian Ocean.[180] It ruled that Count 5 (the conspiracy with Germany and Italy) has not been proved. Within this narrow limit the Tribunal found that a conspiracy had existed and that it had been in existence before the period covered by the indictment (i.e. between 1 January 1928 and 2 September 1945).[181] It reasoned that the far-reaching and intricate preparations for wagging the wars of aggression were the work of many leaders acting in pursuance of a common plan for the attainment of a common criminal objective, namely, to secure Japan's domination by preparing and wagging wars of aggression. For all but two of the accused, the verdict was "guilt of conspiracy to wage aggressive war"[182] The Tokyo Tribunal's verdict, as well as its findings on conspiracy have been criticized for;the lumping together at the door of conspiracy and at the accused, events remotely apart, ranging from those of mid 1921 up to those of 1942;the questionable use of the term "conspiracy" regarding the Cabinet (of Tojo Hideki 1941-44), and excessive reliance on inference for proof of the conspiracy.[183] One of the most vocal critics of the conspiracy charge was Judge Radhabinod Pal who in dissenting opinion rejected it, in that: [184]

---

[177] Opening Statement, Joseph B. Keenan, Chief of Counsel, Trial of Japanese War Criminals, p. 9.

[178] Appleman J A (1954) p. 247.

[179] P. 247, Id.

[180] Minear R H (1971) Victor's Justice. The Tokyo War Crimes Trial, Princeton University Press, Princeton, N.J., p. 29.

[181] P. 29, Id.

[182] P. 31, Id. "Of the two who were acquitted on this count, one, Shigemitsu, was guilty of six other counts of aggressive war and conventional war crimes, and the other was guilty on one count of conventional war crimes. To be sure, no on e was convicted on all counts;but no one was acquitted on all counts either", at p. 31. For criticism of the Conspiracy verdict by the Majority Judgment, See, Dissenting Judgments of Judge R.M. Pal (India) and Judge Henri Bernard (France), in Minear, R H (1971) at pp. 127 – 143.

[183] Minear R H (1971) pp. 130-132.

[184] Cited in Brook T (2001) The Tokyo Judgment and the rape of Nanking, vol. 60, No.3, The Journal of Asian Studies, p. 688.

"The alleged conspiracy which the prosecution has attempted to trace and describe is one of the most curious and unbelievable things ever sought to be drawn in a judicial proceeding.

Along series of isolated and disconnected events covering a period of at least fourteen years are marshalled together in a hodgepodge fashion;and out of this conglomeration the prosecution asks the Tribunal to find beyond all reasonable doubt that a 'common plan or conspiracy' existed to accomplish the objective stated in the indictment".

"[It] is not for us to see whether or not the events and their speed could be justified. We are now only to see whether the happenings could be explained otherwise than by the existence of a conspiracy".

Minear puts the nail in the coffin in concluding that the question of conspiracy lead directly to one fundamental flow, perhaps the fundamental flaw, of the whole Tokyo trial: it was not prepared to consider a verdict of not guilty.[185] For Brook the victor nations wanted conspiracy as a net through which none of Japan's highest politicians, bureaucrats or officers could escape;it also justified the desperate measures of the American total-war response, from fire-bombing to atomic detonation.

Of 22 accused charged with conspiracy at the Nuremberg Tribunal only eight were convicted of that offence.[186]The restricted view on conspiracy limited its application to defendants who belonged to the core of the Hitler clique.[187] The principle criterion for participation in the conspiracy was attendance in meetings in which Hitler divulged his criminal plans.[188] An accused (Streicher) was acquitted of this charge because the Tribunal considered that he had not taken part in the plans for invasions, and had not been a military, political or diplomatic adviser of Hitler.[189] In applying the concept of conspiracy the Nuremberg Tribunal was guided not only by the traditional concept of conspiracy as known in common law but was also influenced by the concept of accessory liability as known in the European continental legal systems.[190] The theoretical concept of conspiracy had "baffled" the French and Soviet Judges, and it was their influence that contributed to a more contained view of conspiracy.[191] Woetzel's submission is indeed correct that there is no real precedent in international law to conclude that the crime of conspiracy is an international delict;and it is difficult to find a basis for this crime in the universal practice of nations.[192] Indeed there is very little basis, if any, for

---

185 Minear R H (1971) pp. 134, 160-180, 209-211.

186 Cf. At the Tokyo Tribunal all but 2 of the 28 accused were convicted of the conspiracy charge. "In Tokyo, the concept of conspiracy did not encounter the same civil law skepticism as in Nuremberg", Sliederegt V (2004) p. 20.

187 Gross L (1984) p. 330.

188 De Vabres Donnedieu (1947) p. 542.

189 Davidson E (1996) The Trial of Germans, An Account of the 22 defendants before the IMT at Nuremberg, The Macmillan Company, N.Y., 1996.

190 Woetzel R K (1960) p. 204, fn. 37.

191 Bloxham D (2001) p. 69.

192 Woetzel R K (1960) p. 2215.

assuming that the concept of conspiracy was part of international law prior to the Nuremberg trial.[193]

When looking at the treatment of conspiracy by the Nuremberg Tribunal it is worth recalling that it regarded a criminal organization as analogous to criminal conspiracy.[194] It however circumscribed the scope of the alleged conspiracy, and ruled that it had to be proved that any member of a criminal organization had joined voluntarily and with an awareness of its criminality.[195] The principle of criminal guilt of organizations is now a dead letter in adjudication by international criminal tribunals. It has not been recognized by the UN ad hoc Tribunal or the ICC, where guilt can only be established for natural persons and not organizations.[196]

III. The Genocide Convention, the ICC and conspiracy to commit genocide

We stated that conspiracy to commit genocide was defined by the Trial Chamber in *P. v. A. Musema* as "an agreement between two or more persons to commit the crime of genocide".[197] The requisite intent for the crime of conspiracy to commit genocide is ipso facto the intention required for the crime of genocide, that is, the *dolus specialis* of genocide.[198] The *mens rea* of the crime rests in the concerted intention to commit genocide, that is, to destroy, in whole or in part, a national, ethnic, racial, or religious group, as such.[199]

The concept of conspiracy relied upon in the Genocide Convention was the Anglo-Saxon doctrine of conspiracy.[200] It is thus important that we point the essentials as formulated by the *Musema* Trial Chamber Judgment. First, conspiracy to commit genocide is committed as soon as there is agreement, and no requirement of an overact attaches for its commission. The travaux preparatoire of the Genocide Convention suggests that the rationale for including such a crime was to ensure, in view of the serious nature of the crime of genocide, that mere agreement to commit genocide shall be punishable even if no preparatory act has taken pla-

193 P. 2215, Id.

194 Kittichaisaree K (2001) p. 248.

195 Bloxham D (2001) p. 20, fn. 14.

196 At the Nuremberg Trial, of the seven organizations charged, four were found to be criminal, namely, the Leadership of the Nazi Party, the "SS" [Shutzstaffeln], the "SD" [Sicherheitsdienst] and the Gestapo [Geheime Staatspolizei], and those found non criminal were the Reich Cabinet, the General Staff and High Command of the Armed Forces, ("OKW"), and the "SA" (Sturmabteilungen).

197 *P. v. A. Musema*, Judgment, ICTR Case no: 96-13-T, 27 January 2000, para. 192.

198 Para. 192, Id.

199 Para. 192, Id.;"The *mens rea* is the specific intent to commit genocide", *P. v. E. Niyitergeka*, para 423.

200 *P. v. A. Musema*, Judgment, para. 187;For the Convention on the Prevention and Punishment of the Crime of Genocide, see, U.N.T.S, No. 1021, Vol. 78, p. 277, Entered into force on 12 January 1951.

ce.[201] Secondly conspiracy to commit genocide is punishable even if it fails to provide the result, that is to say, even if the substantive offence, genocide, has not been actually perpetrated.[202] It is the process of conspiracy which is punishable, not the results.[203] Third, the crime of conspiracy was included in the Genocide Convention to punish acts which, in and of themselves, did not constitute genocide.[204]

Genocide and conspiracy to commit genocide are two distinct offences respectively provided for in Articles 2 (3) (a) and 2 (3) (b) of the Statutes of the ICTR, which is verbatim Article III (a) and (b) of the Genocide Convention. Given that the elements of the crime for offences are different, they constitute two distinct offences. It is a Prosecutor's discretion to charge an accused with one or both crimes in an indictment. This practice has been widely accepted in practice by the UN ad hoc Tribunals. It has valid rationale and is legally sound in that the crimes were meant to be, and are in fact and in law, distinguishable.

With regard to convictions for both conspiracy to commit genocide and genocide, although the law of conspiracy as developed in Anglo-Saxon jurisprudence, and on which the Genocide Convention is based, permits conviction for both, especially where the objective of the conspiracy extends beyond the offences actually committed, the Trial Chamber in *P. v. Musema* did not follow that practice. It ruled that an accused could not be convicted of both conspiracy to commit genocide and genocide on the basis of the same facts.[205] It considered that this was in keeping with the purpose of the Genocide Convention which intended that the crime of conspiracy punish acts which did not constitute genocide, and that no purpose would be served in convicting an accused, who had already been found guilty of genocide with conspiracy to commit genocide, on the basis of the same facts.[206]

From the point of view of full accountability for the 1994 genocide in Rwanda this is contestable. A conviction only on genocide is not reflective of the totality of the acts imputable on both the conspiracy and the substantive offence. The consummated crime of genocide may be based only on executed acts, not necessarily on the agreement to commit that genocide. In the Rwandan context the core or national conspiracy is also much wider than individual set of crimes an accused, who is a party to a conspiracy, may have committed in his or her own sector, commune, or Prefecture. Moreover there is no real prejudice to the accused if convicted for both, since reliance is placed on evidence of overt acts to prove both the conspiracy and the consummated offence of genocide. In the Rwandan situation the importance of convictions, in the sense of restorative justice is not that genocide was committed by a certain accused, but rather the whole process in which the

201 *P. v. A. Musema*, Judgment, para.185;See also, Summary Records of the Meetings of the Sixth Committee of the General Assembly, 21 September-10 December 1948, Ordinary Records of the General Assembly.

202 *P. A.Musema*, Judgment, para. 194.

203 Para. 193.

204 Para. 198 Id.

205 Id.

206 Id.

accused, together with others conceived, prepared, planned, organized, and finally executed the genocide plan to exterminate Tutsi and kill moderate Hutu. This is hardly explained by the restrictive conviction only of genocide, when there is sufficient finding of conspiracy to commit it. In fact this undermines the truth function of accountability. Conspiracy to commit genocide cannot be treated the same way as attempt, in that the latter when successful merges into the consummated crime.

It is worth reiterating that the test to be applied in determining when multiple convictions based on the same set of facts might be entered or affirmed was prescribed by the ICTY Appeal Chamber in *Celebici.* There it laid down that:

> "Reasons of fairness to the accused and the consideration that only distinct crimes may justify multiple convictions entered under different statutory provisions but based on the same conduct are permissible only if each statutory provision involved has a materially distinct element not contained in the other. An element is materially distinct from another if it requires proof of a fact not required by the other. Where this test is not met, the Chamber must decide in relation to which offence it will enter conviction. This should be done on the basis of the principle that the conviction under the more specific provision should be upheld. Thus, if a set of facts is regulated by two provisions, one of which contains an additional materially distinct element, then a conviction shall be entered only under that provision." [207]

Although this test takes into account the interests of justice, and balances fairness to the accused with the jeopardy in the case of double convictions, when examined against the conspiracy to commit genocide and the genocide that took place in Rwanda its result are insufficient to unearth the judicial truth in which genocide was conceived, planned and organized as well as the conspiracy behind it. To facilitate national reconciliation the final consummated act (i.e. genocide) cannot be explained without a showing of only the "agreement" and resolve to carry it out.

One of the questions that needs to be answered in this chapter is whether the concept of joint criminal enterprise as a mode of criminal responsibility available under Article 6 (1) and 7 (1) of the ICTR and ICTY Statutes is as sufficiently suitable as conspiracy in ensuring effective accountability for atrocity crimes. The other associated issue is whether Article 25(3) (d) of the ICC is also a sufficient alternative to conspiracy for the purpose of accountability for atrocity crimes, particularly genocide. A starting point for the discussion on the concept of joint criminal enterprise is the *Tadic* Appeal Chamber Judgment which articulated its scope and parameters.[208] The Chamber considered that the notion of joint criminal enterprise was firmly established under customary international law in 1992, fell

[207] *Celebici,* Appeal Judgment, para. 412-413, approved in *A. Musema (Appellant) V. Prosecutor,* Judgement Appeal Chamber, ICTR Case no: 96-13-A, 16 November 2002, para. 363.

[208] *P. v. D. Tadic,* ICTY Case no: IT-94-I-AC, 15 July 1999, paras. 185-237;See also Decision on *Dragoljub Ojdanic's* Motion Challenging Jurisdiction, ICTY Case no: IT-37-AR72, AC, May 2003 paras. 20-21.

within the scope of having 'committed' a crime and thereby available under Article 7 (1) of the ICTY Statute[209]. It held that the Tribunal Statute:

"does not exclude those modes of participating in the commission of crimes which occur where several persons having a common purpose embark on criminal activity that is then carried out either jointly or by some members of this plurality of persons. Whoever contributes to the commission of crimes by the group of persons or some members of the group, in execution of a common criminal purpose, may be held to be criminally liable."[210]

That joint criminal enterprise is a form of "commission" has been reaffirmed by the Appeal Chamber in *Krnojelac* Appeal Judgment[211], the *Ojdanic* Motion Challenging Jurisdiction,[212] and by the Trial Chamber in *Brdjanin and Talic* [213]. In *Blogojevic* the Trial Chamber précised that it is a form of "commission" rather than a form of accomplice liability, with the term "accomplice" being understood to refer to one who aids and abets the perpetrator.[214] As to the appellation, in *Brdjanin and Talic*, the Trial Chamber observed that the concept has been labelled interchangeable by the Appeal Chamber, as a common criminal plan, a common criminal purpose, a common design or purpose, a common criminal design, a common purpose, a common design, and a common concerted design, the preferred is 'joint criminal enterprise'.[215] Having said that, it is worth noting the categories of collective criminality as encompassed by the doctrine of joint criminal enterprise as laid down by in *Tadic.* There the Appeal Chamber postulated that it had been applied in three distinct categories of cases: first, in cases of co-perpetration, where all co-defendants possessing the same intent pursue a common criminal design;second the so-called 'concentration camp' cases, where crimes are committed by members of a military or administrative Unit acting under the authority of a superior and in pursuant of a common design to violate the laws and usages of war;and the third, in cases where one of the perpetrators commits an act, which outside the common design, was nevertheless a natural and probable consequence of the ef-

209 Para. 220, Id.

210 Para. 189, Id.

211 ICTY Case no: IT-97-25, 17 September 2003, para. 73.

212 Decision on *Dragoljub Ojdanic's* Motion Challenging Jurisdiction, ICTY Case no: IT-37-AR72, AC, 21 May 2003, para. 20-21.

213 Decision on Form of Further Amended Indictment and Prosecution Application to Amend, ICTY case no: IT-94-I, 26 June 2001, para. 24.

214 *P. v. Blogojevic and D. Jokic*, ICTY Case no: IT-02-60-T, Judgement, para. 696.

215 That is also term preferred by the Appeal Chamber, See *Dragoljub Ojdanic's* Motion Challenging Jurisdiction.

fecting of that common purpose.[216] Sliedregt has suggested "collateral liability" as a better name for the latter category.[217]

The Appeal Chamber also outlined the objective elements (actus reus) required for joint criminal enterprise as a mode of 'commission' of one of the crimes provided for in the ICTY Statute. It specified the elements, which were the same for the three categories of the afore-mentioned joint criminal enterprise as, (a) a plurality of persons, who need not be organized in a military, political or administrative structure, (b) the existence of a common plan, design or purpose that amounts to or involve the commission of a crime provided for in the Statute, and (c) the participation of the accused in the common design involving the perpetration also of one of the crimes set forth in the Statute.[218]

It is common ground that a conviction for conspiracy to commit genocide does not require the commission of the substantive offence, genocide. To impute criminal responsibility through joint criminal enterprise requires that the substantive offence to have been actually committed, as well as the conspiracy behind it. In this sense compared to the crime of conspiracy it is a slight limitation in accountability, although it is admitted that it had been effectively used by the Prosecutor at the ICTY at least since 2001 to book an increasing number of high-level perpetrators.[219] Where genocide had however actually occurred, a charge of genocide pursuant to the doctrine of joint criminal enterprise is no doubt appropriate.[220]

It is also pertinent in the context of the discussion in this chapter on conspiracy to commit genocide to make cross reference to Article 25 (3) (d) of the ICC Statute. Three forms of perpetration are envisaged under Article 25 (3) (a) namely, "as an individual", "jointly with another or through another persons". These may conveniently also be referred as direct or solitary perpetration, co-perpetration and intermediary perpetration or perpetration by means respectively.[221] Of interest to us is co-perpetration. To commit "jointly with another person" seems to express no more than two requirements, namely there must be no more than one person committing the crime and they must work together.[222] Thus like conspiracy it must at the least involve two persons. Co-perpetration also available under Article 6(1) and 7 (1) of the ICTR and ICTY Statues, has been broadly interpreted by the Ap-

216 Paras. 196, 204-219, 228, Cf. "A closer inspection of the authorities and practice cited in *Tadic* as giving rise to a customary norm of international law in relation to the third category of joint criminal enterprise, the extended form, reveals that the acceptance of such liability was limited", Powers S (2004) Joint Criminal Enterprise Criminal Liability by Prosecutorial Ingenuity and Judicial Creativity, Journal of International Criminal Justice 2, p. 615.

217 Sliedregt V (2004) p. 100.

218 Para. 220, Id.

219 See, Piacente N (2004) Importance of the Joint Criminal Enterprise Doctrine for ICTY Prosecutorial Policy, Journal of International Criminal Justice, 2 (2004) 446-454.

220 Powers S (2004) pp. 613-614.

221 Ambos K Individual Criminal Responsibility, *Draft* in Treffterer O (ed.) Commentary on the Rome Statute, forthcoming edition;see also Eser A (2002) Individual Criminal Responsibility, in Cassese *et all.* (eds.) (2002) pp. 789 -794.

222 Eser A (2002) in Cassese A *et all.* (eds.) (2002) p. 789.

peal Chamber in *Tadic* as constituting a form of participation particularly necessary in order to cope with atrocity crimes since most of these crimes are committed in pursuance of a common criminal design.[223] Through the doctrine of common purpose developed by the case law of the ICTY, co-perpetration has developed into a separate mode of participation.[224]

As far as the jurisprudence of the two UN Ad hoc Tribunals is concerned, it has been suggested that two criteria are required, first the co-perpetrators must have a common plan, design or purpose which amounts to or involves the commission of a crime provided for in the Statute, though this plan does not need to have been previously arranged or formulated and secondly, the co-perpetrators must participate in the common design whereby this participation may take the form of assistance, or a contribution to the execution of the common plan or purpose.[225] Ambos has submitted that this form of perpetration is characterized by a functional division of the criminal tasks between the different co-perpetrators whom we have said must be at least two, who are normally interrelated by a common plan or agreement;every co-perpetrator fulfilling a certain task which contributes to the commission of the crime and without which the commission would not be possible.[226]

The ICC Statute, in Article 6 (Genocide), incorporates only Article II of the Genocide Convention that lists enumerated acts constituting genocide. It does not incorporate, as does Article 2 (3) of the Statute of ICTR and Article 4 (3) of the ICTY Statute, Article III (a) - (e) of the Genocide Convention which provides for five punishable crimes, namely, the substantive crime of genocide, conspiracy, direct and public incitement, attempt, and complicity to commit genocide. It is worth recalling that the latter article of the Genocide Convention is not only about forms of participation, but constitutes an enumeration of distinct genocide crimes.

The ICC Statute[227] did not incorporate Article III (b) of the Genocide Convention on conspiracy to commit genocide. At the Rome Conference on the Establishment of the International Criminal Court, the Working Group on General Principles agreed to omit Article III of that Convention from the definition of genocide, but on condition that its provisions were actually reflected in article 25, dealing with individual criminal responsibility.[228] Although on first thought it may seem that Article 25 (3) (a) and (d) contains words which could elastically be interpreted to encompass conspiracy, it is the author's view that one cannot read

---

223 *P. v. D. Tadic*, ICTY Case no: IT-94-i-A, 15 July 1999, paras. 185-232.

224 Sliedregt V (2004) pp. 72-76.

225 Eser A in Cassese A *et all.* (eds.) (2002) p. 791;See also *P. v. D. Tadic*, ICTY Case no: IT-94-i-A, 15 July 1999, para. 227 (iii).

226 P. 6, Id.

227 Rome Statute for the International Criminal Court, Adopted by the United Nations Diplomatic Conference of Plenipotentiaries on the Establishment of an International Criminal Court, 17 July 1998, Doc A/CONF.183/9 (1998), See. Http://www.un.org/law/icc/statute/romefra.htm.

228 Schabas W Genocide (Chapter 6), in Triffterer O (ed.), (1999) Commentary on the Rome Statute of the International Criminal Court.

conspiracy out of Article 25 of the ICC Statute.[229] For Cassese the crime of conspiracy to commit genocide as stipulated in Article III of the Genocide Convention was purposely not been incorporated in Article 6 (Genocide) of ICC Statute either because the notion of conspiracy has not been accepted by the Rome Conference or the concept of conspiracy itself had not found the support of all the civil law countries present at that conference.[230] To Schabas the inconsistency with the terms of Genocide Convention appear to have been inadvertent.[231] From the Rome deliberations, it is most likely to have been the result of political compromise.

As noted the ICC Statute fell short of its aim of incorporating Article III (b) of the Genocide Convention within the Statute with respect to conspiracy in that it envisions a form of conspiracy involving the commission or attempted commission of such a crime by a group of persons acting with a common purpose, thus rejecting the common law approach.[232]

Article 25 (3) on individual criminal responsibility provides:

"In accordance with this Statute a person shall be criminally responsible and liable for punishment for a crime within the jurisdiction of the Court if that person:

(a) Commits such a crime, whether as an individual, jointly with another or through another person, regardless whether that other person is criminally responsible;
(b) Orders, solicits or induces the commission of such a crime, which in fact occurs or is attempted:
(c) For the purpose of facilitating the commission of such a crime, aids, abets or otherwise assists in its commission or its attempted commission;
(d) In any other way contributes to the commission or attempted commission of such a crime by a group of persons acting with a common purpose. Such contribution shall be intentional and shall either:
(i) Be made with the aim of furthering the criminal activity or criminal purpose of the group, where such activity or purpose involves the commission of a crime within the jurisdiction of the Court;or
(ii) Be made in the knowledge of the intention of the group to commit the crime."
(e) In respect of the crime of genocide, directly and publicly incites others to commit genocide;
(f) Attempts to commit such a crime by taking action that commences its execution by means of a substantial step, but the crime does not occur because of circumstances independent of the person's intentions. However, a person who abandons the effort to commit the crime or otherwise prevents the completion of the crime shall not be liable for punishment under this Statute for the attempt to commit that crime if that person completely and voluntarily gave up the criminal purpose".

The reading of this is that the forms of criminal participation recognized in Article 25 are the only ones that can impute the commission of genocide. This would exclude conspiracy in its common-law version. That article only recognizes other forms of participation such as ordering, soliciting, inducing, aiding, abetting, or

[229] See also Ambos K Individual Criminal Responsibility' in Triffterer O (ed) (1999).
[230] Cassese A, Genocide, in Cassese A *et all* (eds.) (2002) p. 347.
[231] Schabas W in Triffterer D (ed.) (1999) para. 16.
[232] Pp. 115-116, Id.

otherwise assisting, and directly and publicly inciting others to commit that crime. Article 25 (3) (d) covers anyone who with the aim of furthering criminal activity or purpose, contributes in any way to the commission of a crime by a group of persons acting with a common purpose. The offence of conspiracy to commit a crime is different from the substantive crime itself, that is the object of the conspiracy, because the conspiracy precedes the commission of the crime and is complete before the crime is attempted or completed, and equally the crime attempted or completed does not require the element of conspiracy as one of its ingredients.[233]

Conspiracy is distinguishable from complicity in that no distinction is made in the former between direct perpetrators and indirect perpetrators, perpetrators and co-perpetrators, or perpetrators and accomplices: all the participants are associated in the framework of a common plan and have jointly decided to commit the crime.[234] Pellet has submitted that the existence of a general article on individual criminal responsibility, that is, Article 25, which notable incriminates, in a certain disorder, aids, "contributes", or incites (curiously limited to genocide) and applicable to all crimes of which the Court has competence, made the reproduction of Article III of the Genocide Convention into the ICC Statute unnecessary. [235] With respect, this does not seem to be the case. The non incorporation, in particular, of Article III of the Genocide Convention into the ICC Statute constitutes a limitation in that the former contains a list of punishable acts (i.e. offences), some of which are forms of criminal participation such as attempt [Article III (d)], conspiracy [Article III (b)] and complicity [Article III (e)]. The omission of a clear reference to conspiracy in Article 25 of the ICC Statute means that it can hardly be considered as a valid form of criminal participation, not only for genocide but also for other crimes under the jurisdiction of the Court. Furthermore, it cannot be charged as a separate inchoate offence for the crime of genocide. This view is fortified by the fact that the ICC's Elements of Crimes which, by virtue of Article 9 of the ICC Statute are to assist the Court in the interpretation and application of Article 6, 7, and 8, do not contain elements for the crime of conspiracy to commit genocide.[236]

What the ICC Statute has done is to incorporate into its Statute the list of five genocidal acts contained in Article II (a) - (e) of the Genocide Convention. It has noticeably left out conspiracy to commit genocide contained in Article III (b). The better view is that there is an inconsistency between customary international law and the ICC Statute, in that the former prohibits and makes punishable conspiracy to commit genocide. That is an inchoate crime consisting of planning and organizing of genocide not necessarily followed by the perpetration of the crime, whereas Article 6 of the ICC Statute does not contain a similar provision.[237]

---

233 Desai D A *et all.* (1995) p. 393.

234 Kittichaisaree K (2001), p. 25.

235 Pellet A (2001) Pour La Cour Pénale Internationale, quand même ! - Quelques remarques sur sa compétence et sa saisine, International Criminal Law Review, vol. 1 no: 1-2, p. 91.

236 See, Finalized Draft Text of the Elements of Crimes, Doc. PCNICC/2000/1/Add.2, 2 November 2000.

237 Cassese A in Cassese *et all.* (eds.) (2002) Cf. " the concept of conspiracy is covered indirectly in Article 25 (3) (d) of the ICC Statute", Kittichaisaree K (2001) p. 250.

This constitutes a potential drawback on the prosecution of genocide by the ICC, especially in situations where genocide has been hatched by a conspiracy. The 1994 atrocity crimes in Rwanda are a reference in point. Regrettably, Article 25 (3) of the Rome Statute demonstrates that the lessons of the conspiracy to commit the Rwanda genocide were not taken into account by the drafters of the ICC Statute. As a political compromise it expunged conspiracy to commit genocide as a substantive offence that ought to have been recognized in its own right. Perhaps not all is lost. This gap may possible be narrowed down in four ways. First, generally with the offence of conspiracy, Ashworth has submitted that in so far as its indispensability as an inchoate offence is concerned much ground might be covered by the law of attempt and prosecution of attempt since many conspirators would have carried acts far enough to fulfil the test of criminal attempt, and the procedural advantages of conspiracy still maintained in that the law of principals and accomplices do not require the prosecution to charge defendants separately accomplices or principals.[238] Secondly through national implementing legislation on the ICC, where a whole-hearted incorporation of the Article III of the Genocide Convention is more desirable than a selection of its provisions, as is the case with Article 6 of the ICC Statute. Thirdly through the doctrine of co-perpetration as a form of criminal liability under Article 23 (3) (a) (d) of that Statute. Fourthly and as demonstrated in the accountability process at the ICTY, especially in the case of Milosevic and General Kristic, the doctrine of joint criminal enterprise has become the concept *per excellence* to construct the criminal responsibility of senior military and political figures for crimes planned by them and carried out by others.[239] It may afford an effective alternative in case of genocide, the crime of crimes.

IV. The Rwandan Conspiracy: Investigation and Prosecution strategy

It has been the Office of the Prosecutor's investigation premise, at least from May 1997, that the 1994 atrocity crimes in Rwanda constituted only one over arching and interconnected crime of genocide and not a thousand genocides. The theory held is that the genocide was a wholly consummated conspiracy. The analysis of the Prosecution is that conspiracy to commit genocide, and the substantive crime of genocide, had successive developments from conception, planning, organization, and execution. Along its path, and during its execution, new means and methods may have been devised, but that did not make them separately distinct genocides from a purely criminal investigation perspective. The Siamese-twin character of the perpetrators, the systematic nature of atrocities, the methodical commission of direct public incitement of the populace, the concerted scheming of those in authority or command, and the interwoven criminal connection between

238 Ashworth A (2003) p. 459.
239 Sliedregt V (2004) p. 101.

those in positions of governance or control or national responsibility with those at the prefectoral, communal and sectoral levels point to one direction. That any meaningful inquiry into the 1994 atrocity crimes in Rwanda must consider Rwanda as a single territory-wide crime scene. The Office of the Prosecutor had been of the view:[240]

"That the systematic, generalized and methodical nature of the crimes that were perpetrated throughout Rwanda during 1994 give rise to the inference of coordination, hence conspiracy to destroy in whole or in part the Tutsi, as such. Consequently the Office of the Prosecutor attached high priority to a line of investigation that is likely to develop substantive proof of conspiracy".

The Prosecution asserted that:[241]

"The investigations have revealed the existence of a nationwide plot in which the State authorities and elements of civil society, in particular members of the media, were implicated."

This strategy was explained in these terms:[242]

"This strategy is two pronged, consisting of, essentially in (a) investigation of persons wielding authority of State, during the genocide more precisely, targeting political and military officials at the highest levels and attempting to elicit proof that they conspired among themselves to organize and execute the genocide;and (b) organizing trials on the basis of multi-defendants joint indictments. The prosecution theory of conspiracy was out into practice through joint indictments thematically based upon the accused's sphere of intervention (the media, for example) or regionally specific, on the basis of the accused's sphere of influence (e.g. Butare prefecture)."

For accountability and the judicial process, it is legally prudent to proceed by way of indicting thematic, regional or national homogenous groups of conspiracy to commit genocide. This facilitates the handing both of evidence and witnesses, and provides the best possibility of connecting co-perpetrators with the overt acts that resulted in the genocide, and which forms the building blocks of the conspiracy and the consummated crime. Even if the conspiracy to commit genocide is deemed of the 'grand' type, it is not necessary to obtain a conviction of those with the greatest responsibility to proceed by way of demonstrating a single master conspiracy. Given the likelihood that the Trial Chambers will be inclined to draw a visible line between the architects and the planners of the genocide (i.e. ""the big fish");those who participated as coordinators (i.e. "the medium fish"); and those who subscribed to it (i.e. "the small fish);and hold liable for conspiracy those in the higher bracket, it is advisable for the prosecution to opt for a selective indict-

240 Annual Report of ICTR to the U.N. General Assembly, UN Doc. A/55/435, S/2000/927, 2 October 2000, para. 132.

241 Annual Report of ICTR to the U.N. General Assembly, UN Doc. A/53/429, S/1998/857, 23 September 1998, para. 57.

242 UN Doc. A/55/435, S/2000/927, para. 120.

ment approach. Even though the classic doctrine of conspiracy is elastic enough to consider those who joined much later, including those at the end of the chain as co-conspirators, for atrocity crimes of the magnitude committed in Rwanda, the amalgamation of those with the greatest responsibility with the rank and file hardly adds anything to the accountability of those who held the reigns of authority.

From a policy perspective it is immaterial for effective accountability that the crimes were the targeted result of a core, single or global conspiracy that embraced those with the greatest responsibility, intermediate and low-level perpetrators. Much as atrocity crimes are the result of organized and coordinated violence, and invariably involve an astronomical number of perpetrators. Proof of individual criminal responsibility and of an agreement to conspire makes it more judicious to avoid indicting by way of a master conspiracy of the Nuremberg type. *In P. v. O. Serushago,* the indictment confirming Judge, Yakov Ostrovsy, declined to confirm the count alleging that the accused, a local interehamwe leader, conspired with others to commit genocide in Gisenyi Prefecture. The reasoning was that the accused had been a moneychanger in Gisenyi, had no official status or position in any party or the militia organizations, and was deemed a "small fish" unlikely to have been party to any conspiratorial agreement with senior authorities.

On the birth, or rather the time of conception, of the conspiracy that led to the Rwandan genocide, it has been submitted that, at some point, the exact moment of which is unknown, but between 1 October 1990 and the commencement of genocide on 6 April 1994, anti Tutsi violence in Rwanda turned into a strategy for genocide.[243] For Reytjens there may not have been a resolution to commit genocide at time "X".[244] The evidence most plausible suggests that the idea of genocide could only have emerged gradually;beginning after the 1990 RPF invasion, continuing through 1991 and 1992, and accelerating in determination through 1993 and into 1994.[245] From the former date Rwanda endured three years and a half of violent anti-Tutsi incidents, each of which in retrospect can be interpreted as a deliberate step in a vast conspiracy.[246] In law the exact time at or before a conspiracy begins need not be identified, where this is not possible, and a like principle governs identification of the date of termination of a continuing conspiracy.[247] The prosecution is not required to prove the specific date of its inception so long as the proof establishes as a fact that the conspiracy existed within the dates specified in the indictment.[248]

Conspiracy to commit genocide in Rwanda, involved pre planning and concerted action. Planning implies that one or several persons contemplate designing the

---

[243] OAU, Executive Summary, Report of the International Panel of Eminent Personalities created by the Organization of African Unity to investigate the Genocide in Rwanda, E.S. 22, 2000, See, www.aou.oua.org.

[244] Reytjens P Un Tribunal loin du Rwanda, Le Monde, 4 Avril 1998.

[245] OAU (2000) Executive Summary, Report of the International Panel of Eminent Personalities, E.S. 23.

[246] E.S. 23, Id.

[247] Gillies R (1990) p. 214.

[248] Opening Statement, Keenan J B Chief of Counsel, Trail of Japanese War Criminals, US Dept. of State, W.D.C., 1964, p. 21.

commission of a crime both at preparatory and execution phases.[249] As stated by the Representative of Rwanda to the Security Council, during the debate on the adoption of SC resolution 955 (1994), the genocide "was the result of a large period of planning, during which pilot projects for extermination were successfully tested".[250] The conspiracy to commit genocide in Rwanda may have shifted its locus to the DR Congo, after July 1994, following the full-scale influx of interahamwe and genocidaire after the fall of the interim Government. This does not in any sense negate the fact that it was part of the criminal design of the Rwandan atrocity crimes.

Conspiracy: Indicators and Overt acts

An accurate diagnosis of conspiracy to commit genocide in Rwanda must incorporate a full examination of overt acts, which form the evidential pyramid of that secretive crime. Overacts are not merely evidence that there was a common design on the part of accused persons;they may also be relied upon as a means of detecting the objective of the combination.[251] As stated in *R v. Murphy*:[252]

> "Though the common design is the essence of the charge, it is not necessary to prove that the defendants came together and actually agreed, in terms, to have that design, and to pursue it by common means. If it is proved that the defendants pursued by their acts the same object, often by the same means, one performing one part and another part of the same, so as to complete it, with a view to the attainment of the same object, the jury will be justified, that they were engaged in a conspiracy to effect that object"

Following the shooting down of the Presidential plane on 6 April 1994, the instigators of the genocide had an overall strategy they implemented with scrupulous planning and organization.[253] The concordance of events, their timing, the synchronic 'field' participation of those in positions of authority, leadership, or command, the directives issued to the civilian population from the various levels of the civil administration, and the media campaign aimed at promoting ethnic hatred and incitement were all aimed at a common object. Conspiracy we have stated is a matter of inference;and the Prosecutor's task is to collate the evidence, often circumstantial that can lead to an irresistible conclusion of the existence of a criminal conspiracy. The gist of the offence lies not in doing the act, nor effecting the purpose for which the conspiracy is formed, nor in attempting to do them, nor in inciting others to do them, but in the forming of the scheme or agreement between the parties. The law does not require that the agreement have any particular content, such as detailed plans, which would facilitate the commission of the offence.[254]

---

249 *P. v. J.P. Akayesu*, Case no: ICTR-96-4-T, para. 480.

250 UN Doc. S/PV 3454, 8 November 1994.

251 Bryan J W (1970) p. 89.

252 Holmes, J, R, *Murphy, U.S.A. v. Kissel* (1910), 218 U.S. 601, at 608.

253 OAU (2000) Report of the International Panel of Eminent Personalities, E.S. 37.

254 Colvin E (1991) p. 347.

For the Rwandan genocide the mischievous combinations of the conspiracy to commit it, included the designation as early as 1992, of the Tutsi as the principle enemy and the moderate Hutu as the accomplice, the preparation of lists of potential targets for assasination, the common incendiary discourse of political leaders and civil administrators, the backing of the militia by civilian, military, and political authorities, and mutual supportive conduct of these authorities. From an investigation perspective it is these connecting factors and participation, which lead to a reasonable inference of conspiracy. In the Rwandan situation, where the genocide was not an overnight though, discovering the conspiracy and the dens of conspirators requires, as a must, a retrospective examination of events prior to April 1994 that point to a pre conceived genocidal policy, the preparations for it, the anti Tutsi incitement, express omission to prevent its occurrence, and participatory spiral.

Dens of Conspirators

Given that the primary concern of international justice is accountability for those with the greatest responsibility, it is essential that the search for conspirators must commence with those who had authority, de jure or de facto, within the interim Government;its armed forces, the gendarmerie, and the civil administration. Those in the latter include Prefets, Bourgmesters, and Counsellors, even though we consider that the trial of each and every suspected Bourgmestre or Counsellor is not worthy of expenditure and time of an international criminal tribunal, that must have as its priority accountability for those in an incontestable leadership position. This with the caveat that perhaps a few notorious accused, whatever the rank, may merit exemplary prosecution given the gruesome conduct and the gravity of the crimes that may have been committed.

Furthermore, accountability for the Rwandan atrocity crimes must encompass the leaders of political parties, especially the power ("pawa") factions, and those who set up and ensured that the media was the virulent megaphone of the genocide. The importance of accountability for political leaders lies in the fact that they devised the criminal policies and set up the interim Government, which ultimately bears moral and political responsible for the atrocity crimes. This group of conspirators is incomplete without the inclusion of senior militia commanders and those in charge of the Civil Defence programme. The one enterprise they all subscribed to was the extermination of the Tutsi and the elimination of the moderate Hutu. In the Rwandan context even where some may have acted individually, an inquiry into the actions of each can lead to converging results. It is worth emphasizing that in Rwanda not everybody joined the conspiracy. Others abandoned it after learning of its highly explosive ethnic and criminal content or on appreciating its illegitimacy. There are also others who joined the conspiracy as it moved on. A person who joins subsequently to the plot being hatched is contaminated from the moment of entry.[255]

[255] Williams G L (1961) p. 664.

Meetings

Meetings show that conspirators formally met, communicated with each other, and can be relied upon as evidence of direct participation. They provide a communication forum for the parties and their minds to meet.[256] It is also possible to decipher evidence of planning from meetings. The outcome or results of deliberations or meetings may be indicative of joint evil intention. Knowledge can be inferred by attendance at meetings in which reports were presented and discussed, decisions jointly taken, or government policy arrived at. During the genocide in Rwanda reports by Prefets on the security situation, and massacres, were tabled before the Cabinet. As the principal forum for the conduct of Governmental affairs, it reviewed the precarious security situation faced by the civilian population, and was fully appraised of the victimization of the Tutsi and moderate Hutu. To sustain a charge of criminal conspiracy it is not necessary for the prosecution to prove that the accused persons met and laid their heads together and after a formal consultation came to an express agreement to commit an offence.[257] As stated by in the *Decision on the Prosecutor's Motion for Joinder in the Military Case*:

"It is sufficient that the accused had a common purpose or design, that they planned to carry out that purpose or design and that they executed the plan. All the accused in a conspiracy need to know or be in contact with every other person on the conspiracy. Where there are a series of agreements or relationships, all of which are regarded as essential to the pursuit of a single large-scale scheme, the agreement or relationships may be regarded as a link in the overall chain of relationship".[258]

In Rwanda, between April and July 1994, Cabinet decisions and press communiqués from the Government were transmitted to the population via both Radio Rwanda and RTLM. The subsequent acts, conduct, and public pronouncements of Ministers and other participants to meetings, immediately after, or in between such meetings may lead to an inference of knowledge of certain events or agreement on a certain course of conduct, or common object or design. Since most conspiracies take place in private, the existence of the agreement can frequently only be deduced from subsequent acts, but the mere fact that people happened to do the same things is not without more, proof of a conspiracy.[259] A noted feature of atrocity crimes in Rwanda was Cabinet action, as well as omission. When the Cabinet took the decision to issue the directive on 'civil defence' to the civilian population it was by consensus. When it failed in the duty to protect the victimised population from massacres that it was fully aware of, it was by a deliberate policy of omission. Vested with governance, it was, throughout the 1994 atrocity crimes, an in-

---

256 'In conspiracy it is by no means necessary to prove actual meetings between the conspirators', Harrison D (1924) p. 70.

257 Gupta R L (1965) pp. 207-208.

258 See, Decision of Trial Chamber III, *P. v. T. Bagosora*, Case no: ICTR 96-7, *P. v. G. Kabiligi* and *A. Ntabakuze*, Case no: ICTR 97-43 & ICTR-97-30, *P. v. A. Nsengiyumva*, Case no: ICTR-96-12, 29 June 2000.

259 Mewett AW, Manning M S (1994) p. 335.

formed bystander. In many aspects it was derelict in its constitutional duty to take immediate remedial measures to put a stop to the atrocities.

Butare: The Rallying Point

In a speech delivered in Kinyarwanda in Butare on 19 April 1994, during the installation of Sylvain Nsabimana Butare's new Prefet, and in the presence of Jean-Baptiste Habyarimana the dismissed Tutsi Prefet, the President of the Interim Government, Theodore Sindikubwabwo, addressed an appeal to the inhabitants of Butare, stating that they should not act as they had in the past: a past characterized by apathy, and instead urged them to engage in a manhunt.[260] He stated, "You, people of Butare. You are adopting an it's none of your business attitude;the enemies are among you, get rid of them". He added, "If you cultivate a field and then fail to weed it, what you have done is pointless", and concluded, "analyze each one of my words and you will discover the meaning of the message I am conveying to you".[261] Also present at that occasion were Prime Minister Jean Kambanda, four Cabinet Ministers (i.e. Minister of Information, Minister of Justice, Minister of Family Affairs and Minister of Commerce and Industry), a number of Bourgmesters, and military officers. The President's speech not only empowered Prefets and other civilian administrators but also reinforced their de facto authority. He further informed the population that Ministers would not be giving directives from their offices with curtains drawn, but will descend on the field, and that they would spend some days in their offices and others in the field to work with the population.

By his own admission, in a speech at Butare University on 15 May 1994, former Prime Minister Jean Kambanda's incendiary phrase, "*Wima Igi hugu amaraso imbwa zikayanywera ubu*sa", (i.e. you refuse your spill your blood for your country and yet the dogs drink it for free) became the instantaneous fuel that incited the civilian population and militiamen to commit genocide against the Tutsi and moderate Hutu. In other Prefectures, Civil administrators followed suit and continued the incitement. With regard to speeches, the law does not prohibit a person from forming views however extreme they may be, if the accused confines himself to an academic discussion as to the soundness of his views, and he will not be guilty of any crime, but having decided to go beyond the state of academic discussions, the accused should have regard not merely to the attractive doctrines of political philosophers but to the mundane matter of fact provisions of the Penal Code.[262].

---

[260] Report on the situation of Human rights in Rwanda submitted by Mr. Rene Degni-Segui, Special Rapporteur of the Commission on Human rights, UN Doc. A/49/508/Add.1, S/1994/1157/Add.1, 14 November 1994, para. 10.

[261] Para. 10, Id.

[262] Gupta R L (1965) p. 241;*Manabendra Nath v. Emperor*, 1933 A.I.R., All. 498;35 Cr.L.J. 768

It is no coincidence therefore that on or about 10 June 1994, Niyitegeka the Minster of Information, Kayeshema the Prefet of Kibuye, and others had a meeting at the Kibuye Prectural Office to plan the killing of Tutsi in Bisesero.[263] This was followed by another meeting a week later, also attended by the Prefet, to distribute weapons. At this occasion the Minister sketched a plan for the next day's attack against the Tutsi hiding in Bisesero, and designated the five leaders of the attack, which took place as planned. Again around 18 June 1994 Niyitegeka also attended another meeting at the Kibuye Prefectural Office where he urged Bourgmesters and others to do all they could to ensure participation in the attacks so that all Tutsi in Bisesero could be killed.[264]

With regard to Niyitegeka's participation in meetings and in the conspiracy to commit genocide the Trial Chamber concluded that:[265]

> "the accused and others acted as leaders of attacks against Tutsi… taking into account the organized manner in which the attacks were carried out, which presupposes the existence of a plan, and noting, in particular, that the Accused sketched a plan for an attack in Bisesero at a meeting on or about 10 June, which the people in attendance, including Kayishema and Ruzindana agreed, the Chamber finds that the above facts evidence the existence of an agreement between the Accused and others, including Kayishema and Ruzindana, to commit genocide".

A conspiracy is seldom born of open covenants openly arrived at.[266] The secrecy normally surrounding the formation of criminal plans makes proof of the agreement by direct evidence improbable, and thus usually forces the Prosecution to rely upon conduct of the conspirators from which an inference of an agreement can be drawn.[267] Conspiracy can be sufficiently proved by circumstantial evidence even though the Prosecution is unable to point to any particular moment or incident as marking the inception of the agreement.[268] Is a matter of inference, deducted from criminal acts of the parties concerned, done in pursuance of an apparent criminal purpose in common between them?[269]

Mere association is not sufficient to inference a conspiracy.[270] It should be noted, however, that mere membership as a Cabinet Minister does not make one a co-conspirator. More is required. In *P. v. J. Kamuhamda et all.*, the Trial Chamber stated that the Prosecutor cannot rely on the status of an accused, in that case a Minister of the Interim Government, to establish that he may have contributed or otherwise participated in a common scheme, strategy, or plan to commit a crime

---

263 *P. v. E. Niyitegeka*, Judgement and Sentence, para. 424.

264 Para. 245, Id.

265 Para 428, Id.

266 Direct Sales Co. v. U.S, 1943, 319 U.S. 703, 714, 63 S Ct. 1265, 87 L.Ed.1674, 1683.

267 LaFave W R (1978) p. 73.

268 Orchard G (1974) p. 298.

269 *R. v. Brisac* (1803) 4 East 164, cited in Harrison D (1924) p. 71.

270 *Prin Krishna Chakravarti*, 1935 Cal. 580;30 Cr.L.J. 1322, cited in Gour H S (1968) p. 828.

together with other accused, most of whom were also Ministers.[271] It is worth recalling that one of the reasons the Nuremberg Trial declined to deliver a verdict of guilt against the Reich Cabinet was that the Tribunal found that not a single meeting of the Reich Cabinet was held after 1937, and the Secret Cabinet Council never met at all.[272] The acceptable principles of international criminal law, as enshrined in the Statutes of the UN ad hoc Tribunals and the ICC do not recognize the criminality of organizations. There is no offence for being a member of a political party or for that matter the Cabinet: such membership being insufficient to constitute conspiracy. The mere holding of beliefs or doctrines is not punishable *per se*.[273] Moreover there can be no agreement so long as the object of the conspiracy remains in the minds of the parties.[274] It is not sufficient that the group shared the same ideas;they must have resolved to act together in a criminal enterprise.[275]

That apart it is probable in the case of Rwanda that some conspirators withdrew. For a conspirator to effect a legally valid withdrawal, he must clearly cease to aid the conspiracy in the performance of its activities.[276] The withdrawing conspirator must withdraw not only his material aid, but his moral support as well: he must negate the influence of his prior contributions to group support and resolve.[277] Withdrawal requires affirmative action by a conspirator to disavow his part in the illegal association, and to communicate his withdrawal to his co-conspirators while group resolve can still be meaningfully influenced;while there is still time for other conspirators to withdraw from or influence the conspiracy to be abandoned.[278]

Government Authorities

The high priest of the genocide group was within the Government.[279] When genocide is committed it is often at the instigation by or with the connivance of state authorities.[280] It makes investigative sense therefore to detect conspirators within the various Government agencies or organs, in particular the Cabinet, the Civil Administration, the Rwandan Armed Forces and Gendermerie. The Rwandan interim Government bears full responsibility for having refused to take effective steps

271 *P. v. J. Kamuhanda et all.,* Decision on the Prosecutor's Motion for Joinder, Case no: ICTR-98-54-T, 6 July 2000, para. 71.
272 Trial of Major War Criminals before the International Military Tribunal, pp. 275-279.
273 Aiyar K J (1958) p. 132.
274 Harrison D (1924) p. 68.
275 Elliot C (2001) French Criminal Law, Willan Publishing, Devon, U.K, p. 102.
276 Day B D (1983) The Withdrawal Defense to Criminal Conspiracy: An Unconstitutional Allocation of the Burden of Proof, George Washington Law Review, vol. 51, p. 421.
277 Id.
278 Id.
279 Khan S M (2000) p. 198.
280 Green L C International Criminal Law and the Protection of Human Rights, p. 135, in Cheng B, Brown E D (eds.) (1988) Contemporary Problems of International Law, Stevens and Sons Ltd., London, p. 135.

to prevent the violations of human rights and international humanitarian law, including genocide. From the outset of the atrocities, the Rwandese leaders maintained that massacres would cease *only* with the end of the armed conflict. During his meeting with the Chief of Staff of the FAR (i.e. Rwandan Armed Forces), the UNCHR Special Rapporteur, Rene Degni Segiu (Cote D'Ivoire), was told that the Rwandese authorities would appeal to the general public to stop the massacres and that that would be heeded, but that the condition of a ceasefire agreement was a prerequisite for any such appeal."[281] Conspiracy can be proved from inferences drawn from acts or illegal omissions by the conspirators in pursuance of a common design.[282] Failure to prevent or punish constituted one of the deliberate omissions of public authorities.

Civil authorities and political leaders went out, each often to his or her prefecture, sector, and commune to incite the population, to deliver speeches containing the same messages, to give out similar directives, and to mobilize and organize the local population to commit atrocities. These avowals and incitements were typical of public declarations and statements of persons with civil or political authority. Probable membership in a criminal conspiracy is determined by having regard only to the acts and declarations of the accused as viewed against a background or interpretative context of only the acts, including verbal acts, of the other conspirators.[283] The logic of conspiracy dictates once it is shown that co-conspirators intended to commit a particular act;that it is possible to draw an inference of adherence to a common plan.[284] The uniform course of action could not have been without communication or understanding of what each was supposed to do, in view of the common design to eliminate the Tutsi and moderate Hutu. There was mutual reinforcement. A conspiracy is not merely a concurrence of wills but a concurrence resulting from agreement.[285]

It seems that each of the actors, principals and agents, played their part in one integrated and unified effort to achieve a common purpose: the extermination of the Tutsi and elimination of moderate Hutu;each participant aware of his part, and the part to be played by the other. Conspiracy is not about the prosecution of independent actions, however criminal, but about agreement to work together in order to accomplish a common object. If a person understands the unlawful nature of the attacks taking place, and nevertheless assists in any manner in the carrying out of the common scheme, he thereupon becomes a conspirator to commit the offence.[286]Where there are overacts on the part of the members of the conspiracy they are to be looked at as evidence of the existence of a concealed intention.[287]

281 Report on the Human Rights situation in Rwanda, UN Doc. E/CN.4/1995/7, 28 June 1994, para. 65.

282 Batra T S (1981) p. 558.

283 Ewaschuck E G (1996) para. 19:3030.

284 Goode M R (1992) p. 234.

285 Williams G L (1961) p. 667.

286 Wolcott C J *Bender v. State*, S.C. Delaware 1969, 253 A. 2d. 686.

287 Gupta R L (1965) p. 243;See also *Jitewara Nath v. Emperor* A.I.R. (1937) Cal. 99, 38 Cr.L.J. 818 (S.B.) 10 R.C. 69, 169 I.C. 977.

The 'Big' or 'Global' Indictment

This indictment filed by the Prosecutor, against Bagosora and 28 other accused on 6 March 1998, represented a draconian attempt by the Prosecutor of the two UN ad hoc Tribunals to charge a group of accused with conspiracy to commit genocide.[288] It signalled the apex of investigations which had focused on the conspiracy theory mentioned earlier: one in which it was believed that for the Rwandan tragedy to have taken place in the front yard of a Government, its armed forces, and an entrenched civil administration, there must have been either *a conspiracy of silence* (i.e. a conspiracy of inactivity or inaction), or *a conspiracy of participation* to allow perpetrators to do the killing.[289]

The Indictment, popularly referred to as the 'Global' Indictment, was a mammoth conspiracy indictment, a copycat of the Nuremberg Indictment where twenty-two individuals had been jointly tried before the Nuremberg Tribunal under Count I with the crime of "participation in a common plan or conspiracy". The "*Global*" indictment was confectioned following the Prosecution's conviction that the widespread and systematic atrocities that took place in Rwanda in 1994 were the result of an agreement among core groups of individuals to exterminate the Tutsi and eliminate moderate Hutu. To the prosecution the indictment and its supporting material contained information which had given rise to a substantially new charge of conspiracy, as well as evidence on how the genocide in Rwanda was planned, prepared and executed.[290] As a sign of determination to pursue the mega indictment the Prosecutor Louise Arbour appeared in person for the ex-parte confirmation hearing, before Judge Hossain Khan and held pursuant to Article 18 of the Statute and Rule 28.

Those charged in that indictment comprised three groups of accused. The first group consisted of eleven accused whose indictment has been confirmed earlier, had already made their initial appearance, and who had their cases "ripe" for hearing before the Trial Chambers.[291] The second group comprised five (5) accused against whom indictments had also been confirmed previously, but remained at large;and the third group comprised of thirteen new suspects who were at large and were being indicted for the first time.

Two pertinent legal issues emerged at the indictment confirmation hearing. The question of the legal competence of the Prosecutor to bring a joint and composite *de novo* indictment against all 29 named accused, and that of the jurisdiction of the confirming judge with regard to the overlapping indictments.[292] The Prosecutor submitted that it was her statutory obligation to put forward new evidence, which had recently come to her possession, showing that the 1994 Rwandan genocide

---

288 *P. v. T. Bagosora and 28 others*, Case no: ICTR-98-37-I, 6 March 1998.

289 Muna B (1998) The ICTR Must achieve Justice for Rwandans, Am.U.Int'l. L. Rev., vol. 13, p. 1481.

290 Appellant Brief by the Office of the Prosecutor, para 40.

291 Dismissal of Indictment, *P. v. T. Bagosora and 28 others*, Case no: ICTR-98-37-I, 31 March 1998, p. 11.

292 Pp. 1, 3 & 6, Id.

was pre-planned.[293] This evidence implicated persons already before the Tribunal in a broad conspiracy with others not yet charged.[294] She further submitted that the indictment was in essence a new indictment, as it added substantially new charges against the accused, namely conspiracy.[295] Only four of the 29 proposed accused had previously been charged with conspiracy in their original indictments.[296] The Tribunal's first indictment against Theoneste Bagosora, signed by the first Prosecutor of the UN ad hoc Tribunals, Goldstone on 5 August 1996, and confirmed by Judge Lennart Aspegren on 10 August 1996, did not contain a charge of conspiracy to commit genocide;only that of genocide. The amended Indictment against him, dated 12 August 1999, contains both the charges of conspiracy to commit genocide and as well as genocide, this premised on the Prosecutor's belief that the genocide was the result of a conspiracy. In 1996 it had not occurred to the Prosecution that the genocide in Rwanda was the calculated manifestation of a conspiracy. In mid 1997, as we have stated earlier, the Prosecutor's investigation and prosecution premise firmly stood on conspiracy to commit genocide.

The confirming Judge held that the Prosecutor did not have the legal competence to file a substitute joint indictment on substantially all the same allegations and crimes as alleged in the existing cases against the eleven accused in the first group, whose status was that of accused persons who having made their initial appearance.[297] A reason for this, the Judge held, was that a trial begins when an accused person enters a plea, at the time of his initial appearance, under Rule 62, thereby changing the jurisdictional purview of the question from the confirming Judge to the Trial Chamber.[298] The confirming Judge considered that so much judicial activities had taken place concerning these cases to the extent that jurisdiction lay with the Trial Chambers rather than him. Additionally, he was of the opinion that the Prosecutor could not keep the old pending cases intact against the accused, while at the same time indicting the same accused again and based on the same allegations and crimes.[299] He held that an exparte confirmation hearing on the 'Global' Indictment under Rule 47 would have deprived these accused the opportunity to be heard.[300] He considered the Prosecutor's "short cut" consolidation of these pending cases with entirely new cases untenable in law, in fact and circumstances of the case.[301]

As regard the second group of five accused, still at large, whose indictments were confirmed but whose initial appearance had not taken place, the confirming Judge considered that jurisdiction lied with the Judges who confirmed their indictments.[302] Finally concerning the third group consisting of thirteen new accu-

[293] Para. 1, Id.
[294] Para. 2, Id.
[295] Para. 4, Id.
[296] Para. 4, Id.
[297] Pp. 6 & 10, Id.
[298] Pp. 7, 8 & 9, Id.
[299] P. 9, Id.
[300] P. 9, Id.
[301] P. 11, Id.
[302] Id.

sed, the Judge found that this group was indictable.[303] He held that the present indictment against this group had no legal complications, and was permissible provided the Prosecutor was willing to withdraw the indictments against the accused in the first and second groups.[304]

The suggestion to withdraw the existing indictments against accused in the first and second groups, under Rule 51, before confirmation of the 'Global Indictment' was found by the Prosecutor to be unfeasible and likely to lead to conflicting decisions since various Judges and Trial Chambers would be seized with jurisdiction, there by creating a legal vacuum.[305] The procedure she preferred to follow, in the event of confirmation of the indictment in its composite form, was to seek in the appropriate forum leave to withdraw the indictments against the 16 accused that were the subject of existing indictments.[306] Given the insistence of the Prosecutor of maintaining the 'Global Indictment' as a whole, and the confirming Judge's finding that jurisdiction with the cases of the other accused lay with other confirming Judges or Trial Chambers, the judge dismissed the indictment.

This decision "duly alarmed"[307] the Prosecutor. On 6 April 1998 she appealed to the Appeal Chamber of the Tribunal setting out 20 grounds of appeal, the most important ones of which were that the dismissal of the '*Global*' Indictment by the confirming Judge had prejudiced her ability to discharge her mandate under the Statute;that the confirming Judge had erred in law by declining to exercise the jurisdiction conferred upon him by Article 18 of the Statute and Rule 28 of the Rules of Procedure and Evidence, in finding that the Prosecutor did not have the legal competence to present the new indictment in its current form, pursuant to Rules 47, 48, and 49 of the Rules, for the purposes of indictment review,and confirmation;that he had erred in law in holding that the Trial Chambers and confirming Judges had jurisdiction over accused in the first and second groups;that he had also erred in law and in fact, inter alia in holding that the Indictment contained only one substantial new charge.[308]

In its decision the Appeal Chamber held that execution of the Prosecutor's mandate was clearly not adversely affected by the non-confirmation Decision, as the Rules provided a variety of remedies to cure the effects of the dismissal of an indictment.[309] It clarified that the Prosecutor enjoys sole discretion in the execution

303 P. 12, Id.

304 P. 11, Id.

305 Para. 6, Id.

306 Para. 8, Id.

307 Arbour L (1998) History and Future of the International criminal Tribunals for the For mer Yugoslavia and Rwanda, Am.U.Int'l L.Rev, vol.13, p. 1498.

308 See, Notice of Appeal (Article 24 and Rule 108), *P. v. T. Bagosora and 28 others*, Case no: ICTR 98-I-3, 3 April 1998, See also Appellant brief by the Prosecution in support of the admissibility of the Appeal of the Dismissal of the Indictment against Bagosora and 28 others of 31 March 1998, Case no: ICTR-98-37-I, 30 April 1998.

309 Decision on the Admissibility of the Prosecutor's Appeal from the decision of a confirming Judge dismissing an indictment against T. Bagosora & 28 Others, *P. v. T. Bagasora and 28 others*, Appeal Chamber, Case no: ICTR-98-37-A, 8 June 1998, para. 27.

of her mandate, while the Trial and Appeal Chambers, on the other hand, had the sole prerogative, by applying the Statute and the Rules, to determine the limits of their own competences.[310] Pronouncing itself on the admissibility of the Appeal under Article 24 of the Statute, the Appeal Chamber opined that in the instance case, where the matter affects the rights of accused, the Prosecutor can have no greater power of appeal than an accused person, and to grant the Prosecutor an unfettered power of appeal, while that of the accused is limited would violate the principle of equality of arms.[311] The Appeal Chamber was also of the view that Rule 108 (Notice of Appeal) did not create a right of appeal and did not apply to a decision of a single Judge acting under Rule 47.[312] Consequently the Appeal Chamber rejected the Prosecutor's application for leave to appeal the Decision.[313] In a declaration appended to the appeal decision, Judge Mohamed Shahabudden reasoned that as a matter of construction Article 24 of the Statute does not visualize an appeal being made when there is no case in existence between the Prosecutor and an accused.[314] He clarified that the decision of the confirming Judge, which was being sought to be appealed from, was not made in such a case;it was concerned with the prior question whether there should be such a case.[315]

The question that will always be posed in devising an effective accountability tool is whether the Prosecution should proceed in the case of a conspiratorial criminal enterprise involving numerous accused with one Indictment, as was the case at the Nuremberg Tribunal[316] and with the 'Global' Indictment, or with manageable homogeneous group indictments as is the current approach of the Rwanda Tribunal. In considering the path to take, account must be taken of each defendant's acts, conduct, and statements in relation to the overall evidence of the conspiracy, of the quantitative disparity of evidence that may exist between co-accused, of the evidence of the common scheme, and of the need to demonstrate full judicial accountability. Additionally in the case of a mega indictment or trial, perhaps involving even eight accused, one has to figure whether it is administratively feasible. Reasons of fairness and sound administration of justice in complex international trials require compelling reasons for an entitlement to the joinder of 29 accused in one trial. Given that atrocity crimes often involve a large-scale criminal enterprise, it is perhaps most desirable to proceed by way of homogeneous group trials, in which the evidence is demonstrative of both the hatching of the criminal conspiracy and the consummated crime. A trial involving dozens of accused, before an international criminal tribunal is a complex and lengthy process, if

310 Para. 31, Id.

311 Paras. 34, 35 Id.

312 Para. 51 Id.

313 Para. 53 and Disposition, at p. 21.

314 Declaration of Judge Mohamed Shahabudden on the Admissibility of the Prosecutor's Appeal, *P. v. T. Bagasora* and 28 others, Appeal Chamber,Case no: ICTR 98-37-A, 8 June 1998, p. 2.

315 P. 2, Id.

316 Cf. 'The Trial was more like thirty trials rolled into one than like one trial, since it had been judged desirable to try all ring leaders simultaneously", Calvocoressi P (1947) p. 25.

not an administratively unmanageable affair. One drawback of an omnibus indictment such as the 'Global' Indictment is in deciphering the criminal intent of each and every conspirator. Determining the mens rea of the "smaller fish" who participated only at subsistence level in a complex criminal enterprise, without necessarily agreeing to the transactions of all its incidents is a costly evidential exercise.

Conclusion

This chapter examined conspiracy to commit genocide both as a crime distinct for that of Genocide, and as an accountability tool that is central stage in prosecutions before the ICTR. Generally it can be said that the law of conspiracy remains an import of the common law of conspiracy, despite its codification in a number of jurisdictions and its increased use for the prosecution of offences involving organized or web-like crimes. Conspiracy to commit genocide entails an agreement between two or more persons to commit genocide. The essentials of the law require an agreement between two or more persons for the offence to be committed;that it is a distinct offence in its own right;that it does not merge into the consummated offence;that no requirement of an overact attaches to its commission beyond the making of the agreement;that it is a specific intent crime and that there must be common purpose, design, or scheme between the conspirators. Given the secretive nature of the crime, in practice, the Prosecutor must rely on overt acts to prove it. Conspiracy is a matter of deduction and inference from a collocation of circumstances, including events, physical acts, such as meetings, gatherings, speeches, words, and directives by which conspirators signify their mutual common consent to the agreement.

Since the Nuremberg and Tokyo Tribunals, the most accumulated use of conspiracy to prosecute atrocity crimes has been that by the ICTR. In the latter, numerous accused, particularly those alleged to have had leadership responsibilities have been indicted with conspiracy to commit genocide on the basis of thematic (e.g. media trial), professional (e.g. military trial), prefectural (e.g. Butare, Cyangugu) or national leadership or Governance (e.g. Government Trial) conspiracy agreements to pursue a common criminal design. Highly favoured by Prosecutors, because of its procedural advantages (e.g. joinder of trials, and exception to hearsay evidence), it is submitted that much of the critique on the judicial unfairness of the conspiracy trial is misplaced when examined in the light of the practice of the two UN ah hoc Tribunals and accountability for atrocity crimes. The law as applied by these Tribunals is firmly anchored on the criminal responsibility of the individual, and guarantees the right to a fair trial. It is not associative or collective criminal responsibility. Furthermore the law and procedures adhere to international standards of justice and due process, the Prosecutor is an independent organ and does not receive instructions from any source, and trials are conducted by professional judges.

The approaches of the Nuremberg and Tokyo Tribunals on conspiracy were all encompassing and purely related to the circumstances of the events leading to and including World War II. The allegation was of a 'grand' conspiracy that cast its net widely in terms of the existence of the conspiracy, its time frame, geographical coverage, and those alleged to have been involved. While it makes interesting comparison, the considerations cannot be equated with the prosecution of conspiracy to commit genocide before the ICTR. In the context of the atrocity crimes committed in Rwanda in 1994, conspiracy to commit genocide offers the Prosecutor an appropriate accountability language to detail the conception, planning, organization, and ultimately, the genocide itself. The non-incorporation of conspiracy to commit genocide as a specified crime in the ICC Statute is a serious omission. It has deprived atrocity crimes of a viable vehicle of accountability. The test of time will demonstrate whether the principle of co-perpetration as a form of criminal liability engraved in Article 23 (3) (a) of the ICC Statute and the doctrine of joint criminal enterprise by the jurisprudence of the UN Ad hoc Tribunals as viable alternatives.

The pursuit of conspiracy to commit genocide at the ICTR developed out of the prosecution strategy conceived in May 1977 and based on investigation findings that the atrocity crimes committed in Rwanda in 1994 were the result of a coordinated and organized plot conceived much earlier than 1994, to destroy in whole or in part, the Tutsi, as such. It was also based on a line of investigation that considered the whole Rwandan territory as one crime scene;that for investigation purposes only one genocide had taken place, and that persons who wielded authority and command from the Government, its armed forces, and civil administration, and those with de facto authority including leaders of political parties, shareholders and directors of media organs, and private individuals, mutually charted out the criminal design of extermination.

As a direct result of this strategy was the unprecedented accusation before the ICTR of 29 persons, in what is known as the 'Global' Indictment issued on 6 March 1998. The dismissal of the indictment by the confirming Judge due to lack of jurisdiction in relation to the group of indictees jointly charged, a number of whom had already been indicted and were in custody, others who were indicted but at larger, and yet others who were new indictees, and the Prosecutor's insistence on maintaining the indictment as a whole, eventually led to a change of course in the prosecution of conspiracy at the ICTR. The realistic option made was that of the prosecution of conspiracy to commit genocide through accusations against a smaller and more homogeneous group of accused. From a 'Global' conspiracy to commit genocide, experience has it that accountability through a number of tightly framed core conspiracies can be an equally effective means of accountability. At the ICTR this has permitted the joint trial of persons alleged to have held authority and control. If successfully proved it may explain the genocidal pre-planning that took place in Rwanda. As an accountability tool the prosecution of the consummated crime of genocide, without conspiracy, offers an unfinished explanation of the collective, collaborative, and coordinative nature of the atrocity crimes committed in 1994 in Rwanda.

Chapter 7
Superior Responsibility

This chapter focuses on superior responsibility,[1] an established principle of international humanitarian law. A form of liability that is not only instrumental in imputing criminal responsibility to various categories of persons responsible for atrocity crimes, but also of capital significance against persons in leadership positions often absent at the battlefield or massacre sites. By virtue of this principle a superior is criminally accountable for acts or omissions committed by his subordinate if he knew, or had reason to know that the subordinate was about to commit such acts or had done so; and the superior failed to take the necessary or reasonable measures to prevent such acts or to punish the perpetrator thereof. The doctrine of superior responsibility provides the bait for effective accountability to those with the greatest responsibility and those at intermediate level: "the medium fish".

In this chapter we first undertake a legal analysis of the law, including recent case law. Of particular interest will be the application of the principle of superior responsible to civilians (i.e. 'non–military commanders'), given that international humanitarian law imposes criminal responsibility to them as well, and not just to military commanders. The history of conflicts has vividly demonstrated that both military and para-military commanders and civilian authorities instigate, organize, and orchestrate atrocity crimes. Secondly we illustrate the application of the principle in two contexts; namely, Rwanda and East Timor. This offers an informed account of de jure and de facto superior responsibility. The two situations are reflective of the growing phenomenon of the involvement of irregular armies, paramilitary forces, and militia groups in the commission of atrocity crimes. The Rwanda atrocity crimes of 1994 had as frontline criminals, interahamwe and impuzamugambi militia from the Youth wings of two Political parties, respectively MRND and CDR. That of East Timor in 1999 had pro-autonomy militia groups. These groups were purposely created by the Indonesian Armed Forces, backed by pro autonomy political leaders and supported by civilian authorities. They were an extended arm of the TNI and committed most of the visible violence. Finally the chapter will discuss and draw conclusions on ways superior responsibility may serve as a meaningful accountability tool for the investigation and prosecution of individuals responsible for atrocity crimes.

---

1 The term 'command or superior responsibility" is often used interchangeably to refer to indirect superior criminal responsibility.

Command or Superior Responsibility

International law imposes two modes of criminal participation for atrocity crimes; direct and indirect individual criminal responsibility. An example of the former is Article 6 (1) of the Statute of the Rwanda Tribunal[2] which provides:

"A Person who planned, instigated, ordered, committed or otherwise aided and abetted in the planning, preparation and execution of the crimes referred to in Articles 2 to 4 of the present Statute, shall be individually responsible for the crime".

In the wider sense the mode of participation under the above article is either the direct commission of a crime by the accused (i.e. as sole perpetrator), or as a co-perpetrator (i.e. as an aider or abettor).[3] Active and direct participation in crimes means that the accused committed by his own hand, all or some of the crimes.[4] In addition to responsibility as principal perpetrator, an accused can be also held responsible for the criminal acts of others where he plans, instigates, orders, or aids and abets them to commit those acts.[5]

The principle of indirect superior responsibility on the other hand is expressed in Article 6 (3). This provides:

"The fact that any of the acts referred to in articles 2 to 4 of the present Statute was committed by a subordinate does not relieve his or her superior of criminal responsibility if he or she knew or had reason to know that the subordinate was about to commit such acts or had done so and the superior failed to take the necessary and reasonable measures to prevent such acts or to punish the perpetrators thereof".

Under this article a commander or superior may be held criminally responsible in respect of acts of his subordinates in violation of the crimes specified in the Statute; acts in which he did not directly participate. Superior responsibility must not be seen as responsibility for the act of another, but derives directly from the failure of the person against whom the complaint is directed to honour an obligation.[6] This responsibility establishes liability for omission since it makes the superior liable only for a failure of the proper supervision and control of his or her subordinates but not more, at least not 'directly' for crimes they commit; the crimes are 'directly' imputed to the subordinates, the superior is only responsible for the fail-

---

2 Article 6(1) and 6 (3) of the ICTR Statute is verbatim that of Article 7 (1) and 7 (3) of the ICTR Statute.

3 *P. v. Z. Kupreskic, M. Kupreskic, V. Kupreskic, D. Josipovic, D. Papic and V. Santic*, Judgement, para. 772, Trial Chamber (T. C) Case no. IT-95-16-T, 14 January 2000.

4 *P. v. T. Blaskic*, Judgement, para. 790, (T. C, Case no. IT-95-14-T, 3 March 2000.

5 *P. v. J. P. Akayesu*, Judgement, para. 471, T. C, Case no. ICTR-96-4-T, 2 September 1998.

6 *P. v. Z. Aleksovski*, Judgement, T. C, Case no. IT-95-14/1-T, 25 June 1999, para. 72; Cf. "the concept seems to create, on one hand, direct liability for the lack of supervision, and, on the other, indirect liability for the criminal act of others", Ambos K Superior Responsibility, in Cassese *et all.* (eds.) (2002) p. 824.

ure to prevent them from occurring.[7] The inherent purpose of Article 6(3) is to ensure that a morally culpable individual is held responsible for heinous acts committed under his command.[8] Superior responsibility is an exception to the principles articulated in Article 6(1), and is derived from military law, namely the principle of the liability of a commander for the acts of his subordinates or command responsibility.[9] This principle of command responsibility, strictu sensu, forms part of customary international law.[10] After examining post World War II practice the Trial Chamber in *Blasckic* opined that, after that period a standard was established according to which a commander may be liable for crimes of his subordinates if 'he failed to exercise the means available to him to learn of the offence and under the circumstances he should have known, and such failure to know constitutes criminal dereliction.[11]

In *Celebici* the Trial Chamber observed:

> "The doctrine of command responsibility is ultimately predicted upon the power of the superior to control the acts of his subordinates. A duty is placed upon the superior to exercise this power so as to prevent and repress the crimes committed by his subordinates, and a failure by him to do so in a diligent manner is sanctioned by the imposition of individual criminal responsibility in accordance with the doctrine."[12]

Article 6 (1) and 6 (3) address distinct principles of criminal liability.[13] It is legally permissible to charge an accused with both direct individual criminal responsibility as well as indirect responsibility as a superior (i.e. cumulative charging). It is also possible to charge these two forms of criminal liability in the alternative. With regard to conviction, however, initially the practices of the two UN Ad hoc Tribunals varied. At the ICTR Kambanda was convicted for both direct and indirect superior criminal responsibility. And so was Kayishema, the Prefet of Kibuye. At the ICTY while the Trial Chamber in *Blaskic* was favourable to the concurrent application of both forms of liabilities,[14] that in *Krnojelac* found it inappropriate to

---

7 Ambos K, pp. 850-851, Id.

8 *P. v. C. Kayishema and O. Ruzindana*, T. C, Case no: ICTR-95-1-T, 21 May 1999, para. 516.

9 *P. V. J. P. Akayesu*, Judgement, T. C, para. 471.

10 *P. v. T. Blasckic*, Judgement, T. C, para. 290; For a legal survey of post World War II jurisprudence see paras. 314-332; Green L C (1995) Command Responsibility in International Humanitarian Law, Transnational law and Contemporary Problems, vol. 5/2 pp. 327-370; Burnett W D (1985) Command Responsibility and a Case Study of the Criminal Responsibility of Israeli Military Commanders for the Pogrom at Shatila and Sabra, Military law Review, vol. 107, pp. 87-131; Sliedregt V (2004) Superior Responsibility at the Tribunals and the ICC, Chapter, pp. 137-197.

11 *P. v. T. Blasckic*, Judgement, T. C, para. 322.

12 *P. v. Z. Delalic, Z. Mucic, H. Delic, & E. Landzo*, (*Celebici*) Judgement, T. C, No. IT-96-21-T, 16 November 1998, para. 377-378; cited with approval in *Celebici* Appeal Judgement, Case no. IT-96-21-A, 20 February 2001, para 197.

13 *P. v. J. P. Akayesu*, Judgement, T. C. para 471; Jia B B (2000) The Doctrine of Superior Responsibility: Current Problems, Yearbook of International Humanitarian Law, p. 164

14 *P. v. T. Blaskic*, Judgement, T. C, para 337.

convict for both heads of responsibility for the same conduct.[15] The Appeal Chamber in *Celebici* and *Aleksovski* held that the form of liability not chosen must be considered as aggravating circumstance, because the final sentence to be imposed on a convicted accused should reflect the totality of the culpable conduct.[16] This divergent practice was however put to resolved by the Appeal Chamber in *P. v. D. Kordic & M. Cerkez*, where it held that Concurrent conviction pursuant to Article 7 (1) and 7 (3) of the ICTY Statute in relation to the same count based on the same facts by a Trial Chamber constitutes a legal error invalidating a judgement.[17] The Appeal Chamber opined:

"The provisions of Article 7 (1) and 7 (3) of the ICTY Statute connote distinct categories of criminal responsibility. However the Appeal Chamber considers that, in relation to a particular count, it is not appropriate to convict under both Article 7 (1) and 7 (3) of the Statute. Where both Article 7 (1) and 7 (3) responsibility are alleged under the same count, and where the legal requirements pertaining to both of these heads of responsibility are met, a Trial Chamber should enter a conviction on the basis of Article 7 (1) only, and consider the accused's superior position as an aggravating factor in sentencing".[18]

As observed the doctrine of superior responsibility provides a distinct basis for imputing criminal liability. It should not be regarded as a fall back position or a second option meant to surface only when evidence of direct involvement is feeble or lacking.[19] It ought to be part of a conscious prosecution strategy to hold accountable those in de jure or de facto positions of authority or command that instigate, organize, plan, and permit the commission of atrocity crimes. These persons are more often than not in high and senior positions of command or civilian leadership.

Indictments issued by the UN ad hoc Tribunals and 'mixed' Court arrangements contain allegations of superior responsibility against a number of accused, considered "big and medium fish". In the first and the second amended indictments against Slobodan Milosevic (former President of the Federal Republic of Yugoslavia) of 24 May 1999, in relation to the Kosovo conflict, he was charged together with Milan Milutinovis (President of Serbia), Dragoljub Ojdanic (Chief of Staff of the Yugoslav Army), Nikola Sainovic (Deputy Prime Minister) and Vlajko Stojilkovic (Minister of Internal Affairs) The Prosecutor based her accusa-

---

15 *P. v. M. Knojelac*, Judgement, T. C, Case no: IT-97-25, 15 March 2002, para 173; See also *P. v. M. Naletilic and V. Martinovic* (*Tuta and Stella*) Judgement, T. C. Case No. IT-98-34-T, 31 March 2003.

16 *P. v. Z. Aleksovski*, Judgement, A. C, Case No: IT-95-14, 24 March 2002, para. 183.

17 *P. v. D. Kordic & M. Cerkez*, Judgement, A. C, Case no: IT-95-14/2A, 17 Dec. 2004, para. 35.

18 Para. 34.

19 It has been suggested that it is a "fallback" position, see, Damaska H M (2001) The Shallow Side of Command Responsibility, American Journal of Comparative Law, vol. XLIX, no:3, p. 481; or for that matter, a "second option", see, Bantekas I (1999) A. J. I. L, vol. 93/3, p. 595.

tion of the accused on two theories of liability.[20] Direct individual responsibility and command responsibility as commanders or civilian superiors. D'Amato has submitted that although that allegation of both de jure and de facto authority represents very sound prosecutorial pleading, the indictment used a somewhat inelegant phrase, "superior authority".[21] Following the jurisprudence of the UN ad hoc Tribunals and the Statute of the ICC, the preferred terminology is perhaps "effective command and control or effective authority and control". It is also worth registering that the other indictments against Milosevic, related to the conflicts in Bosnia and Croatia, also contain allegations of his de jure and de facto superior responsibility.[22]

Among those also held liable through superior responsibility are Rodovan Karadzic, the first President of the Bosnian Serb Administration, and General Ratko Mladik, the Serb Republic Army Commander.[23] Since their indictment on 14 November 1995, over 9 years ago, they remain at large in Bosnia and Serbia.[24] The indictment against Jean Kambanda, the former Prime Minister of Rwanda in 1994, also alleged his de jure superior responsibility over members of the Interim Government that included Ministers and both de jure and defacto authority over senior civil servants, including Prefets.[25] In East Timor the indictment against General Wiranto, Indonesia's former Minister of Defence and Security and Commander-in-Chief of the Indonesian Armed Forces, which charged him for crimes against humanity (murder, deportation or forcible transfer of population and persecution) committed in 1999, is also based on superior responsibility.[26] The allegations are to the effect that he had been the highest officer in the chain of command for all the Indonesian military and police forces throughout East Timor, and had superior responsibility with respect to the pro-autonomy militia over which he had

---

20 On allegation of de jure and de facto superior responsibility of Milosevic on the events in Kosovo, see *P. v. S. Milosevic et all.* , Indictment, Case no: IT-02-54-I, 24 May 1999, paras. 55-62; See also Second Amended Indictment, Case no: IT-99-PT, paras. 19-28, 29 October 2001; Scharf M (1999) The Indictment of Slobodan Milosevic, ASIL Insight, http://www. asil. org/insight35. htm; Weller M (2000) The Kosovo Indictment of the International Criminal Tribunal for Yugoslavia, The International Journal of Human Rights, Vol. 4, No. 3/4, pp. 207-222.

21 D'Amato A (1999) A Brief Review of the Indictment Against Milosevic and Others, 27 May 1999, at http://jurist. law. pitt. edu/amato. htm.

22 On Bosnia, *see P. v. S. Milosevic*, Case no: IT-01-51-I, 22 November 2001, paras. 27-31; On Croatia, see *P. v. S. Milosevic*, Case no: IT-02-54-I, 23 October 2002, paras. 29-33.

23 *P. v. R. Karadzic & R. Mladic*, Case no: IT-95-5-18 (Srebrenica), 14 November 1995, paras. 34-40; *P. v. R. Karadzic & R. Mladic*, Case no: IT-96-5-I (Bosnia and Herzegovina), 24 July 1995, paras. 3-9; *P. v. R. Karadzic*, Amended Indictment, 28 April 2000, paras. 60-66; *P. v. R. Mladic*, Amended Indictment, 16-19, Case no: IT-95-5/18-I, 11 October 2002, paras. 16-19.

24 Karadzic and Mladic, Arrest the fugitives, so Bosnia can move on, Carla Del Ponte, International Herald Tribune, 20 June 2003.

25 *P. v. J. Kambanda*, Indictment, Case no: ICTR-97-23-I, 28 October 1997.

26 *P. v. Wiranto et all.* , Indictment, Case no: 5/2003, SPSC, paras. 208-215.

effective control in fact.[27] Among the facts alleged to substantiate his authority over militia is assurances to Ian Martin the Special Representative of the UN Secretary General in East Timor and head of UNAMET that if the independent forces would surrender their weapons to the Indonesian Police he could "guarantee" that the militia would disarm within 2 days.[28] It also alleges that the Commander of the Marshal Law operations command for East Timor, which Wiranto had established on 7 September 1999, as well the head of the Adjutant General's Task Force for East Timor at the TNI Headquarters in Jakarta also directly reported to him.[29] That apart, another indictment, that issued on 7 March 2003, by the Special Court for Sierra Leone against the former President of Liberia, is also anchored on superior responsibility.[30]

An individual incurs criminal responsibility for the failure to act only when there is a legal obligation to do so.[31] With regard to the liability of superiors as respectively outlined in identical Article 6(3) and 7(3) of the Statutes of the ICTR and the ICTY, a person is obliged to act only if it has been established that he was a superior of the perpetrator of the offence, and also knew or had reason to know that a crime was about to be committed or had been committed.[32] Should such be the case, the person against whom the claim is directed is obliged to take all the necessary or reasonable measures to prevent the crime or to punish the perpetrator or perpetrators.[33]

Commenting on Article 7(3) of the Statute of the ICTY, the Appeal Chamber in *Aleksovski* observed that the article:

"provides the legal criteria for command responsibility, thus giving the word "commander" a juridical meaning, in that the provision becomes applicable only where a superior with the requisite mental element failed to exercise his powers to prevent subordinates from committing offences or to punish them afterwards. This necessarily implies that a superior must have such powers prior to his failure to exercise them. If the facts of a case meet the criteria for the authority of a superior as laid down in Article 7(3), the legal finding would be that an accused is a superior within the meaning of that provision".[34]

---

27 Id.

28 Id.

29 Id.

30 Taylor was indicted on 7 March 2003, when he was still incumbent President and Head of State of Liberia. The Indictment was unsealed on 4 June 2003, while he was in Ghana attending the ECOWAS and UN brokered talks with Liberian Rebel Groups. See, also, *P. v. C. Taylor,* Indictment, Case no: SCSL-2003-01-I; Romano CP R, Nollkaemper A (2003) The Arrest Warrant Against The Liberian President, Charles Taylor, ASIL Insight, June 2003, at http://www. asil. org/insight/insight110. htm.

31 *P. v. Z. Aleksovski*, T. C, para. 72.

32 Para. 72, Id.

33 Para. 72, Id.

34 *P. v. Z. Aleksovski*, Judgement, A. C, Case No: IT-95-14, 24 March 2002; para. 76; *P. v. T. Blaskic*, Judgement, A. C, para. 745.

Explaining the two the Trial Chamber in *Kayishema* and *Ruzindana* said:

"The question of responsibility arising from a duty to act, and any corresponding failure to execute such a duty is a question that is inextricably linked with the issue of command responsibility. This is because under Article 6 (3) a clear duty is imposed upon those in authority, with the requisite means at their disposal, to prevent or punish the commission of a crime. However, individual responsibility pursuant to Article 6(1) is based, in this instance, not on the duty to act, but from the encouragement and support that might be afforded to the principals of the crimes from such an omission".[35]

The doctrine of command or superior responsibility has also been incorporated in Article 28 of the ICC Statute. This article does not open a new form of liability, but merely clarifies that criminal responsibility for crimes within the jurisdiction of the Court does exist equally for military commanders and all other superiors acting in relationship with subordinates.

Military Commanders and Civilian Superiors

It is well established that the principle of superior responsibility applies not only to military commanders, but also extends to civilians who wield the requisite authority.[36] This includes political leaders and other civilians in positions of authority.[37] It is not limited to civilians only in very high positions such as Government ministers, governors or mayors.[38] It encompasses all civilian authorities. A commander or superior is someone who possesses the power or authority in either a de jure or a de facto form to prevent a subordinate's crimes or to punish the perpetrators of the crime after the crime has been committed.[39]

Superior responsibility is not limited to individuals formally designated as commanders, but also encompasses both de jure and de facto command.[40]

Legal criteria

Generally three criteria constitute the essentials of the doctrine of superior responsibility: (a) the existence of a superior-subordinate relationship; (b) the superior's knowledge or reason to know that the criminal act was about to be or had been committed; and (c) the superior's failure to take the necessary and reasonable

35 *P. v. C. Kayishema and O. Ruzindana*, Judgement, T. C, Case no: ICTR-95-1-T, 21 May 1999, para. 203.

36 *P. v. C. Kayishema and O. Ruzindana*, T. C, para. 213; Cf. "in the case of civilians the application of the principle of international criminal responsibility enshrined in Article 6(3), to civilians remains contentious", *P. v. J. P. Akayesu*, T. C, Judgment, para. 491.

37 *Celebici*, Judgement, T. C, para. 356.

38 *P. v. Z. Aeksovski*, Judgement, T. C, paras. 74-7.

39 *Celebici,* Judgment, A. C, para. 192.

40 *P. v. T. Blaskic*, Judgment, T. C, para. 300.

measures to prevent the criminal act or punish the perpetrator.[41] These constituent elements are derived from Article 86(2) of Additional Protocol I of the Four Geneva Conventions of 1949, Article 6 of the International Law Commission's Draft Code of Crimes Against the Peace and Security of Mankind,[42] and Article 28 of the ICC Statute. The first has been termed a *conceptual* element in that a superior's position must entail a duty to act, the second a *cognitive* element as a superior must have known or should have known, and the third an *operational* elements in that a superior must have failed to act.[43]

a) Superior-Subordinate Relationship

A superior–subordinate relationship is established by showing a formal or informal hierarchical relationship involving an accused's effective control over the direct perpetrator.[44] The superior must be senior to a subordinate.[45] He or she must possess the power or authority, either de jure or de facto, to prevent or punish an offence committed by his or her subordinates.[46] The concept of effective control over a subordinate in the sense of a material ability to prevent or punish criminal conduct, however that control is exercised, is the threshold to be reached in establishing a superior-subordinate relationship.[47] The material ability to control the actions of subordinates is the touchstone of individual criminal responsibility under Article 6(3).[48] This ability is a question that is inherently linked to the given factual situation of a case.[49]

In *Celebici* Trial Chamber expressed this requirement in this way:

"A position of command is indeed a necessary precondition for the imposition of command responsibility. However, this statement must be qualified by the recognition that the existence of such a position cannot be determined by reference to formal status alone. Instead, *the factor that determines liability for this type of criminal responsibility is the actual possession or non-possession, of powers of control over the actions of subordinates*. Accordingly, formal designation as a commander should not be considered to be a necessary prerequisite for command responsibility to attach, as such responsibility may be imposed by virtue of a person's de facto, as well as de jure, position as a commander".[50] [*Emphasis added*]

---

41 *Celebici*, Judgment, A. C, paras. 189-198, 225-226, 238-239, 256, 263; *P. v. Bagilishema*, Judgement, T. C, Case no: ITCR-95-1-T, 7 June 2001, para. 395; *P. v. L. Semanza*, Judgment, T. C, Case no: ICTR-97-20-T, 15 May 2003, para. 400-401.

42 Report of the International Law Commission on the work of its forth-eighth session, 6 May to 26 July 1966, Official document of the General Assembly, UN Doc. A/51/10 (1966).

43 Sliedregt V (2004) pp. 137-197.

44 *P. v. L. Semanza*, Judgement, T. C, para. 415.

45 *Celebici*, Judgement, A. C, para. 303; *P. v. L. Semanza*, Judgement, T. C, para. 401.

46 *Celebici*, Judgement, A. C, para. 192; *P. v. L. Semanza*, TC, para. 402.

47 *Celebici*, Judgment, A. C, para. 256.

48 *P. V. C. Kayishema and O. Ruzindana*, Judgement, T. C, para. 229.

49 Para. 231, Id.

50 *Celebici*, Judgement, T. C, para. 370.

The key test therefore is effective control.[51] The superior's liability for his or her omission stands and falls on an objective level with his or her effective authority and control: the possibility of control forms the legal and legitimate basis of the superior's responsibility; it justifies his or her duty of intervention.[52] This has been accepted, including in the jurisprudence of the Tribunal, as a standard for determining superior responsibility.[53] That test is mandatory, for all superiors, whether de jure or de facto superiors.[54] However it should be noted that there is no need for both de facto and de jure authority to be established before a superior can be found to exercise effective control over his or her subordinates.[55] It is equally misplaced to consider that a finding of de jure authority is required for criminal responsibility under Article 6 (3).[56]

"Even where a clear hierarchy based on de jure authority is not present, this does not prevent the finding of command responsibility. Equally, the mere existence of a de jure power does not always necessitate the imposition of command responsibility. The culpability that this doctrine gives rise to must ultimately be predicted upon the power that the superior exercises over his subordinates in a given situation".[57]

The mere existence of de jure powers does not always necessitate the imposition of command responsibility.[58] The litmus test in all cases is whether the accused exercised effective control over his or her subordinates; that is not limited to asking whether he or she had de jure authority.[59] It is misconceived to argue that without de jure authority there can be no subordinates, hence no de facto authority.[60] As long as a superior has effective control over subordinates to the extent that he or she can prevent them from committing crimes or punishing them after they committed the crimes, he or she would be held responsible for the commission of the crimes if he or she failed to exercise.[61] This power or authority to prevent or punish does not arise solely from a de jure authority conferred through official appointment.[62]

In *Celebici* the Appeal Chamber held that:

"Customary law has specified a standard of *effective* control, although it does not define precisely the means of control in any sense which falls short of the possession of effective control over subordinates, which requires the possession of material abilities to prevent

51 Para. 377, Id.
52 Ambos K Superior Responsibility, p. 853.
53 *Celebici*, Judgement, A. C, para. 196.
54 *P. v. I. Bagilishema*, Judgement (Reasons) A. C, A. C, Case no: ICTR- 95-1A-A, 13 December 2002, paras. 50, 56.
55 Para. 61, Id.
56 *P. v. C. Kayishema and O. Ruzindana*, Judgement (Reasons), A. C, para. 298.
57 Para. 491, Id.
58 Para. 491, Id.
59 *P. v. I. Bagilishema*, Judgement (Reasons) A. C, para. 61.
60 *P. v. C. Kayishema and O. Ruzindana*, Judgement (Reasons), A. C, para. 294.
61 *P. v. I. Bagilishema*, Judgement (Reasons) A. C, para. 50.
62 Para. 50, Id.

subordinate offences or to punish subordinate offenders, lacks sufficient support in State practice and judicial decisions".[63]

It is worth recalling that under the ICC Statute the superior-subordinate elements are not identical. Article 28 (a) (i) of the ICC Statute provide:

"(a) A military commander or person effectively acting as commander shall be criminally responsible for crimes within the jurisdiction of the Court committed by forces under his or her *effective command and control*, or *effective authority and control* as the case may be, as a result of his or her failure to exercise control properly over such forces,…….

(a) With respect to superior and subordinate relationships not described in paragraph (a), a superior shall be criminally responsible for crimes within the jurisdiction of the Court committed by subordinates under his or her *effective authority and control*, as a result of his or her failure to exercise control properly over such subordinates…

In additional with regard to non-military commanders, Article 28 (b) (ii) also requires that:

The crimes committed concerned activities that were within the *effective responsibility and control* of the superior" [*Emphasis added*].

A few issues need to be commented upon. The first is that the Statute applies not only to military commanders, but also to any person effectively acting as commander. Secondly the requirement of effective command and control for commanders is replaced by that of effective authority and control for non-military superiors. Thirdly for the latter class of superiors there is a requirement for a nexus between the criminal activity of the subordinate and the subordinate's activities that the superior can control.[64] Under the ICC Statute superior responsibility does not substitute, but supplements the other forms of participation prescribed in its Statute, and clarifies that criminal responsibility exists equally for military commanders and all other superiors acting in relationship with subordinates.[65]

We have stressed that the prime requirement is effective control. Substantial influence over the subordinate does not suffice for the purpose of command or superior responsibility.[66] There lacks sufficient evidence of state practice or judicial authority to support a theory that substantial influence as a means of exercising command responsibility has the standing of a rule of customary law, particularly a rule by which criminal liability would be imposed.[67] Substantial influence therefore is not a sufficient measure of control for the imposition of liability to superi-

63 *Celebici* Judgement, A. C, para. 266.

64 Vetter G R (2000) Command Responsibility of Non-Military Superiors in the International Criminal Court (ICC), Yale Journal of International Law, vol. 25, pp. 115, 119-120.

65 Triffterer O (2002) Causality, a Separate Element of the Doctrine of Superior Responsibility as Expressed in Article 28 Rome Statute?, vol. 15, No1, Leiden Journal of International law, p. 186.

66 *Celebici*, Judgement, A. C, paras. 26, 266.

67 Para. 266, Id.

ors.[68] A simple showing of an accused's general influence in the community is insufficient to establish a superior-subordinate relationship.[69] It is also not sufficient that an accused was an influential personality[70], or merely perceived by the community as being someone with authority.[71]

One of the most problematic aspects of determining superior responsibility is that related to proof of de facto authority and control. Self-declared Governments, irregular armies, paramilitary units, and militia groups, whose command structure is often obscure, have often, plagued contemporary conflicts. Superior responsibility is not reserved for official authorities, and any person acting de facto as a superior may he held accountable.[72] The decisive criterion in determining who is a superior according to customary international law is not only the accused's formal legal status, but also his ability, as demonstrated by his duties and competence, to exercise control.[73] Mere absence of formal legal authority to control the actions of subordinates should therefore not be understood to preclude impositions of such responsibility.[74] If this were the case, a Tribunal could find itself powerless to enforce humanitarian law against de facto superiors if it only accepted as proof of command authority a formal letter of authority, despite the fact that the superiors acted at the relevant time with all the powers that would attach to an officially appointed superior or commander.[75] In summary the absence of formal appointment is not fatal to a finding of criminal responsibility.[76]

The ability to exercise effective control is also necessary for the establishment of de facto command or superior responsibility[77] The Appeal Chamber in *Celebici* was of the view that although the degree of control wielded by a de jure or de facto superior may take different forms, a de facto superior must be found to wield *substantially similar powers of control* over subordinates to be held criminally responsible for their acts.[78]

A relevant question that needs probing is whether civilian superiors can only be found liable on condition that they exercise a military style command authority over alleged subordinates. The logic of this reasoning is the fact that superior responsibility takes its origin from military law. In *Bagilishema* the Trial Chamber held:

---

68 Para. 300, Id.

69 *P. v. L. Semanza*, Judgement, T. C, para. 415; *P. v. E. Niyitegeka*, Judgement and Sentence, Case no. ICTR-96-14-T, 16 May 2003, para. 474.

70 *P. v. L. Semanza*, Judgement, T. C, para. 413.

71 *P. v. A. Musema*, Judgement and Sentence, T. C, Case no. ICTR-96-13-T, 27 January 2000, para. 880.

72 *P. v. Z. Aleksovski*, Judgement, T. C, para. 73.

73 Para. 76, Id.

74 *Celebici*, Judgement, TC, para. 354.

75 Para. 193, Id.

76 Para. 197, Id.

77 Id.

78 Id.

"[A] civilian superior will have exercised effective control over his subordinates in the concrete circumstances if both de facto control and the trappings of de jure authority are present and similar to those found in a military context".[79]

It considered these trappings of authority to include; awareness of a chain of command, the practice of issuing and obeying orders, and the expectation that insubordination may lead to disciplinary action.[80] For the Trial Chamber it was by these trappings that the law distinguished civilian superiors from mere rabble-rousers or other forms of influence.[81]

The approach of the *Bagilishema* Trial Chamber was to consider the character of de jure or de jure like relations (in French "quasi-de jure") between the accused and his supposed subordinates, and then determine if the accused's authority (whether real or contrived) was comparable to that exercised in a military context.[82] The Appeal Chamber, however, rejected that reasoning to the extent that it suggested that the control exercised by a civilian superior must be of the same nature as that exercised by a military commander. The Appeal Chamber endorsing the *Celebici* Trial and Appeal decisions ruled:

"The establishment of civilian responsibility requires proof beyond reasonable doubt that the accused exercised effective control over his subordinates. In the sense that he exercised a degree of control over them which is similar to the degree of control of military commanders. It is not suggested that "effective control" will necessarily be exercised by a civilian superior and by a military commander in the same way or that it may necessarily be established in the same way in relation to both a civilian superior and a military commander".[83]

b) Knowledge of Subordinates' Actions

As indicated earlier, Article 6(3) of the ICTR Statute provides that a superior may incur criminal responsibility for criminal acts of subordinates if 'he knew or had reason to know that the subordinate was about to commit such acts or had done so', but failed to prevent such acts or punish those implicated subordinates. The import of mens rea under this article covers two situations. The first arises when the superior "knew" of the crimes that were being committed by those over whom he exercised control, and the second arises when the superior "had reason to know". It should be noted in this regard that command responsibility does not impose strict liability on a superior for the offences of subordinates.[84]

79 *P. v. I. Bagilishema*, Judgement, T. C, para. 151.

80 Para. 43, Id; see also, *P. v. I. Bagilishema*, (Judgement Reasons), A. C, para. 53.

81 Judgement, T. C, para. 43; Judgement (Reasons) A. C, para. 53, Id.

82 *P. v. I. Bagilishema*, T. C, Judgement, para. 152; Also refereed to in *Bagilishema*, Judgement (Reasons), A. C, para. 54.

83 *P. v. I. Bagilishema*, Judgement (Reasons), A. C, para. 52; see, 'the doctrine of superior responsibility extends to civilian superiors only to the extent that they exercise a degree of control over their subordinates which is similar to that of military commanders', *Celebici* Judgement, T. C, para. 378l; Judgement, A/C, para. 197.

84 *Celebici*, Judgement, A. C, paras. 73 & 313.

Although knowledge may be proved through either direct or circumstantial evidence, it may not be presumed.[85] To presume knowledge would be a violation of the principle of guilt.[86] In *Celebici* the Prosecutor's contention of the existence of a rule of presumption in cases where the crimes of subordinates were a matter of public notoriety, occurred over a long period, or over a wide geographical area, was rejected by the Trial Chamber.[87] Actual or constructive knowledge may be inferred from the circumstances of each case, especially in terms of time and place.[88] In determining whether in fact a superior must have had the requisite knowledge, consideration may be had to the number, type, and scope of the alleged acts; the time during which the alleged acts occurred; the number of types of troops involved; the logistics involved, if any; the geographic location of the acts; the widespread occurrence of the acts; the speed of the operations; the modus operandi of similar illegal acts; the officers and staff involved, and the location of the commander at the time.[89] These examples are non exhaustive. The more physically distant the commission of the acts was, the more difficult it will be, in the absence of other indicia, to establish that the superior had knowledge of them.[90] Although a commander's failure to remain appraised of his subordinates' action, or to set up a monitoring system, may constitute a neglect of duty which results in liability within the military disciplinary framework, it will not necessarily result in criminal responsibility.[91]

A discussion of the knowledge requirement of superior responsibility will be incomplete without reference to one of the roots of command or superior responsibility, namely, Article 82(2) of Additional Protocol I. It provides:

"The fact that a breach of the Convention or this Protocol was committed by a subordinate does not absolve his superiors from penal or disciplinary responsibility, as the case may be, if he knew, or had information which should have enabled them to conclude in the circumstances at the time, that he was committing or was going to commit such a breach and if they did not take all necessary measures within their powers to prevent or repress the breach".

Customary international law does not impose in the criminal context a general duty to know upon commanders or superiors, breach of which would be sufficient to render him responsible for subordinates' crimes. [92] The customary standard of *mens rea* with regard to "had reason to know" is that a superior will be criminally

---

[85] *P. v. T. Blaskic,* Judgement, T. C, para. 307; *P. v. Z. Aleksovski*, Judgement, T. C, para. 80; Cf. "A presumption of knowledge in cases of notorious and widespread criminality is an emerging rule of customary law", Bantekas I (2002), p. 595.

[86] Ambos K Superior Responsibility, p. 864.

[87] *Celebici*, Judgement, T. C, para. 384.

[88] Kittichaisaree K (2001) p. 257.

[89] *P. v. T. Blaskic*, Judgement, T. C, para. 307; *Celebici* Judgement, T. C, para. 386. The list is based on that contained in the Final Report of the Commission of Experts for the Former Yugoslavia, UN Doc. , S/1994/674, 27 May 1994, para 58.

[90] *P. v. Z. Alkesovski*, Judgement, T. C, para. 80.

[91] *Celebici* Judgement, A. C, para. 226.

[92] Paras. 230 & 240, Id.

responsible through the principles of superior responsibility only if information was available to him which would have put him on notice of offences committed by subordinates.[93] A duty of inquiry arises when a commander is put on notice or in the circumstances ought to have been put on notice.[94]

Thus failure to conclude or conduct additional inquiry, inspite of alarming information constitutes knowledge of subordinate offences, given the explicit wording of that article which provides as knowledge element, "knew or *had information which should have enabled him to conclude in the circumstances at the time*", that the subordinate was committing or was going to commit a breach of the Geneva Convention or Additional Protocol.[95] "Had information" means that at the crucial time, the commander had in his possession such information that should have put him on notice of the fact that an unlawful act was being or about to be committed by his subordinate.[96]

In *Semanza* the Trial Chamber explained that a superior will be found to possess or will be imputed with the requisite *mens rea* sufficient to incur criminal responsibility where: (i) the superior had actual knowledge, established through direct or circumstantial evidence, that his subordinates were about to commit, were committing, or had committed a crime under the Statute; or (ii) the superior possessed information providing notice of the risk of such offences by indicating the need for additional information in order to ascertain whether such offences were about to be committed, were being committed, or had been committed, by subordinates.[97] As remarked by the Appeal Chamber in *Bagilishema* the decisive question in the second instance is whether the superior possessed information which put him on notice of the risk of crimes being committed or crimes which have been committed and requiring him to carry out an additional investigation or punish his subordinates guilty of such crimes.[98] The "had to know " standard does not require that the accused actually knew that crimes had been committed or were about to be committed; it merely requires that the Chamber be satisfied that the accused had some information on his possession which would put him on notice of possible unlawful acts by his subordinates.[99]

Article 28(a) (i) and 28 (b) (i) of the ICC Statute provides for a different mens rea requirement for military commanders and civilian superiors. For the former it imposes a more active duty[100] upon the superior to inform himself of the activities of his subordinates when he, "knew or, owing to the circumstances at the time, should have known that the forces were committing or about to commit such crimes". Military commanders can be held liable for knowledge or negligence

---

93 Para. 241, Id.

94 Rogers A P V (1996) Law on the Battlefield, Manchester University Press, Manchester, p. 134.

95 *Celebici* Judgement, A. C, paras. 231-232.

96 Paras. 233, Id.

97 *P. v. L. Semanza*, Judgement, T. C. para. 405.

98 *P. v. I. Bagilishema*, Judgement (Reasons), A. C, para. 26.

99 Para. 28, A. C, Id; *Celebici*, Judgment, A. C, para. 238.

100 Kittichaisaree K (2001) p. 256; *Kayishema,* Judgement, T. C, para. 227.

(should have known).[101] On the other hand, for other superiors, Article 28(b) (i) requires that they either "knew or consciously disregarded information which clearly indicated, that the subordinates were committing or about to commit such crimes".[102] This "wilful blindness" standard represents an exception to the positive knowledge requirement in that it is considered satisfied-regarding the existence of a particular fact-if a person is aware of a high probability of its existence, unless he actually believes that it does not exist.[103]

Expressed in the vocabulary of municipal law, this means that negligent complicity in the crime of one's subordinates is no longer punishable; it is only reckless and intentional complicity which remains within the pale of punishable acts under that provision.[104] There is no prima facie duty upon a non-military commander to be seized of every activity of all persons under his or her control.[105] It should also be recalled that 'knowledge' is defined in Article 30(3) of the ICC Statute as "awareness that a circumstance exists or a consequence will occur in the ordinary course of events".

c) Prevent or Punish

A superior incurs criminal responsibility only for failing to take "necessary and reasonable measures" to prevent or punish crimes committed by subordinates.[106] He should only be held responsible for failing to take such measures that are within his material possibility.[107] That is upon a material ability to prevent or punish the crimes in question.[108] Such ability must not be considered abstractly; it must be determined on a case-to-case basis depending on the circumstances.[109] Apart from issuing orders or taking disciplinary action, material ability may entail submitting reports to the competent authorities in order for proper measures to be taken.[110] Surely Tribunals cannot demand the impossible (nemo potest obligari impossibili)![111] In order to establish the responsibility of a superior under Article 6 (3), it must be shown that the accused was in a position to prevent or, alterna-

101 Ambos K Superior Responsibility, p. 848.

102 Cf. "The formulation sets an easier standard for the accused to exonerate himself of her self via the knowledge element", Vetter G R (2000) Command Responsibility of Non-Military Superiors, p. 120.

103 Ambos K Superior Responsibility, p. 870; "Consciously disregarded"......... represents the 'willful blindness' that the *Celebici* court said was actionable", Vetter G R (2000) p. 125.

104 Damaska M (2001) p. 494.

105 *P. v. C. Kayishema and O. Ruzindana*, Judgement, T. C, para. 228.

106 *P. v. L. Semanza*, Judgement, T. C, para. 406.

107 *Celebici*, Judgement, T. C, para. 499.

108 *P. v. Kayishema and O. Ruzindana*, Judgement, T. C, paras. 499, 511.

109 *P. v. Z. Aleksovski*, Judgement, T. C. para. 81.

110 *P. v. T. Blaskic*, Judgement, T. C, para. 302.

111 *P. v. Kayishema and O. Ruzindana*, T. C, para. 499; "It must, however, be recognized that international law cannot oblige a superior to perform the impossible", in *Celebici*, Judgement, T. C, paras. 394-95.

tively, punish the subordinate perpetrators of those crimes. A superior can only be held criminally responsible for failing to take such measures that are within his powers.[112] A demonstration that the superior attempted to prevent atrocities that he knew were about to take place, and which were within his powers to prevent can exonerate a superior.

The power or authority to prevent or punish, does not solely arise from de jure authority conferred through official appointment.[113] The lack of formal legal competence to take the necessary measures to prevent or repress the crime in question does not necessarily preclude the criminal responsibility of the superior.[114] As long as a superior has effective control over subordinates, to the extent that he can prevent them from committing crimes or punishing them after they committed the crimes, he would be held responsible for the commission of the crimes if he failed to exercise such abilities of control.[115] In the assessment whether a superior failed to act, it is necessary to look beyond formal competence to actual capacity to take measures.[116] D'Amato has submitted that mere "paper record" of orders not to commit crimes will not exonerate a Commander who infact tolerated or even approved of those atrocities.[117]

The obligation to prevent or punish is not a set of two alternative and equally satisfying options.[118] They are distinct. If a superior is aware of the impending or ongoing commission of a crime by subordinates, necessary and reasonable measures must be taken to stop or prevent it.[119] Moreover a superior with such knowledge and the material ability to prevent the commission of the crime does not discharge his responsibility by opting simply to punish his subordinates in the aftermath.[120] A superior's duty to punish occurs after the commission of an offence, and is not predicated on future offences.[121]

---

[112] *Celebici*, Judgement, T. C, para. 394-95.

[113] *Celebici,* Judgement, A. C. para. 193.

[114] *P. v. Kayishema and O. Ruzindana*, Judgement, T. C, para. 499.

[115] *Celebici* Judgment, A. C, para. 198.

[116] *P. v. Kayishema and O. Ruzindana,* Judgement (Reasons), A. C, para. 302.

[117] D'Amato A National Prosecution for International crimes. In Bassiouni M C (1999) International Criminal Law (Enforcement), Vol. III, 2nd Edition, Ardsley, N. Y, p. 223.

[118] *P. v. T. Blaskic*, Judgement, T. C, para. 336, *P. v. I. Bagilishema*, Judgement, T. C, para. 49; *P. v. L. Semanza*, Judgement, T. C, para. 407.

[119] *P. v. Bagilishema*, Judgement, T. C. para. 49; *P. v. Semanza*, Judgement, T. C, para. 407.

[120] *Bagilishema*, Judgment, T. C. para. 49; *Semanza*, Judgement, T. C, para. 407, Id.

[121] Bantekas I (2002) p. 592.

De facto and de jure Orders

A guide in determining superior responsibility is to examine the superior's ability, de jure or de facto, to issue orders to prevent a crime or to punish the perpetrator. This sanctioning power should not be broadly interpreted.[122] As stated in *Aleksovski*:

"Although the power to sanction is the in dissociable corollary of the power to issue orders within the military hierarchy, it does not apply to the civilian authorities. It cannot be expected that a civilian authority will have disciplinary powers over his subordinates equivalent to that of the military authority in an analogous command position. To require a civilian authority to have sanctionary powers similar to those of a member of the military would so limit the scope of the doctrine of superior authority that it would hardly be applicable to civilian authorities. The Trial Chamber therefore considers that the superior's ability de jure or de facto to impose sanctions is not essential. The possibility of transmitting reports to the appropriate authorities suffices since the civilian authority, through its position in the hierarchy, is expected to report whenever crimes are committed, and that, in the light of this position, the likelihood that those reports will trigger an investigation or initiate disciplinary or even criminal measures is extant".[123]

Even if orders were given to subordinates, it is essential to show that the orders were carried out in a superior-subordinate hierarchy; and any exchange of words between the alleged superior and subordinates should be that of a superior commanding a subordinate demonstrating effective control of the former over the latter, in that it has to be shown that the superior could prevent or punish them for the crimes committed.[124] The signing of orders will support a charge of command responsibility when they provide evidence of a superior-subordinate relationship, irrespective of the importance of that order.[125]

Chain of Command

A formalized position in a direct chain of command over the subordinate is not required.[126] There is no need to prove that a superior was exercising an authority within a formal chain of command; but what is required is that the superior should have effective control over the subordinates in having the material ability to prevent or punish crimes committed by the subordinates.[127] The fact that one is part of a chain of command should not automatically give rise to a duty to prevent or re-

[122] *P. v. Z. Aleksovski*, Judgement, T. C, para. 78.

[123] Para. 78, Id.

[124] *P. v. Niyitegeka*, Judgement and Sentence, T. C, para. 477.

[125] Bantekas I (2002) p. 582.

[126] *Celebici* Judgment, A. C, para. 305; For a classical understanding of the hierarchical and vertical formation of the Armed Forces see, *Lt. Col. Prithi Pal Singh Bedi etc v. Union of India and Others* [1983] Supreme Court Reports(India) 393, at 419-420.

[127] *Celebici* Judgment, A. C, para. 305.

press violations by a subordinate.[128] Subordination, hierarchy, and chain of command need not be established in the sense of formal organizational structures so long as the fundamental requirement of an effective power to control the subordinate, in the sense of preventing or punishing criminal conduct, is satisfied.[129]

Evidence of the distribution of tasks within a Unit can be applied to ascertain the precise authority of both operational and prisoners of war camp commanders.[130] It is the superior-subordinate relationship that lies at the heart of the concept of command responsibility.[131] Command responsibility is ultimately predicted upon the power of the superior to control the acts of his subordinates.[132] The perpetrator of the underlying offence must be a subordinate of the person of higher rank.[133] The Appeal Chamber in *Celebici* clarified that this carried with it the requirement to prove that the perpetrator was the "subordinate" of the accused, not to import a requirement of direct or formal subordination, but to mean that the relevant accused is, by virtue of his or her position, senior in some sort of formal or informal hierarchy to the perpetrator.[134] This relationship of subordination encompasses indirect and informal relationships.[135] Often, as we shall see in the case of Rwanda, it is unofficial relationships, informal connections, and de facto authority that lied behind the marching orders of the atrocity crimes committed in 1999. In *Celebici* the Trial Chamber, however, cautioned:

> "[We] must at all times be alive to the realities of any given situation and be prepared to piece such veils of formalism that may shied those individuals carrying the greatest responsibility for heinous acts".[136]

Rwanda: Superior Responsibility

The liability of civilian superiors for atrocity crimes committed by subordinates remains one that requires a diligent approach to proof, and the piecing together of the elements establishing effective command and control or effective authority and control. As detailed earlier the crimes committed in Rwanda in 1994 were to a large extent Government sponsored and acquiesced to. Their execution was driven by a top-down relationship between those with the greatest responsibility, the intermediate level coordinators, and those who executed widespread and systematic

---

128 Wu T, Kang Y J (1977) Criminal Liability for the Actions of Subordinates-The Doc trine of Command Responsibility and its Analogues in United States, Harv. Int'l L. J, vol. 38, pp. 28-281.

129 *Celebici* Judgement, A. C, para. 254.

130 Bantekas I (2002), p. 582.

131 *P. v. C. Kayishema and O. Ruzindana*, Judgement, T. C, para. 217.

132 *Celebici*, Judgement, T. C, para. 376.

133 Paras. 646-647, Id.

134 *Celebici* Judgement, A. C. para. 303.

135 Para. 304, Id.

136 *Celebici*, Judgement, T. C, para. 377.

criminal acts at local level. There the dominant feature of superior responsibility for civilians was both de jure and de facto authority, depending upon the relevant legislative texts and the individual's position, political belief, portfolio, origin, network, affiliation, and social standing in the community. The Rwandan situation was also particular in another sense. The society was obedient to the Government and its national prefectoral and communal authorities.

One phenomenon that sparked the flames of atrocity crimes was direct and public incitement through the Media, and by leaders in public meetings attended by the civilian population. In one instance, in Bisesero, Kibuye Prefecture, on 13 April 1994, the Minister of Information of the Interim Government who was with armed attackers, told them to go back "to work", a reference to the killing of Tutsi, which led to an attack being launched against Tutsi in Rugarama.[137] In another meeting at Kucyapa, after a large scale attack on 13 May at Muyira Hill, for the purpose of deciding on the programme of killings for the next day and to organize the killings of Tutsi in Bisesero, the same accused thanked attackers for their participation in attacks and commended them for "a good work"; that is, the killing of Tutsi civilians.[138] He told them to share looted cattle and eat meat so that they would be strong to return the next day to continue to "work", that is, to kill.[139] The next day the Tutsi in Bisesero were pursued and attacked throughout the day.[140] The Trial Chamber held that the accused's words, including the call to "work", were understood by his audience as a call to kill the Tutsi, that he knew his words would be interpreted as such, and that they constituted direct and public incitement to commit genocide.[141] With regard to the above incidents of public incitement, an eyesore of the Rwandan, it is worth noting that mere indication that an accused had a leadership role is insufficient by itself to show that he was in a superior-subordinate relationship with the people in attendance at meetings; in that he could prevent or punish the people at the meeting for their crimes.[142]

It is interesting to highlight the position of Prefets, who in the context of the atrocity crimes committed in Rwanda should be considered among those with responsibility for governance. Prefets were the trustees of State authority in the Prefectures. In the case of the Kayishema, the former Prefet of Kibuye, the Trial Chamber found that he exercised clear, definite control, both de jure and de facto, over assailants at every massacre site set out in the indictment, namely, over bourgmestres and other members of the administration, gendarmes, soldiers, communal police, and other law enforcement agencies identified at those sites.[143] Furthermore, the Trial Chamber held that he had de jure authority over bourgmesters and other law enforcement officers borne out of his overarching statutory duty to maintain public order and security, coupled with the numerous laws and

---

[137] *P. v. E. Niyitegeka*, Judgement and Sentence, T. C, para. 432.

[138] Para. 433, Id.

[139] Para. 433, Id.

[140] Para. 433, Id.

[141] Paras. 435-437, Id.

[142] Para. 476, Id.

[143] *P. v. C. Kayishema and O. Runzindana*, Judgement, T. C, paras. 480, 489, 515.

decrees that evidenced a hierarchical authority and supervisory jurisdiction which the Prefet had.[144] This included the *Loi sur l'organisation de la commune* (Law on the Organization of the Commune), 1963, which provided in Article 59 that as representative of the executive power, the Bourgmestre is under the hierarchical authority of the Prefet. Under Article 46 and 48 the Prefet had the power to take disciplinary sanctions against a Bourgmestre and even to propose his dismissal to the Minister of Interior. Article 85 further provided that where a communal authority fails to execute measures prescribed in the law or decree, then the Prefet may ultimately supplement his communal authority in order to remedy their inaction.

The Prefet's power to requisition communal police and place them under his direct authority in cases of grave public disorder or in times when unrest has occurred or is about to occur was considered by the Trial Chamber in *Kayishema and Ruzindana* as conferring de jure authority, and a superior-subordinate relationship.[145] Similarly Kayishema's ultimate authority of requisition over the gendarmerie nationale in the face of public disorder that prevailed in Rwanda in the pivotal months of April to July 1994 evidenced his de jure authority over the gendermerie.[146] The Trial Chamber also held that Kayishema had de facto control over all of the assailants participating in massacres, by varied acts that included addressing, instructing, directing, leading and rewarding assailants.[147]

The chaotic situation in Rwanda after 6 April 1994 and the practical realities at that time may well have meant that a Prefet not only had no control over certain de jure subordinates, but also that he had no means to effectively prevent the atrocities that were occurring.[148] It is essential to examine the evidence of actual authority or control exercised by the superior over the subordinates. The culpability that this doctrine of command or superior responsibility gives rise to must ultimately be predicted upon the power that the commander or superior exercises over his subordinates in a given situation.[149] It is not enough to pinpoint to the title, position, or rank of the superior. Evidence that needs to be collated is that of superior authority. Most important is evidence of orders, the assignment of tasks, demanding and receiving in return direct reports from subordinates, the power to requisition persons and place them under the superior's direct authority, and the issuance of instructions. In *Niyitegeka* the Trial Chamber held that the Minister of Information in the Interim Government of Rwanda had no de jure or de facto control over Prefets or Bourgmestres.[150] It further opined that there was no evidence that a Minister of Information in Rwanda, by virtue of his position alone, would have effec-

---

144 Para. 481, Id. Cf. Loi sur L'organization de la commune, 1963, Decret Loi organization et fonctionnement de la prefecture, 11 March 1975.

145 *P. v. C. Kayishema and O. Ruzindana*, Judgement, T. C, para. 482.

146 Paras. 483-486, Id.

147 Paras. 501-506, Id.

148 Para. 219, Id.

149 Para. 491, Id.

150 *P. v. E. Niyitegeka*, Judgement and Sentence, T. C, para. 474.

tive control over alleged subordinates, such as Bourgmestres or interahamwe.[151] These are but a few examples.

One clarification is needed: that of situations of negligence. In *Bagilishema* the Appeal Chamber suggested that superior responsibility not be described in terms of negligence at all.[152] It suggested that the test of negligence be left aside in ascertaining superior or command responsibility. A military or a civilian superior may be held responsible if he fails to discharge his duties as a superior either by deliberately failing to perform them or culpably or wilfully disregarding them.[153]

At the ICTR one of the accused, Alfred Musema, Director of the Gisovu Tea Factory, a public enterprise was charged with criminal responsibility under both Article 6(1) and 6 (3). He had been appointed to that position by the late President Habyarimana in 1984, and had been director until 1994. With regard to his authority the Trial Chamber held that he had de jure and de facto power over employees of the Tea Factory.[154] It opined that Musema was the superior of the Tea Factory employees who participated in the attack on 26 April 1999 on Gitwa Hill, which resulted in serious bodily and mental harm to members of the Tutsi group. [155] The Chamber also ruled that he also had de jure and de facto authority over factory employees who had participated in various others attacks against the civilian Tutsi population, such as that at Rwirambo Hill between the end of April and 3 May 1994; that on 13-14 May at Muyira Hill, and finally that of mid May on Mumataba Hill against 2000-3000 Tutsi, an attack that involved 120-130 attackers, among whom were Gisovu Tea Factory employees.[156] The accused, despite his knowledge of the participation of Gisovu Tea factory employees in these attacks by his physical presence at the various sites in which attacks against Tutsi civilians had taken place, and their use of the Tea Factory property on the commission of these attacks, had failed to take any reasonable measures to prevent or punish such participation or use of Tea Factory property.[157]

On de jure authority the Chamber held that Musema exercised such authority over factory employees, while they were on the Tea Factory premises and while they were engaged in their professional duties as employees of the factory even if

---

[151] Para 474, Id.

[152] *P. v. I. Bagilishema*, Judgement (Reasons), A. C, para. 36; "References to "negligence" in the context of superior responsibility are likely to lead to confusion of thought", at para. 35; Cf. This type of responsibility imposes "criminal liability for conduct attributable to serious neglect in the supervision of subordinates", Osiel M J (1999) Obeying Orders. Atrocity, Military Discipline and the Law of War, Transaction Publishers, New Brunswick, p. 192.

[153] *P. v. I. Bagishema*, Judgement (Reasons), A. C, para. 35; Cf. Article 28(2) ICC Statute.

[154] *P. v. A. Musema*, Judgement and Sentence, T. C, paras. 894, 899, 905, 914-915, 919-920, 950. For a critique of the Trial Chamber's decision relating to the application of Article 6(3) in cases of managerial responsibility, see Zahar A (2001) Command Responsibility of Civilian Superiors for Genocide, Leiden Journal of International Law, vol. 14/3, p. 602-603.

[155] Paras. 893-895, Id.

[156] Paras. 898-900, 919, Id.

[157] Para. 950, Id.

those duties were performed outside factory premises.[158] He had exercised legal and financial authority over them, particularly through his power to appoint and remove the employees from their positions at the factory.[159] By virtue of these powers he was in a position, to take reasonable measures, such as removing, or threatening to remove an individual from his or her position at the factory, if he or she was identified as a perpetrator of crimes punishable under the Statute.[160] He was also in a position to attempt to prevent or punish the use of Tea Factory vehicles, uniforms or other factory property in the commission of such crimes.[161]

In *Aleksovski* where the accused, a civilian prison warden at Kaonik prison (a military prison under the jurisdiction of the Travnik military tribunal), was also charged with superior responsibility for the criminal acts of subordinates committed inside as well outside the prison facility, the ICTY Trial Chamber held that although the accused had superior responsibility over subordinate guards inside the prison, the powers of the accused did not extend beyond the confines of the prison compound, and did not extend to acts of subordinates who detained Muslim detainees at trench sites, nor over those who used detainees as human shields at localities outside.[162]

In *P. v. Elizaphan Ntakiritumana* and *Gerard Ntakiritumana* it was alleged that the later, who served as a medical doctor at the Seventh Day Adventist Mugonero Hospital in Gishyita Commune, Kibuye Prefecture, Rwanda, was the superior of hospital employees in respect of genocide, complicity to commit genocide, and crimes against humanity (extermination and murder). The Tribunal held that although Dr Ntakirutimana took charge of Mugonero Hospital in the days before April 1994 and that he played a prominent role during some of the attacks at Bisesero during the period April to June 1994, he had no effective control over any person.[163] It stated that:

"The assumption of the directorship of the hospital (whether or not by way of formal appointment) does not, alone demonstrate that the accused had effective control over hospital staff. Conversely, the fact that the accused was not in any kind of administrative relation with some of the alleged subordinates, does not in itself preclude that he had effective control over the subordinates. Regard must be had to the evidence adduced."[164]

Serushago offers an interesting reading of the *de facto* authority of a civilian superior over militia, namely, interahamwe.[165] A secondary school leaver and money

[158] Para. 880, Id.

[159] Id.

[160] Id.

[161] Id.

[162] *P. v. Z. Aleksovski*, Judgement, T. C, paras. 106, 134, 137.

[163] *P. v. E. Ntakiritumana and Gerard Ntakiritumana*, Judgement and Sentence, T. C, 819-822, Case no: ICTR –96-10 and ICTR-96-17-T, 21 February 2003, para. . 438.

[164] Para. 436, Id.

[165] See, *P. v. Omar Serushago*, Sentence, T. C, Case no. ICTR-98-39-S, 5 February 1999, paras. 28-29; *O. Serushago v. P* (Reasons for Decisions) A. C, Case no. ICTR-98-39-A, 6 April 2000, paras. 16-19.

changer by trade, he was neither a member nor had he any official position within the youth wing of any of the political parties then active in Rwanda in 1994. He was, however, a prominent member of the Interahamwe and enjoyed definite authority in his local Prefecture, Gisenyi. Serushago's father Faizi Sinabyaye, a prominent Gisenyi businessman with 33 children from 4 wives originated from the same area, Karago, Bushiru, Gisenyi as the Habyarimana's.[166] He did some business together with Habyarimana's father-in-law, and served as the MRND Sector Counselor for Gisenyi.[167] These strong connections had enabled Serushago to wield considerable power. In his guilty plea before the ICTR, he admitted that 33 persons had been killed by interahamwe placed under his authority.[168] It was admitted and accepted by the Trial Chamber that he held a de facto power of authority over the interahamwe in Gisenyi, and that within the scope of acts by militiamen between April and June 1999, he gave orders which were followed and which no one could contradict.[169]

In the Media Trial involving three accused, Ferdinand Nahimana, Jean Bosco Barayagwiza, and Hassan Ngeze, the prosecution's theory has been that the media played a key role in the plan to exterminate members of the Tutsi ethnic group and moderate Hutu in 1994. That RTLM and Kangura were the main media forums involved in this conspiracy, and to this extent their shareholders bore superior responsibility for incitement contained either in the broadcasts or publications, and authored by broadcasters, or contributors.[170] The theory of responsibility changed for some of the accused as the events developed, especially after 6 April 1994, given that some were not physically present in Rwanda or at the Radio Station.

The charging premise of the Office of the Prosecutor was that before 6 April, Nahimana had de jure superior responsibility for the incitement on RTLM by journalists and broadcasters including Georges Ruggiu, Kantano, Valerie Bemeriki, Noel Hitimana and Gasper Gahigi, some of whom considered to have fueled ethnic hatred and incitement in Rwanda in 1994.[171] The prosecution's allegation was that at two meetings that took place on 26 November 1993 and in February 1994 the former Minister of Information, Faustin Rucugoza, drew the attention of the members of the Radio Station's Steering Committee that included Felicien Kabuga, Nahimana and Barayagwiza to radio broadcasts that accentuated ethnic hatred and targeted Tutsis, and asked them to stop those broadcasts. These incendiary broadcasts continued, even targeting the Minister in person. He was killed in Kigali on 7th April 1994. For Barayagwiza, the prosecution also alleged

---

166 See, Pre Sentencing Brief, *P. v. O Serushago*, Case no: ITCR-98-39-I, 21 Jan. 1999.

167 Id.

168 *Serushago*, Sentence, T. C, para. 29.

169 Para. 36, Id.

170 For allegations of superior responsibility in the Indictment, see, *P. v. F. Nahimana*, Amended Indictment, Case no: ICTR-96-11-I, 15 November 1999, paras, 5. 20 and 6. 8 – 6. 24; *P. v. J. B. Barayagwiza*, Indictment, Case no: ICTR-97-19-I, 14 April 2000, paras. 5. 1-2, 5. 5, 5. 22 –25, 6. 5 – 6. 19, 7. 13 –7. 15.

171 All have been classed as Category I suspects (No: 5, 14, 23 and 92 in the 1999 Update List of the First Category, issued by the Prosecutor General of Rwanda under Article 9 of the Organic Law No: 8/96.

de jure superior responsibility in the period before 6th April 1994. Like Nahimana it was submitted that he had been a shareholder, a member of the Steering Committee, signed checks on behalf of the broadcasting company and was considered in the RTLM itself as the Number 2.

After 6th April 1994 the prosecution theory, as regards superior responsibility was that they both retained de facto authority and control. Although a General Manager had been officially appointed by that time, it was alleged by the testimony of Georges Ruggiu, a former RTLM broadcaster who pleaded guilty before the Rwanda Tribunal that both Nahimana and Barayagwiza continued to be the bosses. It was further alleged that the former visited RTLM three times after 6th April, and gave encouragement to the journalists to continue those broadcasts. As regards the latter while the General Manager was absent, some problems were still reserved for his action and he was approached to resolve them. On its part the Defence submitted that the accused could not be held accountable as superiors. They were not in charge of the Radio Station nor its emissions or broadcasting policies.

In its Judgement the Trial Chamber held that Nahimana and Barayagwiza through their respective roles on the steering committee of RTLM which functioned as a board of directors, effectively controlled it from the time of its creation through and beyond 6 April 1994, and that the former was, and was seen as, the founder and director of the company, and the latter, was and was seen, as his second in command.[172] In short, Nahimana was "number one", and Barayagwiza "number two" in the top management of the Radio.[173] Furthermore, it held that after 6 April 1994, they both continued to have de jure and de facto authority over RTLM.[174] It convicted Nahimana of direct and public incitement to commit genocide pursuant to Articles 6(1) and 6 (3) of the Statute, and Barayagwiza of the same offence pursuant to Article 6 (3).[175]

The guilty plea of former Prime Minister Kambanda also illuminates some of the trappings of superior responsibility to those in high Governmental or political office.[176] In the Plea Agreement of 28 April 1998 with the Prosecution, he admitted that he exercised de jure authority and control over the 20 members of the Council of Ministers of his Government. In this regard it is of interest to recall the 1991 Constitution of Rwanda, which the Interim Government deemed applicable in April 1994, and over which former Prime Minister Kambanda and Cabinet members took the oath of office.[177] It provided in Article 51 that the Prime Minister directs the action of the Government fixes the attributes of Ministers and determined the nature and competence of services placed under their respective authorities, countersigns laws promulgated by the President, and executes by decrees laws and regulations. Under Article 56 the resignation or the cessation of duties of

---

172 *P. v. F. Nahimana et all.*, Judgement, T. C, para. 31.
173 Para. 79, Id.
174 Paras. 32, 81.
175 Paras. 81, 100-101.
176 *P. v. J. Kambanda*, Judgement and Sentence, T. C, Case no. ICTR-97-23-S, 4 September 1998, para. 39.
177 Constitution of Rwanda, J. O, p. 615, Official Gazette of the Rep. of Rwanda, 10 June 1991.

the Prime Minister for whatever reasons leads to the resignation of the Government. As Prime Minister and Head of the Interim Government he also accepted in the Plea Agreement that he exercised de jure and de facto authority over senior civil servants, such as Prefets, and senior military officers. Effective control over some of his subordinates was demonstrated by the admission that he had participated in the dismissal of the Prefet of Butare because the latter had opposed the massacres, and the appointment of a new Prefet to ensure the spread of massacres of Tutsi in Butare. As Prime Minister he had also issued the Directive on Civil Defense addressed to Prefets on 25 May 1994.[178]

In Rwanda the socio-cultural and political context facilitated the growth of de facto control and authority. Informed observers of the Rwandan events of 1994 suggest that immediately after the death of former President Habyarimana on 6 April 1994, the person who "took charge" of the ensuing events was Bagosora,[179] then a retired army officer and *Directeur de cabinet* in the office of the Minister of Defence Augustin Bizimana, who was abroad on mission at that time. In a demonstration that showed who had real power, on 28 April 1994, three weeks into the atrocities, Ambassador Prudence Bushnell, then Principal Assistant Secretary of State for African Affairs at the US Department of State in Washington D.C, spoke on the telephone to Bagosora, and confronted him with eyewitness accounts of Rwandan Armed Forces complicity in the violence and urged him to end the killings.[180] Bushnell told Bagosora that the world would not buy the story that the killings were a spontaneous reaction by the population to the RPF offensive, because credible witnesses were reporting that the Rwandan military was aiding and abetting civilians in atrocities.[181] She told him that it would behove the Rwandan military to show some "responsible leadership" and willingness to compromise, emphasizing that the United States was looking to him personally to do the right thing.[182] The second highest-ranking official of the State Department did not call Theodore Sindikubwabo, the President and the Head of State. According to the 1991 Constitution, which the Interim Government said was applicable, the President was the Supreme Chief of the Armed Forces, represented the Republic in its external relations, and was the guarantor of national unity.[183] Neither was the Prime Minister Kambada, responsible for directing the actions of the Government, nor General Augustin Bizimungu, the Chief of Staff of the Rwandan Armed Forces, called by United States official. Instead Bushnell chose to call Bagosora, a retired FAR colonel, and at that time a *Directeur de cabinet* in the Defence Ministry.

---

178 The Directive on Civil Defence addressed to Prefets was signed 25 May 1994 (No. 024-0273), and was dissemination on 8 June 1994.

179 Human Rights Watch/FILDH (1999) Leave None to tell the Story, p. 185.

180 Memos reveal Rwandan Delay, The Washington Post, 23 August 2001; Papers show US knew of Rwanda genocide early on, Reuters, 22 August 2001; US Department of State, Cable No 113672 to US Embassy Bujumbura, US Embassy Dar es salaam, 29 April 1994 cited at htpp://www. gwu. ed/~nsarchives/NSAEB53/indexhtml.

181 Id.

182 Id.

183 Articles 39, 44 (5), and 45, Constitution of 1991, Id.

Following the death of President Habyarimana, Bagosora, on 6 April 1994, presided over a meeting of senior officers of the Rwandan Armed Forces and the Gendarmerie which decided that FAR's Chief of Staff, General Nsabimana, who had also been killed in the plane shooting, should be replaced by Colonel Marcel Gatsinzi, as acting Chief of Staff. Bagosora signed the latter's formal appointment, and invited him to assume functions without delay. On 7 April Bagosora chaired another meeting at ESM (Ecole Superiuer Militaire) attended by army and gendarmerie commanders more senior than him. He also issued a press communiqué in the name of the Rwandan Armed Forces on efforts that were being made to stabilize the situation, and incited the armed forces to restore order in the country. That same day he also convoked leaders of the five main political parties to a meeting that decided and agreed on the composition of the Interim Government. All these are indicators of political and military authority. In what appears to be grounded on de facto authority, in the amended Indictment against him, the Prosecutor has alleged that by his rank, office, the personal relations he had with Commanders of the Specialized Units of FAR (i.e. Presidential Guard, Reconnaissance and Para-commando Battalions) implicated in the crimes, and the fact that they were from the same region and shared the same political beliefs gave him authority over these persons and other members of the militia given the regional context in which power was exercised in Rwanda.[184] De Forges has submitted that in Rwanda, the State was highly organized, the military system, by all accounts functioning as all military systems do with a chain of command, but from historical records, parallel to the organized and functioning hierarchies, there was another chain of command that was completely informal and based upon personal contact and in some cases, that informal chain of command was far more effective and deadly than any official chain of command.[185]

Blurred Command Structures

The Rwandan situation was also one that had blurred chains of command. Neither the interahamwe nor armed civilians involved in the 'civil defence programme' had explicitly officially documented command structures in 1994.[186] The command structure of the Presidential Guard, which was officially tasked to provide personal security to the President, and whose soldiers were visible perpetrators of atrocity crimes, is often debatable. General Delaire the UNAMIR Commander was directly informed by his interlocutors that the Presidential Guard was under the Rwandan Armed Forces, or that it directly reported to the President or his Office. Inspite of this he admitted that there was a certain ambivalence concerning the role and the responsibility of the Presidential Guard.[187] On its part the Genderme-

---

184 *P. v. T. Bagosora*, Amended Indictment, Case no: ICTR-96-7-I, 12 August 1999, para. 4. 4.

185 Des Forges A (2001) Justice in the Balance, p. 2-3.

186 *P. v. C. Kayishema and O. Ruzindana*, Judgement, T. C, para. 493.

187 Testimony, R. Dellaire, Transcript, ICTR, pp. 98-100.

rie Nationale, which was an officially recognized paramilitary organization reported to the Minister of Defense in times of peace, but fell under the command of the Rwandan Armed Forces during an armed conflict. The task for a Prosecutor is how to find a hierarchically answerable command structure, and to identify the elements of proof for effective command and control or effective authority and control. Of course legislative enactments provide an indication of de jure command or control and may, if applicable at the relevant time, serve as a starting point for an in-depth inquiry into superior responsibility.

The Indonesian Armed Forces and East Timor

Deciphering command or superior responsibility with regard to the 1999 atrocity crimes in East Timor requires an understanding of the organization and functioning of the Indonesian security forces; namely, (a) the TNI and the POLRI; (b) the pro autonomy civilian administration and (c) the militia groups: a trio, the combination of which was ultimately responsible for the widespread serious human rights abuses and international humanitarian law violations that occurred. All were deeply involved in the violence. In this chapter we are only concerned with indicators that are useful in determining the three legal elements of command or superior responsibility mentioned earlier. That is, superior-subordinate relationship; the knowledge requirement, and the inaction element, that is failure to prevent or punish. The points raised are of importance in the examination of superior responsibility as a form of criminal participation, and a charging toll for the prosecution of accused, military or civilian, with superior or command responsibility. While it is not our intention to detail the military doctrines of the Indonesian security forces responsible for security and law and order in East Timor in 1999, it suffices for the purpose of our analysis of superior responsibility to illustrate their organizational details. This provides a better understanding of at least the de jure chain of command, coordination, communication and reporting lines. It is of importance in analyzing command relationships.

It has been assessed that Indonesia had as many as 20,000 troops in East Timor in 1999; one soldier per 40 inhabitants, a ratio that is 7 to 9 times higher than the ratio in Indonesia.[188] In the beginning of 1999 the combined Armed Forces of the Republic of Indonesia (ABRI-*Angakatan Bersenjata Republik Indonesia*) consisted of four armed services, namely the Army, Air Force, Navy, and the Police.[189] The Army is divided into two forces, the central forces and the territorial

[188] Indonesia's Death Squads, Getting Away with Murder, A Chronology of Indonesian Military sponsored Paramilitary and Militia atrocities in East Timor from November 1998 to May 1999, ETISCO Occasional Paper No 2, East Timor International Support Center, Darwin NT, May 1999; see, also Martinkus J (2001) p. 18; See also Tanter R, Selden M, Shalon S R (2001) Bitter Flowers, Sweet Flowers, East Timor, Indonesia and the World Community, Rowman & Littlefield, Lonham, MD.

[189] On the Indonesian Armed Forces see, Indonesia-A Country Study, Nov. 1992, at www. lcweb2. loc. gov/frd/idtoc. html; Indonesia Intelligence and Security Agencies. www.

forces. The Indonesian Army has central forces, consisting of the Army Strategic Reserves Command, KOSTRAD (*Komando Strategis Angkatan Darat*) and its supporting arms, and the Special Forces Command, KOPASSUS (*Komando Pasukan Khusus*) and its operational groups. These forces are under the direct command of the Commander in Chief. With an estimated strength of 6,000 soldiers KOPASSUS is an elite force, distinctively identifiable by its troops "red berets", and serves as a para-commando or quick reaction force. The force has among other Units, an intelligence outfit, the SGI (*Satuan Tugas Intelijen*). On its part KONSTRAD, with around 25,000 "green beret" troops, is tasked to oversee operational readiness of all Commands and is involved in defence and security operations. Former Indonesian President Major General Suharto was in the mid 1960s KOSTRAD's Commander (*Pangkostrad*). The Indonesian National Police (POLRI) was separated from ABRI on 1 April 1999, and the official name of the army reverted to TNI (*Tentara Nasional Indonesia*) or National Army of Indonesia. The Commander in Chief of the TNI maintains operational control over all the services, with the heads of each of the services acting as administrative in charge.

The territorial forces consist of Regional or Area Military Commands (KODAM- *Komando Daerah Militer*), which have strategic, operational, and tactical responsibilities. Indeed the power of Indonesia's Armed Forces rests on its vast, politically anchored territorial network.[190] The KODAM is headed by a *Pangdam*. Direct chain of command flows from the Commander in Chief directly to the Regional Military Commands, and further below to subordinate territorial commands. For East Timor (Timur Timur) the relevant Regional Military Command was KODAM IX based in Bali, Den Pasar. It was also responsible for that island, Nusa Tenggara Timur, and Nusa Tenggara Barat provinces of Indonesia. Further down that organization structure was the Sub-Regional or Resort Military Command, KOREM (*Komando Rayon Militer*), headed by the *Danrem*. Below this command structure was the District Military Command, KODIM (*Komando District Militer*), and then the Sub-District Military Command, KORAMIL, headed by a *Dandim* and a *Danramil* respectively. The lowest unit of the Indonesian armed forces was the BABINSA (*Bontara Desa)* or village military post. It was composed of non commissioned officers, both Indonesian and East Timorese.

With regard to the presence of the Indonesian Armed Forces in East Timor in 1999, KOREM 164, based in Dili, East Timor was under KODAM IX, the Regional Military Command, based in Bali, Indonesia. Its Commander, the *Pangdam*, reported to the Commander in Chief of the TNI in Jakarta. Below the Sub-Regional Military Command in Dili (i.e. KOREM 164) there were 13 KODIM Commands in each of East Timor's 13 districts, divided into two sectors. Sector

---

fas:or/irp/world/Indonesia; Lowery B The Indonesian Armed Forces (Tentera Nasional Indonesia, TNI), Research paper No. 23, 1998-99, http://www.aph.gov.au/library/pubs/rp/1980-99/99rp23. htm; Raman B (2000) The Indonesian Armed Forces and Politics, South Asia Analysis Group, Institute for Topical Studies, Chennai, 20 May 2000, athttp://www. saag. org/papers2/paper124. html.

190 Mietzer M (2000) Politics of Engagement: The Indonesian Armed Forces, Islamic Extremism and the War on Terror' Brown Journal of World Affairs, Vol. IX, Issue No. 1, 2000, available at www. watsoninstitute. org/bjwa/archives/9. 1/Indonesia/mietzer. pdf.

A, which covered the western half of East Timor, and Sector B for the eastern half. Directly under the District Military Commands, i.e. KODIM were 62 KORAMIL, and beneath them 442 BABINSA covering the whole territory. KOREM 164 also had, directly attached to it, a number of territorial battalions, each with strength of about 700 troops. Among these were Battalion 745, based in Los Palos, Lautem District, and others that covered Dili, Baucau, Bobonaro, Liquica, Manatuto, and Ailieu. Indonesian officers held all command positions in these battalions, with East Timorese soldiers serving in lower ranks and as foot soldiers. During the 1999 events in East Timor both KOPASSUS and KOSTRAD troops were deployed in order to beef up the territorial troops based in East Timor. A number of Bupati (Regency or District Administrators, like that of Los Palos and of Liquica) were honorary members of KOPASSUS.[191]

Bantekas has suggested four stages of command, along a vertical scale, that seek to effectively filter the dictates of the decision makers to the solder on the battlefield.[192] These are the *policy command* level, with the power to commit or withdraw a state's armed forces; the *strategic command* level, in which the highest ranking military officers, namely the Joint Chiefs of Staff, and senior government officials are fully involved in drawing military plans to achieve policy command objectives; the *operational command* level which involves battlefield implementation by senior military officers; and at the end of the scale, *tactical command*, which exercises direct control or subordination over troops assigned to that command.[193]

If one is to go by this classical description of command levels, and transpose it to the Indonesian Armed Forces, it can be advanced that the policy command level in the case of Indonesia entails the involvement of the President, the Cabinet ministers responsible for Defence and Security, and the Commander in Chief of the Armed Forces.[194] The strategic command level is vested in the Commander in Chief and his immediate TNI Flag Staff Generals. In the case of East Timor, KODAM IX in Bali also provided strategic and operational command. It is thought to have had operational control over combat units assigned or attached to it. The responsibility for operational and tactical command also rested with KOREM 164, which had directly under it a number of territorial battalions. Tactical command can be said to have been with the KODIM and the DANRAMIL. The above analysis, however, should be viewed with a caveat, in that there seems to be in the case of the Indonesian Armed Forces, a deliberate cross of operational

Rabasa A, Haseman J (2000) The Military and Democracy in Indonesia: Challenges, Politics and Power, Nat. Sec. Research Division, The Rand, www.rand.org/publications/MR/MR1599/zer. pdf.

191 See, *P. v. L. Martins and others*, Indictment, Dili District Court, Special Panel for Serious Crimes, 22 November 2001, para. 28.

192 Bantekas I (2002), p. 578.

193 Pp. 578-579, Id.

194 Lowry B (1999) Indonesian Armed Forces, (Ttentara Nasional Indonesia-TNI), Research Paper no: 23, 1998-9, Dept. of the Parliamentary Library, Parliament of Australia, 29 June 1999.

and tactical command responsibilities between the various territorial based commands, and the Special Forces Command and their elements, such as the SGI.

When understanding an armed forces organization and structure as complex as that of Indonesia, it is essential to bear in mind that an official organizational chart does not explain all. The commander's effective command and control is measured by actual possession or non-possession of command and control over troops. Moreover evidence, such as that of orders, direct subordination, reporting and communication must be relied upon. In examining the organization of the Indonesian Armed Forces during the atrocity crime committed in East Timor, an appreciation of the extended structure and territorial network of that armed force is also important. It is part of the jigsaw puzzle that must be pieced together. Overall in Indonesia and East Timor the TNI had in 1999 10 KODAM (military regional commands), 39 KOREM (sub regional military commands), 271 KODIM (district military commands), 3, 818 KORAMIL (sub district military commands) and 26,720 BABINSA (village military posts).

The Indonesian Armed Forces has an extended chain of command and elements of its forces include Territorial Forces, Special Forces, Intelligence Units, Air Force, and the Navy. The separate existence of operational, logistic and supplies, administrative, reporting, and coordinating lines of authority at times blur the chain of command. This is compounded by "*Bapak*" relationships, those of loyalty, patronage or allegiance, which may de facto give a junior officer more effective command and control than a senior ranking officer. As has been said, the key to understanding the mindset of the Indonesian army officer lies in understanding his views of integrity and loyalty.[195]

That apart, the Indonesia Police Force (POLRI) was part of the Indonesian Armed Forces, until 1 April 1999, when it was officially separated from the latter.[196] The only link maintained with the Defense establishment was through its parent Minister, the Minister of Defence and Security, who was also the Minister in Charge of the Indonesian Armed Forces and had jurisdiction over POLRI. The chain of command flows from the Chief of Indonesian National Police, *Kapolri*, down to the Regional Police Command (POLDA) headed by the *Kapolda*, and deputized by the *Wakapol.* Each POLDA is administratively sub divided into the district police command (POLRES) commanded by the *Kapolres*, the sub district military command (POLSEK), headed by the *Kapolsek*, and the village police post (BINPOLDA). In addition the Indonesian National Police Force also had a militarized rapid reaction force, the Mobile Brigade (BRIMOB). In East Timor the most senior police officer was the *Kapolda.* He headed the East Timor Regional Police Command (POLDA) based in Dili. The other subordinate organizational units we have mentioned above were also present in the Districts, Sub-Districts, and Vil-

195 Creveling R (1999) Loyalty and Integration in the Indonesian Armed Forces, Foreign Area Officer Association, 29 November 1999, at www. faoa. org/Journal/Indonesia. /rtml.

196 Cf. Article 5 (1), "The Police Force of the Republic of Indonesia is a component of the Armed Forces of the Republic of Indonesia which primarily has the role to keep the security inside the country/at home", Law of the Republic of Indonesia, No. 28 of 1997.

lages. Although as we have stated the Police Force was separated in April 1999, this separation was not reflected in reality. De facto POLRI continued to be under the effective control of TNI officers at various levels along the chain of command. This was the field situation predicted by the dominance of the TNI throughout all districts of East Timor, before and immediately after the popular consultation.

In examining the application of superior responsibility to commanders of the Indonesian Armed forces and the Indonesian Police it is important to recall the terms of the 5 May 1999 Agreements on the question of East Timor, and the modalities for a popular consultation, between Indonesian, Portugal, and the United Nations. The agreements provided that:

"The Government of Indonesia will be responsible for maintaining peace and security in East Timor in order to ensure that the popular consultation is carried out in a fair and peaceful way in an atmosphere free of intimidation, violence or interference from any side"(Article 3).

Officials of the Governments of Indonesia and Portugal will not participate in the campaign in support of either option. (Annex II, E, (c)).

East Timorese Government officials may campaign in their personal capacity. All such campaigning will be carried out strictly in accordance with the Code of Conduct without use of public funds and government resources or recourse to pressure of office. (Annex II, E (c) (c)).

A secure environment devoid of violence or other forms of intimidation is a prerequisite for the holding of a free and fair ballot in East Timor. Responsibility to ensure an environment as well as the general maintenance of law and order rests with the appropriate Indonesian security authorities. The Absolute neutrality of the TNI (Armed Forces of Indonesia) and the Indonesian Police is essential in this regard. (Annex III, Article1). The police will be solely responsible for the maintenance of law and order." (Annex III, Article 4).

The involvement of commanders and subordinates in atrocity crimes was confirmed in a civil suit in United States brought by an unnamed group of East Timorese plaintiffs, against General Johnny Lumintang, the former Deputy Chief of staff of the Indonesian Armed Forces at the time of East Timor's referendum. The Court, on 13 September 2001, ruled that he was responsible for a large pattern of gross human rights violations in East Timor, and ordered him to pay USD $ 66 million in damages to victims.[197] In its decision six plaintiffs, or their estates, were awarded USD $ 10 million each in punitive damages and compensatory damages of between USD $ 750,000 - 1.750,000 each. The Court ruled that the general, who was not represented in the suit, "along with other high ranking members of the Indonesian military, planned, ordered, and instigated acts carried out by subor-

[197] US Judge slaps 66 million dollars in damages on Indonesian general, AFP, 5 October 2001; Timorese activists hail 66 million-dollar US court ruling against Indonesian General, AFP, 5 October 2001.

dinates to terrorize and displace the East Timorese population and to destroy East Timor's infrastructure following the vote for independence".[198]

The indictment against General Wiranto *et all.,* holds him and others criminally liable under superior responsibility pursuant to section 16 of UNTAET Regulation 2000/15.[199] Annex II details the mode of criminal responsibility for each of the Indictees. The Indictment alleges that as Indonesia's Minister of Defence and Security, and Commander of the Armed Forces of Indonesia (*Panglima Angkatan Bersenjata Republik Indonesia*), he had command authority over all branches and personnel of the armed forces, including six senior ranking officers (i.e. the Head of the Special Team/Adjutant General's Task Force, and member of the Task Force to Oversee the Popular Consultation; the Commander of the Marshal Law Operations Command; the Commander of KODAM IX; the two Commanders of KOREM 164, and the Commander of the Intelligence Task Force within the KOREM. Under the indictment he was equally held accountable as a superior and is alleged to have had effective control, whether in person or through his subordinates, over members of militia groups. All the other Commanders cited above have also been held liable for superior responsibility, with a number held accountable for both direct individual criminal responsibility and indirect superior responsibility.

Under the same indictment Major General Adam Rachmat Damiri, the former Commander of the Regional Military Command (KODAM IX) from June 1998 to November 1999, is held liable for individual criminal responsibility pursuant to section 14 of UNTAET Regulation 2000/15, and for superior responsibility under section 16. He is said to have had command authority over all TNI personnel within the regional military command, including the KOREM 164 Commanders and the Commander of the Intelligence Task Force. Colonel Suhartono (Tono) Suratman, the former Commander of the Dili based sub regional military command (KOREM 164), is also held criminally responsible for both forms of liability. He is alleged to have had superior authority over all TNI personnel within KOREM 164, and as having had effective control, whether in person or through his subordinates, over members of militia groups. His replacement, Colonel Mohammad Nuer Muis who took up duties in East Timor, is only held accountable for superior responsibility. Major General Kiki Shahnakri, the Commander of the Marshal Law Operations Command set up on 7 September 1999, is held liable with both individual criminal responsibility and indirect superior responsibility for the crimes of his subordinate military officers and members of militia groups over which he had effective command and control respectively. Lieutenant Colonel Yayat Sudrajat, the Commander of Tribuana VIII Task Force, and the Commander of the Intelligence Task Force within KOREM 164 are also held accountable for both forms of criminal liability. The Tribuana VIII Task Force was the operational name for a KOPASSUS contingent deployed in East Timor during the 1999 events.

[198] General facing 66 million dollar damages over East Timor denies, AFP, 5 October 2001; US Judge slaps 66 million dollars in damages on Indonesian general, AFP, 5 October 2001.

[199] *P. v. Wiranto et all.*, Indictment, Case no: 5/2003, SPSC, Dili.

In *P. v. Wiranto et all.*, Abilio Soares the former Governor of East Timor, is held criminally responsible for his conduct as an individual pursuant to section 14 of UNTAET Regulation 2000/15.[200] It is revealing to note that before the Ad Hoc Human Rights Court in Indonesia he was not charged with direct personal involvement, but only with superior responsibility for the crime committed by his alleged subordinates that included the Bupati of Liquica, the Bupati of Suai, and the Deputy Commander of the Pro Integration Forces (PPI). From the articulation of facts in the various indictments issued by Prosecutors in East Timor, it would seem that the conduct attributed to him in the Wiranto Indictment does not fully cover his responsibility over the alleged acts of implicated Bupati. The latter indictment may have been the product of a charging decision to put him in the net with the "big fish" (i.e. high-ranking TNI Commanders), but it paid a price for the non-inclusion of superior responsibility, much as the prosecution may have considered that it had sufficient evidence to obtain a conviction on the basis only of direct individual criminal responsibility.

In the various indictments issued by Serious Crimes Prosecutors in Dili against the former District Military Commanders of the Indonesian Armed forces in East Timor, the liability is also superior responsibility. This is the situation with regard to the military commanders of Luquica, Suai and Maliana, implicated respectively in the Liquica Church, Suai Church and Maliana Police Station massacres of 1999.[201] As we have observed District Military Commanders had both operational and tactical level command responsibilities. It is inconsistent with military principles for the commander of an operational area not to have authority over all the troops acting within the confined of his area of responsibility.[202] Normally in the army when a person is in command of a specific area of responsibility he commands ipso facto all the military units located in that area.[203]

Change of Guards

A tactic used by the Indonesian security forces to blur command responsibility was the change of guards or duty on a short tenure. This involved the transfer of senior officers to and fro from East Timor, as well as the appointment of military officers to senior civilian duties. For example Colonel Mohammad Noer Muis replaced Colonel Tono Suratman, who was Commander of the Sub-Regional Military Command in Dili from June 1998 on 13 August 1999, two weeks before the popular consultation. Major General Damiri took over as Commander of the Regional Military Command (KODAM IX) in Bali from June 1998 to November 1999. Major General Kiki Syahnakri served as Marshal Law Commander in East Timor only during the month of September 1999. What requires understanding is that most had earlier served in East Timor, had been associated with the pro

200 See, Indictment, para. 270.

201 See Indictments, Case no: 9/2003, Case no: 18/2003, Case no: 8/2003, SPSC, Dili.

202 *P. v. T. Blaskic*, Judgement, T. C para. 451.

203 Para. 451, Id.

autonomy cause, the setting up of paramilitary groups and the militia, or had a KOPASSUS or KOSTRAD background.

Rogue Elements

A familiar argument by those in alleged superior authority or command, and often with the greatest responsibility, is to argue that atrocity crimes were unplanned or spontaneous and perpetrated by "uncontrolled" or "rogue" elements of the armed forces, or paramilitary groups. The claim is that pro Indonesia East Timorese paramilitaries, enraged and surprised by the result of the ballot and supported by elements within the Indonesian military hierarchy, went on a rampage.[204] For one, General Wiranto, the former Commander in Chief of TNI and Minister of Defence and Security has claimed that the mayhem in East Timor was triggered by disappointment over the "unfair" administration of the ballot by the UNAMET. [205] With this submission it is important to assess whether such a defense can be reconciled with the widespread, systematic, and methodical nature of crimes committed. It is also essential to examine the nature and pattern of crimes and those behind their commission. The planned nature, and in particular the fact that all units acted in a perfectly coordinated manner, presupposes in fact that those troops were responding to a single command, which accordingly could only be superior to the commander of each of the units.[206]

Militia Groups and East Timor Violence

By the time UNAMET arrived in East Timor there were over 25 active militia groups with an estimated total strength of about 10,000 men throughout East Timor. Their declared aim was to defend integration with Indonesia. Some of these groups were old para-military groups, which were revived, such as *Halilintir* (Thunderbolt) in Bobonaro, Maliana; *Tim Alfa* in Los Palos, Leutem District and *Tim Saka* in Baucau. Others were created at the end of 1998 and the beginning of 1999. What can be affirmed is that the formation and reengineering of militia groups coincided with the schedule of the popular consultation process. It was also in response to pro independence initiatives, in particular the formation of the CNRT (National Council of Timorese Resistance); the umbrella organization for all East Timorese pro independence organizations.

The establishment and use by the Indonesian Armed Forces of para-military and militia groups in East Timor goes as far back as 1975, when the army helped set up and train, among others, *Halilintir* headed by Joao da Silva Tavares, who in

---

204 See, Nevins J (2002) The Making of 'Ground Zero' in East Timor in 1999: An analysis of International Complicity in Indonesia's Crimes, vol. XLII, No. 4, Asian Survey, pp. 623-641.

205 Former Indonesian Military Chief grilled over Timor Violence, AFP, 16 May 2002.

206 *P. v. T. Blaskic*, Judgement, T. C, para. 467.

1999 became the Supreme Commander (i.e. *Panglima*) of the Integration Fighting Forces (PPI). He had been part of the Indonesian forces that had invaded East Timor in 1975, and thereafter had been named Bupati of Bobonaro District, a post he held for over a decade. Among the paramilitary groups that the Indonesian Armed Forces had established, trained and supported in East Timor were the Peoples Resistance Forces, *WANDA* (Perlawanan Rakyat); the Guards to Uphold Integretion, *Gada Paksi* (Gadu Penegak Integrasi), the Trained People, *Ratih* (Rakiyat Terlatih) and the self initiated Volunteer Community Security, *Pam Swakarsa* all of which were directly and indirectly armed, trained, and funded by Military, Police, and Civilian authorities.[207]

The East Timor militia groups were paramilitary organizations purposely organized on the basis of the command structure of the TNI battalion, but without a General Staff. They were present in all Districts and most of the Sub-Districts. In most cases, militia groups operated under the de facto command of the Indonesia Armed Forces which trained them, supplied them with arms and ammunition, including weapons permits, provided them with logistic support, radio transmitters and communications facilities, and at times ordered them into action. The groups also had a close working relationship with the SGI (*Satuan Tugas Intelijen*) the intelligence unit of KOPASSUS, which was directly in charge of overseeing their activities.

The specific reintroduction of militia groups at the end of 1998 was part of a strategy by the Indonesian Armed Forces to enlist paramilitary elements to support its forces against FALANTIL, and to counter the growth of pro independence support. Calling a military commander or a superior "boss" or "chief" or any equivalent word alone is insufficient to infer subordination without evidence of the superior's overall authority, the subordinate's reaction and behaviour, in particular, his or her subjugation to those orders. It should be recalled that not all militia groups in East Timor had immaculate command structure, or written rules or regulations governing command. Many of the smaller groups at the Sub-District level had as Commanders acting local gang leaders. Militia recruitment targeted unemployed, illiterate and socially isolated young adults; those who could easily be manipulated. Many were also coerced into joining. Some were the subject of forced conscription. The remit of this Chapter does not permit us to detail all militia groups that existed in East Timor in 1999. Nonetheless in order to appreciate the issues surrounding command responsibility for militia, it suffices if we describe a few of them. To begin with the overall umbrella militia organization in East Timor, the PPI or the Integration Fighting Forces was inaugurated on 5 February 1999 in Balibo. The PPI was organized along the structure of the TNI. It had a Commander, a Deputy Commander, 4 Sector Commanders, Company, Platoon and Section Commanders, and at the bottom the militia members. In practice the PPI did not have any operational authority or command over the various militia groups. Each of these groups coordinated its activities and operations directly with the various KOPPASUS units based in East Timor.

---

207 KPP-HAM Report, para. 64.

One of the key militia organizations in East Timor was *Aitarak* ("Thorn") Force Command (Pasukan Komando Aitarak). It was set up in early 1999 ahead of the popular consultation. Based in the capital, Dili, and headquartered at the former Hotel Tropikal, less than two hundred meters from the office of the former Governor of East Timor, its influence and activities covered areas as far as Liquica and up to the border with West Timor. The professed goals of *Aitarak* were to defend the holy Red and White Indonesia Flag (Sang Saka Merah Putih) so that it continued to fly over the earth of Loro Sae (East Timor); take an active part in the 'socializing' the autonomy package agreed upon by Indonesia, Portugal, and the United Nations, and win the referendum in favour of integration within the Unitary State of Indonesia. With militia strength of about 1,500 men, *Aitarak's* command structure resembled that of a TNI battalion, consisting of a Commander (Komandan), and a Deputy Commander (Wakil Komandan, Wadan). Below them were four sections (Seksi) each headed by a section commander (*Komandan Seksi*). The main troops of militiamen were under the direct command of the Komandan or Wakil Komandan, and were divided into four companies (Kompi), and an additional Support Company (Kompi Bantuan, Komban).

Its Commander, Eurico Guterres, also held the position of Deputy Commander of the umbrella militia organization in East Timor, the Integration Fighting Forces (Pasukan Perjuangan Integrasi) or PPI. Militia groups were a part and parcel of the *PAM Swakarsa*, (self-initiated volunteer/community security group). This provided a cover for legitimacy and official recognition by civilian authorities and pro autonomy organizations. It is worth recalling that militia groups also had the direct support of the civilian authorities, in particular the Bupati. These District Civil Administrators, through directives, ordered the establishment of self initiated volunteer community security groups, the *PAM Swarkarsa*, which were headed by civilian administrators, and of which militia members were the core cadre. For example that established by the Bupati of Dili, had the Administrative Mayor of Dili as its Chief; the Chief of Staff of KODIM (District Military Command) as first Deputy Chief; the Deputy Chief of Police of Dili District, as second Deputy Chief; and *Aitarak's* Commander as coordinator of field operations.[208]

Another group, the *Besi Marah Putih* (BMP), or Iron Rod for the Red and White, was set up on 27 December 1998 in Kaikasa, Maubara Sub-District, Liquica District on the initiative among others, of the Bupati of Liquica and the Sub-District Military Commander of Maubara KORAMIL. The BMP received the collaboration and support of TNI Battalion 143 stationed in Vatuboro, Liquica. The organization of the BMP militia consisted of an overall Commander, a Vice Commander, and a Commander and Deputy Commander in each of the Sub-Districts of Liquica. Liquica military and civilian authorities had control over the group and directed its affairs. These authorities also provided food rations and paid allowances from government funds. The TNI and BMP militia undertook joint operations aimed at intimidating, threatening, abducting and interrogating

[208] Order of Upgrading and the Execution of the activities of security and order in the city of Dili, issued by Dominagos M. D. Soares, (Bupati Kepala Daerah TH. II – Bupati and Head of Area Stage II), Dili, 1999.

pro independence supporters. On 22 November 2001 the Office of the General Prosecutor in East Timor charged 21 persons, among whom were the District Administrator (Bupati), Leoneto Martins; the KODIM 1638 Commander, Lt. Colonel Asep Kuswani; the District Police (POLRES) Commander, Lt. Colonel Adios Salova; the Sub-District Military Commanders of Bezertete and Maubara; the Commander of BMP Militia; the Commander of *Aitarak* militia, and others with crimes against humanity with regard to the 6 April 1999 Liquica Church massacre, and an orgy of murders, enforced disappearances, inhuman acts, and deportations that took place between January and September 1999. Those in command or superior positions were also held liable with superior responsibility under Section 16 of UNTAET Regulation 2000/15.

In Ainaro the *Mahidi* (Mati Hidup Demi Integrasi) or the Life or Death for Integration militia was established on 17 December 1999, and officially inaugurated on 1 January 1999 at a ceremony attended by the District Military and Police Commanders of Ainaro, and leaders of the Ainaro District Legislature. Its Commander, Cancio Lopes de Carvalho, the son of the Liurai (Chief) of Cassa, Ainaro, was a public servant in the Justice Department. With around 1,300 members Mahidi received training from the Indonesian Armed Forces, which also supplied SK, AK 47 and G 3 rifles, ammunition and arms permits to members of the group. KODAM 1623 in Ainaro issued de Carvalho, a 9 mm pistol with the required arms permit on 27 July 1998. It operated in Ainaro District, as well as Zumalai Sub-District, Covalima District. In the village of Cassa, its base, it had two Kompis (Company A and B), each headed by a Commander. Another company was based in Zumalia Sub-District. On 21 February 2003 the Office of the Deputy Prosecutor General for Serious Crimes charged De Carvalho and 21 other *Mahidi* militia members with crimes against humanity before the Special Panel for Serious Crimes.[209] Three of its commanders were held liable for superior responsibility.

In Los Palos, Leutem District, *Tim Alfa* (sometime known as Jati Merah Putih, or the Authentic Red and White) was initially established in 1986 by KOPASSUS as a locally recruited armed paramilitary group (Ratih) to fight against FALANTIL. KOPASSUS commanders directed its activities. Tim Alfa was revived in 1999, and at least between April and September 1999, the team and KOPASSUS operated out of the same building in Laruara, Los Palos. They shared logistic means and conducted joint operations, which included unlawful arrests and abduction of suspected pro-independence for interrogation at the TNI barracks, particularly at Battalion 745 base. Joni Marques, the team's de facto Commander, had also received military training in Indonesia. Its team members were paid by the Forum for Unity, Democracy and Justice (FPDK) (Persatuan untuk Demokrasi dan Keadilan*)*, a pro autonomy organization that was controlled by the Bupati as well as the TNI.

In the East Timor enclave of Oecussi, the main militia group that operated there was *Sakunar* (Scorpion). The former Governor of East Timor, Abilio Soares; Aita-

209 *P. v. Cancio Lopes de Carvaho et all,* Indictment, Dili District Court, Special Panel for serious Crimes, Case no: 06/cg/2003/pd dili, 21 February 2003.

rak Commander, Eurico Guterres; and both the Oecussi TNI and Police Commanders attended the inauguration ceremony of this militia group around April 1999. Its leaders were mostly government employees such as school teachers or heads of villages. Its Supreme Commander, Simao Lopes, was a Government employee in the Ministry of Fisheries, and its Commander, Leorentino "Moko" Soares, the Chief of Cunha village. Assailants in West Timor, Indonesia, killed the latter in September 1999, the death of which precipitated into the killing by militiamen of three UNHCR staff on 6 September 2000. On 27 September 2001 the Office of the General Prosecutor for East Timor held five de jure and de facto Commanders of *Sakunar* militia criminally liable for the crimes of their subordinates, in addition to direct individual criminal responsibility for crimes against humanity committed in that enclave between April and September 1999.[210] Among the crimes alleged to have been committed by the *Sakunar* militia, with the assistance of the TNI, is the calculated extermination and killing of the entire population of the villages of Tumin, Nibin, and Kiobeselo, with the exception of 10 survivors. Of the 11 persons charged, only one accused, Florenco Tacaqui, has been arrested and is to face trial before the Special Panel. The rest are presumed to be in West Timor, Indonesia. As lamented by Judge Maria Natercia, the only East Timorese Appeal Judge for the Special Panel for Serious Crimes: "Is it fair to prosecute the small Timorese, and not the big ones who gave them orders?"[211]

The Indonesian Armed Forces and Militia Groups

The mobilization of militias by military and civilian authorities in East Timor in 1999 was in line with various policies of the military leadership and Indonesia's Coordinating Minister for Politics and Security.[212] These groups were under the direct coordination of the Indonesian Armed Forces.[213] Militia commanders were identified, chosen or approved by the TNI. Some commanders were in active service within the army. Others were Government employees. Juanico Cesario Belo, the Commander of *Tim Saka*, and at the same time Sector "A" Commander of the PPI, was a KOPASSUS 1st Sergeant with KODIM 1628 in Baucau. Tim Saka's Commander for Baucau Sub-District was also 2nd Sergent in that same military command. Manuel da Sousa, the Commander of BMP (*Besi Merah Putih*) militia, was like Eurico Guterres of Aitarak a member of *Gadapaksi* (Gada Pemuda Penegak Intergrasi or Youth Guard to Uphold Integration). The entire *Aitarak* membership, of 1,521 men, were also members and received a monthly allowance from the civil administration. Civilian authorities in East Timor exercised a degree of de facto control, among other things, by the fact that they controlled funding.

---

210 *P. v. Simao Lopes et all.* , Indictment, Dili District Court, Special Panel for Serious Crimes, 27 September 2001.

211 Modest Beginnings for East Timor's Justice System, The New York Times, March 4, 2001.

212 KPP-HAM Report, Executive Summary, para. 29.

213 Id.

The salaries and allowances of the militia were paid out of government funds, including that earmarked for development. Members of the Indonesian Armed Forces often organized joint meetings with the militia to discuss or plan attacks against pro independence supporters. For example a meeting between TNI and members of the *Dadarus Merah Putih* (DMP) militia was held in Maliana town on 29th June 1999, before the militia attack on the UNAMET Headquarters there, which left 12 people dead.

The claim by Colonel Suratman, Commander of KOREM 164, that militia groups in East Timor emerged spontaneously "by popular imitative" in response to President B.J. Habibie's January 27th announcement of a popular consultation process for East Timorese, and the brutality of pro independence forces, [214] is contrary to all information at hand, including that officially presented by KPP-HAM to the Attorney General of Indonesia. That investigation found that the violence was not caused by civil war, but was the result of a systematic campaign of violence.[215] TNI control over militia is also grounded on the fact that the violence in East Timor could be "switched on and of".[216] Control over militia groups is also evidenced by the fact that TNI and civilian authorities were capable of giving orders to stop the violence, orders of which were followed by militia groups. This occurred when important dignitaries visited East Timor during the period of the popular consultation. On 11 September 1999, when the UN Security Council delegation visited Dili to observe first hand developments in East Timor, there was almost a complete absence of any violent incident. Decision to stop violence on these days, must have been taken at a high level involving TNI, POLRI, and civilian authorities. No serious act of violence was committed on the day of the popular consultation or during the vote count. It is not discounted that the abrupt lull in the violence may have been due to the possibility that pro integration leadership thought that they had won the popular consultation.

Indonesian Security Forces and the Inaction Element

Failure to act or prevent acts of violence is a telling component of the element of command or superior responsibility. Generally reports of violence that occurred during Indonesia's occupation were always met with blanket denials from Indonesian authorities.[217] The failure of the TNI and Indonesian Police forces to respond to acts of violence committed by pro-integration militia, to prevent them, or to take any measures to investigate or punish perpetrators took a variety of forms. A common feature of the East Timor atrocity crimes was the clear instances when the TNI forces and POLRI stood aside to allow militias into towns to conduct or-

---

214 Suratman T (2000) Merah Petih, Pengabdian & Tanggung, Jawad Di Timour Timur, Juni 1998-Juli 1999, Lembaga Pengkajian Kebudayaan Nusantara, pp. 45-46.

215 KPP-HAM Report, Executive Summary, para. 21.

216 Report of the UN SC Mission to Jakarta and Dili, UN Doc. S/1999/976, 14 September 1999, para. 15.

217 Martinkus J (2001) p. 3.

ganized and coordinated campaigns of arson and terror. [218] The response of Indonesian authorities to criminal acts by pro-autonomy supporters was typically characterized by a *semblance* of concern, but was action less and at times covered up. For the Liquica massacre the Indonesian military initially claimed that only 5 people were killed. A subsequent investigation commissioned by the Indonesian Armed Forces Headquarters, and which included as members, Major General Zacky Anwar Makarim and Major General Kiki Syahnakri, also supported that earlier conclusion.

An example of the worst kind of inaction is that of the *Dandim* Colonel Tono Suratman, Indonesia's military commander in East Timor when approached for assistance by Mario Carascalao, just as his house was about to be attacked by a combined elements of the *Aitaraka* militia, led by its Commander Eurico Guterres, and members of the *Besi Merah Putih* Militia, on 17 April 1999 in Dili, some 400 meters from the Governor's office. When directly approached in this case of imminent threat of death, Suratman laughed, and told Carrascalao to seek the assistance elsewhere, from CNRT. These words were uttered in front of the Irish Minister of Foreign Affairs who was on an official visit to East Timor. In his report to the Irish Senate (Seanad Eireann) on 22 April 1999 stated that the military commander was clearly fully aware of the activities being carried out throughout the territory by pro integration militias and that he was making no effort to curb their rampage or to protect ordinary citizens from brutal militia behaviour. Moreover as they held their meeting at Suratman's residence lorry loads of militia passed by; and that he took not the slightest action to calm the situation nor did de demonstrate any willingness or sense of responsibility to maintain law and order and protect lives following Carsascalo's urgent request for assistance.

Non-action or follow up to effectively investigate or prosecute crimes committed against pro independence supporters was a pattern of governance during Indonesia's occupation of East Timor. Insufficient action to investigate thoroughly with a view to establish facts, identify perpetrators, and bring them to justice was the established practice. It became almost an unwritten policy of the security forces, if not a norm. A few examples spread over time fortify this reasoning.

A grave incident of the past but one that is a resound of recent events, typical of cover up, and which reflected an unwillingness to unearth details of criminal acts is that of the Balibo Five.[219] Five journalists comprising two Australians (Greg Shackleton and Tony Stewart), two Britons (Brian Peters and Malcom Rennie), and one New Zealander (Gary Cunningham), from Australia's Channels 7 and 9 were killed in Balibo, Bobonaro District, East Timor, on 16 October 1975 when Indonesian forces assisted by a number of East Timorese "partisans", among whom were Joao da Silva Tavares, and Tomas Goncalves, launched the first major military assault (*Operation Flamboyan* - "Flame Tree") against the then Portu-

---

218 Report of the UN SC Mission to Jakarta and Dili, UN Doc. S/1999/976, 14 September 1999, para. 14.

219 For a detailed account see, Ball D, McDonald H (2000) Death in Balibo, Lies in Canberra, Allen and Unwin, Australia; Jollife J (2001) Cover-Up. The Inside Story of the Balibo Five, Scribe Publications, Melbourne.

guese colony of East Timor[220]. The journalists were on mission to cover Indonesia's imminent invasion of East Timor. The Indonesian official version of the deaths was that they were killed in crossfire between FRETELIN and anti-FRETLIN Forces. On 12 November 1975 a box of charred bones purporting to be the remains of the five journalists, a number of personal items such as passports and photographic equipment, were delivered to Australia's Ambassador to Indonesia in Jakarta by Lt. General Yoga Sugama of the Indonesian Armed Forces. On 5 December 1975 the remains were buried in the Christian Cemetery of Kebayoran Lama in Jakarta. None of the family members of the deceased were allowed to attend the funeral.

Twenty-five years later evidence has emerged that there was little resistance in Balibo as the majority of FRETLIN forces had departed earlier that day. Surviving eyewitnesses, including some former East Timorese "partisans", have provided new information that on that fateful night, the journalists were executed, their bodies set on fire and the crime's scene altered.[221] The Indonesian Special Forces team thought to have been responsible, known as team *Susi* was allegedly headed by Captain Yunus Yosfiah who later became an Army General, and thereafter Indonesia's Minister of Information. No one in Indonesia has ever been held accountable for the crimes.[222]

The investigation into the death of the journalists was reopened in 2000 when East Timor was under UNTAET.[223] It enabled further information to be gathered which disproved the earlier Indonesian version of events. A request from UNTAET in 2001 to interview members of the Indonesian armed forces who were alleged to have been present at Balibo was turned down by the Indonesian Attorney General's Office on the ground that it did not have jurisdiction. For Indonesia the case had been closed to the satisfaction of the Australian Government. Those who have seriously inquired into this affair believe that the Australian Government knew of Indonesia's planned invasion, and the imminent death of the journalists by Indonesian Armed Forces through successful monitoring and decoding of communications by Australia's Defence Intelligence.[224] Efforts by UNTAET to prosecute those suspected of involvement require the entanglement of a number of hurdles. The first is overcoming the legal issue of prescription, since under Article 118 of the Penal Code of Portugal, applicable in the territory on the date the crimes were committed, is 15 years. Under Article 78 of the Penal Code of Indonesia it is 18 years. Both time periods have elapsed. The second is a determination whether the crimes could be considered war crimes (wilful killing) under the laws

---

220 McDonald H, Ball D Murder in Balibo: What our Spies Knew, Sydney Morning Herald, 14 February 2002.

221 See, Ball D, McDonald H (2000); Jollife J (2001).

222 Id.

223 UN names Balibo murderers, Sydney Morning Herald, 3 February 2001.

224 Ball D, MacDonald H (2000) pp. 117-118, Cf. On Australia's Government knowledge, "The inquiry concluded that intelligence material meeting this description did not exist, although there was intelligence material relating to journalists in Timor", Balibo Killings 1975 and Intelligence Handling. A Report by the Inspector General of Intelligence and Security, September 2001, para. 63, at www. igis. goc. au/balibo_summary. html.

and customs of war. A positive legal finding would render the crimes prosecutable, and not subject to any statutory limitation or prescription under international law. The third is the willingness of surviving members of the Indonesian special forces who were present in Balibo to volunteer further evidence, and the fourth, which seems almost an impossibility is the availability of the suspects to the jurisdiction of East Timor Courts in the face of Indonesia's opposition to the extradition or transfer of any of its nationals to the United Nations in East Timor or the East Timor Government.

Another serious event that Indonesian authorities did not exhaustively carry out to the satisfaction of the international community is the Santa Cruz Cemetery Massacre of 12 November 1991 in which an estimated 200 students were killed and their bodies buried by the TNI at a yet to be discovered location.[225] In relation to that massacre, the UN Commission on Human Rights in 1994 expressed preoccupation on "incomplete information" on the number of people killed and the persons still unaccounted for as a result of that tragic event.[226] On that day a peaceful pro-independence procession of an estimated 3000-4000 unarmed civilians, mostly students and other young adults, had marched to the grave of Sebastiao Gomes,who was killed on 28 October 1991 during an attack by Indonesian security forces on the Motael church, where he and a number of other East Timorese political activists had taken refuge.[227] The demonstrators had also carried anti-integration banners. As the procession was about to enter the cemetery, Indonesian security forces opened fire on the crowd. The shooting lasted for 10 to 15 minutes, and was followed by further shooting, beating, and stabbing inside the perimeter of the cemetery. A number of demonstrators managed to escape, but many were killed on the spot, and a number of wounded demonstrators transported in trucks to the military hospital were ill treated or deliberately killed during the journey or at the hospital's morgue.[228]

While Indonesian authorities reported that only 19 persons had been killed; a National Commission of Inquiry, established by Presidential Decree No.53, put the death toll at about 50 and estimated that over 91 persons had been wounded.[229] The Special Rapporteur on Extra Judicial, appointed by the UN Commission of Human Rights, to collect information on the massacre, estimated that between 150 and 270 people had been killed although some estimated it to be around 400.[230] This was based on documentary evidence and reliable testimonies gathered by the Special rapporteur in East Timor. That apart, he also pointed to discrepancies in

[225] Ten years later, Santa Cruz still leaves a scar, 12 November 2001, Sydney Morning Herald; Tears Still flow over Dili killings, 12 November 2001, The Age.

[226] Report by the Special rapporteur on Extra judicial, summary or arbitrary executions, Mr. Bacre Waly Ndiaye, on his mission to Indonesia and East Timor from 3 to 13 July 1994, UN Doc. E/CN. 4/1995/61/Add. 1, 1 November 1994, para. 5.

[227] Para. 19, Id.

[228] Id.

[229] Para. 21. Id. ; For Text of the Commission's Advance report. See Advance Report of the national Commission of Inquiry into 12 November 1991 Incident in Dili-East Timor, Annex to Report of the Special rapporteur.

[230] Para. 21, Id.

the number of cases of disappearances subsequent to the Santa Cruz killings. While Indonesian authorities acknowledged only 66 cases of disappearances, the Working Group on Enforced or Involuntary Disappearances transmitted to the Government of Indonesia a total of 224 cases of disappearances alleged to have occurred in connection with the Santa Cruz killings.[231]

A court martial set by the Indonesian military to try those involved convicted ten low-ranking members of the security forces for disobeying orders under article 103, paragraph 1, of the Military Criminal Code and received disciplinary sentences.[232] Only one of them was found guilty of assault, in violation of article 351 of the Criminal Code, for cutting off the ear of a demonstrator.[233] No member of the Indonesian security forces was charged with murder or manslaughter for the killings which Indonesian authorities described as an "incident".[234] The reason advanced by the Commander of the Indonesian Armed Forces for not indicting anyone for the above crimes was that "there was no evidence on who killed who". This is the same line of reasoning applied 10 years later with regard to the prosecution of militiamen responsible for the tragic death of 3 UNHCR workers in Atambua, West Timor on 6 September 2000. Furthermore with regard to the Santa Cruz massacre, the court martial meted out sentences of from 8 to 18 months to those convicted. The Special Rapporteur considered these to be inappropriately light sentences given the violation of the right to life that had been committed at the Santa Cruz cemetery.[235]

On their part East Timorese civilians who were involved in peaceful protest during and after 12 November 1991 were sentenced to terms of up to life imprisonment.[236] With regard to prevention the Special Rapporteur concluded that the members of the security forces responsible for the abuses had not been held accountable and continued to enjoy virtual impunity.[237] The Special Rapporteur also found that the investigation which was carried out by the Indonesian police was not thorough; that the forensic examination was flawed (no adequate autopsy was performed on the corpses nor were any ballistic examinations conducted), and that the criminal investigation was inadequate (it failed to clarify the identity of the perpetrators or even the number of victims).[238]

Inaction in the face of serious human rights violations is not only far dated. It is also recent. We had mentioned earlier that the atrocity crimes committed in East Timor in 1999 included widespread sexual violence. And this did not begin after the announcement of the results of the popular consultation. Long before that time women whose husbands were suspected of being pro-independence or who were believed to support that cause, were specifically targeted for intimidation, threat, forced labour, and inhuman acts. The thematic Special Rapporteurs also gathered

[231] Para. 22, Id.
[232] Para 43, Id.
[233] Id.
[234] Paras. 24, 34, 70 & 81 Id.
[235] Para. 70(e), Id.
[236] Para. 70 (g), Id.
[237] Para. 74, Id.
[238] Paras. 49-64, Id.

information that directly pinpointed to TNI officers as perpetrators of sexual violence.[239] Owing to the widespread nature of violations, it is clear that the highest level of the Indonesian military command in East Timor knew, or had reason to know, that there was widespread violence against women in East Timor.[240] Yet no action has been taken by Indonesian authorities to prevent or to prosecute the perpetrators in compliance with international law.[241] None of the 18 persons charged by the Attorney General of Indonesia before the Ad hoc Human Rights Court has been held accountable for sexual violence.

Another series of incidents reflecting not only inaction but also acquiescence by Military Commanders, of crimes committed in 1999, is that surrounding Battalion 745 of the Indonesian Armed Forces.[242] On 20 September 1999 the Battalion, which was based at Fuiloro village, Leutem District, moved by convoy to Dili, on its way out of East Timor to West Timor, Indonesia. En route that day, on 21 September, members of that Battalion forming part of the convoy shot and killed two civilians at Buile village and two other persons at Buruma village, Baucau. They again shot and killed two persons at Caibada village, Baucau; and two other persons in Becora, Dili. This included an East Timorese who was walking along the road and a Dutch freelance journalist Sander Thoenes.[243] The latter was shot and his body mutilated. At that time the battalion was the sole armed user of that road. When the convoy, led by a Battalion Commander arrived at KOREM 164, the sub Regional Military Command in Dili, the Commander, Colonel Mohammad Nuis allegedly addressed members of the convoy, and instructed them not to tell anyone about what had just happened on their way to Dili, not even their wives.[244] Inspite of the urge by both the Netherlands and UNTAET for accountability for the murder of the journalist, and criminal investigation leads on the suspected involvement of a serving Indonesian officer who was part of that convoy, investigations by Indonesia were closed in June 2002, without holding anyone responsible[245].

That no action was taken is further demonstrated by the attitude, reaction, and overall conduct of Indonesia's security forces in 1999. In a Report prepared by UNAMET, its staff submitted that on 10 September 1999 *Aitarak* militia were al-

---

239 Report on the Joint mission to East Timor undertaken by the Special Rapporteur on extra judicial, summary or arbitrary executions, the Special Rapporteur on the question of torture and the Special Rapporteur on violence against women, UN Doc. A/54/660, 10 December 1999, para. 62.

240 Para. 62, Id.

241 Id.

242 See, Batallion 745, A brutal Exit, http://www.csmonitor.com.

243 On the alleged killings committed by Battalion 745, including the murder of Sander Thoenes see, *P. v. Wiranto et all.* , Indictment, paras. 143-157; Martinkus J (2001) pp. 360-364.

244 *P. v. Wiranto et all.* , Indictment, para. 158.

245 Indonesian team probing journalist's murder ends East Timor visit, The Age, 9 March 2002; Fury as Indonesia 'army killer' returns to East Timor, Electronic Telegraph, 12 May 2002; Indonesia prosecutors drop case against suspect in Thoenes murder, AP, 13 June 2002; Indonesia's failure to prosecute killers of Dutch journalist a victory for impunity, Press Release, TOPAL, http://www. topal. gn. apc. org/pr 020620. htm.

lowed to freely pass TNI and POLRI checkpoints into the environs of the UNAMET compound.[246] Militia members perpetrated acts of violence in full view of heavily armed police and military personnel who either stood by and watched or actively assisted the militia. [247] As stated by the three thematic Rapporteurs of the UNHCHR,

"Even applying the strict standards of the International Court of Justice to establish State responsibility for the acts of armed groups in a context of external intervention (dependency of the group on the state) and the exercise of effective control of the group by the State-a standard which cannot reasonably be applied to a State's own acts and omissions of governance of its own people-there is already evidence that TNI was sufficiently involved in the operational activities of the militia, which for the most part were the direct perpetrators of the crimes, to incur the responsibility of the Government of Indonesia. What still remains to be determined is how much of TNI and to what level in the hierarchy was there either active involvement or, at least, culpable tolerance of the activities".[248]

Conclusion

Increasing superior responsibility is being recognized as a viable charging tool for those in positions of effective command and control or effective authority and control over subordinates: both military and civilian superiors. Persons wielding such authority often include those with the greatest responsibility involved in the architecture of atrocity crimes, as well as intermediate level perpetrators. The Indictments against Kambanda, Karadzic, Milosevic, Mladic, Taylor and Wiranto, all high civilian or military officials, contain this form of criminal liability. Superior responsibility remains a principle with its own standing in international law. The three legal criteria accepted by the UN ad hoc criminal tribunals, and which constitute customary law and the essentials of that norm are: a superior-subordinate relationship, the superior's knowledge or reason to know that the crime was about to be or had been committed, and his or her failure to take the necessary and reasonable measures to prevent the criminal act or to punish the perpetrator.

The law as reflected in decisions of the international criminal tribunals squarely lays down that effective command and control or authority and control, whether de jure or de facto, to prevent or punish an offence committed by a subordinate is the mandatory litmus test for demonstrating the existence of a superior-subordinate relationship. Popularity, wide acclaim, including substantial influence over others is not sufficient in the eyes of the law. For the knowledge element the Statutes of the UN Ad Hoc Tribunals require a showing that the superior either knew of the crime that was being committed by his or her subordinate, or had rea-

[246] Report of the UN High Commissioner for Human rights, UN Doc. EW/CN. 4/S-4/CRP. 1, 17 September 1999, para. 15.

[247] Para. 16, Id.

[248] Report of Special rapporturs, para 72.

son to know that the crime was about to be or had been committed.[249] The latter arises only if information was available to the superior that would put him on notice of offences committed or about to be committed by subordinates. There is no strict liability involved, and neither is that knowledge to be presumed. The inaction element of superior responsibility requires a superior to have failed to take the necessary and reasonable measures to prevent the crime or punish the subordinate perpetrator thereof. This entails possession by the superior of a material ability to prevent or punish. Such ability neither requires formal or legal competence to do so, nor de jure authority.

In this chapter, we have used the Rwandan atrocity crimes of 1994 to illustrate the trappings of both de jure and de facto superior responsibility. There for the latter, the socio-cultural system, the civilian administrative set up, and the political context largely contributed to the ascendancy of de facto superior responsibility as a form of criminal participation. A system of parallel rule, one official and the other subterranean was already entrenched in Rwandan politics by the time atrocity crimes were ignited in 1994. With regard to civilian superiors in *Musema* we saw how a CEO's effective authority and control, demonstrated by control over human and material resources of a company, including, the power to hire and fire, or otherwise discipline employee subordinates implicated in crimes, can entail a finding of de jure superior responsibility. In *Sergushago* de facto superior responsibility arose out of the sheer strength of personal relations between a Head of State, the President of Rwanda and Sureshago's father, a local businessman. Both originated from the same locality.

In the case of East Timor's widespread and systematic violence we examined the organizational framework and the chain of command of the Indonesian security forces in East Timor in 1999. It is important to note that a formal chain of command does not by itself automatically prove effective command and control giving rise to a duty to prevent or repress the crimes of subordinate troops. A showing of orders, instructions, the issuance of directives that are acted upon, subordination, and reporting, compounds proof of superior responsibility. We have attempted to show the camouflage of superior responsibility by way of change of guards, as well as the establishment of militia groups as a criminal front office, intended as a cover-up of the responsibility of superiors. Also as concerns East Timor we high-lighted a number of daring examples of inaction or connivance that almost became an unwritten policy of impunity for the accountability of superiors over the crimes of subordinates.

---

[249] Art 6 (3) ICTR & Art. 7 (3) ICTY Statutes. Cf. Article 30 of the ICC Statute prescribes the knowledge element for *military commanders*: either knew or, owing to the circumstances at the time, should have known that the forces were committing or about to commit such crimes; and for *other superiors* (civilian): either knew, or consciously disregarded information which clearly indicated, that the subordinates were committing or about to commit such crimes.

Chapter 8
Guilty Pleas

This chapter analyses the guilty plea as a tool of accountability for atrocity crimes. It offers a comprehensive review of the plea of guilty as practiced by the International Criminal Tribunal for Rwanda. Reference will also be made to the practice of the ICTY, given the application of almost identical Rules of Procedure and Evidence and a common Appeals Chamber. First the chapter reviews the guilty plea as a judicial process. Second, it spells out the legal requirement of a valid guilty plea before the UN ad hoc Tribunals. Third, the chapter discusses plea-bargaining, highlighting the pitfalls and merits of the traditional plea-bargaining process, and offers an in-depth examination of Guilty Plea Agreements as practiced by the two UN ad hoc Tribunals. The role of the Courts and that of Defense Counsel is also looked at. Fourth, the chapter embarks on a critical analysis of guilty plea cases before the ICTR. An appreciation of the process in which a plea of guilty operates in an accountability strategy for those responsible for atrocity crimes is best exemplified by the examination of cases before the ICTR, in which the accused pleaded guilty. To date, four accused have done so. Jean Kambanda, the former Prime Minister of Rwanda, who by pleading guilty became the first former Head of Government to have pleaded guilty for genocide before an international criminal tribunal;[1] Omar Serushago, one of the de facto leaders of the interahamwe militia in Gisenyi Prefecture;[2] Georges Ruggiu, a Belgium-Italian radio broadcaster them with RTLM[3] and Vincent Rutaganira, Counsellor of Mubuga, Gishyita commune, Kibuye[4] The controversial sentencing of Kambanda to life imprisonment, despite his guilty plea, is debated. A question to be answered is whether a tribunal errs in proceeding via a guilty plea rather than a full trial in a case involving a "big fish", such as an accused Prime Minister or Head of Government, implicated in the crime of genocide; the "crime of crimes". The final part of the chapter contains conclusions.

---

1 *P. v. J. Kambanda*, Judgement and Sentence, T.C, Case no. ICTR.97-23-S, 4 September 1998.

2 *P. v. O. Serushagp*, Sentence, T.C, Case no: ICTR-98-39-S, 5 February 1999.

3 *P. v. G. Ruggiu*, Judgement and Sentence, T.C, Case no: ICTR-97-32-I, 1 June 2000.

4 ICTR Case no: ICTR-95-IC-I; Rutaganira Changes His Plea to Guilty, ICTR Press Release, ICTR/INFO-9-2-413 EN, 8/12/04. Rutaganira first pleaded not guilty on 26/03/2002, and changed it to a guilty plea n 8/12/2004.

I. Guilty Pleas and the Justice Process

As a part of the criminal process the guilty plea existed in one form or another since the 13th and 14th centuries.[5] At that time the judicial use of torture was officially tolerated in obtaining a guilty plea, since it was thought capable of enhancing testimonial validity. [6] This was later abolished with the advent of other methods of legal proof, and the abolition of the Star Chamber in 1641.[7] The guilty plea made significant headway as part of the English criminal practice in the 19th century,[8] from where it was exported to other commonwealth jurisdictions.

The concept of the guilty plea *per se* is the peculiar product of the adversarial system of the common law that recognizes the advantage it provides to the public in minimizing costs, in the saving of court time, and in avoiding the inconvenience to many, particularly to witnesses.[9] It has been said that confessions are of powerful probative value; none better as proof of crime.[10] The practice of guilty pleas does not have a direct counterpart in the civil-law tradition, where an admission of guilt is simply part of the evidence to be considered and evaluated by the Court.[11] In that system the guilty plea is an element of proof, whose probative value depends upon the condition in which it was obtained, and entirely left to the sovereign appreciation of the Judge.[12] The confession is the "queen of proof"[13] (confessio est regina probationum) and does not interfere with the official nature of the determination of guilt, which is left to the free determination of the judge.[14] It may also be considered as a mitigating factor, again, subject to the judge's discretionary faculty.[15]

An analysis of guilty pleas suggests that the approaches of domestic courts are not always the same as that of UN ad hoc criminal tribunals. The Rules of Procedure and Evidence of the latter are much broader than either the common law or civil law, and almost reflect an international amalgamated system without adopting any one system as such. These Rules do not employ the popular expression "confession" as does the criminal procedures and the laws of evidence in many

---

5 Fitzgerald OE (1990), The Guilty Plea and Summary Justice, Carswell, Toronto, p. 21.
6 Fine R A (1986) Escape of the Guilty, Dodd, Mead and Company, N.Y., pp. 115-116.
7 P. 116, Id.
8 Fitzgerald O E (1990) p. 21.
9 Joint and Separate Opinion of Judge McDonald and Judge Vohra, *P. v. D. Erdemovic*, A.C, Case no: IT-96-22-A, 7 October 1997, para. 2.
10 May R (1991) Admissibility of Confessions: Recent Developments, Journal of Criminal Law, vol. LV, p. 366.
11 Separate and Dissenting Opinion of Judge Cassese, *P. v. D. Erdemovic*, A.C, para. 8.
12 See, Art 428 'L'aveu, comme tout element de preuve, est laisse a la libre appreciation des judges, French Code of Criminal procedure, Gradel J, Casorla F (2001) Code de Procedure Penale, Quarante Deuxieme edition, Dalloz, Paris, p. 5000.
13 Dalloz (1981) Repertoire de Droit Penal et de Procedure Penal, Vol.1, 2 ed., Aveu- par B. Boulac, cited in Fitzgerald O E (1990) fn 88, p 22.
14 P. 24, Id.
15 Merle R, Vitu A (1984) Traite de Droit Criminel, les Circumstances attenuantes, Edition Cujas, 6eme ed., pp. 946-954.

common law jurisdictions.[16] Nonetheless, they provide for guilty pleas as part of the judicial process. Many national criminal justice systems, as exemplified by the United States, operate on the basis that only a small percentage of all cases go to trial.[17] The experience of the ICTY suggests a wholehearted embrace of guilty plea process in that 17 accused have pleaded guilty in that Tribunal's first ten years existence.[18] That of the ICTR on the other hand demonstrates that the vast total of cases have and will proceed by way of trial rather than by plea of guilty. Of about 83 accused persons indicted before the ICTR as of 31 December 2004 only four accused have pleaded guilty. Although the number of accused who have pleaded guilty before the ICTY is more than that at the ICTR, the predominant manner of administering justice is still through trials rather than by way of guilty plea. The reality of international criminal jurisdiction seems to be inevitable complex trials.

In some national jurisdictions, such as the U.S.A, the guilty plea and its associated plea bargaining process are at times associated with laziness of administrators of the justice system(i.e. Prosecutors and Defense Counsel) and their desire to take "short cuts" in order to expedite the delivery of justice. The remark made over a century ago, by an Indian policeman during the British colonization of India, that 'it is much more agreeable to sit in the shadow rubbing red pepper into the defendant's eye's in order to make him confess the crimes than to go about in the hot sun looking for evidence against him that you cannot find and that may not even exist'[19] has no relevancy at all in the practice of international criminal tribunals.

Guilty Plea: Meaning

A guilty plea is an admission by an accused of the material averments charged in the indictment, and relieves the prosecution of the requirement of formal proof.[20] As laid down by Lord Atkin, in the Privy Council case, *Paraka Narayana Swami v. Emperor:*

"*A* confession must either admit in terms the offence or at any rate substantially all the facts which constitute the offence....... It has to be a direct acknowledgement of the guilt of the offence in question and such as would be sufficient by itself for conviction. If it falls short of such a plenary acknowledgement of guilt it would not be a confession even though the

16 E.g. Section 24 - 30, Indian Evidence Act.

17 Bishop J B (1989) Prosecution without Trial, Butterworths, Sydney, p. 184.

18 Combs N A (2004) Guilty Pleas in International Criminal Law: Constructing A Restorative Justice Approach For Bridging Justice and Truth, Dissertation, Leiden University.

19 Du Cann C G L (1960) Miscarriages of Justice, Frederick Muller Ltd., London, (statement recorded by Sir James Stephen) pp. 149-150; Also cited in Fine R A (1986) p. 115.

20 Fitzgerald O E (1990) p. 103-104.

statement is of some incriminating fact which taken along with other evidence tends to prove his guilt. Such a statement is admission but not confession."[21]

A guilty plea must be a complete admission of all the necessary legal ingredients of the charge, of all the essential elements of the offence, and should be of sufficient foundation on its own to support a conviction without there being any need for corroboration of the facts so admitted.[22] It is now well settled that a statement by an accused person admitting an incriminating fact, even a conclusively incriminating fact, does not constitute a confession by itself, and in order to constitute confession, the statement must in clear terms admit the commission of the offence by the accused or at least substantially all the facts constituting the offence.[23]

By pleading guilty to the charge against him, the accused makes a formal admission in open court of all the facts that otherwise would need to be proved against him, thereby providing the complete evidential basis for his own conviction.[24] This constitutes a waiver of a number of fundamental rights guaranteed under internationally recognized human rights conventions and incorporated in the Statutes of the UN ad hoc criminal tribunals and the ICC.[25] These enshrined rights which are waived on a plea of guilty include the right to plead not guilty and to require the prosecution to prove the charges in the indictment beyond a reasonable doubt at a fair and impartial public trial, the right to prepare and put forward a defence, the right for an accused at his trial to examine, or have examined, the witnesses against him and to obtain the attendance and examination of witnesses on his behalf at a trial under the same conditions as witnesses against him, and the right not to be compelled to testify against himself or to confess guilt. The administering of a guilty plea by a Trial Chamber does not amount to a trial, the waiver of the right to trial being a condition precedent to a guilty plea proceeding. If the accused, by pleading guilty, decides to waive his right to a trial, this waiver may only be admitted under very stringent conditions.[26]

The law and practice of the UN ad hoc criminal tribunals recognize the value of guilty pleas to its judicial process, in that they assist to avoid lengthy and costly

---

21 *Pakaya Narayana Swami v. The King Emperor*, 66 Ind.Appl 66: AIR 1939 PC 47; 180 IC 7; 40 Cri. J J 364. Referred to and approved in *Veera Ibrahim v. State of Maharashtra*, AIR 1976 SC 1167; See Dutta K K (1979) Treatise on Criminal Law, Eastern Book Co. N. Delhi, Chapter XII, pp. 243-249.

22 Fitzgerald O E (1990) p. 105.

23 Dutta K K (1979) p. 249; Cf. "Confession, is a statement made by an accused which must either admit in terms of the offence, or at any rate substantially all the facts which constitute the offence", Sarkar S (2003) 424.

24 Fitzgerald O E (1990) p. 103-104.

25 Article 20 (Rights of the Accused), ICTR Statute; Article 21, ICTY Statute; Article 67 ICC Statute.

26 Separate and Dissenting Opinion of Judge Cassese, *P. v. D. Erdemovic*, Case no: IT-96-22-A, 7 October 1997, para. 97.

trials, the eyesore of its judicial process.[27] As stated by the ICTY Trial Chamber in *Sikirica, Dosen and Kolundzija:*

"A guilty plea facilitates the work of the International Criminal Tribunal in two ways. First, by entering a plea of guilty before the commencement of his trial, an accused will save the International Tribunal the time and effort of a lengthy investigation and trial. Secondly, notwithstanding the timing of the guilty plea, a benefit accrues to the Trial Chamber, because a guilty plea contributes directly to one of the fundamental objectives of the international tribunal: namely, its truth finding function.[28]

This common law institution of the guilty plea finds a ready place in an international criminal Tribunal adjudicating cases which, by their very nature, are very complex and necessarily require lengthy hearings if they go to trial under stringent financial considerations arising from allocations made by the United Nations, itself dependent upon the contributions of states.[29] International criminal proceedings are expensive, extremely arduous, and time consuming, and by pleading guilty an accused undoubtedly contributes to public advantage.[30] By pleading guilty the accused may find his pleading guilty beneficial to his own condition.[31] It may help him salve his conscience and atone for his wrongdoing; it helps him avoid the indignity and the possible demoralization of undergoing a trial, as well as the psychological ordeal of trial (both for witnesses and himself, should he decide to testify as a witness); it helps him eschew the public expose that may ensue from trial, and the adverse consequences for his social position, and finally the accused may expect that the court will recognize his cooperative attitude by reducing the sentence it would have imposed had there not been a plea of guilty.[32]

Guilty Plea: Legal Requirements

With regard to the legal requirements of guilty pleas, Rule 62 (B) of the Tribunal's Rules of Procedure and Evidence provides:

---

27 "The accused's guilty plea has spared the Tribunal a lengthy investigation and trial, thus economizing time, effort and resources", *P. v. Georges Ruggiu*, Judgement and Sentence, T.C, para. 53.

28 *P. v. D. Sikirica, D. Dosen & D. Kolundzija*, Sentence and Judgement, T.C, Case no: IT-95-8-S, 13 November 2001, para 149; A guilt plea is always important in establishing the truth in relation to a crime, *P. v. S. Todorovic*, Judgement and Sentence, T.C., Case no: IT-95-9/1-S, 31 July 2001, para. 81.

29 Joint Separate Opinion of Judge McDonald and Judge Vohra, *P. v. D.Erdemovic*, A.C, para. 2.

30 Para. 8, Id.

31 Separate and Dissenting Opinion of Judge Cassese, *P. v. D. Erdemovic*, AC, para. 8.

32 Para. 8, Id.

Initial Appearance of Accused and Plea

If an accused pleads guilty in accordance with Rule 62 (A)(v), or requests to change his plea to guilty, the Trial Chamber shall satisfy itself that the guilty plea:

i. is made freely and voluntarily;
ii. is an informed plea;
iii. is unequivocal; and
iv. is based on sufficient facts for the crime and accused's participation in it, either on the basis of independent indicia or of lack of any material disagreement between the parties about the facts of the case.
Thereafter the Trial Chamber may enter a finding of guilt and instruct the Registrar to set a date for the sentencing hearing.

In their Joint Opinion in *P. v. D. Erdemovic*, Judge McDonald and Judge Vohra, laid down the minimum preconditions to be satisfied before a guilty plea can be validly entered, namely that:[33]

"(a) *The guilty plea must be voluntary.* It must be made by an accused who is mentally fit to understand the consequences of pleading guilty and who is not affected by any threats, inducements or promises.
(b) *The guilty plea must be informed*, that is, the accused must understand the nature of the charges against him, and the consequences of pleading guilty against them. The accused must know to what he is pleading.
(c) *The guilty plea must not be equivocal.* It must not be accompanied by words amounting to a defence contradicting an admission of criminal responsibility".

The Statute of the ICC also recognizes in Article 65, the admission of guilt. At the commencement of the trial where the accused makes an admission of guilt, the Trial Chamber is required to determine whether, (a) the accused understands the nature and consequences of the admission of guilt, (b) the admission of guilt is voluntarily made by the accused after sufficient consultation with the defence counsel, and (c) the admission of guilt is supported by the facts of the case that are contained in the charges brought by the Prosecutor and admitted by the accused; any materials presented by the Prosecutor which supplement the charges and which the accused accepts; and any other evidence, such as the testimony of witnesses presented by the Prosecutor or the accused.[34]

A Voluntary Plea

Voluntariness involves two elements; firstly an accused person must have been mentally competent to understand the consequences of his actions when pleading, and secondly the plea must not have been the result of any threat or inducement, other than the expectation of receiving credit for a guilty plea by way of some re-

---

33 Joint and Separate Opinion of Judge Mc Donald and Judge Vohra, *P. v. D. Erdemovic*, A.C, para. 8.

34 Article 64 (8) (a); Article 65 (1), ICC Statute.

duction of sentence.[35] The reason for the exclusion of a confession, judicial or extra judicial, from evidence, if it is not voluntary, is that by the exercise of unfair means an accused may have been forced or induced to say something which is untrue.[36] Thus the plea must be made by a defendant who is compos sui, that is to say whose mental health is not in doubt.[37] The plea must not result from a deranged state of mind whereby the defendant accuses himself of imaginary crimes in order to satisfy a psychological propensity for delusive self-punishment.[38]

A voluntary confession of guilt, if it be full, consistent, and probable, is justly regarded as evidence of the highest and most satisfactory nature, because it is presumed that self-live, the main spring of human conduct, will usually prevent a rational being from making admissions prejudicial to his interest and safety unless when caused by promptings of truth and conscience.[39] Voluntarism is at best an economic tautology, in that if individuals are presumed, in a positive sense, to make decisions on a loss minimization (or utility maximization) basis, then the decision to pursue the least costly course of action from among a given set of alternatives must, in any meaningful sense of the word, be voluntary.[40]

The exclusion of guilty pleas coercively obtained has valid rationale, ethical and legal. Coercion vitiates the waiver of procedural rights and the reliability of the guilty plea as a substitute for proof beyond a reasonable doubt.[41] The law is not afraid of having the truth elucidated, but rather it is jealous of not having the truth.[42] A confession forced upon the mind by the flattery of hope, or by the torture of fear comes in so questionable a shape, when it is to be considered as evidence of guilt that no credit ought to be given to it.[43] It is a violation of due process to contrive a conviction resting solely, or in part, upon confessions obtained by violence or psychological coercion.[44]

A word with regard to the undertaking by the Office of the Prosecutor of the safety and protection to the family of cooperating accused, including accused who plead guilty. Such offer of protection to accused substantially cooperating with the Prosecution cannot be considered an inducement or undue promise, invalidating a validly entered guilty plea. Plea agreements entered into between accused persons, their Defense Counsel, and the Prosecutor often acknowledge that protection has been and will continue to be offered by the Prosecution to the immediate family of the accused given the personal risks involved in collaborating with authorities.

---

35 Joint and Separate Opinion of Judge Mc Donald and Judge Vohra, *P. v.D. Erdemovic*, A.C, para. 10.

36 Mitler V (1978) Chaudhuri's The Law of Confessions and Evidence of Accomplices, Law book Company, Allahabad-1, p. 138.

37 Separate and Dissenting Opinion of Judge Cassese, *P. v. D. Erdemovic*, A.C, para. 10.

38 Id.

39 Mitler V (1978) p. 211.

40 Adelstein R P (1984) The Negotiated Guilty Plea. An Economic and Empirical Analysis, Garland Pub. Inc., New York and London, p. 54.

41 Fitzgerald O E (1990) p. 150.

42 *Williams, JR. v. Mansfield*, (1881) 14 Cox.C.C.639.

43 *Rex v. Warwickshall* (1788) 1 Leach C.C. 263, 2 East P. C.658.

44 Maguire J H (1959) Evidence of Guilt, Little, Brown and Company, Boston, p. 122.

Protection against reprisals and other risks, as well as witness protection programs are commonly offered in most jurisdictions to those who plead guilty, and who intend to testify against co-perpetrators for the prosecution. For testifying accused, the risk of harm and injury to their kin is real, and it is permissible, if not an obligation, for the Prosecutor or the Tribunal to offer such protection. It is in the interest of the judicial process and accountability.

An Informed Plea

An informed plea requires the accused to understand the nature of the charges against him and the consequences of pleading guilty to them.[45] The accused must know to what he is pleading to.[46] Furthermore if charged with alternative offences, he must understand the nature and distinction between alternative charges and the consequences of pleading guilty to one rather than the other.[47]

An Unequivocal Plea

The precondition that the guilty plea must not be equivocal means that it must not be accompanied by words amounting to a defence contradicting an admission of criminal responsibility.[48] An accused is not to be taken to admit an offence unless he pleads guilty to it in unmistakable terms with appreciation of the essential elements of the offence.[49] The requirement that a plea must be unequivocal is essential to uphold the presumption of innocence and to provide to an accused against forfeiture of the right to a trial where the accused appears to have a defense, which he may not realize.[50] The accused cannot be allowed on the one hand to admit to his guilt, and by the same token nullify this plea by claiming that he acted in self-defence or under a mistake of fact, or some other reason, which would exculpate him.[51]

The accused should plea to a charge in unmistakable and unambiguous terms without qualification or condition.[52] A qualified or conditional plea should not be accepted unless after due inquiry the Court is satisfied that the accused intended to enter an unequivocal guilty plea and that the accused's explanations raise no de-

---

45 Joint and Separate Opinion of Judge Mc Donald and Judge Vohra, *P. v. Erdemovic*, A.C, para. 14.

46 Para. 8, Id.

47 Para. 14, Id.

48 Paras. 8, 29 & 30, Id.

49 Halsbury's Law of England (1990) Lord Hailsham of Marylebone (ed.), 4th Edition, Vol.11 (2), Butterworths, London, para. 977.

50 Joint and Separate Opinion of Judge McDonald and Judge Vohra, *P. v. D. Erdemovic*, A.C, para. 29.

51 Separate and Dissenting Opinion of Judge Cassese, *P. v. D. Erdemovic*, A.C, para. 10

52 Fitzgerald O E (1990) pp. 36-36.

fence to the charges.[53] Whether a plea of guilty is equivocal must depend on a consideration, *in limine*, of the question whether the plea was accompanied or qualified by words describing facts which establish a defence in law.[54]

II. Plea Bargaining

The process of arriving at guilty pleas in adversarial legal systems such as those of Australia, Canada, and the United States is normally through a process, termed plea-bargaining, between a Prosecutor on one side and the accused and his Defence Counsel on the other. Herman has submitted that in the United States plea-bargaining, which is a form of negotiation, results in one or more of the following:

"(1) the prosecutor agrees not to charge a defendant; (2) the defendant pleads guilty or *nolo contendere* (I will not contest it) to a reduced charge or lesser included charge; (3) the defendant pleads guilt or *nolo contendere* to a particular charge in exchange for the dismissal of other charges; (4) the defendant pleads guilty or *nolo contendere* as charged or to a lesser charge in return for a sentencing concession by the Prosecutor, or (5) the defendant enters into a conditional plea of guilty or *nolo contendere*, reserving the right to appeal the judgment and to withdraw his plea in the event that the appellate Court affords him relief on the adverse determination of a specified pre trial motion."[55]

Generally it can be said that plea-bargaining involves an offer by the Prosecution of a lesser charge (charge bargaining) or recommendation for a reduced sentence (sentence bargaining) in return or rather exchange for the defendant's guilty plea. Miller, McDonald, and Cramer have identified two types of plea bargaining processes in the United States, namely; explicit plea bargaining, which involves overt negotiations between two or more actors (prosecutor, defence attorney and judge) followed by an agreement on the terms of the bargain; and implicit plea bargaining that involves an understanding by the defendant that a more serious sentence may be imposed for going to trial rather than pleading guilty.[56]

Formal plea-bargaining involves concessions that may range from the dropping of a number of charges, an agreed sentence recommendation, and an agreed summary of facts, the objective of which appears to be to restrict the magistrate to meting out a sentence based on a limited set of agreed facts and designed to exclude some of the more inflammatory aspects of a case.[57] In national systems the

53 P. 35, Id.
54 Joint and Separate Opinion of Judge McDonald and Judge Vohra, *P. v. D. Erdemovic*, A.C, para. 31.
55 Herman G N (1997) Plea Bargaining, Lexis Law Publishing, Charlottesville, Virginia, pp. 1-2.
56 Miller H S, Donald, W F, Cramer J A (1978) Plea bargaining in the United States, National Institute of Law Enforcement and Criminal Justice, US Dept. of Justice/ George Washington University, W.D.C, p. xiii.
57 Seifman R D, Freiberg A (2001) Plea Bargaining in Victoria: The Role of Counsel, Criminal Law Journal, vol. 25, pp. 70-74.

Prosecutor's purpose in plea-bargaining is mainly to save time by dispensing of cases in the fastest and most efficient manner, and to maintain or improve his chances of conviction.[58] Whether or not a defendant pleads guilty is dependant on two critical variables; the perceived likelihood of conviction, and the differential between the penalty likely to be imposed on a plea of guilty and that which would follow one of not guilty.[59]

Plea-bargaining is an institutionalized procedure in United States where 90 % of all criminal trials are resolved through that process.[60] It is a procedure more fundamental than trials.[61] It has been submitted that plea-bargaining occurs when the Prosecutor induces an accused criminal to confess guilt, and to waive his right to trial in exchange for a more lenient criminal sanction that would be imposed if the accused were adjudicated guilty following the trial.[62] The prosecution offers leniency either directly, in the form of a charge reduction, or indirectly, through the connivance of the judge in the form of a recommendation for reduced sentence that the judge will follow.[63] By plea bargaining the combat of the adversarial struggle to test the accusation is gone and a mixture of bartering and bureaucratic cooperation replaces it.[64] Opponents of plea-bargaining deplored such a process, in that "bargaining" connotes a haggle in a market place descending into the courtroom.[65] They equate it to horse-trading.[66] Plea-bargaining it is claimed turns the Court into a street bazaar where justice is hawked, bartered, bought, and sold.[67] For some it is a complete disaster,[68] a mixed blessing, if blessing at all,[69] harmful,[70] and a short and incomplete answer. For an accused to plead guilty, it has been argued, is to commit legal suicide.[71]

---

58 Nasheri H (1998) Betrayal of Due Process. A Comparative Assessment of Plea Bargaining in the United States and Canada, University Press of America Inc., Lanham, Maryland, pp. 28-29.

59 Sanders A, Young R (2000) Criminal Justice, Butterworths, London, p. 397.

60 Herman G N (1997) p. 1; See *Brady v. United States,* 397 U.S. 742, 752 n.10, 90 S.Ct.1463, 1471, n.10, 25 L.Ed.2d 747 (1970).

61 Wright M (1999) Criminal Procedures. Prosecution and Adjudication, Aspen Law and Business, N.Y., p. 466.

62 Langbein J H Torture and Plea Bargaining. In Glazer N (1984) The Public Interest in Crime and Punishment, Abt Books, Cambridge, Mass., pp. 249-250.

63 Pp. 250-251, Id.

64 Gorecki J (1979) A Theory of Justice. Proving the Truth, Columbia University Press, N.Y., p. 56

65 Nasheri H (1998) p. 68.

66 Stuntz W J, Scot R E (1991-1992) Plea Bargaining as Contract, Yale Law Journal, vol.101, III, p. 1912.

67 Gerber R J (1998) A Judicial View of Plea bargaining, Criminal Law Bulletin, vol.34/1, p. 31.

68 Schulhofer S J (1991-92) Plea Bargaining as Disaster, Yale Law Journal, vol.101, p. 2009.

69 Gerber R J (1998) p. 16.

70 Gorecki J (1979) p. 103.

71 Sanders A, Yang R (2000) p. 395.

The pros and cons of plea-bargaining have been extensively debated, and for our purposes it only suffices to briefly recite that controversy. Those against plea-bargaining, consider that it is a 'bluffing' practice aimed at securing a guilty plea, and one that is repugnant to the fair and proper administration of justice.[72] It has also been deplored for its 'invisibility' as a process, for its reliance on improper inducements or coercion[73], for its inappropriateness in rewarding those who are genuinely guilty, for undermining the right to silence, and for being an encouragement to lazy Prosecutors and Defense Counsel.[74] Plea-bargaining it is advanced, provides extraordinary opportunities for lazy lawyers whose primary goal is to cut corners and to get on to the next case.[75] They argue that confessions of guilt heal all flaws in a prosecution.[76] It leads lawyers to consider themselves as judges and administrators rather than advocates; it subjects them to serious financial and other temptations to disregard their client's interest; it diminishes the confidence in attorney-client relationship, and it tends to make figureheads of judges.[77]

That apart it has been advanced that victims consider it offensive; that it results in an uncertain sentence for an accused; that adds to the likelihood of coercion on a defendant to surrender his right to trial; that interferes with the opposing interests of the prosecution and those of the defendant, and that it abandons the moral lessons of the trial.[78] The Plea Agreement is the source of coercion and embodies in itself involuntariness.[79] Plea bargaining drives a gaping hole through the assumptions of the criminal justice system, that in part the public spectacle of wrong doing, capture and punishment will deter crimes.[80] It impairs and defeats public interest in effective law enforcement and at the same time denies defendants the benefits of a vigorous defence and inflicts underserved punishment on innocents who could win acquittal at trial.[81] Guilty pleas should be perceived as conspiracies that obstruct justice rather than as components of its administration.[82] In plea-bargaining the affected parties are represented by agents who have inadequate incentives for proper performance, prospects for effective monitoring are limited or non-existent and the dynamics of negotiation can create irresistible pressure for

72 McDonald W F, Cramer J A, Rossman H H (1980) Prosecutorial Bluffing and the case against Plea-Bargaining, in McDonald W.F, and Cramer, J.A. (Eds.), Plea Bargaining, Lexington Books, Lexington, Ma., pp. 1, 3, 21.

73 Alschuler A (1983) Implementing the Criminal Defendant's Right to Trial: Alternatives to the Plea bargaining System, vol.50, University of Chicago Law Review, p. 958.

74 Seifman R D, Freiberg A (1998) p. 64.

75 Alschuler A (1983) p. 958.

76 Du Cann C G L (1960) p. 149.

77 Alschuler A (1983) pp. 931 et seq.

78 Gerber R J (1998) pp. 19-25.

79 C.f. " The Plea agreement is the source of the coercion and itself embodies involuntariness", Langbein J H (1984) p. 255.

80 Gerber R J (1998) pp. 25-26.

81 Schulhofer S J (1991-92) Plea Bargaining as Disaster, Yale Law Journal, Vol.101, p. 2009.

82 Gorecki J A (1979) p. 51.

defendants falsely to condemn themselves.[83] The sentencing differential in plea-bargaining elicits confessions of guilt that would not be freely tendered; and at times can result in unjustified leniency.[84] It is coercion in the same sense as torture, although surely not in the same degree.[85]

On the other side of the coin proponents of plea-bargaining consider that it is not only worthwhile, but also indispensable, and its abolition would unearth a worst judicial scenario.[86] Their point of view is that the law governing plea bargaining policies the process, and that if there was no plea bargaining the number of trials would increase, the error rate of trials would rise, the total number of convictions would fall probably substantially, the average sentence would be both higher than the current average bargained-for-sentence and lower than the current average post trial sentence.[87] Simply put, there is no escape from it.[88] Whatever the merits or demerits plea bargaining, in the words of Warren Berger, former Chief Justice of the US Supreme Court, constitutes "an essential component of the administration of justice".[89] That Court has upheld its constitutionality.[90] Plea-bargaining is not an adjunct of the American criminal justice system, it is *the* system.[91] The United States Courts which are untroubled by it, have constructed a body of contract based law to regulate the plea bargaining process, taking for granted the efficiency and decency of the process being regulated.[92] As we shall demonstrate, the guilt plea process as practiced by the UN Ad hoc Tribunals does not contain the kind of abuses narrated above, which seem to be abundant in the typical plea bargaining process in United States.[93]

---

83 Schulhofer S J (1991-92) p. 2009; Darbyshire P (2002) The Mischief of Plea Bargaining and Sentence Rewards, Criminal Law Review, pp. 902-904.

84 Langbein J H in Glazer N (1984) p. 254.

85 P. 254, Id. Cf. "The law of plea bargaining has not only recapitulated much of the doctrinal folly of the law of torture, but it is also repeating the main institutional blunder of the law of torture", at p. 259.

86 Stuntz W J, Scott R E (1991-92) Plea Bargaining as Contract, Yale Law Journal, vol.101, III, pp. 1912, 1931; "Plea bargaining is preferable to mandatory litigation", Easterbrook F H (1991-92) Plea bargaining as Compromise, Yale Law Journal, vol.101, p. 1975.

87 Stuntz W J, Scott R E (1991-92) p. 1932; Easterbrook F H (1991-92) p. 1975.

88 Rothway H J (1996) Guilty: The Collapse of Criminal Justice, Random House, N.Y, p. 144.

89 *Santobello v. N.Y.* 404 U.S. 257, 260 (1971), Berger, W, "if every criminal charge were subjected to a full –scale trial, the States and the Federal Government would need to multiply by many times the number of judges and Court facilities", at p. 260.

90 *Santobello v. United States*, 404 U.S. 257, 92 S.Ct.495, 30 L.Ed.2d.427 (1971).

91 Gerber R J (1998) p. 17; Stuntz W J, Scott R E (1991-92) p. 1912.

92 Stuntz W J, Scott R E (1991-92) p. 1910.

93 See also, Combs N A (2002) Coping a Plea to Genocide: Bargaining of International Crimes, University of Pennsylvania Law Review, vol. 1151, No.1 p. 147.

III. Plea Agreements and UN Ad Hoc Criminal Tribunals

Guilty pleas before the ICTR have so far involved intensive direct discussions and negotiations between the Prosecution, Defence Counsel and the concerned accused on the intended plea, legal elements constituting the offences charged in the indictment, and verification and common accord on material facts, rather than charge or sentence bargaining; the latter being at the absolute discretion, even unpredictability, of a Trial Chamber.

Initially considered a distasteful practice in the ICTY, it has now been wholeheartedly embraced, and was that Tribunal's dominant method of case disposal between October 2002 and January 2004.[94] In its early days, a proposal by U.S.A. to incorporate a provision in the Tribunal's Rules of Procedure and evidence authorizing the Prosecutor to grant defendants full or partial testimonial immunity in exchange for their cooperation was rejected.[95] To date it has matured to encompass charging concessions, as well as sentence concessions in the form of an agreement between the Office of the Prosecutor and the accused and his Defence Counsel, for the former to recommend to a Trial Chamber a specific sentence or a range of sentence in 'exchange' for the guilty plea, substantial cooperation and the full disclosure of criminal conduct of the accused.[96]

In a number of cases before the ICTY in which accused had agreed to and pleaded guilty, the Prosecutor offered concessions by withdrawing or opting not to prefer charges. In *Erdermovic* the Prosecutor agreed not to proceed with the alternative count of murder as crimes against humanity under Article 5 (a) of the ICTY Statute. In *Todorovic* the Prosecutor, on the accused guilty plea to persecution as a crime against humanity pursuant to Article 5 (h) of the ICTY Statute, withdrew 26 of the 27 counts charged in the Amended Second Indictment of December 1998.[97] In *Plavsic* the Office of the Prosecutor agreed in the Plea Agreement with the accused and her Counsel to move to dismiss with prejudice at the time of sentencing the remaining Counts in the Indictment, on the accused pleading guilty to persecution based on political, racial, and religious grounds.[98] In another case, again on entering a guilty plea to persecution as a crime against humanity, the Prosecutor withdrew 6 counts against Dusko Sikirica, 2 counts against Damir Dosen, and 4

[94] Combs N A (2004) p. 232.

[95] P. 232, Id.

[96] Cf. "Neither Tribunals have been engaged in charge bargaining", Combs N A (2002) p. 140.

[97] See, Decision on the Prosecution Motion to withdraw Counts of the Indictment and Defense Motion to withdraw pending Motions, *P. v. Todorovic*, Case no: IT-9-5-9/1, 26 February 2001; Cf. "Todorovic's plea, the first to result from bargaining, seemed in many respects idiosyncratic", Combs N A (2004) p. 235.

[98] Plea Agreement, *P. v. M. Krajinik and B. Plavic*, Case no: IT-00-39 and 40-PT, 30 September 2002, para 3 and 9 (a); Decision Granting Prosecutor's Motion to Counts 1, 2, 4, 5, 6, 7, and 8 of the amended Consolidated Indictment, *P. v. B. Plavsic*, Case no: IT-00-39 and 49/I-S, 20 December 2002.

counts against Dragan Kolundzija, charged in the Indictment against them.[99] In *Samac*, in exchange for pleading guilty to two counts of torture as a crimes against humanity the Prosecutor withdrew several charges including the most serious, persecution as a crime against humanity, even though it was supported by substantial evidence.[100] Along the same veins, Nancy Combs discovered that in a barely-noticed charge bargain, that involving Dragan Nicolic's amended indictment the Prosecutor in anticipation of his plea, withdrew charges that the accused had allegedly raped a girl about 13 years of age nearly every night for two months.[101]

As indicated earlier, in a number of Plea Agreements between a guilty pleading accused and the Office of the Prosecutor the latter "in exchange" for a guilty plea, full and substantial cooperation, a full accounting of the accused criminal behaviour and fulfilment of all obligations, has agreed to recommend to a Trial Chamber a specific or a range of sentence, containing the minimum and maximum, from which if imposed by a Trial Chamber will not be appealed. On the basis of this exchange and undertaking, the Prosecutor, for example, agreed to recommend a sentence not exceeding 12 years for Todorovic; a sentence of between 10-17 years for Sikirica, 5 to 7 years for Damir Dosen and 3-5 years for Dragan Kolundzija;[102] a term of 10 years for Miroslav Deronjic,[103] that within the range of 15-20 years for Momir Nikolic,[104] and a term of 8 years for Predraj Banovic.[105] These recommendations are in no way binding on a Trial Chamber. It is fully competent to sentence an accused as it sees fit. Plea agreements also contain a common clause to the effect that pursuant to Rule 101 an accused could face a sentence, if convicted, of a term of life imprisonment, up to and including the remainder of his life.[106]

One of the earliest recourse to a Plea Agreement in proceedings before the UN ad hoc Tribunals was the guilty plea of Drazen Erdemovic.[107] Although there was

---

99 Sentence and Judgement, *P. v. D.Sikirica, D. Dosen and D. Kolundzija*, Case no: IT-95-8-S, 13 November 2001, paras. 13, 39; Cf. 'the withdrawal of charges in Jelisic and Kolundzija was a result of evidentiary deficiencies –not instances of plea bargaining', Combs N A (2002) p. 12.

100 Combs N A (2004) p. 236.

101 P. 240 and fn. 829-830, Id.

102 See, Sentencing Judgement, *P. v. D.Sikirica, D. Dosen and D. Kolundzija*, Case no: IT-95-8-S, 13 November 2001.

103 Plea Agreement between M. Deronjic and the Office of the Prosecutor, *P. v. M. Deronjic*, Case no: IT-02-61-PT, 30 September 2003, para. 11.

104 See, To the Joint Motion for Consideration of a Plea Agreement between Monir Nikolic and the Office of the Prosecutor, Amended Plea Agreement, *P. v. M. Nikolic*, Case no: IT-02-06-PT, 7 May 2003.

105 Pre Sentence hearing, *P. v. P. Banovic*, Transcripts, Case no: IT-02-65/1, 3 September 2003.

106 Cf. Amended Plea Agreement, *P. v. M. Nikolic*, para. 13.

107 Joint Motion for Consideration of Plea Agreement between Drazen Erdemovic and the Office of the Prosecutor, *P. v. D. Erdemovic*, Case no: IT-96-22-PT*bis*, 8 January 1998; see also, *P. v. D. Erdemovic*, Case no: IT-96-22-T*bis*. Sentencing Judgement, 5 March 1998, paras. 18-19; For a critique, see Yee S (1997) The Erdemovic Sentencing Judgement: A Questionable Milestone for the International Criminal Tribunal for the Former

at that time no provisions governing plea agreements in the Statutes and the Rules of Procedure and Evidence, use of such an agreement was permissible, since the practice had roots in national jurisdictions.[108] A plea agreement of the kind used before the Tribunals is simply an agreement between the parties, reached on their own initiative without the contribution or encouragement of a Trial Chamber.[109] The agreement has no binding effect on a Trial Chamber.[110] The purpose of such an agreement is to clarify the understanding of the parties as to the nature and consequences of the accused's plea of guilty, and to assist the parties and the Trial Chamber in ensuring that the plea entered into by the accused was valid, according to the Rules of Procedure and Evidence.[111] In *P. v. J. Kambanda* the Appeal Chamber held that the conditions for accepting a plea agreement are firstly that the person pleading guilty must understand the consequences of his or her actions, and secondly that no pressure must have been brought to bear upon that person to sign the plea agreement.[112]

In international criminal tribunals the guilty plea of a cooperating accused has the added value of providing information and evidence against co-perpetrators, and those presumed to possess the greatest responsibility for the crimes committed. Rule 101 (B) (ii), of the Rules of Procedure and Evidence, recognizes that substantial cooperation with the Prosecutor as a statutory mitigating factor. Drazen Erdemovic, the first accused to plead guilty before the ICTY, provided the Office of the Prosecutor with names and identities of other perpetrators; valuable testimony and details of four incidents (the killings at the Pilica collective farm, those at the Piliça cultural hall, the killing of an unidentified civilian male of military age in Srebrenica, and a killing in Vlasenica on 13 July 1996 by soldiers who, under orders, had cut the throat of a prisoner) which the Prosecutor did not previously know; the identification of his commanders and fellow executioners, as well as information on the Drina Corps, the structure of the BSA, and the Units that were involved in the takeover of Srebrenica such as the 10th Sabotage Detachment and the Bratunac Brigade.[113] Omar Serushago, one of the leaders of the 5 interahamwe militia groups in Gisenyi Prefecture in 1994 who pleaded guilty before the ICTR, provided the Office of the Prosecutor with invaluable recorded testimony of probative value against top politicians, senior governmental officials and military

Yugoslavia, Georgia Journal of International and Comparative Law, vol. 26/2, pp. 263-309.

108 See, Rule 11 (Pleas), Federal Rules of Criminal Procedure for the United States District Courts.

109 *P. v. D. Erdemovic*, Sentencing Judgement, para. 19; "The Court shall not participate in any such discussions", Rule 11 (e) (1) (c), Federal Rules of Criminal Procedure.

110 Para. 19, Id. Cf. In the United States, the Court may accept or reject the agreement, Rule 11(e) (3) and Rule 11 (e) (4), Federal Rules of Criminal Procedure.

111 Para. 18, Id.

112 *P. v. J. Kambanda*, Judgement, A.C, Case no: ICTR-97-23-A, 19 October 2000, para. 61.

113 *P. v. D. Erdemovic*, Sentencing Judgement, Trial Chamber, 5 March 1998, para. 14 (iv).

and gendarmerie commanders.[114] He had been privy to meetings where the elimination of Tutsi and moderate Hutu was discussed.

George Ruggiu, the RTLM broadcaster and journalist, who pleaded guilty to direct and public incitement to commit genocide and crimes against humanity (persecution) provided the Prosecution with insider information on the editorial policy of RTLM, and those who where behind its confection, the financing of that radio, the managerial decision making process, the contents of announcements and their meaning as perceived by the civilian population, the links between political parties, the military and the media, the connection between the Presidency and RTLM, the background and profile of various Kinyarwanda speaking broadcasters suspected of inciting the population to commit crimes against the Tutsi and moderate Hutu, and the overall role of the media in the extremist Hutu strategy to commit genocide.[115]

Plea agreements of the kind admitted in the practice of the UN ad hoc criminal tribunals assist to ensure defence counsel's effective participation, not persuasion, in a guilty plea process. Inducing an accused to plea guilty to international crimes such as genocide, crimes against humanity, and war crimes is intolerable in an international judicial arrangement intended to apply the highest standards of justice and recognized human rights norms. In certain national systems, when persuading, the Defence Counsel acts not as the defendant's adviser, but also in the interests of all those involved in the disposition of the case; especially the judge and the prosecutor, and he impresses the defendant that the judge would cooperate, and the prosecutor will recommend a light sentence, reduce the charge, or dismiss some of the multiple charges against the defendant.[116] In the UN ad hoc criminal tribunals, plea agreements have been used to ascertain the voluntariness of a guilty plea, as well as its factual and legal requirements.[117]

Another purpose of a Plea Agreement is to assist the Chamber by ensuring that there is no material disagreement between the parties on the facts in support of the indictment. A common accord and understanding between the Prosecution and the Defence on both the legal elements of the offences charged and the material helps to cement the requirements of Rule 62 (v) (d) of the Rules of Procedure and Evidence. Under this rule one of the requirements of a valid guilty plea is that it should be based on sufficient facts for the crime and the accused's participation in it, either on the basis of independent indicia or lack of any material disagreement between the parties about the facts of the case. Plea agreements assist the Chambers in ascertaining the factual basis of a plea. The major procedural safeguard

---

114 See, *P. v. O. Serushago*, Prosecutor's Pre Sentencing Brief, Case no: ICTR-98-39-I, T.C, 5 February 1999.

115 See, Les Confessions de "M. Georges", Ubutabera, No.72, 11 October 1999; Insider Evidence, Judicial Diplomacy, Chronicles and Reports on International Criminal Justice, at http://www.diplomatiejudiciare.com/UK/Tpiruk/Nahimana12.htm.

116 Gorecki J (1979) p. 53.

117 *P. v. J. Kambanda*, Judgement and Sentence, T.C, Case no: ICTR 97-23-S, 4 September 1998, paras. 4, 6, 7.

against conviction of the factually innocent is judicial inquiry into the factual basis of the plea.[118]

In the Plea Agreement with Ruggiu and his Defence Counsel accord had to be reached between the Prosecution and the Defence on whether Belgians were actually "killed" in Rwanda or were only "targeted"; whether RTLM had announced that there would be a "prize" or rather a "reward" for anyone who killed one; and whether in particular broadcasts, it was Belgians who were explicitly referred to or that they were referred to as "whites" who combated with the RPF. Similarly there needed to be agreement on the interpretation to be derived from use of anti Tutsi words and phrases in Kinyarwanda, purposely repeated over the radio during the events in Rwanda. In relation to direct and public incitement to commit genocide it was essential that agreement be reached as to the specific broadcasts that constituted direct incitement in the context of the use of the Kinyarwanda language and the particular circumstances prevailing in Rwanda. This joint interpretation and decoding of the various broadcasts was an essential part of the negotiating process of that guilty plea. In discussions on the draft Plea Agreement, it was also agreed, lessons learnt from the Kambanda Plea Agreement that allusion should not be made to other persons whom the accused thought were responsible for the planning and execution of atrocity crimes, since this might be perceived as "passing the buck" of responsibility and undesirably lead to an assumption that the plea was unequivocal. By their use in the practice of both the ICTR and the ICTY, Plea Agreements provide the necessary transparency of the results of factual understanding and negotiations between the Prosecutor and the accused and his Defence Counsel.[119] Plea Agreement have at times expressly recorded that no agreement, understanding, or promises had been made between the parties with respect to sentence which, it is acknowledged, is at the entire discretion of the Trial Chambers.[120]

The Plea Agreements entered into between accused persons and the Prosecutor have also involved a common accord and understanding on the range of sentence to be recommended by the Prosecutor. While this has been the case with guilty pleas administered by the ICTY, this has not been the case at the ICTR. In *P. v. D. Erdemovic* the accused and the Prosecutor, while acknowledging that sentencing is at the sole discretion of the Trial Chamber, jointly agreed that 7 years incarceration was an appropriate sentence.[121]

The procedures related to Plea Agreements have now been regulated by Rule 62 *ter* "Plea Agreement Procedure", adopted 28 February 2001 at the ICTY which provides:

---

[118] Miller H S *et all.* (1978) p. xx.

[119] Although at times jointly transmitted to a Trial Chamber under seal, this is waived after pronouncement of judgment and sentence, and they become part of the public court or tribunal records.

[120] *P. v. J. Kambanda*, Judgement and Sentence, T.C, para. 48.

[121] Plea Agreement between D. Erdemovic and the Office of the Prosecutor, January 1998, paras. 8,16.

Rule 62 *ter*
Plea Agreement Procedure

A. The Prosecutor and the defence may agree that, upon the accused entering a plea of guilty to the indictment or to one or more counts of the indictment; the Prosecutor shall do one or more of the following before the Trial Chamber:
   i. apply to amend the indictment accordingly;
   ii. submit that a specific sentence or sentencing range is appropriate;
   iii. not oppose a request by the accused for a particular sentence or sentencing range.
B. The Trial Chamber shall not be bound by any agreement specified in paragraph (A).
C. If a plea agreement has been reached by the parties, the Trial Chamber shall require the disclosure of the agreement in open session or, on a showing of good cause, in closed session, at the time the accused pleads guilty in accordance with Rule 62 (vi), or requests to change his or her plea to guilty.

It is of utmost importance to stress that in the law and practice of the UN ad hoc Tribunals, a Plea Agreement is not binding on a Trial Chamber.[122] Irrespective of the terms of a Plea Agreement, sentence is ultimately a matter for the Trial Chamber to determine.[123] The Prosecutor, accused persons and their Defence Counsel have also repeatedly acknowledged this.[124]

In the *Erdermovic* Appeal Decision Judge Cassese, partly critical of that process opined:

"Both the Statute and the Rules deliberately do not make provision for plea bargaining-or al least, of any endorsement of acknowledgement by the Chambers of out-of-court plea bargaining. This means, among other things, that the framers of the Statute and the Rules aimed at averting those distortions of the free will of the accused, which may be linked to plea-bargaining A plea bargain implies that the accused relinquishes his right to a proper trial, namely proceedings in which he is presumed innocent until his guilt is proved beyond reasonable doubt".[125]

At the ICTR the Prosecutor's prime interest in a plea of guilty has been evidential rather than docket clearance. It has been in the substantial cooperation of an accused in a full recount of criminal behaviour and participation, and truth about the events, including the involvement of co-perpetrators. The generation of information and new evidence, the clarification of facts, the confirmation of incidents, and the interpretation of phenomena is what the Prosecution has sought as the legal savings of a guilty plea. The basis of negotiations has been full truth in substantial cooperation, and appearance as a prosecution witness. The Prosecutor of an international Tribunal is not a carpet merchant resolved to trade a lesser sentence just

---

[122] "[T] he Trial Chamber reiterates that it is in no way bound by this Agreement. It is the Chamber's responsibility to determine an appropriate sentence, ", *P. v. S. Tadorovic*, Judgement, Case no: IT-95-9-S, 31 July 2001, para.16.

[123] Para. 16, Id.

[124] Paras. 16, 79, 86, Id.; Plea Agreement between the Prosecutor and J. Kambanda, December 1998, para. 40.

[125] Separate Dissenting Opinion of Judge Cassese, *P. v. D. Erdermovic*, Case no: IT-96-33-A, 7 October 1997, para. 10.

for the purpose of clinching a guilty plea. She or he must continue to be a Prosecutor throughout the guilty plea process, and must forcefully argue that due credit should be given to an accused who substantially cooperates. Given that as a general rule, a guilty plea by an accused at separate proceedings or at the same proceedings involving a co-accused is not admissible against a co-accused,[126] the Prosecutor's approach has been to count on the post guilty plea cooperation of an accused so as to testify against co-perpetrators or others. In this regard both Ruggiu and Serushago have testified in the Media Trial. The calling of an accomplice to testify against a co-accused when charges are outstanding against the first accused, or the first accused's guilty plea has not yet been accepted, or the first accused has not yet been sentenced on the guilty plea, has been universally condemned.[127] It is essential to note with regard to cooperation, the determination whether the cooperation should be considered substantial and therefore whether it constitutes a mitigating factor is for the Trial Chamber to determine, not the Prosecutor.[128] That apart, the Statute and the Rules leave it open to the Trial Chamber to consider the mitigating effect of a guilty plea on the basis that the mitigating weight to be attached to the plea lies in the discretion of the Trial Chamber.[129] It has been submitted this wide discretion of Judges in sentencing inhibits plea-bargaining by making a guilty plea a potentially perilous exercise for defendants.[130] In the UN ad hoc Tribunals judges do not participate, directly or indirectly, in guilty plea discussions and negotiations between the Office of the Prosecutor, the Defence Counsel, and the accused. The integrity of the process and respect of the highest standards of international justice and human rights justify that distance.

The profile of accused who have pleaded guilty at the UN ad hoc Tribunals is a varied one. It has included all classes of perpetrators, those who were in leadership, authority or command positions, intermediate, and low level perpetrators. We have already mentioned those who pleaded guilty before the ICTR, namely Kambanda, Serushago, Ruggiu and Rutaganira. At the ICTY those in positions of authority or command include Plavsic, former Acting President of the Serb Republic of Bosnia Herzegovina, and Admiral Miodrag Jokic, Commander of the Ninth (Boka) Military Naval Sector (Ninth VPS). Those who also pleaded guilty include Goran Jelisic, Commander of Luka camp; Todorovic, the Chief of Police in Bosanski Samac; Sikirica, the Commander of Security; Dosen, a shift commander, and Kolundzija, also a shift leader with limited control over 6-12 guards at Keraterm camp which held between 1000-14000 detainees, in Prijedor, north western Bosnia-Herzegovina. It has also included Ranko Cesic, who acted under the police authority in Brcko and served at Luka Detention Camp, an accused with

---

126 *P. v. Berry* (1957), 118 C.C.C. 55 at 50, 26 C.R. 218 at 223 (Ont.C.A.); *R. v. Lessard* (1979), 50 C.C.C. (2d) 175 (Que. C.A.).

127 Fitzgerald O E (1990) p. 108.

128 Judgement, *P. v. G. Jelisic*, Judgement, A.C, Case no: IT-95-10-A, 5 July 2001, para. 126.

129 *P. v. G. Jelisic*, Judgment, A.C, para. 121.

130 Combs N A (2002) p. 74.

a relatively "small case" and whose profile as a marginal perpetrator was more suited for referral to national jurisdiction, namely, Bosnia-Herzegovina or the Special Chamber in Sarajevo, under Rule 11 *bis* of the ICTY Rules that govern trial by the Tribunal.[131]

Guilty Plea: Jean Kambanda

Jean Kambanda, born on 19 October 1955 in Gishamvu commune, Butare prefecture, Rwanda, graduated as a commercial engineer at the *Ecole des hautes Etudes Commerciales* in Liege Belgium in 1984. He joined a housing Bank in Kigali where he rose to become one of its directors before being named at the eruption of atrocity crimes as Prime Minister of the Interim Government of Rwanda. He served in that capacity from 9 April 1994, the day he was officially sworn in, until about 17 July 1994. He was a member of the central committee of MDR Party.

Coincidence had it that Kambanda had an air ticket to travel to Dakar at 07:00 hrs, on 7 April 1994, to attend a banking seminar, but was forced to cancel his trip because of the shooting down on 6th April of Presidential Habyarimana's plane over Kigali. On the 8 April 1994 Kambanda was fetched from his residence in Kigali by Froduald Karamira, of the MDR "pawa" (power) faction, and taken to the ESM, the Senior Staff College of the Rwandan Armed Forces, where a meeting of political party leaders and senior military commanders had already decided on his nomination as Prime Minister, as well as the composition of members of the Interim Government.[132]

Following a request for provisional measures to the Kenyan Government made by the Prosecutor on 9 July 1997, Kenyan police authorities arrested Jean Kambanda, in Nairobi, on 18 July 1997. The arrest was part of the Prosecutor's NAKI (Nairobi-Kigali) Operation which resulted in the arrest of seven persons, some considered to have had significant responsibility for the atrocity crimes in Rwanda. On the basis of a request by the Prosecutor, under Rule 40 (B) of the Rules of Procedure and Evidence of the Tribunal, for the transfer and provisional detention of the suspect, the Tribunal's President Judge Laity Kama, on 16 July 1997, ordered the transfer and provisional detention of Kambanda to the Detention Facility of the Tribunal, in Arusha, Tanzania. Kambanda was taken to Jomo Kenyatta International Airport in Nairobi, and transported by a UN aircraft, in the company of UN security personnel and staff of the Prosecutor's Office to Arusha the same day of his arrest.[133] The other arrestees travelled on board a United Nations bus by road to Arusha, also on the same day.

---

131 *P. v. R. Cesic*, Status Conference Transcript, Case no:IT-95-10-1, 25 July 2003, pp. 55-57.

132 The repartition of ministerial portfolios in the Interim Government was as follows: MRND (9) including the President, and the Defence and Interior; MDR (3) including the Prime Minister, PL (3), PSD (3) and PDC (1).

133 *P. v. J. Kambanda*, Transcript, Examination-in-Chief, J. Kambanda, Appeal hearing, Case no: ICRT-97-23-A, 27 June 2000, p. 23.

Before the expiry of the maximum period foreseen under Rule 40 *bis* for the provisional detention of a suspect without charges by the Tribunal,[134] Kambanda was indicted on 16 October 1998 with six counts; namely, genocide, conspiracy to commit genocide, direct and public incitement to commit genocide, crimes against humanity (murder), and crimes against humanity (extermination).[135] Both direct and indirect criminal responsibility under article 6 (1) and 6 (3) of Statute were attributable to his criminal conduct. Between 18 July 1997 and 2 June 1998 Kambanda voluntarily accepted to be questioned on record by the Prosecutor, without the presence of Defence Counsel, at Tribunal safe houses in Arusha and Dodoma, Tanzania, and in The Hague. During questioning by investigators from the Prosecutor's Office cautions were administered, and he waived his rights some 15 times while under questioning in Dodoma, and 14 times during the interviews conducted at the ICTY Detention Facility in The Hague.

At his initial appearance on 1 May 1998, before Trial Chamber I, composed of Judges Laity Kama, Lennart Aspegren, and Navanethem Pillay the indictment against him was read over by the Tribunal's Registrar, Agu Okali. At that hearing, Kambanda, pursuant to Rule 62 of the Rules of Procedure and Evidence, pleaded guilty to all six counts charged. He acknowledged that he had signed on 29 April 1998 a Plea Agreement with the Prosecutor, signed by his Counsel and himself. Together with this agreement, a signed Joint Motion was tabled before the Chamber, outlining the parties' common understanding on the requirements of the law and the procedure involved in a plea of guilty before the Tribunal.[136] Under the Plea Agreement Kambanda stated that he was pleading guilty because he was in fact guilty, and acknowledged full responsibility for his actions. He declared that he had decided to plead guilty even before his arrest by members of the Kenya Police Force in Nairobi, and his immediate transfer to the Tribunal's Detention Facility in Arusha on 18 July 1997.

As for his motivations, he indicated that he had a profound desire to tell the truth, and that it was only the full truth that can restore national unity and foster reconciliation in Rwanda. He further added that he wished to contribute to the national reconciliation process, and hoped that his gesture will motivate others to tell the truth about their involvement in the mass killing of Tutsi and moderate Hutu, and that it will contribute to the building of trust between Rwandans. He also condemned without hesitation the massacres committed in Rwanda between April and July 1994, which he admitted amounted to genocide against the Tutsi. It is worth noting that in subsequent proceedings before the Appeal Chamber, Kambanda continued to admit the genocide of the Tutsi, but also pressed for the recognition by the Tribunal of the atrocities committed by the RPF. [137]

---

134 Rule 40 *bis* (H), Rules of Procedure and evidence; *P. v. J. Kambanda*, Extension of the Provisional Detention, ICTR Case no: 1CTR-97-23-DP, 16 September 1997.

135 *P. v. J. Kambanda*, Indictment, Case no: 97-23-I, 16 October 1997.

136 Joint Motion for Consideration of a Plea Agreement between J. Kambanda and The Office of the Prosecutor, Case No. ICTR-97-23-I, 29 April 1998.

137 "I am one of the few people in my group to admit that there was genocide in Rwanda; and before you, I confirm and admit that there was genocide in Rwanda", *P. v. J. Kam-*

In discussions between the parties, the Plea Agreement of 29 April 1998 had been preceded by an earlier draft agreement dated 17 April 1998. A few changes proposed by the parties, including the accused were incorporated in the final agreed text.[138] Given the legal imperatives for a valid guilty plea, which require the voluntary admission of substantially of all the facts constituting the offences charged, the plea agreement contained a detailed narration in twenty-two paragraphs of the agreed facts. [139] These formed one of the material considerations on which Trial Chamber based its judgement and sentence on the guilty plea.[140]

At the initial appearance held on 1 May 1998, the Trial Chamber inquired and verified the validity of Kambanda's guilty plea (i.e. that it was an informed plea made freely and voluntarily, without any pressure or threats or promises), and that he fully understood the nature of the charges against him, as well as the consequences of his guilty plea, and that his guilty plea was unequivocal. The whole object in fact of putting questions to an accused person who offers to confess is to obtain an assurance of the fact that the confession is not caused by any inducement, threat or promise having reference to the charge against the accused person; and the question as to whether the accused is making the statement voluntarily or not must be directed to that end.[141] There is also a requirement for the Court to make an–on-the-record determination that there is a factual basis for the plea as a condition precedent to exercising the Court's discretion to accept or reject the plea.[142]

At the conclusion of the initial appearance, the Trial Chamber found Kambanda guilty of all six counts in the Indictment. With the accord of the Trial Chamber both parties submitted pre sentencing briefs.[143] The Prosecution pointed out two aggravating factors, namely, the gravity of the offences committed by the accused, and his abuse of authority and office. As mitigating factors the Prosecution detailed his personal circumstances, the substantial cooperation extended to the prosecution, including the fact that he had provided a ninety hour tape recorded statement,[144] his prompt guilty plea communicated immediately after his transfer,

---

banda, Transcript, Examination-in-Chief, Jean Kambanda, Appeal Chamber hearing, p. 58, 27 June 2000.

[138] Transcript, Cross Examination, Jean Kambanda Appeal Chamber hearing, *P. v. J. Kambanda*, pp. 110-114.

[139] *P. v. J. Kambanda*, T.C, Plea Agreement between J. Kambanda and the OTP, paras. 21-40.

[140] *P. v. J. Kambanda*, Judgement and Sentence, T.C, para. 39.

[141] Mitler V (1978) pp. 80-81.

[142] Herman G N (1997) p. 11.

[143] See, Prosecutor's Pre Sentencing Brief *P. v. J. Kambanda.*

[144] "I consider the statements that I made when I cooperated with the OTP are true, and I can repeat them, but I am not going to endorse that particular act. That is, I can endorse my statements, but not this gesture", Jean Kambanda, Transcript, Examination-in Chief, Appeal hearing, *P. v. J. Kambanda*, p. 104-105, 27 June 2000; " I've never said that the statements I made were…were made under duress because I explained the context in which I operated and if, I, myself, requested to make statements without the presence of counsel, these were verified today, nobody asked me to do that, because I had a purpose", p. 108.

and implied remorse in the guilty plea. With regard to the meaningful cooperation extended by the accused as a mitigating factor, the Prosecutor suggested that it be pinned down to any future reduction of sentence that he may become entitled. Attention was drawn on the promptness of the plea. Such a guilty plea, it was submitted, carries weight partly because it spares the victim the anxiety of awaiting trial and the trauma of giving evidence, partly because it obviates the risk of unjustified acquittal and partly because it does, in many cases, involve a genuine acceptance of responsibility for the crime, which may well be the first step towards rehabilitating the offender.[145] An early guilty plea is an enhancing discount factor.[146] With regard to the sentence the Prosecutor's view was that a specific sentence should be recommended. There was in fact no explicit or implicit sentencing bargaining between the parties. Principally, taking into account the extreme gravity of genocide and other offences committed by the accused, the Prosecutor recommended life imprisonment. She also requested the Trial Chamber to put on record that in view of the substantial cooperation of the accused with her Office, any future application or consideration of pardon and commutation of sentence(s) under Article 27 of the Statute, should be considered favourably on the basis of past, current, and future significant cooperation extended to her Office.

The Defence Counsel on the other hand urged in mitigation of sentence, Kambanda's admission of guilt, his remorse and the substantial and on going cooperation with the Office of the Prosecutor. Testifying against the ultimate defendant is in the interest of a greater law enforcement triumph and ought to be negotiated with a major discount in mind.[147] The Counsel submitted that the accused had no ministerial experience, did not know the ins and outs of government, and was coopted into a ministerial team not of his making or political coloration.[148] He argued that Kambanda possessed "diminished responsibility", was "'trapped' and had been a "puppet" with no will of his own, controlled by certain military authorities.[149] The Defence Counsel reiterated the promptness of his guilty plea, which sprang from remorse and the desire to tell the truth, and for which he merited a sentence discount. Remorse in itself is already a price to pay; one is always haunted by past events after reparation has been made.[150]

The Defence Counsel also challenged the Prosecutor's recommendation of life imprisonment, as being inconsistent and illogical, bearing in mind the mitigating circumstance, and the substantial cooperation extended by the accused. On its part the Defence recommended a term of imprisonment not exceeding two years, arguing that any greater sentence would be a disappointment to those who are waiting to hold hands with the accused with a view to healing and national reconcilia-

145 Bingham J (2000) The Business of Judging, Oxford University Press, Oxford, p. 307.

146 Samuels A (2000) The Discount factor for Guilty Pleas: The Judicial Principles, Justice of the Peace, vol.163, p. 792.

147 Uviller H R (1996) Virtual Justice. The Flawed Prosecution of Crime in America, Yale University Press, New Heaven and London, p. 191.

148 *P. v.J. Kambanda*, Pre Sentencing hearing, Transcript, Case no: ICTR-97-23-I, 3 September 1998, p. 23-25.

149 P. 25 Id.

150 P. 26, Id.

tion.[151] It is probable that an extraordinary suggestion of a light sentence by the Defence Counsel was based on a very liberal interpretation of Article 83 of the Penal Code of Rwanda,[152] as applying to persons accused of genocide and crimes against humanity,[153] when in law, the applicable law was in fact the Rwandan Organic Law on the organization of Prosecutions for offences constituting the Crime of Genocide and Crimes Against Humanity.

Article 14 of that law provides that penalties imposed for the offences relating to Article 1, namely, genocide and crimes against humanity shall be provided for in the Penal Code, except that persons in Category I are liable when convicted to a mandatory death penalty. Furthermore Article 5 stipulates that persons falling within that Category are not eligible to any reduction in sentence even when they confess or plead guilty.[154] As regards the requirement under Article 23 (1) of the Statute and Rule 101(B) (iii) of the Rules of Procedure and Evidence that recourse shall be made to the general practice of prison sentences in Rwanda, the Tribunal has often stated that that practice is only of reference, that it represents one of many factors, and that it prefers to lean more on its unfettered discretion each time it has to pass on sentence on persons found guilty of crimes falling within its jurisdiction, taking into account the circumstances of the case and the standing of the accused person.[155]

In its judgement and sentencing decision of 4 September 1998 the Trial Chamber first took into account the substantial cooperation already extended and that which Kambanda was willing to continue to extend to the Prosecutor, the fact that the guilty plea was likely to encourage other individuals to recognize their responsibilities in the tragic events in Rwanda in 1994, and that a guilty plea is generally considered, in most national jurisdictions, including Rwanda, as a mitigating factor. The Chamber, however, observed that the aggravating circumstances, namely, the intrinsic gravity, widespread, atrocious, and systematic character of the crimes for which Kambanda was responsible, that he had committed the crimes knowingly and with premeditation, and that as Prime Minister of Rwanda he was entrusted with the duty and authority to protect the population, and that he abused this trust, thus negating the mitigating circumstances, especially since he occupied

---

[151] Pp. 34-35, 38 Id.; See also, Judgement and Sentence, T.C, para. 60.

[152] Decree-Loi no.22/77, 8 Aout 1997 in Reyntjens F, Gorus J (eds.) (1980), Codes et Lois du Rwanda, Volume II, Faculte du Droit, Universite Nationale du Rwanda, Butare.

[153] *P. v. J. Kambanda*, Pre Sentencing hearing, Transcript, pp. 34; Article 83, Penal Code of Rwanda reads, "Should mitigating circumstances exist, sentence shall be modified or reduced as follows; capital sentence shall be replaced by a prison sentence of not les than five years. Life imprisonment shall be replaced by a temporary imprisonment of not less than two years".

[154] See also Article 14; J. Kambanda was listed in Category 1, No.39, Publication of the list no.1 of the first category prescribed by article 9 of the organic law no.8/96 of 30 August 1996 (O.G. no.17 of 1/9/1996), Official Gazette of the Republic of Rwanda, 30 November 1996, p. 6.

[155] *P. v. J. Kambanda,* Sentence and Judgement, T.C, paras 22-25; Sentence P. *v. C. Kayishema and O. Ruzindana*, Sentence, T.C., Case no: ICTR- 95-1-T, 21 May 1999, para. 7.

a high ministerial post at the time he committed the crimes.[156] The crimes were committed during the time when he was the head of Government, and he and his government were responsible for maintenance of peace and security.[157] He had abused his authority and the trust of the civilian population, had personally participated in the genocide, and had failed to take necessary and reasonable measures to prevent his subordinates from committing crimes against the population.[158]

With the above factors in mind the Trial Chamber sentenced Kambanda to life imprisonment.[159] As required by Statute and Rules of Procedure and Evidence, this was to be served in a state designated by the President of the Tribunal, in consultation with the Trial Chamber concerned, and the said designation conveyed by the Tribunal's Registrar to the Government of Rwanda. The Trial Chamber ignored the conventional wisdom of national courts that an accused that pleads guilty receives a lesser sentence than one who is convicted after trial.[160] As stated by Lord Widgery:

"Everyone knows that it is so and there is no doubt about it. Any accused person who does not know about it should know about it. The sooner he knows the better".[161]

As former Prime Minister, by pleading guilty, he had to take the "wrap".[162] His Counsel had argued in Court that by accepting to plead guilty, the accused had demonstrated that he is a man of courage, honesty, compunction, and vision. At the time of Kambanda's guilty plea only two cabinet Ministers in the Interim Government of which he headed had been arrested.[163] Rwanda's Minister of Justice considered that the guilty plea constituted a great step towards justice, and its Minister for Foreign Affairs expressed satisfaction in the gesture made by the accused, and in his public acknowledgement that genocide did indeed take place in Rwanda in 1994.[164] For Simeone Rwagasore, former Supreme Court President, Kambanda was "a guy who joined a moving genocide train".[165] The plea temporarily dislodged several accused, who on 6 May 1998 wrote to the UN Secretary

156 *P. v. J. Kambanda*, Judgement and Sentence, T.C, paras. 61-62.

157 Para 44, Id.

158 Id.

159 Part IV, Id.

160 Wright M (1999) p. 473.

161 *In Cain*, [1976] Crim.L.R. 464.

162 Ex-Rwandan Leader Admits Genocide, The Washington Post, 2 May 1998; "I didn't expect a life sentence. I expected something like 10 to 15 years", J. Kambanda's Defence Counsel, See, Rwanda leader gets life prison for genocide, Associated Press, 4 September 1998.

163 These were Pauline Nyiramasuhuko, former Minster of Family Affairs and Andre Ntagerura, former Minister of Transport.

164 Interview, Minister of Justice, M. Faustin Ntezilyayo, BBC, 1 May 1998; Declaration of Foreign Minister, Anastace Gasana, Radio Rwanda, 1-2 May 1998; " Rwanda has hailed the convictions", Rwanda Tribunal Hands Life Sentence to Former Premier, IHT, 7-13, September 1998.

165 "un type qui a pris le tran de genocide en marche", Interview with Author, Kigali, 11 December 2002.

General rejecting the historical plea as illegal. Kambanda's guilty plea was equally a matter of profound public interest. Confessions are important to the public, and the offender, in that they relieve the collective guilt of society.[166] They also deny an accused the status of a legendary hero.[167] On their part the Rwandan public, which heard the Trial Chamber proceedings live over Radio Rwanda, there were mixed feelings over the fairness of the life sentence against a man of that rank who for the first time in world history, accepted culpability for the crime of genocide before an international court.[168] Some "hailed" the conviction,[169] while others expressed "shock". Yet to others it was a historic event.[170] Gerald Gahima, Rwanda's former Prosecutor General, considered the plea a "big deal."[171] In remarks on the significance of Kambanda's guilty plea, the Tribunal's Registrar, Adama Dieng, had this to say:

"The confession, conviction and sentencing of the former Prime Minister of their country for genocide was a cathartic moment in the post-genocide healing process in Rwanda. At a global level, the Kambanda judgement-the first ever conviction in history of a head of government for genocide –set an important precedent for the judicial accountability of powerful political and military leaders for human rights crimes and the efficacy of international criminal justice in general. It happened before the case of former Chilean leader Augusto Pinochet and the indictment of Mr. Slobodan Milosevic, former President of the Federal Republic of Yugoslavia by the International Criminal Tribunal for the former Yugoslavia."[172]

Sentence: Just, Severe or Excessive

The sentencing outcome of Kambanda's guilty plea remains a controversy. His Counsel considered the sentence a "cowardly" decision", one that "shocked" Kambanda; and which shut the door on future cooperation with the accused.[173]

---

166 Romanowski A K (1988) Crime and Confession: An Analysis of the Relationship between Contrition, Sentence and Recidivism, University of Michigan, 1988, (PhD.), U.M.I., Anne Arbor, MI., p. 53.

167 Angiolillo P F (1979) A Criminal as Hero. Angelo Duca, The Regents Press of Kansan, Lawrence.

168 Okali A U Rwanda Genocide Verdicts Set Legal Precedents, Opinion, International Herald Tribune, 7-13 September 1998. Rwandese Express Mixed Feelings Over Kambanda Sentence, The Newsline, Kigali, 3 October - 3 November 1998.

169 "Rwanda has hailed the convictions", Rwanda Tribunal Hands Life Sentence to Former Premier, International Herald Tribune, 7-13 September 1998; Rwandese happy on sentence of Kambanda, Sunday News, 6 September 1998; Rwanda welcomes PM's life sentence, The New Vision, 5 September 1998.

170 Rwanda leader gets life in prison for genocide, Associated Press, 4 September 1998.

171 Ex Rwanda Leader Admits Genocide, The Washington Post, 2 May 1998; Former Prime Minster pleads guilty to genocide, The Guardian 2 May 1998.

172 Statement by the Registrar, A. Dieng on the Report of the International Crisis Group, ICTR Doc. ICTR/INFO-9-3-01.EN, Arusha, 1 June 2001.

173 Ex Rwandese Prime Minister gets life sentence for genocide, Daily News, 5 September 1998; "Cf. Although some international defendants rely on sentence based calculations

The question how a prison sentence of two years as suggested by the Defence Counsel would have helped the healing process and national reconciliation in Rwanda was also one that later on commanded the attention of the Appeal Chamber.[174] It has been said that the International Tribunal, in addition to its mandate to investigate, prosecute, and punish serious violations of international humanitarian law, has a duty, through its judicial functions, to contribute to the settlement of the wider issues of accountability, reconciliation, and establishing the truth behind the evils perpetrated.[175]

With regard to the sentence imposed the Prosecutor, Arbour, applauded the life sentence as "a landmark".[176] Muna, the Deputy Prosecutor, considered it "very tough".[177] In most cases of a guilt plea, there is a direct correlation between the guilty plea and sentencing result. Usually a defendant will waive his right to trial and enter a plea of guilty, if the cost to him of the sentence received upon the plea is less than the expected disutility of the sentence associated with the trial prospect.[178] It failed to provide an incentive for others to plead guilty.[179] A mere erroneous estimate of a sentence or sentencing range does not render the plea involuntary, and an erroneous legal opinion regarding the binding effect of the Government's or Prosecutor's promise to make a recommendation as to the defendant's sentence does not render the plea involuntary.[180] Mere dissatisfaction with the sentence imposed is not a ground to permit withdrawal of a guilty plea.[181] It has been advanced that under *Turner*, a statement that on a plea of guilty a judge would impose one sentence but on a conviction following a plea of not guilty he would impose a severer sentence is one, which should not be made since this could amount to undue influence.[182]

Generally it is implicit in an accused's plea of guilty that he will benefit from the plea of guilty, the plea simpliciter assuming an independent role as a factor in sentencing.[183] The practice in many jurisdictions is that a guilty plea calls for leniency given that the plea is of assistance to the administration of justice, it spares

when deciding whether or not to plead guilty, for a substantial proportion, currently in the dock, sentence inducement have only limited persuasive value", Combs N A (2005) Combs N A (2005) Procuring Guilty Pleas, *Draft*, forthcoming publication.

174 *P. v. J. Kambanda*, Appeal hearing, Transcript, 27 June 2000, pp. 160-161.

175 *P. v. D. Erdemovic,* Sentencing Judgement, Case no: IT092-22-T*bis*, 5 March 1998, para. 21.

176 Ex Rwanda Prime Minister jailed for life for genocide, The Guardian (Tanzania), 5 September 1998.

177 Id.

178 Adelstein R P (1984) The Negotiated Guilty Plea. An Economic and Empirical Analysis, Garland Pub. Inc., New York and London, p. 27.

179 Jorgensen N H B (2002) The Genocide Acquittal in Sikirica Case before the International Criminal Tribunal for the Former Yugoslavia and the Coming of Age of the Guilty Plea, Leiden Journal of International Law, vol. 15/2, p. 407.

180 Herman G N (1997) p. 20.

181 *R. v. Antoine* (1984) 40 C.R. (3d) 375 (Que.C.A.), affirmed [1988] 1 S.C.R. 212, 84 N.R. 80.

182 Sanders A, Yang R (2000) Criminal Justice, Butterworths, London, p. 422.

183 Bishop J B (1989) Prosecution Without Trial, Butterworths, Sydney, p. 186.

victims and witnesses from the ordeal and discomfiture of trial, and the accused's disclosure of information often leads to the arrest or conviction of others.[184] To the extent that the guilty plea demonstrates genuine remorse on the part of the accused, it is viewed as a first step towards rehabilitation, and in order to encourage or reward this, sentence will be mitigated.[185] Even if it is not motivated by remorse but engineered by more pragmatic conditions, such as overwhelming strength of the case of the accused, the guilty plea may be considered as a mitigating factor, if it saves the prosecution the expense of a lengthy and complicated trial, this being a matter of pure administrative convenience.[186] It is also worth observing that it is possible for circumstances not to warrant a reduction of sentence in recognition of a guilty plea, and this may occur where the protection of the public makes it necessary that a long sentence, possibly the maximum sentence, should be imposed; in cases where the guilty plea is "tactical" (i.e. where the offender delayed his guilty plea until the final moments, in a case where he could not hope to put up most of a defence), or where the accused had been caught red- handed, and a guilty plea was practically certain.[187]

In analyzing the guilty plea, as part of a Prosecutor's strategy to enlist the substantial cooperation of an accused, one cannot avoid a discussion on the life sentence imposed on Kambanda upon his guilty plea. The limitations of reading the minds of the trial judges, as well as the plenary sentencing discretionary authority of the Trial Chamber notwithstanding. The saying among German lawyers that for each judgement there are three sets of reasons: the oral reasons, the written reasons, and the real reasons is very valid in this instance.[188] In its judgment and sentence the Trial Chamber noted that Kambanda had offered no explanation for his voluntary participation in the genocide; nor had he expressed contrition, regret or sympathy for the victims in Rwanda, even when given the opportunity to do so by the Chamber.[189] During the 3 September 1998 pre sentencing hearing the Presiding Judge, Laity Kama, as part of accepted criminal procedure, gave the last word to the accused before delivery of the sentence by the Trial Chamber. He asked Kambanda:[190]

Presiding Judge: Do you have anything further to add concerning the sentence that we should inflict upon you, do you have anything to say, if you do so, if you do have anything to say, I will give you the floor. If not, I will let you go?

---

[184] Pp. 190-191, Id.

[185] Fitzgerald O (1990) p. 139.

[186] Pp. 139-140.

[187] *R. v. Cullen*, (1989), 11 Cr App. Rep. 182; *R. v. Hastings* (1966) 1 Cr App Rep. 167.

[188] Weigend T (1983) Symposium: Comparative Criminal Justice Issues in the United States, West Germany, England and France, Sentencing in Western Germany, 42 Md Law Review 37, Univ.of Maryland, fn.167.

[189] *P. v. J. Kambanda*, Judgement and Sentence, T.C, para. 51.

[190] *P. v. J. Kambanda*, Transcript, T.C, Case no: ICTR-97-23-I, 3 September 1998, pp. 42-43.

Accused: Mr. President, I have nothing further to add.

Presiding Judge: You have nothing further to add? I understand that. You may withdraw. Counsel Inglis, must I understand that you have nothing further to add because the last word is always with the Defence?

Defense Counsel: Nothing.

A valid inquiry into the Trial Chamber's sentencing decision, and the adverse inference it may have drawn from the above, is whether there was any valid legal basis for doing so. In other words whether they were entitled to draw such an inference on the basis of Kambanda's demeanour; not offering any explanation for his voluntary participation in the genocide, regret or sympathy.[191] A fair procedure would have been for the Trial Chamber to ascertain that Kambanda appreciated the implications of an adverse inference being drawn, especially since he had occupied a high ministerial post during the 1994 events in Rwanda. A defendant is entitled to remain silent, and the privilege against self-incrimination is not only a rule of evidence applied in judicial proceedings, but a fundamental criminal law principle.[192] In the author's view the Trial Chamber did not draw an inference of guilty, but only interpreted his conduct and demeanour, which it was entitled to do. In its Judgement and Sentence the Chamber noted that:[193]

"Kambanda has offered no explanation for his voluntary participation in the genocide; nor has he expressed contrition, regret or sympathy for the victims in Rwanda, even when given the opportunity to do so by the Chamber".

---

191 See, "An adverse inference can be drawn only where the silence can be sensibly attributed to the defendant's having no answer or none that would stand up to cross examination", Howard M N (ed.) (2000) Philson on Evidence, 15th Edition, par 32-15, Sweet and Maxwell, London.

192 McNicol S B (1992) Law of Privilege, The Law book Company, N.S.W, North Ryde, pp. 136, 188. The right to silence is a " specific immunity…possessed by accused persons undergoing trial, from having adverse comments made on any failure 9a) to answer questions before the trial, or (b) to give evidence at trial", Lord Mustil, *R. v. Director of Serious Fraud Office ex parte Smith* (1993) AC 1, 31. "his rights, if it be such, is sometimes treated as indistinguishable from the citizen's right not to indiscriminate himself, the well-known privilege against self-incrimination. It is, I think, sometimes different, but related; a first cousin once removed perhaps." Bingham, J. 'Silence is Golden-or is it?, p. 285, in The Business of Judging, ibid. 'The two are distinguishable, in that "privilege" implies the according of a special favour or concession, whereas "right" denotes an interest guaranteed as an expression of basic values", Wolchover D (2001) Silence and Guilt. An Assessment of Case Law on Criminal Justice and Public Order Act, 1974, Lions Court Lawyers, UK. On the right to silence and the privilege of self incrimination, See, Easton S M (1991) The Right to Silence, Avebury, Aldershot, England; Stone E (1998) Calling a Spade a Spade: the Embarrassing Truth about the Rights to Silence, Criminal Law Journal, Vol.22, No.1, pp. 17-35.

193 *P. v. J. Kambanda*, Judgement and Sentence, T.C, para. 51.

Additionally it is worth observing that at the pre sentencing hearing Judge Pillay had asked, in relation to the accused's possible contribution to justice, truth, and national reconciliation, whether he had made before his arrest, any public statements on the truth of the events in Rwanda.[194] To the Prosecution's knowledge no such public statements had been made.[195] Although Defence Counsel had submitted the accused was ready to undertake "constructive responsibility" for truth and national reconciliation in Rwanda, it may well be that the non-offer of a public explanation, regret or apology to victims cast a shadow of doubt on contrition and remorse. It is also probable that there was no showing of good cause for the non-explanation, especially after the voluntary acknowledgement of responsibility in the Plea Agreement. Contrition is a genuine or sincere feeling of remorse for sins or wrongful behaviour often resulting in guilt, humility, sorrow and earnest repentance; where as remorse is a deep torturing sense of guilt felt for one's actions, usually involving regret, pity, compassion and penitence.[196]

It has indeed been established that a guilty plea may also be taken as an indicator of genuine remorse, a mitigating factor, especially when accompanied by an expression of regret to the victim or responsibility of some kind.[197] In order to accept remorse as a mitigating circumstance in its determination of sentence, the Trial Chamber must be satisfied the accused expressed remorse and that the remorse is sincere.[198] In *Todorovic* during the pre sentencing hearing, the accused expressed his "profound repentance and remorse", and stated that if given a chance he would "invest every effort in the new multi-ethnic Bosnia" so that the "inter-ethnic wounds" should heal as soon as possible.[199] The Chamber accepted the accused's words and his demeanour as reflecting remorse.[200] In *Kolundzija* the Tribunal Chamber was of the opinion that the accused's benevolent attitude towards detainees at Keraterm detention Camp, and his expression of regret and remorse, for all the acts committed, which were intended to contribute to a new beginning, was sincere.[201]

On the other side in the case of Jelsicic the Chamber held that the accused had demonstrated no remorse before it for the crime committed, and accorded 'only relative weight' to his guilty plea to 31 counts of violation of the laws or customs of war and crimes against humanity.[202] The Chamber ruled that the repugnant, bestial and sadistic nature of his behaviour, the cruelty of his acts, cold-blooded

---

194 *P. v. J. Kambanda*, Pre sentencing hearing, Pre Sentencing hearing, pp. 16-18.
195 Para. 18, Id.
196 Romanowski A K (1988) pp. 56-57.
197 *R. v. Skilton* (1982) 4 Cr. App. R. (S) 339.
198 *P. v. Todorovic*, Judgement and Sentence T.C, Case no IT-95-9/1-S, 31 July 2001, paras. 89-90 and fn 90.
199 Para. 91, Id.
200 Para. 90, Id.
201 *P. v. D. Sikirica, D. Dosen and D. Kolundzija*, Sentence and Judgement T.C, Case no: IT-95-8-S, 13 November 2001, paras. 229-230.
202 *P. v. G. Jelisic*, Judgement, T.C, para 127.

commission of murders and mistreatment of people attest to a profound contempt for mankind and the right to life.[203] It sentenced him to 40 years imprisonment.

In its sentencing decision the Trial Chamber accepted that most national jurisdictions consider admissions of guilt as matters properly to be considered in mitigation of sentence, but was of the view that remorse is not the only reasonable inference that can be drawn from a guilty plea.[204] What is certain about the sentencing decision is that there was no precedent to guide it.[205] It is possible that the above may have had an indirect influence on the final determination of the sentence. The accumulated effect of all the mitigating factors raised, including the prompt guilty plea itself, would in most national jurisdictions have resulted in some sentencing discount, the gravity of the crimes and position of an accused not withstanding.[206] The effect of the decision to award the maximum punishment under the Statute and the Rules of Procedure and Evidence; that is, life imprisonment to a confessing accused no doubt created a disturbance of the sentencing equation in the guilty pleas of substantially cooperating accused before the ICTR. For Muna, though "exemplary", it dissuaded others from coming forward to plead guilty.[207] When asked to comment on the sentence by Tanzania's Daily News correspondent, Sukhdev Chhatbar, President Kama had this to say: "Don't put me in conflict with the Prosecutor. Everyone has his responsibility, and the Judges took their responsibility". Much later, commenting on the sentencing decision, Judge Pillay thought that the Prosecutor might have inadvertently put the onus on the Trial Chamber to reduce the sentence.[208] In its decision the Trial Chamber had stressed that the principle must always remain that the reduction of the penalty stemming from the application of mitigating circumstances must not in any way diminish the gravity of the offence.[209] It pointed out that the Rwandan Organic Law No.8/96 of 30 August 1996 went even further since under that law persons falling under Category I, like Kambanda, cannot benefit from a reduction of sentences even after a guilty plea.[210]

Kambanda: Appeal

Courts have supervisory responsibility to ensure that the guilty plea process is just, and a trial court ought to assure itself that the plea is not coerced.[211] In the guilty plea process the primary concern of Courts is elimination, as far as possible, the

[203] Paras. 126, 130 and 139, Id.

[204] *P. v. J. Kambanda*, Judgement, para. 51.

[205] 'The passing of sentence must be governed by reason and guided by precedent, not coloured by emotion or a desire for revenge', Bingham J (2000) p. 309.

[206] See also Combs N A (2002) pp. 25-158.

[207] Philadelphia Inquirer, 5 September 1998.

[208] Interview with Author, The Hague, 19 June 2003.

[209] *P. v. J. Kambanda*, Judgement and Sentence, para. 35.

[210] Para. 37, Id.

[211] Fitzgerald O E (1990) p. 150.

likelihood that innocent defendants will be erroneously convicted.[212] A Trial Chamber however, does not have the duty to advise the accused of the legal ingredients of the crimes or each and every element of the charge with which he is charged.[213]As concerns the Prosecution, it generally has an interest in a full and fair defence and as a litigant has an interest in ensuring that any conviction obtained is un-impeached, and that therefore not challenged on appeal.[214]

Once a trial court, which has an absolute discretion, has entertained a guilty plea it will not be lightly interfered with on appeal.[215] A guilty plea entered in open Court is presumed to have been voluntary so that the accused (appellant) must establish that his plea was wrong and that it would be unjust to uphold the plea.[216]

As submitted by Fitzgerald:

> "An accused who attempts, only on appeal, to obtain permission to withdraw faces a considerable challenge. Withdrawal may only be permitted if the accused can establish a compelling case, for example, that the accused was unrepresented by Counsel and lacked understanding of the process; or the trial judge, crown Counsel; or Defence Counsel committed an egregious error resulting in a miscarriage of justice; or the guilty plea was unsupported in law or in fact".[217]

An appellate Court, however, has the power to allow a change of plea at any stage, particularly where the accused demonstrates that he did not appreciate the nature of the charges or did not intend to admit guilt; where the accused could not in law be convicted, or where the Court feels there is some other ground for exercising its jurisdiction.[218] On appeal a heavy onus lies on the accused to establish the existence of these grounds.[219] An appeal process of the International Tribunal is not designed for the purpose of allowing the parties to remedy their own failings or oversights during trial or sentencing.[220] When the accused makes a confession of his guilt and he sticks to it throughout the trial there is no better evidence for his conviction than his own confession.[221]

Although a number of appeal notices from the judgement and sentence of the Trial Chamber had been filed earlier,[222] on 8 December 1999 the Appeal Chamber

---

212 Adelstein R P (1984) p. 54.

213 Separate Opinion of Judge Shahabuddeen, *P. v. D. Erdemovic,* Case no: IT-092-22, 5 March 1998.

214 UN HQ Press Conference, Louise Arbor, Prosecutor, New York, 5 May 1999.

215 *R. v. Gagne* (1956) 117 C.C.C. 97 (Alta, C.A.) Canada, cited in Fitzgerald O E (1990) p. 82.

216 *R. v. Hughes* (1987), 76 A.R. 294 (C.A.).

217 Fitzgerald O E (1990) p. 80.

218 P. 59.

219 Pp. 59-60.

220 *P. v D. Edermovic,* Judgement, A.C, 7 October 1997, para. 15.

221 Mitler V (1978) p. 211.

222 A number of notices of appeal had been filed subsequent to the Trial Chamber judgement and sentence. Notice of Appeal of 4 September, filed on 7 September 1998; Supplementary Notice of Appeal dated 22 September 1998 filed on 8 October 1998; Second Supplementary Notice of Appeal dated 24 November 1999.

ordered the Appellant to file one consolidated notice of appeal. In its consolidated notice of appeal, filed on 8 February 2000,[223] the appellant primarily asked the Appeal Chamber to quash the guilty verdict and order a new trial on the ground that the Trial Chamber had erred in law by not taking into consideration the denial of the right to be defended by a counsel of one's own choice; by not taking into consideration the appellant's unlawful detention outside the Detention Unit of the Tribunal; and by accepting the validity of the plea agreement without a thorough investigation that the guilty plea was voluntary, informed and unequivocal. The Appellant further asked the Appeal Chamber leave to add another sub-ground of appeal; namely, that the Trial Chamber did not satisfy itself that the guilty plea was based on sufficient facts for the crimes and the accused's participation in it, either on the basis of independent indicia or lack of any material disagreement between the parties about the facts of the case, as required by amended rule 62 (V) (a) (d) of the Tribunal's Rules of Procedure and Evidence.

In the alternative to the above grounds of appeal, Kambanda prayed for the Appeal Chamber to set aside and reverse the entire sentence on the ground that the Trial Chamber had erred in law by not observing and applying the general principle of law that a plea of guilty as a mitigating factor carries with it a discount in sentence, by not taking into account the provisions of article 23 (1) and (2) of the Tribunal's Statute and rule 101 (B) (ii) and (iii) of its Rules of Procedure and Evidence which require that mitigating circumstances, personal circumstances of the accused, substantial cooperation with the prosecutor and the general practice with regard to prison sentence in the courts of Rwanda in the determination of sentence, and in failing to pronounce and impose a separate sentence for each count in the indictment, each count being a separate charge of an offence. As further alternate grounds of appeal, the appellant submitted that the sentence of life imprisonment was excessive[224] and that the Trial Chamber had erred in law and fact in considering the non-explanation of the accused when asked whether he has anything to say before sentence as militating against any discount.

The Prosecutor objected to the Appellant's Consolidated Notice insofar as it contained a new ground of appeal, not supported by good cause, and prompted by a new Rule 62(v) (d) which had in fact come into being on 8 June 1998, well before the guilty plea, but three months after submission of the appellant notice of appeal filed on 7 September 1998.[225]In its decision on the appellant's consolidated notice of appeal, the Appeal Chamber, on 13 June 2000, ruled that the interests of

[223] *P. v. J. Kambanda* Consolidated Notice of Appeal, (Appellant), Case no: ICTR-97-23-A, 8 February 2000.

[224] "It is normal that I did not appreciate the sentence because it was based on facts which I do not appreciate", Appeal Hearing, Transcript, P. V. J. Kambanda, 27 June 2000, p. 141. Asked by Judge Shahabuddeen whether he would have been satisfied if the Trial Chamber has acceded to his Counsel's request for sentence of two years, Kambanda responded: "personally, I would have been satisfied with two years having gone scoot free, but politically no., I would not be satisfied", p. 160; "My approach was meant to enable me not to go to prison", p. 161.

[225] Prosecutor's Objection to the Appellant's Consolidated Notice of Appeal, *P. v. J. Kambanda*, Case no: ICTR-97-27-A, 1 March 2000. paras. 3, 28, 34.

justice required the hearing of the testimony of the appellant on whether the guilty plea was voluntary, informed, and unequivocal, and whether it was based on factual elements likely to establish the crimes and the participation of the accused in its commission as provided for by Rule 62, and on condition that his testimony is limited to the factual allegations of the matters before the Appeals Chambers.[226] The Appeal Chamber also ruled that facts related to the appellant's choice of Counsel, as well as alleged illegal detention were not to be pleaded before it.[227]

In its Judgement rendered on 19 October 2000, the Appeal Chamber concluded that the Appellant was represented free of charge by assigned counsel and that he had received effective representation, and that incompetence on the part of counsel for the Appellant had not been substantiated.[228] With regard to the invalidity of the guilty plea, the Appeal Chamber noted that the Appellant had several opportunities to raise any issues of fact on the basis of which he now alleges that his guilty plea was invalid, but failed to do so until after receiving a life sentence for the guilty plea. [229]It further stated that, in the absence of a satisfactory explanation of his failure to raise the validity of the guilty plea in a timely manner before the Trial Chamber, the Appellant has waived his right to later assert that his guilty plea was invalid.[230]

However as the Appeal Chamber was the venue of last resort for the Appellant who was facing life sentence on the basis of his guilty plea, the Chamber, and given the general importance of the issues raised for the work of the Tribunal, deemed it essential to consider the question of the validity of the guilty plea; namely whether it was voluntary, informed, unequivocal, and based on sufficient factual basis supporting the guilty plea.

In *Jelisic* the Appeal Chamber has this to say on appropriate sentencing;

> " [A] sentence should not be capricious or excessive, and that, in particular, it may be thought to be capricious or excessive if it is out of reasonable proportion with a line of sentences passed in similar circumstances for the same offence. Where there is such disparity, the Appeals Chamber may infer that there was disregard of the standard criteria by which sentence should be assessed, as prescribed by the Statute and set out in the Rule."[231]

In *Kambanda* the Appeal Chamber considered that there was no merit in the claim that the guilty plea was involuntary[232] If the Appellant pleaded guilty instead of going to trial in the hope of receiving a lighter sentence, he cannot claim that the plea was involuntary merely because he received a life-term after pleading guilty

---

226 Arret (Relatif a la requeste de L'appelant en Admisson de Nouveax Moyens de Preuve), *P. v. J. Kambanda*, C.A, Case no: ICTR- 97-23-A, 13 June 2000.

227 While in detention in Dodoma, Tanzania, under the custody of the ICTR, the International Committee of the Red Cross visited Kambanda.

228 *P. v. J. Kambanda*, Judgement, Case no: ICTR-97-23-A, A.C, 19 October 2000, paras. 31, 34.

229 Para. 55 Id.

230 Id.

231 *P. v. G. Jelisic*, Judgement, A.C, para. 96.

232 Para. 64, Id.

to several counts of genocide and crimes against humanity.[233] It further found out that the plea was informed, both parties having accepted that the imposition of life imprisonment was a possibility.[234] With regard to the claim that the guilty plea was equivocal, the Appeal Chamber agreed with the statement of Judge McDonald and Judge Vohra, in their Separate Opinion in the *Erdemovic* Case, that "[w]hether a plea is equivocal must depend on a consideration, *in limini*, of the question whether the plea was accompanied or qualified by words describing facts which establish a defence in law".[235] It considered that the Trial Chamber had several opportunities to question and observe the Appellant, and that it was satisfied that his guilty plea was voluntary, informed and unequivocal.[236] The Appeal dismissed the contention that there was an insufficient inquiry by the Trial Chamber of the factual basis of the guilty plea.[237] In this regard it noted that there was no disagreement between the parties as to the facts of the case or as to the Appellant's participation in the crimes alleged in the indictment and agreed to in the Plea Agreement.[238]

It its judgement the Appeal Chamber also ruled that the Statute was sufficiently liberally worded to allow for a single sentence to be imposed for multiple convictions, this being within the discretion of a Trial Chamber.[239] On the claim that the Trial Chamber erred in law in failing to properly take into account mitigating factors, the Appeal Chamber was of the view that all statutory and non statutory mitigating factors had been taken into account by the Trial Chamber, that the sentence imposed fell within the discretionary framework of that Chamber, there having been no showing that it abused that discretion.[240] It found no reason to disturb that decision.[241] The Appeal Chamber unanimously rejected the Appellant's eight grounds of appeal, and affirmed Kambanda's conviction on all six counts of the indictment and the sentence of life imprisonment imposed upon him.[242]

The guilty plea process requires effective assistance of Counsel. The Statute of the ICC is categorical on that. Article 65 (1) (b) requires that the admission of guilt be voluntary made by the accused *after* sufficient consultation with defence counsel. In *R. v. Turner* guidelines were laid down as to counsel's advice to the accused:[243]

233 Para. 63, Id.
234 Para. 76, Id.
235 Judgement, Joint Separate Opinion of Judge McDonald and Judge Vohra, *P. v. D. Erdemovic*, para. 31.
236 *P. v. J. Kambanda*, Judgement, A.C, para. 87.
237 Para. 95, Id.
238 Para. 93, Id.
239 Paras. 103, 109, 111, Id.
240 Paras. 126 & 124, Id.
241 Para. 126, Id.
242 P. 39, Disposition, Id.
243 *R. v. Turner* [1970] 2 QB 321, 54 Cr. App. Rep. 352, CA; See also *R. v. Bird* (1977) 67 Cr. App. Rep. 203; *R. v. Cullen* (1984) 81 Cr. App. Rep. 17.

(1) Counsel must give the accused the best advice he can, in strong terms if necessary, and this may include advice that a plea of guilty may attract a lesser sentence, always emphasizing that the accused must not plead guilty unless he has committed the acts constituting the offence charged;
(2) The accused, having considered that advice, must have a complete freedom of choice whether to plead guilty or not guilty.
(3) The judge should never indicate the sentence which he is minded to impose, except to say, if it be the case, that whether the accused pleads guilty or not, the sentence will or will not take a particular form (e.g. a probation order of a fine, or a custodial sentence): and the accused should be informed where any such discussion has taken place.

The responsibility of pleading guilty or not is that of the defendant himself, but it is the clear duty of defending counsel to assist the defendant to make up his mind by putting forward the pros and cons of a plea, if need be in forceful language, so as to impress on the defendant what the results of a particular course of conduct is likely to be.[244] The Defence Counsel is the sole advocate of the accused, with responsibility for making certain that the defendant understands the rights waived upon pleading guilty, and the defendant's understanding of the available pleading options and their implications.[245]

It is incumbent on Counsel to emphasize that the client should only plead guilty if he or she is guilty, and if Counsel genuinely believes that it is to the Client's advantage to plead guilty, Counsel is entitled to put that view strongly and persuasively.[246] Defense Counsel may not permit an accused to plead guilty where the accused denies his guilt.[247] The overall competency standard for entering a plea is whether the defendant has sufficient present ability to consult with his lawyer with a reasonable degree of rational understanding, and has a rational as well as factual understanding of the proceedings against him.[248]A defendant has the right to effective assistance of Counsel in deciding whether to plead, how to plead, and in entering the plea.[249] The test of ineffectiveness is whether Counsel's representation fell below an objective standard of reasonableness, and whether there is a reasonable probability that, but for Counsel's ineffectiveness, the defendant would not have pleaded guilty and would have insisted on going to trial.[250] A confession should be excluded because the defendant was denied access to legal assistance.[251]

All guilty pleas before the ICTR have not been on the basis of Defense Counsel prompting, influence, inducement or persuasion. They have solely been made by the accused on the basis of a voluntary decision, promptly made following arrest, transfer and detention or after a certain period of reflection and soul searching

[244] Archbold, Chap. 4, Arraignment, Pleas Change of Plea, paras. 4-91.
[245] Miller H S *et all.* (1978) p. xxix.
[246] Seifman R D, Freiberg A (2001) pp. 66-67.
[247] *R. v. (S.)* (1995), 99 C.C.C. (3d) 376, 24 O.R. (3d) 199, 82 O.A.C. 132 (AC).
[248] Herman G N (1997) p. 12.
[249] P. 13, Id.
[250] P. 20, Id.
[251] May R (1991) p. 370.

while at the detention facility. The role of Defense Counsel as reflected in discussions related to plea agreements has been that related to clarification of the legal elements of the crimes alleged; that of verifying the factual elements of the plea; the interpretation of those facts in the light of the circumstances prevailing at the time of the commission of the offences; an explanation to the accused of the waiver of his or her rights, the guilty plea procedure, and legal and other consequences of pleading guilty, and finally advice and strategies for sentence mitigation.

A discussion of the Kambanda guilty plea is incomplete without an examination of the guilt plea of Biljana Plavic before the ICTY. It offers interesting comparison, but sharp contrast in the discretionary faculty of the Judges of the two UN Ad hoc Tribunals as regards their appreciation of aggravating and mitigating factors in sentencing, as well the overall value of such pleas. Even though the Appeal Chamber in *Celebici* observed that as a general principle, sentence comparisons with other cases, which have already been the subject of final determination for the purpose of assessing an appropriate sentence in a specific case are often of "limited assistance",[252] and in *Jelisic* it cautioned that it was not useful to compare one case to another, unless the cases relate to the same offence committed in substantially similar circumstances,[253] it is difficult to resist a comparative inquiry into the sentencing decisions of Kambanda and Plavsic given the high positions they both occupied during the commission of atrocity crimes in Rwanda and in the Former Yugoslavia respectively, the position of trust which they both abused, and the huge disparity in sentencing following their guilty pleas. With regard to the offences they pleaded guilty to (i.e. Genocide and Crimes against Humanity for the former and persecution as Crimes against Humanity for the latter); both are grave crimes of an extreme character and offensive to mankind. In so far as persecution is concerned, the Trial Chamber in *Todorovic* held that the crime of persecution was inherently very serious, being the only crime enumerated in Article 5 of the ICTY Statute which required a discriminatory intent, and which by its nature may incorporate other crimes.[254]

In particular regard to crimes specified in the Statutes, Judge Shahabuddeen in his Partial Dissenting Opinion considered that:

> "The Statute provides no hierarchy of penalties for the various crimes which it deals, and so it would not be correct to proceed on the basis that any one crime is intended to be mechanically visited with greater punishment than another. However, in fixing the penalty for genocide, a Trial Chamber would have to pay regard to the character of the offence and in particular to the fact that it is generally considered to be "the crime of crimes". It is indeed very grave".[255]

That said the gravity of the offence is the primary consideration in imposing sentence, and the determination of the gravity of the crime requires a consideration of

---

252 *Celebici*, Judgement, A.C, Case no: IT-956-21-A, 20 February 2001, para. 717.

253 *P. v. G. Jelisic,* Judgement, A.C, para. 101.

254 *P. v. Todorovic*, Judgement and Sentence, T.C, paras. 32, 113.

255 Partial Dissenting Opinion, Judge Shahabuddeen, *P. v. G. Jelisic*, A.C, para. 26.

the particular circumstances of the case, as well as the form and degree of the participation of the accused in the crime.[256] The other consideration is that penalty is individual and must fit the individual circumstances of the accused.[257]

Plavsic had served as Serbian representative to the Presidency of the Socialist Republic of Bosnia and Herzegovina from the end of 1990 to the end of 1992, and as acting Co-President of the Serbian Republic of Bosnia and Herzegovina from 28 February to 12 May 1992. She voluntarily surrendered to the ICTY on 10 January 2001 and first pleaded not guilty to the indictment against her of the same date, during her initial appearance on 11 January 2001.[258] An amended consolidated indictment was confirmed on 23 February 2001. On 2 October 2002, the 72 years old accused, pleaded guilty to Count 3, persecution as a Crime against Humanity. The guilty plea was entered pursuant to a Plea Agreement between the Prosecutor and the accused, dated 30 September 2002, in which the Prosecutor agreed to move to dismiss the remaining counts of the consolidated Indictment following the plea of guilty by the accused.[259]

The Trial Chamber accepted that persecution as a Crime against Humanity is a crime of utmost gravity, involving as it does a campaign of ethnic separation which resulted in the death of thousands and the expulsion of thousands more in circumstances of great brutality. It also accepted that the superior position of an accused is an aggravating factor.[260] However with regard to Plavsic's position as a high ranking wartime leader of the Bosnian Serbs, and once a member of the collective and expanded Presidency of the Serbian Republic of Bosnia Herzegovina and the Republic of Srpska, she was not in the very first rank of the leadership; others occupied that position.[261] The Chamber was of the view that although she did not conceive the plan which led to the crime in question, and had a lesser role in its execution than other, nonetheless she was in the Presidency; the highest civilian body during the campaign of violence, and encouraged and supported it by her participation in the Presidency and her pronouncements.

As mitigating factors the Trial Chamber took into account her voluntary surrender, guilty plea, good character, record of no prior conviction, expression of remorse and post conflict conduct.[262] Former US Secretary of State Madeleine Albright, and Carl Bildt, the former Prime Minster of Sweden (1991-94) and Co-Chairman of the Dayton Peace Conference [which resulted in the 1995 General Framework Agreement for Peace in Bosnia and Herzegovina (Dayton Agreement) after the cessation of hostilities in Bosnia and Herzegovina] testified to the accused's positive post conflict role. The Chamber it seems accorded weight to the testimony of these witnesses of "high international reputation" jointly convened

---

[256] *Celebici* Judgement, A.C, para. 731.

[257] Para. 717, Id.

[258] See, *P. v. B. Plavsic*, Sentencing Judgement, Case no: IT-00-39 and 40/1, 27 February 2002.

[259] Decision granting Prosecutor's motion to dismiss Count 1, 2, 4,5,6,7 and 8 of the Amended Consolidated Indictment, *P. v. B. Plavsic*, 20 December 2002.

[260] *P. v. B. Plavsic*, Sentencing Judgement, para. 57.

[261] Paras. 55, 57, 68 & 127, Id.

[262] Para. 65, Id.

by the parties. One wonders why the Prosecution decided to shoot its own feet by recommending on one hand a maximum sentence of 25 years, and on the other hand calling on its behalf highly credible witnesses to reinforce the mitigating factors, especially national reconciliation, a major purpose of the very establishment of the Tribunal. That apart the Chamber also accepted Plavsic's statement in support of the motion to change plea, as well as at the sentencing hearing, as an expression of remorse to be considered as part of the mitigating factors.[263] It gave significant weight to the expression of remorse, expressed by her policy for her actions and the positive impact she made in the reconciliation process.[264]

In *Plavsic* the accused offered no cooperation to the Prosecutor. The Chamber held that cooperation with the Prosecutor is a mitigating factor, but that it does not follow that failure to do so is an aggravating factor.[265] In other words an accused's unwillingness to give evidence is not a factor to be taken into account in determining sentence.[266] In *Kambanda* the initial cooperation offered consisted of invaluable information and substantial cooperation. Assisting authorities is an enhancing discount factor, more so when it is done at personal risk.[267] That aside, in *Plavsic* the Trial Chamber accorded significant weight to the guilty plea, the expression of remorse, and positive impact on the post conflict reconciliation process, and sentenced her to 11 years imprisonment, sentence that horrified Bosnian Muslims.[268] And to compound matters, the Tribunal sent her to serve her sentence in Sweden's Kronberg Prison in Stockholm that features sauna, solarium, massage room, horse-ridding paddock, and where its wardens treated her with a birthday cake on her 73rd birthday.[269] In her case, the Prosecutor, had recommended a sentence of between 15 and 25 years, and had suggested that in the absence of a guilty plea, a sentence of imprisonment for the remainder of the life of the accused would have been appropriate.[270] The Chamber also ruled that the Prosecution had given insufficient weight to the age of the accused, and the sufficient mitigating factors concerned with her plea of guilty and post conflict conduct.[271] Neither party appealed the sentence.

Although sentencing is a matter of judicial discretion, and must be based on each accused's personal and individual circumstances, it would seem by a number of measurements, when compared to Kambanda's case, and the sentencing decisions of both Tribunals, that Plavsic, admittedly a top ranking official, reflected

263 Para. 73, Id.

264 Paras. 76 & 81, Id.

265 Para. 64, Id.

266 Para. 64, Id.

267 Samuels A (1999) The Discount for Guilty Pleas: The Judicial Principles, Justice of the Peace, vol. 163, p. 792.

268 Combs N A (2000) p. 244, fn, 851.

269 Bosnian war criminal served Birthday cake in Swedish Jail, BBC, Monitoring International Reports, 30 July 2003' Swedish jailers defend decision to treat war crimes convict to birthday cake, Associated Press, 30 July 2003; see also Combs N A (2004) p. 244.

270 *P. v. B. Plavsic*, Sentencing Judgement, paras. 59 & 128.

271 Para. 128, Id.

leniency. If anything the sentence disparity cannot be satisfactorily explained in terms of an apology and remorse by Plavsic and none by Kambanda. Plavsic's guilty plea was not only a change of plea, but a belatedly one. Although it took place before her trial began, she changed plea eight months after her initial "not guilty" plea. The accused's unwillingness to cooperate, which would have required her to reveal additional truth, and information on the participation of others high-ranking personalities that constituted the political and military leadership that planned and organized ethnic, national, and religious violence in the Balkans to an extent undermined the reconciliation process, which admittedly she is said to have very much contributed earlier to. The scant 5 pages factual basis of her guilty plea represented the briefest sketch of the atrocities that were committed and of her role in them.[272]

True Kambanda's remorse was found lacking, and his written reconciliatory overtures deemed unconvincing, he was found to have occupied a high government position, as head of the Rwandan Government during the genocide. Indeed this was so, but it should also be observed that it was a Government chosen for him, and put in place by extremist Hutu in the army and the "pawa" factions of the dominant Rwandan political parties. If the sentencing divide between the two accused is an 11 years sentence for Plavsic, and life imprisonment for Kambanda, then judicial discretion needs questioning. Kambanda's guilty plea was prompt, at the first occasion, and although holding 'high office' as Prime Minister of the Interim Government, and with certain recognized authority, he was not in the words of Rwegasore, Rwanda's former Chief Justice, "the centre of gravity of the genocide".[273] Both he and Plavsic are on the same footing for making public statements in support of the violence that engulfed their countries. Kambanda's initial cooperation led to the unearthing of the conspiracy to commit genocide involving key members of the Government, leaders of political parties, and senior Military Officers. No cooperation in unveiling the truth or in furnishing information or leads on the involvement of others in high office was offered by Plavsic.

Furthermore the Trial Chamber in *Plavsic* considered the accused's age (72 years) a mitigating factor. By comparison, at the ICTR, senior pastor Elizaphan Ntakirutumana a 78 years old Seventh Day Adventist priest, who was the head of the West Rwanda Association of that congregation based at Mugonero Complex, Gisyita Commune, Kibuya Prefecture, was sentenced to 10 years imprisonment on 21 February 2003, after being found guilty of one count each of Genocide in relation to the Mugonero and Bisesero Indictments.[274] Ntakirutimana had no high official government function, did not play any leading role in the crimes, did not personally participate in killings, and did not fire on any refugee or carry a weapon. The Chamber, however, found that by conveying individuals who attacked his Tutsi "flock" which had sought refuge at the Mugonero complex, his conduct was

272 Combs N A (2004) p. 263.

273 Interview with Author, Kigali, 11 December 2002.

274 *P. v. Elizaphan and Gerald Ntakirutimana,* Judgement and Sentence, Case no: ICTR-96-10- and ICTR-96-17-T, 21 February 2003, paras. 35-36.

dishonourable as a man of the cloth.[275] Ntakirutimana had fought his transfer from the United States to the ICTR in United States Courts, pleaded not guilty, abused the trust of his "flock", demonstrated no remorse, and made no contribution to the healing and reconciliation process. Here too the reasons for the sentencing contrast with Plavsic require further explanation. No one is suggesting a sentencing grid, since punishment must be based on the gravity of the offence and the particular circumstances of the individual accused, but it has to be perceived as fair, just, and most important uniform.[276]

Omar Serushago

Omar Serushago, born on 24 April 1961, in Rumbavu commune, Gisenyi Prefecture, and one of the former heads of the interahamwe militia in the Prefecture of Gisenyi, was indicted on 8 October 1998, with five charges; namely, genocide and crimes against humanity (murder, extermination, torture, and rape).[277] He had voluntarily given himself up to Cote d'Ivoire Police authorities in Abidjan on 9 June 1998. Serushago was transferred to Arusha on 11 July 1998 by a UN Beech-craft, which had on the same trip flown to Mali so that UN Security personnel, in the company of members of the Prosecutor's Office tracking team to take custody of Mathieu Ngurumpatse, then stopped in Abidjan, Cote d'Ivoire for Serushago, then to Lome, Togo for Edouard Karemera, and finally to Cotonue, Benin for Joseph Nzirorera, all Indictees, before flying back to Arusha.

On 29 September 1998, an indictment against him was reviewed and confirmed by Judge Yakov Ostrovsky.[278] In the indictment confirmation hearing the judge had ruled that there was insufficient basis in the indictment and supporting material to sustain the allegations that the accused had conspired with others to commit genocide, and had consequently dismissed that count.[279] On 14 December 1998 Serushago pleaded guilty before Trial Chamber I, composed of Judges Laity Kama (Presiding), Lennart Aspegren, and Navanethem Pillay, to four of the five counts with which he was charged. He pleaded not guilty to count five, pertaining to crimes against humanity (rape). On the oral request of the Prosecutor under Rules 73 and 51 of the Rules of Procedure and Evidence, the Chamber granted leave for the rape count to be withdrawn.[280] Serushago acknowledged to the Trial Chamber that his Defense Counsel and he had signed with the Prosecutor a Plea

---

275 Paras 897, 902-904, Id.

276 Cf. "A sentencing grid could well be a disaster to arrive at a fair and uniform sentencing practice", Howard P K (1994) The Death of common sense: How Law s suffocating America, Warned Books, pp. 35-36.

277 Decision on the Review of the Indictment, *P. v. O. Serushago*, Case no: ICTR- 98-38-I, 29 September 1998.

278 Id.

279 Id.

280 Decision Relating to a Plea of Guilty, *P. v. O. Serushago*, Case no: ICTR- 98-39-7, 14 December 1998.

Agreement, within which he admitted to having committed the crimes for which he was charged in the indictment and to which he pleaded guilty.[281]

Under the terms of the plea agreement, entered into between the accused and his Counsel on one hand, and the Prosecution on the other, Serushago acknowledged that he was the direct author of the murder of 4 persons, abducted at a house and killed at "*Commune rouge*", the local killing fields, in Gisenyi, and that between April and June 1994, he had acted in concert with his group of interahamwe who had killed at least 33 persons, all murdered in his presence or with his knowledge. After verifying the validity of the guilty plea, the Trial Chamber found Serushago guilty of the crime of genocide, and of crimes against humanity. In its decision the Chamber noted that there existed sufficient facts to substantiate the crimes brought against the accused in the four counts to which he had pleaded guilty, and that the participation of the accused in the commission of the crimes was established considering the absence of any disagreement between the parties on the relevant facts.[282]

At the pre sentencing hearing the Prosecutor submitted[283] as aggravating factors, first, the gravity of the offences committed, and the role of the accused as one of the interehamwe executioners in Gisenyi. Serushago had committed atrocities at the instigation or on the orders of senior political and civil administration leaders as well as military or gendarmerie commanders, without hesitation or reluctance. He had never challenged the manifestly illegal orders. His participation had included the manning of the "Corniche" roadblock assigned to him, where he and his group searched for and arrested Tutsis and moderate Hutu in order to eliminate them. During the events in Rwanda he had been given and had used a Toyota Pick up truck to carry out criminal activities, including the distribution of ammunition, in particular cartridges, to interahamwe at the various roadblocks. Secondly, the Prosecutor submitted that, Serushago had superior de facto authority over members of his group, and to whom he gave orders to search for, abduct and kill Tutsi. When he took decisions no one could contradict him. The group had followed his instructions and had executed at least 33 victims at "*Commune rouge*".

Serushago's individual and personal circumstances were reflective of the multi-facet commission of the genocide in Rwanda. He was born of a Tutsi mother and was married to one. Before April 1994 he was a moneychanger in Gisenyi. With only secondary school education he had no official status in any political party or its affiliated youth wing. His involvement in militia activities was prompted by his father, who came from Bushiru (Karago and Giciye communes), the same native area as that of the President Habyarimana. His father had been approached by MRND party leaders to solicit his son's participation in the recruitment of youth for secret interhamwe training in 1993. Seruahago thus assisted in the mobilization of youth for the training organized at Mukamira Camp in Gisenyi in 1993. At that

---

281 Joint Motion for Consideration of Plea Agreement between Omar Serushago and the Office of the Prosecutor, *P. v.O.Serushago*, Case no: ICTR-97-39-, 8 December 1998.

282 Id.

283 Prosecutor's Pre Sentencing Brief, *P. v. O.Serushago*, Case no: 98-39-, 20 January 1999.

occasion he received a rifle, an R4, with fifty cartridges from General Augustine Bizimungu, then Rwandan Armed Forces operational commander of the Gisenyi-Ruhengeri sector, in order to combat the enemy, "Inyenzi-Tutsi". In one incident, at the end of April 1994, he had given this rifle to his younger brother and body guard, who used it to kill a Tutsi who had been abducted by their interahamwe group, and brought with others from the Gisenyi military camp for execution at "*Commune rouge*" (i.e. red Commune).

As mitigating factors the Prosecutor emphasized Serushago's substantial cooperation with the Prosecutor before and after arrest, his guilty plea and remorse. Cooperation that is considered substantial includes voluntary surrender, confession or a guilty plea, genuine remorse or contrition, and stated willingness to provide evidence with probative value against other individuals for crimes falling within the jurisdiction of the Tribunal.[284] Serushago had meaningfully assisted the Prosecutor in the NAKI operation a year before his arrest. The cooperation extended by Serushago included information on his own criminal conduct, which was unknown to the Prosecution. He had also voluntarily given himself up to Cote D'Ivoire authorities in Abidjan on 9 June 1998. Serushago was not in the list of Category I suspects issued by the Prosecutor General of Rwanda under the Organic Law.

Under this law the sentence for a confession and a plea of guilty by a Category II offender prior to prosecution, is imprisonment for 7 to 11 years (Article 15 (a)), and//or a confession and a guilty plea, after prosecution, is imprisonment for 12 to 15 years (Article 16 (a)). Recognizing the Trial Chamber's absolute sentencing discretion in determining a just and appropriate sentence in the particular circumstances of each case, the Prosecutor recommended a term of imprisonment of not less than 25 years. His Defence Counsel, Mohamed Ismail, former President of the Tanganyika Law Society urged the Chamber to consider the accused's background as offering an explanation into his involvement in the crimes he had admitted. He submitted that Serushago was non political in that he did not hold any political position or aspire to hold one, that he was not a person of hierarchy, and that he did not undergo any military training, even though he was given a firearm. The Defence suggested as mitigating factors the accused's surrender to authorities, substantial cooperation, including an offer to testify against other perpetrators, the fact that the accused offered protection to a number of people, and turned a blind eye to a number of Tutsi to allow them to successfully cross the border into the Democratic Republic of Congo, that his middle age allowed rehabilitation and transformation into a useful member of society, his prompt guilty plea, and finally his expression of remorse.[285]

Taking into account several mitigating factors, notably Serushago's substantial cooperation with the Prosecutor even before his arrest, which had made it possible for the Prosecutor to organize, with success, the arrest of several high ranking in-

---

284 *P. v. D. Erdemovic*, Sentencing Judgement, Case no: IT 96-22 29 November 1998, para. 55.

285 *P. v. O. Serushago*, Pre-sentence hearing, T.C. Transcript, Case no: ICTR-39-I, T.C, 29 January 1999, pp. 21-38.

dividuals during the NAKI operation in Nairobi, in July 1997, his open and public expression of remorse, including pardon which he had sought from victims of his crimes and from all the people of Rwanda, as well as the appeal he made for national reconciliation, the Trial Chamber on 5 February 1999, sentenced him to a single term of 15 years of imprisonment. On appeal the Appeal Chamber considered that the Trial Chamber had given full consideration to all of the issues related to sentencing, taking into account the nature of the offences in question and all the elements referred to in Article 23 of the Statute and in Rule 101 of the Rules, and that the sentence imposed was within the discretionary framework of the Trial Chamber, for which, there was no reason to depart from.[286]

Georges Ruggiu

The guilty plea of Georges Ruggiu, the only non-Rwandan so far indicted by the International Criminal Tribunal for Rwanda, was a historical and non-routine event. It involved a case of a change of plea, from not guilty to a plea of guilty. George Ruggiu, born on 12 October 1957, of Belgium-Italian nationality, was a French-speaking broadcaster and journalist at RTLM. He was arrested on 23 July 1997 by Kenya Police authorities in Mombassa, as part of the NAKI operation. On 29 July 1997 he was transferred to the Tribunal's Detention Facility in Arusha, Tanzania. On 9 October 1997 Judge Lennart Aspegren confirmed the indictment against him. On 24 October 1997 at his initial appearance before Trial Chamber I, he pleaded not guilty to the two counts against him; namely, direct and public incitement to commit genocide and crimes against humanity (persecution). Following complaints from the accused of several incidents at the Detention Facility, the Prosecutor sought orders under Rule 64 of the Tribunal's Rules of Procedure and Evidence, for the modification of his conditions of detention. On 12 June 1998, the Tribunal's President authorized the Registrar to take appropriate measures to ensure the separation of the accused from other detainees. On 28 June 1999 Ruggiu sought further modification of his conditions of detention, on the grounds, interalia, of threats to his personal safety, and for which he requested to be completely separated from other detainees. On 14 July 1999 the Tribunal's acting President authorized the transfer of the accused to a separate detention facility, a "safe house", in Arusha.[287]

While in detention, on 26 April 1999, he accepted to be questioned by the Prosecutor of Bari, Italy in relation to the violation of Italians laws on arms exportation. Following a preliminary informal discussion between the accused, his Counsel, and the Prosecution, in Arusha from 27-30 June 1999, Ruggiu voluntarily accepted to be questioned on record by the Prosecutor, in the presence of his Defence Counsel. This took place from 29 July to 23 November 1999. On 11

[286] Reasons for Judgement, *P. v. O Serushago*, Case no: ICTR-98-39-A, 6 April 2000.

[287] Decision on Defence's Application for the Modification of Conditions of Detention of the Applicant, Mose E (J), P. *v. G. Ruggiu*, Case no: ICTR-32-I, 14 July 1999.

April 2000 the Defence applied for leave to change the earlier plea to guilty.[288] This followed an evolving process of lengthy and painful reflection in which the accused accepted and recognized his personal guilt in the charges brought by the Prosecutor.[289] On its part the Prosecution sought leave to amend the Indictment through the introduction of more clarity to the allegation and the two counts charged.[290]

At a hearing on 15 May 2000 the Trial Chamber granted leave for the Defence to change the plea. Courts have developed a four part balancing test to determine a change of plea before sentence; namely, (i) whether the defendant established a fair and just reason to withdraw his plea, (ii) whether he asserts his legal innocence of the charge, (iii) the length of time between the guilty plea and the motion to withdraw, and (iv) whether the Prosecutor would be prejudiced.[291] Following authorization for a change of plea, the accused pleaded guilty to the two counts set forth in the amended Indictment against him.[292] Ruggiu confirmed to the Trial Chamber that he and his Defence Counsel had signed a Plea Agreement with the Prosecutor in which he admitted having committed all the acts to which he pleaded guilty as charged.[293] Under the Plea Agreement the accused explained that he had decided to change his plea voluntarily, and that it was an informed and unequivocal one. He further informed the Trial Chamber that he had full understanding of the inherent consequences of his decision. He explained to the Chamber that his change of heart was a result of long reflection during which he became fully aware of both the consequences of and scope of the offences he committed in 1994 while in Rwanda, and that his decision was final. As is common practice, the Plea Agreement also contained a narration of facts admitted by the accused. Ruggiu acknowledged that Radio Television Libre des Mille Collines (RTLM) was one of the key instruments used by the extremist elements of the MRND (Movement Republicain National pour le Developpement) and the CDR (Coalition pour la Defence de la Republique) political parties to mobilize and incite the population to massacre the Tutsi and political opponents, mostly moderate Hutus.

From a mere spectator Ruggiu had, over a span of three years, progressively become active involved in Rwandan politics. Through his social contacts and association with Rwandans in Belgium, and later in Rwanda, he became gradually engulfed in the Rwandan quagmire. On his third trip to Rwanda, on 3 November 1993, he actively pursued a job offer to work for Radio Television Libre des Milles Collines. Prior to that, while still in Belgium, in June 1993, he had bought 2 shares in RTLM at a nominal value of 1000 Belgium francs. In early December

---

288 (Motion for Leave to Change Plea), Requete Postulant L'autorisation de changer de plaidoyer, *P v. G. Ruggiu*, 11 Avril 2000.

289 Id.

290 Prosecutor's Request for leave to file an amended indictment, *P. v. G. Ruggiu.*

291 Weaver K D (2002) A Change of Heart or A Change of Law? Withdrawing A Guilty Plea under Federal Rule of Criminal Procedure 32(e), The Journal of Criminal Law and Criminology, pp. 274-275, vol. 92/1-2, pp. 274-275.

292 *P. v. G. Ruggiu*, Amended Indictment, 2 May 2000.

293 Plea Agreement between Georges Ruggiu and the Office of the Prosecutor, *P. v. G. Ruggiu*, Case no: ICTR- 97-32-DP, 10 May 2000.

1993, while on his way on foot into Kigali town, he ran into President Habyarimana's convoy, which stopped, and he was invited by a member of the President's escort into the President's vehicle. The President inquired about his professional activities in Rwanda. Ruggui informed him about his disappointment with having received no firm job offer with RTLM. The President immediately intervened, and within a few days he received a letter of appointment. He commenced work as an announcer and journalist with RTLM on 6 January 1994 and continued in that position until 14 July 1994. He was issued a Rwandan identity card by the Kicukiro commune, Kigali, in which the entry on his ethnic origin was marked "white race".

While at RTLM, on 7 April 1994 he had read in French the official communiqué on the death of President Habyarimana. During the events of 1994, Rwandan military authorities provided him with a vehicle, a driver-bodyguard armed with an AK 47, and a 9mm pistol for personal protection. During his eloquent and virulent broadcasts over RTLM, during the period of the genocide, he had called upon members of the civilian population to be "vigilant", that "inyenzi-inkotanyi" infiltrators would be identified, and that it was the business of the population to prevent infiltration. He had congratulated the interahamwe and the gendarmes who were engaged in the combat against the "Inyenzi". In broadcasts over that radio he, like other RTLM kinyarwanda speaking journalists, employed the term "Inyenzi"; a term then understood by the population not only in its literal sense (i.e. cockroach), but in the socio political context of Rwanda, which meant the RFP and the Tusti.

The widespread use of that term conferred the de facto sense of persons to be killed. Its use was discriminatory to the Tutsi population, because it meant singling them out for extermination. In that context the term was derogatory, widely used to dehumanize Tutsi, and to incite violence against them.

Ruggiu also admitted to having urged the population, including interahamwe manning roadblocks, on several occasions, to "work"; an expression that also came to mean "kill" the Tutsi and Hutu political opponents. The word "work" (in kinyarwanda, "gukora)" was used by Hutu extremists to signify to "kill". Ruggiu had also called upon the population, particularly the military and the interahamwe militia, to finish off the 1959 revolution. It is also worth noting that Ruggui's incendiary broadcasts over RTLM were also targeted against the Belgium Government, Belgians, and UNAMIR's Belgium contingent.[294] He waged a media war against Belgians.[295] In some of the broadcasts he directly imputed the responsibility for President Habyarimana's death to Belgium. Ruggio was listed as No 92 in the updated list of Category I suspects issued by the Prosecutor General of Rwanda.[296]

---

294 See also, Braekman C (1994) pp. 165-168.

295 *P. v. G. Ruggiu,* Judgement and Sentence, para. 44.

296 Publication of the Updated List of the first category prescribed by Article 9 of the Organic law no 8/96 of 30 August 1996 (O.G. no.17 of 1/9/1966), Official Gazette of the Republic of Rwanda, 31 December 1999.

On 1 June 2000 the Trial Chamber sentenced Ruggui to 12 years of imprisonment, for each of the two counts charged, the sentences to be served concurrently. The accused did not appeal against sentence. In reaching its decision the Chamber considered as aggravating factors the inherent gravity of the offences committed and the 'critical' role played by the accused in the incitement of ethnic hatred and violence, which RTLM vigorously pursued. It held as mitigating factors 9 attendant circumstances, namely, the accused's guilty plea, his substantial cooperation with the Prosecutor, the absence of any previous criminal record, his generally good character imbued with ideals before he became involved in the events in Rwanda, his offer of regret and remorse, the assistance he offered to several victims in 1994, his subordinate position within RTLM, and the fact that he did not personally commit any acts of violence nor did he use the pistol given to him. In the words of the Trial Chamber, he did not strike a blow or fire a shot.[297] Ruggiu's guilty plea, as opposed to that of Kambanda, contained a feeling of overwhelming and ensuring sense of regret and remorse, which the Trial Chamber accepted as a significant change in the accused's attitude towards victims of the Rwandan genocide and crimes against humanity.[298] Acknowledgement of mistakes and crimes is a healthy application of reason and sentiment, which illustrates the beginning of repentance.[299]

Vincent Rutaganira

The fourth and latest accused to plead guilty before the ICTR was Rutaganira, the Counsellor of Mubuga sector, Gishyita commune, Kibuye Prefecture. He had voluntarily surrendered to the ICTR early 2002. Rutaganira confessed for having between 14-17 April 1994 or thereabouts aided or abetted by omission the attacks at Mubuga Church (Gishyita) that resulted in thousands of deaths and numerous injured within the church. Following a plea agreement between the Prosecutor and him and his Counsel, dated 7 December 2004, he agreed to plead guilty to one count of crimes against humanity (extermination). In return the Prosecutor sought leave to withdraw a number of charges that had been levied against him in an amended indictment that had been issued on 6 May 1996. This included genocide, conspiracy to commit genocide, crimes against humanity (murder, other inhuman acts) and violations against common Article 3 of the four Geneva Conventions and Additional Protocol II. On 14 March 2005 the Trial Chamber sentenced him to a term of 6 years imprisonment. It considered as mitigating factors his guilty plea, voluntary surrender; good conduct in detention, ill health and his age (60 years). At this stage it is too early to predict the impact of this guilty plea given the accused's low ranking status. Moreover, it is not certain that the sentence imposed reflects a real change of heart in the Tribunal's attitude towards punishment, since those imposed under Rwandan Law though not binding are a point of reference.

---

297 *P. v.G. Ruggiu*, Judgement and Sentence, para.77.

298 Paras. 69-72, Id.

299 Para. 55, Id.

East Timor

P. v. Joao Franca da Silva, alias Johni Franca[300] represents the most significant guilty plea case involving crimes against humanity committed in East Timor in 1999. Jhoni Franca, Commander of the *Kaer Metin Merah Putih* in Lolotoe, Bobonaro, East Timor was arrested on 5 February 2001, and indicted with four other accused, including an Indonesian army officer (the *Dandramil*) (i.e. the Sub-District Military Commander) on 6 February 2001.[301] Pursuant to an amended indictment filed on 25 May 2001, the accused was charged with 8 counts of crimes against humanity offences committed between May and September 1999, under UNTAET Regulation 2000/15; namely, four counts of imprisonment or other severe deprivation of physical liberty in violation of fundamental rules of international under Section 5.1; torture under Section 5.1 (f); two counts for other inhuman acts of similar character intentionally causing great suffering or serious injury to the body or mental or physical health under Section 5 (k); and persecution of pro independence supporters in Lolotoe Sub-District, Bobonaro District, East Timor. These charges imputed both direct individual criminal responsibility, as well as superior responsibility for the acts of his subordinates in violation of Sections 14.2, 14.3 (a) to (c), and 16 of UNTAET Regulation 2000/15.

Trial before the Special Panel for Serious Crimes of the Dili District Court commenced on 5 March 2002. The Panel heard the Prosecutor's opening statement, and subsequently the testimony of 3 witnesses in April and in May 2002, following a number of incidents of trial rescheduling. On 21 October 2002 Jhoni Franca changed his plea, and pleaded guilty to the four charges of imprisonment or other forms of severe deprivation of physical liberty of fundamental rules of international law, and torture, as crimes against humanity. On 22 October the Special Panel, after verifying the validity of his guilty plea in the light of Section 29A of UNTAET Regulation 2000/30, convicted Franca on the five charges of the indictment. With the consent of the Panel, the Public Prosecutor withdrew the remaining three counts relating to other inhuman acts and persecution. The Panel also decided to sever the case from that of the other co-accused. Pursuant to Section 29A of UNTAET Regulation 2000/30, the Special Panel sought to verify the validity of the guilty plea by asking the accused, (a) if he understood the nature and the consequences of the admission of guilt; (b) if his guilty plea was voluntarily made, and if he did it freely and knowingly without pressure or promises; (c) if his guilty plea could not be refuted by any line of defence; and (d) if he had consulted with his legal representative regarding his guilty plea. The Panel after considering the above, including the accused admission of the contents of the indictment and the materials submitted to the Court, found that all the essential facts required proving the crimes to which the admission of guilt relates had been established.

---

300 *P. v. J. Franca da Silva alias Jhoni Franca*, Judgement, SPSC, Dili District Court, Case no: 04a/2001, 5 December 2002.

301 *P. v. Joao Franca da Silva alias Jhoni Franca.*, Indictment, SPSC, Dili District Court, Case no: BO-6-99-SC.

The Transitional Rules of Criminal Procedure in East Timor require the Prosecutor as a statutory obligation to deposit with the Court the statements of witnesses made before investigators. The Panel in its consideration of the guilty plea thus relied on the accused's admissions in open court, the testimony of the 3 witnesses who appeared and the statements of witnesses, both for the prosecution and the defence. Based on prior agreement the Prosecution and the Defence mutually proposed that the accused be given a penalty of 7 years imprisonment.[302]
With regard to sentencing, the Panel considered as mitigating factors the accused guilty plea, his substantial cooperation with the Court by freely admitting to his participation in the crimes, no previous conviction, the fact that he lived in a coerced environment in which there was pressure and solicitation from the regime in power for the accused to join the militia[303], his young age and amenability to integration into society, and his public expression of remorse. He has asked for forgiveness, said that he was sorry, apologized to the victims for his acts, to all other victims of the events that occurred in 1999, and to the people of Lolotoe.[304] As aggravating factors the Special Panel, considered the defenseless status of the victims, and the accused's role as the decision-maker, a superior, and an authority during the commission of the crimes.[305] Taking all these into account the Pane, on 5 December 2002, sentenced him under Section 10.1 of UNTAET Regulation 2000/15 and Article 64 (1) of the Penal Code of Indonesia, to 5 years imprisonment.

Conclusion

The law and practice of the UN ad hoc Tribunals confirms the acceptance of guilty pleas as a tool for accountability. Its case disposal and judicial saving advantages as well as truth telling function have now been acknowledged. What has recently been stressed is the need to, (a) ensure a more transparent guilt plea process, (b) involve victims, (c) present complete factual information on the accused involvement in the alleged crimes rather than an arbitrary selection from the context of a larger criminal plan.[306] Judge McDonald former ICTY President has also urged that the guilty pleas should not short-circuit the establishment of a historical record of what transpired, and that victims and witnesses should be able to confront the perpetrators through that process.[307]

---

302 *P. v. J. Franca da Silva* Judgement, para. 141.

303 Para 146, Id.; Cf. "The fact that some joined while others were able to resist, does not mean that there was no coercive environment", para 146.

304 Para. 147, Id.

305 Para. 151-152, Id.

306 *P. v. M. Deronjic*, Dissenting Opinion of Judge W. Schomburg, Case no: IT-02-61-S, 30 March 2004, para. 4.

307 McDonald G K (2003) Assessing the Impact of the ICTY p 25-27 in Ratner S R et al. 2003 International War Crimes Trials: Making a Difference? Proceedings of an Interna-

As of 31 December 2004 four accused out of over 80 Indicted have pleaded guilty before the ICTR. At the ICTY 17 had done so during the first ten years of its mandate. The legal requirements for a valid guilty plea have also been clearly spelled out in Rule 62 of the Tribunal's Rules of Procedure and Evidence, as well as in the jurisprudence of the Ad hoc Tribunals. It is a statutory requirement that the guilty plea be voluntary, informed, unequivocal, and that there is sufficient factual basis for the crime and the accused's participation in it, either on the basis of independent indicia or on lack of any material disagreement between the parties about the facts of the case.

The chapter drew attention to the controversy that lie behind the plea bargaining process in United States, where the guilty plea process is an institutionalized procedure, and where the guilty plea is more frequent and fundamental to trials, almost to the ratio of 9 guilty pleas to 1 trial. Plea bargaining, strictly speaking, as used in that system is not a "copy cat" of that adhered to by the UN Ad hoc Tribunals. The Tribunal's practice has avoided thus far many of the abuses associated with the American plea-bargaining.[308] In order to ensure the transparency and integrity of the judicial process involving guilty pleas, to avoid unethical deals, and to assist the Trial Chamber in its determination of facts and issues before it, a Plea Agreement procedure, Rule 62 *ter*, has been incorporated in the ICTY Rules. This has helped ensure that there is no "hole and corner" bargaining.[309] Guilty pleas before the Tribunals have not been on Defence Counsel prompting or suggestion, but rather at the accused's own volition, as per the plea agreements, the application of Rules, and the Trial Chambers appreciation of the guilty plea before it.

The chapter reviewed in detail the guilty plea of Jean Kambanda, the former Prime Minister of Rwanda in 1994, the first former Head of Government to have pleaded guilty to genocide and crimes against humanity before an international Tribunal. His plea constituted a public acknowledgement that genocide did take place in Rwanda, and that the Government in place had a significant role. It throws in disarray revisionist arguments that the atrocity crimes committed were not planned but spontaneous. It "punched a hole" in that submission.[310] While his admission of guilt was welcomed by most, the sentence imposed upon him, life imprisonment, the maximum penalty the Tribunal can impose on an accused, remains a divided issue.

The Trial Chamber departed from the conventional wisdom of allocating a sentence discount for the guilty plea, on the basis that the crimes committed by the accused carry an intrinsic gravity and were particularly shocking to the human conscience, that he had committed them knowingly and with premeditation, and that as Prime Minster of Rwanda he was entrusted with the duty and authority to protect the population, and he abused this trust. As regards remorse, which must

tional Conference at the University of Texas School of Law, Austin, Texas, November 6-7, 2003.

308 Combs N A (2002) p. 147.

309 McDermond, J.A, *P. v. Wood*, 2 W.W.R. 135 (Alta, C.A), (1976).

310 Former Rwanda Prime Minister admits to genocide, The Electronic Telegraph, 2 May 1998.

have influenced the sentencing outcome, the Chamber observed that it was not the only reasonable inference that can be drawn from a guilty plea.[311] It noted that he had offered no explanation for his voluntary participation in the genocide, nor expressed contrition, regret or sympathy for the victims in Rwanda, even when given an opportunity to do so by the Chamber.[312] It is probable that his non-regret may have cost him a reduction below the maximum sentence. One may also suggest that this question was also a matter that occupied the mind of the Appeal Chamber in its deliberation, and final decision, which affirmed the sentencing decision of the Trial Chamber.

That as it may be, the Kambanda sentencing decision for a significant period did put a hand-break on guilty pleas at the ICTR. It has been suggested however that high-level defendants at the ICTR are so convinced of their innocence, so ideologically committed to their characterization of the Rwandan conflict, and so concerned about their role in the history books that virtually no sentence reduction will persuade them to plead guilty.[313] The recent guilty plea of Vincent Rutaganira may be an indication of a changing situation, although in terms of profiling he is of the lower ranks. In the context of the Tribunal's Completion Strategy future guilty pleas, if any, will confirm whether as a judicial process it is being fully subscribed to. As we have plainly indicated guilty pleas at the ICTY have been actively pursued by the prosecution, and have become a fully fledged judicial phenomenon. Such pleas have been greatly facilitated by pull factors, in particular the significant charging and sentencing concessions agreed to and offered by the Office of the Prosecutor "in exchange" for the admission of guilt and full disclosure of incriminating facts. Often it has been accompanied by substantial cooperation.

In addition a more accommodating or lenient sentencing attitude by the Trial Chambers has increased their attractiveness, even though the Judges have of recent exercised their judicial discretion to impose sentence higher than the range of sentence recommended by the Prosecutor in the plea agreements. That a light sentence had been issued, in one case, is reflected Judge Patrick Robinson's Separate Opinion in the Sentencing Judgement in *Banovic*[314]. She opined that in all the circumstances of that case, of a guilty plea, including aggravating and mitigating circumstances, the criminality of the accused, involving as it did 5 murders relating to the beating of 5 persons, and the beatings of 27 others, warrants a longer term of imprisonment than 8 years.[315] *In Nikolic* the Trial Chamber rejected the Prosecutor's recommendation of a 15-20 years sentence and instead imposed a term of 27 years.[316] In another guilty plea, that of Milan Babic the Trial Chamber sentenced him to a term of 13 years imprisonment instead 11 years, which they con-

---

311 *P. v. J. Kambanda*, Judgment and Sentence, para. 52.

312 Para. 51, Id.

313 Combs N A (2005) Procuring Guilty Pleas, *Draft*, forthcoming publication.

314 *P. v. P. Banovic*, Sentencing Judgement, Separate Opinion, Judge P. Robinson, Case no_ IT-02-65/1-S, 28 October 2003; Plea Deals being Used to Clear Balkan War Tribunal's Docket, New York Times, 18 November 2003.

315 Id.

316 *P. v. M. Nokilic*, Sentencing Judgement, T.C, para 183.

sidered, would not do justice.[317] In another case, that of Deronjic where the Trial Chamber exactly followed the Prosecutor's recommendation and imposed a 10 years sentence, one of its judges, Wolfgang Schomburg considered it inadequate, and opined that such a high-ranking perpetrator deserved a sentence of not less that 25 years imprisonment.[318]

From the perspective of a Prosecutor, guilty pleas from cooperating accused when fully exploited offer enormous evidential value. Rule 101 (B) (ii) recognizes an accused's substantial cooperation with the Prosecutor as a statutory mitigating factor. However, it should be underlined that what constitutes "substantial cooperation" is not defined in the Rules, and whether the cooperation should be considered substantial and therefore whether it constitutes a mitigating factor is for the Trial Chamber to determine.[319] This chapter has discussed Serushago and Ruggui's guilty pleas as an acceptable illustration of the evidential value added of the guilty plea. The former contributed in an effective way to the Prosecutor's sting arrest operation, NAKI, in Nairobi in July 1997, which led to the arrest of more than a handful of suspects alleged to have had leadership roles in the Rwandan atrocity crimes. In addition, he has also appeared as a prosecution witness before the Tribunal. The latter, as a radio broadcaster and journalist, provided inside information, editorial policies and the corridors of authority at RTLM, the most vocal instrument of the Rwandan genocide. He too has appeared as a Prosecution witness. In contrast, while Kambanda's earlier substantial cooperation contributed to the reinforcement of the Prosecutor's conspiracy theory, the evidential value of his statement has not been judicially tested. It is possible that he is torn between two worlds. On one hand to stand by his 90-hour tape recorded statement which he asserted on Appeal he stood by, and on the other, his reluctance for anyone to get credit for his testimony, including the disappointment of a stiff sentence. If he does eventually appear, and is cross-examined, it sure will be a confrontation for the truth behind the atrocity crimes committed in Rwanda in 1994.

---

317 *P. v. M. Babic*, Sentencing Judgement, Case no: It-03-72-S, 29 June 2004, paras. 101-102.

318 *P. v. D. Deronjic*, Dissenting Opinion of Judge Schomburg, Case no: It-02-61-S, 30 March 2004, paras. 2, 9.

319 *P. v. G. Jelisic*, Judgement, A.C, paras. 124, 126.

Chapter 9
Conclusion

Accountability Matrix

The preceding chapters reviewed the arrangements for accountability in Rwanda and East Timor. They provided a comparative examination of judicial responses to the commission of atrocity crimes. Accountability requires a balance, on the one hand, between the obligation of the international community to punish and prevent genocide, crimes against humanity, and war crimes; crimes that shock its conscience and rupture its order, and on the other hand, the basic responsibility of national jurisdictions to effectively deal with such crimes. The impunity gap for atrocity crimes can only be narrowed down and contained by cooperation between International Criminal Courts or Tribunals and states and between states. It cannot be shortened by competition, exclusive or unilateral arrangements. Complementary measures represent the best chances for effective accountability.

The earlier chapters closely detailed the various attempts at profiling perpetrators, with an assent on those with the greatest responsibility, the top target group of international and 'mixed' Criminal Tribunals. Given the predictable involvement of other categories of perpetrators, this book also looked at the legal and policy issues surrounding the accountability of intermediate and low-level perpetrators. Such persons form the backbone of criminality. Often they are numerically more pronounced, and within the radius of national, rather than international, accountability. In reviewing the accountability processes at the International Criminal Tribunal for Rwanda and in East Timor, an inquiry was made on the investigative and prosecutorial approaches and solutions adopted. As the author has pointed out some of these solutions were inconsistent, others infinite, yet others offered the only unique by-pass for effective accountability. The book also gave due attention to legal and policy issues related to conspiracy to commit genocide, the ICTR's arch prosecution strategy for the prosecution of the "big" and "medium fish", alleged to have planned, masterminded and fuelled the genocide in Rwanda in 1994. Two other key subjects were dealt with in the book, namely, superior responsibility and the guilty plea not only as judicial processes, but also as valuable instruments of accountability.

The entry point for commencement of accountability for atrocity crimes is an analysis of the pattern of violence. This involves a review of historical, political and socio-economic developments, including census data that has a bearing on the events or situation. This facilitates an interpretation of the violence, and of all associated factors, including the crimes committed. It also assists in grasping the policies or plans, be they of a Government, an entity, or organization that lay behind the orchestration of such egregious crimes. In the Rwandan context, for example, appreciating how the 'enemy' was defined and identified, tracing the development of ethnic hatred and incitement to violence through the media and the public discourse of political and civil administrators, and the mounting extremist Hutu opposition to the Arusha Peace Agreement are all factors that contributed to the design of the prosecution strategy and investigation focus. As regards East Timor, the 5 May 1999 arrangements for the popular consultation and the resulting events, especially pre and post ballot violence were capital to the designation of the early investigation priorities, and the timeframe it should cover.

Atrocity crimes invariably involve a unique triggering event, or a series of connected events spread over a period of time. In the case of atrocity crimes committed in Rwanda, it is acknowledged that the shooting down of President Habyarimana's plane, which took his life as well as that of the President of Burundi and others, on 6 April 1994, was the most immediate criminal act that sparked the violence. The non-investigation of this incident by the United Nations and the ICTR seriously undermines the revelation of part of the truth about the genocide. It is argued that such an investigation is within the mandate and temporal jurisdiction of the Tribunal, and can be handled as a project based once-off investigation with the technical assistance of UN specialized agencies or independent experts. If for U.S.A. September 11th, 2001 constituted an act of war, the shooting down of President Habyarimana's plane also falls within the same radius. To lay hands off is to accept that the crime should remain both unresolved and unanswered. It is also to reject its direct relevance to the "crimes of crimes", genocide that ensued. Accountability for atrocity crimes requires pre-situational investigations, their time-frame to be determined on the basis of a triggering incident, events or situation, whether immediate, past, or historical. *Matrix A* provides a diagnostic listing of points of inquiry for the design of investigations and their prioritization in the case of atrocity crimes.

Persons who bear prime responsibility for the committing serious Human Rights and International Humanitarian Law violations should face justice. *Accountability requires the investigation and prosecution of all parties involved, without distinction as to rank, status, position or political, ethnic, religious affiliation or the conflict divide.* We have noted that from the Security Council's designation in the first half of the 1990s, of the UN ad hoc Tribunals as the authoritative and dominant forum of accountability, the new international criminal order ushered in by the ICC establishes that institution as complementary to national criminal jurisdictions. It confers the first option for accountability to those jurisdictions. It further contains a built in mechanism for it to complement any shortfall in accountability due to a state's "unwillingness" or "inability" to genuinely investigate and prosecute alleged perpetrators. With respect to atrocity crimes allegedly committed by Rwandan Patriotic Army (RPA) soldiers, accountability is a pending, but resolvable affair between the ICTR and the Rwandan Government, which equally has an obligation to investigate those crimes and prosecute those allegedly involved.

Atrocity crimes allegedly committed by RPA soldiers *ought* to or *should* be accounted for through the ICTR. They fall within its jurisdiction. That Tribunal cannot be perceived to be selective in the choice of perpetrators-much as genocide is the "crime of crimes". As a measure of fulfilling its mandate the ICTR must investigate and prosecute. However that is by far the equivalent of imposing that accountability *must* end up at that Tribunal. Given the mindset of the emerging international criminal order, Rwanda should be given the first option, but one that should be subject to stringent oversight requirements and a tabulated yardstick monitored by the Prosecutor. Here the ICC Statute can serve as a guide. Such an option, if agreed to, should (a) focus on those at authority or command level, (b) be exercised within a realistic timeframe, (c) conducted diligently, and according to international standard of justice, (d) subjected to monitoring and informed observation, and (e) demonstratively realized well before the end of the Tribunal's Completion Strategy (i.e. 2010). It being understood that the ICTR's primacy of jurisdiction over national courts of Rwanda, or that of all other states remains intact, and its accountability responsibility to pursue its investigation of RPA soldiers, inside or outside Rwanda, unreservedly continue. This requires that it pursues those investigations will full vigour, and all states, including those in the Great Lakes Region are obliged to fully cooperate within.

A key question for any accountability process is whether the mandate of a given international or mixed tribunal is *full* accountability or a limited and highly selective one. In the case of the ICTY and ICTR, it was recognized on their establishment that they could only realistically deal with a relatively smaller number of accused than those to be handled by the affected states. That the Tribunals should essentially concentrate on the organizers, planners, and leaders responsible for atrocity crimes. This approach has been endorsed by the Security Council in its consideration of the Completion Strategies of the Tribunals, which require them to prosecute the most senior leaders suspected of being most responsible for crimes within their respective jurisdictions, and the transfer of intermediate and lower-level accused to competent national jurisdictions.[1] If we were to rewind the clock, the current list of indictees before the ICTR include a number of accused who are best suited for national, rather than international, accountability. The Tribunal was the fate for some only because of its initial strategy of localized massacre site investigations. It was not the result of an emphatic pursuit of those at the highest level of leadership responsibility. Achieving the appropriate level of responsibility that satisfies international accountability is a by-product of the profiling of perpetrators.

1 Statement of the President of the Security Council, UN Doc.S/PRST/2002/21, 23 July 2002; UN SC res. 1503 (2003), UN Doc. S/RES/1503 (2003), 28 August 2003; See also Rule 28 A, ICTY Rules of Procedure and Evidence.

The model of accountability adopted by the United Nations Security Council for atrocity crimes committed in East Timor in 1999 is cushioned on a dual track: in East Timor and Indonesia. Both venues have their own institutional frameworks and pursue accountability on the basis of independent set of goals. Although it was intended that they would cooperate, this has so far been one directional. East Timor providing assistance to the Office of the Attorney General of Indonesia; but with receiving no reciprocal cooperation in return. In East Timor the specificity of accountability is that it is dispensed through a 'hybrid' or 'mixed' Court arrangement that is an integral part of the national system of administration of justice. It is not long distant, as that of the ICTR or the ICTY, respectively based in Arusha or The Hague. Special Panels for Serious Crimes (SPSC) within the Dili District Court have exclusive jurisdiction over atrocity crimes. These are composed of both international and East Timorese Judges in the Trial and Appeal Chambers, the former constituting the majority. In Indonesia accountability is through a specially promulgated Ad hoc Human Rights Court, within the North Jakarta District Court, composed of career and non-career Judges.

Accountability by Indonesia for the East Timor atrocity crimes has been expressive of an intention to shield perpetrators, especially members of the Indonesian Armed Forces. The enabling law, the Presidential Decree on the Formation of Ad hoc Tribunal for Human Rights Violations in East Timor, first promulgated by President Abudurrahman Wahid on 23 April 2001, and amended by President Megawati Soekarnoputri on 1 August 2001, have personal, temporal and territorial jurisdictional limitations; the investigation process non comprehensive; the Indictments proffered by the Attorney General's Office weak in the articulation of facts and allegation of criminal responsibility, and even worse the prosecutions have not been diligent. They were not conducted with earnestness or vigour. No account was taken of the public interest of victims in East Timor. In terms of the requirements of accountability, the above deliberate lacuna is tangible evidence of genuine "*unwillingness*" or "*inability*" to take accountable action; one whose correction necessitates the imposition of an authoritative and mandatory response by the Security Council. As we have said, the international criminal order envisaged under the ICC is one that emphasizes the prime responsibility of national jurisdictions for the investigation and prosecution of atrocity crimes. Accountability by the ICC is complementary to that of signatory states. It overtakes that process only in the case of an "*unwillingness*" or "*inability*", genuinely by the concerned state to account. Although accountability by Indonesia, for the East Timor atrocity crimes is not under the ICC framework, it has offered a valuable dress rehearsal; one that would surely have warranted an assumption of accountability by that Court.

A major hurdle of accountability for atrocity crimes, when national, is the capacity to cope with an astronomical number of alleged perpetrators. *Full* accountability, as that desired by East Timorese, required the judicial processing of all categories of perpetrators (i.e. the "big, medium, or small, fish") with priority to the first two groups. In both East Timor and Rwanda, this proved to be a gigantic, if not an insurmountable task. Rwanda's approach, a categorization of perpetrators into four categories of suspects that takes into account the level of responsibility (national, prefectoral, communal, and sectoral) and the nature of the offence committed, is meant to ensure accountability for the societal or 'mass' character of the 1994 atrocity crimes. In East Timor, where perpetration was more by identifiable rank and file pro-integration militia, the approach was to use prosecutorial discretion in the charging decision; to indict those at lower level under the Penal Code of Indonesia rather that with Crimes against humanity. The criteria used included an appreciation of the leadership and command level of the suspect; whether the criminal conduct constituted a single offence or a series of criminal offences committed over a significant period of time, taking into account the jurisdiction (pre and post ballot) of the Special Panel for Serious Crimes; whether the suspect acted alone or in concert with others non-arrested persons; the inherent gravity of the offence and conduct of the perpetrator; the notoriety of the conduct of the suspect; the sufficiency of evidence for immediate trial; prolonged pre trial detention, and cooperation with the Prosecution.

In the discussion on the main targets of accountability for atrocity crimes, this book has noted that various terminologies have been employed to designate those that should be held judicially answerable by international or 'mixed' judicial instances. These persons have been referred to as masterminds, arch criminals, ringleaders, and high-ranking or top leaders. As discussed earlier, the UN Secretary General's preference in the case of Sierra Leone for the use of the term "most responsible" was overruled by the Security Council, which preferred the appellation those with the "greatest responsibility". It is the author's submission that this is more a question of emphasis rather than substance. Both terms are explanative, not juridical. In the final analyses they encompass the same notion; namely a highly select number of individuals in high positions of authority, command or leadership.

Profiling perpetrators, that is, determining through indicators and markers the category, class or individual levels of responsibility for the accountability of atrocity crimes, inevitably involves an analyses of the evidence, multi-facet interpretation of facts, examination of the policy or plans behind the crimes, an inquiry into the authority, command and control wielded, and an ascending, if not vertical, allocation of responsibility, de facto or de jure. Some of the specific profiling criteria so far developed include the classification of suspects into four categories adopted by Rwandan authorities; the 'list of names' adopted by Indonesia for those suspected of having committed serious human rights and International Humanitarian Law violations in East Timor, and of late, the 'deck of 55 cards' featuring 52 most wanted Iraqi leaders of the past regime, issued by the United States Armed Forces, following War in Iraq.

Matrix B provides a three dimensional scheme aimed at profiling perpetrators. It incorporates five measurements; namely (a) function, position or status, whether official or non-official, (b) agency, organization, or entity, (c) governance level, (d) role, and (e) the gravity of the crimes. It must be stressed that each situation engulfed by atrocity crimes has its own characteristics. Even with that caveat, the matrix proposed should be of assistance in prosecutorial decision making, devising the appropriate strategies and investigation plans, and determining the level of responsibility to be held accountable. It is worth emphasizing that international accountability is more limited, and requires high selectivity in the choice of targets for investigation and prosecution, than is domestic accountability. National accountability may require, as we saw in the case of East Timor and Rwanda, *full* accountability. This is not the case for international accountability. The unfortunate fact is that policy makers know about this, but not those victimized by such atrocious crimes.

In the analysis of accountability for crimes committed in Rwanda in 1994, the book detailed in Chapter 6 the prosecutorial policy as well as the law of conspiracy to commit genocide. Defined as 'an agreement between two or more persons to commit the crime of genocide', conspiracy does not require an overt act to constitute an offence. In its greater part the law of conspiracy is a child of the common law of conspiracy. The three elements of that offence are, (a) an agreement, (b) at least two or more persons by whom agreement is effected, and (c) a common object or design. Much as an overt act is not a legal requirement, it is indispensable for the Prosecution to rely on overt acts in order to reinforce proof of common object, knowledge, planning, concerted action or conduct, and inference of the conspiracy, a crime that is often nurtured in secrecy. Overt acts provide the evidential building blocks to prove the conspiracy. Conspiracy is a matter of deduction and inference. This can be drawn from evidence, including circumstantial. It can be deciphered from a given set of circumstances, and joint consort in meetings, common discourse, joint participation or co-perpetration; all acts that are important to signify mutual consent to the agreement.

Conspiracy to commit genocide does not merge into the substantive crime of genocide. They are distinct. That is the import of Article III (b) and III (c) of the Genocide Convention, the verbatim expression of which is Article 2(3) (a) and 2(3) (b) of the ICTR Statute. Thus the cumulative charging of both is permissible, and desirable for accountability in the case of atrocity crimes. This has been affirmed by the practice of the ICTR. A lesson on conspiracy to commit genocide and genocide derived from the ICTR's accountability process is that a full accounting of the genocide in Rwanda requires the charging of both offences. Conspiracy to commit genocide is an ideal crime for unveiling who its architects were, in explaining the conceptual framework within which genocide, and its main feature, "societal" participation, was committed in Rwanda in 1994.

A genocide verdict, in the case of the existence of a conspiracy, hardly offers a comprehensible explanation of the totality of acts imputable for the conspiracy and the substantive offence. The consummated crime of genocide may be based only on accomplished acts, not necessarily on the agreement to commit genocide. For the Rwandan atrocity crimes, the core, national, or other conspiracies were much wider than the individual set of crimes an accused, who was a party to one of the conspiracies, may have committed in his or her own prefecture, sector, commune or cell. Moreover an accused if convicted for both, suffers little prejudice, since during trial reliance is placed on evidence of overt acts to prove both the conspiracy and the genocide. In the Rwandan context the importance of convictions in its judicial and restorative meaning is not that genocide was committed by a certain accused; but the whole process, in which the accused together with others conceived, prepared, planned, organized, and finally oversaw the execution of the genocidal plan to exterminate Tutsi and kill moderate Hutu. This is hardly explained by the myopic conviction only of genocide, when there is also sufficient evidence to render a guilty verdict on conspiracy to commit it. In fact this undermines the truth and restorative function of justice, and its facilitation of the national reconciliation process.

Accountability before the ICTR constitutes the most extensive use of the crime of conspiracy before an International Criminal Tribunal, the Nuremberg and Tokyo Tribunals included. It has been the Prosecutor's investigative premise, since May 1997, that the genocide in Rwanda was a wholly consummated conspiracy. The line of investigation pursued was anchored on the presumption that the crimes were the result of prior planning and coordinated and concerted action involving high ranking Government authorities, senior military commanders, leaders of political parties, senior civil administrators, members of the media, and elements of civil society. Charging accused persons with conspiracy to commit genocide and genocide also legitimatised joint trials at the ICTR. This led to the joint trials of between 3 and 6 accused in the Cyangugu, Butare, Media, Military I, and Government I Trials among others. The experience of the Rwanda Tribunal, especially the dismissal of the 'Global' Indictment involving 29 suspects and accused by the confirming Judge, suggests caution in proffering a 'grand' conspiracy as an accusation for complex trials involving atrocity crimes. A more viable option, one that is warranted by a more transparent administration of justice, is to proceed by way of a conspiracy accusation against a more homogenous group of accused, either selected on the basis of concerted territorial or geographic co-perpetration, or common design or purpose. This too permits the joinder of defendants – a net procedural advantage to the prosecution in the case of accountability by way of a conspiracy charge.

In Chapter 7 the book examined superior responsibility. This form of criminal liability is most pertinent for those in positions of authority or command, whether de jure or de facto. Be it civilian superiors or military commanders. It provides bait for effective accountability to a varied class of perpetrators, particularly those with the greatest responsibility, and those at intermediate level. Superior responsibility is a distinct doctrine of criminal responsibility, the other being direct individual criminal liability. To establish indirect superior responsibility, generally requires three criteria: (a) the existence of a superior-subordinate relationship, (b) knowledge that the superior knew or had reason to know that the criminal act was about to be or had been committed, and (c) the superior's failure to take necessary and reasonable measures to prevent the criminal act or punish the perpetrator thereof.

The existence of a superior-subordinate relationship requires demonstration of a formal or informal hierarchical relationship involving a superior's effective control over the subordinate. It requires the possession by the superior of authority or power, de jure or de facto, to prevent or punish an offence about to be committed or committed by the subordinate. It is now well established, in the jurisprudence of the two UN ad hoc Tribunals that by effective control is meant the material ability to prevent or punish the criminal conduct.[2] The factor that determines liability for this type of criminal responsibility is the actual possession or non-possession of powers of control over the actions of subordinates.[3] The law does not require the existence of both *de* jure and de facto authority; either suffices. It should be recalled that a formal legal status or the mere existence of de jure authority does not automatically entail the imposition of criminal responsibility. The mandatory test is the exercise of effective control or command.

In contemporary conflict situations that have been engulfed with atrocity crimes, like those of Rwanda and East Timor, we have noted the pronounced involvement of para-military armed groups, such as militia or other armed wings of political parties or other entities, whose command structure is often of a de facto and undocumented character. Even if so de facto authority is also sufficient to impute superior responsibility provided the superior is found to wield substantially similar powers of control over subordinates as a de jure superior.[4] The second element required for establishing superior responsibility is knowledge. Article 30 of the ICC Statute defines knowledge as "awareness that a circumstance exists or consequence will occur in the ordinary course of events". The requirement for the UN Ad hoc Tribunals is that the superior knew of the crimes that were being committed by those over whom he exercised control, or he had "reason to know" that the subordinate was about to commit such crimes or had done so.[5] By the latter is meant the possession of information, which put him on notice of the risk of crimes being committed or crimes which had been committed and which require him to carry out an additional investigation or to punish his subordinates guilty of such crimes.[6] The third element is the superior's failure to take necessary and reasonable measures to prevent or punish crimes committed by subordinates. Measuring such ability is not an abstract affair; it ought to be based on the superior's material ability and assessed on a case-to-case basis taking into account the circumstances of each situation. One has to inquire beyond the formal competence to prevent or punish and to take into account the superior's actual capacity to do so.

Accountability, through superior responsibility, requires amassing evidence on all of the above legal criteria. Of assistance is proof of orders by commanders or those in authority and control. A de jure or de facto authority or command to issue orders to prevent or punish perpetrators and a showing that orders are carried out in a superior-subordinate hierarchy is of value in substantiating the superior responsibility of military commanders. For a civilian superior, possession of the power of sanction is not essential. Transmission of reports to appropriate authorities suffices.[7] Furthermore while a formal chain of command may be of assistance

2 *Celebici*, Judgement, T.C, paras. 256, 370; *P. V. C. Kayishema and O. Ruzindana*, Judgement, T.C, para. 229.

3 *Celebici*, para. 370, Id.

4 *Celebici*, Judgement, A.C, para. 197.

5 Cf. See Article 28 (a) (i) and 28 (b) (ii) of the ICC Statute for the knowledge element required of military, and of civilian and other superiors respectively.

6 *P.v. I. Bagilishema*, Judgement (Reasons), A.C, para.26.

7 Para.26, Id.

in assessing the level of authority or command of a superior, it is not required that a superior exercise such effective control within a formal chain of command. The key determining factors, as explained earlier, is effective authority and control over the subordinate, in the sense of preventing or punishing the criminal conduct. Matrix C highlights the legal criteria for superior responsibility, the determining factors, and the possible defences to such liability, as borne out from the experiences of the accountability processes in Rwanda and East Timor.

In Chapter 8 the book inquired into the guilty plea as an instrument of accountability for atrocity crimes. Although the judicial process under the two UN ad hoc Tribunal is through the inevitable complex trial, guilty pleas have provided a window of opportunity to expedite a number of trials. This more at the ICTY than at the ICTR. To the Tribunals the advantages of such pleas include judicial economy, sparing witnesses the trauma of cross-examination, and truth telling. For the prosecution the most lucrative value, if forthcoming as a result of the guilty plea, is insider information and the testimony of a cooperating accused. To the prosecution this overrides the case disposition advantage of a guilty plea. The conditions for a valid guilty plea have been specified in Rule 62 (A) (v) of the ICTR Rules of Procedure and Evidence, and are now firmly spelled out in the jurisprudence of the ad hoc Tribunals. The plea must be made freely and voluntarily made, it should be an informed and unequivocal one, and must be based on sufficient facts for the crime and the accused's participation in it, either on the basis of independent indicia or of the lack of any material disagreement between the Prosecutor and the accused about the facts of the case.

Essentially all guilty pleas before the ICTR have involved intensive direct and intense negotiations between the Prosecution, Defence Counsel and the concerned accused on the intended plea, whether prompt or not; on the legal elements constituting the offences charged in the indictment, and verification and common accord on material facts, rather than charge or sentence bargaining. The latter being at the absolute discretion, even unpredictability, of a Trial Chamber as demonstrated by life sentence imposed upon Kambanda by the trial Court and confirmed on Appeal. At the ICTY the guilty plea process has matured to encompass charging and sentence concessions between the Office of the Prosecutor and the accused and his Defence Counsel, for the former to recommend to a Trial Chamber a specific sentence or a range of sentence "in exchange" for the guilty plea, full disclosure of criminal conduct, most of the times, substantial cooperation. Such practice is not in a strict sense plea-bargaining as practiced in United States domestic Courts.

The exigencies of judicial integrity, fairness, and due process has led to the adoption of Plea Agreements between the Prosecutor and accused persons and Defence Counsels, as the legislated mechanism in the procedures of the UN ad hoc Tribunals (i.e. Rule 62 *ter*) for the administration of guilty pleas. Plea Agreements assist Trial Chambers in ensuring that the legal requirements are adhered to, and that there is no material disagreement between the parties on the material facts constituting the crimes alleged to have been committed. They provide the written assurance required to show that there was no inducement, persuasion, or promise made, and that the guilty plea has been the responsibility of an accused, not Defence Counsel. Their duties rest in the provision of effective assistance throughout that process. These agreements have helped ensure that the guilty plea is not 'a distortion of the free will of the accused'. There is however, a need to ensure their transparency, to allow witnesses and victims to testify, at least at the sentencing stages, and for the Trial Chambers to provide the judicial oversight necessary for the full truth to be revealed, instead of a half baked version of facts.

As of 1 January 2005 only 4 accused, of a total of over 80 accused indicted by the ICTR had pleaded guilty. The latest, Vicent Rutaganira was sentenced on 14 March 2005 to a term of 6 years imprisonment. At the ICTY 17 had done so within that Tribunal's first 10 years. The profile of such accused at the former Tribunal has ranged from a de facto interahamwe leader at Prefectoral level, to the former Prime Minister of Rwanda. In the annals of international accountability he is the first Head of Government to have pleaded guilty to genocide and conspiracy to commit genocide in an International Criminal Tribunal. The profile of those who have pleaded guilty before the ICTY ranges from four prison wardens to a senior member of the Presidency of the Socialist Republic of Bosnia and Herzegovina. As such the guilty plea can be an effective tool of accountability for all classes of perpetrators, those with the greatest responsibility, intermediate, and even those at lower levels. In analyzing the Kambanda's guilty plea it is evident that the sentencing outcome, life imprisonment to a cooperating accused, although within the discretion of a Trial Chamber, has acted as a disincentive to other accused in leadership positions to plead guilty. The inverse practice at the ICTY, which centres on charging and sentencing concessions by the Prosecutor "in exchange" for the guilty plea, full disclosure of personal involvement, substantial cooperation, and a more accommodating sentencing attitude has lubricated a motivation among accused at that tribunal to plead guilty. Matrix D provides a three dimensional framework on the guilty plea that includes the four legal requirements for a valid plea and the sentencing considerations. What is unknown in the matrix is weight to be given to each of these factors, and the sentencing outcome. That is within the judicial discretion of each Trial Chamber. It is also uncertain to predict.

A pertinent question related to prosecution strategy, and effective accountability, for those with the greatest responsibility is whether the best of justice and truth was served by proceeding by way of a guilty plea, in a case involving the highest government official in the Interim Government of Rwanda (i.e. the former Prime Minister) rather than by way of a full trial? Related to that is issue is whether Kambanda's guilty plea contributed to national reconciliation. It has been submitted that Kambanda's cooperation with the Office of the Prosecutor provided a unique opportunity for the Prosecutor to evidentially penetrate into the deliberations of the Cabinet of the Interim Government, and the conduct and demeanour of its members during the 1994 atrocity crimes. It reinforced the Prosecutor's theory of conspiracy, one that entailed both active support for victimization of the Tutsi and moderate Hutu, and a deliberate policy of omission, which the Interim Government adhered to, and its members subscribed to. The guilty plea met the legal requirements of a valid plea, and was interpreted by Rwandans as an initial step towards national reconciliation. To the extent that it included an acknowledgement by the former Head of Government that genocide did indeed take place in Rwanda in 1994 it was a positive development. A full trial through adversarial confrontation may also have achieved the same, but only after a considerable lapse of time. Kambanda's guilty plea provided at least an acknowledgement that the genocide was committed and for which the Interim Government was responsible. What remains is the judicial testing of his 90-hour recorded statement, should he chose to appear for the prosecution, and be cross- examined on it by the Defense.

Matrix

Matrix A

Pattern of Violence

Widespread (i.e. large scale multiplicity of victims)	Systematic (i.e. methodical)	Indiscriminate	Planned	Organized

Individuals, groups or collectivity targeted

Children young adults Adults Elderly men Women

Unlawful acts

* Genocidal acts * Murder/willful killing * Extermination(i.e. mass killings) * Acts of persecution * Enslavement * Deportation/forced transfer of population * Torture * Sexual violence/rape * Imprisonment/unlawful confinement * Cruel treatment inhuman acts * Plunder of public property * Collective punishment * Taking of hostages * Acts of terrorism * Summary/extra judicial execution

Identification of policy or plan (deliberate or incidental)

Elements of preconceived plan or policy
(e.g. directives, guidelines, instructions etc.)

Omissions

Identifying the duty to act, and acts of failure to prevent or punish

Discriminatory basis of the violence

Ethnic Political Racial National Religious Cultural
Gender Other

Forensic findings

Personal identification of bodies Cause(s) of death Manner of death

Physical Destruction

Infrastructure Household/dwellings Other property Historical sites/monuments

Instrumentality of Violence

Acts of intimidation Threats/Hatred/Incitement Speeches

Triggering event(s)

Most immediate	Recent past	Past	Historical
e.g. shooting down Presidential plane, 6 April 1994 (Rwanda)	October 1990 civil war	1959 'social revolution'	colonialism

Nature of event(s)/conflict

International Non-International Mixed (internationalized) civil strife

Authority/ organization/Entity/Group (de jure or defacto

Government Armed Forces Gendarmerie/Police Civil Administration
Political parties Para-military/militia Media (Radio and Press)
Business/Financial Religious Congregations

Matrix B
Profiling Perpetrators
(Markers)

Function Position Status	Agency Organanization/ Entity	Governance – level	Role	Gravity of crime(s)
Head of State Head of Government Minister(s)	Government Cabinet	National National	Planners Organizers Instigators Leaders Conspirators Financers Conspirators Accomplices	Widespread and /Systematic Heinous Zealous Gender crimes Discriminatory Persecutory
Deputy Minister		National		
Commander – in – Chief	Military/Gendarmerie	National		
Chief of Staff		National		
Commanders				
Governor	Civil Administration	National		
Prefets		Regional		
Mayors/Bourgmestres		Communal		
President/Chairperson Secretary General	Political Parties	National/ regional national		
Head of Media/Press	Media	National /Provincial		
Commanders and Deputy Commanders	Para-military/militia Para-military/militia	National/provincial/district/co mmunal national/provincial/district		
Top civil servants	Government	National /provincial		
Senior Civil servants	Government	National/provincial/district		
Head of Para-statal	Government	National /provincial		
Commanders Deputy Commanders	Civil Defence Civil Defence	National/provincial/district National/provincial/district		
Commanders	Prisons/camps	National/provincial/district		
Professional's	Liberal professions	National/provincial/district		
Religious leaders	Religious congregations	National/provincial/district		
Councilors Community leaders	Government/municipality local communities	District/communes communal cell (i.e. nyumba kumi)		

Matrix C

Superior Responsibility

Element	Criteria/Factors for consideration	Defences
Superior-Subordinate Relationship (de jure or de facto)	• Superior's effective authority (de jure or de facto) and power to control acts of subordinates. • Possession or non-possession of authority and control. • Evidence of direct subordination. • Superior's hierarchical position. (formal or informal). • Issuance of orders and their obedience. • Evidence of subordination to orders. • Power of appointment and dismissal. • Authority and control over resources, including finances. • Reporting	• Unstructured, blurred or "invisible" chain of command. • Rogue elements. • Change of guards. • Influence is not authority • Spontaneous acts or uprising. • Proxy groups and entities. • Irregular forces or groups. • Parallel system of rule and governance (e.g. Akazu)
Knowledge element "knew or had reason to know"	• Actual or constructive knowledge. • Actual possession of information. • Notice of risk of crimes. • Conscious disregard of information. • Location and physical distance of superior. • Extent of criminalization/atrocities. • Type and number of troops involved. • Geographical and territorial spread of criminal acts. • Spread of operations. • Modus operandi or operations. • Officers, staff and subordinates involved	• Knowledge should not be presumed.
Inaction element Failure to prevent or punish	• Legal obligation/duty to act. • Material ability to prevent or punish	• Semblance of concern. • Monitoring system made non-functional by events/situation.

Matrix D

Guilty plea

Pre conditions for valid guilty plea

(a) Voluntary
(b) Unequivocal
(c) Informed
(d) Based on sufficient materials facts/lack of disagreement between the Parties (Accused/Prosecutor

Sentencing factors

(a) Inherent gravity of the crime
(b) Individual circumstances of the accused
(c) General practice regarding prison sentences in the concerned state

(d) Aggravating and mitigating factors

Aggravating factors

Superior authority.
Abuse of authority.
Cruel, sadistic and bestial conduct. Zealousness and willing participation.
Accused prominence in the community.
Superior's participation in subordinates Crime.

(Beyond reasonable doubt)

Mitigating factors

Cooperation with the Prosecutor.
Voluntary surrender.
Remorse.
Benevolent attitude/assistance to victims. Public apology and regret
Age (young or advanced ages).
Possibility of rehabilitation.
No previous conviction.
Diminished mental responsibility.
Duress
Non-possession of official position/status

(Balance of probability)

(e) Any other relevant information, sentencing practice of the UN Ad hoc Tribunals/Courts

Note: The weigh to be attached to these sentencing factors is within the discretion of the Trial Chamber to determine.

Annex

Annex I

A Summary of the position or rank of accused persons indicted before the International Criminal Tribunal for Rwanda (as of 31 December 2004)

Organization/Agency or Entity	Accused's position /function
Government	
The Executive	Prime Minister
The Cabinet	Ministers
Military/Gendermerie	Chief of Staff (Rwandan Armed Forces) Chief of Staff (Gendarmerie Nationale) Commander (Presidential Guard) Commander (Para Commando Battalion) Commander (Military Operations) Commander (Reconnaissance (RECCE) battalion) Commander (Military Police) Deputy Commander (RECCE Battalion)
Civil Administration	*Prefets* *Bourgmesters* Directors (Departments) Counsellors Public Prosecutor
Political parties	President MRND Secretary General, MRND Secretary General CDR Vice President, Interahamwe
Media	Directors/Shareholders RTLM Editor in Chief, Kangura Radio Journalist Musician/Composer
Religious congregations	Rector (Christ Roi College) Pastor, 7th Day Adventist Military Chaplain Priest, Roman Catholic
Business/Finance	Businessmen Traders
Liberal Professions	Medical Doctor
Others	*Interahamwe* militia Youth Organizer

Annex II

Allegation of direct individual and superior responsibility under Regulation 14.3 and Section 16 of UNTAET regulation 2000/15

Indictment: P.v. Waranto and 7 others

Accused	Individual criminal responsibility	
	Direct	Indirect superior responsibility
General Wiranto	-	X
Maj. General Makarim	X	X
Maj. Gneral Syahnakri	X	X
Maj. General Damiri	X	X
Brig. General Suratman	X	X
Colonel Muis	-	X
Lt. Colonel Sudrajat	X	X
Governor Abilio Soares	X	X

Note: Offences charged:

(1) Crimes against humanity (murder), section 5.1 (a) Reg. 2000/15.

(2) Crimes against humanity (deportation or forcible transfer or population) Section 5.1 (d) , Reg. 2000/15.

(3) Crimes against humanity (persecution), section 5.1 (h), Regulation 2000/15.

Annex III

Prefets and *Bourgmestres* suspected of genocide and crimes against humanity as Rwanda's List of Category I suspects/accused

Area of Jurisdiction	Number
Prefets	
	2
Butare	1
	1
Kibuye	1
Kigali City	1
Kigali Rural	1
Gikongoro	1
Gisenyi	
Ruhengeri	
Total	**8**
Bourgemestres	
	15
Butare	4
	10
Byumba	6
Cyangugu	4
Gokingoro	9
Gisenyi	5
Gitarama	9
Kibungo	10
Kibuye	2
Kigali	10
Nyamata	2
Ruhengeri	
Rushashi	
Total	**86**

Source: Updated list of the first category prescribed by Article 9, Organic Law no.: 8/96 of 30 November 1996, Official Gazette of the Republic of Rwanda, year 38, 31 December 1999.

Selected Bibliography

Documents and Reports: United Nations

(a) Rwanda

Report by the Special Rapporteur on extrajudicial, summary and arbitrary executions on his mission to Rwanda, UN Doc. E/CN.4/1994/7 Add.1, 8-17 April 1993.

Report of the United Nations High Commissioner for Human Rights on his mision to Rwanda of 11 –12 May 1994, UN Doc. ECN.4/S-3/3, 19 May 1994.

Final Report of the Commission of Experts for the Former Yugoslavia, UN Doc. S/1994/674, 27 May 1994.

Report of the Secretary-General on the situation in Rwanda, reporting on the political mission he sent to Rwanda to move the warring parties towards a cease-fire, UN Doc. S/1994/640, 31 May 1994.

Report on the situation of human rights in Rwanda submitted by Mr. Rene Degni-Segui, Special rapporteur of the Commission on Human Rights, UN Doc. E/CN.4/1995/7, 28 June 1994.

Report of the Secretary General on the investigation of serious international humanitarian law violations committed in Rwanda during the conflict, UN Doc. S/1994/867, 25 July 1994.

Preliminary Report of the Independent Commission of Experts established in accordance with SC resolution 935 (1994), UN Doc. S/1994/1125, 4 October 1994.

Final Report of the Commission of Experts established pursuant to SC resolution 935 (1994), UN Doc. S/1994/1405, 9 December 1994.

Rapport sur la situation des droits des l'homme au Rwanda, UN Doc. E/CN.4/1995/71, 24 Janvier 1995.

Rapporteur of the Commission on Human Rights, UN Doc. E7CN.4/1996/68, 29 January 1996.

Report of the Independent Inquiry into the Actions of the United Nations During the 1994 Genocide in Rwanda, 15 December 1999, http://www.un.org/News/ossg/Rwanda_report.htm

(b) East Timor

Report by the Special rapporteur on Extra judicial, summary or arbitrary executions, Mr. Bacre Waly Ndiaye, on his mission to Indonesia and East Timor from 3 to 13 July 1994, UN Doc. E/CN.4/1995/61/Add.1, 1 November 1994.

Question of East Timor, Report of the Secretary General, UN Doc. S/1999/513, 5 May 1999.

Report of the Security Council Mission to Jakarta and Dili, UN Doc. S/1999/976, 14 September 1999.

Report of the High Commissioner for Human Rights on the human rights situation in East Timor, UN Doc.E/CN.4/S-4/CRP.1, 17 September 1999.

Report on the Joint mission to East Timor undertaken by the Special Rapporteur on extra judicial, summary or arbitrary executions, the Special Rapporteur on the question of torture and the Special Rapporteur on violence against women, UN Doc. A/54/660, 10 December 1999.

Question of East Timor, Progress Report of the Secretary-General, UN Doc. A/54/654, 13 December 1999.

Report of the International Commission on Inquiry on East Timor, UN Doc. A/54/726, S/2000/59, 31 January 2000.

Report of the Special rapporteur on the Independence of Judges and Lawyers, UN Doc. E/CN.4/2003/65/Add.2, 13 January 2003.

Situation of Human Rights in Timor-Leste, Report of the UN High Commissioner for Human Rights, UN Doc. E/CN.4/2003/37, 4 March 2003.

(c) Sierra Leone

Report of the Secretary-General on the establishment of a Special Court for Sierra Leone, UN Doc. S/2000/915, 4 October 2000.

Report of the Planning Mission on the Establishment of the Special Court for Sierra Leone, UN Doc. S/2002/246, 8 March 2002.

Documents and reports: other Institutions/Organizations

Report of the International Panel of Eminent Personalities created by the Organization of African Unity to investigate the Genocide in Rwanda, 2000, Organization of African Unity, See www.oau.oua.org

Indonesia's Death Squads, Getting Away with Murder, A Chronology of Indonesian Military sponsored Paramilitary and Militia atrocities in East Timor from November 1998 to May 1999, ETISCO Occasional Paper No 2, East Timor International Support Centre, Darwin NT, May 1999.

Report of the Indonesian Commission of Investigation into Human Rights Violations in East Timor, referred to as KPP-HAM Report), 31 January 2000; at www.jsmp.minihub.org/Resources.htm
mh.com.au/news/0104/29/etimor02.htm

Human Rights Watch World Report, 2001, http://www.hrw.org/wr2kl/asia/etimor.html

The War within the War: Sexual Violence against Women and Girls in Eastern Congo, Human Rights Watch, June 2002.

Covered in Blood: Ethnically Targeted Violence in Northern Democratic Republic of Congo, Human Rights Watch, July 2003.

International Centre for Transitional Justice (2003), Intended to Fail: The Trials Before the Ad Hoc Human Rights Court in Jakarta by David Cohen, ICTJ, N.Y.

International Crisis Group, The Rwanda Tribunal: Justice Delayed, www.crisiweb.org/about/030/. Cfm

A Review of Peace Operations. A Case for Change, East Timor Report, Conflict Security and Development Group, IPI, Kings College, London, 28 February 2003, http:/ipi.sspp.kcl.ac.uk/rep006/index.html

International Crisis Group, The Special Court for Sierra Leone: Promises and Pitfalls of a "New Model", 4 August 2003, www.intl-crisis-group.org

International Crisis Group, The International criminal Tribunal for Rwanda: Time for Pragmatism, ICG Africa Report No.69, 26 September 2003, www.crisweb.org

Watch Indonesia and German Commission on Justice and Peace (2004) Justice for Victims, A Legal Opinion on the Indonesian Human Rights Trials Concerning the Crimes Committed in East Timor in 1999, Bonn/Berlin, Germany.

Books & Articles

Adedeji A (1999) Comprehending and Mastering African Conflicts. The Search for Sustainable Peace and Good Governance, Zed Books, London and N.Y.

Adelstein R P (1984) The Negotiated Guilty Plea. An Economic and Empirical Analysis, Garland Pub, Inc., N.Y & London.

African Rights (1994) Death, Despair and Defiance, London.

Aiyar K J (1958) Law Relating to Criminal Conspiracy in India and Pakistan, Eastern Book Company, New Delhi.

Alfredsson G, Macalister-Smith P (1996) The Living Law of Nations, N.P. Engel Publishers, Kehl.

Alschuler A (1983) Implementing the Criminal Defendant's Right to Trial: Alternatives to the Plea bargaining System, University of Chicago Law Review, vol.50 pp. 931 et seq.

Ambos K (1998) The International Criminal Court and The Traditional Principles of International Cooperation in Criminal Matters, The Finnish Yearbook of International Law, vol. IX, pp 413-426.

Ambos K (2000) The Status, Role and Accountability of the Prosecutor of the International Criminal Court: A Comparative Overview on the Basis of 33 National Reports, European Journal of Crime, Criminal Law and Criminal Justice, vol.8/2, pp. 89-118.

Ambos K, Wirth S (2002) The Current Law of Crimes Against Humanity. An Analysis of UNTAET Regulation 15/2000, Criminal Law Forum, 13: 1-90.

Ambos K, Othman M (eds.) (2003) New Approaches in International Criminal Justice: Kosovo, East Timor, Sierra Leone and Cambodia, Max Planck Institute for Foreign and International Criminal Law, Freiburg im Breisgau.

Ambos K (2003) Current Issues in International Criminal Law, Criminal Law Forum 14: 225-260.

Ambos K (*Draft*) Individual Criminal Responsibility (Article 25). In Triffterer O (ed.) Commentary on the Rome Statute of the International Criminal Court, Observers Notes. 2nd Ed., Article by Article, Nomos Verlagsgesellschaft, Baden-Baden.

Andrews J A, Hirst M (1997) Andrews and Hirst on Criminal Evidence, IIIrd Edition, Sweet & Maxwell, London.

Angiolillo P F (1979) A Criminal as Hero. Angelo Duca, The Regents Press of Kansan, Lawrence.

Anyidoho H K (1999) Guns over Kigali, Woeli Publishing Services, Accra.

Appleman J A (1954) Military Tribunals and International Crimes, The Bobbs-Merrill Company, Inc., Indianapolis.

Arbour L (1998) History and Future of the International criminal Tribunals for the Former Yugoslavia and Rwanda, Am. U. Int'l L. Rev., 13: 1498-1508.

Arbour L, Esser A, Ambos, K and Sanders A (eds.) (2000) The Prosecutor of a Permanent International Criminal Court, Max Planck Institute of Foreign and International Criminal Law, Freiburg im Breisgau.

Arbour L (2004) The Crucial Years, Journal of International Criminal Justice, vol. 2: 396-402.

Ashworth A (2003) Principles of Criminal Law, Oxford University Press, 4th edition, Oxford.

Askin K D (1999) Sexual Violence in Decisions of the Yugoslavia and Rwanda Tribunals: Current Status, A.J.I.L, 93: 97-123.

Ball D, McDonald H (2000) Death in Balibo, Lies in Canberra, Allen and Unwin, Australia.

Bantekas I (1999) The Contemporary Law of Superior Responsibility, A.J.I.L, 93: 573-595.

Barboza J (1999) International Criminal Law, Recueil des Cours, Academie de Droit International, T. 278, pp. 1-196l.

Bass G J (2000) Stay the Hand of Vengeance. The Politics of the War Crimes Tribunals, Princeton University Press, N.J.

Bassiouni M C (1999) International Criminal Law, (Enforcement), Vol. III, 2nd Edition, Transnational Pub. Inc., Ardsley, N.Y.

Bassioni M C (1999) Crimes Against Humanity in International Criminal Law, 2nd ed. Kluwer, The Hague.

Bassiouni M C, Wise E M (1995) Aut Dedere Aut Judiciare. The Duty to Extradite or Prosecute in International Law, Martinus Nijhoff Publishers, Dordrecht.

Batra T S (1981) Criminal Law in India, Metropolitan Book Co. Put. Ltd, New Delhi.

Bauman J (1994) Conspiring Drug Kingpins: Twice in Jeopardy? U.Chi. L. Rev. 61: 197 et seq.

Beigbeder Y (1999) Judging War Criminals. The Politics of International Justice, MacMillan Press Ltd., London.

Berry C P, Berry J A (eds.) (1999) Genocide in Rwanda. A Collective Memory, Howard University Press, W.D.C.

Bingham J (2000) The Business of Judging, Oxford University Press, Oxford.

Bishop J B (1989) Prosecution Without Trial, Butterworths, Sydney.

Black's Law Dictionary (2000) Gardner B A (ed. *et all.*) 7th edo., West Group, St Paul. Minn.

Bloxham D (2001) Genocide on Trial, Oxford University Press, Oxford.

Bourloyannis C (1992) The Security Council of the UN and the Implementation of International Humanitarian Law, Denver Journal of International Law and Policy vol. 20, no. 2, pp. 335-355.

Braeckman C (1994) Rwanda. Histoire d'un genocide, Librairie A. Fayard, France.

Braathen E, Boas M, Saether G (2000) Ethnicity Kills? The Politics of War, Peace and Ethnicity in Sub Saharan Africa, Macmillan Press, London.

Bring O (2001) International Criminal Law in Historical Perspective, Comments and Materials, Juridiska Fakulteten, Nr. 66, Stockholms Universitet.

Brook T (2001) The Tokyo Judgment and the Rape of Nanking, The Journal of Asian Studies, vol.60 no.3 pp 673-700.

Brownlie A (1998) Principles of Public International Law, 5th Edition, Clarendon Press, Oxford.

Bryan J W (1970) The Development of the English Law of Conspiracy, Da Capo Press, New York.

Brook T (2001) The Tokyo Judgment and the Rape of Nanking, The Journal of Asian Studies, vol.60 no.3 pp 673-700.

Burnett W D (1985) Command Responsibility and a Case Study of the Criminal Responsibility of Israeli Military Commanders for the Pogrom at Shatila and Sabra, Military law Review, 107: 87-131.

Burtov D, Mack P (2001) In God's Name. Genocide and Religion in the Twentieth Century, Berghahn Books, N.Y. and Oxford.

Cahin G (2000) L'action Internationale au Timor Oriental, Anuaire Francais de Droit International, Vol. XLV1, pp. 139-175.

Calvocoressi P (1947) Nuremberg, The Facts, the Law and the Consequences, Chatto and Windus, London.

Card R (2001) Card, Cross and Jones Criminal Law, 15th ed., Butterworths, U.K.

Castonguay J (1998) Les Casques Blues au Rwanda, Editions L'Harmattan, Paris.

Cassese A (1999) The Statute of the International Criminal Court: Some Preliminary Reflections, E.J.I.L, vol. 10, pp. 144-171.

Cassese A, Gaeta P, Jones J R W D (eds.) (2002) The Rome Statute of the International Criminal Court: A Commentary, Oxford University Press, Oxford.

Cassese A (2004) The ICTY: A Living and Vital Reality, International Journal of Criminal Justice, vol. 2:585-597.

Cheng B, Brown E D (eds.) (1988) Contemporary Problems of International Law, Stevens and Sons Ltd., London.

Chopra J (2000) The UN's Kingdom of East Timor, Survival, The International Institute for Strategic Studies, vol. 42, no. 3, pp 27-39.

Chrétien J P (ed.) (1995) Rwanda. Les Medias du Génocide, Karthala and Reporteurs sans Frontières, Paris.

Cohen D (2003) Intended to Fail, The Trials Before the Ad Hoc Human Rights Court in Jakarta, http://www.ictj.org/downloads?Intended_to_Fail--Final.pfd

Cohen D (2002) Seeking Justice on the Cheap: Is the East Timor Tribunal Really a Model for the Future? Asia Pacific Issue, East West Centre 61:1.

Colvin E (1991) Principles of Criminal Law, Thomson Professional Publishing Ltd, Canada.

Combs N A (2002) Copping a Plea to Genocide: The Plea Bargaining of International Crime, University of Pennsylvania Law Review, vol. 151 no. 1, pp. 1-158.

Combs N A (2004) Guilty Pleas in International Criminal Law: Constructing A Restorative Justice Approach For Bridging Justice and Truth, Dissertation, Leiden University.

Combs N A (2005) Procuring Guilty Pleas for International Crimes: The Limited Influence of Sentence Discounts, *Draft,* forthcoming publication.

Cooper B (ed.) (1999) War Crimes The Legacy of Nuremberg, TV Books, N.Y.

Creveling R (1999) Loyalty and Integration in the Indonesian Armed Forces, Foreign Area Officer Association, 29 November 1999, at www.faoa.org/Journal/ Indonesia./rtml

Crocker C A, Hampson F O, Aall P, (1996) Managing Global Chaos, Sources of and Responses to International Conflict, U.S.I.P. Press, Washington D. C.

Damaska H M (2001) The Shallow Side of Command Responsibility, American Journal of Comparative Law, vol. XLIX, no.3, 455-498.

D'Amato A (1999) A Brief Review of the Indictment against Milosevic and Others, 27 May 1999, at http://jurist.law.pitt.edu/amato.htm

Darbyshire P (2002) The Mischief of Plea Bargaining and Sentence Rewards, Criminal Law Review, pp. 899- 910.

David A K (1993) The Movement Towards Statute-Based Conspiracy Law in the UK and the US, Vanderbilt Journal of Transnational Law, 25: 951 et seq.

Day B D (1983) The Withdrawal Defense to Criminal Conspiracy: An Unconstitutional Allocation of the Burden of Proof, George Washington Law Review, vol. 51, pp. 420 et seq.

Davidson E (1996) The Trial of Germans, An Account of the 22 defendants before the IMT at Nuremberg, The Macmillan Company, N.Y.

Desai D A, Jain M L, Menon N R D (eds.) (1995) Ratanlal and Dhirajlal's Law of Crimes, N.R.D, Bharat Law House Put. Ltd., New Delhi.

Des Forges A (2001) Justice in the Balance, Conference on Military Commissions and International Criminal Tribunals in a Violent Age, UC Berkeley War Crimes Studies Centre/Human Rights Centre, University of California HRW, March 2001.

Desportes F, Le Gunehec F (1998) Le Nouveau Droit Pénal, Tome I, Droit Pénal Général, Cinquième édition, Economica, Paris.

Destexhe A (1995) Rwanda and Genocide in the Twentieth Century, Pluto Press Ltd, London, E. Haven, CI.

Dix G E, Sharlot M M (1973) Criminal Law. Cases and Materials, West Publishing Company Ltd., St Paul, Minn.

Dobkowski M N, Wallimann I (eds.) (1998) The Coming Age of Scarcity. Preventing Mass Death and Genocide in the Twenty-first Century, Syracuse University Press, Syracuse.

Drost P N (1959) The Crime of State, II, Genocide, A.W. Sijhoff, Leyden.

Du Cann C G L (1960) Miscarriages of Justice, Frederick Muller Ltd., London.

Dunn J (1996) Timor. A People Betrayed, ABC Books, Sydney.

Djilas A (1993) A Profile of Milosevic, Foreign Affairs, vol. 72 no. 3 pp 81-96.

Donnediue de Vabres H (1947) Le Proces De Nuremberg Devant Les Principes Modernes du Droit Penal International, Receil des Cours, Academie de Droit International, T. 70/ I, pp. 477-580.

Drumble M A (2000) Punishment, Post Genocide: From Guilt to Ham to Civis in Rwanda, Yale Law Journal, 75/2: 1211-1326.

Dutta K K (1997) Treaties on Criminal Law, Eastern Book Company, New Delhi.

Easterbrook F H (1991-1992) Plea bargaining as Compromise, Yale Law Journal, 101: 1996-1978.

Easton S M (1991) The Right to Silence, Avebury, Aldershot, England.

Egonda-Ntende F (2001) Building a new Judiciary in East Timor: The first steps and missteps, Commonwealth Juridical Journal, vol. 14 no. 1, pp 22 et seq.

Elliot C (2001) French Criminal Law, Willan Publishing, Devon, U.K.

Ewaschuk E G (1996) Criminal Pleadings and Practice in Canada, 2nd Ed., Canada Law Book Inc., Ontario.

Fendrick, W J (1999) Some International Law Problems Related to Prosecutions before the International Criminal Tribunal for the Former Yugoslavia, Duke J of Comp. & Int. Law, vol. 6, pp. 103-125.

Fine R A (1986) Escape of the Guilty, Dodd, Meal & Company, N.Y.

Finch G A (1947) The Nuremberg Trial in International Law, A.J.I.L, vol. 41, pp. 20-37.

Fitzgerald O E (1990) The Guilty Plea and Summary Justice, Carswell, Toronto.

Gaur K D (1992) A Textbook on the Indian Penal Code, Oxford and IBH Publishing Co. Pty Ltd, New Delhi.

Gerber R J (1998) A Judicial View of Plea bargaining, Criminal Law Bulletin, vol.34/1, pp. 16-31.

Gillies P (1990) The Law of Conspiracy, The Federation Press, 2nd Edition, Leichhardt, NSW, Australia.

Glazer N (1984) The Public Interest in Crime and Punishment, Abt Books, Cambridge, Mass.

Goldstein A S (1981) The Passive Judiciary, Prosecutorial Discretion and the Guilty Plea, Louisiana State University Press, Baton Rouge.

Goldstone R J (1998) Healing Wounded People-War crimes and Truth Commissions, C.F. Muller Verlag, Heidelberg.

Goldstone R J (2004) A View from the Prosecution, Journal of International Criminal Justice, vol. 2: 380-384.

Goode M R (1975) Criminal Conspiracy in Canada, The Carswell Company Ltd., Toronto.

Goor M J, Harwood S (1992) Controversies in Criminal Law, West View Press Inc., Boulders, Colorado.

Gorecki J (1979) A Theory of Justice. Proving the Truth, Columbia University Press, N.Y.

Gourevitch P (1998) We Wish to Inform You That Tomorrow We Will Be Killed With Our Families: Stories From Rwanda, Farar, Strauss and Giraux, N.Y.

Gour H S (1968) The Penal Law of India, Vols. I-III, 8th edition, Law Publishers (India) PVT Ltd, Allahabad.

Gradel J, Casorla F (2001) Code de Procedure Penale, Quarante Deuxieme edition, Dalloz, Paris.

Grant T D (2000) East Timor, the U.N. System, and Reinforcing Non-Recognition in International Law, Vand. J. Transnat'l. L. 33: 273 et seq.

Green L C (1995) Command Responsibility in International Humanitarian Law, Transnational law and Contemporary Problems, vol.5, no.2, pp. 319 et seq.

Greenlees D, Garran R (2002) Deliverance:The Inside Story of East Timor's Fight for Freedom, Allen and Unwin (Australia) Pty Ltd.

Gross L (1999) Selected Essays on International Law and Organization, Transnational Publishers, Inc., Irvington-on-Hudson, N.Y.

Guichaoua A (2004) Migrants, refugies et deplaces en Afrique Centrale et Orientale, Editions Karthala, Paris.

Guichaoua A (1995) Les crises politique au Burundi et au Rwanda (1993-1994), Université des Sciences et Technologies de Lille, Lille, France.

Gupta R L (1965) Law of Abetment, Criminal Conspiracy and Constructive Liability, Law Book Company, *Allahbad-I.*

Gurule J (1996) Complex Criminal Litigation, Prosecuting Drug Enterprises and Organized Crimes, Michie Law Publishers, Charlottesville, Virginia.

Halsbury's Law of England Lord Hailsham of Marylebone (ed.) (1990) 4th Edition, Vol.11 (2), Butterworths, London.

Hankin A H (2002) The Legacy of Abuse. Confronting the Past, Facing the Future, The Aspen Institute/N.Y. University School of Law, N.Y.

Harold J R (1996) Guilty: The Collapse of Criminal Justice, Random House, N.J.

Harrison D (1924) Conspiracy as a Crime and as a Tort in English Law, Sweet and Maxwell, London.

Hazel R (1974) Conspiracy and Civil Liberties, A Memorial Submitted to the Law Commission, A Lobden Trust Memorandum, Occasional Papers on Social Administration, Willmer Brother Ltd., Birkenhead, England.

Herman G N (1997) Plea Bargaining, Lexis Law Publishing, Charlottesville, Virginia.

Holroyd J (2000) The Reform of jurisdiction over International Conspiracy, The Journal of Criminal Law, vol.64/3, pp. 323-331.

Howard P K (1994) The Death of Common Sense: How Law Suffocating America, Warned Books, USA.

Howard M N (ed.) (2000) Philson on Evidence, 15th Edition, Sweet and Maxwell, London.

Human Rights Watch (1996) Shattered Lives. Sexual Violence during the Rwandan Genocide and its Aftermath, New York.

Human Rights Watch/Federation Internationale des Ligues des Droit de L'Homme (1999) Leave None to Tell the Story, NY.

Ickler N L (1983) Conspiracy to Violate Rico: Expanding Traditional Conspiracy Law, Notre Dame L. Rev. vol. 58, pp. 587 et seq.

Iriola R A (2001) Primer on Legal Issues surrounding the Extra territorial apprehension of criminals, A.J.I.L. vol.29/1, pp. 1-28.

Jackson R H (1971) The Nuremberg Case as presented by Robert H. Jackson, Chief Counsel for the US, Cooper Square Pub. Inc, N.Y.

Jacoby J E (1977) The Prosecutor's Charging Decision: A Policy Perspective, National Institute of Law Enforcement and Criminal Justice, US Dept. of Justice, W.D.C.

Johnson P C (2000) Criminal Law, Cases, Materials and Text, 6th Edition, West Group, St Paul, Minn.

Johnson P E (1973) The Unnecessary Crime of Conspiracy, California Law Journal, vol. 61/5, pp. 1137-1188.

Jollife J (2001) Cover-Up. The Inside Story of the Balibo Five, Scribe Publications Melbourne.

Jones A (2002) Gender and Genocide in Rwanda, Journal of Genocide Research, vol. 4/1, pp. 65-94.

Jorgensen N H B (2002) The Genocide Acquittal in Sikirica Case before the International Criminal Tribunal for the Former Yugoslavia and the Coming of Age of the Guilty Plea, Leiden Journal of International Law, vol. 15/ 2, pp. 389-408.

Khan S M (2000) The Shallow Graves of Rwanda, I.B. Thauris and Company Ltd, London.

Kiernan B (1996) The Pol Pot Regime, Race, Power, and Genocide in Cambodia under the Khmer Rouge, 1975-1979, Silkworm Books, Thailand.

Kittichaisaree K (2001) International Criminal Law, Oxford University Press, Oxford.

Klein N S (1966) Multilateral Disputes and the Doctrine of Necessary parties in the East Timor case, Yale Journal of International Law, pp. 305 et seq.

Klein S A (1957) Conspiracy-The Prosecutor's Darling, Brooklyn Law Review, vol. XXIV, no.1, pp. 1-11.

Kress C (2002) The 1999 Crisis in East Timor and the Threshold on the Law of War Crimes, Criminal Law Forum, 13: 409-470.

Krug H N (1998) Genocide in Rwanda: lessons Learned and Future Challenges to the UN Human Rights System, Nordic Journal of International Law, 67:165-213.

LaFave W R (1978) Principles of Criminal Law, Cases, Comments and Questions, West Publishing Company, St Paul, Minnesota.

LaFave W R, Scott Jr. A W (1986) Substantive Criminal Law, West Publishing Co., St Paul.

Lattanzi G, Lupo E (2000) Codice Penale, Vol. 111, Dott A. Guiffre Editore.

Levie J H (1954) Hearsay and Conspiracy, A Re-examination of the Co-Conspirators' Exception to the Hearsay Rule, Michigan Law Review, vol.52, no.8, pp. 1159-1178.

Linton S (2001) Rising from the Ashes: The Creation of a Viable Criminal Justice System in East Timor, Melbourne University Law Review, 25:122-180.

Linton S (2001) Prosecuting Atrocities at the District Court of Dili, Melbourne Journal of International Law, 2:301-345.

Maguire J H (1959) Evidence of Guilt, Little, Brown & Company, Boston.

Mamdani M (2001) When Victims Become Killers, Colonialism, Nativism and the Genocide in Rwanda, Princeton University Press, Princeton, N.J.

Martin I (2001) Self-Determination in East Timor, The United Nations, the Ballot and International Intervention, International Peace Academy Occasional paper Series, Lynne Reinner Publishers Inc., London.

Martinkus J (2001) A Dirty Little War, Random House Australia.

May R (1991) Admissibility of Confessions: Recent Developments, Journal of Criminal Law, vol. LV, pp. 366-373.

McDonald G K, Swaak-Goldman O (eds.) (2000) Aspects of the International Criminal Law, Vol.1, Kluwer Law International, The Hague.

McDonald W F, Cramer J A (eds.) (1980) Plea Bargaining, Lexington Books, Lexington, Ma.

McNicol S (1992) Law of Privilege, The Law Book Company, North Ryde, N.S.W.

Minear R H (1971) Victor's Justice. The Tokyo War Crimes Trial, Princeton University Press, Princeton, N.J.

Melvern L (2000) A People Betrayed. The Role of the West in Rwanda's genocide, Zed Books, London.

Merle R, Vitu A (1984) Traite de Droit Criminel, les Circumstances attenuantes, Edition Cujas, 6eme ed.

Meron T (1993) Rape as a crime under International Humanitarian Law, A.J.I.L, 87: 424-428.

Metzl J F (1997) Rwandan Genocide and the International Law of Radio Jamming, A.J.I.L, 91: 628-651.

Mewett A W, Manning M S (1994) Mewett and Manning on Criminal Law, 3rd Edition, Butterworths, Toronto.

Meyerfeld J Who Shall be Judge?: The US, the ICC, and the Global Enforcement of Human Rights, Human Rights Quarterly, vol. 25, pp. 93-129.

Mietzer M (2000) Politics of Engagement: The Indonesian Armed Forces, Islamic Extremism and the War on Terror' Brown Journal of World Affairs, vol. IX, no.1, www.watsoninstitute.org/bjwa/archives/9.1/Indonesia/mietzer.pdf.

Miller H S, McDonald WF, Cramer J A (1978) Plea Bargaining in the US, National Institute of Law Enforcement and Criminal Justice, US Dept. of Justice, Georgetown University, W.D.C.

Mitler V (1978) The Law of Confessions and Evidence of Accomplices, Law Book Company, Allahabad-1.

Mitler V (1978) Chaudhuri's The Law of Confessions and Evidence of Accomplices, Law Book Company, Allahabad-1.

Morris V, Scharf M P (1998) An Insiders Guide to the International Criminal Tribunal for Rwanda, Transitional Publishers, N.Y.

Morris V, Scharf M P (1995) An Insiders Guide to the International Criminal Tribunal for the Former Yugoslavia, Transitional Publishers, N.Y.

Morris M (1999) The Trials of Concurrent Jurisdiction: The Case of Rwanda, American Diplomacy, at www.unc.edu/depts/diplomat/amdipl_6/morris.html; Also in Bassiouni M C (1999) International Criminal Law, (Enforcement), vol.III, pp. 567-584.

Mueller C B (1984) The Federal Co-conspirator Exception: Action, Assertion, and Hearsay, Hofstra L. Rev. 12: 323.

Muna B (1998) The ICTR Must achieve Justice for Rwandans, Am. U. Int'l Rev., 13:1480-1484.

Mustafa F (1993) Islamic law of Confessions-A Comparison with Western and Indian Laws, Islamic and Comparative law Review, vol. XIII, no.1, pp. 27-37.

Nasheri H (1998) Betrayal of Due Process. A Comparative Assessment of Plea-Bargaining in the United States and Canada, University Press of America Inc., Lanham, Maryland.

Neier A (1999) Rethinking Truth, Justice and Guilt after Bosnia and Rwanda, in Human Rights and Political Transitions: Gettysburg to Bosnia, pp. 39-52, N.Y.

Neier A (1999) Human Rights in Political Transition: Gettysburg to Bosnia, Zone Books, N.Y.

Nevins J (2002) The Making of 'Ground Zero' in East Timor in 1999: An analysis of International Complicity in Indonesia's Crimes, Asian Survey, vol. XLII, no. 4, pp. 623-641.

Newbury C, Newbury D (1999) A Catholic Mass in Kigali: Contested Views of the Genocide and Ethnicity in Rwanda, Canadian Journal of African Studies, Vol.33/2-3 pp. 292- 315.

Orchard G (1974) "Agreement" in Criminal Conspiracy, Crim.L. J, pp. 297-304, 331- 339.

Osiel M J (1999) Obeying Orders, Atrocity, Military Discipline and the Law of War, Transaction Publishers, New Brunswick/London.

Oswald B M (2000) The INTERFET Detainee Management Unit in East Timor, Yearbook of International Humanitarian Law, pp. 347 –361.

Othman M C (2003) East Timor: A Critique of the Model of Accountability for serious Human Rights and International Humanitarian Law Violations, Nordic Journal of International Law, vol. 72, no: 4, pp. 449-482.

Othman M C (2002) The Protection of Refugee Witnesses before the International Criminal Tribunal for Rwanda, International Journal of refugee Law , vol. 14/4, pp. 495-508.

Pellet A (2001) Pour La Cour Pénale Internationale, quand même! – Quelques remarques sur sa compétence et sa saisine, International Criminal Law Review, vol. 1, no. 1, pp. 91-110.

Pillay N (1998) The Rwanda Tribunal and Its Relationship to National Trials in Rwanda, Am. U. Int'l L. Rev., 13: 1473-1480.

Pillay N (1997) The Status of the International Criminal Tribunal for Rwanda, Conference paper, Securing State Cooperation and Compliance: The International Criminal Tribunal for Rwanda, Parliamentarians for Global Action, Cape Town, S. Africa.

Proceedings of the IMT sitting at Nuremberg Germany, The Trial of German Major War Criminals, Part 22, Published under the authority of the Attorney General of his Majesty's Stationery Office, London, 1950.

Prunier G (1997) The Rwanda Crisis. History of a Genocide, Hurst, and Co., N.Y.

Rabasa A, Haseman J (2000) The Military and Democracy in Indonesia: Challenges, Politics and Power, Nat. Sec. Research Division, The Rand, www.rand.org/publications/MR/MR1599

Ratner S R et all. (2003) International War Crimes Trials: Making a Difference? Proceedings of an International Conference at the University of Texas School of Law, Austin, Texas, 6-7 November 2003.

Richardson H J (2000) Recent Developments in East Timor: A critical Thought on Self Determination For East Timor and Kosovo (Symposium), Temp. Int'l and Comparative L. J., 14: 101 et seq.

Rodley N (2002) The Definitions(s) of Torture in International Law, Vol. 55, Current Legal Problems, 55:467-494.

Rogers A P V (1966) Law on the Battlefield, Manchester University Press, Manchester.

Romano C P R, Nollkaemper A (2003) The Arrest Warrant Against The Liberian President, Charles Taylor, ASIL Insight, June 2003, at http://www.asil.org/insight/insight110.htm

Romanowski A K (1988) Crime and Confession: An Analysis of the Relationship between Contrition, Sentence and Recidivism, (PhD), University of Michigan, U.M.I., Ann Arbor, MI.

Rothwax H J (1996) Guilty: The Collapse of Criminal Justice, Random House, N.Y.

Rudasingwa T (1998) The Rwanda Tribunal and its relationship to National Trials in Rwanda, Am.U.Int'l L.Rev, 13: 1484- 1493.

Samuels A (1999) The Discount for Guilty Pleas: The Juridical Principles, Justice of the Peace, vol. 163, pp.792-793.

Sanders A, Yang R (2000) Criminal Justice, Butterworths, London.

Sandoz Y (1978) L'application du droit humanitaire par les forces armees de L'organisation des Nations Unies, International Review of the Red Cross, pp. 274-284.

Sardar M I K M (1978) Law Terms and Phrases Judicially Interpreted, Law Publishing Co., Lahore.

Sarkar S, Manohar V R (2003) Sarker on Evidence, Wadhwa and Company Nagar, 15 th edition.

Schabas W A (2000-2001) Hate Speech in Rwanda: The Road to Genocide, McGill L.J, vol. 46, pp. 141-170.

Schulhofer S J (1991-1992) Plea bargaining as Disaster, Yale Law Journal, 101:1979 et seq.

Seifman R D, Freiberg A (2001) Plea Bargaining in Victoria: The Role of Counsel, Criminal Law Journal, 25:64-74.

Sellers P, Okuizumi K (1997) International Prosecution of Sexual Assaults, Transnational Law & Contemporary Problems, vol. 7, no. 3, pp. 45-80.

Scharf M P (1997) Balkan Justice. The Story Behind the First International Warcrimes Trial since Nuremberg, Carolina Academic Press, Durham, N. Carolina.

Scharf M P (1999) The Indictment of Slobodan Milosevic, ASIL Insight, http://www.asil.org/insight35.htm

Scheffer D J (2003) The Future of Atrocity Law, Suffolk Transnational Law Review, vol. XXV/3, pp.399 et seq.

Sok An (2003) The Proceedings for the Trial of Senior Khmer Rouge Leaders, Paper presented at the Conference on The Rule of Law and Legacy of Conflict, USA-U.N. Association, Gabarone, Botswana.

Sorbo G, Vale P (1997) Out of Conflict. From War to Peace in Africa, Nordiska Afrikainstitutet, Uppsala.

Sliedregt V (2004) The Criminal Responsibility of Individuals for Violations of International Humanitarian Law, T.M.C Asser Press, The Hague.

Smith J C, Hogan B (1988) Criminal Law, Butterworths, London.

Sprecher D A (1999) Inside the Nuremberg Trial. A Prosecutor's Comprehensive Account, Vol. II, University Press of America, Maryland.

Stefani G, Levasseur G, Bouloc B (1997) Droit Pénal Général, Dalloz, Paris.

Stone E (1998) Calling a Spade a Spade: the Embarrassing Truth about the Right to Silence, Criminal Law Journal, vol.22, no.1, pp. 17-35.

Storey A (2001) Structural Adjustment, State Power and Genocide: the World Bank and Rwanda, Review of African Political Economy, 89:367-369.

Strohmeyer H (2000) Building a New Judiciary for East Timor: Challenges of a Fledging Nation, Criminal Law Forum, 11: 259-285.

Strohmeyer H (2000) Collapse and Reconstruction of a Judicial System: The United Nations Mission in Kosovo and East Timor, A.J.I.L, 95: 46-53.

Stuntz W J, Scott R E (1992) Plea Bargaining as Contract, Yale Law Journal, vol. 101/3, pp. 1909-1967.

Suhrke A (1998) Dilemmas of Protection: The Log of the Kigali Battalion, International Peacekeeping, vol. 5, no.2, pp. 1-18.

Swinarski C (1994) Studies and Essays on International Humanitarian Law and Red Cross Principles in honour of Jean Pictet, ICTR, Martinus Nijhoff Pub. Geneva.

Tanter R, Selden M, Shalon S R (2001) Bitter Flowers, Sweet Flowers, East Timor, Indonesia and the World Community, Rowman & Littlefield, Lonham, MD.

The Trial of German Major War Criminals, His Majesty's Stationery Office, London, 1946.

The Trial of German Major War Criminals, His Majesty's Stationery Office, London, 1946.

The Trial of War Criminals: Documents, US Dept of State, W.D.C., 1945.

Trial of the Major War criminals Before the International Military Tribunal, Vol.1, published at Nuremberg, Germany, 1947.

Triffterer O (2002) Causality, a Separate Element of the Doctrine of Superior Responsibility as Expressed in Article 28 Rome Statute? Leiden Journal of International Law, vol.15, no1, pp. 179-205.

Triffterer O (ed.) (1999) Commentary on the Rome Statute of the International Criminal Court, Observers Notes. Article by Article, Nomos Verlagsgesellschaft, Baden-Baden.

Turner J W C (1964) Russell on Crime, Vol. I, 12 Edition, Stevens and Sons, London.

Twagiralimana A (1998) Hutu and Tutsi, The Rosen Publishing Group, Inc. N.Y.

United Nations (2000) The United Nations and East Timor, Self Determination through popular consultation, UN Dept. of Public Information, N.Y.

United Nations (1996) The UN and Rwanda (1993-1996), UN Dept. of Information, Blue Book Series, N.Y.

US Dept. of State (1946) The Trial of Japanese War Criminals, Documents, W.D.C.

US Department of State (1945) The Trial of War Criminals: Documents, W.D.C.

Uviller H R (1996) Virtual Justice. The Flawed Prosecution of Crime in America, Yale University Press, Hew Heaven and London.

Verny E (2002) Le Membre d'un Group en Droit Pénal, Librairie Général de Droit et de Jurisprudence, Paris.

Verwimp P (2000) Development, Ideology, the Peasantry and Genocide: Rwanda represented in Habyarimana's Speeches, Journal of Genocide Research, vol. 2/3, pp. 325-361.

Vetter G R (2000) Command Responsibility of Non-Military Superiors in the International Criminal Court (ICC), Yale Journal of International Law, 25:115-120.

Wald P M (2002) General Radislav Krstic: A War Crimes Case Study, Thomas F. Ryan Lecture, Georgetown University Law Centre, Washington D.C.

Weaver K D (2002) A Change of Heart or A Change of Law? Withdrawing a Guilty Plea under Federal Rule of Criminal Procedure 32(e), The Journal of Criminal Law and Criminology, vol. 92/1-2, pp. 273-305.

Weigend T (1983) Symposium: Comparative Criminal Justice Issues in the United States, West Germany, England and France, Sentencing in Western Germany, Md Law Review, Univ.of Maryland, 42: 37.

Weisbord R G (2003) The King, the Cardinal and the Pope: Leopold II's genocide in the Congo and the Vatican, Journal of Genocide Research, vol.5, no.1, pp. 35-46.

Weller M (2000) The Kosovo Indictment of the International Criminal Tribunal for Yugoslavia, The International Journal of Human Rights, vol. 4, no.3/4, pp.207-222.

Wharton's Criminal Law (1996) vol. 4, 15th Edition, Charles E. Torcia, Clark Boardman Callaghan, Deerfield.

Williams G L (1961) Criminal Law. The General Part, 2nd Edition, The Law Book Company of Australia, Sydney.

Williams G (1978) Textbook of Criminal Law, Stevens and Sons, U.K.

Wilson W (1998) Criminal Law, Doctrine and Theory, Longman, London.

Woetzel R K (1960) The Nuremberg Trials and International Law, Stevens and Sons, London.

Wolchover D (2001) Silence and Guilt. An Assessment of Case Law on Criminal Justice and Public Order Act, 1974, Lion's Court Lawyers, U.K.

Wright M (1999) Criminal Procedures. Prosecution and Adjudication, Aspen and Business, N.Y.

Wright R S (1980) The Law of Conspiracy and Criminal Agreements, Willy & Sons Ltd., London.

Wu T, Kang Y J (1977) Criminal liability for the actions of subordinates: the doctrine of command responsibility and its analogues in United States law, Harv. Int'l L.J, vol. 38, pp. 272 et seq.

Yee S (1997) The Erdemovic Sentencing Judgement: A Questionable Milestone for the International Criminal Tribunal for the Former Yugoslavia, Georgia Journal of International and Comparative Law, vol. 26/2, pp. 263-309.

Zahar A (2001) The Command Responsibility of Superiors for Genocide, Leiden Journal of International Law, vol. 14/3, pp. 591-616.

Zaklin R (2004) The Failings of Ad Hoc International Tribunals, Journal of International Criminal Justice, vol. 2, pp. 541-545.

Media sources

Associated Press
BBC
Daily News (Tanzania)
Franfurther Allgemeine Zeitung
International Herald Tribune
Internews
Lusa
New York Times
National Post (Canada)
Reuters
Sydney Morning Herald
The Age
The East African
The Guardian (Tanzania)
The Electronic Telegraph
The Times
The Jakarta Post
The Washington Post
Le Monde
The New Vision (Rwanda)
Ubutabera

Glossary

actus reus	the wrongful or forbidden act or deed that constitutes the physical component of an offence
Akazu	("little house") used to refer to group of individuals very close to President Habyarimana
Amicus curia	friend of the court, a non-interested party who informs the Court on a point of fact or law.
Bourgmestre	Head of civil administration at Commune level
Bupati	Regency head/District Administrator.
Gukora	to work, also used to refer to destroy or to kill
Icytso/Ibyitso	accomplice, extended meaning: RPF sympathizer, Tutsi or Hutu favourable to, or as a sympathizer of the RPF or somebody in agreement with its opinion or policies
Impuzamugambi	Those who have the same goal, name of Youth wing of CDR
Inkotanyi	literal meaning (an ardent warrior), RPF, RPF soldier;extended meaning Tutsi in general or as a group
Interahamwe	Those who attack together, name of Youth wing of MRND
Inyenzi	cockroach; extended meaning: group of refugees set up in 1959 to overthrow the new regime; sympathizer of RPF, Tutsi as a group
Inyenzi-Inkotanyi	inkotanyi who were Tutsi, as well as Tutsi in general

Kangura	"Awaken" in the imperative form, name of anti Tutsi newspaper that published the Ten Hutu Commandments; published in Kinyarwanda and French
mens rea	"guilty mind", i.e. criminal intent or recklessness, which is a an essential element of an offence
Pawa	'*power*', a slogan coined in October 1993, by Froduald Karamira, Vice President, MDR to emphasize anti-Tutsi extremism
Prefet	Head of civil administration at Prefecture (province)
res gestae	"thing done", the events at issue or other events contemporaneous with them

Sources:

P. v. F. Nahimana et all. Case no: ICTR-99-32-T, Judgement and Sentence, 3 December 2003.

Dr M. Ruzindana, Expert Testimony, ICTR, Transcript, *P. v. J. B. Barayagwiza, F. Nahimana & H. Ngeze*, ICTR case no: 99-52-T (Joinder), 96-11-T, 97-27-T, 97-19-T, 20 March 2002.

Black's Law Dictionary (2000) Gardner B A (ed. *et all.*) 7th ed. West Group, St Paul. Minn.

FSC
www.fsc.org
MIX
Papier | Fördert
gute Waldnutzung
FSC® C083411

Kolibri 360 GmbH
Ferdinand-Jühlke-Straße 7
99095 Erfurt, Deutschland
produktsicherheit@kolibri360.de